MYTHASTROLOGY II
Planets in Houses

MythAstrology II
Planets in Houses

Raven Kaldera

Ellhorn Press
Hubbardston, Massachusetts

Alfred Press
12 Simond Hill Road
Hubbardston, MA 01452

MythAstrology II: Planets in Houses
© 2024 Raven Kaldera
ISBN 978-1-7345032-4-1

All rights reserved.
No part of this book may be reproduced in any form or by any means without the permission of the author.

Printed in cooperation with
Lulu Enterprises, Inc.
860 Aviation Parkway, Suite 300
Morrisville, NC 27560

*Dedicated to Urania, Muse of Astrology,
and all her sisters,
who unblocked the flow.*

Contents

Introduction 1

☉ The Sun ☉

- 1☉ Sun in the 1st House: Saulé..................................5
- 2☉ Sun in the 2nd House: Midas................................9
- 3☉ Sun in the 3rd House: Seshat..............................13
- 4☉ Sun in the 4th House: Akka.................................17
- 5☉ Sun in the 5th House: The Nine Muses 21
- 6☉ Sun in the 6th House: The Handmaidens of Frigga 26
- 7☉ Sun in the 7th House: Surya, Saranya, and Chhaya 30
- 8☉ Sun in the 8th House: Selket...............................35
- 9☉ Sun in the 9th House: Jason................................39
- 10☉ Sun in the 10th House: Rama............................43
- 11☉ Sun in the 11th House: Mithras.........................48
- 12☉ Sun in the 12th House: Beiwe...........................53

☾ The Moon ☾

- 1☾ Moon in the 1st House: Ezili Dantor....................61
- 2☾ Moon in the 2nd House: Lakshmi.......................64
- 3☾ Moon in the 3rd House: Nisaba..........................69
- 4☾ Moon in the 4th House: The Son of Seven Mothers 73
- 5☾ Moon in the 5th House: Jizo...............................78
- 6☾ Moon in the 6th House: Anahita........................81
- 7☾ Moon in the 7th House: Yue Lao........................85
- 8☾ Moon in the 8th House: Morgan Le Fay.............89
- 9☾ Moon in the 9th House: Lancelot and Galahad 93
- 10☾ Moon in the 10th House: Sita............................97
- 11☾ Moon in the 11th House: Ninshubur 103
- 12☾ Moon in the 12th House: Iphigenia................106

☿ Mercury ☿

- 1☿ Mercury in the 1st House: Iris...........................115
- 2☿ Mercury in the 2nd House: Clever Manka 119
- 3☿ Mercury in the 3rd House: Nabu......................123
- 4☿ Mercury in the 4th House: Wenchang Wang...126
- 5☿ Mercury in the 5th House: Bragi......................131

6☿ Mercury in the 6th House: Diancecht, Miach, and Airmed 135
7☿ Mercury in the 7th House: Nuwa and Fuxi 139
8☿ Mercury in the 8th House: Odin and the Mead of Poetry 143
9☿ Mercury in the 9th House: Odysseus 148
10☿ Mercury in the 10th House: Indra 152
11☿ Mercury in the 11th House: Puss in Boots 156
12☿ Mercury in the 12th House: Father Raven 160

❦ Venus ❦

1♀ Venus in the 1st House: Aušrinė 169
2♀ Venus in the 2nd House: Benzaiten 172
3♀ Venus in the 3rd House: Sunu and Xuannu 177
4♀ Venus in the 4th House: Xochiquetzal 180
5♀ Venus in the 5th House: Pygmalion and Blodeuwedd 184
6♀ Venus in the 6th House: Hebe 188
7♀ Venus in the 7th House: Sif 193
8♀ Venus in the 8th House: Kamadeva and Rati 197
9♀ Venus in the 9th House: Atalanta 201
10♀ Venus in the 10th House: Ezili Freda 205
11♀ Venus in the 11th House: Milda 209
12♀ Venus in the 12th House: Sigyn 212

❦ Mars ❦

1♂ Mars in the 1st House: Achilles and Patroclus 219
2♂ Mars in the 2nd House: Bishamonten 223
3♂ Mars in the 3rd House: Ogma 228
4♂ Mars in the 4th House: Chantico 231
5♂ Mars in the 5th House: Perseus 235
6♂ Mars in the 6th House: Heimdall 239
7♂ Mars in the 7th House: Hercules and Omphale 243
8♂ Mars in the 8th House: Neith 247
9♂ Mars in the 9th House: Scathach 251
10♂ Mars in the 10th House: Kartikeya 254
11♂ Mars in the 11th House: Gilgamesh and Enkidu ... 258
12♂ Mars in the 12th House: Hercules and Dejaneira 263

✴ JUPITER ✴

1♃ Jupiter in the 1st House: Perun 271
2♃ Jupiter in the 2nd House: Hotei 274
3♃ Jupiter in the 3rd House: Manannan mac Lir 278

4♃ Jupiter in the 4th House: Daikoku 283
5♃ Jupiter in the 5th House: Uzume 287
6♃ Jupiter in the 6th House: Fukurokuju and Jurojin 291
7♃ Jupiter in the 7th House: Draupadi 295
8♃ Jupiter in the 8th House: Baron Samedi 299
9♃ Jupiter in the 9th House: Njord 302
10♃ Jupiter in the 10th House: The Wufang Shangdi 305
11♃ Jupiter in the 11th House: Forseti 310
12♃ Jupiter in the 12th House: The Fisher King 314

✢Saturn✢

1♄ Saturn in the 1st House: Babalu-Ayé 323
2♄ Saturn in the 2nd House: Ebisu 327
3♄ Saturn in the 3rd House: The Seven Swans 331
4♄ Saturn in the 4th House: Baba Yaga 335
5♄ Saturn in the 5th House: Gerda 340
6♄ Saturn in the 6th House: Shennong 344
7♄ Saturn in the 7th House: Penelope 348
8♄ Saturn in the 8th House: Dhumavati 353
9♄ Saturn in the 9th House: Aeneas 357
10♄ Saturn in the 10th House: Okuninushi 361
11♄ Saturn in the 11th House: Varuna 365
12♄ Saturn in the 12th House: Cailleach 369

Uranus ♅

1♅ Uranus in the 1st House: Tatterhood 377
2♅ Uranus in the 2nd House: Inari 382
3♅ Uranus in the 3rd House: Nanabozho 386
4♅ Uranus in the 4th House: Antigone 389
5♅ Uranus in the 5th House: Kokopelli 395
6♅ Uranus in the 6th House: Hanuman 399
7♅ Uranus in the 7th House: Maeve 404
8♅ Uranus in the 8th House: Number Eleven in the
    Village of Death 409
9♅ Uranus in the 9th House: Sun Wukong 413
10♅ Uranus in the 10th House: Daedalus 417
11♅ Uranus in the 11th House: Momotaro 421
12♅ Uranus in the 12th House: Iktomi 425

☐NEPTUNE☐

1♆ Neptune in the 1st House: Vishnu 433
2♆ Neptune in the 2nd House: Aegir and Ran 437
3♆ Neptune in the 3rd House: Kui Xing 440
4♆ Neptune in the 4th House: Orestes 444

5♆ Neptune in the 5th House: Brahma 448
6♆ Neptune in the 6th House: Kamrusepa 452
7♆ Neptune in the 7th House: Izanami and Izanagi 456
8♆ Neptune in the 8th House: Yarilo and Marzanna 461
9♆ Neptune in the 9th House: Merlin 465
10♆ Neptune in the 10th House: The Fisherman and
   His Wife 470
11♆ Neptune in the 11th House: Damon and Pythias 475
12♆ Neptune in the 12th House: The Nine Undines 478

☠ PLUTO ☠

1♇ Pluto in the 1st House: Pele 487
2♇ Pluto in the 2nd House: Maman Brigitte 491
3♇ Pluto in the 3rd House: Veles 495
4♇ Pluto in the 4th House: Oedipus 499
5♇ Pluto in the 5th House: Tlazolteotl 505
6♇ Pluto in the 6th House: Nephthys 509
7♇ Pluto in the 7th House: Circe 514
8♇ Pluto in the 8th House: Set 519
9♇ Pluto in the 10th House: Etain 524
10♇ Pluto in the 10th House: Yama 528
11♇ Pluto in the 11th House: Theseus and Pirithous 531
12♇ Pluto in the 12th House: Cerberus 536

Introduction

Years ago, I wrote the first *MythAstrology*, about planets in signs. Even then, I intended it to be only the first book in a series, but other writing projects interfered (about thirty of them) and it took two more decades before this book finally came to fruition. I pecked away at it occasionally in my spare time, and finally chipped away the wall between myself and completion. It is meant to be a companion book to the first *MythAstrology*, but used for the same purposes. Some readers will just want to look up their house placements and those of their friends and loved ones. Some will be astrologers looking for ways to explain those confusing messes of symbols and lines and jargon to the client in front of them.

The astrological houses, as opposed to the signs, are often bewildering to beginning astrologers. Sure, it's easy to say that "this is the house of X", but what does that entail when combined with a planet or sign that seems antithetical to the energy of X? Combining the first two—planets and signs—seems intimidating enough without adding yet another layer of barely-understood complexity. (And this is before getting into the even-more-complex issue of aspects, which hopefully will be a third book in this series somewhere down the road before I'm dead.)

When I wrote about planets in signs, I used the archetypal characteristics of a long list of Gods and heroes to describe the situations created by those combinations. *This is who they are; they behave in this way because of who they are; their behavior shows their nature.* With many of the chapters in this book, the focus is not on the essential nature per se but on how that nature reacts when thrown into a particular place and time. The houses are the stages on which the planets act out their dramas, and those stages affect how they are acted out. One does not do an act the same way on a crowded street as one would in one's own bathroom. The focus is on where and when rather than who and what: *they behave this way because their environment forces them into it, and yet their behavior varies due to their inner nature.*

This means that you will find some of the same players in *MythAstrology* I, only the focus will not be on their basic natures but on specific adventures in their histories. Hercules represented Neptune in Aries in the first book, but here he gets to play a Mars archetype (not so far off, considering that Mars rules Aries). Looking at the story of Hercules in Omphale's Court, one could practically title it "Mars Has A Seventh-House Adventure". The emphasis is on what they do, and it is in their actions that the nature of the house is played out. Some of the chapters, however, are about specific mythic figures that did not make it into MythAstrology I—Njord and Hebe, for example. You'll also find a more global and less classical-western array of legends here, because I now have access to more sacred stories. Besides, the line between myth and folktale is really a large grey area.

Please keep in mind that this book is only one artificially separated piece of what is actually an interlinked whole. The signs of the planets in question aren't taken much into account in this book (being that if I had done so, it would have been three times as long), so the reader is encouraged to add that omitted but very important layer of information. An Aries Sun behaves quite differently in the very public tenth house than a Pisces Sun, for example, and will make different decisions. Indeed, in many ways it's dangerous to leave out the effect of the sign, which is why I write this with more trepidation than I wrote MythAstrology I. If these myths don't resonate as closely for you, it's probably because of sign variance, and that should be taken into account.

Welcome again to the world of cosmic stories!

☀ The Sun ☀

1☉ Sun in the 1st House: Saulé

The Sun has always been the most important character in the sky—beautiful, golden, life-giving, and generally extremely impressive. It's no wonder that most mythologies started out with a sun deity before they came up with a wide array of other Gods. (Some seemed to start out with Gods of fertility or hunting, human activities which needed help and propitiation, or else general "creator gods", but when it came to personifying the natural world, everything started with the Sun.) In the area of central Europe which became Lithuania and Latvia, the Sun was a goddess named Saulé, whose bright face warmed the world and made it fertile.

The first house rules the body, which includes its general physical characteristics, but is often more concerned with what we do with it. How do we dress and adorn the body to make a statement of who we are to the world? How do we wear our hair, the "rays" of our physical being? How do we move the body and choreograph facial expressions to communicate or hide messages about ourselves? How do we put ourselves forward or step back in reserve? How do we draw immediate attention or deflect it away? For some people, it is a daily costume and a daily "act", as they conceal their inner self out of fear, awkwardness, or a need for privacy. For others, it is an easy, near-effortless flow where their inner self naturally exudes out into the world.

For those with the Sun, the core of identity, right there in the first house, it's something of both. Any planet in the first house doesn't just "leak" out through the mask of the Ascendant, it becomes part of the mask's paint job, like a label pasted across the forehead. When it's the Sun, the brightest object in the sky, it subsumes the Ascendant nearly entirely. If the Ascendant is in the same sign as the Sun, they become one; if different, it becomes just another costume the Sun dons. The core of Self is right there where everyone can see it, and since the Sun is always a performer to some extent, the many "costumes" which communicate that person's statement to the world are a natural extension of the facets of personality rather than a shield to hide behind.

Of all the solar deities in the world, Saulé is the goddess with the most extensive wardrobe descriptions. Other Sun deities settle for being clad in golden robes or a reference to rich garments, but Saulé's clothing and accoutrements are like the lists made by a queen's maid who is packing the royal lady for a visit. Sometimes she is lovingly described in silk gowns of gold or silver or white or red as a sunset; sometimes her dress is described as being woven of threads of all these colors. She wears a golden shawl, golden slippers, golden scarves, a gold belt, golden rings on her fingers, golden ribbons in her hair, gold tassels on her clothing, and either a sparkling golden crown or a wreath of red roses on her head. When the Sun appears in the first house, the individual is going to express themselves both naturally and elaborately—and yes, those two adjectives can happen together—to show off the glory of who they are. While the costume and the effect will have more to do with the Sun's sign and any conjuncting planets, it will be sincere, and it will make a big impression.

Even Saulé's vehicles for crossing the world were many and sumptuous—and what self-expressive person who could afford it hasn't driven multiple cars to suit their mood (or at least seriously considered it)? Sometimes she rides two golden or bay-colored horses—one for herself and one for her various golden tools, or else three horses of gold, silver, and diamond-color. Sometimes it's a gleaming copper chariot with copper wheels, sometimes a silver sleigh made of fishbones. At night she ditches all of these and gets into a silver or golden boat, sailing to sleep under the waters in a silver cradle surrounded by white seafoam. (In other stories, she sleeps in a tree full of red flowers.) All this detail isn't just poetic license through the ages, but rather Saulé making sure that you notice everything she is and does and has. The first-house Sun person is not a wallflower; they want to be *seen*. Saulé is said to dance on a silver hill on the special solar holidays of the spring equinox and the summer solstice, because performing for the people and their applause is important. Even a first-house Sun in a shyer sign will enjoy an appreciative audience and subtly seek it out.

In ancient times all women were expected to spin (and often the children, and sometimes crippled men as well), as the making of clothing was an endless task. It was even expected of goddesses, and Saulé supposedly spun the sun's rays on a golden spindle. Drop spindles with amber whorls have been found in archeological digs in the Baltic area; some even show signs of use, meaning they were not merely symbolic. Here in one of the world's largest amber-producing areas, they still call amber blobs *Saulé's Tears*, because even the tears of such a majestic lady would be a substance of beauty and value. Similarly, when the first-house Sun grieves, they don't withdraw to a cave until all traces of sorrow are no longer visible to the audience. They weep or rage openly, and expect everyone around them to be understanding ... because, of course, it's so obvious that they should be sad. There's often a sense that onlookers should feel a sense of privilege for being able to observe the first-house Sun's sincere presentation of their woes.

Saulé married the Moon (Ménuo), and drove to see him every night in her golden chariot (or whatever car she felt like driving), dancing and emitting fiery sparks on the way. They had six children as a result. The three daughters were Earth and the Morning and Evening Stars; the three sons were Mercury, Jupiter, and Saturn. The two Venusian star-daughters assist Saulé in getting ready in the morning and settling down at night. (This is sometimes an issue with first-house Sun people, who often end up with important jobs and/or important positions in the community; their family gets pressed into being assistants or audience or both.) However, her inconstant husband ended up falling in love with his dawn-star-daughter Aušrinė (Venus in the first house) and having an affair with her, and Saulé—being the all-seeing Eye—found out about it. Furious, she told Perkunas/Perun the thunder God (Jupiter in the first house) to chop her husband up into pieces, which he happily did, and this is why the Moon appears in pieces over the month. Another version has Saulé scratching his face with her nails badly enough that Ménuo now only shows one side to the Earth. They divorced, and share the sky at different times so that they can see their children without having to deal with the ex-spouse.

More than anything else, the first-house Sun wants to be seen as *special*. Saulé's anger at her unfaithful husband is not so much about a marital betrayal as it is about being rejected for her younger, prettier daughter. It meant that she was not the most special person any longer, the greatest light in the sky. When the loved one rejects the specialness of the first-house Sun, the claws come out and the loved one can get badly scratched. The Sun is associated with the sign of Leo, and even a Sun which is naturally pleasant and "sunny" can lash out in genuine hurt and say something they don't really mean. It's not calculated—with this Sun, it's always an instinctive reaction to pain, and often they are just as genuinely contrite afterwards.

Wearing one's Self on one's golden sleeve can be a vulnerable position, something which many observers don't understand. What, that glorious VIP, vulnerable? And yet what's out front may be a bigger target for slings and arrows, especially from envious people who wish they had the first-house Sun's charisma and ability to command attention. What can clearly be seen is that, in reality, this creates more risk of being rejected. There is real courage in the first-house Sun's willingness—or need—to show themselves to the world again and again, clinging to the belief that if they cast enough warmth with their smiles, people will love and honor them … and help them when they are in trouble. One legend tells of how a sorcerer-king imprisoned Saulé in a tower, and she was rescued by her planet-sons who used a giant sledgehammer to break her out. (The sledgehammer apparently lay in Prague for centuries, venerated by the local people, and was written about by a medieval Christian cleric.) While the first-house Sun does not like to think of themselves as weak or needing help in general, when the chips are down, they want those loved ones who cluster about them to come to the rescue. They don't want their motivation to be duty, either; they want the rescue to come about because everyone loves them and thinks they are marvelous, and would of course do anything for the One who gives them such an amazing show every day. In fact, one folk custom for Saulé was to pause all work for a few minutes just after sunset, the "grey hour", to bid her good night and honor the work she had put in with her daily ride.

At its best, first-house Sun people can be warming, joy-bringing, and protective of those around them. Saulé was known to be a protector of orphan children, who needed her warm light to keep them from the cold of abandonment, and she was prayed to in order to find them loving, secure homes. Saulé was also said to lead the newly Dead safely to the Underworld—all burials had to be finished before sunset because Saulé carries away the keys to the Land of Shades, which is then locked for the night and the dead soul may get lost and wander away. Saulé also supposedly took away as much blight, illness, disintegration, and decay as she reasonably could, sinking it into the Underworld instead of letting it fester on the Earth. On the other end of the spectrum, women in labor prayed to Saulé not to "take away the keys", indicating that she could also open the door to allow new souls into the world.

This is the goal of the matured first-house Sun—to have earned the honor of those around them by their works and not just assuming privilege; to spread warmth and goodness and improvement around their world and banish as much blight as they can; to protect the unfortunate and those trapped in darkness; and do all these shining works with as much open sincerity as possible. That's a great challenge, because this is so often a position of greatness … just like the greatest light in the sky.

2☉ Sun in the 2nd House: Midas

The Sun's metal has always been gold, throughout time and history. Any culture that works with metals cannot fail to note the similarity of the Sun's rays to the beautiful, soft, yellow metal, and it may be that this more than anything else has influenced the value of gold in the world. Even today, when we have metals that are much rarer, it is gold that is the choice metal of jewelry due to its beauty and resistance to corrosion, and gold that is the money standard as well. The association of gold with not only ornament but money is ingrained into us. "Gold" as a word is used to connote nearly every nuance around money, from weregild to Gold Standard to the modern tongue-in-cheek version of the Golden Rule … that whoever has the gold makes the rules.

You'll notice, of course, that all these connotations symbolize not only material goods but Value. This is the higher octave of meaning of the astrological second house. While it is unquestionably the house of material goods and money, its deeper meaning is that of Values: what do you value, and above what? How do you prioritize? What would you sacrifice to save something else? In what areas are you generous, or even profligate? Did you decide these things on your own, or did you just adopt someone else's standards on the matter?

With the Sun in the second house, issues around money are always going to come up as central to the individual's life, whether they like it or not. Even moving into a communal monastery to get away from money (as one client with a Pisces Sun in the second house actually did) is still a reaction to the basic premise of how one deals with one's gold. What the second-house Sun person needs to understand is that the real issue is one of Values, not just one of material wealth or the lack of it.

In ancient Greece, Midas was the King of Pessinus, a city-state in Phrygia—and a King, we must remember, is a solar archetype. Unlike other mythical (and historical) kings, who are often the sons of other kings, or gods, or various important personages, Midas is the son of a peasant. According to the myth, the old king of Pessinus had died without leaving an heir, and the people were all instructed to come into the center of the city and pray, and the new King would arrive in the back of a wagon. As luck would have it, a poor countryman named Gordius unwittingly creaked his old wagon into the square just as this prayer-conflagration was going on, with his wife by his side and his son in the back of the wagon. The youth Midas was immediately proclaimed king, even though he was the son of a mere peasant.

This rags-to-riches story is echoed in the lives of many second-house Sun people, who start out the sons and daughters of shoemakers and aluminum siding salesmen, and who end up with mansions and expensive cars. The house that houses the Sun is the arena where the ego wishes to manifest, and for many of these people, wealth is more than just security. It's a show of how much you are worth to the world, and as such they may invest a lot more effort in obtaining wealth than someone for whom money is just a means to an end, or a way to keep the wolf from the door. Although they may be willing to work very hard to earn their golden prize of social worth, there is also sometimes a streak of luck in their early endeavors, as the Sun shines on them here—getting just the right job at the right time, the right promotion, the right lottery ticket. Like Midas, they can start out with a knack for finding the path of least resistance towards affluence. It is also certain that even if they do not get a rags-to-riches story (perhaps due to an afflicted Sun), they will dream about one, and desire it, and resent not getting it.

Once installed in Pessinus, Midas is a kind but hedonistic ruler, enjoying food, drink, and the good life. His pride and joy is his children—a daughter named Zoe (Life) and a son named Lityerses—and his rose gardens. When the drunken mentor of Dionysos, a fat old demigod known as Silenus, becomes lost and wanders away from the traveling Bacchanalia, the people of Pessinus bring him to Midas, believing that the good King will know what to do. Knowing that this fat old drunk has divine patrons who have been known to give gifts, Midas feasts Silenus generously for ten days and then returns him to Dionysos.

The wine-deity Dionysos (Pluto in Scorpio) is not a second-house figure like the wealthy, sensual, calculating Midas. As a god of altered states, one who has died and been reborn, one who travels with a sexual orgy of wild women who rip their sacrificial victims to pieces and eat the flesh, he is much more a figure of the opposing eighth house of sex, death, and the mysteries. When he faces Midas, it is a moment of the opposing of two ways of being, and the Opposition, in astrology, is a point not only of antagonism but objectivity. Dionysos sees through Midas's genial facade, thanks him for the good treatment of his friend, and offers him a gift ... which is really a test of the supposedly generous King's values.

Midas, unfortunately, fails the test utterly. One wonders if his poor upbringing has planted the seed of want in him, a seed which his kingly wealth nourishes but cannot satisfy. Like the televangelist Tammy Faye Bakker, who grew up poor and after achieving fame and riches would buy shopping-cartfuls of cheap cosmetics at the local five-and-dime, Midas's greed gets the better of him—he asks that everything he touches be turned into gold. Dionysos smiles wryly, and grants the gift ... and leaves shaking his head.

Midas rushes home, touching oak twigs and stones and watching them become solid gold artifacts. His clothing becomes cloth of gold; his famed roses become delicate golden versions of themselves. However, when he tries to eat and drink, he discovers that the food and wine also becomes solid gold the second it touches his lips, and he realizes that if this goes on, he will starve. In later versions of the story, he touches his daughter Zoe and she becomes a golden statue. Desperate, he flees the palace in search of Dionysos, begging him to lift the golden curse.

One assumes, reading the myth, that he didn't realize how literal this gift would get. For the individual with the second-house Sun, the golden touch is the ultimate gift. The idea that any project you apply yourself to will yield up fruit and add to your financial nourishment seems like the best faery gift in the world to them, especially if they have spent years working hard tilling poor soil. If they actually get their wish for riches, the danger for them is that the lifestyle needed to create (and sustain, and show off) those riches may harden and starve out other areas of their lives. The high-powered job needed to afford the big car and the condo and the expensive things eats up all the individual's energy, and they find precious little time to actually enjoy themselves on anything but a superficial level. Deeper meaning is prioritized away in favor of maintaining the life that they cannot imagine living without.

Again, it's a test of Value, and one that astrologers see again and again with second-house Suns. Their good fortune depends on how they handle their Golden Touch, and what values its use demonstrates. If those values are in the right place—is the monetary gain a means to an end, or the end itself? Is the money given away generously and with an open heart? Are there no ulterior motives about impressing people by looking like Lord or Lady Bountiful? Is it better to buy a lot of cheap or a little of quality? Do purchases reflect thoughtfulness and sustainability of the Earth, or are they shiny impulse buys?—then their streak of luck will stay with them, but when it falls, so do they. It's a fascinating thing about this placement: you can literally see how the good fortune of the person waxes and wanes with changes of their value system.

In the myth, Dionysos grants Midas's request by ordering him to bathe in the River Pactolus. As the desperate king did so, his power passed into the river and the sands became gold. All that he had transformed changed back, leaving him no richer. After this, he moved to the country and lived a simpler life, rejecting the ostentatious collecting of wealth. In spite of this—or perhaps because of it—he was considered wiser than before, and people flocked to him to ask for advice. Midas himself makes friends with the rustic goat-god Pan (Pluto in Aries)—hardly an upscale deity—and finds solace in listening to Pan's simple pipe-music.

This is the other side of the second-house Sun experience—the riches-to-rags story. It's not the side that gets written about in inspirational stories about prosperity consciousness. Sometimes it's the guy who makes poor choices, and ruins himself—again, a failure of values. Sometimes it's the guy who made it big and then one day decides to walk away from it all, because there's something deeper than just money calling to him. Either way, this section of the life-myth forces a re-prioritization, where everything is turned on its head. Simplicity calls, or perhaps it steamrolls over the protesting King, compelling a more spartan life, or everything will go terribly wrong. The idea, of course, is to choose some measure of Simplicity, before she calls on you in her more severe—and less consensual—guise.

One day, Pan challenges Apollo, the God of the Sun (Mercury in Leo), to a music competition. Apollo, skilled on the lyre, wins—but Midas, defending his friend, claims that Pan's music is still better. Apollo becomes angry and curses the recalcitrant King, making him grow donkey's ears. Humiliated, Midas hides his ears under a turban and warns his family not to talk about them.

Rather than reading this part of the myth as mere malice on Apollo's part, it would be better to think about what it means for a solar king to be cursed by the God of the Sun himself. Midas has already screwed up once, showing himself to have less than stellar judgment, yet here he decides to stand up not for the bright solar ideal, but for his friend Pan, who symbolizes his newly-found prioritizing of Simplicity, and the solace of his heart. His new honesty is touching and laudable ... but the Sun is still the place of the Ego, and that means Reputation, and Looking Good. It is not an uncommon moral detour for second-house Suns who discover material simplicity to start preaching its benefits out of ego, which is in its own way just as iffy as collecting material wealth out of ego. "See how wonderfully ascetic I am" isn't really much better than "See how wonderfully rich I am," except perhaps that one uses up fewer resources in proving one's poverty to the masses. Either way, the ego needs to be cut out of the value system, or the whole thing won't work.

Still acting out of pride, Midas shows his ears only to his family and his barber. The barber is sworn to secrecy, but the secret burns within him until he finally whispers it into a hole in the ground. A thick bed of reeds springs up where the hole had been, and they constantly whisper, "King Midas has ass's ears," until eventually everyone knows about it anyway. Midas finds out and considers killing the barber. In a crisis of conscience, he decides instead to weather the storm, ears and all, and not punish anyone for his own bad fortune. At this point, now that he has given up acting from the ego, Apollo appears and removes the ass ears. The king is hailed as an even wiser man, and eventually after death becomes one of the Judges of the Underworld ... a strangely eighth-house fate for this second-house figure. It is not that the ego has to be cast aside—the Sun is the ego incarnate—but that it must be in service to the greater good, where its golden touch can spread the wealth rather than merely making a surface show of being the archetype of Golden Abundance.

3☉ Sun in the 3rd House: Seshat

In *MythAstrology I*, we met Thoth/Djehuti (Moon in Gemini) who is the God of Scribes in Egyptian mythology. Now it's time to introduce you to another deity from the Land of the Eternal Sun: Seshat, Djehuti's wife.

Writer, librarian, architect; she embodies the interesting and varied intellectual life of the Sun in the third house of communication, words, and the mind.

When the Sun lands in Mercury's house, the identity will be centered around the mind and the ideas it generates. That's not to say that third-house Sun people don't have emotions—everyone has a Moon, and it is weak or strong individually dependent on the chart—but they will do a great deal of living in their head. They won't do it silently, though; this is the house of communication, and these people like to talk about what's in their head as much as they like to think about it. In fact, any given thought or idea may feel incomplete if it is not shared. Writing, speaking, and teaching all come naturally to them; this doesn't guarantee that they are good at it, only that it feels natural for them to do it, as often as possible, which over time tends to make someone fairly accomplished at something. Even as children, they will talk all the time and compulsively explain things to other children, often holding forth to a fascinated audience.

Their interests are widely varied, and they need a lot of mental activity and change of scenery, or they get bored. Books and other media are their friends—one of Seshat's titles was "Mistress of the House of Books". Her priests oversaw the library where the scrolls were kept, paying special attention to the scrolls with magical spells in them. It is said that Seshat invented hieroglyphic writing and taught it to Djehuti, who then passed it on to humanity.

Seshat is not a solar deity per se, but as a contrast to her lunar-associated husband, she is often shown wearing a dress made out of the yellow skin of a leopard, a definitely solar animal. She bears a papyrus plant on her head, the material from which parchment was made. She is also shown writing on the stem of a palm leaf, or on the leaves of a persea tree—like third-house Suns who can't resist scribbling down thoughts on anything that is to hand. On the other hand, she was a meticulous record-keeper, recording all the speeches made by pharaohs, as well as their reigning years, their deeds, and how many years they had left to rule.

This is also the house of short trips, as opposed to the ninth house, its opposite number, which rules long travels. Think about short trips—you go to the local store, the pharmacy, the neighbor, the library. You circulate around the town. It probably never occurs to you, unless you're in a very specific sort of career, how that local town or village or neighborhood is laid out, how that happened, and why the buildings look as they do. The third house also involves this kind of city planning, the laying out of buildings and roads, making things inviting or impressive or survivable in extreme weather. It's not a part of the third house that we think of, but it does require a fair amount of intellectual knowledge and experimentation. This is also an area where Seshat ruled in her day; she was the patron of architecture, building, and space planning—the divine measurer.

It was said that she assisted the pharaoh in the "stretching of the cord ritual", done to lay out and mark temples and other important buildings. Sacred architecture was done to specific standards, alignments, and precise dimensions, which Seshat had created. She was also in charge of the people who re-measured the land after the flooding had receded, making sure that everyone had the piece of dirt they'd had before the waters rose. Most of us don't live somewhere that floods every year, wiping out boundaries and markers and buildings, which then have to be redone all over again … and again, and again. It's no wonder that Egypt became superb at ritually surveying and measuring everything, and Seshat was the lady who figured it all out. Third-house Suns like to measure things, to sort them into categories, and to play and experiment with those boxes. It's why they often like mathematics as much as they like words—it is a language unto itself, really, and it's also another area Seshat rules, along with accounting, astronomy, and astrology. Some scholars think that her leopard-skin dress was supposed to represent the spotted sky, covered in stars, alluding to her affinity with that science.

Third-house Sun people see competence primarily as a matter of experience—how many times have you actually done the thing you're talking about? While they love to read about all manner of activities, it's also important to them that they have done at last some of them, and become expert at a few. The word "expert" makes them tingle, because it presupposes hours of perfecting some skill or knowledge. Their curiosity is endless, and like Seshat they prefer to be jacks-of-all-trades, although they usually manage to be masters of at least some of them.

The third house rules the lungs, arms, and hands; the lungs are obvious because they create the breath for talking. The hands and arms are for all the activities done "by hand"—not so much creativity (that would be the fifth house) but artisanship, following a pattern precisely and making something happen from the pattern. Strangely enough, Seshat's one duty with the death Gods is in assisting Neith (Mars in the eighth house) to help people regrow limbs after they are dead, specifically the arms and hands.

Instead of being Djehuti's wife, Seshat was sometimes identified as his sister. It wasn't unusual for Gods in Egypt to marry their brothers, but the brother/sister relationship that Seshat and Djehuti revert to at times is noteworthy, as the third is the House of Siblings. Third-house Sun people tend to revert to sibling-type relationships with friends and partners, whether or not they have actually had siblings in their childhood. If their early sibling relationships were unsatisfying, they may try to create better ones with their peers as adults; where the unhappy fourth-house Sun keeps trying to recreate the parents they didn't have, the unhappy third-house Sun keeps trying to recreate the sibling relationships they wanted but which were denied them. This can have a charming playfulness, but can also come with some "sibling rivalry" or refusal to be serious.

Another danger of the third house Sun is just not being able to control their tongue. The mouth opens, the words pour out, and a filter may or may not be in place. This can accidentally hurt someone, especially if the individual is particularly skilled in sarcasm, or it can get a person blacklisted because they said words which should have remained unsaid, at least if they wanted to keep their job or look good in public. The sad thing is that these are not usually outbursts aiming to actually hurt someone or something; it's just that the brakes didn't come on and the contents of their head spilled out over everything. Third-house Sun people often have a way with words and a fair amount of verbal charisma, but they also have the tendency to spill things which can't be so easily shrugged off or patched with charm. In this day and age of the semi-anonymous Internet, it's even more tempting to let fly, if only because the person isn't standing in front of you, but it's important for them to have some self-preservation and bite their tongues once in a while. It's better to have a group of trusted friends, all with a non-disclosure rule, where these concepts can be vomited up and bantered around.

The Sun illuminates parts of you and makes them special, depending on where it is in your chart and what sign it is embodying. Here, it illuminates the intellect and the mind, putting out a constant flow of new ideas. Archaeologists have not discovered any temples specifically dedicated to

Seshat, but she was still symbolically present in all the temples through the hieroglyphs, the architecture, the record-keeping—and also the per-ankh, the learning institutions which were often attached to temples. Instead of living in one settled place, she was literally living "in heads"—being worshiped by thought and writing and learning in many places, just as those with this Sun placement live both in their head and in many places at once.

Third-house Suns are idea people; they go through more in twenty minutes than most people have in a whole day, and probably discard most of them as boring or irrelevant, but fun to throw out there. A few, though, are surveyed and measured by Seshat's cord and taken up as worth sharing, spreading, perhaps even manifesting. The floodwaters of confusion retreat, the Sun shines, and the ideas sprout. Community blossoms and people swear brotherhood and sisterhood. The words pour forth and do magic ... because all words are magic. It's something that the third-house Sun was born knowing.

4☉ Sun in the 4th House: Akka

For the Sámi people of the far north—Arctic Norway and Finland—Akka is the name of a group of goddesses who deal with matters of hearth and home. In non-Sámi Finland, Akka is the name of the Mother Goddess, the wife of Ukko the god of thunder and sky who brings forth fertility. It is unknown whether the Sámi name for these goddesses came from the Finnish goddess, or vice-versa. For now we'll be discussing the five Akkas of the Sámi to illustrate the nature of the house of Hearth and Home.

The fourth house is ruled by the Moon, associated with Cancer, and when the Sun lands here it takes on a decided lunar feel ... and yet it is still the Sun, the center of the chart. This brings the matters of family to a crucial point for individuals with this placement. The Sun is the center of identity, and much of their struggle will revolve around how much of that identity is bound up with their family patterns and cultural upbringing. They may happily build their selves around these; they may rebel and do the exact opposite as an antithesis position; they may fluctuate back and forth—but those early years, and/or the relationships of blood kin, will continue to overshadow their lives for a long time.

The fourth house starts with the Nadir, the most private part of the conscious psyche. Where the Midheaven has to do with standing tall in public, the Nadir is what you keep hidden from everyone. And in that vein, family patterns like to hide here as well; while monetary inheritances are the business of the eighth house, genetic and psychological inheritances come down to us through the fourth, for better or worse. Denying those inheritances—pretending that you don't have the genes you have from your birth parents, and/or pretending that the treatment given to you by the people who raised you didn't have any effect—is neither true nor useful. At the same time, you are a unique person with choices, and the more you know about both of these kinds of inheritances, the better you can mindfully pick and choose what is possible, and compensate for what cannot be thrown away. Denial, however, simply leaves you blind and vulnerable.

The first of the five Akka goddesses is Maderakka ("Mother Akka"), the goddess who gives us our bodies. She received souls from Veralden-Radien, the ruler of the heavens, and crafted bodies for each of them, placing them inside their mothers. Women and girls belong to her, and so do boy babies until they reach their fifth year. She is the keeper of the genetics of those bodies, and science is finding out more and more about just how much our genes affect us. It's not just about genetic illnesses any more, or even inherited neurological problems; the studies of twins separated at birth tell us that all sorts of behaviors are expressed through our genetics. This is true for everyone, but with the Sun in the fourth house, something about your genetic inheritance is important enough that it shapes who you are as a person. This can be a matter of inherited illnesses which create disabilities, or special gifts carried in the bloodline which demand to be used. Genetic information bubbles up through this house, and if the center of the chart is here, it will be affected in some crucial way.

Maderakka has three daughters—Sarakka, Juksakka, and Uksakka. Her eldest daughter Sarakka is the most popular of all the Akkas, at least among women. She rules over sexuality and love, but specifically as it relates to procreation. She is the patron of all physical women's mysteries, such as fertility, menstruation, pregnancy, and childbirth. Women were given a healing porridge directly after birth which was called "Sarakka porridge", showing her connection to the cooking fire and later the kitchen. Like her mother, she also watches over girls and women from birth to death. If Sámi couples wanted a girl child, they would hang the feathers of the snow grout, which was Sarakka's favorite bird, over the empty cradle.

Here we come to the fourth-house sun's issues of parenting, and especially that of the mother. There is a lot of argument between astrologers as to whether the fourth house represents the mother and the tenth house the father, or vice-versa. The best explanation I ever heard is that the fourth house represents the parent who set the tone for the home, and the tenth house represents the parent who introduces you to the outside world. These can be the same person, and either or both parents can be the one whose aura and desires run the home. The relationship with this parent, and with the family in general, will have a profound effect on the fourth-house Sun person's identity, more so than another child in the same home with a different Sun placement. They will be working out the relationship between themselves and that parent for much of their adulthood, perhaps well after the parent has passed on. Whether they identify with them or do everything they can to get away from them, it will be a hugely formative connection.

Later on in life, that work may take on the form of creating their own family, and either trying to be the parent who raised them (or at least make them proud), or be the parent they wish their parent had been. This can be a way of remaking the concept of family with conscious purging of the dysfunctional patterns which have been passed down. Either way, their role in the family they create will also become a defining part of their identity. If they choose not to create a biological family—and this can be a way of getting as far away as possible from a dysfunctional childhood—they will end up creating or joining some sort of chosen family, and then taking on a specific (and probably parental) role in that replacement family group. It may be healthier or not, but it will be a way of working it all out.

Juksakka ("Arrow-Akka") is a very different goddess when compared to her sister Sarakka. She is a goddess of hunting, which is a male preserve among the Sámi, and looked after the reindeer, protecting them from wild animals. If Sámi couples wanted a boy child, they would hang arrows over the empty waiting cradle, so the fact that the hunter is a girl may raise some eyebrows. Juksakka looked out for boy children until they reached puberty and passed under the watchful eye of a male deity. She was known to be a tomboy, a very masculine goddess whose symbol was two crossed arrows. This is strangely similar to Neith (Mars in the eighth house), although the two are a continent and an ocean apart and their cultures never touched. This androgynously-leaning goddess was said to be able to change the gender of the child in the womb, or even during the birthing process if she felt it was necessary for some reason, which made many prospective parents pray to her for this "cheat" if they wanted a boy or a girl.

If we set aside the complicated gender situations of both this goddess and parenting in general, we can see that this is the complementary role to Sarakka and her porridge. It is the role of the guardian and protector, regardless of whether that was someone in a female body or a male one, or if the two roles were held by one parent. This will affect the fourth-house Sun in a serious way: did they feel safe and protected as a child? Everyone is affected by this question in some way, but this Sun placement may find their identity shaped by this question. Becoming someone who protects the helpless or defends the family system will feel very important to them.

Uksakka ("Door-Akka") is the least-well-known of the sisters; she is the goddess of midwifery, who brings the child through the "door" of the womb. She is honored on house-doors as well, with her symbol scratched over them or buried beneath them. The home as womb, or the womb as home, is not an uncommon trope in tribal religions and in the human collective unconscious. The fourth-house Sun is a homebody, and owning their home will be something they want from a young age. (I know one fourth-house Sun child who started saving for their first home while still in their teens.) They want a homespace where they can have control over the decorations, the rules, and who comes in and out; they may put up with living in someone else's space for a time, but if they can't "nest" and have a large say in how things are done, they will come to resent the situation and eventually move on. If they are half of a couple who live together or plan to do so, letting them have control over the major part of the homespace will be a gift to their sense of security. Once they have that safe space, it will take a lot to lever them out of it. They would rather stay home and watch a movie they've already seen than go out to see a new one. Owning a home—and especially if it comes with owning land—will strongly affect their sense of who they are; they may not feel that they are "real" in some way until there is earth beneath their feet which they can call their own.

Finally, we come to Jabmeakka, who some say is the sister of Maderakka. Her name means "Dead Akka" and she is a goddess of the underworld who cares for the souls of dead children. As a keeper of the Dead, she is linked to the past and the ancestors. The fourth is the house of the past itself, and here we have to bring up the other contributions of one's ancestors, which can be a whole buffet of cultural traditions and assumptions. This Sun placement is often very bound up in ancestral traditions; they may continue ones they were taught, or go seeking ones which their family line had become separated from, to revive them and take them on as a part of daily life. This may include religion, but it will be less a draw to the faith itself and more of a way to use the faith practices to tie them more firmly to the ways of their ancestors. In some cases, it can be a subtle form of ancestor worship itself, which is known to be the oldest of religious practices. Others with this placement may stick to secular traditions, but if they have children they will be sure to pass them on. The Dead have a strong place in the home of a fourth-house Sun.

The fourth-house Sun placement is not easy; the Sun doesn't like to be down there in the bottom house, in the half-dark, working through all the patterns which have been laid down in the past. Puzzling it all out through emotional work or experimentation can take years, and most fourth-house Suns really come into their own in the second half of their lives, after the Saturn return. By then, the giant figures of parents loom less large, they have hopefully found the place where they can root, and those roots will help them to grow into the caring and protective figure they are meant to be.

5☉ Sun in the 5th House: The Nine Muses

When the Sun, the planet of identity, falls into the fifth house of self-expression, it makes a beeline for the aspect of this house which calls to it most strongly: creativity. Certainly the other rulerships of this house can manifest, and often do, but the Sun falling in its own house will always want, first and foremost, to create great works to offer to the world. In fact, it's said that if other aspects of this house seem to be more important in the individual's life, it may mean that some terrible experience has discouraged them from the creative powers which are their birthright, and they are "making do" with the other aspects. When the Sun shines clearly from this house, however, it longs to create, to make manifest, and to show that work to others.

This is the sacred act of passing on inspiration like a holy virus. Yes, that's a strange metaphor, but it is really how it works with the fifth house. Inspiration is ideally like a chain—one work inspires the next artist, who does something different with it, and that passes to another viewer, and so on down the centuries and millennia. Fifth-house Sun people are often polyartists—not satisfied with only one medium, they might draw, write, sing, play an instrument, dabble in filmmaking, whatever brings them joy. This is so prevalent with this placement that one deity could not do the job of describing the journey. Instead, the goddesses who laughingly came forward, all at once, were the Nine Muses of Mount Helicon.

The Muses were the handmaidens of Apollo (Mercury in Leo), who oversaw the arts and sciences; it is no accident that these nine ladies of the Sun's house serve a Sun God. Their father was Zeus (Jupiter in Aries)—which made them half-sisters of Apollo—and their mother was the Titaness Mnemosyne, which means *memory*. This is telling, as in a largely illiterate society, memory would be stored in images, symbols, songs, and performances. Poets and speakers would invoke the Muses at the beginning of their shows; many extant pieces of writing begin with the familiar "Sing, O Muse!" including Homer's own poetry.

Each Muse inspired creators in their specific field, but they also inspire an emotion or state of mind which is bound up with that field, like strands of cord twisted together. Each of these "secondary gifts" can be accessed through creative work by a fifth-house planet, but the Sun has the biggest "pipeline" of all. They just have to remember that it's there, to be used.

The eldest of the Muses is Calliope, the Muse of Epic Poetry, called the trailblazer of the Muses. She is the mother of Orpheus (Mercury in Pisces), the tragic singer whose talent mesmerized the King and Queen of the Dead themselves. Her work is the tales of heroes and tricksters and adventure stories—the tales that thrill, expand the mind, and also inspire listeners to wonder: "Could I do that? Could I be a hero?" As such, Calliope's gift is courage, which is the first state of mind that a fifth-house Sun needs to cultivate. This is the house of risk-taking, and when a fifth-house Sun gives up and lives a small, narrow life of caution, it's a sad thing. One can't take part in that viral chain of inspiration if one fears social opprobrium too much to show off what one does, and yet at the same time those arrows of outside criticism (and, sometimes, jealousy) can hurt a great deal. Calliope speaks of the bravery it takes even to start the work, and much more so to hold it up to the window of the world. But like the Sun itself, if it doesn't shine, nothing will grow.

The second sister is Clio, the Muse of History. This is much more than dry texts recited in classrooms; her name comes from the word *kleio*, meaning *to make famous*. We don't often think about how historians shape culture by foregrounding one happening and downplaying or erasing another. Clio was the Muse closest to her Mother, Memory; she could grant immortality in writing or consign someone to oblivion. She follows courage-bestowing Calliope quite naturally, because she asks: *Now that you're down with putting it out there, can we think about what message it will send? How will it affect the future?* The fifth house is often very concerned with the Now, and Me, and Clio gives the Sun here an echo of the opposing eleventh house of Eventually, and All of Us. On top of that, it must be said that in every Sun in the Sun's house, no matter how modest they pretend to be or how insecure they actually are, there is a deep desire to be liked and admired, to *matter* in the eyes of others. Being remembered—being a part of someone's history—is deeply satisfying to them in way that a wouldn't occur to a sixth-house Sun, for example.

The third sister is Erato, the Muse of erotic writing, and here we touch on the fifth house's rulership of romance—not committed relationships, but the early stages, when your breath catches and your heart leaps and the love-drugs start going off in your brain. And, of course, when the body yearns to touch another body with erotic intent. Fifth-house Sun people are often at their most creative when they are engaged in a romantic period with a lover; partners often become Muses for them, whether directly by stimulating conversation or indirectly by lifting the mood. For some with this placement, the love-drugs wearing off means leaving and finding a new romance; older and wiser fifth-house Suns learn to hoard and use activities done with a partner which bring up an echo of that original feeling, so as to keep restimulating it with a long-term lover.

As with the other Muses, the feeling can also be brought out by erotic art, writing, music, film, etc. which then inspires the making of more of it. A fifth-house Sun can live single and celibate, but the flow of the erotic/romantic is so useful to their inspiration that most will dare the ocean of love even if it's filled with sharks. It's important, though, to see the partner as the three-dimensional human that they are, and not just treat them like an inspiration dispenser. Erato didn't just inspire happy, fluffy love stories. At least as many are complicated, difficult, even tragic, and the most inspiring can still go wrong if not handled well.

The fourth sister is Euterpe, the Muse of music. Her favorite instrument tended to be flutes, both single and double, and sometimes the lyre as well. Music is a tool of emotional inspiration par excellence, and although it is normally ruled by Venus (and especially Taurus), it is still a popular fifth-house channel. Euterpe's gift is not so much any one emotion, as music can deliver any number of those quite effectively, but of clearing the mind itself. Whatever it is that you are feeling, if you don't want to be feeling it, music can help clean it out, if only for a short time. I don't know how many people I know with mild or severe mood disorders who use music as their secondary or even primary mood-altering tool. Having the center of your identity in the house of Joy can mean that if you can't seem to find that joy, you may come to believe that there is something very wrong with you at your core. A simple case of the blues—or, even worse, actual depression—can take on an almost cosmic importance with this placement. Euterpe reminds this Sun placement that her gift is always there, and unless you're actively fighting against it, it generally always works. At the same time, the musicians (and music-purveyors) of this house often have a talent for finding the right piece to wrap around someone's head in order to clear it up.

The fifth sister is Melpomene, the Muse of tragedy, and the mother of the Sirens—mermaids who lured sailors to their deaths with plaintive songs. Her name actually means "to celebrate with song", because she was originally a goddess of funeral songs. Through tragedy, one celebrates the bittersweet nature of Life, and here we have to bring up again the issue of the fifth-house Sun losing their joy. One of the pitfalls documented about this Sun placement is that no matter how creative they are, no matter how many works they make, they can't stop thinking that they ought to be able to do more, or do it better, or in general shine brighter. When they come up against the limits of reality, it's disheartening. (Read that word again, and remember that Leo, the traditional ruler of this house, ruled by the Sun, rules the heart.) Melpomene's gift is to find beauty in sorrow, in tragedy, and to make something to share that raw loveliness with others who are also experiencing it. For the fifth-house Sun, the old saying is true: *Nothing entirely bad can happen to a writer. Everything is material.*

The sixth sister is Polyhymnia, the Muse of sacred poetry and eloquence. In modern times, she tends to be most noted for her inspiring of political speeches, but that's because many modern people think of sacred music as frozen in time, not something which is continually reinvented to praise and honor the Divine. The ancient polytheists understood that the Divine wants fresh new creations, not just the familiar but static old ones. Polyhymnia bestows that state one could call "open to Divine inspiration", where one is calm, clear, and ready to have the One Right Word come into your mind, the one which will turn the key and make the difference. If the fifth-house Sun is to keep from becoming shallow in their creativity, they need to cultivate this state.

The seventh sister is Terpsichore. Her name means "delighting in dance", and she is the Muse of dancing. She also ruled choral song, the sort of singing groups of people would dance to in ancient times. Part of creativity is being able to involve the body in some way. Even a passively absorbed art where one sits quietly and watches or listens should ideally have some resonance with the body—making the audience shiver, or laugh, or sit up straighter. The fifth-house Sun isn't as head-focused as a Mercury, but it can be less body-centric than is healthy (unless the individual is partaking of erotic activities), and Terpsichore's gift is to make you want to move. Dance isn't the only art that seizes the body, and this Sun placement needs to remember that freeing up the body can sometimes get past a block in the mind. That's especially important for a Sun placement where creative blocks can feel like being choked to death.

The eighth sister is Thalia, the Muse of comedy, which reminds us that this is the house of children. Some fifth-house Suns enjoy teaching children or adolescents, and they know instinctively that comedy (and even broad, crude slapstick) will get through to them quicker than almost any other approach. Other fifth-house Suns have very strong inner children, and want to be the kid-energy in the room. One of the archetypes of Leo—which traditionally rules this house—is the Clown, and the Moon and Jupiter here also produce comedians, but for different reasons. The fifth-house Moon does it primarily because things hurt, and it's a defense mechanism. The fifth-house Jupiter does it as an outgrowth of a "jovial" nature. The fifth-house

Sun does it because it's a way of getting the audience's attention which can work when the serious stuff falls flat. The Clown's point is to make them all smile, and that's the metric of success. Just as Melpomene gives the gift of finding beauty in misfortune, Thalia's gift is finding humor there. It's the job of the fifth-house Sun to send it on down the chain of inspiration for the next person in need.

Finally, the last sister is Urania, the Muse of astrology, who has a special place in this book. Originally, she ruled astronomy, but at the time the two were one discipline. As well as being the nod to the sciences—whose progress also depends, in its own way, on inspiration—she was the diviner who could tell the future. While Clio wants the inspired individual to affect the future, Urania wants us to see it—and creative thought is a classic method for that. (I've always thought she had a link to science fiction.) When one's core identity is bound up with keeping that creative flow going, it's only a step away from using that flow to express not only one's self in the Now, but one's self as it might be in the future ... which is one step away from giving expression to the Voice of the Universe.

6☉ Sun in the 6th House: The Handmaidens of Frigga

Just as all nine of the Muses stood forth for the fifth-house Sun, so the bevy of industrious ladies who serve the Norse goddess Frigga (Moon in Capricorn) all stood forth at once for this diligent Sun placement. The sixth is the house of Labor and Maintenance, all the hard work which we may not want to do but which does need to get done if we are to be healthy and productive. With the planet of Identity here, the person with this Sun placement really does tend to base their ideal of who they are one what kind of work they do ... and this isn't necessarily a bad thing. The important part is that they choose work to base it on which brings them joy and at which they can excel.

The sixth-house Sun person isn't afraid to work, whether that is doing your taxes or washing your dishes or changing the oil in your car. Note the "your" in that sentence—this is also the House of Service, and I've rarely met someone with this placement who wasn't a "helpful helper" in some way, taking pleasure and pride in making other people's lives easier and more comfortable. (One sixth-house Sun person I know is referred to by his loved ones as "the human multi-tool", and the running joke is that if you tell him to make himself at home in your house, he will fix your doorknob and stop your toilet from running.)

Frigga is the Queen of Asgard, the realm of the sky Gods in Norse/Germanic mythology, and she is a goddess of marriage, home, children, hospitality, and peacemaking. At the same time, women in Nordic countries did not just sit enthroned and carry about cups of mead all day. They had to do a great deal of labor in order to keep their land and family healthy and happy, as much as their husbands or brothers did. Therefore, Frigga gathered around her a group of goddesses who signified home industry and all the myriad duties of a woman. While it was generally said that she had twelve handmaidens, the list wasn't set in stone and sometimes various others were switched in and out, so I will compromise by naming thirteen of them. Each holds a particular facet of the experience of the sixth-house Sun, and an important rule for their survival.

First I'll start with the goddess Eir, whose name simply means "healer". She is the physician of Asgard, and as this is the house of Health, it is imperative that people with this placement have a good relationship with their physical body and can put together a routine for its care and maintenance. Eir speaks of prevention, that a little work on a regular basis can forestall major issues down the line. She has a healing well in her courtyard which is used to soothe her patients, and as the Sun in this Virgo-associated house often bestows sensitive nerves and an easily-irritated sensory system, it is important to take time for calming activities or even just rest.

Next in line is Fulla, Frigga's younger sister, whose name means "abundance". Her main job is assisting Frigga in whatever she needs, and also keeping her jewelry box and shoes in order. (The sixth-house Sun often makes an excellent assistant.) This would seem like a rather mundane task, except that the All-Mother's jewels and shoes have magical powers, and must be kept in a specific way. Sixth-house Suns like to organize things, whether they are good at it or not (and with practice they can become very good at it). However, these diligent individuals can sometimes overestimate their energy for Getting Things Done, and they need to define "abundance" in a somewhat more realistic manner lest they set themselves up for failure.

In a similar vein, we can look to the goddess Syn, Frigga's sacred door guard. Her name means "denial", in the sense of denying someone entrance.

Some sixth-house Sun people are so service-oriented that it becomes very difficult for them to say "No" to someone who honestly needs their help, even if they are exhausted or need to get to other work. They tend to be the ones who, when the support group moderator says, "Someone needs to stack up all the chairs," decide their name must be Someone and automatically volunteer to do it. Syn reminds them that they can't help the whole world, and they need to prioritize their own time and easily-frazzled nerves as well.

Gefjon is a large, capable giantess-goddess whose name means "giver" (again, another reference to service) and who bore four large sons out of wedlock. She was a farmer and plough-woman, and she asked the local lord for a piece of land to make her living on. He told her that she could have as much land as she could plow in a day. Gefjon then turned her four giant-sons into oxen and ploughed the then-peninsula of Zealand off the mainland, turning it into an island and claiming it. She shows the ingenuity and problem-solving ability of this Sun placement, who can quickly assess a problem and put together tools and skills for a solution. Gefjon is also the guardian of unmarried women, which gives a nod to people with this placement being more likely to put their work ahead of family and relationships.

On the other end of work motivation, the goddess Var is the Keeper of Oaths. Her name means "vow", and she is the Lady of Commitment. She can strengthen the commitments of people who have made promises which are hard to keep, and support them in their determination. Ancient people swore by her name when they made a contract, and she was expected to punish them if they discarded it without very good reason. The sixth-house Sun is usually very good at keeping their commitments, although they do tend to overcommit and drop things due to overwork.

Snotra, whose name means "courtesy", is the goddess of hospitality and social rules; it is her job to see that guests are made welcome. In practice, hospitality is more than making polite conversation; it is making sure that everyone has clean sheets and clean towels and a place to park where they won't be ticketed, not to mention enough to eat. Snotra notes the details in service which make people light up and feel cared for, and this can be a real sixth-house Sun talent. In a very real way, when it comes to service, Goddess is in the details, and this Sun placement knows that very well.

Saga is the goddess of history and storytelling, very literally the librarian of Asgard who keeps all the details of the "sagas" which are named for her. People with Suns in this Virgo-associated house love to keep written details about all sorts of intellectual subjects, and can be excellent researchers as well. Libraries are a happy place for them. (Often, so are spreadsheets.)

Gna, whose name may either come from "to soar over" or the onomatopoeic sound of a horse's neigh, is Frigga's messenger. She jumps on her horse and rides away to do the All-Mother's bidding … and let me just say that no one runs your errands as precisely as a sixth-house Sun. At the same time, Gna reminds us that it's important for this Sun placement to get out of their house and workplace periodically and travel somewhere, if only on a work trip. It's good to get a "change of wallpaper", and not feel guilty about the fact that the dishes may not be done when you get back.

Huldra, whose name means "herder", is a Goddess of flocks and herds, which is another job that involves hard work and keeping track of a lot of moving parts. She is a Goddess of hard labor, and strengthens the backs of those who must do it. She echoes the strength it takes to live one's life in the house of Work, keeping one's identity there are well. She gives patience and persistence to keep plugging on with it, no matter what happens.

The next Goddess is Vor, who is a sorceress and diviner. A lady of magic and divination may seem out of place in this very practical house, but sometimes it does seem like the sixth-house Sun works magic. They have a gift for figuring out what someone needs and doing it for them, sometimes even before the person themselves has figured it out. In terms of telling the future, they often worry about it a good deal, noting ways in which things can go wrong. This placement, with its focus on details, can get bogged down in the worry that nothing will go as perfectly as they want it to. Vor points out that one can't control the future, but only prepare for it … which is something this sometimes-apprehensive Sun placement does almost compulsively. They need to learn to relax—not easy for them—and to breathe and let the future be what it is, relying rather on the knowledge that they will be able to handle whatever comes along.

Hlin, whose name means "refuge", is both a Goddess of protection (rather like the way police say "Protect and Serve") and of release from mourning. People with this Sun position can be protective, but it's still a service—they do it not out of emotion, but out of duty. When it comes to helping others who are mourning, we tend to think of the person who says, "There, there," and lets people cry on their shoulder. We forget about the person who comes in with a casserole when there's a death in the family, and does their dishes so that they can grieve without having to worry about it. If we think about that at all, we tend to denigrate it in comparison to the more emotionally nurturing sort of grieving aid. And yet, when someone is grieving and doesn't have anyone to help them manage the everyday sixth-house matters, they can easily fall messily by the wayside. This kind of service may be quiet and often disregarded, but it is terribly missed when it doesn't come.

Finally, the last two goddesses are Lofn, whose name means "permission", and Sjofn, whose name means "affection". Lofn is the goddess of bringing together unlikely lovers, and Sjofn bestows love on a family. While work is sacred to this Sun placement, it is crucial to their mental health that they also take time—and give themselves permission—to indulge in affectionate time with those they love, and who love them. They can forget that their bodies and hearts can be soothed through loving contact, and that this can sustain them and give them energy for the next round of work and maintenance, which will start with the new morning.

It can be difficult for the loved ones of a sixth-house Sun to understand why they persist in basing who they are on how much they get accomplished, but telling them not to do it isn't really helpful. This is who they are—this is the center of their natal chart, and that needs to be appreciated. Their dedication to Duty, and the way they use it as a sign of love, may also confuse more emotional types. Isn't Duty cold and sterile? Not with the warmth of the Sun shining over it. Instead, the Sun's energy can light it up and make it truly a work of excellence ... in love, or whatever else they apply their assiduous souls to manifest.

7☉ Sun in the 7th House: Surya, Saranya, and Chhaya

The seventh house is traditionally called the House of Marriage, but it might as well be called the House of Committed Long-Term Relationships. It covers not only romantic commitments but also business partners (as long as there are only two) and its less friendly moniker is the House of Open Enemies. (This reminds us what happens sometimes when the House of Marriage files for a divorce.)

Not an official name, but one I have definitely observed, is the House of Projections. The first cusp of the seventh house is the Descendant, which always opposes the Ascendant, your personal outward projection. Besides just being an indicator of whose "outsides" you find attractive, the Descendant holds your understanding of the principle of "I-Thou"—that we are separate from, and yet in a balanced dance with, other people with whom we interact one-on-one at any time. Just as the first house displays your own mask and its accessories, so the seventh house is where you shove the qualities you'd prefer not to admit you have. How that works in the House of Partnerships is, of course, that you select partners who have those qualities and project them, letting them "carry" that energy for you. It can be fascinating, looking at your partner's seventh house (and any planets close to the Descendant) and see what you're "carrying" for them, what qualities you embody.

At least, that is, while the seventh-house person is still not very mature. Eventually they will have to own those planetary qualities in themselves and learn to use and appreciate them. Sometimes, when that happens, they lose interest in the partner who has been "carrying" those qualities for them. Sometimes it draws them even closer, comrades in a dance who can now be equals. Either way, it is a necessary process—no one can healthily outsource large pieces of themselves forever.

The Sun is the brightest point in the chart, the identity itself. What happens when the Sun lands in the house of projections? What can sometimes happen, at least in the beginning, is that the seventh-house Sun person desperately searches for a partner who will validate their identity, and perhaps even create it, telling them who they are. The partner may become the Sun around which they revolve, at least from a "remind me who and what I am" standpoint. The partner is the one who shines, and the seventh-house Sun person is the rock star's biggest fan.

In India, the Sun God is Surya, known as the Eye of the Universe, the Origin of All Life, and the symbol of spiritual emancipation. He is one of the oldest Vedic Gods still worshiped in India, perhaps *the* oldest surviving Vedic God. Certainly he has some of the oldest surviving hymns in that region, but then who can ignore the Sun? He is also the father of numerous other Gods, ones who came of age long after the Vedic system had been replaced. However, in this chapter we are going to look at one particular myth of Surya—that of his marriage with his wife Saranya. The issues of the seventh-house Sun are played out by different characters in the story, but the most poignant tale about Surya is a story of marriage.

Surya definitely starts out the story as the "beloved" of the seventh-house Sun, the shining solar force who is always extroverted, always "on stage"—the Sun rules Leo, the sign of performance. His wife Saranya (Cloud) was given to him in marriage by her father Vishwakarma, the architect of the Universe. To her, Surya must have been the bright Sun, the really important one, the one who got to shine. They had several children together—Manu, the future progenitor of humans; Yama the future God of the Dead (Pluto in the tenth house); Yamuna the river goddess. However, Surya had been made into the fiery Sun God in childhood in order to be able to literally burn up demons, and he was hard for Saranya to be around. He burned her eyes and scorched her skin, and after a time this constant burning made him far less attractive to her.

This is a general seventh-house problem—not only do partners carry the positive aspects of the projected planet, they carry the negative ones as well. Over time the solar "rock star" partner becomes the arrogant one, the egotist, the one who never lets anyone else shine. Saranya decided to deal with this in a unique way. As a cloud goddess, she was a mistress of illusions. She created a woman who looked exactly like her in every way, but was quiet and submissive, and named her Chhaya (pronounced *cha-hi-ya*) which means Shadow. She instructed her double to stay and take care of her children, and went back to her father's house.

Being a seventh-house Sun person in the unwitting grip of a solar-type partner can be stifling. It's not the partner's fault—all too often they have no idea what's going on in the mind of their beloved, and just keep going along naturally. But the seventh-house Sun individual can only be pulled along by their lover, and their lover's conception of who they are and who they should be, for so long before rebelling. The solar traits of their own chart press upward and want to be released. Sometimes the presence of the solar partner even exacerbates this—in a sense, the partner teaches them how to manifest those traits. If they don't want to rock the relationship—and for a seventh-house Sun, destroying their partnership can feel like death itself—they may construct a compliant, supportive persona whom they don when around their beloved. They are the Shadow when they are with them, and then lead a completely separate life where they can be themselves. The solar partner doesn't know that real intimacy has ceased, and they are interacting with a Shadow of their partner.

Surya actually didn't notice that Saranya wasn't there any more, at least not for several years. He had more children with Chhaya—a son named Mani, another river-daughter named Tapti, and Shani the planet Saturn. However, Chhaya was not able to keep her promise to Saranya and care for Saranya's children as if they were her own. She favored her own children and ignored or criticized Saranya's brood. This, too, can happen if the seventh-house Sun demands that their children live in the same illusory shadow as them, in order to please their other parent ... and some of the children are willing to go along with it, and some are not able to do so.

Yama, the future God of the Dead, was an aggressive child and constantly got into arguments with Chhaya. Once he became so angry with her neglect and disrespect that he threatened to kick her, and she cursed his foot to fall off. He went to his father in angry tears and asked him to intervene; Surya could not entirely stop the curse, but limited it to a little flesh from Yama's foot falling off and burrowing into the ground to the Underworld as an offering. Then Surya confronted Chhaya about her mistreatment of the older children, and during their argument he realized that she was not actually Saranya. Furious, he demanded to know where his wife was, and Chhaya threw herself at his feet and begged for mercy, weeping that she had no idea where Saranya had gone. Sooner or later, these illusions will come out; either the seventh-house Sun person will get tired and leave, or the solar partner will break up with them, or as a best-case scenario they will figure out that this is not a real relationship with true intimacy, and will try to do something about that.

Meanwhile, Saranya had gone home to her father's house, but did not stay there long as Vishwakarma kept nagging her to go back to her husband. (Family members and friends may, from the outside, see the seventh-house Sun's marriage as perfect, and subtly or openly encourage them to be the Shadow rather than themselves. "You don't know how lucky you are!" is often heard.) Finally Saranya fled to the wild meadows and turned herself into a horse. The horse is a very solar symbol—many Sun deities ride in chariots pulled by horses; Surya's chariot is pulled by seven of them, one for every day of the week. With this, Saranya is owning her wild solar self, finally.

Vishwakarma did not know where his wayward daughter had gone, but he suspected that he knew what the problem was. He told Surya what Saranya had feared to say—that his brilliance was driving his wife away. Surya wasn't unaware that people turned their heads and looked away from him, but he had hoped Saranya would be different. Seeing his sorrow, Vishwakarma offered to fix the problem—to stretch him out on a lathe and cut off most of his burning rays, so that Saranya could bear to be near him. Surya agreed, hesitantly, but all the Gods came and cheered the plan. It would change the shape of the Universe, but it would allow the Sun to be closer to people and the Gods. Surya took a deep breath and allowed himself to be stretched on the lathe, and Vishwakarma cut away five in six parts of his brilliance. With what was removed, he made many divine tools—Vishnu's divine discus, Shiva's trident, Kartikkeya's spear, and (eventually) Yama's staff. After this was done, Surya tracked down his wandering wife. Seeing her running in the fields, he turned himself into a stallion and approached her—*I am willing to be where you are, to meet you on your terms*—and they had a fine reunion. From this, twins were born—the healing Ashwinis, the future physicians to the Gods. From reunion with willingness to see each other as they really were, there came healing.

When they took human form again, Saranya was thrilled to see that her husband had cut down enough of his flaming rays that she could actually look upon him. The seventh-house Sun person needs to be able to see past the idealization or demonization of their partner to the flawed but hopefully lovable human being they are underneath. However, this requires the partner to be open and honest about those flaws, acknowledging them and not trying to hide them under a façade of distracting glitter. As with all matters of the seventh house, this must be a dual effort. Yes, this does mean that the seventh-house Sun person can only go so far in healing these problems on their own ... and that's part of the lesson. Choosing the right partner is excruciatingly important for them, and they may go through a few glittery mistakes before they find the one who is willing to fully see them and help them to actualize their own self without trying to define it for them.

Surya did not abandon Chhaya, though. He took both consorts—Cloud and Shadow—and treated them both well, demanding full honesty from both of them. This can be seen as a way of the partner saying, "I love it when you shape yourself to be someone I want, and I also love who you are when you are living only for yourself. I see both and appreciate both, and you get to choose which you will be, so long as you are honest with me and yourself about it." That's the message the seventh-house Sun really needs to hear, and they should not settle for anything less.

8☉ Sun in the 8th House: Selket

When you died in ancient Egypt, one of four beautiful winged goddesses would come for you and escort you to the realm of Death, where your heart would be weighed and judged. They were Isis (Moon in Libra), Nephthys (Pluto in the sixth house), Neith (Mars in the eighth house), and Selket (also possibly pronounced *Serket*). Which one of them came for you would depend on who you are and what you had done in your life. Egyptian society was not egalitarian; there were great differences of class and wealth among the population. It was Isis's job to usher royalty and their attendant nobles to the other side. Nephthys took the souls of the good working men and women who labored to sustain everyone. Neith took the souls of honorable warriors dead in battle or of their wounds. Then there was Selket, the scorpion-goddess, whose job was dealing with everyone else.

If you were a scoundrel, a rogue, a villain, you were her job. If you were a beggar, a thief, a member of the poverty-stricken underclass who made their living through questionable means, you were hers. She accepted the darkest souls with compassion and equanimity, and if they were obstreperous, well, she was also a stinging creature who could keep them in line. A couple of the very early pharaohs, before the joining of Upper and Lower Egypt, took her as a patron and named themselves after the scorpion that is her symbol.

The eighth is the House of Death, and that includes suffering, loss, darkness, and rebirth—the whole difficult gamut of dealing with endings. Before plants can grow, life needs to die and rot into the soil (which is one reason why Gods of the Underworld are often associated with wealth, even more than underground metals for mining—they gave the riches which nourished life). It's also the House of Mystery, because while there's a lot we can see about that process from a natural, physical standpoint, there is always the mysterious question of where the soul goes after it leaves the body, and what happens then.

The Sun, on the other hand, is supposed to be the giver of life, and it is the energizing life center in a chart. What does it mean to have the life-center in the House of Death? The first image that comes into my mind is when the Sun is actually a giver of Death, not Life … and anyone who has been in the Sahara desert understands what this means. The Sun beats down on the soilless ground and kills everything.

Well, no, almost everything. Some very tough forms of Life remain in the realm of Sun-Death. The scorpion is one of them. It needs to be fierce, because it's a rough time out there on the burnt sands. People with this placement have a strong survival instinct and a lot of willpower. They know that there is suffering in the world, and on some level they understand that it may be their lot to face more of it than other people. Regardless of the sign, this house placement toughens people up, or it washes them out and they don't survive.

If for some reason they come up against suffering they can't get through, the Sun's next step is to illuminate it, to get the message out to other people so that maybe something useful can come of it. This Sun placement often creates whistle-blowers, people who are not afraid to speak up about what they see, and call the attention of others to it. They are not frightened by having the spotlight shone on them with unpleasant intent, any more than the scorpion is terrified by the deadly desert Sun. Sure, it's better to hide under a rock, but when you have to come out and face the light, you come out and do what is necessary. Besides, the eighth is also the House of Transformation, and how do you transform anything if it can't be revealed?

Eighth-house Sun people aren't afraid of talking about the darkness because they aren't afraid of walking into it in the first place. Humanity shoves a lot of Life into the collective basement and stops talking about it. Things which frighten us, things which disgust us, things which make us vaguely uncomfortable in ways we'd rather not look at—these all go into our personal dark, dank basements, and into the collective basement of society's unconscious. Once down there, they may fuse to each other, and continue to rot. The eighth-house Sun tears the roof off and sheds light on them, examining them with a calm, interested attitude—like Selket collecting the souls of her scoundrels and rogues and thieves. Rather than judging and rejecting, this Sun placement has the urges of a detective and wants to know *why*. Why does this work the way it does? What does that mean? And, most importantly—if we knew enough about it, could we change it? The thought process always comes back, sooner or later, to transformation.

Exposing the hidden darknesses is part of the deal, and one of those hidden darknesses is power. This Sun placement struggles with the concept of power—when is it healthy or unhealthy to wield it? What recourse do you have when it is used against you? Is the power to harm and the power to heal merely two sides of the same coin? Two of Selket's titles were "She who tightens the throat" and "She who causes the throat to breathe". She was both the one who inflicted poison with her scorpion's sting, and the one who protected others from death by poison. In a desert country inhabited by multiple poisonous species, she was the one who could reverse death by Nature's misadventure. Said to have protected the infant Horus from poisonous creatures, she was invoked for the same protection, especially for pregnant women and children. This kind of example of the two sides of power will be fascinating to the eighth-house Sun, and sooner or later they will find themselves staring into its dark hole with a flashlight, trying to learn everything they can.

This is also the house of other people's money, and it's usually assumed that this financial aspect of the house is related to Death and inheritances, but if we look at the fact that this is also the house of power—over one's self and others—the point of "other people's money" becomes clear. The power to give others money and withhold it is very potent indeed, and the eighth-house Sun tends to be extremely aware of its influence, especially when they are in debt to others, or others are in debt to them. This may prompt explorations into ways to transform the situation, if only for themselves, such as working (not playing, not with this house) the stock market or investments. Other people's money and resources can be a hand around one's windpipe or it can release choking poverty, if the arcane art to managing it is learned. Money can be either a venom or an antidote.

Selket was associated with the art of embalming, which involves opening, studying, and altering a dead body. Her title "Lady of the Beautiful Tent" refers to the embalmer's tent, which was outside because they needed good ventilation for dealing with the various fluids used for preservation. These were compared to Selket's venom, which in various amounts can preserve or break down tissue. As one of the four guardians of the canopic jars—used to hold the internal organs of mummies—Selket, along with one of the four sons of Horus, was in charge of the guts. This is where everything is digested and then let go, and the eighth house—traditionally ruled by Scorpio—also rules the colon and rectum and the physical act of letting go, so that one's waste can go into the earth and nourish it again. Here we are back to letting go again, to transformation.

The eighth house also dealt with the reproductive organs and sex, in our culture almost as dark and dangerous and mysterious a place as death. Here, however, it is not about the kind of fun sex for pleasure associated with the fifth house—it is the sex that gets into people's heads and connects them to each other and to the universal forces. It's sex where every orgasm is understood as a "little death", and the overall act links you into Life, regardless of whether or not it is used for procreation. That urge to get inside other people also leads the eighth-house Sun individual to the study of psychology. Again, it comes back to power—sexual power, the power of knowledge which helps you to understand the minds of others, and your own. This path often leads down the road to self-awareness and learning to control one's self and one's desires. The ultimate form of power, the eighth house current tells us, is not power over others but power over yourself.

While Selket had no temples, she had a fair number of priests, all of whom were doctors and/or magicians. Medicine in ancient Egypt was heavily laced with magic, and both were pits of darkness where practitioners tried hard to shine a light. Eighth-house Sun people may be drawn to medical research—the still-hidden elements of the practice—or the practice of magic itself, which still retains much of its mystery. As a mistress of death and rebirth, Selket gave magical and medicinal advice for protecting the people.

What is the definition of poison, and is it entirely an evil thing? Such an eighth-house question. The concept of "poison" expands beyond physical venomous substances—many of which, of course, have been made into useful medicines—and moves into anything which may cause unwellness in a system. Selket tells us that what can kill can cure, and that the best way to handle any kind of poison is to apply yourself to transmuting it into its other side, which heals the problem. It's the eighth-house alchemy, moving anything from life to death and from death to life, from night to day, from shadowed to illuminated. All you need is a sharp pair of eyes and the willingness to stare the mysteries in the face.

9☉ Sun in the 9th House: Jason

The ninth house was originally called the House of Long Journeys Over Water, highlighting its association with long-distance travel (as opposed to the third house, which rules short trips around one's local area). Of course, these days, what "long-distance" means may be very different from the experiences of ancient peoples; they didn't even know some parts of the globe existed, but we can get there in a matter of hours if we have the money. So today, the less physical aspects of this house are more emphasized—religion, the reading of philosophy, higher education. Certainly some planetary manifestations of this house may lean much more towards these quieter aspects, but that's missing the point. What these all have in common is expansion of the mind and the worldview. This urge, more than anything else, is present in someone with the Sun in the house of travel—the quest to see the next shore, just because it exists and you haven't seen it yet. Whether it is done with a boat or a plane or a pile of books is irrelevant.

Unlike Odysseus (Mercury in the ninth house) who is a shrewd and crafty Mercurial character caught up in the journey he did not choose and must squeeze his way out of, Jason willingly chose his quest. He is a solar hero—honest, straightforward, and an enthusiastic leader of men. Born into a family dispute, his uncle deposed his father and killed all the nieces and nephews, ordering that no more of those children would be born. Alcimede, the former queen, was pregnant and gives birth to her last son Jason in secret, sending him away to be raised by the wise centaur Chiron (Saturn in Sagittarius). The centaur teacher—a very appropriate starting "extra" in this house associated with Sagittarius—teaches Jason the arts and sciences of the world, and raises him to love the idea of the quest to new and strange places. To paraphrase a famous television quote, the whole point of this Sun placement is, indeed, to boldly go where no man has gone before. (Or at least where one hasn't personally gone—somehow, whenever one turns up new territory, one finds people who already live there, and this too is one of the happier lessons of this placement.)

Meanwhile, Jason's usurping uncle Pelias has been given a prophecy: that he must beware of the man with only one sandal. When Jason is of age to actually fight some battles, he travels to the court of Pelias to demand his birthright. On the way there, he meets an old woman struggling to cross a stream, and offers to help her across. The old woman is Hera (Jupiter in Libra), who has chosen Jason as one of her favorite potential heroes, and on the way across the stream with her, she makes sure that he loses one sandal. So it is that he turns up at Pelias's court bedraggled and half-barefoot, informing his uncle that he is the rightful heir and the throne is his. (The ninth-house Sun is often more interested in the long-term goal than short-term diplomacy, unless other Sun qualities or aspects say differently.)

Pelias assesses Jason in an instant as a would-be adventurer, and knows immediately how to get rid of him. He tells Jason that in order to prove his worthiness for the throne, he must go on a valiant quest to bring back the Golden Fleece of Colchis to his city of Iolcus. Undaunted, Jason agrees and prepares to put together a contingent of heroes for the journey. In fact, his readiness to go on the trip subtly hints at the fact that he would be happier on a wild quest than sitting around in a throne room; he is a leader of adventurers, not a bureaucrat. This, too, is a ninth-house-Sun problem. With their mental gifts and courage, they are often thrust into leadership roles, only to abandon them when they become too boring and limiting. The explorer may lead a small band of experts through the jungle—of academia, of research, of religious fervor—but they become bored and jittery when too much responsibility presses in on them.

This Sun placement also grants the ability to assemble a large amount of knowledge into a reasonably organized work, and the assembly of the Argonauts shows a remarkable ability to plan the different kinds of skill which would be needed on the quest's team. The team included such major lights as Hercules (Neptune in Aries), Orpheus (Mercury in Pisces), Castor and Pollux (Sun in Gemini), Atalanta (Venus in the ninth house), and many others. The ship itself was built by Argus, the best shipbuilder in the area, and named after him. Jason didn't just throw himself onto the nearest boat and run toward the goal; he researched and planned the trip. This sets him apart from many other heroes who are either thrust into a situation they did not choose or expect, or leap heedlessly into the adventure. In fact, people with this placement are very good at trip planning; more to the point, they are also good at "selling the trip". Their knowledge and enthusiasm convinces others to buy that tour to Africa or learn to love that course of study or start to believe in that religious idea. They make the best tour guides, regardless of what area of mind expansion they are showing to the gaping tourists.

The story of the Argonauts itself is simply a Greek soap opera, moving from one exciting adventure to the next one. It is full of mistakes, victories, people who are kind for no reason and people who are cruel for no reason. The real turning point comes when the Argonauts arrive in Colchis to get the fleece, and Jason is given three apparently impossible tasks in order to win it from Aeetes the King. However, Aeetes's daughter Medea falls in love with him and helps him to find solutions to the problems.

These three tasks can be seen as symbols of three of the four greatest challenges for the ninth-house Sun. The first task was to yoke together a pair of fire-breathing oxen and plough a field with them. This reminds us of the ninth-house Sun's overenthusiasm—there are so many places to see and things to do in the world that they often get too caught up in the adventure to actually pay attention to the life they are living. As soon as they get to one place and have scoured it for its share of mind-expansion, they are planning for the next trip, the next achievement, the next degree, the next spiritual exploration. Medea gave Jason an ointment which made him temporarily invulnerable to fire and steel, made from a red flower which grew from the blood of Prometheus (Saturn in Aquarius). With this, Jason was able to grab the oxen and control them without getting burned, which can be seen as learning to be invulnerable, if necessary, to the siren call of the next adventure when what you really need is to slow down for a moment.

Jason plowed the field and sprinkled the helmet-full of seed given to him by Aeetes, which turned out to be dragon's teeth. When sowed in the earth, they became terrible skeletal warriors who sprang up fully armed from the earth and attacked Jason. Fortunately, Medea's potion protected him, and he was able to start hacking and fell them all without being harmed. The skeleton warriors come from the earth, which in astrology is the element of the solid practical world with all its needs and obstacles. One can see the warriors as all those distracting pragmatic details which the big-picture ninth-house Sun would rather not have to deal with at all. Did we pack enough toilet paper for the trip? Did anyone remember the sunscreen? What is the deadline for this paper to be done? Can we really get a hundred people to carry candles in and out of the church without setting each other's hair on fire? To the ninth-house Sun, these are mere irritations and can be ignored … until enough of them have become problems to rise up and swamp the situation. Each must be dealt with, fully encountered and properly put to bed, or they will continue to sabotage the quest.

The third task was to fight the dragon who was the sleepless guardian of the Golden Fleece. Jason attempted to get by it, to no avail. He tried to kill it, but the dragon's hide was too hard. Finally he made a wrong move and the dragon pounced on him and swallowed him in one gulp. Medea frantically tried all the spells she knew, and managed to put the dragon to sleep. Once it slept, Jason was able to ooze out of its mouth and grab the Fleece. This dragon is the worst obstacle of all, because it is so hard for the ninth-house Sun to see that it's actually a problem. It is the dragon of fanaticism. What this placement is really seeking for, at bottom, is Truth. The problem is that Truth is scattered in many places, and some of its pieces look like the opposite of others. It is very easy, in this house of religion which can encourage someone to make a religion out of anything, to assume that you have found the one great Truth, and everything else is a lie. Fanaticism, and the cherished hope that the real truth has finally been found once and for all, can devour the ninth-house Sun person entirely if they are not careful. The answer is to put the dragon to sleep, to deliberately choose to suspend one's belief and drag oneself out of the emotion, forcing oneself to see the competing truths of others as just as valid to those who hold them as yours are to you.

However, it is the final lesson which Jason fails, and it has nothing to do with reaching the goal. Jason, the Argonauts, and Medea with them all flee Colchis with the Golden Fleece, pursued by Medea's brother with the Colchian army, and a storm sent by Zeus (Jupiter in Aries) to punish them for theft. They are blown off course and have more adventures getting home, including a stop at the island of Circe (Pluto in the seventh house), Medea's aunt, to be ritually cleansed of the sin of their theft.

Coming home, the Fleece is presented to Pelias, but he has no intention of giving up his throne. Medea schemes to get the prince killed, and manages to pull it off by tricking his daughters into cutting up their father and cooking him, in the hopes that it would magically bring back his youth. Pelias's son is horrified and exiles both Jason and Medea, and they settle in nearby Corinth. After some years and a couple of children, Jason decides that he wants a new romantic adventure and begins to woo a local princess. When Medea remonstrates with him and reminds him what he owes her, he bluntly says (because bluntness is common for this Sun in the Sagittarian house) that it isn't her he owes, but Aphrodite (Venus in Libra) who made her fall in love with him.

This is the last and most important lesson for this Sun placement. It is one thing to treat one's career, one's research, one's recreation, even one's religion as an adventure where one pursues the goal, achieves it, and then moves on to the next one ... but it is an entirely different thing to treat one's relationships that way. Human beings can often be much more difficult to abandon cleanly and still move on with your head and heart and life intact. Medea, of course, is a special case, but she does not deserve to be thrown aside after she has effectively given up her life for Jason. She goes into a whirlwind of revenge, murders their two children, and flies away. Jason goes weeping to the shore where the wreck of the Argo—the wreck of his hopes— still stands, and is killed by a falling timber.

Love can be an adventure, but unlike Venus in this house, the Sun can become too ego-driven, too focused on their goal and unable to see the pain of the people around them ... until it comes at them with the force of a Fury. The best preventative is to treat one's loved ones not as a means to the goal ahead, but as a special study all their own. Learning them inside and out, and fully understanding their thoughts and needs and unique flaws, can reframe them as winds to be skillfully sailed with rather than the hapless boat steered to a shore it did not plan for. The art of making a commitment and finding the adventure in that long-term story can keep this Sun placement from leaving loved ones behind in the race for the far horizon. Because in the end, when you reach the furthest shore, it's a sad and sorry goal if there is no one left to see it with you.

10☉ Sun in the 10th House: Rama

In Hindu mythology, the great god Vishnu (Neptune in the first house) takes on multiple mortal forms throughout his lifetime, in order to understand what it is to live in the world in a living-and-dying body. The first six of his incarnations were animals, but the seventh was his first mortal form—a prince of the kingdom of Kosala, named Rama. Hindu Vishnu-followers who particularly love him in the Rama incarnation consider this to be a name and form just as divine as Vishnu in his primal God-manifestation, an avatar as powerful as Jesus is to Christians. His story is told in the *Ramayana*, one of the major ancient sacred texts of India, but the final ending we will explore here comes from other Sanskrit stories, written in later. The origin of his name is argued by scholars; but some draw it from a term meaning "dark" and some from a term meaning "charming". While Sanskrit etymology is always messy and complicated due to historical length and fanciful record-keeping, this duality still has reverberations in the background of the tale.

However, all deification aside, this chapter will focus on the humanity—and human errors—of Prince Rama, who was a god living in mortal form with mortal short-sightedness. His is the story of the Sun—bright, powerful, and the center of all decisions—in the tenth house of public reputation, and the gifts and price that it brings. To place the Sun—the very core of the personality—into the tenth house is to wrap that core up with ambition, responsibility, and a focus on career over other parts of life.

Tenth-house Sun people are drawn to leadership, and this incarnation of Vishnu—unlike his later incarnation of Krishna (Venus in Sagittarius) where he comes into the world as a poor cowherd—is a prince of noble blood, expected to rule and to uphold the laws and tenets of his society, right or wrong. The culture of India at this time was rigid, repressive, caste-bound, and sexist; it was also unstable and fluctuating, filled with constant internecine wars between rival ruling houses. One slip—such as challenging the social rules—could cast down a ruler, and someone more conservative would step over his dead body and take his place. Being publicly correct, in this culture, was of great importance. This may be echoed in the life of a tenth-house Sun individual, who may instinctively sum up the best way to "get ahead" in life, and end up forced onto a track laid out for them by social expectations rather than their own innate preferences.

According to the various tales about his early life, Rama grows up as a reserved, polite, self-controlled youth who has learned not to show his feelings. This is not unusual for a tenth-house Sun story; the tenth is not exactly a house which is comfortable with emotions, and planets here would rather act toward the long-term goal than get bogged down in feeling anything which might get in the way.

At some point Rama wins the hand of Sita, daughter of a neighboring king, who is supposedly Vishnu's wife Lakshmi in disguise (and whom we will meet in the chapter on Moon in the Tenth House). He shows himself to be a model prince from a public-behavior point of view, and his stepmother realizes that she will have to do something if she wants her own children to have the spotlight. She convinces his father to exile him for fourteen years to the forest. Sita follows him into exile, and Rama spends his time protecting the forest hermits from wandering demons. The tenth-house Sun individual is not afraid of responsibility, and even when placed in a less-than-optimal situation, will generally step up to take care of perceived problems in a matter-of-fact way. They will do what needs to be done in the present, although their eyes are always on the goal ahead. However, they do prefer to be the one giving rather than taking orders, and will bide their time with gritted teeth until they can be in a place of power. Even in exile, Rama gathers competent subordinates around him and attacks problems with a hand-picked team.

Rama kills so many demons that he draws the attention of Ravana the demon king, who comes to face him down. Ravana sees the pretty Sita and becomes attracted to her, and carries her off instead of staying to fight Rama. Jumping into action, the exiled prince (along with his younger brother Lakshmana) makes a deal with the monkeys and bears of the forest to raise an army and march against Ravana, which results in a long war. At the end, Rama rescues Sita, who has resisted Ravana's advances the entire time she has been held captive. Action and strategy have won the day, and the goal is achieved! It's the tenth-house Sun's perfect ending ... except that the story has really only just begun.

After Sita is rescued, Rama grimly informs her that while he rescued her out of a sense of duty—the demons could not be allowed to get away with their kidnapping—he does not believe that she has actually been able to resist Ravana's advances, and thinks she has been unfaithful to him. More importantly, he fears that the rest of the kingdom will believe that she has been unfaithful to him, and his ability to come back to his father's city and claim his rightful place will be impaired by her standing as a "ruined" woman. This is Rama's first big stumbling block; his reputation as a perfect prince must not be stained, even if Sita had no choice in the matter.

Sita protests, and agrees to walk through a fire in order to prove her innocence—an ordeal known as the "test of Agni". As she walks through the blaze, the fire turns to flowers, showing that she speaks the truth. (In some versions, Agni the Fire God (Jupiter in Sagittarius) actually appears and validates her honesty and chastity.) Rama decides that this ought to be enough proof for the onlookers, and accepts her back. At the end of his exile, they return to his father's city and he is installed as a ruler. It is said that he excelled in the performance of his position and was always correct in his judgments, which is what a tenth-house Sun would think of as the best compliment ever.

However, while that is where the older parts of the Ramayana end, the story itself goes on in a final manuscript called the *Uttara Kanda*, or "epilogue story", and here it becomes much darker and uglier. When this book was added (possibly as late as the fifth century), Hindu culture and politics had changed from the era of the middle stories, becoming even more rigid and caste-based, and Rama the "perfect ruler" had to be seen to be more than a hero and a ruler with decent judgment. He had to be seen as someone who would be willing to do acts that might be considered cruel or unethical, and justify them with the end-goal of preserving his place at the top of this society. This, too, is a problem that the tenth-house Sun must often face—if your goal is to get to the top of the heap, what do you do when you get there and realize that the heap is rotten? If you won the game with your ability to be strong and decisive, what happens when you must cross the line into cruelty or lose it all? Sooner or later the driven tenth-house chase to the top comes to that threshold, and a choice must be made.

Fear of failure is a driving force with this Sun placement; they feel that they must succeed no matter what they have to sacrifice along the way—their partner, their friends, their compassion, their ethics, their own heart. Sometimes this comes from parental pressure to prove their worth—Rama was raised as a prince with strict expectations for his correct behavior. Some tenth-house Sun individuals actually grow up in situations where the parent made bad choices while acting from their emotions and undid their chances of achieving their ambition. This can offer subtle proof to them that the heart should be kept out of all career (and perhaps life) decisions; we see that Rama's father exiled his son for fourteen years in order to keep the peace with a vengeful wife, which may have hardened the rejected prince's resolve to keep all relationships strictly in line, never deciding with anything as unreliable or illogical as emotions. Since this Sun placement cannot conceive of not throwing all one's resources towards bettering one's lot, hard choices sometimes have to be made. After all, this house is traditionally associated with Capricorn and Saturn, neither of which are particularly comfortable with foregrounding their affairs of the heart, but both of whom are quite familiar with the long, slow slog up the mountain.

First, Rama must decide the case of a hermit named Shambuka who has been doing ascetic practices in the forest, and whom the people are beginning to treat with spiritual respect as if he were a Brahmin. The Brahmins of the kingdom feel threatened by this low-class individual, and petition Rama to execute him, which he does. This part was written in to cement rigid birth-class rules, without which Rama would not have his high-ranking Kshatriya (warrior-class) position. Political editing aside, one of the decisions of being in charge is whether to consolidate your position by creating convenient rules to prevent being deposed, or to allow for fate and the free will of others. Here Rama takes a step backwards into his fear of failure, of losing what he has gained. Second, his brother Lakshmana, who has been both loyal and invaluable to him during his war with the demons, is placed by Rama into a convoluted predicament where he must either kill himself or possibly see the whole kingdom cursed. Instead of doing anything to untangle the situation, Rama puts the potential welfare of the kingdom ahead of his brother's life, and sacrifices Lakshmana.

His third mistake, however, is his worst. Rumors fly about Sita and her fidelity, even after the test of Agni, and Rama decides to reverse his earlier decision and exile his wife. Even though he knows she is innocent, he feels that she is a political liability and thus she is sent to the forest. It must be said that this Sun placement is notorious for finding partners unworthy, even when they've walked through fire to prove their honor and their commitment to supporting their ambitious partner's career goals. Like Calpurnia, Caesar's wife, they may be expected to be "beyond reproach", and have little room for human error. It will be crucial to learn patience on this front, or the tenth-house Sun individual will just keep replacing and discarding partners, looking for the impossibly perfect one of whom no one might ever say anything less than praiseworthy

In the forest, living in the hermitage of the sage Valmiki, Sita gives birth to twin sons who are named Kusha and Lava. She raises her sons alone until they reach the age of twelve, when they are discovered by Rama's subordinates, largely because Sita has taught the boys to sing Rama's praises.

Their father is pleased with his sons and takes them back to live with him. Sita, completely abandoned at this point, asks the Earth to swallow her up and it does so.

Some versions of the story end there, leaving Rama alone on his throne with his sons, but other versions—rebuttals to the *Uttara Kanda* rebuttal—have Rama realizing how poorly he has treated Sita and falling into great grief, after which he drowns himself. After his suicide, he becomes Vishnu again and remembers himself, and is reunited with Sita/Lakshmi. Rather than trying to decide which is the "right" ending, let's step away from "correct" for the moment and notice that this dual ending lays out the tenth-house choice. Which is more important, the love of the public or the love of the personal partner? When you realize that you have erred badly, is it better to go on pretending nothing is wrong—perhaps because there are responsibilities you're stuck with—or to drown in all the emotions and realizations you've put aside for all these years? And then there's the hardest question of all—has the process of being able to shine, Sun-like, in your career actually forced you to don a mask which is not your own ... and what are you going to do about that?

Unless there are major planetary afflictions, the Sun in this house is likely going to forge ahead to fame, fortune, and success in the world; this is especially true if it is also conjunct the Midheaven. (And if there are afflictions, it will be very difficult for them not to feel guilty about not achieving something large and impressive.) Like Rama, they are born to make it to high places. That's not their big challenge. The issue is getting to the goal without compromising one's heart, soul, and ethical understanding. This is a far more important and more honorable quest to take on than any big desk and CEO's chair in the world.

11☉ Sun in the 11th House: Mithras

There are very few Gods who specialize in friendship. (I ought to know, I'm writing this book and the eleventh house has consistently been the hardest to fill.) The sacred nature of the eleventh house starts with the simple concept of the best friend—the one person in the world who talks to you, skips rocks in a pond with you, or whatever it is that feeds both your souls. While one can make friends within a family, the eleventh house's magic is more about the stranger which one makes chosen family with no blood ties. Then the next step is to have a group of friends who are one's chosen family, and who may indeed be closer to your heart than the human beings you were forced onto at birth. After this, it is one's relationship with the group, the tribe, the community, but especially the interest group where one knows one belongs as securely as one's own kin and perhaps more so. Then the next step beyond that is universal brotherhood—being able to see all humankind as brothers and sisters, as friends whom you simply have not yet met. The light of friendship travels outward to encompass the world.

This area of life is so important astrologically that one-twelfth of the human experience is wholly dedicated to it, according to the cosmic clock ... and yet Gods who focus on this part of the human experience are few and far between. Some may have started out as deities of friendship for all we know, but were soon distracted by other pursuits and routed into other jobs.

One who kept his orientation as a God of friendship and camaraderie was Mithras, even as his odd and shifting history reworked his character over and over. No matter who adopted him, he never lost that appellation. There is a great deal of argument over the history of Mithras which I don't wish to get into, so I will merely sketch the major theory and leave it at that. Mithra, whose name meant "contract" or "oath", was a native Persian deity thousands of years ago who was later absorbed into Zoroastrianism when it spread across that land. As far as we can tell, he was originally a deity of justice who was called upon to witness oaths, but even then friendship and brotherhood came into his titles. He was not a Sun God per se, but was associated with the sunrise and the morning light. When Zoroastrianism reorganized all the original Indo-Iranian Gods and categorized them into the good/evil camp, Mithra became the solar assistant and judge of Ahura Mazda, the God of Light (Saturn in Leo). He was the deity who protected the righteous dead souls from being dragged down to the punishment-world by demons. He was called "The Mediator", because he could mediate between Ahura Mazda and his enemy Ahriman. At the same time, he was also considered a God of Loyalty.

It is important to point out here that many of these attributes, while not listed as friendship per se, are certainly foundational values which make true, enduring friendship possible. Oath-taking is about keeping your word, and deeper than that, it's about trust. Without trust, you can never have anything more than a shallow bond at best, so showing oneself as a trustworthy person is one step on the path for this Sun. Being a mediator means being able to see both sides, also necessary if any peace is to be kept between friends. Loyalty is what makes friendship endure through difficulties; indeed, the balance between loyalty and mediation is a dance which must be constantly adjusted, but without which friendship will fall apart. It's the crux of the question "Do I abandon my friend when he is thinking or acting wrongly, or do I hold on, even if only to be an example of right?" This lesson will be learned by the eleventh-house Sun early and often, because as soon as they can toddle over to another toddler, they will want to make friends.

Nearly as powerful and apparently more popular than Ahura Mazda himself, Mithra then traveled to Babylonia and became established there. The Babylonians added a strong astrological foundation to the Mithra story, claiming that he made the Zodiac go around and could move the heavens. Eventually the story grew of him beheading a sacred bull and bathing in its blood, a concept unknown to the Persians. The Babylonians were excellent astrologers for their era, and they noted the precession of the equinoxes, when the Age of Taurus/Scorpio became the Age of Aries/Libra—the warrior and the law-giver, both of which are Mithraic attributes. Mithras killed Taurus the Bull in the sky, heralded the moving of one age to another, and became identified with the constellation the Greeks called Perseus, standing above the Bull. The Babylonians were the first to call him by the title which was later translated to *Sol Invictus*, the Unconquered Sun. (I feel that there is something appropriate about the Sun deity in the house associated with Aquarius becoming the one who moves the heavens astrologically.)

Mithra's worship traveled eastward to India where the God of friendship and morning light became Mitra, and was combined with the Vedic deity Varuna and the Vedic Sun God Surya (Sun in the seventh house). Unlike other cultures, India decided that Mitra was a complete pacifist, because no friendship could be sustained during fighting. Unfortunately, all mention of Mitra ends with the Vedic period, although anyone doing a yoga Sun Salutation will be saying *Om Maitreya Surya*, which is the last vestige of Mitra's name.

Nearly a thousand years later, the worship of Mithras grew up in Rome as an import from the reaches of the bustling empire. The Roman Mithras had his own specific characteristics and uniquely Roman flavor. He was much more martial, as befitted Roman culture. He was worshiped by men only; no women were allowed into his temples. (The Romans did not believe in cross-gender friendships as they felt such fraternizing could only lead to disgrace for both parties.) He was still a deity of camaraderie among friends, and because of this practically the entire army converted to Mithraism over a period of about three hundred years. Mithras's worship became a mystery cult in Rome, where men—and especially soldiers—went through ordeals and secret rites, promising to put the cult of Mithras ahead of family and all others.

This is the point where the dynamic of friendship—even that of a group of friends—gives way to membership in a group where everyone has one large thing in common. The eleventh-house Sun has a unique and driven relationship with groups. Unlike the similar-but-different Aquarius Sun who can dabble on the edges of groups, join and get thrown out and be rebelliously independent, the eleventh-house Sun needs to be part of a multi-human endeavor. They will be propelled toward the issue of being "in" or being "out" at a young age, and sorting out the feelings and reality around that will be a struggle for them, probably for the rest of their lives. They will go through the experience of joining inappropriate groups in the way that their peers are experimenting with the lesson of inappropriate romantic relationships. They will agonize over what has to be sacrificed to fit in, of the pain of being outcast, of each group not quite being the perfect chosen family they see in their heads.

It's not uncommon for this Sun placement to want to base their whole identity on belonging to a particular group, because the Sun is all about identity. It's also not uncommon for them to buy the story of an exploitative group, hook, line and sinker. Eleventh-house Sun people are often at risk for getting sucked into cults, not so much for the spiritual aspect as for the social one. Imagine for a moment the Roman army—thousands of men all standing in rows shouting "Hail Caesar!", all in uniforms and armor, each one knowing that the men standing around them will have their back in a conflict. That's also part of the eleventh house. Many motivations are used to force men to go out onto a battlefield and kill each other. For most of them, the one that works best is putting them into situations where they bond with their teammates, and don't want those comrades to die because they weren't there to watch their backs.

This Sun placement's biggest danger is holding loyalty to a group—especially one they have based their identity on—higher than their own well-being, even long after the group has ceased to be a comfortable place for them. Mithras is the God of Loyalty, and this Sun placement doesn't want to give up on that chosen-family experience too quickly. *If I just act rightly according to their standards, I'll fit right back in,* they reason. Inevitably, at some point they must go through the pain of breaking from a group, or being ejected from one, and for them it is as bad as a breakup with a lover. Perhaps worse, for now they have to create a new identity, based on something else.

The worship of Mithras was officially outlawed in 391 B.C. when all pagan religions were banned in Rome. Most of the army had already converted to Christianity, because the Emperor converted and expected his military to follow him, and they were all so used to practicing the same religion—Mithraism—that it seemed natural for them to convert wholesale. (That, too, is an eleventh-house lesson. Be careful where your group decides to take everyone.) But Mithras's story goes on a little further, even though his cult was officially outlawed. We are talking about a god of light, justice, and brotherhood whose Roman legends had him go into a cave each year and come out reborn and renewed. Demons slew him and he rose again. The Zoroastrians had made him a celibate god, more interested in morality than sex or romantic love; they had made his mother Anahita (originally a fertility goddess) into a virgin goddess who conceived him without sex; they had given him twelve disciples. He was called Mankind's Savior and the Light of the World. His initiates were welcomed with bread and wine. His birthday was on December 25th, four days after the winter solstice which was the sun's birthday in many other cultures.

If this all sounds terribly familiar, it's because Mithraism was the largest competitor for early Christianity, and so they borrowed Mithraic imagery and dogma in order to make it more attractive to converts. (That included the birthday.) One of the aspects they borrowed was the God who could be your friend, which they applied to Jesus. If you've ever seen or heard "You've got a friend in Jesus" … well, now you know where it came from. So in many ways Mithras's legacy lives on.

The eleventh-house Sun person lives and dies by their participation in groups and their relationships with friends. If they have a committed love relationship, they will probably select their lover or spouse from their group of friends or their affinity group, and expect them to understand that going out with the boys or girls is just as important as staying home with the squeeze, of not more so. However, the final outpost of this house is expanding the concept of friendship and brother/sisterhood to the whole world, and if anyone is mentally set up to do this, it's the eleventh-house Sun. Once they've worked out their issues with friend-loyalty and group-loyalty, they may become attracted to causes which work for peace and opportunity for all humankind. Assuming, of course, that they can do that work in a group. A nice, comfortable group of good people who are different the same way they are different. Because the other truth this Sun placement understands is that alone, we are twigs to be broken. Together, we are a force to be reckoned with. And that is the ultimate understanding of Sol Invictus, the Unconquerable Sun.

12☉ Sun in the 12th House: Beiwe

I started out the Sun section with a statement about how the Sun is the most visible and potent object in the sky, and that cultures all over the world revered and honored it for its power and awe-inspiring majesty. I led that into an assumption that the Sun—the seat of Identity—is also the central and most important influence in the astrological chart. But what happens when the Sun is cast down into darkness, into a place of defeat and hiding? Certainly many myths speak of the Sun going underground during the night, perhaps battling demons and devouring spirits, but every morning it arrives in glory again, a triumph of the light against the closing darkness. It's a reliable beacon of hope, of victory, of Unconquered Self … except where it isn't.

The twelfth house is the hardest Sun placement of all, because it is against the nature of the Sun to be cast into darkness and hidden there. This is the house of the unconscious, of confinement, of the mystic shut in their dark cave of meditation. There's little room for glory, and no one to applaud … and yet one in twelve people will have this placement which forces the knowledge of Self down into the depths. They will struggle to find that solid core of "I am!", and will be forced to use unusual means to find it.

Likewise, there are places in the world where the sun doesn't come up every morning as promised. In fact, at the poles of the Earth it vanishes for six months at a stretch. Granted, it also rules overhead for six months as well, but it is a cold, weak Sun which cannot grow a flower through the ice. The importance of the Sun, essential to the health of our bodies and minds (not to mention our food), has an entirely different meaning in the areas where its easy return is definitely not guaranteed ... and its appearances may not be enough to keep us healthy and sane.

Still, humans are resilient, and have learned to live in all sorts of difficult places. The Sámi people of the Arctic circle in Norway and Finland (and formerly into Russia, although those borders are closed to the passage of those nomadic people now) started by following and living off of the wild reindeer herds, and eventually learned to partially domesticate and train them. Their language shows them to have been living in that cold area long before the Indo-Europeans thundered across two continents; there is speculation that they may have been there since the end of the Ice Age, following the herds northward with the withdrawing ice. They extract survival out of a bleakly inhospitable land, and manage to find happiness and contentment in the midst of that white tundra where little grows and the Sun vanishes entirely for months at a time in midwinter. They are not ignorant, however, of the price they pay for living without Sun ... and it is why Beiwe, their Goddess of the Sun, is also a goddess of sanity.

For a long time, it was assumed that circumpolar Arctic-area natives had adapted handily to their semi-darkness and weren't bothered by it; southern people who went to live there were the ones who complained about being seasonally depressed. Later, when Seasonal Affective Disorder was made an official diagnosis, researchers rushed to test those who had lived with uneven Sun for many generations, and found that indeed there were significantly higher levels of mental illness in the winter than indigenous people living in sunnier areas. Now studies show that SAD occurs among 5-40% of Arctic peoples, depending on the area, and it is woven into their folklore. Beiwe is prayed to for relief of the crushing winter depression—which goes to the point of psychosis for some individuals—and it seems that even in ancient times, they understood that it was due to the Sun being trapped in darkness and never showing her shining face.

People with twelfth-house Suns are generally no more likely to suffer from physical SAD than any other Sun placement (although I did know a blind-from-birth twelfth-house Sun whose depression was diagnosed as a kind of permanent SAD—he literally could never see the Sun and his pineal gland got no light), but on a metaphorical level, it makes a good comparison. Individuals with this placement are notorious for depression and anxiety; it's also common for them to not really know who they are. They may have poor boundaries and take on the opinions of whoever is loudest (and most Sunlike), or they may just withdraw and live in a cloud of confusion. The unconscious is the place where we stuff things we don't like about ourselves—down into the dark basement where we don't have to look at them over the breakfast table—and if your core identity is down there, it's going to get those undesirable things stuck all over it. This means that when you try to figure out who you are, all that outcast material pops up. In the less mature stages, this can lead a twelfth-house Sun to run away and attempt to craft an identity out of fantasy archetypes they've read about. (Fantasy is the realm of Neptune, ruler of the twelfth house.) Of course it's depressing to live secretly thinking your identity is wound up with everything you fear and dislike. That's enough to give anyone anxiety, and make them resort to dreams and fantasy to stay afloat.

The Sámi goddess Beiwe was closely associated with reindeer, which were the lifeblood and survival of the inland Sámi tribes (the ones on the coast had fishing as an alternate food source). It was she who made the plants grow so that the reindeer would fatten on summer leaves and make it through the winter. She rode across the sky in a chariot of reindeer antlers pulled by sacred white female reindeer, and one like them was sacrificed to her every winter Solstice. Before being killed, a white thread would be sewn through the ear of the sacred reindeer, to mark her out for Beiwe. In summer, wreaths of the precious leaves would decorate tents and houses in her honor.

While solar deities are usually powerful creatures, it's not unheard of for them to be besieged or even captured at least once in their lifetimes. However, the Sámi traditions around Beiwe (or Beaivvi, or Biejja; her name is simply the word for "sun") have her being assisted by the people at every turn. There seems to be a cultural assumption that Beiwe's seasonal darkness is literally her becoming weak and frail, unable to climb high in the sky. Her cycle becomes lower and lower, until she ceases to rise at all. In fact, unlike other solar deities who are symbolized by some sort of circle (often with a dot in the middle to indicate the Earth around which it circles, like the astrological Sun symbol), Beiwe's symbol is an oval around the Earth-dot. It's painfully clear that she cannot ride the circular path. When winter begins to fade and the Sun's glow is barely seen (Sámi winter darkness stretches from mid-November to mid-March), everyone does what they can to "feed" Beiwe and strengthen her for the long, slow climb upwards. Butter, which can melt in the Sun, is smeared on trees and doorposts to fatten her. The sacred reindeer sacrificed to her on the winter Solstice has been turned into pieces of dried meat, and these are threaded through with thin branches and made into an oval Sun-ring bright with ribbons, which is then hung in the trees to feed her. Songs are sung to give her strength. The season of "winter-spring" (one of eight Sámi seasons, this one from the first hint of light until the snow begins to melt) is the time of Beiwe's convalescence from her great winter illness, and she needs all the aid she can get if anything is to grow at all. This is a Sun, it seems, who needs a lot of help.

That last line could definitely sum up this Sun placement. The Sun is the Ego, and the twelfth house is the place of all the forces which dissolve egos. The way for this Sun to figure out who they are is to bravely excavate the dark basement and treat everything found there with compassion. This Neptunian quality is both a tool for and a goal of the twelfth-house Sun, but it is imperative to turn it on oneself as often as one turns it on others. This doesn't mean people with this placement can just give themselves a break from all bad behavior; even this Sun-in-darkness is still a Sun, and may have feelings of privilege—*I'm special, why don't people see that? They are so unfair not to make allowances for me!*—except that whole dialogue is unconscious and the Sun person may not even be aware of those mutinous mutterings from the basement which periodically send up flares of nasty behavior.

Instead, the submerged ego must be accessed by twelfth-house means—art, poetry, music, natural beauty, inspired writing, meditation, spirituality; any or all of the right-brained methods which ignore the rational left-brain entirely. Instead of describing their Self as "I am a person who does XYZ or has ABC qualities," it's better for this Sun placement to start out with, "I am (image), (image), (image)," and then work on making the images both more realistic and more forgiven for what they look like in the light of day. These methods feed this weak Sun and give it the strength to see itself, set boundaries, and take charge. They are the butter smeared on the doorpost, the dried meat hung in the tree, the prayers to bring the Sun out of convalescence and into the sky.

Another symbol I found striking when researching Beiwe and her images was thorns. During the dark time, Beiwe was represented by a globe made from flexible wooden saplings and covered with thorns; it would be smeared with the blood of the sacrificial reindeer. This is the house of sacrifice, and having the Sun here can mean that the individual feels like it is right and proper that they should be a martyr and sacrifice themselves for others. After all, if they have no self, or if their self feels worthless, why not make a sacrifice of it? Many end up working in institutions or with people who are very ill, which is actually a very good way to deal with this Sun placement, as long as it is done out of real compassion and not a feeling that this is all you are good for—or an instinctive, mindless reaction to the pain of another, used as a crutch to ignore your own internal problems. (Other people's thorns are so much easier to deal with than one's own.) Another thorny danger for this Sun placement is addiction, numbing the pain emanating from the unconscious-dwelling weeping Sun with drugs or alcohol. As the Sun is slowly prayed up from the wintry underworld, it will be better able to value itself from a realistic perspective, and thus value its own self-care.

This is a Self which needs special care and feeding, special attention to be drawn out of its darkness, and special thoughtfulness to keep it free of the chains of addiction, depression, and seductive Walter Mitty-type fantasy. If they can create any sort of a physical spiritual discipline—it needs not have any resemblance to something traditionally religious; it could just be mindful walks in the woods or a t'ai ch'i practice, anything which quiets the mind and allows the subconscious to be seen without judgment—then like Beiwe, the Sun will reward them with growth and fertility and the magic of summer after a long, cold, interminable winter.

THE MOON

1☽ Moon in the 1st House: Ezili Dantor

eople who write about astrology sometimes really underestimate the Moon. Yes, it's parent and child ... but parents can be loving and supportive or terrible monsters, and children can be cheerful and playful or sadistically torturing each other. Yes, it's feelings, but being emotionally sensitive can mean hiding and crying when you're hurt, or punching someone in the face. Yes, it's about our intuition, but intuition is just a tool like any other, used to do good and bad things. The Moon is our emotions, and not just the nice, socially acceptable ones, like the silver disk serenely moving through the sky. The Moon can also be screaming, wild weeping, fury, and terror.

When it's right out there in the first house, every one of these possibilities might also be out there on the person's face where everyone can see them, at any given time. If they're feeling it, you know. People look at someone with a first-house planet and assume things about them, usually projecting their idea of that planet's qualities. In the case of the Moon, what they are projecting is probably Mother, and it will vary depending on the mother experience of the beholder. The Moon person, on the other hand, might or might not be a nurturer, and if they are, it will have more to do with what is aspecting that Moon than any external person's assumptions. Many Mother Goddesses are associated with the Moon, but they are not all tranquil versions of each other. They are different in numerous ways. Some are different enough that they might not resemble your idea of a Mother Goddess at all ... just as someone who wears their feelings on their face might not resemble your idea of what that looks like.

In the Haitian Vodou religion, the Ezili are a family of *lwa*, or divine spirits. Ezili Dantor is a female *lwa* who is a mother, and indeed is called the Mother of Haiti. She wears her motherhood out in front, but she is no cookie-baking mom. The *lwa* usually take on the archetypes of people in specific periods of history, and this needs to be accepted in order to understand them. Dantor usually appears in iconography as a Black Madonna with her child in her arms. She is a very dark-skinned Black woman, the kind who would have been a slave or a working-class mother in the era that set her appearance. She sees and understands poverty, and the grind of caring for children when there is barely enough to feed and clothe them, or not enough at all. What she has, she earned by the sweat of her brow.

Ezili Dantor has different faces, different aspects, depending on what part of her story she is enacting. First is the white-clad Rada Dantor, the calm, peaceful mother with her child on her lap. Like the serene Moon, all is well with her and her family. They are surrounded by her love. No one shows love as openly and instinctively as the first-house Moon. You can feel it radiating from them. This Dantor protects single mothers; she may take many lovers, but basically raises her children alone. However, even a loving mother can become furious, especially when she sees the injustice of children born into slavery being torn from their mothers, sees the mothers themselves raped and made to breed more children who would be reduced to what they could bring in the marketplace. Dantor wept against the injustice, over and over, with the wholehearted weeping only a first-house Moon can pull out. And then she got angry.

The Vodou religion practices deity-possession in order to honor the *lwa*, and the first recorded public possession by Ezili Dantor was at a Haitian ceremony on August 14th, 1791. This ceremony would spark the Haitian revolution that would overthrow the government, freeing all enslaved people. Within a week hundreds of plantations had been burned and the wrath of the enslaved ripped across the island. It was said that Ezili Dantor oversaw the whole revolution. She had been a kind mother nursing her child, but now she was a fierce revolutionary, a warrior who carried twin knives and danced with them in a furious, stomping dance. No longer dressed in white, she now wore blood-red, and was now called not a Rada spirit, but a Petro spirit. Her eyes turned flaming red; she was the energy of the protective mother bear, the one who will defend her children to the death. Dantor the warrior is bloodthirsty and vengeful; when she attacks, it is not fairness which is first in her mind, but hatred for the oppressors who dared to attempt to own others against their will. She still fights the oppressors, especially those who harm mothers and children. Not every emotion is pretty, especially in the face of wrongdoing. The Moon on the front lines can be frightening and devastating, fueled by their own or other's pain. If you want to see a first-house Moon become a bear protecting their cubs, threaten their loved ones, not they themselves. Especially their more helpless loved ones.

Dantor the warrior avenges the innocent dead whose voices cry out from the earth, where they may have been buried without marker or ceremony. In both her Serene-Mother and Warrior-Mother guises, she sacrifices herself—for her children, for her family, for the oppressed, for all victims. Neptune's sacrifice is passive martyrdom or compassionate healing. The Moon's sacrifice is working yourself into a screaming emotional riot and flinging yourself into the war, taking out as many as you can until you fall from exhaustion. It is opening your body to give birth, again and again, or putting yourself between your child and the wolf, or the bully, or the abuser. Dantor's warrior aspect is made unique by the scars on her face—two or three across her cheek. It may be a memory of African scarification, or it may represent her struggle as an enslaved woman, which could leave the scars of abuse. Either way, they symbolize strength—she has come through something hard, and survived it with her fortitude intact. Tough and wild, she is still a mother. Even when this Moon placement is angry, they still have the urge to protect those they see as suffering.

Somewhere along the line in her story, Ezili Dantor has her tongue cut out. There are various tales about how and why that happened—some say it was done by other Haitian revolutionaries who wanted to keep her from betraying them, some say it was the enemy when she was captured and let fly that same tongue at them. Horrifying as this is, it is also relevant to this Moon position. Just because your emotions show on your face and in the movements of your body doesn't mean that you can articulate them properly, especially in the heat of the moment. Unless there is a strong, harmonious Moon-Mercury connection, the Moon person can sometimes find themselves tongue-tied or incoherent when they try to explain rationally what is going on with them. While this can happen with any Moon, when it's in the first house, it's just more embarrassing and hard to hide.

When you call upon Ezili Dantor's third aspect, the veteran after the war, she doesn't speak. Occasionally she is said to let out a cry—"ke-ke-ke-ke-ke!"—but no words come out. She shows what she wants through her face, her dance, the force of her brave spirit. This aspect of Dantor is sometimes known as the Queen, or the Mother of Haiti. She is now not only mother to her own children, but to many others as well. The first-house Moon is drawn to care for people, whether or not they are related. Dantor the Queen has some wealth, for the first time, and because she is victorious, she can bestow victory—as long as you are on the side she respects, which is not the side of oppressors and exploiters. She is a giver of discipline, in the sense that she is willing to point out where you have gone astray, and point you back to the right path.

This is a Moon placement which desires a strong emotional connection, and can become frustrated with someone whose feelings are constantly hidden. It's important for them to remember that just because someone doesn't show their feelings does not mean they are not strong or passionate. The first-house Moon person may have trouble connecting to a very reserved individual, however, and may sometimes make attempts to trigger a more emotional response from them, which can go poorly. The Moon person isn't doing it to annoy them; it's actually an attempt at deeper intimacy and connection, but it probably won't come across that way to the individual who is being emotionally prodded. The Moon person needs to understand the perhaps more subtle emotional responses of others, and be willing to ask how someone is feeling ... and believe them when they express it in a quiet way. While Ezili Dantor is powerful and passionate—and effective—in expressing her emotions, not everyone can dance like her.

The Mother of Haiti is not a comfortable divine spirit, although she is fiercely loyal and protective of the ones she loves. Having a first-house Moon isn't comfortable, either for the person who has it or the people around that person. Still, like Dantor, they are open and sincere ... because they have to be. They are often lousy at deception, although a few may be able to disguise the truth in a flood of distracting feelings. Most prefer not to bother, and just wear it on their sleeve. Like Dantor, when they say they care, you know it. When they say you're about to step too far, you know it. When they say that they will do something no matter how hard it is, no matter what they have to sacrifice ... you can bet your shining crescent that it will happen.

2☽ Moon in the 2nd House: Lakshmi

The Moon is an emotional planet, and it is not always comfortable in the extremely material second house. Of course, the higher "octave" (meaning) of the second house of money and resources is one's values, and the Moon's emotions are often irrevocably entwined with that ... but there is so much in the House of Wealth which can be devastatingly distracting to the Moon. It was Lakshmi, the consort of Vishnu and the Hindu goddess of wealth and fortune who stood forth to untangle that mess and highlight the Moon's swerving path through this gold-laden house.

We've met the second house through the Sun with Midas and his golden touch; here the love of wealth is less bound up with the identity and is more about emotional security. The Moon, ruled by Cancer, wants emotional security more than anything else, regardless of its sign. It simply has twenty-four different ways of going about that—twelve signs, twelve houses—and in this house, money can become the symbol, or literal blanket, of that safety. Possessing anything goes right to the heart of this Moon placement—they are strongly emotional about anything they possess, and they feel possessive of anything they are strongly emotional about. This is the house of self-worth, and that may be precariously balanced on their financial and material means.

Lakshmi is known in modern times as the goddess of wealth, prosperity, good fortune, fertility, beauty, grace, charm, and worldly power. While these attributes may seem to span Jupiter and Venus as well, it was she who stood forth for this Moon—standing on her trademark giant lotus flower, with another smaller lotus in each hand. (The lotus is a watery flower associated with the Moon in Western occultism.) One of her creation legends say that she was born from the foam of the ocean of milk churned by the Gods—an image both lunar and echoing Cancer, the Moon's ruler. One hymn to Lakshmi chants out: "Every woman is an embodiment of you. You exist as little girls in their childhood, as young women in their prime, and as elderly women in their old age." This reminds us of the Moon as representing the feminine in all its forms. (Of course, this Moon is no more or less feminine than any other, and as many men as women have it, and it works its gifts and difficulties in all genders.)

According to Hindu tradition, there are eight different sources of wealth, not all of it monetary, and these are referred to as the *Ashta Lakshmi*, or Octet of Lakshmi—her eight faces and eight gifts. The first one is, of course, Dhana Lakshmi, the giver of material possessions. The second house is not just money but objects of worth—at least to the owner—and this Moon placement may collect so many items which either seem valuable to them or represent memories in their life that it can become a real problem. Not all or even most people with this Moon become hoarders—it's actually more common with Neptune here—but it is very hard for them to let go of those objects, even when they are falling apart or the house is crammed and there's no room for anything new. Even when they are valuable and supposedly being kept for that rainy day when extra money is needed, this Moon will have a very hard time actually selling them. They may find it too difficult to let go of the items, even when the cash is necessary to save someone or something else.

Dhanya Lakshmi, the next category of riches, is agricultural or plant wealth ... in other words, food. It's not that this Moon placement overeats, but they may hoard food—full freezers and pantries, possibly even beyond the time when it has gone bad. If the Moon remembers a childhood of food insecurity, or strictly regulated diet which felt emotionally like deprivation, or even just a lack of nurturing to "feed the heart", this placement may fill the cupboards with nourishment, "just in case." They may also equate their weight or dietary habits to their worth in the world, which this aspect of Lakshmi gently separates out, showing that one does not define the other.

The next two of the Octet—Gaja Lakshmi, the giver of animal wealth, and Santana Lakshmi, the giver of children—both echo the attitude of the second-house Moon toward living things in their care. While the original "animal wealth" referred to livestock and could theoretically be lumped in with agriculture, modern Western individuals—many of whom have pets in place of children—would pray to Lakshmi for the right dog and the money to pay its vet bills rather than cows or goats. Pets and children, for the second-house Moon, can become emotionally lumped in with all their other property. They care for their charges assiduously and can be quite possessive of them, because the living things they "own" are also part of the web they weave for emotional support and reassurance.

Pets die (and while this Moon will mourn them, they are also likely to quickly replace them) but children begin to reject being an adult's possession somewhere around or just after puberty. This can lead to family battles, as the children's natural stage of rebellion strikes the second-house Moon in the security wound and they grab for more control or weep with betrayal, depending on the sign of the Moon and its way of handling fear. Many cultures consider one's children, and their particular successes or failures, as an extension of the parent's achievements and thus reflective of their value as a parent. (In some cultures, the child is also financial security to be relied upon in old age, a strongly lunar concern which may worry this Moon placement.)

Vidya Lakshmi is the giver of knowledge and wisdom in the arts and sciences, very like Sarasvati (Mercury in Libra) in some ways. Career skills and earned knowledge can be the source of money, and this Moon placement can be very possessive of skills and trade secrets on which their income rests. They may refuse to train replacements or potential rivals if they fear it will eventually impact their paycheck. If they are artists, they may have a very hard time actually giving up their creations to the world. It's not that they fear how they will be received so much as they just don't want to let their property out of their hands, especially if they have strong emotional attachments to these creative "children". The second house is ruled by Taurus, whose keyword is "I have", and it is very important to any planet in this house to *have*.

However, as we go down the list, things change. There are actually multiple Ashta Lakshmi lists which differ a fair amount, so I will pick the most enlightening ones for this lunar placement. Dhairya, Veera, or Vijaya Lakshmi (Courageous, Valorous, or Victorious respectively) is the face of the goddess who grants the ability to overcome hurdles in life and achieve success. All the difficult behaviors we've listed so far for this Moon come down to fear, pure and simple. When there is courage to move ahead without the security blanket, it—and all the items which make it up—no longer hold power over them. Lakshmi's gift of courage is the first tool needed to make their way to peace.

The second tool is offered by Vara Lakshmi, the goddess who bestows boons—gifts you didn't expect or know you needed until they fell into your lap. Every planet in the second house must, sooner or later, wrestle with the fact that their financial luck is better when they give than when they hoard. The more they can give, the more will come back to them ... in all forms of wealth. To be able to give means having enough to share. That can mean feeling that one has enough to share and still make do—and that may be a very subjective situation which can be reframed to "feel like enough". Or one can take the even braver road of "There isn't enough, but it doesn't matter; I trust that I will survive even after giving." Of course, this Moon needs to make sure that they don't just give too much impulsively because they happen to feel sorry for someone this week. Emotional spending on one's self can become emotional spending on others. To be the boon-giver they must have a realistic assessment of what they really have, what it is worth, what they can spare, and what they can do without. This may be a rough realization for the second-house Moon, and they may need objective outside perspective to help them see it clearly.

The oldest form of Lakshmi—long before she became a goddess of wealth and fertility and good fortune—is the member of the Octet now known as Adi Lakshmi, who has nothing to do with materialism or even worldly success. She brings spiritual wealth—silence, bliss, and centered peace. Her hand makes the *mudra* which means Fearlessness. To realize that the goddess of riches started out as a deity of spiritual peace strips the assumptions off of the second-house Moon and shows their ideal goal. Once you have that inner peace, there is no need for the security blanket. Possessions become simply something that is useful, makes your life more beautiful, or can be given away to create joy in others. Only things which are comfortable being your possessions need to stay in that category. Their loss may be sad, but it is not devastating, and does not affect your peace of mind. One's worth becomes based on other metrics, and the golden chains no longer bind the heart.

This brings us to Lakshmi's relationship with her husband Vishnu (Neptune in the First House). Whether or not the second-house Moon person sees their spouse as their possession depends on that spouse and how they handle the situation. A spouse who gives in and goes along with the Moon partner's fears and possessiveness generally ends up in that category. A spouse who calmly but firmly sets boundaries and reminds their Moon partner that they are a separate human being with their own agenda and agency, and that it is not fair to treat them otherwise without their consent, can prevent themselves from becoming part of the bank-balance-and-self-worth package.

Vishnu the Preserver is a deity of (among other things) maintaining life through spiritual peace. He has a strong sense of transcendence beyond the physical, and he does not belong to Lakshmi. Instead, she belongs to him—sitting before him and listening to his words, rubbing his feet, cradling his head tenderly in her lap while he sleeps. This is more than just the Hindu cultural ideal of a perfect wife; other divine deity-pairs are equals or the goddess is more prominent or dominant. Lakshmi, however, chooses to bow her head to Vishnu. That doesn't mean second-house Moon people should all be submissive to their partners; this isn't that literal. What it does mean is that this Moon needs to bow its head periodically to the concept of the real truth being beyond what anyone can own. This is often difficult for the emotional Moon to remember, but is desperately needed.

In the end, when the individual with this Moon gets their values sorted out in light of the bigger picture, they can learn to embody wealth of all sorts which is guided by kindness and caring to everyone involved. It's important that the way they make money feels good to them; their work must reflect their values and create obvious improvement in the world. This needs to be valued over how much it pays, or the paycheck will begin to push them back into the place of fear. Lakshmi's generosity can only shine forth through a clear lens … and turn lunar white to shimmering gold.

3☽ Moon in the 3rd House: Nisaba

One of the earliest known Sumerian deities was the goddess Nisaba, originally a goddess of grain and fertility approximately three millennia before the current era, symbolized by a single stalk of grain. One of her titles was "Lady Whose Body Is The Flecked Barley". She was the daughter of Anu and Unas—gods of Earth and Heaven. In early Sumer, almost everyone simply farmed, and there was very little in the way of writing or literacy. Tax collectors and merchants began to make clay tablets for keeping tallies of animals and goods, with pictographs and *tally* marks. Eventually this slowly became an alphabet, with cuneiform phonetic letters. This grew out of a need for keeping better records, and the first writing we find was just that—keeping track of food.

Slowly, writing grew and spread, and the goddess of grain also took charge of the process of recording food which was grown or traded, and became a sacred scribe. She who made the grain grow became the one who saw to its distribution. As writing spread from simple accounting to stories, communications, and all sorts of other records, Nisaba became the goddess of writing and literature. Her later title was "Lady of the Place of Writing". As scribal schools came into being—mostly men, but we have clear records of female scribes as well—new scribes would finish off their practice writings with "Praise be to Nisaba!" Other titles of hers were "Professor of Great

Wisdom" and "Unsurpassed Overseer". Her patron, and boss of a sort, was Enki the inventor god (Mercury in Aquarius).

However, just as much as she was a goddess of knowledge, writing, and literature, she was also very much a mother. The most well-known lay about Nisaba is not about her clay tablet and stylus, but about her close relationship with her daughter Sud. The god Enlil comes to Nisaba and asks her for the maiden Sud's hand. The rest of the story is about Nisaba's careful negotiation to make sure her darling daughter will have the best from him, including a long and carefully documented list of the different kinds of food which he sends over to their city as a down payment on his bride. The union is finally agreed upon and Sud is blessed by her mother and sent to Enlil's city, where she is made his favorite queen and has everything she needs to prosper.

Nisaba's motherly care for her scribal charges is also evident from their writings about her; she was spoken of as if she was a favorite teacher and they were her prize students. There's a good reason why teaching is a frequent career for people with the Moon in the third house of communication and writing. The Moon is the planet of the parent-child relationship, and in Mercury's traditional (and very intellectual) house, this can stretch to caring for the minds of students. It's not unusual for teachers to have almost parental relationships with long-term favorite pupils, but the connection is a little different when it's mind-to-mind. The Moon is just a bit more distant and a lot less smothering in the third house; teachers know that they have to let the students pass out of their grasp and fly, and that's the goal they are striving for.

A third-house Moon puts the planet of emotions in a rather scattered intellectual place. People with this placement have many, many interests—whatever catches their eye and then their heart. Note the "heart" part—the Moon is the center of our hearts, and whatever they learn, whatever they do has to appeal to them emotionally. As this is a fairly cerebral house, this Moon may be utterly enchanted by all sorts of subjects wound around with letters and numbers. Whether it is literary or mathematical, they may love it—and love teaching it to others who might learn to share their love for their special interest. This placement gives emotional depth to learning, and the minds of these individuals may be deeply intuitive. They may have a knack for putting emotions into words, and helping others to do the same, pulling the feelings out of them verbally.

At the same time, their way of showing caring is more like a teacher and less like a cuddly parent. They can be detail-oriented and precise about their caring—Nisaba makes sure that her beloved daughter is going to have all the riches she can in her marriage, and she wants every bit of it listed in detail, because it's her way of showing love. Her blessing on her daughter is long and laden with wishes, but it's words, because words are her power. Partners and children either love this aspect of the third-house Moon, or are vaguely sad because they would rather just have a hug and not have to talk everything out or hear the parent or partner natter on. If the partner or child isn't particularly verbally oriented, they may not be able to respond in the way the third-house Moon person might prefer, and this Moon may have to struggle to keep their mouth shut and their arms open.

They are still sensitive, though; this is definitely a Moon, and it can be just as parental or childlike as any other Moon. In fact, since this is the house of siblings, people with this Moon placement can sometimes revert to a playful child, treating friends or partners like brothers and sisters. This placement sometimes creates a childhood where one or both parents were more like a sibling than a parent, or where the Moon person had to parent younger siblings.

Like a curious child, they like to ask "Why?" about everything. *How does it work? Why does it work?* Their inner machinist wants to take everything apart and check it out, but unlike the more detached Mercury or Uranus placements, the Moon will have strong opinions about whatever they find, and how it affects people. They are often the scholar with a very strong emotional attachment to their nerdery, and as such they are better at explaining it to people outside the circle of knowledge and interest than those who rely on less other-oriented planets.

The biggest drawbacks to this entwining of mind and heart are, first, a tendency to think that they are being rational when they are actually reacting from emotion, and second, interpreting their environment through their emotions so that when they are having a good day everything is wonderful about the situation, and when they're having a bad day, the same situation is terrible. Oh, and while we're at it, how about being mentally distracted by the squirrels? There is a scatteredness to the Moon's presence in the third house, like the brilliant but slightly dotty teacher who is always misplacing their glasses on top of their heads.

Nisaba went from being a goddess of knowledge to being a goddess of wisdom, and as such she was asked to bestow her gift on rulers. Scribes also attested that their right to their job and status was gifted to them by Nisaba. She was said to write on a tablet of lapis lazuli covered with "heavenly writing", which might be astrological or astronomical symbols, upon which she wrote with a golden stylus. Over time, she also became a patron of architecture, which relied on a great deal of mathematics, geometry, and keeping good records. She was not only the scribe and accountant of the Gods, but the architectural planner who gave the blueprint to more physical deities to construct.

The original husband of Nisaba was Haia, a minor deity who seems to be a god of official clay seals, but when the Assyrian invaders conquered the land, their religious culture was forced on the people by their king Hammurabi. The Assyrians thought little of women and less of goddesses, and all the powerful Sumerian divine ladies were either forcibly married to random Assyrian warrior Gods and made into subordinate consorts, or they were entirely replaced. The Assyrians didn't really have a proper deity of writing and literature, so they pulled out a son of Marduk who had originally been a herald or announcer figure, and proclaimed him as the god of writing, largely so that they could marry Nisaba to him and make her a lesser figure. The process wasn't quick or overnight, and many Sumerians continued to honor Nisaba alone as the patron of literacy and numeracy, ignoring her new husband, but eventually Nabu was accepted as not only her equal but her superior.

This is sometimes a problem for this Moon. Their position halfway between intellectual ability and the wish to connect with people sometimes makes them less willing to advocate for themselves when they are sidelined by aggressive bosses or co-workers. They simply want to do their interesting jobs, and may not have much ambition, but they are hurt when their intellect and efforts are belittled. They may be content to stay in more low-paying jobs, especially in teaching or research, because they have an emotional attachment to the job, but they may never feel comfortable asserting themselves to demand promotions or pay raises. They can be vulnerable to "We don't have the money right now, and we'll all have to pitch in and make sacrifices," as long as there is at least some pretense at "...because we're all a family here." Eventually they will break out of their hesitation, and then all their emotions will come flying out of their mouth, of course. This can be helpful or a hindrance, depending on how well they remember their people skills, and how careful they are to say the right thing. These people do know how to say the right thing, make no mistake (public speakers with this placement are excellent at swaying the audience), but any Moon will sometimes slip and revert to less-than-eloquent statements when they are feeling especially insulted.

Nisaba's subordination to Nabu was one of the strongest and most obvious historical examples of the Assyrian patriarchal divine gender subordination. However, later during her eclipse (but before the Christianization of the area which washed away both Nisaba and Nabu) she gained some notoriety as a goddess of exorcisms. These were spoken Words of Power which could cast out evil and cleanse a soul. Any third-house planetary placement eventually comes up against the issue of Words of Power—finding the One Right Word which will shift the situation—and here Nisaba shows her verbal power in spite of any forced subordination. *This is the voice which teaches the future. Do not underestimate its power.*

The final line of the story of Nisaba and Sud ends with a beautiful and very third-house line of praise for Nisaba: "The scribal art, the tablets decorated with writing, the stylus, the tablet board, the computing of accounts, adding and subtracting, the shining measuring rope, the head of the surveyor's peg, the rod of numbers, the marking of the boundaries; all of these are fittingly in your hands." There is little praise more perfect for this Moon of the mind.

4☽ Moon in the 4th House: The Son of Seven Mothers

In European folktales, we see a definite lack of mothers. They all seem either to die in childbirth, or in the child's youth, giving rise (of course) to the unpleasant stepmother. Fathers are generally distant and uncaring, or at least ineffectual and too busy to bother with their wayward children. The accepted explanation of this lack of parental care for the main characters is that it gets them out of the house and into adventures, because the home is such a terrible place that they can't wait to run away.

In Asian folktales, the situation is entirely different. The bond between parent and child is mandated by society, as children are supposed to take care of their parents in old age, and probably take regular advice from them throughout life. Instead of rescuing strange maidens from towers, many of these young heroes rescue their parents, as in the folktale we examine here.

The Moon, the planet which rules the parent-child relationship, loves to be in its own house of home and family. That doesn't mean that everything will be all posies and butterflies, but it does indicate a very strong family bond. The fourth-house Moon child is not the abandoned one—in fact, there may even be a little too much parental energy.

In this folktale from India, we start with a King who has seven wives. Unbeknownst to him, every one is pregnant. He goes out one day on a hunting trip and sees a beautiful young woman who lives with her mother in a hut in the woods; in some versions of this story, she takes the form of a white deer and then turns into a white-haired maiden. The King falls madly in love with her, and asks her to marry him. She agrees, but says that she must be his only wife. Her would-be suitor agrees instantly, but she has one more requirement, and it is a cruel one. She demands that the eyes of his other seven wives be torn out and given to her mother. The King agrees, and has all seven of his wives blinded, thrown into a deep dungeon, and nearly forgotten.

In reality, the beautiful deer-woman is a rakshasa, a kind of shapeshifting demon of chaos, and her mother is a rakshasa-sorceress who makes a rope of the eyes the way another housewife might make a rope of garlic, to use in her evil magic. The seven wives each give birth one at a time, and as they are not fed enough to make sufficient milk to keep a child alive, each wife offers her baby up to her sister-wives to eat, that they might all survive. The seventh wife's baby is not eaten; all seven of the sister-wives agree to raise the child as their own, and take turns feeding it what meager milk they can make. It is just enough to keep the boy alive, and he grows up cared for by seven blind women in a dark dungeon.

The Moon is the planet of emotions, and the fourth house denotes not only the home but the parent who sets the tone for it; this is usually (although not always) the mother. With the Moon here, there is a strong identification with the domestic parent. They may seem very large and omnipresent to the child—seven mothers' worth of parent, for example. Everything revolves around them, and they give the child the impression of what home is and probably will be for much of their life. An afflicted Moon here can mean a parent who is anxious, neurotic, depressed, or abusive. In adulthood, the individual with this Moon placement may remember their childhood home only through the parent's eyes—if Mama said that everything was terrible and gloomy, then that's the story that will remain in their minds.

The boy grows large enough to tunnel out of the dungeon, but the seven mothers cannot leave as their blindness and helplessness prevents them from making it past the guards. This, too, can be a manifestation of this Moon—the mother may be unable or unwilling to see things as they are, perhaps blinded by her upbringing, or so helpless and wounded that the child must care for and rescue her. The boy hunts for his mothers, bringing them meat from the nearby forest, and working local farm jobs to acquire food for them. He grows to be a young man, but is still tied to his confined mothers. One day he runs into the white deer rakshasa Queen. She questions him and he innocently gives away that he has seven blind mothers in a dark cave. The Queen, realizing that he is the son of her imprisoned sister-wives, tells him that she knows how he can get his mothers back their eyes, and sends him off to her own mother with a letter from her ... telling her mother to kill him and use his body parts as she pleases.

Evil stepmothers are often mythological shorthand for the actual mother at her worst. It was easier to imagine that a child's actual mother would never dream of harming them, so the abusive mother is moved further away and made into a stepmother. In real life, the fourth-house Moon individual might have a wonderful or terrible mother, or either by turns, depending on how afflicted the Moon is. However, even good mothers are sometimes railroaded by their own emotions and give bad advice, perhaps in an unconscious bid to keep them dependent. This may be something they learned from their own parents, as the white deer rakshasa Queen involves her own mother. The fourth is the house of ancestry, and of the patterns we inherit through the generations, for good or ill. That the rakshasa mother holds the eyes of the "good" mothers suggests that older parental patterns may be "blinding" the well-meaning mother, and attempting to keep the child ensnared as well. Figuring out these patterns, and freeing one's self from them, is the work of any fourth-house planet. The Moon, though, with its heart-deep loyalty to the family, makes it especially difficult to see and discard them.

On his way down the road for his first real journey, the young man meets a young woman. In some versions of the story she is a princess from a neighboring kingdom; in others she is simply the daughter of a rich local man. She is intelligent and perceptive, and invites the young man to stay and speak with her for a few days. He tells her his errand, and gives her the letter from the Queen, which he cannot read but she can. She realizes that he has been set up to be killed, and secretly rewrites the letter, telling the Queen's mother to help the young man in any way that she can.

This is the point in the story where outside perspective enters—perhaps the fourth-house Moon individual's love interest or good friend. Eventually someone will notice the unhealthy patterns—and the blinding loyalty to family—and point out that this is not right. In the case of a partner or spouse, they may even attempt to insert themselves between the Moon person and their family, perhaps because they want the Moon person's loyalty to shift to them, or perhaps because they resent being expected to fill the nurturing role that the parent held, exactly as the parent has done it, and they want to break their partner's attachment to that pattern. At any rate, the rakshasa mother reads the letter and agrees to give the young man the rope of his mothers' eyes, and he is able to return and restore their sight, allowing them to escape.

It's the dream of every fourth-house Moon: to rescue one's parents from pain or imprisonment in a bad place, to be the ultimate good child and deserve their everlasting love. In real life, however, it's never that simple—and sure enough, the white deer rakshasa Queen sees the young man and realizes that her stratagem has failed. This time she tells him of her mother's white cow, which gives lakes of milk, and sends him again with a letter telling her mother to slay him. In spite of all the attempts to rescue the parent, the negative side comes back up and creates problems. Fortunately, the young man stops again at the young woman's house and stays with her for a time, and she again reads and rewrites the letter, telling the rakshasa mother that her daughter needs the magical cow and the young man will deliver it to her. He acquires the cow, and his mothers will have food and some extra money. The Moon person's external-perspective partner has saved the day again—and there is nothing like time spent in a different home to broaden a fourth-house perspective.

The cycle repeats once more, because three is a magic number in folktales. The Queen tells the young man of her mother's field of million-fold rice, which only ripens at night, and gives him a third letter. She knows that the rice is guarded by a horde of demons, and hopes they will kill him. Again the rich man's daughter reads and rewrites the letter and sends him off, but the young man is brought up short by seeing eighteen million demons swarming around the field. The rakshasa mother tells him to walk straight to the middle of the field and pick the tallest ear, and then leave without looking back. If he stares at the demons or looks behind him in fear, he will become a heap of ashes.

That's a problem with family demons. It takes a very strong person to look them in the eyes, and a stronger one to walk away from them. The fourth-house Moon is often too wound up in the family drama to be able to easily face down the demons that they carry; the planet of emotions cries out and it feels like death. And—you guessed it—the young man manages to pluck the ear of rice, but he is too frightened by the demons and cannot help looking back in anxiety, and becomes a heap of ashes. The rakshasa mother is moved to help in spite of herself—she magically revives him, gives him a good scolding, and sends him on his way.

Here the good mother/bad mother situation shifts a bit, reflective of reality where nothing is black and white. While old family patterns can be destructive, they can also be helpful. Inherited family wisdom can be inaccurate falsehoods, or it can be useful, grounded insight passed down by the elders that the younger generation would actually do well to follow. The demon might not actually be such a demon, or not wholly one. It's important for the sensitive Moon to refrain from the temptation of seeing their parents and family as good or bad, especially if that shifts with their own feelings on any given matter.

The young man gives the million-fold rice to his mothers and they grow so much that he is able to bring a proper bride-price to the wealthy young woman who has saved him three times, and they are married. After their wedding, she invites his father and stepmother to their home, and it is she who tells the young man's father the whole story, including that his white-deer wife is a rakshasa. His seven wives are seated on thrones behind her, and as she speaks the rakshasa Queen's spell is broken. The young man's father has the rakshasa executed and reinstates his wives.

It is telling and important that the one who speaks the final truth and breaks the spell is not the son of seven mothers, but his wife. The fourth-house Moon can be so buried in and bound up with the family's emotions that they do not know where the family ends and they begin. It can take a caring outsider to break that spell and show them a different perspective. Of course, the Moon person can always reject their partner's view, but with this placement, it's crucial to have that alternate view. It might be a spouse or a therapist or just a good friend, but seeing the situation through other eyes can be the curse-breaker for the family spell.

In the end, the young man creates his own family, with his trusted truth-speaking wife beside him, and that is the final goal of this placement. It isn't that you have to recreate the original home; it is important not to let that imprison you. But you have to build the hearth you, the adult with your own needs and desires, want to have ... and it has to be safe, whatever that means. Determining what truly "safe" means to you may be another story entirely, but being able to relax within your four walls with the memory of the seven mothers, the wicked stepmother, and the ambivalent grandmother no longer tugging at your coattails is the sign that you have finally, truly, come home at last.

5☽ Moon in the 5th House: Jizo

When we look at the Sun and Venus in the fifth house, we focus on the aspect of this house which is creativity. Here, with the Moon which rules both parent and child, we focus on its aspect of children. It's not that fifth-house Moon people aren't creative—they certainly are, and their creativity gives them emotional peace and satisfaction, often becoming an outlet for their overwhelming feelings. It's just that the parent-child relationship is so strong with this house that it shone out as the place to focus. I thought that a Mother Goddess would stand forth for this placement, but instead the one who came into focus was the Japanese god Jizo, the protector of dead children.

Granted, Jizo does have some femininity in his history. He started out as two separate figures in China who were eventually combined into one, both of them named Ksitigarbha. The first was a Chinese tale of an Indian Brahmin maiden who prayed her dead mother out of the Chinese Hell—a tale of filial piety showing the parent-child relationship from the other side. After this, she vowed to dedicate the rest of her life to helping suffering dead souls. The second Ksitigarbha was a Buddhist monk and bodhisattva of great compassion, who found that his mother had been reborn as a dog, and kept her with him, treated kindly until she died. Folk Buddhism went through a period of replacing female goddesses with male monk-saints (rather out of a phobia of women) and this accounts for a series of very androgynous monk-figures who took on the female attributes of their original stories, such as Kwan Yin (Moon in Cancer) and Avalokiteshvara. When Ksitigarbha came to Japan, he/she was renamed Jizo, which literally means "womb of the Earth" to drive home his androgynous beginnings. He was made the protector of children, especially those who have passed on. He is still portrayed as a Buddhist bodhisattva, but his features are round and childlike to be closer to the little ones he loves.

It's a beautiful way to point out that the love of children is not gender-specific. It's said that fifth-house Moon people either have the hearts of parents or the hearts of children, and even the ones who are parents have a knack for getting down on the ground and playing kid-games with their little ones. This Moon often works with children as a career, or makes toys, games, or other treasures which make children's lives more magical. Like the bald Jizo who still resembles a child, they understand and remember what it is to be young and wide-eyed. While some stay childlike and immature, others go on to become parents or child-caretakers, because this Moon ensures that the desire for children wells up within them.

Before we go further with Jizo's story, we need to confront one of the most horrible beliefs ever created by Buddhism. Sometime in the fourteenth century, some Japanese Buddhist monks began to write about the Children's Hell, which was one of the many hells the dead would be sentenced to in order to suffer. The Children's Hell was a stretch of ghostly bank along the river which separated the realms of Hell from the road to Heaven. According to the teaching, the soul of any child who died before the age of ten was condemned to suffer in this hell for the sin of having caused their parents pain by dying.

The baby-souls were forced to pile stones up into towers, over and over until their period of penance was over. Periodically, a crowd of *oni* (ogre-demons) would fly by and knock down all the towers, and the children would have to start over. After knocking the towers down, the *oni* would chase and torment them. Parents were told that if they wanted to shorten the period of their dead child's suffering, they should pay the temples for special prayers and ceremonies; if they paid for enough prayers and made enough offerings over several years, their child's penance would be ended and they would be allowed to cross the deathly river and find their way to Heaven.

Most scholars agree that this horrifying myth was started as a way for financially languishing Buddhist temples to extort money out of grieving parents, creating one of the ugliest blame-the-victims spiritual extortions in world history. Belief in the children's hell lasted for centuries, and is still taught and believed in some parts of Japan today. As well as making offerings, stones are piled up to help the children with their penitential task, with many stones bearing baby bibs and hats to keep them warm during their suffering. However, eventually the bodhisattva Jizo stepped forward and proclaimed that he would spend the rest of his days in the children's hell, helping them as he could, caring for them as both mother and father. Apparently he could not end their periods of penance, but when the *oni* came after them, he would hide them all in his voluminous robes until it was safe to come out again.

After this, Jizo became one of the most beloved deities in all of Japan. He is called upon to protect all children, living or dead, that they might be safe from any accident or illness which might send them to the Children's Hell. He is seen as a kindly, patient, childlike figure with a protective staff, and tiny statues of him litter the roadsides where parents have placed them for the safety of their children. Sometimes they are interspersed with little towers of stone, others with plaques thanking Jizo for saving their child from some terrible illness. Sometimes the hats and bibs—always bright red to keep away evil influences—are placed on the Jizo statues themselves. Little toys are scattered about the feet of the rows of Jizos as offerings. Children who get lost are encouraged to find a roadside Jizo statue and stay with it, as Jizo will then find a way for them to be rescued quickly and returned to their home.

The fifth-house Moon often has very strong emotions which threaten to sweep them away. Especially as children, situations which other children might stoically endure or quickly forget can feel like an unendurable hell to them. As they grow older, they may grow out of this overreactive tendency or not (depending on the rest of their chart and how stable it is), but how their caregiving parent responded to those emotional spells will have made a strong impression on them. The Moon is often where our "mother problems" appear, and later in life the fifth-house Moon person who sensed rejection from a parent during an episode of emotional deregulation may project that onto their own relationship with their own children, and overcompensate by smothering them.

As this is the house of romance, some fifth-house Moon people unconsciously look for romantic partners who are childlike (and perhaps needy), taking care of them and protecting them from the *oni* of adult responsibilities and challenges. Others prefer to remain emotionally childlike, and seek a partner who will be the "grownup" in the relationship, being patient and caring and protective and all-compassionate like Jizo. Whether this works or not will depend largely on whether the child-partner is slowly encouraged to have mastery experiences and come into their own as a responsible adult who simply takes small vacations as a "child", or whether they are kept unhealthily dependent. There is also the danger of the "parent partner" getting exploited and held hostage by the emotional storms of the "child partner". It is important for the fifth-house Moon person, if they end up in the unhealthy version of either side of such a relationship, to remind themselves that they are not actually stuck in hell and can free themselves at any time. It is good to be patient and compassionate, but there is no kindness in enabling bad behavior.

People with fifth-house Moons have the ability to project a kindly, engaging, and non-threatening demeanor, with a childlike innocence to their charisma. It is said that people find something vaguely familiar about them, in a warm and positive way. When the Moon shines luminously in the house of the Sun, the result is a soft glow which beckons others to its circle of light. Like Jizo whom almost no one in Japan can resist, to whom children instinctively flock, their soft light draws in everyone's inner child to a creative and comforting story-time of love.

6☽ Moon in the 6th House: Anahita

The Moon, like Venus, is a watery and emotional planet, flowing like a river to the ocean. The sixth house is a very unemotional place, a dwelling of work and service and maintenance. The Moon isn't particularly happy here, but it manages to find ways to flow through these limited channels. This is reflected in the goddess who stepped forward to illustrate this slightly uncomfortable combination: Anahita, the Lady of the ancient Persians.

Scholars argue about Anahita's origins; one theory is that she is a syncretic deity made up of a couple off different goddesses combined together, and then later altered to fit into Zoroastrian beliefs. It is known that she was originally a river goddess; some speculate that she may be related to the Hindu river-goddess Sarasvati (Mercury in Libra), but she has few of that artistic lady's attributes. She provided the waters which flowed through underground streams and created wells and springs. These watered both people and livestock, so she was the goddess of domestic animal health and, eventually, the healing of humans. They watered the fields, so Anahita grew into a goddess of fertility; she also ensured the milk-flow of nursing mothers and milk-giving animals, and was a goddess of pregnancy and childbirth.

Over and over, her attributes echo the idea of liquid flowing through small and precise channels, as opposed to the great unending ocean. Anahita's main symbol was the white moonlike lotus flower, which is found in ponds and lakes. One of her hymns states that she was the mistress of the Heavenly River, which was said to flow down through a hundred thousand golden channels to a mythical sacred mountain, where it entered a holy lake and from there was sent through still more channels to various places on the earth. The description is rather like a precise plumbing diagram of cosmic size, all for purposes of purification. The sixth house is associated with Virgo, a sign which is very much bound up with cleanliness and purification, and cleaning is part of the maintenance ruled by this house. Anahita was said to purify the man's seed and the woman's womb, as well as the wells, springs, rivers, and other water sources. She was kind and maternal, but also very much a cleansing goddess.

The sixth is the House of Labor, and it is interesting that the earliest descriptions of Anahita have her clad in the skins of beavers, her favorite animal. Beavers gained her favor partly because they were river and lake creatures, of course, but they are also a symbol of diligence and hard work. No other mammal their size puts so much work and trouble into creating their home, not to mention making a huge effect on the landscape. Beavers move earth and water to create structures, and this is the watery Moon in the earthy and structural Virgo-associated house.

The interplay of water, earth, and structure in a beaver dam can give us a good clue as to how the sixth-house Moon best handles the problems of stressful emotions which threaten to flood everything. The Moon is the planet of emotion and it wants to run freely, but the most common negative feeling this Moon usually manifests is anxiety. Anyone who has an anxiety disorder—meaning that it has been out of control enough to seriously affect one's functioning and quality of life—knows that if you let it, anxiety spills over everything and floods you into paralysis or panic or both (the latter situation of which is particularly horrible). Anahita herself was said to ride a chariot through the skies which was drawn by four horses named Wind, Rain, Clouds, and Sleet—good examples of the movement of heavenly water in a less-than-pleasant manner.

Anxiety can be like a drowning river, and while tools to fish yourself out are excellent, tools to prevent the flood from taking over in the first place are preferable. The key is structures, especially routines. The Moon isn't much for routines as a whole, but this Moon placement will do better if it has regular routines which create a familiar anchor, a series of wholesome and familiar actions to take which force mindfulness and pry the spinning mind and heart off of the obsessing situation. Routines can be the carefully-built dam wall which keeps the water in one area, and like all beaver dams they require continual upkeep.

This is the house of health, and the first instinct of this Moon position is to build routines of health; this can be excellent because they do maintain the body, but they can also go overboard if the Moon individual is not careful and start to become obsessive about them to the point of reversing the overall healthful effect. The Moon in this house doesn't do these things out of a rational approach to wanting the body to be healthy; the Moon does them because they make the Moon person feel better. Mercury rules this house, and so the heart and mind need to work together, creating those structures in a way which honors and helps the heart while still allowing the mind to focus and motivate to get things done when needed. This focus on healing sometimes turns outward as well; Anahita was a goddess of healing, and her temples had physicians of both genders. Medicine and health care can be very interesting to the sixth-house Moon person.

Another common set of routines for this Moon placement is cleaning, which can be extremely cathartic, but again needs a mental brake put on it to keep it from becoming obsessive and overdone. Work can also provide a routine, at least most of the time, which can both create the secure anchor and also make the individual feel productive and competent. This placement is a little different from the Sun here, in that while the sixth-house Sun needs to be objectively productive and competent, the sixth-house Moon only needs to *feel* that they are productive and competent, and thus can get the effect with less actual effort. For them, it is less about how much actual work got done, and more about whether it felt like a lot, or that the end result was emotionally satisfying.

At the same time, the sixth-house Moon does like to be of service to others, and often ends up in service careers—perhaps caregiving jobs due to the parental lunar nature. Duty is very important to them, and they will go far out of their way to help loved ones. They do not tend to be particularly emotionally effusive, so those who need more of an outward show of affection and adoration may feel unsatisfied with this Moon placement's quiet service. ("Do you love me?" "I did your dishes, fixed your toilet, put gas in your car, bought you cough drops, and changed your cat's litter box. Would I do that for someone I didn't love?") Affection here comes through as service, making someone's life better. Occasionally this can even be the opposite of what makes someone feel loved, as in their enthusiasm for helping, they may give unsolicited and unwanted advice or aid. On the other hand, they may also be so caught up in their all-important work that they starve their loved ones for their time and energy, expecting them to understand that the work comes first, and be all right with that. Complaints abound of how they have time for their co-workers when they are in crisis, but not their own family.

The Moon reflects the individual's parenting experience in childhood, and usually has to do with the mother. With this placement, the mother would have (perhaps inadvertently) taught the child about how to handle anxiety, for better or worse. If the mother was often freaked out and had few tools to get herself out of it, the child will learn that this is how anxiety is handled, and will not know any different. It may take a while to break out of the mother's example of how to handle one's nervous complaints. (For that matter, focusing on routines of either health or cleaning may have been picked up from the mother.)

In her later depictions, Anahita was given the robes and crown of a queen, and made a major deity of Zoroastrianism; while she was eventually dropped from that faith when they cast out everything which was not patriarchal, the springs and wells and streams next to the temples are still treated as sacred. She is still invoked in some places for purification, and a stone near one of her former temples is still touched to bring fertility. The Semitic version of Anahita's name was found on some tablets with exorcism prayers to cast out demonic influences; she was as interested in cleansing a soul as a body or a river. Anahita shows us the purifying power which can be wielded by a maternal goddess, and so does this cleansing-house placement of the white-flower Moon.

7☽ Moon in the 7th House: Yue Lao

The Moon is not a reasonable planet. It *feels*, and that is its job. It wants, and needs, and blisses, and cries, and rages, and generally *responds* rather than *acts*. Even something which looks like an action, if it comes from the Moon, will usually be a response to some trigger from the environment, warranted or not. The Moon is the inner child and the inner parent, and it carries the growth from good nurturing in childhood and the scars from the less skillful variety. There are hundreds of lunar deities, all over the world, sometimes two or three to a culture (because different places had their own local story about the Moon). In China, with its great area and thousands of years of written history, there are several.

One of these is Yue Lao, who is both a lunar God and a god of marriage. He is unique among Moon deities, as he appears as an old man with a long white beard, dressed in lunar colors. He is quiet and humble, and good-natured; he carries a red book in which are inscribed the names of all the couples who are destined to be together. (And more than couples—traditional Chinese patriarchal culture allowed men to have more than one wife, although a woman having more than one husband was unheard of. However, it does show that Yue Lao is fine with complicated humans having multiple committed relationships, at once and over time, because that is how humans operate.)

Yue Lao is said to have an unending skein of red thread, and he spins out a certain length and ties the ends to the ankles of people who are destined to come together into a committed relationship. These threads can only be seen by him and by other deities, unless he helps someone to see them. They are part of the threads of destiny which are woven by the Fate-Gods, but only the parts which show where couples are bound together. Yue Lao's full name is *Yue Xia Lao Ren*, which literally means "the old man under the Moon", but he is commonly only referred to as Yue Lao. He is a lunar god and tends to appear to people only in the moonlight, which is considered special for lovers in China. (It is also said that Yue Lao is himself married, but that he never tells anyone whom his wife is, in order to keep her privacy safe. It has been speculated that he takes mortals to marry, and has had a string of mortal wives, which is why he is so passionate about matchmaking humans.)

People with seventh-house Moons are going to feel strongly about being married, or at least having a committed partner. In some cultures, having a spouse is paramount, and it's easy for seventh-house Moon people to choose inappropriate spouses just to have someone to be with, which they will often later regret and have to extricate themselves. In cultures where people are told that "needing" to be married is a weakness, they may feel guilt at their constant desire to be in partnership. Their hearts yearn to be partnered, and even if the partnership isn't right, they may submerge their feelings in order to stick with it, or become oversensitive to or over-adaptive to the desires of the other partner, putting their own aside and pretending they don't exist.

The Moon, as we've said above, is the planet of childhood nurturing, and as such generally represents the nurturing parent. It's not uncommon for seventh-house Moon people to realize later in life that they've been looking for a spouse who is like their mother in certain important ways, even if that mother was deeply flawed and caused them pain. They may inadvertently recreate their parental trauma over and over, or project that trauma onto any argument or bad experience they have with their spouse. They may also be looking for the mother they didn't have—someone who will give them caring, nurturing, and security in the ways they wish they had been given (which, of course, will be impossible for a mere mortal to fulfill). However, constantly judging partners by subconsciously comparing them to parents or even ideal parents prevents them from seeing the person as the unique adult they are, and being with them as two unique humans in a unique relationship which must be co-created.

The most famous story of Yue Lao stars a rich and hotheaded young Chinese man named Wei Gu, who was strolling one evening in the city of

Songcheng, when he saw an old man reading a book by the light of the newly-risen Moon. He walked up and asked the old man what he was reading, and Yue Lao replied that he was reading a book which had lists of all the people who would ever marry each other. Wei Gu expressed his disbelief that such a thing could exist, and the old man told Wei Gu to follow him. They walked together to the mostly-deserted marketplace and Yue Lao pointed out an old woman carrying her three-year-old little granddaughter in her arms. The old man told Wei Gu that this little girl would be his future wife.

Wei Gu was angry, thinking that a trick was being played on him ... and also not wanting to believe that he would not be able to marry quickly but would have to wait until this little girl grew up. To prove the old man to simply be a liar and manipulator, he took out his knife and slashed out at the child, thinking he would kill the girl and thus prove this old man's prophecies entirely wrong. The old woman screamed and ran away with her bleeding granddaughter, and Wei Gu felt that he had made his point to the old man, who looked at him with disgust and vanished into the moonlight.

When I find a myth (or an entity in a myth) which comes forward for a particular astrological combination, it's not unusual for side characters in the story to also be a part of illustrating the nature of that pattern, because the "main character" draws those side characters for a reason. In this case, the emotional volatility of Wei Gu also reflects part of this lunar placement. The Moon is emotions—including strong emotions—and does not care about being rational. The seventh house, on the other hand, is the House of Projections, and until we mature, we tend to project our seventh-house planets onto others and subtly ask them to "carry" those qualities for us. We can then disown them in ourselves, and spend years pretending that we don't have them (and we're talking about both positive and negative qualities of that planet). That means we don't get the chance to acknowledge and work with them until we stop projecting. Those qualities will still bubble up in us, though; a partner "carrying" them doesn't eliminate them in ourselves.

The seventh-house Moon can easily be projected on another person, or multiple people in our lives with whom we have close one-on-one relationships. "I'm not the one with the crazy emotions—that's them. I'm logical and always make sense. I don't know why I keep attracting these lunatics with out-of-control feelings." At the same time, the seventh-house Moon person may be acting just as emotionally and irrationally as their partner, but they can conveniently ignore that and blithely decide that they are the one who is acting reasonably. Wei Gu feels threatened by this lunar figure, so he lashes out at the child (another lunar figure, as the Moon is the inner child), trying to destroy her. This is analogous to the wounded, frightened individual whose heart points out an uncomfortable truth which they reject, and they lash out at their own terrified child self or at the vulnerabilities of those close to them. There may be a lot of "they made me do it" in their justifications, but of course it wasn't an outside party which made them do it, but their own dissociated, projected, painful heart.

Wei Gu went on to court other women, but the engagements always fell through, and he ended up spending many lonely years by himself. Over time, he learned to be a better person and regretted the foolish and violent urges of his youth, many of which seem to have driven away potential brides. Finally, nearly two decades later, he was approached by a man who was trying to find a good husband for his daughter. She was sweet and pretty, but her father was having trouble arranging a marriage because her legs trembled and she had trouble walking. When Wei Gu met with father and daughter, he asked if she was born this way, with a nervous disorder. The girl's father told him that she was born a healthy child, but at three years of age she was attacked by a madman who slashed at her, and only her grandmother's quick efforts in getting her away saved her life. He showed Wei Gu the scar on the girl's lower back, and Wei Gu realized with a sinking heart that he had been the cause of the girl's misery. He offered to marry her and give her all she needed to manage her disability, more out of guilt and a wish to atone than anything else, but once they were married she became the light of his life, and they had a happy relationship until he grew old and died.

The seventh-house Moon may also be attracted to individuals who seem like wounded children, and can "carry" the Moon person's wounded inner child (and allow the Moon person to nurture them and take the "parental" role); this is slightly healthier than choosing a partner who echoes a difficult parental relationship, but is still problematic. If someone is carrying your inner child archetype for you, they can't be allowed to heal and put it down, at least not while your actual inner child is still ignored and crying. However, Wei Gu's ownership of his past deeds does show that one can reparent—or at least nourish—one's wounded inner child on one's own, once the situation has been recognized. Even if you weren't the one responsible for what happened, you are now responsible for what must be done.

Later, when Wei Gu had children who were of marriageable age, he called out for Yue Lao to come and advise him on who they should marry, but the Old Man Under the Moon was still angry at Wei Gu—he is a lunar deity, after all, and they are also quite emotional—and refused to help, telling him only to allow them to follow their hearts. This is the Moon's message to the seventh-house Moon person—follow your heart and don't outsource it to others. If the seventh-house Moon individual has been outsourcing their heart to others—projecting their feelings and denying their own emotional volatility—for years, they may not know what it is they actually want. The true core of their own desires may be largely an unexplored country for them, and it may take a great deal of owning their feelings and learning honest introspection before they can figure it out.

When they have matured, the seventh-house Moon can be a wonderful partner, both to another person and to themselves. They will always want a give-and-take of nurturing, but it can become more mutual and less desperate. They will be able to show their inner child, and it won't just be when they are wailing—many people with this placement can be quite playful with a partner, and encourage playfulness in them. They will be able to see their partner's inner child without jumping automatically to parent them. They will never be someone for whom partnerships are casual or a low priority, but they can bloom under the moonlight, and become the calm, beneficent elder who knows the secrets of committed emotional intimacy.

8 ☽ Moon in the 8th House: Morgan Le Fay

The tales of King Arthur (Mars in Libra) may have once been legends of an early Celtic chieftain, but by the medieval period they had long since lost that tribal flavor and had gained all sorts of fairytale romantic themes and characters. One of the most memorable of them was the sorceress Morgan Le Fay, a strongly ambivalent character who is a heroine and healer in some versions and a wicked adversary in others. In all of them, she is a strong and independent character with one foot in the Mysteries, and that alone may put off some people … for the same reason they are made apprehensive by the eighth house of sex, death, and the Mysteries.

The Moon has something of a difficult time in the Pluto-ruled, Scorpio-associated eighth house. Anything in this house will, by definition, have some increased emotional intensity around it, because of Pluto's rulership. Putting the planet of emotions here has at least partially the effect of a Moon/Pluto aspect, intensifying feelings and making the "darker" emotions more accessible. People with eighth-house Moons often find themselves struggling with less socially acceptable feelings like wrath, jealousy, possessiveness, envy, contempt, outrage, ecstasy, deep sympathy, and deep sorrow ... perhaps by turns. Depending on the Moon's sign and aspects, this can be a challenge they learn to breathe through and work with, or it can become a serious problem of emotional regulation which can wreck their lives, not to mention the lives of others around them. They may seem to fly back and forth between angel and demon, as far as those on the outside can tell.

The figure of Morgan Le Fay changed radically over time in just this way, going back and forth between blessing and curse. The name "Morgan" comes from the old Welsh name *Morcant*, meaning "the circling sea" or "sea-born", which echoes this emotional and watery lunar placement in Scorpio's likewise emotional and watery sign. "Le Fay" is a medieval slurring of the French words for "the fairy", although Morgan was definitely born a human woman and there are no tales of her specifically consorting with the Fey Folk. Instead, it was meant to show that she was herself fey, a sorceress and seeress who did not stay within the boundaries of proper society. It was said that she could fly, become invisible, and shift her shape. Water-spirits in Welsh and Breton mythology are also called "morgens", which could be another reason for the "fairy" title. On the astrological side, children with eighth-house Moons are often highly imaginative, with great curiosity about dark or taboo (Plutonian) subjects; they may frighten themselves—and others—with the fanciful and morbid places that their minds go to when they let their imagination roam, so they often come across as somewhat "fey".

In most of the stories, Morgan and her older sisters Morgause and Elaine were the children of Arthur's mother Ygraine by her first husband, Gorlois of Tintagel; this makes them Arthur's older half-sisters. Uther Pendragon desires Ygraine and makes war on her husband to get her, killing him in battle and then taking her as a prize. As a young child, Morgan sees her father killed and her mother forcibly married to Uther, and then she and her sisters are sent away to a convent. (Individuals with eighth-house Moons often see or are affected by Death at a young age; it is not uncommon for it to reshape their early lives.) When she is old enough to leave the convent, she begins her study of the magical arts, especially astrology and healing, which resonates with the eighth-house urge to explore the hidden and mysterious. Eventually she convinces Merlin (Neptune in the ninth house) to teach her magic, before he is imprisoned for years by the nymph Nimue.

In the earlier stories, Morgan is more of a healer and ally of Arthur; she was said to be one of nine wise women who did magic on the Apple-Isle of Avalon (which may have been Glastonbury before its waters dried up and it was an island no more) and when Arthur is mortally wounded, he is taken to Morgan of Avalon to be healed. In later tales, she becomes more of an enemy; there are many reasons listed for her famous hatred of Guinevere the Queen. When her older sister Morgause seduces Arthur for a night and bears his son Mordred, it is Morgan who raises her nephew to eventually destroy his father. It has been postulated in research and later fiction that Morgan and Mordred represent the last vestiges of the old pre-Christian pagan religions in England, and that their implacable opposition to Arthur's court and policies was in response to his attempts to make England a wholly Christian country and ban the old religion's adherents. Guinevere was supposedly Arthur's impetus for doing so, and thus would have made enemies among the paganfolk, although Merlin the Druid tried to mediate the situation for as long as he could.

Morgan Le Fay follows in the footsteps of many semi-divine sorceresses who are benevolent and malicious by turns, including Circe (Pluto in the seventh house) and Medea. Some scholars believe that these classical tales filtered into the lexicon of educated early-medieval writers and shaped their characterization of the Arthurian sorceress. The eighth-house Moon can often relate to the concept of ricocheting back and forth between benevolence and maliciousness; even if they have excellent self-control and do not act on their more unpleasant emotions, they may still be beset with dark feelings and desires which torment them internally. The house of Death can be quite morose and sometimes even gruesome for any planet there, especially the sensitive Moon. This placement does give strong sensitivity to one's environment; they will be easily able to sum up the attitudes of other people, and if the Moon is afflicted, they may use that intuition to manipulate others in order to protect themselves.

The eighth is the house of sex, and Morgan Le Fay is frequently accused of being promiscuous; one of the many stories in which she is mentioned calls her "the most lustful woman in all of England". Some of that is simply due to being a female figure who chooses their own mates and does not confine themselves to one partner in wedlock. In the era of the legends, most marriages were arranged or of convenience, and all sex was supposed to take place only monogamously after a wedding, and primarily for procreation. As a throwback to the old pagan beliefs which were far less prudish, Morgan Le Fay carries the brunt of medieval Christian fears of sexual independence. She seduces many of the knights of the Round Table, as well as (apparently) hundreds of other men, becoming an embodiment of the nymphomaniacal woman who is so frightening to sexually repressed men.

On the other hand, the eighth-house Moon does have a strong emotional relationship to sex. Some may be demisexual, with the genitals only engaging when there is already a strong emotional connection. On the other extreme, some may be fine with casual sex and actually find that the neurochemical stimulation from intense sexual activity calms and centers their strong emotions, acting as a better tranquilizer and/or antidepressant than any pill. Of course, with that mental-health byproduct, they are going to want as much of it as possible, and may not be willing to confine it to only one person. At worst, this side effect can lead to sexual addiction. At the least, sex will be a powerful and passionate experience for them, and not one to be taken lightly or casually. What they need is a sexual relationship with someone who can join deep into the darkness of the psyche, as a partner and companion and not just a lover. Without this, they may substitute hypersexuality for deep connection.

This is also the house of transformation, and the final goal for this placement is transforming the emotions into something clean and controlled, yet also flowing and fully experienced. Once the eighth-house Moon person has worked through their obsessions, bad memories, and fluctuating feelings—once they have emotionally matured and no longer fear the insides of their heads—they can often help others to walk that path as well, transforming their pain to understanding. In nearly all the tales, at the end of the story Morgan Le Fay retreats to the Isle of Avalon with the wise women, to study and heal and no longer bother with the politics of the outer world.

The Arthurian romances were extraordinarily popular all over Europe, and were even brought to southern Europe by Norman warriors during the Crusades. In Italy, the "Fata Morgana" became a name for mirages made of mist which appear in the Strait of Messina. To the less mature eighth-house Moon, the emotions are waves which crash down and cannot be held, and then when they recede, are like mirages which cannot be grasped. As they master the magic needed to become proficient at emotional intelligence, what was once a mirage can become a tool. If you don't think that this process is magic, ask the eighth-house Moon … they'll tell you all about such sorcery. Or perhaps they will simply smile Morgan Le Fay's knowing smile, and say nothing.

9☽ Moon in the 9th House: Lancelot and Galahad

The Arthurian legends may not be exactly ancient—although they do seem to stem from a number of merged ancient stories of heroes and kings—but over time, they have become a powerful set of myths with strong moral lessons in them. While they still retain the Christian overlay, their roots lie deep in old European pagan stories, and many outline the violent clash between the two cultures colliding. In the first MythAstrology book, Arthur (Mars in Libra) appears; you've just met Morgan Le Fay as the eighth-house Moon, and later in this book you will find other Arthurian figures such as Merlin (Neptune in the ninth house) and the Fisher King (Jupiter in the twelfth house). Now, however, we will look at the story of the two greatest knights of the Round Table—father and son—who both sought the Holy Grail, although only one succeeded where the other failed.

The archetypal knight on the quest, riding across the world to find something of value or rescue someone from pain or defeat an oppressor is a strongly ninth-house figure. It resonates with Jupiter, that house's ruler, and adventurous, idealistic Sagittarius associated with it. The Arthurian knights are especially linked to this astrological thread, because they are steeped in a philosophy of using one's strength for good. Some fail periodically, some fall away from the quest, some die giving their heart to it. The archetype of the knight-errant endures, however, and it gave history the legacy of the code of chivalry, which few historical knights ever actually followed.

The ideal of chivalry was set up in order to "civilize" warriors who had been given lands and money and titles, but who were still largely armed thugs with little in the way of manners or kindness. There is a decidedly female-worshiping component to it, visible in the way that Lancelot dedicates all his deeds to Guinevere, Arthur's wife who eventually becomes his lover. (One of the greatest proponents of chivalric and "courtly love" stories in the twelfth century, in a way the woman who started it all, was Queen Eleanor of Aquitaine.) Shadows of this can be found in the ninth-house Moon as well; the Moon rules femaleness and people with this placement are often drawn to a feminine conception of the divine, if it is at all culturally accessible. At the least, they may have idealized views of women, even if they are female themselves.

The Arthurian legends had numerous authors in Germany, France, England, and Italy, with just as many versions of the tales. The patchwork which has come down to us eventually fused into a well-known story, but it is by no means the only version. Each main character has a number of different births, deaths, parents, spouses, children, and stories. The Arthur-Guinevere-Lancelot triangle appears in some tales and not others, for example. Here we will follow the most common version, the one which has come down to us today through story and media.

Lancelot starts out looking like the "perfect knight", holding to the code of chivalry, but the story quickly begins to reveal his character. He is idealistic and chivalrous, but he is also driven by emotion—quick to love, quick to anger, quick to action. He is relentless on his quests to rescue Guinevere (when she is captured) or anyone else; he leaps into danger without thinking and ignores wounds and pain. Some of the stories note how he goes from joyous to furious, shredding whatever is in his hands, his eyes going from dancing to glowing coals of anger. He is emotionally devoted as much to his knighthood and its endless quest as he is to his lady love; perhaps more so.

Any Moon needs to be moved by emotion to act, but the ninth-house placement aims the individual's strong feelings at areas of life which may seem more theoretical than visceral to other Moons, but which are displayed in idealistic technicolor to those with this placement. Religion becomes a spiritual mission in which they can bury their heart. Higher education (including any course of adult study) becomes a quest for information; they are hunters on the scent of elusive prey. Travel becomes both a way to soothe the heart and to pursue new experiences with fascinating people and places. Philosophy becomes a journey to find the Truth, always the best bait for anything associated with truth-seeking Sagittarius. Their world view is shaped by these emotions, which means that they can be somewhat irrational about them. Moons are always irrational, by definition, and this Moon can lead to distorted thinking around these areas, or it can lead to a deep faith—Jupiter's currency—which guides them through all the failures and disappointments and keeps them going toward the horizon. This placement doesn't have goals so much as it has horizons; each accomplishment naturally spurs them on toward even more distant adventures.

As another example of the lunar influence, the most popular version of Lancelot's childhood is that his father was an ousted lord and his mother fled with her young son, but he was captured in a moment of her inattention by a faery enchantress, Nimue the Lady of the Lake. She brings him up on her hidden island, teaching him lore, arms, music, and all other chivalrous pursuits. When he is fifteen, she brings him to Arthur's court where he becomes a knight over the next few years. Like his son Galahad after him, Lancelot comes to the court certain that he will become a knight, and a powerful one; people with this placement often have an uncanny ability to guess the outcomes of situations. They have strong intuitions which grasp metaphor and symbol with ease, leading them to see many layers in spiritual and philosophical concepts.

The problem, as with any Moon placement, is that sometimes you just aren't feeling it, and that's when the Moon strays away. When Guinevere rejects Lancelot because Elaine, the daughter of the Fisher King, has had a brief night with him while he was under an enchantment, he flees into the wilderness and becomes a hermit. His brothers hunt him out and find him weeping for his love and tearing out his hair, saying that he will give up knighthood altogether if he cannot be near Guinevere. They convince him to return, and Guinevere forgives him. Even the ninth-house Moon's dearest quest can be abandoned if their heart is not in it, which is one of the reasons why they are notorious for dropping out of college or changing religions—they "lost heart" in the process, as it were. Usually it means that the idealized illusions were torn away, and they need time to retreat until they can find a way to ride that quest without the comfort of the ideals ... or, more likely, they find another quest to hare off on, one which has not yet had time to disappoint them.

The love affair between Lancelot and Guinevere is what finally splits the Round Table and destroys Arthur's dream. Guinevere is accused of adultery and treason (cheating on the King is a treasonous charge) and sentenced to be executed. Lancelot rescues her again, killing several knights who had been his compatriots in the process. Sides are taken, and rebellion begins, and chaos descends. It is a shattering finale, ending with Arthur dead, peace broken, and Guinevere so guilt-ridden that she chooses to enter a convent rather than be with her lover. This is in stark contrast to the tale of Galahad, Lancelot's illegitimate son by Elaine, who was raised in the palace of the Fisher King.

While Parsifal, whose tale is told in the twelfth-house Jupiter chapter, may or may not ever find the Grail, Galahad manages to do it. Like his father, he comes as a young man to court with his magically powerful mother, certain that he will be a knight, and is soon known for his gallantry and purity. While "purity" in the post-Christianity story tended to mean celibacy, it can be looked at as a purity of focus. Lancelot becomes distracted in his quests by love, anger, pride, despair, and all the other lunar traps. Galahad is able to retain a single-minded focus on finding the Grail, and is not derailed by his heart, which remains drawn like a lodestone to his horizon.

Galahad first arrives at Arthur's court and ends up in a duel with Lancelot, who does not know that the young man is his son. He realizes it well into the duel, and is so shocked that for the first time, he is defeated. Galahad reveals himself with a shower of omens, and is accepted into the company as the only man ever to defeat Lancelot. It is a foretelling of how he will surpass his father in other ways as well. Galahad proves himself by rescuing not only lovely ladies but other knights, including his friend Parsifal. He pardons and releases his enemies after defeating them, whenever he can manage to do it. With his two companions Bors and Parsifal, he searches for the Grail until the clues finally lead him home to the Fisher King's palace. His mother Elaine had died in the meantime, and he had not come home since that time. When he returns as an adult and a knight, however, it is revealed to him that the Grail has been kept all this time in the castle where he grew up, guarded by his mother and some of his women, but he was never allowed to know of it.

The Moon rules the parent-child relationship and the home; due to its fourth-house association, Galahad's defeat of his absent father can be seen as the Moon battling the family pain ... and winning, at least in this story. After the duel, Lancelot accepts his son and brings him into the circle of the Round Table, a ninth-house Moon's dream. Finding the Grail in the very home in which he grew up is another lunar message: In the end, all quests end at home, whether that is coming back to the place and family where you grew up, or creating another version of that family which does homage to the culture and world view of the original one, with—like Galahad being more disciplined, focused, and determined than Lancelot—all the unhealthy bits removed.

Lancelot is the Moon/heart divided and distracted by its ambivalent feelings; Galahad is the Moon/heart which manages to stay constant. Both men, ironically, end up with strangely religious lives and deaths at the end. After the death of Arthur and the retirement of Guinevere, Lancelot goes back to being a hermit monk in the wilderness, praying to see his love again ... but only finally seeing her at her funeral, after which he dies. Galahad is spoken to by God while gazing upon the Grail; he is offered a boon, and asks to be allowed to choose the moment of his death. The wish is granted, and he decides to die now, at the perfect end of his quest. In some stories he simply dissolves into white flower petals and is taken up to heaven; in others he dies at that moment and is buried next to the Grail. Neither ending lives in the real world, because the ninth-house Moon believes, on some level, that they can outrace the reality of the undignified and grubby ending. While life doesn't often go that way, it seems like this lunar placement manages it more often than not.

10 ☽ Moon in the 10th House: Sita

Back in the chapter on the tenth-house Sun, we met Rama the prince. Here, where the Moon moves into the position of public image and ambition, we meet his wife Sita. Her side of the story has a very different cast to it than Rama's political and personal choices, because in Hindu culture women were considered to be lesser beings than men. A woman's job was to support her husband and raise "his" children, and a noblewoman's job was to do all that without getting her sari dirty or speaking an ungracious word. Sita has far less power in her life than does Rama, but here we will look at that inequality not merely as an inconvenient historical fact but also of a mirror for the different experiences of Sun and Moon in this most professional and career-oriented of houses.

We watched Rama's rise to power through action and self-control—and, it must be said, ignoring or denying the internal emotional life. The Sun can pull that off. The Moon can't; not without great pain and damage to itself. The Moon is the seat of the emotions, so by definition it has to deal with those messy, blurry, irrational feelings.

All signs are more comfortable in some signs and houses, and downright uncomfortable in others. This is one of the hardest placements for a Moon, because it's all about external actions, hard-driving decisions, and outside opinions. The Moon rules home, family, and domesticity; this house is about the exact opposite, and in opposition to the Moon's own house. In comparison to the Sun, the Moon has an automatic handicap when placed here, like Sita in Hindu culture when compared to Rama. Many astrological opinions foist this placement off with comments about how it might indicate being a housewife as a career, or having a career in child care or other types of nurturing. While this is not uncommon, there's a lot more to the experience of the Moon in this house than just channeling lunar energies into a specific career.

Let's start with Sita. In some sources she is the daughter of Janaka, a king of Videha in ancient India. In others, she is a magical child found in the furrow of a newly-plowed field, and thus is the daughter of Bhumi Devi, the Earth Mother. She is later adopted by King Janaka and his wife. The tenth is certainly an "earthy" house, regardless of the sign on its cusp; it is associated with Saturn and Capricorn, so her status as the daughter of Earth is appropriate. In fact, she may actually be a later version of a Vedic fertility goddess of the same name, who was associated with the Earth's abundance. She is also considered to be an incarnation of Lakshmi (Moon in the second house), the consort of Vishnu (Neptune in the second house), a goddess who is often prayed to for wealth and material gain. By taking her as a wife, Rama "marries fortune" in some sense.

Sita is not to be merely taken, however; Rama must win her hand in a special contest. The magical bow of Shiva (Sun in Scorpio) was kept in a nearby temple; it was so heavy that most mortals could not lift it, and anyone impure of heart could not even approach it. Janaka had observed his adopted daughter Sita shifting over the altar on which it was kept while cleaning the temple, and realized that she was special. He wanted a son-in-law who would be as strong—both physically and morally—as his daughter, and thus held a competition. Rama was the only one who was able to bend and string the bow, and thus he won Sita's hand.

Like Venus in the same house, this Moon placement sometimes indicates an individual who may gain social status through marriage—"famous by proxy". Their public "job" is to be the anchor of the high-flying partner with the big career, and in many cases it can be a real career in and of itself. As the Moon is about family, it's also possible that they were born to their status and inherit it from their family ties. On the other hand, they may choose to be the one with the big career. It's not that a tenth-house Moon lacks ambition; it's just that under it all is one motivation—they want to be *liked*. They want the limelight and the approval for purely emotional reasons, and if success turns out to be a failure on that front, they may well pack up and go. This means that there are fewer big successes with the Moon in this house than with the Sun, but likely also fewer people who have morally or personally compromised themselves.

The Moon here is not immune to compromise, but they tend to do it for emotional reasons—perhaps the needs of the people touch them, or they feel loyalty to the business or the career path. When Rama was exiled for fourteen years by his father, Sita followed him faithfully into exile, and was near him for all his great deeds. At one point, Ravana the demon king sees her and falls in love. He sends a glowing golden deer past the hut where Rama, Sita, and Rama's brother Lakshmana live, and Sita decides that she wants it for a pet. Rama and Lakshmana go out to hunt the deer, and Ravana kidnaps Sita while they are gone, carrying her off to his palace. While her husband and brother-in-law are gathering a magical army to fight a war against Ravana, the demon king continually attempts to woo Sita. She refuses all his advances, including the physical ones; one story tells that he tried to unwrap her sari to rape her and the Gods made it endless, so that no matter how much he unwrapped, she could not be made naked.

It is the moment when the heretofore passive Sita shows her strength and endurance. The Moon knows what it wants, and what it wants is to feel good, about itself and the others in its life. This can lead a Moon with this placement to follow rigid social rules and worry about reputation just like the Sun, but their reasons, again, are all about being liked. Sometimes those reasons can cross the line into wanting others to prove that they love and value you; if that is not forthcoming, this Moon placement can be surprisingly implacable. At one point Hanuman the warrior monkey (Uranus in the sixth house) slips into Sita's prison and offers to secretly carry her back to Rama. She refuses to go, because she wants Rama to be the one to rescue her ... as publicly as possible. She wants her worth to be clearly visible to everyone watching, which is a strong desire for this Moon.

Rama does eventually rescue Sita, but then informs her to her dismay that he believes her to have been unfaithful to him with Ravana ... or at least that the people will believe she has been unfaithful. Sita reacts angrily, asking how he dares to question her when she promises she has been chaste. Part of her rebuttal goes into her family and its honor and importance, reminding him that she is as royal as he is, and her word is thus more trustworthy. This is the tenth-house Moon summoning up her credentials, hoping that public status—and especially that of family—will make a difference. Eventually she agrees to the "test of Agni", where she must walk through fire in order to prove her innocence. The fire turns to red flowers as she walks through it, and in some versions Agni himself (Jupiter in Sagittarius) appears to bolster her word. Thus, in the older part of the Ramayana, the story ends with Rama and Sita returning in triumph to Rama's father's city, and living happily ever after for the rest of their lives. Due to her loyalty and persistent refusal to be violated, Sita is said to be the "perfect wife" of Rama, the "perfect ruler". Here the Moon is still sensitive and vulnerable to the opinions of outsiders, and is willing to do her job in a way that gives her credit. In Sita's culture, this means going back to being compliant and supportive.

However, as we saw in the tenth-house Sun chapter, the story doesn't end there. In the *Uttara Kanda*, or "epilogue story", a later addition which may date to the fifth century, Rama hears his subjects murmuring rumors about whether Sita was really chaste with Ravana, and decides that he must banish her in order to keep the approval of the public. The final story was added because the politics of the era had shifted, and rules around caste and gender were getting even more rigid than they had originally been; writers wanted to show that any deviation from the repressive rules should be severely punished, even if it came through no fault of the transgressor. History aside, this mirrors an ongoing problem with the ambitions of this Moon placement. The lunar qualities of caring, nurturing, paying attention to feelings, and valuing family, are generally disregarded and devalued in the traditional workplace. (If they were, the situation with child care, maternity leave, workplace satisfaction, and taking time off to be with your kids would be very different.) People who come to their jobs from a lunar rather than a solar motivation are often pushed aside to make room for more conventionally driven co-workers who would rather scramble to the top than have time to bond with their kids. It's not uncommon for this Moon placement to put in years of loyal service while seeing the promotions go to Sun or Mars or Saturn types. Unlike these other hard-driving planets, the Moon here is more likely to use softer tactics, such as reassuring people and making them feel comfortable, in order to get ahead. That can be effective in some fields, but not most of them.

Sita goes to live in a hermit's hut and bears twin sons, whom the hermit names Kusha ("grass") and Lava ("cow-hair") because these were the materials used to wipe the birthing fluids from their bodies. In spite of the wrongs done to her, Sita raises her sons to value their father, in an act of sacrifice vaguely reminiscent of Chaucer's "Patient Griselda", another "morality" tale where a wife is badly abused to prove her fidelity to her cruel husband, and endures it with patience and dignity. In a way, this is the tenth-house Moon going back to its domestic roots, being a parent and nurturer. However, this Moon does tend to get emotionally attached to their work, and the loss of Sita's queenly job is painful to her. There's not much tenth-house improvement to be had while living in a hermit's hut in the wilderness, and she feels it keenly, even as she doggedly hangs on.

When the boys are twelve years old, they come to the attention of Rama's underlings due to their singing of praise-songs about their father. Rama takes them in, but leaves Sita in the forest, still unwilling to have her political liability in his house. Alone and abandoned, she gives up on life. Given this Moon story, it may not even be so much about being rejected by Love as it is being shown that you no longer have worth in the eyes of the important people and society.

In one later version Sita enters an ashram, but in the more telling versions she calls out to Bhumi Devi, the Earth Mother, to swallow her up. The Earth opens and she is taken back to her mother; after her death, she remembers herself as Lakshmi and is reunited with Rama/Vishnu after he drowns himself in repentance. (One hopes that they had a long conversation about what living a mortal life showed them about their relationship, and that much was learned from it.)

Centuries later, there is a veritable mound of Hindu philosophical justifications for Sita's ill treatment. *Sita was destined to suffer because she was cursed by a mated pair of parrots she separated. Lakshmi wanted to experience suffering. Sita was punished because she ate the wrong food. Everything was already predetermined and there was no way to escape her fate.* One can almost feel the desperation of the sages, trying to explain away political apologias for merciless leadership. The truth is both simpler and more complex, but it points inevitably to the nagging suspicion that if culture—then and now—did not elevate the Sun at the expense of the Moon, Sita would have had more recourse, and the Moon would do at least a little better when relegated to the tenth house.

The tenth-house Moon story doesn't have to go as badly as Sita's, of course. Part of the problem is that this Moon can become so emotionally attached to the company or the boss or the people in their field that they aren't able to walk away cleanly and start a new career path. When they are shoved aside or devalued, they hang on to the situation, perhaps seething but pretending to be patient and kind, perhaps cast off but unable to move forward in another direction because of an attachment to resentment. They need to choose a career which will fill their heart, and if it turns out to be inadequate, they need to learn to walk away and choose another. In the end, like the example of Gandhi who had this Moon placement, the goal needs to be big enough to be worthy of their great hearts. The process must be able to nourish them through all the hungry places in the road, and give them enough satisfaction to pass on to a hungry world.

11 ☽ Moon in the 11th House: Ninshubur

If you read the *Enuma Elish*—the myth of the descent of the Sumerian goddess Inanna to the underworld (Venus in Scorpio)—you notice that the success or failure of Inanna's risky trip turns on the blade of a knife. That knife's name is Ninshubur, and she is the *sukkal* of Inanna. *Sukkal* is a term which has been variously translated as "servant", "vizier", "messenger", "ambassador", or even "sidekick". Ninshubur is far from a mere maidservant; she is Inanna's second-in command. Inanna herself describes Ninshubur as the one she goes to for advice, and the one who defends her with weapons, a sort of bodyguard as well. One scholar of linguistics has posited that the exact spelling of "sukkal" which is used to refer to Ninshubur is a specific version which suggests someone who is highly important to the ruler they serve, who is dear to them. While some writers have jumped on this as hopeful evidence of a romantic lesbian relationship, we can't confirm or deny that. What we can be certain of, from Inanna's long declamation of all the ways Ninshubur has been faithful to her beyond all expectations, is that we are definitely talking about a pair of best friends.

When the Moon—the wholly subjective and irrational planet of emotions—enters the airy, transpersonal eleventh house of friends, groups, and all of humanity, it brings all of its emotional nature to those areas of life. They get emotional needs fulfilled by being around like-minded people, and often have wide social circles, with graduated rings of friends, friends of friends, acquaintances, and many others who know their name. People with this placement want to belong to something; they long not for the family but for the tribe. This is especially the case if their family relationships are unsatisfying for whatever reason; they are quick to give up on blood kin and create their own chosen family where they are accepted for themselves. Once they have ensconced themselves in that tribe, they will go to the wall for them.

The eleventh-house Moon is capable of making deep and intimate friendships, which they will defend to the death, sometimes even against lovers and spouses who expect to be put first. The eleventh is the house of the future, ruled by Uranus and associated with Aquarius, and they may have strong emotions about relationships being custom-designed instead of defaulting to the expectations of society. That includes ranking one's nearest and dearest not by their role in your life, but by the love that grows between you. In that system, a best friend can be at the top of the list even if lovers and spouses are present.

Ninshubur comes into other myths before the Enuma Elish, always at Inanna's side. When Inanna is pursued by magical spirit-warriors after stealing words of power, it is Ninshubur who fends them off, showing herself to be a warrior. At the beginning of the tale of Inanna's descent to the Underworld to visit her sister Ereshkigal the Queen of Death (Pluto in Libra), Ninshubur is given the responsibility of the emergency plan. If Inanna does not come back in three days, Inanna's best friend is to gain assistance by any means necessary to storm the Land of the Dead and rescue her.

When Inanna (of course) does not come back after three days, Ninshubur implements the emergency plan—with all the overemotional performance the Moon is capable of giving. She throws herself on the doorstep of one powerful God after another, screaming and tearing her clothing, lacerating herself, begging them to rescue Inanna even though she has gone where they have no power. Many people think of the Moon as being serene and kindly and maternal, but as we saw with Ezili Dantor (Moon in the first house), the Moon's emotions can just as easily be rage, anguished weeping, furious anxiety, or terror. Ninshubur does this not as a performance, but because she is in terror for the life of her best friend, and wants everyone to see those emotions in the hope of getting some help. That's the way the Moon goes about things—if I am emotionally loud enough, someone else might be moved and give me aid. The eleventh-house Moon is a little cooler, by nature, than other Moons, but for their best friend they will cry like a seventh-house Moon for their spouse.

Eventually, Enki the inventor deity (Mars in Aquarius) relents and concocts a rescue plan. Inanna comes triumphantly up out of the Underworld, flanked by demons who will seize anyone who is not in mourning for her, and they will take her place. It is Ninshubur who runs on ahead, telling all the temples to mourn for Inanna and act glad to see her, which they do. She fails only once, and does not get to Inanna's lover Dumuzi (Sun in Pisces), who has taken over her throne, in time to warn him before the demons arrive. Dumuzi is taken away to the Underworld, and Ninshubur's part in the story is over. Her actions have saved Inanna, because she was determined to get her friend back from the dead.

The eleventh-house Moon person often desires to live with their friends, opening their home to them. People with this placement are more likely to want to live in community than any other Moon, and may end up in an intentional community, or at least a houseful of roommates. It may be a learning curve regarding what friends are appropriate to let in; Moons by their nature are often moved more by sympathy than logic and this Moon placement may fall for a sob story, at least the first few times. Eventually they will learn to be more discerning, or at least that just because someone needs a roof over their head at the moment does not mean your sacrifice for them will work out well.

They may also end up parenting their friends, perhaps being the one who makes sure they are fed and cared for. Regardless of gender, the Moon desires to take care of people, and in this house it will be the chosen family who is the object of their ministrations. If the Moon is afflicted with a lot of squares and oppositions, it can create repeated disappointing circumstances with friends, and an eleventh-house Moon who becomes cynical and withdrawn. This is exacerbated by the fact that this Moon often hopes to get as much nurturing and support back from their friends as they give out, an expectation which is rarely negotiated up front, and the friends may not know this was the unspoken deal. One solution to this is, of course, simply to make new and better friends. Another solution is to turn to this house's rulership of one's relationship with humanity itself.

This Moon, more than any other, is capable to expanding its caring and sympathy to the rest of the world, seeing people as one great tribe, and sinking all those caregiving desires into the unending needs of the larger group. This is also the house of long-term goals, and as this Moon gains great emotional satisfaction from creating big goals and then accomplishing them, it's not unusual for them to replace disappointing friends with putting their caring efforts toward much larger crowds of people. This does not replace the sympathy and caring they still secretly hope to receive in their turn, but it does give them a fair amount of emotional comfort to even see crowds of strangers helped. After all, strangers are just friends one hasn't yet found a way to connect with, at least according to the eleventh-house Moon.

Ninshubur was not just a character in a sacred story, otherwise discounted in Sumerian religion. The more that archaeologists translate cuneiform and identify statues, the more they find that she was one of the most popular deities in the pantheon to pray to. As the *sukkal* of a major deity, she was the intermediary between the greater Gods and humanity. Just as the gatekeeping vizier is the way in to the king or queen, so Ninshubur was the one who could get prayers to other Gods. Similarly, she brought messages from the Gods and thus mediated between two groups, mortal and immortal.

Being the mediator between groups of people is also something the eleventh-house Moon person will understand. They are often members of so many groups that they become the crossover member, the one who speaks for the other demographics they may belong to, in any company they may be in at the moment. Becoming the representative, the one with sympathy and understanding for both sides who explains the foreign point of view, becomes a natural role for them.

Gods who are gatekeepers, and Gods who are messengers, not infrequently carry various Uranian traits—perhaps they are tricksters, or move against social norms in some way. *How far would you go for the friends you love?* asks Ninshubur. That leads to the question of how far you would go for your tribe, and this Moon placement will go further for them than most others, sacrificing for the group which holds their emotional interest. That leads in turn to asking how far you would go for the sisterhood-and-brotherhood of the human race, which isn't going to be on most peoples' radar ... but it is the ultimate goal for the Heart in the house of the People.

12 ☽ Moon in the 12th House: Iphigenia

The ancient Greek epic story of the Iliad is mostly remembered as a war epic, a story of clashing armies and tall wooden horses. However, it is also full of female figures, and those figures were fleshed out in other Greek stories and plays throughout the ancient world. One of those figures, Iphigenia, goes from being a passive figure to being an active figure depending on which story is told. Yet each version of the story has its own truths and its own merits. Sometimes life happens to us and we are overcome, and sometimes we find in ourselves the quiet strength to turn around our fate.

Iphigenia is the daughter of Agamemnon, the Greek commander, and his unhappy wife Clytemnestra. In order to understand Iphigenia's childhood and how it shaped her, it is necessary to understand her mother ... which is a truth that could be said about any Moon placement. The Moon rules the nurturing parent, which is usually (but not always) Mother, and no Moon grows up without being shaped by that early nurturing experience (or lack thereof). And so with this Moon, we start with the Mother.

Clytemnestra is a tragic figure in Greek mythology. She is the twin sister of Helen of Troy (Sun in Gemini), but unlike Helen who was the daughter of Zeus (Jupiter in Aries), Clytemnestra (also Sun in Gemini) is fully mortal, plain and unbeautiful, and devalued next to her gorgeous sister. She is casually married off at thirteen to one of her father's older retainers, and bears a baby by him. When the family enemy Agamemnon bursts in one day with all his soldiers and slaughters the family, he kills her husband, tears the infant from her arms, bashes out its brains on the wall, rapes her, and then tells her that they are married. Her vain attempts at rebellion get her locked up in prison for years, with Agamemnon periodically stopping in to force pregnancies onto her body. It is no surprise that she cherishes her daughters, but when she has a son, she decides to kill him to strike at her husband. Her son Orestes (Neptune in the fourth house) is smuggled out of Mycenae by his older sister Electra, so that his mother's anger will never be heard by him. Clytemnestra is allowed to keep her daughters with her as a consolation.

Iphigenia is the eldest of these daughters. She spends most of her childhood living in her wounded mother's prison, a concept which may speak volumes to the twelfth-house Moon individual. It is said that Iphigenia was Clytemnestra's favorite, her consolation, and the only thing that kept her from killing herself in the early days of her imprisonment. Twelfth-house planets have a hard time with boundaries, and it is certain that one of the classic twelfth-house Moon childhoods is the one where the mother-child bond becomes so close that there are no good boundaries. The child may become the mother's confidante, or lose their identity in her desires or expectations. Sometimes the mother is depressed or lonely or mentally ill and the child is her solace; sometimes there are outside circumstances that force them unnaturally close—"If we must suffer, at least we are suffering together!" Either way, the twelfth-house Moon child does not have the inner resources to break away and rebel easily. Her boundaries are too permeable, she is too emotionally impressionable by the strong feelings of others, and she has little access to her own feelings. Buried in the depths of the unconscious twelfth house, they might as well be on another planet as far as she is concerned ... and the feelings of her parents are so much louder anyway.

Another classic twelfth-house Moon childhood is one where there is no mother, and the child is "mothered" by an institution—an orphanage, or foster parents, or older and more rigid grandparents. In some cases, one or both of the parents was ill and spent much of their time in hospitals; either way, anything that resembled childhood was bound up with imprisonment. Iphigenia grows up never knowing what it is to be emotionally free, or that such a thing is even possible.

In the Iliad, Agamemnon goes off to attack Troy and finds that there is no wind for his fleet to sail on. According to the local priests, Artemis the Moon Goddess (Moon in Sagittarius) is angry at them, and is withholding the wind until a properly valuable sacrifice is made to her, preferably one of blood. Agamemnon decides to sacrifice one of his own daughters; after all, he has more of them and they are unimportant anyway in his eyes. He sends for Iphigenia, telling Clytemnestra that she is to be married to the hero Achilles (Mars in the first house), and to dress her as a bride. However, when she arrives, she is escorted to the funeral pyre and burned alive.

This is where the twelfth house shows its rulership by Neptune and Pisces, both of whom are concerned with sacrifice. Iphigenia becomes the archetype of the Sacrificed Maiden, and this reflects in the life of the twelfth house Moon child. They are required, again and again, to sacrifice their needs for that of the adults around them. Their boundaries are sacrificed by adults who appreciate their permeable, feeling nature, and much of the rest of their lives are sacrificed by the ones that don't. Like Iphigenia, they may passively go along with it, overwhelmed by the seeming rightness of other people's needs. In fact, that self-sacrifice and blindness to their own emotions may go on for decades, or a lifetime, moving from person to person, neediness to neediness, sacrifice to sacrifice.

At this point, the story splits into two endings. In one version, Iphigenia simply dies and is sent to Artemis as a victim. In the other, Artemis substitutes a doe at the last moment on the funeral pyre and carries Iphigenia secretly to Tauris, where she leaves her as a novice with the priestesses of the Artemis cult in that area. The priestesses take Iphigenia in as one of them and train her to do their job, part of which is making unwilling sacrifices to Artemis of various foreigners who wander into the country. Where once she was the sacrificed maiden, now the tables are turned and she is the one wielding the knife, all in the name of the implacable lunar goddess.

We tend to think of lunar goddesses, and lunar things in general, as being about soft, nurturing, receptive feelings. That is an insultingly incomplete way to look at it, especially when it comes to our own Moons, who are both inner parent and inner child. Sometimes the inner parent is a devouring mother or an evil father, and sometimes the inner child is an inconsolable, selfish brat. That's just the way of it: the lunar feelings can be terrible and aggressive just as often as they can be soft and passive. Since children tend to be encouraged by their caregivers to behave passively and accept what those caregivers think is right, all the years of resentment pile up in the unconscious, but never make it to the surface. The feelings are imprisoned; there is not enough quiet, autonomous solitude to create access to the twelfth house and the buried Moon.

Then, one day, it starts to burst out. A dam can only hold so much water, and then it begins to crack. From the point of view of the Moon individual, those feelings may seem to come out of nowhere and make no sense. *Those can't be mine; I don't know anything about them. I've never felt them before.* The emotions rise up and strike out, often at those who have been fooled into believing in her self-sacrificing exterior; sometimes those who have become dependent on her maintaining that exterior. They are violent, and vicious, and implacable, and all the things associated with the Artemis side of the lunar equation. She is no longer the Good Child; now she is the Avenger.

Many years go by, and Iphigenia becomes tired of her role as Giver of Death. She cannot escape from Tauris without aid, because her home is far away in an unknown direction (Tauris is generally considered to be a peninsula off the northern edge of the Black Sea). As the Chosen One of Artemis, she is not allowed to run off, so she finds herself just as permanently stuck in this role as in the last one. Similarly, the twelfth-house Moon may find herself once again the Sacrificial Maiden, only now instead of being sacrificed to the needs of others, the rest of her life is sacrificed to the screaming, pent-up needs. Relationships, commitments, goals—all fall under the knife. The emotions rule with no brakes and few outside factors to sway them. It is, in its own way, just as much of a prison as the first sort, but the difference is that it is a necessary step towards real emotional understanding.

Awkward and painful as it is, it has to happen; if Iphigenia goes home again before living the experience of Tauris, she will revert to being the imprisoned daughter of her mother. Once she has enough of her own feelings excavated—once she has dug herself a wide tunnel into the dark places of the unconscious, and made it a two-way street—then she can never again be made completely passive and unknowing.

One day two young men come to Tauris, and are captured by the locals to provide another couple of sacrifices. Iphigenia recognizes one as Orestes, the baby brother that she left behind, now grown to manhood. The other is his best friend Pylades, and between them they are plotting to steal the statue of Artemis that stands in the temple at Tauris. Orestes is being pursued by the Furies for his crimes, and desperately wishes to propitiate enough deities to be left in peace. At this point, Iphigenia does the first active thing that she has ever done: she plots to aid them in their theft and escape, and escapes with them, returning to Greece with the sacred statue in tow. She sets up a temple with the statue (either in Brauron or Laconia, depending on which account you believe) and is once again the priestess, but no longer sacrifices unwilling mortals to the divine desires.

The brother-sister relationship is often used in myths to indicate equality as well as close kinship, as opposed to the parent-child bond which is unequal kinship. Iphigenia is moved by her brother's plight, but at the same time she sees a way to benefit herself as well. It is the first time that she has made a decision that takes her own needs, as well as those of a suffering other, equally into consideration and finds a solution that works for everyone. It is unlikely that she could have found this balance with anyone that she perceived to be intrinsically more important emotionally than her (triggering a passive sacrificial response) or attempting to push their own feelings as being more important than hers (triggering a violent response); the brotherly equality of Orestes allows her to find a balanced compassion that is neither martyrdom nor reflexive defensiveness.

Iphigenia brings with her the statue as a reminder of her necessary experiences in Tauris, which is what will keep her from slipping into passive unconsciousness once she goes home again. Artemis was revered as a light-bringer, and here her divine presence stays with Iphigenia in order to continually shed light on what was once sunk in darkness. The twelfth-house Moon must move through these stages in order to gain that light into the dark place, and become acquainted with even their most hideous feelings, and value them equally with the emotional needs of others. Only then will they find themselves able to help the suffering of others with a compassion that does not give their own souls away.

☿ Mercury ☿

☿ Mercury in the 1st House: Iris

If there's one word to describe the first-house Mercury, I think that it would be "colorful". That's also an adjective we could lay down for other first-house planets—Venus, Jupiter, the Sun, even Uranus—but people tend to forget how colorful Mercury can be when it is unleashed and worn on the sleeve, or the face. (Consider the singer Freddie Mercury, who literally named himself after the planet in his first house, close to his rising sign, once its meaning was explained to him by an astrologer.) This is the planet of the mind, of ideas and concepts, and communicating those ideas to others in the world.

In Greek mythology, Iris was the goddess of the rainbow. The daughter of two minor sea Gods (Thaumas, the "dangerous ocean", and Electra, whose name meant "amber"), she was a messenger deity like Hermes, and flew across the sky with her rainbow wings. She was eventually given a caduceus to carry, like that of Hermes (Mercury in Gemini), because by that time the caduceus—originally a symbol of commerce and trade—had become so associated with Hermes that it had come to simply mean "messenger". What Hermes did for Zeus (Jupiter in Aries), Iris did for Hera (Jupiter in Libra), although Zeus apparently has the right to "requisition" her for message-bearing tasks when Hermes is occupied with other errands.

Mercury is associated with the third house, which not only rules communication but also short trips and errands of all sorts, and the first-house Mercury can look like they are always in motion, restlessly moving from this perch to that room, from this town to that one. They are the sort who text or call from their cars, running between errands, almost continuously, and rarely settle down. Like Iris, they unfurl their rainbow wings and are off again, zipping between quick destinations. The invention of the mobile phone probably thrilled all first-house Mercury people, because travel and communication could be easily and smoothly combined into one experience; one didn't need to stop moving in order to have a conversation.

Rainbows shift and change, and like the play of colored light in the air, the first-house Mercury can be something of a chameleon, adapting their outward affect in order to get their message across in whatever they feel is the best way. While Iris was mostly just sent to deliver messages, it was part of her job to attempt to convince the recipients of the wisdom of following the will of Zeus or Hera. Sometimes that worked, and sometimes it didn't; one of the classic failures is when she delivered Zeus's message to the mourning Demeter (Sun in Cancer) who was starving the world of humans until her daughter Persephone (Pluto in Pisces) was returned to her. No matter how Iris persuaded, getting through Demeter's depression and sullen rage was impossible.

This is sometimes a problem with first-house Mercuries—while most people can be convinced through the right kind of eloquence, when the problem is overwhelming emotions, the first-house Mercury is sometimes at a loss to mirror back the sort of deep feeling that would make a difference. That's because it requires tapping empathically into that feeling, and is not a mental process. It might have helped if Iris had thought to sit down with Demeter and mourn with her, validating her emotions, before trying to convince her of anything. For a child of two water deities, Iris is very airy and not much in touch with the feeling element. It has been theorized that her oceanic parents had to do with an early concept of rainbows being caused by light refracting through water droplets; all rainbows need water to exist. It would behoove the first-house Mercury to make a study of empathy and how to mirror people's feelings and not just their words, and when that is appropriate to incorporate into one's persuasive mask. All too often the first-house Mercury holds themselves a little distant from the people they are trying to persuade, and thus are less effective; a little dip into the water of others' feelings can be good for the message.

Iris is sometimes sent on errands of mercy; when King Creon of Thebes refused to let the bodies of his rebellious nephews be buried, Iris was sent by Hera to anoint their corpses with sacred dew, preserving them until the situation had blown over and they could be secretly buried. In other tales, Iris takes pity on the individual to whom she is supposed to deliver an implacable warning. When Leto was in labor with Zeus's children, Hera punished her by withholding her daughter Eileithyia, the goddess of childbirth, and laid a spell that no continent would hold the laboring woman, forcing her to go from place to place in pain without rest or cease. Iris took pity on Leto, and made arrangements with the island of Delos (who was originally Asteria, another of Zeus's mistresses, transformed into an island, and who had little love for Hera) to take Leto. Then she flew back to Hera and blandly informed her mistress that Asteria had disobeyed her command, and there was nothing that could be done about it. Mercury in the first house may spend a fair amount of time, when communicating uncomfortable information, thinking about plausible deniability and how impressions can be subtly manipulated to gain certain ends.

The child with Mercury in the first house probably talked early and precociously, learning at a young age that words were fascinating playthings which could be arranged in odd and, yes, colorful ways which made people around them smile. They may have quickly picked up the concept that those symbols on the cereal box denoted sounds, and that several of them together were words in sign form; I know multiple first-house Mercury people who practically taught themselves at least rudimentary reading skills before their parents got around to noticing and helping further.

One of the hardest lessons that the first-house Mercury will learn is to stop talking and actually listen to other people. They tend to tune out what the other person is saying in a conversation, because they are busy composing their own witty reply in their head, and waiting impatiently for the other person to finish so that they can let it fly. This leads the other person to feel like they are not actually being heard, especially when the Mercury person makes the mistake of not listening well enough to make sure their repartee actually responded to the comment. It's all very well and good to say brilliant things, but they need to actually be relevant. Also, it may take this Mercury a long time to realize that listening to people gives you information which can be used later; perhaps it can even be used seconds later, in order to make a change in the other person's mindset. Ironically for someone who gulps down huge chunks of information and seeks for more, it may take them a while to figure out that the most important information is what the person you're talking to is thinking and feeling.

If Mercury is afflicted in the chart, they can come across as less charming and more nerdy, of the sort who monopolizes conversations, or monologues for long periods about their special interest, not noticing that everyone else is squirming and looking for an excuse to get away. Mercurial afflictions can also put awry the chameleon ability, so that the individual doesn't shift and respond to the audience but rather to the subject matter. This can make them a good lecturer but a poor conversationalist.

The most revolutionary idea that a first-house Mercury can have is the realization *that they can change their attitudes about something*, and therefore make a significant change in who they are and how they interact with the world. It's not so much about changing how you feel about something as it is about reframing it, changing the ideas around it … and those may likely affect how you feel. It's putting the chameleon ability to good use by using it on yourself. Can you play with your ideas around the situation, shift and change them into something that is more positive? Of course, there's a catch with this process. Mercury, as a planet, is not necessarily always concerned with either truth or morality; that's the place of other planets in the chart. So the attitude-changing trick needs to be handled with one foot firmly in the realm of the facts, or they can start shifting it to colors that aren't actually there. Getting outside perspective from a more objective person can help a lot with this.

Iris actually had duties which were relevant to Truth; messengers must walk a fine line between being convincing and still continuing to be honest. She was given the task of fetching a pitcher of water from the River Styx whenever the Gods or their favorite humans needed to take a solemn oath; drinking the water after speaking the words would put to sleep anyone who had sworn untruthfully, with intent to deceive or secretly break the oath. The first-house Mercury needs to drink regularly from this ewer, because it is so tempting to just keep talking and let the words go where they will, sometimes weaving themselves into tall tales.

The restless, colorful minds of those with this placement were designed to get ideas and information to the world, often across boundaries of cultural and ideological difference. However, to carry out this sacred messenger duty, they need to keep remembering that if the audience responded poorly to the message because the messenger was sloppy in their delivery, that dishonors the truth which has been given to them. At the same time, distorting the message past truth for the sake of palatability also dishonors it. Like Iris who skillfully manages the twists and turns of the wind currents with her rainbow wings, they need to fly the fine line between eloquence and manipulation, and deliver the best melding of their own Truth and Story.

☿ Mercury in the 2ⁿᵈ House: Clever Manka

or this placement of Mercury, the planet of words and thought (and cleverness!), what spoke to me was the Czech folktale about Clever Manka, a woman who always knows what to say, and how she made her fortune. The folktale starts out not with Clever Manka herself, but with an argument between two adjacent rural neighbors (a rich farmer and a poor shepherd) over some boundary matter. They brought the matter to the local burgomaster, the wealthiest man in town who was often called upon to adjudicate differences between locals. The burgomaster decided that there was no way to objectively tell who was right, so he decided whimsically to order the two men to come up with an answer to a riddle, and the one with the best answer would win.

The burgomaster loved riddles, and also loved adroit answers to them, which is in itself a very Mercury trait. When the planet of mind and communication is found in the second house of money and resources, the individual finds it easy to apply their clever mind to the task of making money. They may be drawn to Mercurial careers such as writing, journalism, communications, mathematics, or any job that is primarily intellectual … or, they may put their brains toward making the career they find themselves in more productive and lucrative. This placement is also found in people who do public speaking as part of their careers, or general problem-solving—which is where Manka comes in.

The poor shepherd went home and told his family that he couldn't think of an answer to the riddle, and so they were probably going to lose in court, but his daughter Manka, a young woman of exceeding cleverness, came up with an answer to the riddle: *What is the swiftest thing in the world? What is the sweetest thing? What is the richest thing?* She told her father what to say and he went the next day and repeated her words.

The farmer had decided to use the moment to compliment the burgomaster, hoping to please him; he said that the swiftest thing was the burgomaster's best horse, the sweetest thing was the burgomaster's rulership, and the richest thing was the burgomaster's treasure chest. The man of authority heard him and smiled dryly, but said nothing. Then the shepherd said, "The swiftest thing is thought, for nothing can run faster than a man's thoughts. The sweetest thing is sleep, for when one is tired and sad, nothing is sweeter than leaving this world for the one of dreams. The richest thing is the Earth, for all wealth inevitably begins there."

The burgomaster was much impressed and ruled in his favor, but he had noted that the shepherd was not the brightest, and he asked where he had learned this answer. The shepherd told him of his clever daughter who had read the riddle, and the burgomaster decided to test her. In one version of the story, he tells the shepherd to have his daughter send him a gift which no one has yet seen; Clever Manka sends him an egg which is about to hatch. In another version, the burgomaster sends her a dozen freshly laid eggs and tells her to make them hatch in three days, to see if she is honest and will attempt to swap them out for newly hatched chicks. Manka sends back a handful of millet with a message that she will hatch the chicks in three days if he can make the millet sprout, grow tall, and develop a harvestable head in a week.

Second-house Mercury people are known for their quick wit (for thought is the swiftest thing!) and ease with repartee, not to mention their ability to sell anything to anyone. They have a knack for summing up the product and the customer, and discerning the approach which will get them the sale. Manka's ability to speak back to the burgomaster in the riddles he loves, with just the right amount of audacity, shows that she has already discerned how best to catch his attention, and is probably planning her next move, which would be to impress him enough to gain economic advantages for her family. The rich farmer tried obsequiousness and it failed; Manka knows that she must find the right words to meet the word-obsessed burgomaster where he is.

Second-house Mercury people also tend to have a fascination with natural world and how it works; the second house is associated with the earthy, practical sign of Taurus, and they may enjoy learning about how both nature and man-made processes actually work. Many become scientists or mechanics for that reason, although the pragmatic nature of this Mercury means that they will always be looking for a way to turn the information gathered into useful implementation. This resonates with Manka's ability to quickly understand natural processes and relate them to the wordplay being exchanged—thought, sleep, Earth, eggs. Quick intuitive categorization, with this placement, comes after studying the progression of the natural order.

The burgomaster decides that he wants to meet Manka, but he sets her one last test. He tells her father that she should come to him when it is neither day nor night, neither clothed nor unclothed, neither riding nor walking. Manka takes the challenge and sets out for the burgomaster's manor during the time just before dawn when the sky has lightened but the Sun has not risen. She wrapped her naked body in a fishnet—which did not count as clothing—and brought along a goat. She hopped along with one leg over the goat, one hand grasping its horns, and the other clutching a stout stick to help her hop down the road. When she reached the burgomaster's manor, he was delighted and let her in. After talking with her for many days, he decided that she was so clever he must marry her. Manka's cleverness had brought her up in the world, if only by marriage (a common way to rise in the ranks in medieval times). They have a big wedding, the burgomaster showers her with expensive gifts, and they have many happy months together.

However, the story is not over yet. The burgomaster told Manka that while he knew she was clever, she must stay out of his business. If she attempted to interfere when he was making a business decision or judging a case, he would send her back to her parents. (This is never the right thing to say to a second-house Mercury, who is always thinking about how situations could be made more productive.) Manka kept to her word until the day when she saw her husband make a sloppy decision. Two farmers had come before him; one had a pregnant mare which had wandered over into the yard of the other one, and foaled under his cart. When the second farmer found the foal under the cart, he claimed it as his own. The burgomaster heard them out, but was distracted by another case which he had heard earlier and which was still on his mind, so he hastily ruled in favor of the farmer with the cart. Manka remonstrated with him about it, but he told her to stay out of it.

The second house is not just about money and resources; its "higher octave" is that of values. This house rules the judging of worth, in oneself and in all things. With any planet in the second house, if the individual does not have their values on straight, situations related to that house will go sideways and not turn out as they should. Once they act from correct values, wealth and resources begin to accrue. (It's the Universe's way of making sure that materialism does not supplant good judgment in every case.) Manka now has a chance to take her husband to task for his failure in this area, even though it may cost her everything, including all the wealth and position she has gained. Mercury will be heard, though, and she puts her mind to solving the problem.

Manka tells the farmer with the horse to put a fishing net across the road and pretend to fish in it, where her husband can see it. She also tells him what to say when it is noticed. The burgomaster does indeed comment in confusion on the grimly "fishing" man outside his house, and the man tells him, "If a cart can have a foal, then the road can have a fish." At this point, the burgomaster realizes that he has made a mistake and apologizes, restoring the farmer's foal to its rightful owner.

He does not leave the problem at that point, though. The farmer has promised not to tell that it was Manka who planned this solution, but the burgomaster has a mind as clever as Manka's, and he manages to be Mercury-persuasive enough to get the information out of the man. Furious, he goes back to his house and tells Manka that she has done the one thing he has ordered her never to do, and that he is sending her back to her family, and will divorce her in short order. He does relent enough to say that she may choose one thing to take back with her, deciding what is most valuable out of all the gifts he has given her, as he does not want to cast her entirely back into poverty.

Manka reminds him that they have had many months of happiness together, and asks for one last fine dinner with him before she goes back home. He agrees, and she arranges for an excellent feast with a great deal of wine, and coaxes him into drinking entirely too much. The burgomaster has a fine time in spite of himself, and passes out drunk while wondering if perhaps he has been foolish in his anger. As soon as he is asleep, Manka has the servants carefully load him into a cart and bring him to her parents' house, where she puts him into a spare bed and climbs in next to him to sleep. In the morning when he awakes, the burgomaster is confused and demands to know where he is. "Why, you told me that I could take the gift I most valued with me," Manka tells him, "and since you are what I value more than anything, I decided to take you!"

Her husband, it is said, immediately saw what an idiot he had been to throw this marriage away, and simply replied, "My dear, why don't we go home and have breakfast?" So it was that from then on, when a hard decision was brought before the burgomaster and he had no idea what to do, he said, "Let's go ask my wife. She is a very clever woman."

The second-house Mercury will, sooner or later, be put into a position where they must choose between using their minds to act in the service of building wealth, or in the service of holding to a fair standard of values. This is the moment when they must look clearly at what is truly of worth in their lives, and act accordingly. Mercury by itself is an amoral planet; it needs to be bounded and curbed by kinder, deeper understandings within the individual. Once the intellect is harnessed not only to ingenuity but to the greater good, it can take the world along.

☿ Mercury in the 3rd House: Nabu

The third house is Mercury's own—a place of talking, writing, public speaking, teaching, learning, and many other intellectual activities. When the planet of the mind lands in the house of the mind, it exudes brilliance freely ... and can concentrate the personality of the individual into a very mind-focused place, unless there are other areas of the chart which counteract this. The deity who stepped forward to pontificate about this placement of Mind was Nabu, the Babylonian God of literacy. Nabu was actually identified with the planet Mercury during the time of his worship, which makes sense as an extremely third-house deity. His name translates to "speaker", which is the basis of this whole house. We humans are language-based people from as soon as we can mimic the sounds and gestures of the adults around us, which is why this house rules elementary education and early learning, as opposed to the ninth house of adult education across from it.

Those with this Mercury placement usually have quick-witted minds and the ability to process information quickly. Their sharp thoughts leap from subject to subject, and unless their Mercury is in a slower and more methodical sign, they often leave most people behind in their ability to multi-task ideas and concepts. Nabu was the patron of scribes in Babylon; they were usually highly educated men whose mastery of the mysterious cuneiform language seemed magical to most people. Babylonian scribes often wrote his name between the columns of cuneiform on their tablets in order to invoke his blessing on their words, since he had invented that alphabet in the first place. His symbols were the clay tablet and stylus, and later in the period of his worship it was said that he recorded the fates decreed for men by the

Gods. Third-house Mercuries love information technology, and often end up working in that field in some way. If it can make information come faster, or put it into written form more accurately, they are all over it.

Nabu was pictured as a bearded man wearing priestly garb, the fringed skirt and wrap, and a horned headdress. This figure eventually informed the symbol we use for the planet Mercury today. As well as being a patron of writing, Nabu was also said to have invented all the rational arts—mathematics, accounting, astronomy, astrology, and architecture. His legacy, after his time, was that by showing writing as not just a practical form of accounting but as an art in and of itself, his worship paved the way for the heights that writing would achieve in the future.

While the third-house Mercury does tend toward the verbal, and whatever they do they will probably write about it, they may also aim their fine minds at all sorts of scientific and mathematical fields, which they may find fascinating. This is a good placement for science journalism, as they may have a talent for both understanding esoteric concepts and translating them to those with less knowledge or mental acuity. However, they do understand the persuasive power of writing as an art form, and some will be drawn to advertising or other magnetic forms of writing which seek to change minds.

Nabu was originally a local god from Ebla who was absorbed into the Babylonian pantheon as one of the ministers of the warlike God Marduk (Mars in Gemini), but he ended up becoming so popular that he was "promoted" to being one of Marduk's sons. Eventually he became more popular than his "father", a fact which created a great deal of political rivalry among their priests. Nabu won the fight, and he was elevated as co-patron along with Marduk; the two of them ruled dually as Education and War in the Babylonian pantheon. In fact, Marduk's winged dragon Sirrush was eventually taken away and given to Nabu to ride. One could see it as the ultimate Revenge of the Nerds, if one wanted to look at it that way, and proof that the pen is indeed mightier than the sword. He was worshiped until the second century, when cuneiform was abandoned entirely in favor of inked figures on parchment.

Part of his popularity was that he had grown in status to be called "he who knows all and sees all". From being the God who read and wrote it all, he came to be the one who knew it all, and everyone wanted to worship him. This is sometimes a problem in miniature for third-house Mercuries, in that they may start believing their own press and thinking that they do indeed know it all, not just about their own expert areas but just in general, and that people should listen to them on any subject they might deign to speak on. Some manage to create small cults of personality based on their admittedly impressive intellectual credentials; others just manage to alienate everyone around them. The more mature third-house Mercuries are able to acknowledge the finitude of their wisdom, and are able to humbly admit what they don't know.

A major problem with this placement is living in the head all the time—and, in most cases, not even understanding why that might be a problem. One individual with this placement who was accused of this behavior said flatly, "If you lived in my head, you'd want to be there all the time too." This can make them dismissive of emotional relationships, except for wanting someone to talk to … and even then, they'd prefer someone educated who had similar interests and would be willing to talk about them for hours on end, which could be accomplished by friends and colleagues. Other areas in their charts have to be very developed in order to drown out this powerful Mercury.

Partners may complain that they are all talk and no action, planning and theorizing about all sorts of projects but not actually finishing many of them. They may also complain that getting them to talk about their feelings will get a variety of unsatisfactory responses, from dismissive comments to distracting patter to a blank stare followed by a change of subject. What they may not understand is that if this Mercury is powerful enough in the chart, they may have no idea how they are feeling, not having checked in with their emotions in quite a while. It is telling that Nabu's earliest consort is a minor goddess named Tashmetu, whose name means "listening". In more immature third-house Mercuries, it may seem to partners that all they are really wanted for is to be an audience.

The intellectual arrogance that comes with this placement, along with its brilliance, can sometimes lead third-house Mercuries to think themselves above the rules due to their intelligence, and commit petty crimes or manipulate others with their clever talk for their own benefit. Ironically, during the great multi-day celebration for Marduk and Nabu in ancient Babylon, the king himself would be warned about this. On the last day, the statue of Nabu (which had been carried in and out of the city in procession for all the people to see and follow) would be returned to the main temple, and the king would be seized by the high priest, forced to kneel before the statue, and made to swear that he had not abused his powers in any way. Afterwards, the priest would slap his face until tears came to his eyes, showing his contrition for any unfair advantages which he had taken. Nabu understands the temptation of taking advantage of those who are slower than you are, but also understands that it is not acceptable in anyone with power and influence.

Over time, Nabu came to be more than a God of knowledge, and became a God of wisdom. This is the ideal goal for a third-house Mercury, because their mental field can remain broad but shallow, without practical or philosophical depth. He also became, for a time, a deity of oracles and prophecy, with his priests reading the signs for those who came with questions. On a mortal level, this is not about the intellectual deciding that they know everything, but finding that the disparate pieces of knowledge come together in a greater pattern which reveals itself … and links them to something greater.

It's not unheard of that scholars who started out simply as collectors of information eventually branched into wondering—and exploring—how the Universe itself worked, and connecting with something greater than simply facts and figures. In fact, it's almost irresistible—the ultimate knowledge breakthrough. As long as they can walk into that place of mystery without the arrogance of Knowing It All, and can be open to the places where they won't be able to figure it all out, the future of information is theirs.

4☿ Mercury in the 4th House: Wenchang Wang

The fourth house of home, family, and ancestry is a rather uncomfortable place for the intellectual Mercury. Anything in this house tends to foreground the dynamics of the family, be heavily colored by the past, and be extremely subjective in its manifestations. This is not a situation which Mercury finds easy or pleasant. The mind-planet wants to keep a safe distance from all that fourth-house stuff, which makes its nice clean ideas all fuzzy and distorted with Emotion. This house is, after all, traditionally ruled by the illogical Moon and associated with Cancer.

The heavenly bureaucracy of China has levels upon levels of deities, all conveniently sorted into hierarchies and ready to be of service, like technical support people behind desks ready to tell you how to live your life. Higher education being huge in Chinese culture for more than a thousand years, there are multiple Gods whose jobs are to help writers, scholars, and anyone else who is at a loss for words. The head of that department is a deity named Wenchang Wang, whose name literally translates to "King of Flourishing Literature". Authors pray to him for relief of writer's block (all right, I did too, during the writing of this book), and scholars for new ideas to write down, or new ways to express old concepts.

Wenchang Wang usually appears as a kindly old professor holding a pen and a book, the cover of which is emblazoned with the words "Heaven determines literary achievement." That's a Chinese saying which essentially means that one is either born with the intelligence and mental acuity to become a scholar, or one is not, and while one can (and should) strive to do better, there is a certain amount of "luck of the genetic draw" to being a world-class author or scholar. One could also point to one's Mercury placement and its afflictions, which is likewise theoretically given by Heaven, at least according to Chinese theology. This touches on the fourth house's deeper meaning of one's ancestral inheritance, another unfair and subjective situation that objective Mercury dislikes. However, this placement can actually indicate intelligence that is inherited down the family line.

The fourth is the house of Ancestry, both one's genetic inheritance and the old patterns taught by family (as opposed to the eighth house which rules inherited physical objects and money). It was probably someone with Mercury in the fourth house who first wrote down the idea that some people reincarnate down family lines, becoming their own great-grandchildren. Chinese (and especially Taoist) religion not only holds with that, but also believes that people incarnate down professional lines, because they are drawn to doing the same work they did before.

This certainly happened to Wenchang Wang. It is claimed that he was an actual war hero, a man named Zhang Yazi who lived under the rule of Emperor Fu Jian in the province of Zitong. In his retirement, he became such a fine writer, scholar, and government bureaucrat that he then reincarnated seventy-three times over the next few centuries, each time living as a benevolent Chinese government official. After all these lifetimes of helping people, he was officially deified and became the Literature Help-Desk of Heaven. Government officials being scholars as well, it is said that Wenchang Wang holds the memories of every family he grew up in, as well as every person who worked under him—business concerns being very much a sort of family in Chinese culture. This will resonate with the fourth-house Mercury person, who is often fascinated with their ancestry, and may keep the genealogical records for the family.

The fourth-house Mercury is also fascinated with history and everything in the past ... although they may balk when directed to look at the part of the past which is their own childhood, and the inheritance which they gained from their families, for better or worse. It's so much easier to read about ancient Roman centurions and medieval knights than to look at one's own mental mess and sort out healthy from unhealthy ideas. This, however, is crucial to the work of this Mercury placement. In the end, the distant past is most useful as examples of how these patterns are passed down, to be used for the sorting out of one's own personal familial inheritance. This can be painful to the fourth-house Mercury person, especially if it requires discarding pleasant stories of one's noble family culture and how benevolent one's family members were ... or, in the case of overreaching in the other direction, how unalterably horrible they all were.

The fourth-house Mercury may get caught up in obsessing over family drama, replaying it over and over in their heads like a book they wish they could rewrite. Loyalty looms huge for them; they may feel that they have to choose to be loyal to the family or to themselves. If they have been fed stories of how children ought to be faithful to their parents and hold them in esteem, no matter what they do, it may send them into a tailspin of visible fact versus inherited pattern. While caught up in that tailspin, nervous Mercury may throw themselves into detrimental behaviors. Out of all the Gods of intellect and learning and words, Wenchang Wang is the one most associated with filial piety. The legend goes that his mother breastfed him for several years, as she knew that he was a special child. When she became desperately ill, he cut pieces of flesh from his own thighs and fed them to her, and she recovered.

Wenchang Wang's sacrifice illuminates the obsession with family loyalty which can possess the mind with this Mercury placement. *Will they be as loyal to me as I am to them, or will they fail me, not caring enough by my standards? How far do I go in my loyalty? If I must abandon them, can I make it up by being wholly loyal to a new family?* It's not unusual for them to start and/or join multiple families throughout their lives, plunging into and then failing at the mental ideal of perfect family faithfulness. Wenchang Wang, it was said, was just and uncorrupted, never doling out harsh punishments to the people over whom he ruled. He helped unfortunates through hardships, had compassion for loneliness, forgave people their mistakes, and left peace and stability wherever he went. The fourth-house Mercury would like to be like that, because it is a mental ideal, but the actual manifestation sometimes escapes them.

This Mercury placement tends to think of their home as the sanctuary where they read their books, play with media, write their thoughts, and get on the phone with people. Their book collection holds up the ceiling in places. (King of Flourishing Literature!) Take away access to all that, and it doesn't feel like home. It's common for them to move house repeatedly, either in their childhood or their early adulthood. It may take several years for them to find the right place to store all their books and take real solace in the inner world of their mind. As well as the genetic component, this placement also has a high rate of home education, from a simple emphasis on books and learning to full-on homeschooling, so it's not surprising that they picture home as their own private college library.

However, Mercury ruling the parents who set the tone for the home often indicates that they stressed academic achievement over emotional well-being, and may have been overly critical—or possibly elusive, coming and going in and out of the child's life. If Mercury is afflicted, verbal viciousness may have been part of their home life—words used as weapons. This does not give these individuals much in the way of emotional education, unless there are other parts of the chart which offset that tendency. It is not until later in life that they will undertake the work of sorting out those inherited ideas and figuring out which thoughts are actually their own.

This Mercury tends to be a little more traditional in their ways of thinking than other Mercuries. It's not so much that they dislike anything new; rather it's that they become attached to ideas the way that other people become attached to their teddy bears or comfort blankets. Favorite ideas are pulled out periodically, stroked, petted, cuddled, and then lovingly put back; it's part of how this Mercury person self-soothes. Being forced to throw them away, even in the face of clear logic and hard facts, will be difficult. They will do it—sadly, but with finality—although it will take them a while to part with especially beloved concepts. If they can find a way to stretch their minds so that both the old idea and the new one are held in balance, they will happily come to that compromise. Because of this, they often become quite skilled at combining old and new, historic and modern, logical and emotional, facts and tale-telling, in innovative and imaginative ways. It's worth the mental cogitation to be able to keep even a reworked version of their old story.

To an outsider, the unhealthy patterns they retrace look like a product of the emotions, but they are actually generated by the mind—thoughts which create feelings rather than feelings which create thoughts. Once they realize this fact, it will be much easier for them to change their thought patterns and internal mental stories, and thus shift their emotions and actions by doing so. The fourth house is about roots, and the past-tainted mind needs to regrow new mental roots rather than just chopping off the old ones, which just grow back. This can be a long process, but it will "reground" them.

The King of Flourishing Literature was worshiped in China by rich and poor alike, and became so popular that many temples were built to him in southern China. In fact, it was said that "in the north there is Confucius, in the south there is Wenchang Wang." On his birthday—the third day of the second month of the Chinese calendar—everyone went to his temples to hear hours of poetry and prose recited by all the local scholars. His greatest gift is to help others find the right words, and this too can be a gift of the fourth-house Mercury, who often becomes not just a writer or researcher, but a teacher as well.

Wenchang Wang has two assistants and one well-known subordinate, Kui Xing the savior of humble students (Neptune in the third house). His two assistants are known as Tianlong (Heaven-Deaf) and Diya (Earth-Mute), and this, in sideways fashion, sums up two big issues of the fourth-house Mercury. When they are up in the heavenly ideal, they can be deaf to Mercurial reason; when they are forced to come down to earth, the flow of inspiration may turn off and the words have a harder time coming out. Mercury is associated with Gemini, with its light and dark twins; regardless of the sign, there's always that duality to bring together. Wenchang Wang, however, manages to balance both. *Study the past, with all the stories and fine words stripped away. Look upon what is, and do not judge harshly, but with equilibrium and objectivity. The key to both present and future is there, but it is cloaked in kindness. This is the best loyalty you can give.*

5☿ Mercury in the 5th House: Bragi

In Norse/Germanic mythology, Bragi is the Skald of Asgard—singer, poet, performer, and god of eloquence. The son of Odin (who also shares the gift of eloquence and the written word), his story actually starts long before his birth, with the creation of a god named Kvasir. The Aesir sky-gods and the Vanir earth-gods had a war and then a truce, and as part of the truce each deity on both sides spit into a cauldron over a fire, combining their fluids. From this magical spell of peace, a god named Kvasir was born. It was said that he came forth with wisdom and poetry in his soul; his very blood was magical. Everyone loved him and he was, as they said, "welcome in every home."

Of course, nothing this good can last, and Kvasir was murdered not long after his creation for the blood in his veins. The story of what came afterward is told in the story of Odin and the Mead of Poetry (Mercury in the eighth House), but the last chapter of that story concerns Odin (Saturn in Pisces), who had just drunk the Mead of Poetry made from Kvasir's blood, making love for three nights to the beautiful giantess Gunnlod. After his escape from her bedchamber, she found herself pregnant and bore a child who seemed to be born with poetry on his tongue. While it does not say so explicitly in the story, it is fairly clear that the child Bragi was the reincarnation of the soul of Kvasir, passed through the body of his sire.

When Bragi was old enough, he went to join his father in Asgard, the home of the sky Gods at the top of the World Tree, and was proclaimed its official skald. Like Kvasir, it was said he was loved by all and welcome in every home. This is very like the gifts bestowed by having Mercury, the planet of mind and words and speech, in the fifth house of creativity.

A fifth-house Mercury gives the individual the gift of persuasive speech and creative word choice. Their wit is sharp and so are their eyes, missing little of the attitudes and actions around them. Their minds move fast, and as this is the house of play, they enjoy playful banter and clever word games. This placement puts Mercury in the Sun's house, traditionally ruled by Leo, and their faith in their intellectual powers comes with a streak of overconfidence. After all, the modern word "brag" comes from this god's name, largely because of the custom among the Germanic tribes of passing the oath-horn (called a *bragarfull*) and speaking out boasts of deeds they intended to perform. The custom gave them courage to do the hard thing—if you've spoken it in front of the whole hall, it would be shameful to back out in cowardice.

Bragging, in those days, was not considered a bad thing. Modesty was not as valued before the advent of Christianity, and it was expected that one would declare intent and use the witnessing of the people to encourage one to come through on it. In addition, if one gave one's word and kept it, this built up more of a magical power called *maegen*. If you had enough *maegen*, you could state your intent and the Universe would sweep obstacles out of the way. The only shame in bragging was if you backed out and failed. Fifth-house Mercury individuals may gamble on being able to woo someone with their words ... and maybe it will work, and maybe it won't. This is the house of risks, though, and they are generally willing to give it a shot.

While Bragi's main job was being the official entertainer of Asgard, he did not spend all his time there. He traveled frequently—not unusual for a Mercury figure—singing at many people's hearths and thus spreading news and wisdom. His words were seeds sprouting in new fields, pollen borne on the wind to change the lay of the land. A fifth-house Mercury is an excellent storyteller and salesman, persuading people to buy things—and ideas—to which they might have been resistant before Mercury started describing them. This placement has the ability to lily-gild an idea until it shines, and to figure out the best way to paint it in order to make it attractive to the person in front of them.

The ancient poets of most European cultures didn't just sing songs or intone lays. They were expected to convincingly act out all the parts in the story, at least verbally, so that the audience was able to understand and relate to the characters. This Mercury placement bestows a great talent for mimicry and a fair amount of acting ability; they are especially good at copying accents and doing vocal impressions. Like Bragi who would have accompanied his own songs and stories on an instrument, they may be interested in dabbling in music. Usually, however, their favorite music is less about emotion and more about catchy riffs and clever tunes. They are more interested in lyrics than strictly instrumental music; the notes are a useful backdrop, but the real power is, of course, in the words.

We think of Mercury figures as being youthful—and while Mercury on or ruling the Ascendant does tend to give a young appearance—Bragi is often shown as an older man with a long beard, sometimes having gone grey. Some of this is a way of showing his experience; a younger-looking man might not be believable as the Bearer of Wisdom to every hearth he might grace. He is sometimes shown telling tales to children, though, and this Mercury placement loves to tell "when I was little" stories, passing on the past and putting the young listeners in their own younger place. In fact, while this is the house of children, Mercury here is far less interested in nurturing children than in teaching them, and a parent with this placement may lean harder on the teacher archetype rather than a more parental one. They are often very proud of their children's (or students') intellectual achievements, and are more impressed by the child who wins the spelling bee than the one who makes the touchdown.

The fifth is the house of romance, and Mercury woos with words rather than gestures or acts. It was said that Iduna (Neptune in Virgo), the goddess of youth and health who grew the golden apples of immortality, had rejected all Aesir suitors who were attracted by her beauty. Bragi approached her with words and love songs rather than doing glorious deeds of battle, and she fell in love. The two are sometimes painted as a mismatched couple—she is golden and youthful, he is the old graybeard; she stays home and gardens while he often wanders with his harp. However, unlike Njord (Jupiter in the ninth house) and Skadi (Pluto in Sagittarius) who divorced after discovering their differences, Bragi and Iduna seem to get along quite peaceably. Both of them are peacemaking deities, bringing *frith* (order and harmony) to the world. Iduna has little use for warriors, and while Bragi will sing of their great deeds, he also quietly works for peace behind the scenes.

In the *Lokasenna*, an angry and drunken Loki (Saturn in Gemini) accuses him of being the most cowardly of all the Aesir Gods, afraid to go onto the battlefield. This is after Bragi has offered Loki gifts to make peace with him. Iduna intervenes, overtly to make peace, but also to make it clear that she agrees with her husband's diplomacy-over-fighting policy. The fifth-house Mercury placement is more of a talker than a fighter; they may throw verbal zingers at someone when they are angry, but it is more to shame them publicly than to hurt them, and if a fight starts, Mercury will take a back seat to more assertive planets, if there are some.

This Mercury placement wants communication from a partner more than anything else. Good conversation and interesting ideas are what will keep the fickle fifth-house placement attracted. Like Bragi, they may appreciate a partner who will hold down the home fires while they go out and come back, and who will trust that no matter where they go or whose hearth they end up at, they will surely come home when the wind changes direction. After all, there's a lot of fun and creative opportunities out there, and real love shouldn't be a chain holding you back. The other option is that the partner goes along on the journey, willing to be a cheerful companion to Mercury's wandering.

One drawback, of course, is that sometimes Mercury ends up with more than one partner, partly because one is just not enough mental stimulation, and partly because the house-of-romance placement sometimes makes them fall in love with different minds ... or, in some cases, fall in love with the mental idea of who someone might be, with no concrete relation to the actual person. If everything can be negotiated aboveboard, this can work well to keep their restless mind-and-heart complex satisfied, but Mercury is a slippery trickster planet, and not above telling the occasional white lie ... which can escalate into full-blown deception. With this storytelling placement, it's not impossible for them to create a tale where everything they do is reasonable and justified.

Unlike many placements of Mercury or the Mercury-ruled signs, this combination doesn't have the classic problem of separating the mind and the heart. The fifth house is ruled by Leo and the Sun, which rule the heart itself. Mercury here needs a romance which is intellectual enough—and with enough pretty stories—to engage their mind, and at the same time needs a mental relationship with enough love (or loving friendship) to capture the heart as well. Both work in tandem for them, and a partner needs to offer enough on each count to keep them coming back.

It is said that in order to magically enhance his eloquence, Iduna carved the runes on Bragi's tongue. This gives the gift not just of ordinary fluency, but of the quality known as "God-Mouth"—the ability to channel divine inspiration through one's words. The rune most associated with Bragi is the Anglo-Saxon rune ᚩ. Pronounced Os, it is the glyph of a man extending his arms as if holding forth to an audience, and can even literally be used to mean "God-Mouth". There are a number of Mercury signs and placements which are associated with Words of Power, and this is one of them. At its best, this Mercury can tell a story with the Right Words which reflect greater truths and reverberate through the audience, bringing down the aura of the Gods ... like the sacred skald who sings at the top of the World Tree.

☿ Mercury in the 6th House: Diancecht, Miach, and Airmed

Mercury is a fast and brilliant planet. Ruling the mind, the brain, communication, and all things to do with words and numbers, Mercury wants the shortcut, the quick way there, the miracle, the eureka moment that will solve all problems. When Mercury has a great idea and it works, sometimes this sprinting planet decides that it's There, that the solution has been ultimately achieved. Sometimes that's true ... and sometimes it isn't.

The sixth house, on the other hand, is both ruled by Mercury (through its rulership of Virgo) and just a tad uncomfortable for it. The sixth is the house of patient, slogging labor, which Mercury isn't too fond of (unless it's in an Earth sign, in which case it can adapt better), and it's the house of Service. Mercury isn't opposed to rendering service, as long as it involves using its brilliant talents, but Mercury wants those talents recognized. Above all, this is the house of Health, which puts its emphasis on the body—Virgo is an Earth sign. Mercury's attitude towards health tends to be that of fixing broken machinery, but we'll look at that more in a moment.

What Mercury doesn't rule is ethics, morality, or honor. For that, one needs planets like the Moon which teach empathy, or Saturn who holds rules and codes in place. Mercury wants the discovery at all costs, which can be dazzling or disastrous.

In Irish mythology, one of the Tuatha de Danaan was Diancecht the divine physician. His name means "swift power", which sums up Mercury in a heartbeat. He was considered—or at least he considered himself—the best of doctors. The son of the great Dagda (Uranus in Taurus), it is said that he ministered to his patients by soaking them in a sacred well—the Slainge Well, growing in an orchard full of healing apples. He and his children chanted spells over the well, and harvested healing herbs from the fields nearby.

Accounts vary as to how many children he had, but generally he is credited with six total—three sons who became warriors, and one, Miach, who followed in his footsteps as a healer. He also had two daughters, one a poet and one a herbalist. The youngest daughter, Airmid, along with her father and Miach, made up a trio who would chant together over the well and call up spells of healing.

Diancecht performed miraculous cures on many heroes, including healing Mider's eye when it was struck out. When great Nuada lost his arm in a battle, Diancecht replaced it with a magical arm of silver which worked like an arm of flesh. He boasted, when asked, that he could cure anything except a decapitation or amputation; breaking the spinal cord was beyond him, as was reattaching a missing limb, but anything else he could do.

The divine healer's reputation was made when he saved Ireland from a terrible fate. The Morrigan (Mercury in Scorpio) bore a son who reeked of destructive power, and Diancecht declared that the child should be destroyed. The other members of the Tuatha de Danaan agreed, and the child was killed. Diancecht opened the infant's body for an autopsy and discovered three serpents inside its heart. If they had grown to full size, they would have burst out of the child's body and poisoned all of Ireland. He cast the serpents into a fire and burned them to ash, in case even their dead bodies could do evil. He flung the ashes into the nearest river, but then the river boiled up and the poison slew everything in it. The ashes were washed out to sea, and Ireland was saved.

People with this Mercury placement often find themselves in service careers, and/or in fields of science or medicine. With an excellent ability to keep track of small details, they may go into research, especially in areas where it is imperative to know how a complicated organism works. Of course, this can turn into seeing the body like defective machinery, as we mentioned earlier, and they may get upset when it doesn't respond the way they thought it would. They like stability and consistency in their work, and are often uncomfortable when things shift and change. Sometimes this can become mental stagnation, and an unwillingness to focus on self-awareness and mindfulness. All that "swift power" likes to run straight to the goal and ignore the process, unless it becomes scientifically influential in some way.

This is the house of Duty and Service, and Mercury here does want to put the mental faculties in the service of helping others. In general, the sixth-house Mercury person will be law-abiding and dutiful ... until they're not. Usually that's because they succumbed to fear and reacted in a way that even they did not expect. Because Mercury is good at mental footwork, they can then find a way to desperately justify what was done, perhaps in the name of the general "good of humanity". Maybe they are right and maybe they aren't, but they will cling to that mental construct for a long time.

The big weak spot with a sixth-house Mercury is mental anxiety. Mercury is often detached from the emotions, but one's mind can circle and circle around a particular fear, adding layer after layer of scary story about what might happen onto what might not even be that big a problem on its own, or at least not as huge as it becomes after all the mental obsessing. Because this is the house of health, all that mental rumination moves into the physical flesh and creates medical issues. People with this placement are good at "thinking yourself sick". They can also be good at the opposite skill—thinking themselves well—but that takes more conscious focus, while thinking yourself sick is easy to do unconsciously.

They may also have problems with secret insecurity from all that negative storytelling, and if their physical symptoms manifest while in the presence of someone or some situation they are unconsciously uncomfortable with, they can start blaming that person or situation. *I get a headache every time I'm near you; it must be that you are the one causing it.* Information about the environment is certainly available via the barometer of the body, but one has to know how to read it correctly, without the force of denial involved.

In the myth, Diancecht's son Miach also becomes a physician, and slowly gains enough skill that he becomes better than his father. In a twenty-seven-day healing ritual, Miach managed to grow Nuada a real arm, to replace the silver arm that Diancecht had built for him, thus outdoing his father entirely. He not only replaced the eye of a patient, he replaced it with a cat's eye so that the man could see in the dark. He also learned to cure people by using combinations of 365 herbs, laid out in the form of a human body. (This may be an echo of an old shamanic tradition which assigns a group of herbs from any given ecosystem to the 365 acupuncture points of the body, and uses a combination of plants and points for healing.) Miach brought so many people back from the edge of death that his father became extremely professionally envious, concerned that Miach would take his place as the divine physician. He also worried that the Gods of Death might strike back at them, as Miach had stolen so many from their grasp.

Diancecht agonized about the problem until his anxiety could not bear it any longer, and finally he decided that Miach must die. His son refused to stop doing what Diancecht considered to be dangerous cures, and so the father crept up behind the son with a sword and attempted to cut off his head. It took four strokes, because Miach simply magically healed the first three, but the last one clove his brain in half and he died.

Miach's sister Airmed, the "she-leech" and herbalist, buried her brother. While she wept on his burial mound 365 herbs grew up through the grass under her, in the shape of a human body. She began to gather them all up into her mantle and would have taken them home and laid them out again to study, but Diancecht came upon her and saw what had happened. Furious and afraid, he seized her mantle and threw all the herbs into the air, destroying the knowledge Miach had so carefully collected from his experiments. From then on, there was no bringing the nearly dead back to life, and no more cures more miraculous than any Diancecht could create.

Miach was not the only healer to risk being struck down for reviving too many people; the Greek Asclepias (Mercury in Virgo) was actually killed by the Olympian Gods for having too much power. When the sixth-house Mercury goes into a tailspin, it's about not knowing the rules, and becoming anxious that perhaps they are not being followed. Diancecht's clinging to his primacy to the point of murder also shows how easy it is, when confined in one's mind, to justify anything that makes the fear stop. It also shows that mental obsession can lead to destructive places.

In actual life, those with this placement are more likely to harm themselves, perhaps by experimenting with dangerous alternative health cures which cause more problems than they alleviate. Again, the mind looks ahead to the goal and forgets that the body cannot always follow. On the other hand, the majority of people with this placement are more like Diancecht at his best—giving of themselves in the service of the world. As long as they can remember that the world consists of people who must be treated gently—and that includes themselves—they have the potential to leave a legacy of broken things, people, and ideas which have been mended and made whole.

7☿ Mercury in the 7th House: Nuwa and Fuxi

Long ago in Chinese mythology, it was said that the first marriage was made between two Gods, the goddess Nuwa and the god Fuxi. They were not as humans are today, being more like Indian *nagas*—human-looking above the waist and serpents below. They are often shown together with their serpent-tails intertwined below and their hands clasped above. They had both survived a great flood and risen from the waters, and when they had climbed back out onto the land, they had fallen in love. They were not sure if they should be married to each other, because they were also brother and sister, so Nuwa asked the Gods of Heaven if it should be so. The Gods of Heaven, wanting the world to be repopulated, signaled their approval by bringing up a mist and letting it fall, and Nuwa proclaimed that they would be married.

As wedding gifts, they did not give each other riches or flowers or jewels. Instead, Nuwa invented the carpenter's square and gave it to Fuxi, saying that it reminded her of his mind—straightforward and always thinking about how to build things. In turn, Fuxi invented the compass, with the map of the stars of heaven upon it and gave it to Nuwa, saying that it reminded him of her mind—spiraling with ideas up to the heavens. With this exchange of gifts, each became the guardian of earthly building and heavenly creating, because they had come together in a marriage of minds ... which is exactly what Mercury wants when it lands in the seventh house of marriage.

We don't generally associate committed relationships with the intellect, as they are usually shown as a meeting between the watery emotions of love and affection, and the earthy, practical matters of combining households, having children, and getting the legal paperwork done. Mercury is an airy sign of the mind, and not terribly attached to watery feelings; it can get on well enough with practical organization (Mercury does rule Virgo as well as Gemini), but really prefers to live in the head. This is a classic placement for the sapiosexual, the person who is most turned on by intelligence in a potential partner, and the heart may not turn on until the mind is engaged.

The fact that Nuwa and Fuxi are brother and sister before they are husband and wife is also resonant with Mercury here. Mercury rules the third house, which is not only the house of writing and thinking, but of sibling relationships, and Mercury brings a little of that wherever it goes. People with this placement enjoy having a sibling-like friendship; they may enjoy romantic gestures, especially if they play out like a storybook, and sex is a fun and interesting pastime, but during ordinary daily life they tend to revert to the sibling-esque relationship which can be their "default setting". For that matter, romance may be more of a mental flight of fancy for them, rather than a way of connecting deeply with the partner. It's a mask they put on, a role they assume, to please the other person or because they find it fun. Real intimacy, for them, lies in conversation and in shared intellectual interests.

This can be off-putting to a more emotional type when they realize it, and it may also be harder for the seventh-house Mercury person to get the sort of closeness they want. They are quite capable of deep connection, but for them it has to come through the mind first; that's where the doorway is, and appealing to their body or emotions alone will never get you through the door. Once they have experienced the moment of two brilliant minds meeting in a shared mental context, their hearts will soar.

Minds aren't terribly monogamous, though. The seventh-house Mercury may have such a hard time finding someone with whom they have that mental connection that they aren't necessarily likely to turn down someone else whom they also click with in that way. If that person isn't their sexual or romantic cup of tea, it may just turn into the kind of friendship that makes romantic partners vaguely jealous even though they realize it's completely chaste. If they are, then Mercury (which is not a planet of morality in any direction; that's what Saturn is for) may slide into an affair over the spreadsheets and stacks of books. Mercury isn't the most honest planet, either; all Mercuries are good at intellectually justifying all sorts of questionable behavior, and with this placement it's not that uncommon for "little slips" to be glossed over or never mentioned, until they get caught. Then the verbal justifications will come, unless they have matured past that sort of prevarication.

Once married, Nuwa and Fuxi set about codifying how marriage and families ought to work, including the roles and responsibilities of each family member. They had no one to teach these rules to, so they decided that they needed to create a race of beings to teach. Once the seventh-house Mercury realizes that the psychology of people and their relationships is actually a fascinating and changeable subject, they may apply themselves to perfecting their relationships through communication, discussion, and experimenting.

Assessing and understanding people's thoughts and feelings can become a favorite hobby for people with this placement; they may be drawn to the idea of relationship counseling or writing about how marriages can be made better. Teaching is just as interesting to Mercury as learning, and with this placement they will want to teach and learn from a number of people, starting with but not limited to their spouse, and pass it on. They may be more of a teacher than a parent to their children; while they enjoy interacting with the young, the adult conversational relationship is really their preferred mode, and they will likely prioritize marriage over children for that reason.

At any rate, after their marriage Nuwa and Fuxi set out to create humanity. One account says that after they had lain with each other, Nuwa gave birth to a ball of ground meat, and the bits were scattered about the land, changing into human beings. Another story has them making humans out of clay; they made the noble families out of yellow clay, but then became tired and simply turned out the lower classes by dragging a string through rough brown clay. Classist as this myth is, it does highlight one of Mercury's problems: they get bored easily, and their quicksilver minds can become distracted before a tedious task is finished. In the seventh house, this can indicate that a mutual project, once it becomes boring, can be put aside even if this disappoints the partner.

Seventh-house Mercury people do generally love working with a partner on an intellectual project, though. It's a more appealing bonding activity than nearly everything except talking together for hours, jumping from subject to subject, which will always top the list of favorite mutual pastimes. As their human charges grew up, Nuwa and Fuxi together invented hunting with tools of bone or bamboo, fishing with nets, music, cooking, and the domestication of animals, and taught it to early humans. They taught them about the rhythms of time—that one should work in the daylight and sleep at night—and they invented the Kangjie system of writing characters. Fuxi also created a few divination methods—it seems to have been his Mercurial hobby—including the creation of the original eight trigrams of the I Ching. He wrote them down on the shell of a tortoise, which began the practice of throwing the shells of hunted tortoises into the fire and reading omens from their cracks.

Nuwa, on the other hand, was busy trouble-shooting a great problem. The Gods had warred with each other, and a deity had struck one of the four pillars of the sky, breaking it and causing the whole sky to shift, tearing a gaping hole in it. The earth below cracked, causing havoc in the world. Floods, fires, and dangers from wild animals driven from their habitats threatened humans, and Nuwa needed to figure out how to save their greatest marital project so that all the invention and teaching would not go to waste. She took five colors of stone from the riverbeds—blue, black, white, red, and yellow—and melted them to use as plaster, repairing the hole in the sky, which is why the clouds have so many colors. She caught the largest turtle in the ocean and killed it, and used its severed legs as new pillars to prop up the sky. (However, she could not fix the tilt completely, so the polestar is still off to one side. Nor could she fully flatten out the earth, so one side of China is higher than the other.) She filled the cracks in the earth with pebbles to reinforce it, put out the fires, and stopped the floods by moving a great amount of smoldering ashes to absorb the waters. She drove the wild animals back to the mountains and forests, and the world became peaceful again.

Distracting one's self with big projects is actually a good thing for this Mercury placement, especially if they aren't yet partnered, because they can mentally obsess about their relationships past, present, and future until they drive themselves half crazy—or, if they are partnered, their significant other. While relationship analysis can be very helpful, constant talking about it without actually making the time and space to spend positive time together is not an improvement. The spouse of the Mercury person may need to distract them, ideally with a mutual project or trip, but pushing them towards their own mental projects (which aren't about relational connections) can work as well. This is someone who needs to be encouraged in their hobbies, or they will expect their relationship to fulfill all their intellectual needs.

Mercury in this house is just as prone to the great seventh-house trap of projection as any other planet here. The brain of a seventh-house Mercury is no worse than the brain of any other Mercury placement, but because they tend to be influenced by the ideas of others (and attracted to smart, articulate people), they may get it into their head that they aren't as intelligent as the brilliant ones they love and admire. They may think of their partners as the truly clever ones, while they are just stumping along doing their best. In that sense, it will not be until they fully own the strength of their own minds that they can feel equal to their partners. Until that time, they may tend to defer to their partner's mental concepts, considering them to be better and more valid than their own. They may even use this as a chance for some laziness, letting their partner do all the hard mental work in the relationship, such as keeping a budget or paying bills or deciding what project to prioritize.

When they have matured and learned to cogitate their own ideas instead of leaning on those of others, they can be wonderful partners who value reason and talking problems through rather than screaming and conflict. Having Mercury in Venus's house can make them invested in learning their partner's love language, and being able to communicate with it. Nuwa and Fuxi went on to become the first Emperor and Empress of China, ending up as culture heroes, even if they were half snake and not quite human. The seventh-house Mercury must earn its place as king or queen of their partner's heart, but they have a good chance of doing that, once they figure out that minds, as well as bodies, can make love.

8☿ Mercury in the 8th House: Odin and the Mead of Poetry

We already met the Norse/Germanic God Odin once as Saturn in Pisces in the previous book *MythAstrology I*. However, deities—like people—have multiple aspects and may embody different planetary energies at different times. The tale of the Mead of Poetry is well before the period in Odin's story when he learned how to gain wisdom through sacrifice. At this point in his life-tale, he is a much younger Odin, doing a lot of wandering and a lot of verbal persuasion, focused on becoming more eloquent and well-spoken. In other words, this is the Mercury period of his life, and he sought out the Mead of Poetry for the purposes of becoming better with words.

However, the Mead of Poetry was a very ambivalent tainted substance with a significant body count. It starts with the god Kvasir (Mercury in the fifth house), created in a magic cauldron by the combined spittle of all the Aesir (sky) and Vanir (earth) Gods, and beloved by everyone. He wandered the Nine Worlds, teaching peace and good order to everyone he came across. His very blood was magical, and there were those who coveted that power. One such pair were the dwarven brothers Fjalar and Gjalar, who had been banished from the Duergar realms by Ivaldi, Emperor of the Dwarves. It was said that it was for murder, and considering their next act, that is not surprising. When Kvasir came to their hut, they invited him in under the pretense of desiring to learn, and then killed him and drained his blood into a magical cauldron named Odhroerir, and two magical jugs name Son and Bodn. They mixed honey with the divine blood and fermented it into a beautiful mead, one sip of which would give the drinker more eloquence, at least for a time. To thin it, they added water from a sacred well in Svartalfheim, the world of dark elves and Duergar. However, the Mead of Poetry is cursed because of Kvasir's murder, and all who are around it (much less drink it) may come to bad ends.

Fjalar and Gjalar then decided, as the Duergar do, to see how much wealth they could get from selling this unique magical substance. They offer some of it to Ivaldi in order to regain entrance into the Duergar realm; he accepts it, but refuses them entrance, so the brothers wander off again to find a better offer. During their journey northward, a messenger from the Aesir Gods catches up with them, asking about Kvasir. They tell the messenger that Kvasir choked on his own knowledge and died, and hurry away. On their way through Jotunheim, the Giant-Realm, they come across an elderly giant named Gilling who is a fisherman. Gilling and his wife give the brothers food and space to sleep, but the next day they go out in Gilling's boat with him and drown him. His wife, who has seen this from the shore, screams and wails so loudly that the brothers go back to shore and drop a millstone on her head.

Gilling's son, however, is a powerful giant named Suttung, who lives inside a mountain but has many fields surrounding it. When he hears what has happened to his parents, he pursues the brothers, catches them, and ties them to a rock in the bay at low tide to drown them as they drowned his father. The dwarf-brothers begged for their lives, and offered to trade Suttung the Mead of Poetry if he would spare them. Suttung took the mead, but may well have let the dwarves drown anyway. He hid the sacred fluid in the deepest cavern inside his mountain Hnitbjorg, and bade his lovely daughter Gunnlod to stay in that cavern to guard it.

This was the dangerous mead whose reputation made its way to the top of the World Tree where the Aesir dwelled, and to the ears of Odin. He knew immediately that he wanted that sacred substance, even if it was wound around with Death. In fact, that might have made it look even more attractive to him. The placement of Mercury in the eighth house gives the individual a fascination with all things morbid, and a deep desire to find out the dark secrets which lie under supposedly ordinary-looking daily realities. This is the mind of the researcher, the detective, the one who is drawn to forbidden knowledge. The eighth is the House of Mysteries and the House of Death. If it's mysterious and has the scent of Death hanging around it, they are drawn like flies to honey, finding out everything they can.

Like Mercury in Scorpio, the eighth-house Mercury has the mind of a spy, quietly watching and assessing and figuring out how to get the best out of the situation. They are not afraid of subterfuge, if it will get them what they want, and Odin is no different. He disguises himself as a common laborer giant and goes to Suttung's land at harvest-time. The mountain giant is hiring extra hands to get the harvest in, and Odin asks for work, calling himself *Bolverk* (Grief-worker), which one thinks should have been a clue to Suttung, but perhaps such names were ordinary for giants. While he helps with the field work, Odin watches the mountain fortress and tries to figure a way in; the only entrance is guarded and no one but Suttung's family and most loyal retainers may enter. However, he eventually notices a small hole in the side of the mountain, no bigger than a hand-width. The eighth-house Mercury is always logging clues and calculating trajectories, and circling in on the goal. Odin learns from the other field workers that Suttung has a treasure locked up in a deep mountain cave, and he suspects that the tiny hole is ventilation for that cave—and he is right.

One night he changes into a snake and worms his way through the hole into the mountain. However, when he comes out on the other end and resumes his human form, what he faces is not merely the three containers of magical mead, but the lovely Gunnlod who is their guardian. Odin has only a moment to decide what to say, and Mercury comes up with a long story about how he had heard of her beauty and wanted nothing more than to see it. Whether Gunnlod is fooled or not, we do not know, but she eventually relents and takes Odin to her bed.

Have we mentioned that the eighth is the house of sex? If there's something even more interesting to a planet in this house than a Death-scented mystery, it's a dangerous, mysterious sexual liaison. Odin spends three nights with Gunnlod, leaving every day through the hole in the wall and working for her father, then secretly returning to her bed. While she sleeps, he gets up and drinks one of the jugs of the Mead of Poetry, then the second jug the second night. On the third night, she catches him just finishing off the cauldron Odhroerir, and cries out. He turns back into a serpent and gets through the wall as fast as he can, and then turns into an eagle and flies toward Asgard on great wings. By the time Gunnlod has fetched her father and they find the extent of the theft, Odin is well on his way to the world of the sky Gods.

However, the Mead of Poetry has been working on him as well. By the time he drinks the cauldron dry, Kvasir's trapped soul is no longer in the sacred liquid; it has passed through Odin and into Gunnlod through the act of sex, and she eventually bears Kvasir's reincarnation Bragi (also Mercury in the fifth house). Having the same house for both sex and the mysteries means that dealings in this house will lead to a combination of both, and the act of procreation being bound up with the act of reincarnating the ancestors is definitely one of those Mysteries. At the same time, the Mead is still cursed, and it has been making Odin sick the whole time. He tells the birds on his path to fly ahead of him and tell his people to be ready with containers for the moment he lands.

In many aboriginal traditions, it is well known that one of the great feats of a master shaman is to transmute poison with one's own body. This was known as "snake medicine" to some Native American tribes, and it was told that if a shaman took snake poison into themselves, they could transmute it to a harmless—and even magical—substance. One myth stated that a poisonous snake bit a shaman and the snake died the next day. Greek mythology also has stories of serpent-power allowing for the neutralization of poison, and in Hindu belief, the great poisonous serpent who threatened the world was made harmless by Shiva (Sun in Scorpio) drinking its venom and transmuting it with his own body, burning his throat blue in the process. Odin's use of the snake-form in this myth, and his drinking of a spiritually tainted potion, clearly echoes this common concept.

Odin is known as a shaman-king, eventually dying and being reborn, and doing great magics. In this story—perhaps his first major shamanic feat—he transmutes the poisonous mead with his own body and makes it harmless, casting away the evil of the murders that made it. The eighth is also the house of transformation, and this entire story comes down to the act of transforming something which was evil to good, an alchemical passage of metaphorical lead to gold. When Odin reaches Asgard, his people are waiting with tubs and buckets, and he vomits up the Mead of Poetry, cleansed and ready to be given out a drop at a time to worthy skalds and statesmen. Those who prayed to Odin for inspiration and had their prayers granted were said to be given a drop of the magical mead, which was all that was necessary for a mortal.

Let's look again at those fascinatingly morbid subjects which the eighth-house Mercury keeps digging up. They may be frightening, or disgusting, or so sad they make you want to weep, or otherwise filled with all the discomfort most people don't want to look at. Or perhaps they are willing to look at it through their spread fingers for a moment, but not stare deeply at it and try to understand what, and why, and how these situations came to be … and how they can be transformed. Like the Scorpio Mercury, the eighth-house Mercury has the ability to do this. It also has the talent of shaping the words around those terrible subjects so as to make them more palatable and understandable to those with more sensitive natures, easing them into the frightening ideas so that they might actually listen.

Mercury is a planet which doesn't concern itself much with ethics—that is up to other planets to step in and take care of—and this talent for transforming the way we talk about darkness can be extremely positive or extremely negative … or extremely ambivalent. Gently making it clear to someone why they should get cancer screenings instead of refusing to think about such a horrible eventuality is a good thing. Normalizing cruel behavior is not. There are many points in between. Research can help cure sickle cell anemia or justify operating on prisoners for science. It is this Mercury placement's job to decide what they are to do with their talent, hopefully pulling in advice from other planetary influences … especially ones living in other people, so that they can hear more perspectives and not just get lost in the darkness of the cave where they are cleverly stealing information. The miracle of the eighth house is that there is nothing which cannot be reclaimed by transforming it … into something. What? That's a mystery worthy of this Mercury's full attention.

☿ Mercury in the 9th House: Odysseus

The great epic poem by Homer—named *Odyssey* after its main character—is one of the greatest adventure-travel stories ever, even thousands of years after it was compiled. Part of its draw is the character of Odysseus, who is no ordinary sword jock. He is called the Crafty One, the Polytropos ("Versatile"), Odysseus the Cunning, the Man of Many Devices (or, in some translations, the Man of Twists and Turns). He was known for his intellectual brilliance and his ability to talk people into all sorts of crazy plans. This makes him a perfect Mercurial figure rather than a Martial warrior—he was the man who used his head first and only resorted to combat when words no longer sufficed. When he does resort to violence, it often seems merely one of his "devices" which he is using make a point or manipulate the situation.

Mercury is in charge of learning, and in the house of higher education, this placement never stops plundering information. Those with this placement have an unending hunger for knowledge, and if there are no universities or mega-libraries to hand, they will self-educate in any way they can find. Understanding is the goal, and they are not afraid to go extremely far afield to collect those tempting tidbits of knowledge. At the same time, the more they learn, the more resources they have to deal with the new horizons they will inevitably be chasing. For many of them, it isn't even that they actively seek out new wisdom, but that they somehow end up wandering into a new situations when they didn't plan to. This is, after all, the house of Adventure, and thus Odysseus's story doesn't happen in a library, but is one of the earliest Great Adventure novels that survives.

In Homer's first book *Iliad*, Odysseus was the son of Laertes, the King of Ithaca, and his queen Anticlea. He married Penelope (Saturn in the seventh house) and they had just had an infant son, Telemachus, when Agamemnon starts trumpeting his call to all his allies to join him in attacking Troy. Odysseus very much does not want to go fight in Troy, and decides to pretend that he has gone mad. He ropes himself to a plow and begins to sow his fields with salt, muttering nonsense as he does it. Unfortunately for him, Agamemnon and his herald are not fooled; they grab his infant son away from Penelope and lay him in front of the oncoming plow, and Odysseus turns aside, revealing his sanity. After being roped into the venture against his will, he is promptly sent off to hunt down Achilles (Mars in the first house) who is also a draft dodger, and persuade him to come to Troy.

Throughout the *Iliad*, Odysseus is the problem-solver—the one who coaxes everyone back into battle when they lose hope, including the sulking Achilles. When Achilles is killed, Odysseus manages to remove his body in the chaos of the failed treaty. His final act of cleverness is to come up with the idea of the Trojan Horse—a giant horse filled secretly with soldiers which is left outside the gates of Troy as a religious offering; when the horse is brought inside by the reverent Trojans, the soldiers wait until after nightfall and then spill out, taking the city from within. Troy would not have fallen without Odysseus's quick thinking.

The ninth house is the place of one's greater world view, and having the planet of thought here denotes a mind which is especially good for seeing the bigger picture, the whole of the situation, mentally assembling all the details but not being distracted by them. They can figure out how the system works as a whole, and since this is also the house of foreign cultures, that means factoring in the cultural assumptions of other groups. Odysseus deduces that the Trojans will fall for the big horse, not because the Achaeans would have done so, but because he has observed Troy and the mindset of its people.

While the Greeks admired Odysseus as a culture hero, the Romans—who called him Ulysses—despised him, as their code of honor was more rigid and they revered straightforward soldiers who fought in rows. The Greeks' love for Odysseus became, in Roman eyes, evidence of Greek untrustworthiness. In Roman writings, Ulysses is mentioned as an evil deceiver. This echoes Mercury's ambiguous ethical code; unlike straightforward Mars or rule-abiding Saturn or even the emotionally-based values of the Moon or Venus, Mercury is capable of shifting its viewpoint and morals conveniently to fit whatever escapade is in his sights. The mind can hold many different ideas, and in the house of philosophy, Mercury is not above switching creeds when it suits him to do so, and then finding a philosophy to justify it.

In the *Iliad*, Odysseus is one of a cast of thousands; in its sequel the *Odyssey* he is the star of the show. One the way of out Troy, they stop at an island owned by a great one-eyed Cyclops named Polyphemus, who is a son of Poseidon (Neptune in Cancer). Polyphemus captures and imprisons them, and begins to eat them one at a time. Odysseus offers the Cyclops the large jug of wine he had brought along for the whole crew in exchange for being the last one eaten; Polyphemus agrees, drinks all the wine, and then falls into a drunken sleep. Odysseus blinds him with a stick he has hardened in the fire, and then herds his men out while the Cyclops flails about. The other Cyclopes come at Polyphemus's cries, but Odysseus has told the Cyclops that his name is Nobody, so they are confused when he cries out "Nobody has blinded me!" and the men get away. After they flee the island, Polyphemus cries out to Poseidon and prays that Odysseus will be punished by never making it home alive. Poseidon calls up a huge storm that blows the ship off course, and the rest of the story is about the twenty years Odysseus spends adventuring while trying to make it home. Poseidon continues to thwart him, while Athena (Sun in Aquarius) attempts to help.

Odysseus's adventures while traveling are many, and some of them have their own characters and will be discussed in other chapters. He finds an island of cannibals and is almost eaten again; he stumbles across a sorceress who transforms his crew into animals and is delayed for a year; he calls up the ghosts of a dead prophet and his own mother; he gets his ship pinned between a terrible sea monster and a howling whirlpool; he is shipwrecked and captured by a nymph for seven years; he is shipwrecked again and finds himself on yet another island; and on it goes. The Ninth House was traditionally referred to as the House of Long Journeys Over Water, and his story is classic for that. In each strange port, he is able to assess how to get what he wants from the people involved, even if it takes a while to extract himself. In some places he very nearly goes native, which is also the sign of a strong ninth house. His curse of long journeying echoes this Mercury's continual mental wandering; his homecoming would almost be an anticlimax if it wasn't so difficult.

When Odysseus finally gets home, it has been two decades and no one recognizes him except for his faithful dog. Penelope has been beset by suitors who are eating her food and pressuring her to pick one of them to marry, and his son Telemachus—now a teenager—is resentful and ready to do violence. This reflects one of the more problematic sides of the ninth-house Mercury; even when they're home among their family and loved ones, their mind is often elsewhere. Many end up with jobs where they travel frequently, literally leaving their loved ones behind. Others simply leave mentally on internal journeys (sometimes into stacks of books) and their frustrated family members have to subsist on crumbs of attention, or else get on with their lives and stop trying to get regular interactions out of their wayward Mercury person. Sometimes the ninth-house Mercury comes home and realizes they've been gone too long, and everyone else has moved on without including them in the plans.

This situation can be made worse by the ninth-house Mercury's tendency to be aloof and abstract, more interested in discussing some higher concept than dealing with the grubby daily details of which plumber to call or when to pay for the children's schooling. The ninth house hates to be confined and Mercury refuses to be pinned down, and having a mundane conversation can be painfully boring for them. However, it is in pitching in with these details that love and care is shown to one's people, dreary and tiresome as that is to this far-ranging mind. This Mercury placement needs a partner who is—more than anything else—*interesting*. If they seem to be at an intellectual disadvantage, they may eventually be relegated to an occasionally-humored necessity.

Odysseus unmasks himself to his son, and the two of them plot to get rid of the suitors. When Penelope decides that her choice will be whichever suitor can draw Odysseus's huge bow—hoping that none of them will be able to—Odysseus joins the line in disguise and lifts the bow last. He promptly begins to shoot all of Penelope's suitors, with his son finishing off the rest. After the bloodbath, he forces the serving-women who had been sleeping with and encouraging the suitors to clean up their corpses, and then kills the serving-women in turn. Penelope is unsure that he is actually her husband, but he manages to convince her. However, the families of the slain suitors come after him to seek revenge, and it requires the help of Zeus (Jupiter in Aries) and Athena to convince them all to make peace.

Here we come to the other part of the ninth-house Mercury's dark side. We've already mentioned the Mercurial ability to shift one's code of behavior when it's convenient to do so, but the ninth house holds an entirely different mental trap, and that is fanaticism. Sometimes it happens that this Mercury goes so deep into a mental concept that it possesses their whole mind, and then woe betide anyone who challenges them. Mercury's mental slickness can turn into an "ends justify the means" situation, and can become surprisingly cold and uncaring, seeing emotionally complicated situations as just something to be cleared out of the way, by force if necessary. Odysseus is not interested in viewing it as more than black and white; these men are the last point in the way of the triumphant return he has been doggedly envisioning for years, and they must be destroyed. Their grieving families do not come into his equation.

This is also the house of religion, where fanaticism is often a temptation hovering in the background. Even if the "creed" is just an unwavering belief in one's own righteousness rather than tying it to a higher power it can still lead to the extreme of thinking that you can do what you want because you're more knowledgeable than the benighted people in front of you. Athena's interference—Odysseus is her favorite hero, after all—is the force of rationality and strategy who brings him back to an assessment of the future, and taking the annoying motivations of others into account. Zeus is the god of leadership, who points out that if you are actually superior to people you considers your subordinates, your relationship to them should be that of protector and teacher, not abuser. Finally, Penelope calms her husband, using her Saturnian sense of rules and proprieties, and convinces him to make peace at whatever cost with those he has wronged.

Mercury loves being in this house, and often bestows many gifts, including skilled storytelling, ingenuity, and joy in expanding one's mental boundaries, but in order to come down to earth and be part of the world of hearts and bodies and love, it requires these forces to stay in balance. This Mercury placement has trouble keeping that balance, and in fact doesn't enjoy it much—keeping one foot on the ground is a major distraction from free flight—but part of its maturation is learning to bring that knowledge back to those waiting on land, so that it can be truly shared with the world. This is the ultimate end, after all, of the Long Journey Over Water.

10☿ Mercury in the 10th House: Indra

Mercury is an airy planet, as the element of Air is associated with Mind and Words. It is changeable, variable, running to and fro as its interests shift, not steady or sturdy at all ... and one would think that in the tenth house of career, it would be equally as unstable. Yet for some reason, something about the (Saturn-ruled) atmosphere of the tenth house makes Mercury settle out and plant its feet, becoming more dependable and consistent. How do you turn the wind into a competent career CEO, the one at the top of the professional mountain?

As it turns out, historically, the wind very much likes to be at the top, and there have been many Gods of sky and wind and storm, who eventually find their way to divine kingship. The Greek Zeus/Roman Jupiter (Jupiter in Aries) is the most notorious example; another might be the Slavic Perun (Jupiter in the first house) or the Gaulish Taranis. The Indo-European pantheons tended to revere their wind deities, at least during the older periods, and make them Kings over the other Gods ... and not least because a storm God can throw some serious lightning.

During the Vedic era of India, from 1500 to 500 B.C.E., their version of the Indo-European storm deity was Indra, one of the stars of the Rig Veda, and he was indeed the King of Heaven. Indra was a god of wind and storm, a chaotic figure who chose to be a beacon of law and order, to battle the other powers of chaos on their own ground. He kills the great *asura* (daemon) Vritra, who hoarded the rains to cause drought, stole the cloud-cows, and even hid Surya the Sun God (Sun in the seventh house) for a time. (Vritra was a daemon of cold who coiled around a mountaintop, which leads some scholars to associate him with the snows of the Himalayas, "locking up" the water for the rivers.) Indra's famous battle with Vritra looses both the rains and the rivers, and brings fertility to the dry land below. Like Thor (Mercury in Taurus), Indra has a hammer named Bhaudhara which he throws as a thunderbolt, and it returns automatically to his hand. He uses the rainbow as his archery weapon, and rides a four-tusked white elephant. He was allied with the Rudras, all storm-spirits who originally followed Indra's command, during the glory days of the Vedic era when he ruled over all the other Gods as their King.

Tenth-house Mercury people are intellectually driven and ambitious; like Indra, they will fight what they have to in order to get ahead in the world. They tend to out-think their opposition rather than engaging in undignified scuffles. They may also get a reputation for cutting their enemies to pieces over media, and they can be experts of the public-image spin. They are good at looking intelligent in public—this is not to say that they aren't intelligent, but they can master the skill of knowing just how intelligent to look in order to achieve their goals, and how exactly to pull that off. Like the God of the Storm, they know when to make thunderous noise and when to blow softly.

It is true that tenth-house Mercury people often look for careers in Mercurial areas, such as writing, journalism, teaching, publishing, sales, telecommunications, transportation, and any sort of media one can think of. Law may take their fancy because of its emphasis on public speaking and paperwork; politics—like the King of Heaven—may also beckon. They may especially love jobs which allow them to travel for work, even if it's to different jobsites in the same area. This doesn't change in high-ranking positions either. They don't like to be confined to a desk day in and day out, preferring to fly from one situation to another in person, keeping an eye on their small empires and watching for new opportunities whenever possible.

One of Indra's titles is "the thousand-eyed", because it was thought he could do surveillance over the entire area through the eyes of all the birds that fly. Not only are birds themselves ruled astrologically by Mercury, but being the "one who watches" resonates with Mercurial people as well. Tenth-house Mercury bosses want to know what's going on, and may actually watch their subordinates carefully; tenth-house Mercury workers may be the one with the ear to the ground, catching up on the water-fountain gossip. They know who is dating whom and who has a professional rivalry with whom, and they are not above using such data for their own advancement, at least if it can be done without other people finding out. After all, information is power as far as they are concerned, regardless of where it comes from or what sort it is. Unused information is simply something they haven't figured out yet where to place for best effect.

This isn't to say that the tenth-house Mercury is always necessarily manipulative and heartless, although Mercury by itself is an amoral planet and requires the presence of more feeling or law-abiding planets to refrain from unethical behavior. But even if they stick to a code of honor, you can guarantee they've thought about it and mentally played with the idea, if only to dismiss it eventually. If they don't see the use of dubious information as being problematic, and it could be used to their benefit, they will probably use it ... although they may have a backup plan for plausible deniability on hand in case something goes wrong.

The fourth and tenth houses are considered to represent parental influences; there is argument over which is the mother and which the father, but I like to follow the idea that the fourth-house parent sets the tone for the home, while the tenth-house parent is the one who teaches the child about the outside world, and introduces them to its customs and functions. Sometimes that's the same parent; sometimes both parents share representation in both houses. Mercury in the tenth indicates a parent who seemed brilliant to the child—intelligent, articulate, a good communicator, but perhaps distant like the wind and sky. Even if that parent was frequently present, they may have been busy "in their head" and not really seen or connected with their children. They may have laid down the expectation that their children would also be smart, articulate, and well-educated; less intellectual children might have had trouble with this decree. If Mercury is badly aspected, the parent may have had some sort of mental illness which took them even further away emotionally.

Indra is the deity most associated with the mysterious drink called *Soma*, whose actual identity is lost to time. Different plants have been suggested as the potential source of the *Soma* drink, as has the idea that it was a plant now gone extinct due to overharvesting. Some sources claim that it was a psychedelic; others say that it was a stimulant. Either way, Indra consumes it in epic quantities, and this is part of his power. Legends go on about how the sacred drug was stolen and brought to human beings. (One gets the image of the tenth-house Mercury on a caffeine high, rolling through their career projects like the wind, flattening everything before them as they go.) However, in the post-Vedic era, Indra was dethroned and became subordinate to the rising Hindu Gods, and was then pictured as a hedonistic and often intoxicated God. A great deal of emphasis was put on his continual affairs with married mortal women, whose earthly husbands sometimes cursed him. This is a cautionary tale to the tenth-house Mercury, whose wandering attentions and distractions can destabilize him and bring down everything he has worked for, if he is not careful. Mercury's desire to experience it all, and an assumption that "success" means the ability to do whatever you like, can lead to dissolution and a great crash, if they are not careful. Indra's dethronement, like so many other divine falls, may be simply historical politics, but it still sounds a warning bell.

This storm God is not a two-dimensional character, however; as is appropriate for a Mercurial figure, he is complex and has many functions. Besides being a lightning-thrower, a rain-bringer, a cloud-disperser, and a river-helper, he is also a deity of flocks and herds (especially but not limited to cattle). When *asuras* steal the sacred cattle and lock them inside a mountain, Indra sings the songs which will release them, showing his mastery of Words of Power; he is also said to put the milk into the cows and make it flow. (Herding is a very tenth-house Mercurial career, as it involves driving hoofed wealth constantly from one place to another, as is echoed in the Greek stories of Hermes/Mercury in Gemini.) Indra rides the chariot of the winds, and sometimes slams into other chariot-riding-deities such as the dawn goddess and the Sun god Surya, mostly to prove that he is the fastest thing in the sky. This resonates with the tenth-house Mercury, who may make it to the top of his career by the simple virtue of just being faster than everyone else. This is the original "work smarter, not harder" career advice.

That's another thing about the tenth-house Mercury—they may not limit themselves to just one career, or they may choose a career which requires mastering skills from several others. They are versatile and adaptable, and can often make connections between different fields of study while the narrow-focus people are stuck in their short view. People with this placement thrive on mental challenges, and will sometimes set them up for themselves just to see if they can outsmart the odds—where everyone can see it and be impressed, of course. They constantly look for new education, although they are as likely to be self-educated as to take classes run by someone else.

One of the hymns to Indra calls on him as the deity who rejuvenates the immobile into something mobile and prosperous, which excellently sums up the tenth-house Mercury. If something is stuck in the mud, they are here to shift it by the shrewdest means possible, and get it moving in the direction they want. *You can wait for the wind to change,* they say, *or you can figure out a way to change it yourself.* Either way, it's best to get out of the path of that white elephant.

11☿ Mercury in the 11th House: Puss in Boots

While the first MythAstrology book was largely the stories of deities, in this book I am also plundering traditional folktales, and one of my favorite folktales of all time is Puss in Boots. When I was very young, I was enchanted by the story of the swashbuckling, charismatic cat, although I didn't really understand why the cat went to all that trouble. However, now as an adult I understand why this is a story of friendship between two unlikely characters, a tale of the triumph of the eleventh house.

The first version of Puss in Boots was written in Italy in the sixteenth century—and in that version the cat was a fairy in disguise—but the version we know today was adapted by Charles Perrault a century later in France. Cats are often seen as magical animal helpers in European mythology, as opposed to other places in the world where they may be jackals or foxes or monkeys. The concept of the magical animal helper, however, is found everywhere and goes back as far as prehistory. Its roots can be found in shamanic practices of contacting animal spirits through trance journeying. Cats also have a strong stereotypical history as familiars—helper spirits—for witches and rural sorcerers.

In Perrault's version of the story, a poor miller dies and leaves only the family cat to the youngest son, who is downtrodden, hopeless, and limp. The cat begins to speak to him, saying that if he can use the last of his money to buy the cat a pair of nice boots and a large sack, she will take care of him. The young man is entranced with the idea of a talking cat and gladly buys her the boots and the sack. Many later versions have the cat as a male animal, largely because of the swashbuckling masculine attire, but Perrault's version has a female cat, in spite of boots and cape and all. Like Uranus, Mercury is one of the gender-shifting planets who doesn't stick to any one side of a binary. (Except, of course, for "mind/heart".) So it's appropriate that this Mercury character bends gender and eventually shifts it entirely, over time. The gender of the magical cat can be switched back and forth over time and the story continues on, unbothered.

Stories of animal helpers and fairy helpers have a number of themes. In many of them, the magical creature is caught by a human and offers aid as payment for escape. However, the story of Puss in Boots has no such animosity or captivity. The cat decides to help the young man because she likes him in spite of his being a ne'er-do-well, and they strike up a friendship across species lines. Cats are notoriously independent, almost to the point of being barely tamed, and it is notable that in most animal helper stories in other parts of the world, it is a wild animal which agrees to help the human in question. Cats straddle that line between wild and free, and this echoes in the theme of the eleventh house.

In the House of Friendship, we choose the line between freedom and commitment. This house is ruled by the ambivalently chaotic planet Uranus, and the sign of Aquarius. Both sign and planet are infamous for demanding freedom (both for themselves and, once they have evolved past simple rebellion, for others) and also wanting to be part of a group. Close, but not too close; people with this energy want the freedom to run away, and if confined they will strike out. (Rather like a cat who is done with being petted.) In the House of Friendship we freely choose our bonds, and shrug them off or remain loyal depending on their worth and our whims. Mercury is a planet which lives by whims, much as Mercury tries to claim that it is always rational.

The first day after having acquired the boots and bag, the cat uses the bag to catch and kill a couple of rabbits, keeping both she and her young friend fed for a couple of nights. The second day she catches more rabbits, but does not bring them home. Instead, the cat goes to the palace of the local king—a widower with one adult daughter—and offers the rabbits as a gift "from my master, the Marquis of Carrabas." The princess is quite taken with the cat and offers her a dish of cream. After this, she trades her time between catching rabbits to feed her hapless friend—who is apparently unable to find work and fend for himself—and delivering gifts of dead game to the king's palace, all in the name of the fictional Marquis.

In between these adventures, the cat also takes on a local ogre who is a shapeshifter. He had been known to eat people, but didn't care for the meat of cats, and so left Puss in Boots alone. The cat praises and flatters the ogre, and convinces him to show off his shapeshifting skills. First she has him turn into lions and bears and other large intimidating creatures, and acts properly frightened. Then she asks if he has the skill to turn into something tiny, such as a mouse. He does so, and Puss leaps on him and kills him in an instant. Puss then goes to the peasants who work the ogre's fields, and tells them that the ogre is dead and that the lands have been claimed by the Marquis of Carrabas. She threatens them with being chopped into mincemeat if they do not tell this fact to anyone who might drive by and ask.

This is all part of Mercury's smooth tongue and clever mind. In the eleventh house, the planet of eloquence uses its powers to influence groups of people to do their bidding ... and to protect those whom they claim as friend and tribe. One of the problems with this placement is that they may be a little too ready to stretch the truth if it will provide that protection or get those people moving in the same direction. They can be chameleons, turning a different face to everyone, but they don't do it just to be liked. Mercury has a purpose, and the face they don will be the one to make a particular impression and further their goals.

Remember that it isn't Mercury, in any chart, which provides ethics and moral codes; other planets take on that duty. Mercury is slick, sliding from idea to idea and approach to approach. Mercury justifies its actions through mental stories, and this placement of the slippery planet can sometimes lead to someone being called "two-faced" by betrayed group members once they compare notes and realize that their Mercurial friend has been a different person to each of them. This doesn't mean that Mercury can't be a loyal and protective friend. It's just that the way Mercury naturally leans toward making people happy or throwing off danger is to edit people's reality and subtly shift them onto a path of least resistance toward the goal. The more troublesome they are, the fewer qualms Mercury has about manipulating them out of the picture. Puss's flattering but coldblooded approach to getting rid of the ogre underlines the ruthlessness inherent in a planet which has the mind but not the heart.

Puss goes home every night and regales the young miller's son with tales of what she has done. (Mercury in the house of friends needs people to talk to, tell stories to, bounce ideas off of, and generally communicate about their clever plans, ideas, and theories. While they tend to prefer highly verbal and intellectual friends, if they can't get those, they will talk to anyone in their friend group who will hold still and listen.) The miller's son is properly impressed, although he doesn't quite understand where Puss's plans are going. Then Puss tells the youth to take off his clothes and bathe in a particular river visible from the road on a particular day. As soon as the miller's son goes into the water, Puss promptly hides his clothing and waits behind a bush. The naked man realizes that his clothing has vanished, and lurks embarrassed in the water, not daring to come out.

What he doesn't know is that Puss has bribed the king's coachman with a gift of dead game, asking him to drive this road on their way home from the castle of a neighboring lord. As the king views all the fields, he asks who owns them, and the peasants all tell him that they are owned by the Marquis of Carrabas. This is another of Mercury's manipulations; when a Mercurial person thinks it knows what's best for you, and perhaps has doubts about your instant willingness to go along with their plan, they are not always above "arranging" the situation to get the reluctant friend to the "right" place, and any discomfort is shrugged off in the name of progress.

When the king and his daughter come down the road in their coach, Puss runs out crying that robbers have attacked her master and stolen all his clothing. The king, remembering that the "Marquis of Carrabas" had given him many gifts and fed his table many times, immediately offers to bring this potential ally to his home and reclothe him. Puss proudly leads the bewildered miller's son out of the pond to be swaddled in a royal cloak and whisked off to the king's palace. Apparently the youth cleaned up well and didn't embarrass himself (probably with Puss whispering in his ear as prompter), for the princess finds herself attracted to him, and the king decides he is a good match for his daughter. So the former impoverished miller's son becomes a prince, and Puss gets all the cream she wants and no longer has to hunt rabbits.

While this story could be interpreted only as a clever and manipulative character trying to gain undeserved riches, there is a deeper point to it. Puss's goal is to lead her friend out of poverty, pure and simple, and set him up for a better life. The deep goal of the eleventh house is more than hanging out with buddies and interest groups; it is humanitarian work in the world, whether on a tiny basis or a great one. It is brotherhood, which overturns assumed class barriers. Puss's actions turn the class system on its head and bring economic justice for at least one hapless peasant. *All you need are the right words*, says Mercury.

The eleventh is the house of idealism, and this may be overly idealistic thinking, but it is the kernel at the center of every piece of advertising. The saying goes that the master's tools will not dismantle the master's house, but this Mercury placement retorts that with the right verbal seduction, the master will hand over the keys, the tools, and the work crew without understanding what he's doing until it's too late to stop anything. *The magic words*, says Mercury, *can change the world … and free my people.*

12☿ Mercury in the 12th House: Father Raven

In the creation myth of the Inuit, the native peoples of the arctic and subarctic portions of the North American continent, the first man to be created was Tulungersaq (Father Raven). He was not, at this time, a bird;

he was a man, but alone in the dark. Earth, as we know it, had not been created, and even the Upper World was pitch-dark, with only a ground of dead clay. No one knows how Father Raven came to be; perhaps he manifested out of the life-energy of the world. Still, there he sat in the dark, not knowing who or what he was, or anything else save that he sat on hard clay.

His fingers touched his face, nose, mouth, and body, and he knew that he was a unique being, different from the clay. He found a strange little knob on his forehead. He did not know what it was for, but when he touched it he realized that he was an independent being who could move around and affect his environment. Creeping carefully over the clay in the dark, he explored his empty world until he found the edge of a great hole, a place where the clay ended and he could go no further. Testing its depth, he took bits of the clay and threw them over the edge, but there was no sound heard, no bottom. Frightened, he moved away from the abyss to look for something more comforting.

The twelfth house is a dark and primal place at its best, the basement of the soul. Mercury, the planet of thought and speech and travel, flies closest to the Sun and prefers bright, well-lit, clear paths. In a sense, all our Mercuries are born in darkness—we all emerge children whose neural paths need to slowly develop—but something about a twelfth-house Mercury locks the powers of thought into the dark place of the unconscious for much longer, and for greater frequencies, than that of most people. For them, all mental processes start in the unconscious. That means that it takes quite a while longer for the idea or the response to come into the light and be articulated. In childhood, this process may happen as a speech delay, or be read as a lack of brightness by people whose mental processes are quicker and closer to the surface.

The twelfth-house Mercury has a lot of groping in the dark to do before the words will flow anything close to freely. Since planets in the twelfth house all have boundary issues, it may be difficult for them to figure out where their mind starts and another's mind begins, which means that they are quick to absorb the mental constructs of others ... and just as quick to inadvertently morph them into something entirely different once they pass through their nonlinear processes. Sometimes what they reflect back out isn't at all the same as what went in, and both they and whoever they are trying to communicate with become confused. For some twelfth-house Mercuries, it's like struggling against a constant child's game of Telephone, whispered in the dark.

In all our unconsciouses, there is a deep hole. It is where we throw things that we don't like—the garbage-dumpster of the sub-basement. At its bottom—and it does have one—is the place where our minds join to what is not our minds, but something greater. As Father Raven found, throwing things into it merely loses you those things, and eventually you will have to go in after them. For people with twelfth-house Mercuries, this dark hole is frighteningly close; their ability to deny it and live only on the surface is fairly impaired. However, it also means that when they are ready to go down there, it is only a few feet away.

As Father Raven dug in the clay, he found a small round object. Holding it close to him, he discovered that it was an egg, and the warmth of his body hatched it out. A tiny sparrow came forth, took to the air, and whirred about him. It lighted on his hand and he felt glad, for he finally had a friend. Deciding that if one friend could appear, he could make another one, he dug up clay and sculpted a man out of it. The man came to life and began to dig around restlessly, churning up huge amounts of clay. Father Raven tried to stop him, and realized that this man was very different from him; he had a fiery temper and was not afraid to use violence on those who stopped him. He seemed intent on digging everything up, and had no peace. Father Raven decided that this friend was a failure, and threw him over the edge into the abyss. From then on the clay man was known as Tornaq, the evil demon that plagues the earth.

The tiny sparrow and the evil self-created demon are telling symbols of what one finds when one goes exploring in the dark places of one's psyche. The sparrow is fragile and helpful; Father Raven discovers that it can see in the dark and is willing to guide him about. The sparrow is the delicate breath of instinct, intuition, which is really all we have when we go excavating down there. Tornaq, on the other hand, is a problem. He embodies all the urges that we would prefer to pretend that we did not have. "That's not me; I'm not like such-and-such. That's the total opposite of me." He is willing to keep digging things up that we would prefer stayed buried. Inevitably, we throw him into the hole and hope that he vanishes ... after all, that hole has no bottom, right?

As Father Raven explored the world, this time with the little sparrow to help him, he discovered that trees and bushes and rocks had appeared while he was not looking. He found water, and traced it in a circle, and realized that he was on an island. There was nowhere else to go but into the abyss, and while the thought terrified him, it also consumed him. "But if I leap, I will merely fall forever," he said. The sparrow flew into the abyss and came back, and reassured him that there was something down there, forming from the lumps of clay that he had thrown down. "Then I shall fall and die," Father Raven said hopelessly.

At that point, an idea came to him ... the idea that he might be able to shift his shape, as he had shaped the clay into a man. "It would have to be something with wings to fly," he thought to himself. So he bade the little sparrow alight on his hand, and there he explored it with his fingers, and saw how it was made—wings, beak, feathers, bones. He built himself wings from tree branches, and when he tied them on they become great black wings. The lump in the middle of his forehead became a beak, a great raven mask. Thus he transformed into a raven and flew down into the abyss.

This myth charts the process by which the twelfth-house Mercury needs to proceed. There is only so much exploring in the dark that he can do in the upper levels of his mind; sooner or later he realizes that it has boundaries and becomes cramped. The really important things are down there, in that hole. Some twelfth-house Mercury people simply remain in their terror and never venture into the deep unconscious—after all, most other people don't go there, or don't seem to go there very often; why should he? Yet this is what this placement is built for: a bridge between the mental depths and the mental interface with the world, over which things can be hauled up and exposed to the light. To ignore this is to walk away from one's destined path, which will always be looming just behind your heels anyway, a great hole that it will take a huge amount of denial (and a very shallowly lived life) to blind one's self to.

To go down, though, one has to become something other than what one is. One has to change, to shift the shape of one's perceptions, and in order to do this, it is necessary to remember the things you created and threw into the hole, whether you like it or not. Your ability to shape yourself depends on connecting again with those painful memories. Tornaq the demon is not only the unacceptable parts of ourselves. He is part of who we are before we realized that we would have to cut off pieces of ourselves in order to be accepted, and thus he is linked to an earlier wholeness. In order to reshape yourself, you need to know your own shape as it is now, including the hidden parts.

Then you have to do that shaping carefully, bit by bit, according to what your intuition tells you. Father Raven gently studies the sparrow in order to craft his own wings out of branches, and then suddenly discovers that the lump in the middle of his own forehead will change him into a raven ... in other words, that the power was within him all the time, but he couldn't have reached it without coming to know the ways of the sparrow. For a twelfth-house Mercury, since concepts tend to come up in images rather than words, this might mean using a nonlinear method of excavating one's soul—art, poetry, dance, meditation, or anything that bypasses the linear left brain. The left brain will simply wander around in the dark forever in these people's heads; it is the intuitive right brain that knows the way down.

In the myth, the land at the bottom of the abyss was so far away that by the time Father Raven got down to the bottom, he was completely exhausted. However, as soon as he was rested he set about making trees, rocks, and animals from the globs of clay previously thrown down, and thus created the Earth. Some of the plants produced pods from which popped human beings, and he took a liking to them, as they were the most like him. Many adventures followed, in which he taught the people of the Arctic and subarctic continent how to live, until finally he flew back to the Upper World, there to watch over them forever.

A twelfth-house Mercury has the potential of creating a rich inner existence once he has plumbed his depths with courage and intuition, but the ultimate end result must be that he brings those riches back up where they can be communicated to others. This combination shares with Mercury in Pisces both the poetic gift and the accompanying inarticulation, but the former is a little more deeply buried and the latter a little more problematic. Solitude is a balm and a comfort, giving the individual the time that they need to visit their inner depths and work out the answers. If a twelfth-house Mercury clams up in the middle of a discussion, or starts talking nonsense or changing the subject, let them know that it's all right to talk about this later, and that you're willing to give them space to do some more excavating, and some more internal flights. The trip down that hole is exhausting every time, even if it's more than worth it. It also requires facing down the demon Tornaq each time, and dealing with the destruction that he has wrought.

The last thing that Father Raven did before returning to the Upper World was to cast coals of fire into the sky, making the sun and moon and stars. This lit up the darkness of Earth, and when he returned to the Upper World, he discovered that it had lit up the heavens as well. It is only in journeying to the depths of the unconscious that the twelfth-house Mercury that light comes to the groping darkness above, and illumination is cast upon the dome of the mind. Then the Sun can shine, and all the solar, rational, and left-brained processes can finally be given the chance to speak with clarity.

1♀ Venus in the 1ˢᵗ House: Aušrinė

Somewhere along the line, human beings looked up and noticed that there was a very bright star in the sky both in the morning and the evening. Eventually some early astronomers figured out that they were the same heavenly body, showing itself at the points of transition between Moon and Sun. Many cultures decided that this beautiful spark which heralded dawn and dusk should be associated with a deity of love and loveliness. (Certainly not all—some Mesoamerican cultures saw the planet Venus as a harbinger of war, which is very interesting.) The rock itself is named after the Roman love goddess, and astrologically we do know it as the planet of love and beauty. Therefore, it seemed right that a goddess who directly embodied that spark in the sky should step forth for the Venus house placement which brings a human being as close as it is possible to come to embodying the planet themselves.

I say "embodying" because the first is the House of the Body, and it is anecdotally true that a high percentage of individuals with this Venus placement have exceptional physical beauty. It's vanishingly rare to find one who is ugly, and even those with plainer faces have a great deal of charm and grace. They can smile at you and suddenly you are drawn in by their charisma. Not all beauty is skin deep, but this placement has an unfair chance of getting both types. From a young age, they learned that they could charm extra privileges and attention out of the adults around them, and it's a rare one who didn't pull it off whenever they could.

In Baltic mythology, the Sun goddess Saulé (Sun in the first house) has two daughters, Aušrinė and Vakarinė, the Morning and Evening Stars. This old mythology still divides the planet's appearance into two separate bodies, and makes them sisters. Aušrinė, whose name means "dawn star", is so beautiful that she stirs the envy of her mother, the Sun. Accounts of what happened vary, but while at first Aušrinė simply dances for the people on a great stone at the Spring Equinox (the dawn of the year), eventually she and her sister become her proud mother's servants. Aušrinė's job is to get her mother ready for her daily ride, helping her onto her horse and arranging her elaborate hair and clothing. Similarly, Vakarinė helps her mother down off her horse and gets her ready for bed at night. For a time, this is their existence—handmaidens of the shining Sun.

However, Aušrinė's beauty and charm was her undoing. First, people began to watch for her more often than they looked at her mother the Sun, which earned the jealousy of Saulé. This may be a theme that first-house Venus people will relate to—as far as they are concerned, they are just going along minding their own business and being naturally charming, since when you have a planet in the first house, it's easy to follow its example and takes a fair amount of effort to avoid embodying it—and suddenly all these people are expressing envy and resentment, as if the Venus person had done something to offend them. Women with this placement have recounted having few female friends, because the other girls fear they will enchant their male partners. Men with this placement have noted the envy of other men who don't understand why women flock to them and bosses give way before their charm.

Children with first-house Venuses may go further than just exploiting their charming smiles to get that extra piece of cake out of their parents. They may come to depend on that talent to the point where they do not develop other skills for more difficult circumstances; if they can't charm their way out of it, they may feel entirely helpless. Adults may see their good looks and attribute adult qualities to them. One example of this is beautiful girl children who are turned into "little beauty queens" in semi-adult and even slightly sexually suggestive outfits and makeup which give the illusion that they are older than their years. ("Lolita syndrome" is real, and damaging.) If too much emphasis is put on their looks at too young an age, they may grow up to be obsessed with keeping a certain standard of physical beauty. How they look may become the basis of their self-value, and they may spend hours working out, picking out clothing, and generally obsessing over every wrinkle and scar. Being attractive becomes the tool they use to get by in the world, and as society devalues age and puts youth on a pedestal, the quest to keep their good looks may become desperate as they get older, regardless of gender. Many may learn that smiling and playing dumb lets them avoid confrontation, and may cultivate a "bimbo" (or "himbo") affect to pull out when that policeman pulls them over.

Those are the internal problems; the external ones are more unnerving. Sometimes other people can become obsessed with them, projecting an ideal of love and romance onto the first-house Venus. If they are young, they may not even understand why someone would look at them and see an idyllic version of that archetype—the Venus written across their face—but then they have to cope with pursuers, stalkers, and people getting angry because the first-house Venus person does not return their obsessed devotion and refuses to behave like the Venus puppet in their head. Sometimes this can start barely after puberty; even when it waits until adulthood, it is tricky. Such attentions can be extremely flattering at first, and they may get sucked into unsuitable relationships because they wear their heart on their sleeve and the adorer thinks it's for them.

In the case of Aušrinė, her own father the Moon falls in love with her and they begin an affair. The story does not say whether Aušrinė is willing, unwilling, pressured into it, or simply passively goes along. Neither does it matter, because a first-house Venus person might find themselves in any of those positions when approached by someone more powerful who is projecting desires upon them. At the same time, there are stories which hint that Perkunas the thunder god (Jupiter in the first house) also desires to marry her, so she is doubly sought and pressured. Most people feel that they could use more Venus in their lives, and may pursue the valued thing which promises to give them just that.

Yet another story tells how a mortal man named Joseph becomes fascinated with the shining star in the sky, calling it "the second Sun", and chases it until he comes to an island where Aušrinė, the "Mother of Winds", lives with her herd of sacred cattle when she is not in the sky during the morning. (She appears as a maiden on the earth, a star in the sky, and a white mare swimming in the ocean.) Joseph is so obsessed with her that he offers to become her cattle-herder and serve her if only he can be near her. After a few years, he steals a single hair on her head (a very stalkerish act) and puts it into a nutshell, throwing it into the ocean. A ray of light bounces from the sea to sky and accidentally sends Aušrinė to live permanently in the sky, along with Joseph who continues to follow her about (becoming Mercury, who is never far from Venus).

But back to the family drama. When Saulė finds out about the affair, she is furious with her husband and divorces him for sleeping with their daughter, telling Perkunas to chop him into pieces ... which the jealous thunder god does with enthusiasm. She is offended that people might consider Aušrinė to be more attractive than herself—including her husband, to add insult to injury—and is angry with her daughter, but over time Aušrinė wins herself back into her mother's favor. The charm of the first-house Venus is hard to resist, and even when someone is peeved with them, their endearing smile can often win back the person's affections. Aušrinė remained loyal to her mother and continued to assist her in the mornings, and after a time all was forgiven. Still, there is a children's rhyme about her which links her to being a goddess of not only dawn but dew, dawn's water (and Venus is a watery planet); she is shown as the girl who laid her string of pearls on the grass and the Moon only lit them up, but the Sun snatched them away.

The first-house Venus has other pitfalls as well—being lazy and waiting for things to come to them, calculatedly using their charms in a downright treacherous way, being too willing to fold in order to be liked—but at its best, this is a placement which welcomes Life with open arms. This Venus placement's goal is to experience joy, to spread joy, and to diplomatically form connections between other people. When the Venus person realizes that bringing others together is more important in the long term than simply collecting a buzzing crowd around themselves, they will be able to turn their considerable charms into a beacon of light which can lead the way. Just like the Morning Star in the sky.

♀ Venus in the 2ⁿᵈ House: Benzaiten

Most people are aware of the stereotype of the starving artist, poverty-stricken and living in a garret, barely eking out a living. Even musicians who are big stars often fall into a rags-to-riches archetype, because they knew those rags well. Some of these ideas come from the fact that the arts don't always survive well in a capitalist society, and that they aren't always easy to sell. Arts and music are sacred to Venus, and while Venus blesses her starving artists in garrets, she also blesses those who figure out a way to make it pay. The Venus placement which has a real talent for that are those with Venus in the second house of finance.

Benzaiten—also known as Benten, the Chinese pronunciation—is one of the Seven Lucky Gods of Japan, and the only female goddess in the modern "standard" set. It's pretty well known that Benzaiten developed as a

Chinese version of Sarasvati (Mercury in Libra), as several of the Hindu Gods came to East Asia through Buddhism. Benzaiten is portrayed as a beautiful young woman playing a *biwa*, a Chinese stringed instrument, in the same way that Sarasvati plays a *veena*, the Indian lute. Her name means "Heavenly Shrine Goddess", referring to Buddhist shrines which were often decorated with pictures of Hindu/Buddhist deities, reworked to look East Asian. Another of her titles is Myoonten, "Goddess of Lovely Sounds". However, as Gods split off and shift, they take on other attributes and expand their rulerships to include new areas. Sarasvati is primarily a goddess of knowledge, as well as the arts, and is thus more of a Mercury figure, although we've placed her in Venus-ruled Libra. Benzaiten, as we shall see, shifted herself more Venus-ward, and into the second house.

Sarasvati was originally a river goddess (although her river dried up and its exact location has been lost to time), and this fact is reflected in Benzaiten. She became associated with any fresh water—rivers, lakes, streams—and is sometimes shown floating on water in a lotus. Her shrines were built next to rivers, lakes, and springs. Rather than Sarasvati's peacock, Benzaiten's associated animal is a white snake, of the sort found in water in east Asia, a little more reminiscent of the white swan which is Sarasvati's other bird. Sometimes Benzaiten is shown as a coiled white snake with a human head; sometimes the white snake merely accompanies her. As a water goddess, she was given the God of the Sea as a husband in some areas of Japan, and is sometimes seen riding a sea-dragon named Ryuujin to symbolize this. The idea was that all rivers eventually flow to the ocean, so the goddess of fresh water must eventually come to join with the Sea. She was said to be able to calm the Sea with her songs, and thus sailors prayed to her to gentle her husband so that he would not drown their boats. Over time, she became the goddess who could calm the excesses of any male deity, and thus the archetype of the gentle lady who could enchant her husband into abandoning his wrath.

It is said that Benzaiten is responsible for influencing the entire historical course of Japanese art, because so much of it is in styles with flowing lines like water ... or serpents. Comets in the sky were considered to be a sign from Benzaiten, because they were bright serpents flowing through the heavens. The bestowing of money and riches, however, is where she differs from Sarasvati the most. The Hindu goddess encouraged knowledge and artistic endeavor for its own sake; Benzaiten was recruited into being one of the Seven Lucky Gods of Japan, and thus she was in charge of making sure that those starving artists, musicians, and students actually made some wealth from their endeavors. Every prayer to her for skill and talent was matched by one for money. With the other Seven Lucky Gods, she rode a great treasure-ship bringing wealth to the masses. Accepted into the Shinto pantheon as a *kami*, she was seen there as one of the daughters of Amaterasu the Sun Goddess (Sun in Leo).

Benzaiten is the patron of artists and musicians (of course), as well as students who ask her for good study habits, but she is also the patron of geishas. These women were more than mere prostitutes; their primary purpose was not only sex but being a charming companion. They were often highly educated, so that they could make interesting conversation with the men who bought their contracts, and knew how to sing and dance and play musical instruments—geishas were often painted like Benzaiten, holding a lute and singing. They also had to be excellent actresses, in order to entertain their patrons. As high-born Japanese ladies might or might not have been highly educated, depending on whether their families felt that they ought to be more than just polite, submissive brood mares, it is ironic that the most Benzaiten-like women in Japanese society were ones who were for sale … although only to the highest bidders.

Venus in the second house is sometimes subtly disparaged as a placement, because it is said that these individuals bind up love with money in their minds, wanting to marry rich partners or seeing their partners as assets to be bought. In ancient Japan, marriage was very much an economic arrangement, and Benzaiten was prayed to by women and men alike who wanted an appropriately wealthy spouse; women also prayed to her during pregnancy to given them sons, who were preferred over daughters. However, the second house is traditionally ruled by Taurus, which is ruled by Venus, so this is actually one of Venus's own houses, and she is very comfortable there. The uncomfortable part is when people realize that Venus is very concerned with how much one's love should cost. This doesn't have to be in money or resources—although we must acknowledge that the individual with this placement may not be able to help being concerned with that—but how much positive behavior on the part of the beloved should be paid to keep their love and affection.

We need to keep in mind that the highest octave of this house is as the ruler of one's values, and thus of one's own self-worth. Venus here asks the individual how much kindness, respect, thoughtfulness, and attention they are worth, and expects them to adhere to that standard in the face of all those pink emotions. Everyone with this aspect is going to "sell" themselves to a partner in one way or another, and those with poor self-esteem will sell themselves short when it comes to behavior which shows that they are valued. The ones who demand money and resources have given up on getting their "weight", as it were, in loving behavior, and have cynically decided to settle for financial security. Benzaiten asks them, pointedly, what it would mean to hold out for the right price, instead of settling?

Since she is also a goddess who helps people study and work at their craft, promoting excellence, when people with this placement reply that they are not worth very much, her answer is: Then better yourself, and become someone worth the price you desire. This does not necessarily mean becoming more physically beautiful (although a Venusian goddess will at least want you to dress reasonably aesthetically and see to your personal hygiene) or more rich (although with Venus in this house, it's less difficult to create wealth from carefully trained and applied talent than for other placements); there are numerous ways to become a more valuable human being in the often unfair relationship market. Even in modern times in the West, dating could still be considered a market, with certain people at an advantage over others. Benzaiten insists that people bargain well for themselves, advocating for their needs and refusing to be devalued.

This Venus placement loves to surround themselves with beauty and luxury, and they may replace gaining valuable love with gaining valuable lovely items to line their nest. They have a knack, however, for finding those items at a good price, and may gravitate to buying and selling them as a career. With a keen eye for both beauty and value, they may create art which is designed to appeal to an audience rather than be merely a mode of self-expression; like love, they should be careful to give their hearts at least some room to make beauty simply for its own sake. Not everything needs to be commercially viable, and allowing for idiosyncratic beauty may produce something ahead of its time, which can be brought out when public styles change.

Taurus is a possessive planet, and Venus in the house traditionally ruled by Taurus—regardless of the sign it is in—may end up with a possessive streak. During the Edo period, it was quite popular for jealous women to pray to Benzaiten to gain power over their rivals. It is tempting for individuals with this placement to think of their lovers in the same emotional category as their beautiful possessions, and treat them accordingly. Care must be taken to remember that they are independent entities with their own agenda. What you attempt to cage may get away anyway, and if it has escaped a cage, it is less likely to want to return. It is hard for them to hold things or people lightly; once they have "sold" their love for the right price, they expect the product "bought" to stick around. It might be better for them to find partners who enjoy the implied value of possessiveness, rather than ones who are made uncomfortable by its curtailing of their freedom.

Over time, as the imperial Japanese state rose in power, Benzaiten gained another area of influence—she was prayed to for the financial health of the state itself. Farmers began praying to her for good harvests, and merchants prayed to her that their goods would be appealing to customers. While she was still a goddess of knowledge and the arts, she took on more and more of a political nature, in the sense of being one of the pillars by which Japanese society stayed economically afloat. This, too, can echo in the life of someone with this placement; they might start out as someone plying their skill and making fine art, music, or writing ... and then, somehow, the pull of money brings them into a leadership position where they are in charge of some large enterprise, with the welfare of many employees depending on them.

This is the second and not the tenth house, however, so while someone with this placement may do fine in such a position—especially if the business is working around a Venusian product—they need to keep their sense of self-worth invested in their skill at bringing the beautiful thing into the world, rather than being important in their position of authority. Benzaiten reminds us all that the best way to use wealth is to invest it in beauty, and that creating a better environment for people to live in brings happiness all around, which is its own kind of beauty and has its own worth to the heart.

♀ Venus in the 3rd House: Sunu and Xuannu

The third house rules writing and education, both of which are intensely important in Chinese culture ancient and modern. The Chinese people have more Gods of writing, studying, and examinations than any other culture in the world; even some of the Gods who rule other areas of life sometimes get a side dish of studying various mental arts. That also includes deities of the erotic arts, who are not exempt from proving their intelligence and knowledge.

Sunu and Xuannu (pronounced "shan-noo") are two divine sisters in Chinese Taoist mythology. (Supposedly there is a third sister as well, Cainu, but absolutely nothing is known of her.) Their names may translate to "White Lady" and "Dark Lady" respectively, or possibly "Simple Lady" and "Mysterious Lady". Daughters of the Empress of Heaven, they started out as indigenous Chinese deities, but were absorbed into Taoism when that religion swept across of the country. Both sisters were, among other things, goddesses of sacred sexuality. They taught the Taoist Arts of the Bedchamber, and supposedly wrote a book by that name. Other books on sexuality which were clearly written by human beings were dedicated to them, or featured them speaking in dialogue in the books. Some of these books were banned by the Chinese government repeatedly throughout the centuries as being too explicit and likely to undo "proper" marital relations, but given what we know of Sunu and Xuannu, they probably felt it was a compliment. After all, not many such erotic goddesses are also authors.

The third house is a very intellectual place, ruling communication, writing, thinking, speaking, teaching, and everything else we do to connect our brains to other people's brains. Venus, the fairly emotional and watery planet of love and beauty, doesn't exactly have a bad time in this house, but it tends to become colder and less connected to feelings. Love becomes less about an emotion and more about an idea, something to be studied, and most especially to be talked about. In fact, the "first love" of people with this placement is often learning, and that can be a love they carry throughout their lives, falling in love with their intellectual interests.

Venus is the planet of art and aesthetics, and Venus here often indicates talent in art or music. Sunu's gift is that she is a musician, supposedly the first being to play the harp. It is also said that she and Xuannu both lay with the famous and semi-mythical Yellow Emperor Huangdi, in order to teach him the Taoist erotic arts. When he found out that she was a musician, Huangdi gave her an instrument he had designed but which no human being could properly play—the ancestor of the Chinese zither. Sunu promptly redesigned the instrument, cutting the fifty strings down to a less unwieldy twenty-six, which it remains today. Even in the arts, the third-house Venus is clever and innovative.

Xunannu—the dark and mysterious sister—was often used as a messenger by the Gods, sent to help rulers whose countries were in danger. Her tried-and-true way of helping them? Handing them a stack of books and telling them to start studying. The first time that Huangdi called upon her, she appeared to him riding on a cinnabar phoenix, in robes made of bird-feathers in nine colors. Her clothing is lovingly described in detail, because Venus cares about fashion aesthetics; so is her hairstyle (a nine-dragon-and-flying-phoenix topknot), her lips (like cherries), her face (like a lotus calyx), and her body (snow white, elegant, and relaxed). Clearly she made a dazzling impression on the Emperor who would eventually be her lover/student. He moaned about the enemy's army which threatened him, and she gave him a long list of works to read. Some have truly impressive Chinese titles such as *The Book by Which the Five Emperors of the Numinous Treasure Force Ghosts and Spirits Into Service*, *Charts for Grabbing the Mechanism of Victory and Defeat of the Grand Unity from the Ten Essences and Four Spirits*, and *Instructions in the Essentials of Divining Slips*. One is not sure what the Emperor thought of the goddess who was asked for aid and handed him a pile of books to study, but this is the sort of behavior one has to expect from the third-house Venus. One moment they are smiling charmingly and trading witty banter, and the next they are pulling a book off the shelf to have a conversation about … and Heavens help you if you can't keep up, as this Venus placement is immediately bored by anyone who can't carry on an interesting discussion.

Apparently the Emperor seized upon the books and won his battle, and only then did he earn the company of the author-goddess sisters. Later, the general Song Jiang called upon Xuannu in similar circumstances, and unsurprisingly, she gave him three books to study which would enable him to call upon great powers and prevail. Xuannu is said to have conversed with those who gained her attention on anything from warfare and strategy to gaining longevity to spiritual breathwork to politics to alchemy to diet and calisthenics. Apparently she and her sister had intellectual conversation as their favorite form of afterplay. Later Taoist texts attempted to desexualize Xuannu and make her simply a goddess first of intellectual and spiritual esoteric knowledge, and eventually even warfare due to her visits to desperate generals, but even after these attempts seekers were describing her appearing to them with words redolent of falling in love with her. The few Taoist masters who were willing to grant the sisters erotic prowess claimed that the sexuality they taught was strictly energetic/alchemical exercises to grant long life, not actually for pleasure at all ... but Venus knows better.

The third-house Venus definitely has the gift of persuasion; they know instinctively how to pitch their voice in a way that invites and reassures, and perhaps challenges when that's what will move the audience. They make excellent salespeople and diplomats for this reason. It was said that the singing of Sunu the musician could pacify wild beasts, inspire plants to grow, and even change the round of the seasons. When she sang and played, it could bring warming winds in the winter and snow in the summer. Men who heard her immediately fell in love, swooning before her.

If making people swoon isn't enough, the third-house Venus loves to flirt. In fact, they flirt more than any other Venus placement ... because for them, it's a fun mental exercise, a form of communication. It's not necessarily expected to go anywhere, and they assume that the person they are flirting with will immediately understand that. Unfortunately, it's one of the places where they may have some misunderstanding, and bad feelings from the target of their affectionate speech (or the target's indignant partner), but they can often smooth it over and unruffle people's feathers by turning on the diplomacy and persuasion. This placement is also known for being rather wary of commitment; when love is a wonderful idea and an enchanting game, why ruin it with the day-to-day ordinariness of mundane life? Sunu and Xuannu are known as goddesses who can be prayed to for fertility and a good marriage, but neither of them ever actually married themselves, staying single (but most certainly not celibate). They supposedly inspired the custom in rural Chinese culture that people with the same surname could not marry, because diversity was important. (As it is to this placement of Venus.)

It seems at least a little appropriate that a pair of sisters stepped forward to represent this Venus placement, as the third house is associated with Gemini, the Twins. Gemini is notorious having two sides to their personality, usually a "light twin" and a "dark twin". These are opposites in many ways—peaceful versus feisty, active versus passive, and so forth. The third-house Venus can flip back and forth like this, light and dark "twin", Sunu and Xuannu, but never doubt that both are part of their magic.

One of the best-known esoteric gifts they taught, strangely enough, was the gift of invisibility. In fact, Xuannu had six handmaidens who each hid one piece of the soul, plus the body, when this skill was mastered. It would seem that the power of invisibility would not be in character for either these charming and impressively dressed divine sisters or the charming and flirtatious third-house Venus, but you might be surprised. This changeable and faerie-glamour Venus placement likes to hide behind a lot of different faces until they get to know and trust you … which will not happen through romantic adventures but through intellectual conversation. To hide their inner selves until they've talked to you enough, they need a spell of invisibility, and it conceals their soul behind a screen of banter and charm.

It's not unusual for lovers to talk to each other a great deal during the early part of a relationship (unless one or both is really not interested in talking or listening, and those people have no place in this chapter, or in the bed of this Venus placement). In fact, that getting-to-know-you part is sometimes referred to as "the telling of the tales". What is key to understanding this placement, however, is that this is the sweetest part for the third-house Venus, and even after all the erotic arts have burned out, they hope that the telling of the tales will continue in some way. After all, if people keep their minds sharp and continue to learn, they can't run out of interesting conversation, can they? At least that's the hope given by Sunu and Xuannu, the bestowers of lovemaking and books.

4♀ Venus in the 4ᵗʰ House: Xochiquetzal

The Aztec goddess Xochiquetzal was the patroness of love and beauty in her pantheon. Her name meant "Flower-feather", and she was known to be the most beautiful of all the Aztec deities. She was a fertility goddess, a patroness of young mothers, and could be called upon for help in pregnancy and childbirth. However, she was just as interested in sex for merely pleasurable purposes, and unlike some of the other Aztec Gods, was all about fun over reproduction; indeed, she was also a patron of prostitutes. She is always depicted as a young and attractive woman, richly attired and garlanded with wreaths of flowers. At her festivals, people wore elaborate floral and animal masks. During one of her rituals, children were dressed as hummingbirds and butterflies and wove in amongst all the celebrating crowds.

She was also the patroness of artisans, because they made beautiful things, and she appreciated that. Xochiquetzal was known to collect beautiful objects with which to decorate her home—a heaven named Tamoanchan where it was always cool (important for the Gods of Central America) and where a great flowering tree grew, every leaf an amulet of love. Similarly, the fourth-house Venus individual will also love to collect beautiful objects, and a love of physical luxury is one of the hallmarks of this placement. Since this is the house of the past, one's childhood home, and one's ancestry, the family may have passed down a love for domestic beauty, or specific cultural practices regarding how the home is decorated or furnished.

Really, it isn't so much that it domesticates Venus to be here as it is that the fourth house is Venusified. Venus doesn't become a wonderful homemaker just because it happens to be placed in the house of home—more like a home decorator. Venus is the planet of beauty as well as love, and that means aesthetics are very important to any Venus placement, even if it is outvoted by a line of other planets. What those aesthetics look like will be affected by Venus's sign (as well as other planets which may be in conjunction), but regardless of whether the style will be Scorpionic gothic black, Piscean fantasy, Cancerian cottagecore, or Virgoan neutrals and clean lines, Venus will be wanting to redecorate. That's because Venus needs harmony and a pleasant atmosphere, and with this placement, Venus will depend on the homespace to provide that. If it's ugly (by that Venus's standards), it will be a constant irritant and the opposite of what is needed.

Unfortunately, this can create a situation where the fourth-house Venus person has everything just so—perhaps at a fair amount of expense for their budget—and no one else who happens to be living in the house is allowed to touch or move anything. (And all Gods help them if they track in dirt! It's not like Virgo's insistence on purity and cleanliness, it's that it *looks ugly*, and now Venus has to scrub—which Venus does not enjoy doing—and make it lovely again.) While some individuals with this placement work at making everything pleasant for their families and take people's needs into account, others may lean toward the home-as-showplace and the domestic others had better cooperate with that.

This need for domestic harmony also makes this Venus placement a little more reluctant to get involved with just anyone on a long-term basis, especially if that person is going to be yet another decoration in their house eventually. Will their lover's moods clash with the wallpaper, never mind the tacky tchotchkes they are likely to drag in? It may take the fourth-house Venus longer to find the right person, and they will prioritize someone who lets them make the decorating decisions and doesn't rage around the house.

That same need can make them reluctant, once they have chosen a partner for better or worse, to get into long arguments or hold boundaries against anger. This is one of the Venus placements which sometimes has trouble holding their own against particularly aggressive partners (and would-be partners), especially if the argument is happening in their home sanctuary. Drama in the home can feel physically painful for them to endure, and they may give in just to make it stop. Unscrupulous partners may take advantage of this. Xochiquetzal herself started out as the wife of Tlaloc the rain god, but was then kidnapped by Tezcatlipoca and forced to marry him. While the historical backstory of this probably has a lot to do with warring priestly factions, and the winner's god symbolically annexing the prettiest goddess, people with this Venus placement are at definitely at risk for being bulldozed by domestic partners who are willing to keep it up until someone breaks down and gives in. It will be in their best interest to weed out anyone who evidences this behavior, before they are allowed to take up residence in the fourth-house Venus's gilded nest.

The fourth-house Venus isn't completely unable to focus on ordinary domestic tasks; after all, Xochiquetzal was also a patroness of those very homely jobs—spinning, weaving, cooking, gardening, embroidery, and so forth. Women prayed to her in order to be skilled at these tasks and keep their families fed and clothed. The fourth-house Venus person can learn and even enjoy these skills, provided that they don't involve wallowing in too much dirt, but they will want to find ways to make them attractive, perhaps focusing on how they beautify rather than their practicality. One fourth-house Venus woman I knew turned sweeping into "a dance with my broom".

Xochiquetzal was a temptress, sometimes teasing people into doing things they later regretted. She once seduced her brother Yappan, who had taken a vow of celibacy. He was punished for breaking his vow, but she suffered no consequence, because she was just following her nature and testing his resolve. It was also said that she once seduced a priest and when he broke his vows, she turned him into a scorpion. On the other hand, she could also absolve people of their sins. Every eight years her festival became one of cleanliness and absolution; people would flock to her temple and kneel on the floor with a handful of grain-straws, one for each sin they had committed. The straw emphasized this aspect of her as a goddess of earth and fertility. Priests walked about and pierced the tongues of the penitents with a long needle, and they would pull each straw through the hole in their tongue, praying not only for their deeds to be forgiven, but for her aid in preventing them from happening again. The bloody straws were left on the floor, and the priests would sweep them up and burn them all, destroying the record of past misdeeds.

Here we have to look at the darker side of the fourth house. All three of the "water houses" are actually fairly dark in their own way; people think of the fourth house as happy domesticity, forgetting that its first cusp is the nadir, which indicates the dark things we don't look at, but which nevertheless form our foundation. As the house of all the intangible things we inherit from our family and childhood, including dysfunctional behavior, the fourth can be a difficult place for any planet to live. Pretty wall-hangings aren't the only thing which families can bequeath to their descendants. They may also pass down rules about beauty standards which may or may not be difficult or impossible to live up to, and with which the individual with this placement will struggle for a long time. They may impart standards of home life which require peace at all costs, including sacrificing one's needs so that others will not be made angry or uncomfortable. Fourth house planets in general can obsess about the past and worry that things will not go well unless attention is paid to the values taught in childhood, and in this case the fear emanating from Venus can be, "Unless I do this home-and-family thing perfectly, I will not be loved."

To do this, of course, requires a lot of silence and tongue-biting on the part of everyone who lives there ... except, perhaps, the person whose moods and needs rule the home. That may be the Venus person, or it may be someone else with whom they feel they cannot be honest or speak up for themselves. Xochiquetzal's painful absolution ritual echoes the tongue stopped in silence, but in the end the penitent is freed from whatever binds them. It will be painful for the fourth-house Venus to speak up and create disharmony—and perhaps even ruin the home atmosphere for a time—but it is the lesson they must learn in order to truly be at home in the place they have chosen. Love which is only given in exchange for silence and endurance is not love at all. Eventually, those with this Venus placement learn that the only way they can guarantee their place of peace is to defend it, and not to let it be overrun.

5♀ Venus in the 5th House: Pygmalion and Blodeuwedd

Yes, when you look at the chapter title, it wouldn't be unreasonable to scratch your head in surprise. Aren't those two mythic figures from two different ancient cultures, two entirely different stories? Yes, they are. But this was one of the harder Venuses to pin down mythically, largely because the giant gap between most astrologers' take on this placement and what I've seen among actual human beings. Mostly what you read about Venus in the fifth house is "Everything is great! These are wonderful and blessed people whom everyone loves and who never have any romantic problems! Venus loves being in the house of romance! It's all rainbows and unicorns!"

Except that I don't really see that as being the case. Certainly this placement does give some wonderful gifts, but no placement is perfectly hunky-dory with no problems. I sifted through story after story to find something that summed up the reality behind the pink fluff, and came down to these two. Both told a single truth about this particular Venus, but neither seemed to sum up the entirety of it. After puzzling over it for a time, I decided to utilize both of them to talk about the Planet of Love in the House of Creativity, because they touch on different aspects. At the same time, they are bound together in one way: Pygmalion is the creator, and Blodeuwedd is a created being.

Most astrologers also foreground the "romance" aspect of this house, because everyone loves a good romance. Either that, or they focus on it being the House of Children. These are both true, and Venus here definitely wants to love and be loved, to have the fireworks and the hearts and flowers or whatever symbols are special to them. Many have the problem of being "in love with love", love junkies looking for that rush which we now know is chemicals in the brain. The problem comes when it wears off and the lover in front of them isn't giving them the love drugs any more. Then they will have to decide if they want to find another way to get little puffs of those chemicals, or resign themselves to a more mature and lower-burning kind of love … or leave.

Venus here also loves the idea of children. Note the word "idea"—the actual reality of squalling babies with poop-filled diapers, rampaging toddlers breaking the china knick-knacks, and older children throwing rocks through windows can sometimes be too much for them. Real children are much more messy and difficult than Venus had expected, and while some manage to scrape up enough love (or enough willpower and duty from other areas of their charts) to be good parents, others may find themselves withdrawing from or criticizing their children for being far less than ideal little creatures.

That's especially a hazard if they have tapped into the creativity part of this house. Some fifth-house Venuses concentrate on romance; others become artists or artisans, throwing all their energy into making beautiful things—art, music, acting, performing, interior design, writing, crafting. Some do both, of course, but often they find that they can really only give full attention to one of them. The truth is that the creative pursuits can be far more interesting, and hold their attention for far longer, than any hapless human being … unless that human being can be made into one of their creations.

The classic magical myth about this is Pygmalion, a Greek sculptor who had been burned by various human lovers and decided to swear off women. He sculpted a life-size marble statue who was his ideal of what a woman should be, and built an imaginary relationship with her, where he talked to her and embraced her and named her Galatea. At the temple of Aphrodite (Venus in Libra) he prayed that his creation would come to life and love him back. Aphrodite took pity on him (or was amused at the idea) and granted his wish; when he went home and kissed his beautiful statue, she came to life under his touch and went on to be his dream woman and have a lovely relationship with him. In real life, of course, the fifth-house Venus isn't sitting around imagining a relationship with an inert love doll. They have a real person with them (or a couple of them, this placement isn't the most monogamous or faithful), but they may well be constructing the relationship between them and the love object (note that word, "object") just as fancifully as Pygmalion created his ideal woman. Venus in the house of the Artist tends to want every love connection to be a work of art, like the ones which unfold in their heads, and they may attempt to railroad the other person into being the opposite number in their internal theater play.

Everything goes fine as long as the other person is willing to play the part, or happens to naturally fit into it, at least partly. Most people are more than two-dimensional characters, though, and are inevitably going to have a number of ideas, hobbies, opinions, and personality traits which don't fit into the part the fifth-house Venus has spun in their heads. When they stray out of it too many times, this Venus placement may lose interest. As I've mentioned already, this placement is not particularly invested in security or stability—the fifth is the house of gambling and risk-taking, and unless they get badly burned, they aren't averse to seeking elsewhere. (This problem can show up with children as well, with the Venus person encouraging their creativity by signing them up for all sorts of activities, whether the child wants them or is right for them or not.)

From the other side of the problem, the Welsh myth of Blodeuwedd is alluded to in the story of Gwydion (Pluto in Gemini). His son Llew was under a curse that he could marry no mortal woman, so Gwydion and the sorcerer Math set about building him an artificial one. They made her out of flowers of oak, broom, and meadowsweet and enchanted her so that she would come to life. She was beautiful, and they named her Blodeuwedd (pronounced *blod-eye-weth*) meaning "Flower-Face". Then they quickly married her off to Llew and assumed everything would be fine.

Somehow it was entirely lost on Gwydion and Math that just because they had created her and put her into Llew's bed that she would automatically love and obey him. She went along with it for a while, but during a period when Llew was traveling, she met a passing warrior named Gronw and fell in love with him. The two of them plot together to murder Llew, which is harder than it sounds, as he has a spell on him that he can only be killed under specific circumstances. Those are arranged and Llew is badly wounded, although not killed. Math and Gwydion rescue him and turn Blodeuwedd into an owl, a cold-eyed hunting creature of the night.

Venus in the house of the Sun comes across as warm and shining, and perhaps they are, but day always turns to night. In creating their dream relationships and then trying to insert flawed humans into them, they forget that they are also a flawed human who may not fit into the ideal. They often come into relationships with good intentions, and the assumption that they will of course be able to handle happily-ever-after. Then their love-nature rebels, sometimes in spite of all their efforts, because the self they have created to show the ones they love does not encompass all of them.

All planets, signs, placements, and aspects have a dark side; some are larger and more obvious than others, but the shiny happy ones have them too. The fifth-house Venus person's cold-eyed internal owl comes out in their difficulty with seeing either themselves or their partners on a deep level (at least at first) and making assumptions about how everyone involved will be able to hold to their part. When they are no more able to do it than the partner is—when the inner Blodeuwedd comes out and demands recognition and a say in how the relationship goes—they are just as surprised as when the partner failed to be who they expected. They have two choices at this point. They can drop the flawed relationship and walk away—and for all their warmth, the fifth-house Venus can be terribly cold when they decide to leave—or they can learn to rewrite the story.

What this Venus placement wants more than anything is the story. They want to live inside a magical tale of love, where they get to be the hero or heroine. They are willing to share the spotlight and be part of a pair of protagonists, but they need to see the magic in it. On the flip side, they can be extremely vulnerable to partners who are good at spinning the story, telling the archetypal fairy tale that they will be part of, as long as the partner can keep it up. Like Pygmalion, they can fall in love with a partner who isn't fully there or fully willing to show themselves honestly. Like Blodeuwedd, they can proceed like one newborn to love … until it all falls down, and then they will become the owl hunting for the next romantic story. The more fiction they have read or seen in media—and this placement is very drawn to artful fiction—the more likely they are to need a story in order to be in a relationship and feel alive.

Of course, there are thousands of love stories out there (I know, I've been reading myths and fairytales for years trying to put this book together) and many of them star lovers who are separated due to difficult circumstances, and who must fight to be together. Others have lovers who sometimes turn into strange beasts, or have other trials and tribulations. It can be helpful for the fifth-house Venus to mentally recast problems and differences as just one of the darker, grittier versions of a love story, which must be worked through with the same determination the characters had. *These problems which beset us, they are the evil troll, the twisted spell, the cruel mother-in-law, the terrible war that takes us away from each other, and we can overcome them together instead of suddenly being adversaries.* It is also helpful for them to understand that there is no fading into the distance of happily-ever-after; the next story is always on the horizon as soon as the lovers return home after solving the last quest.

The fifth-house Venus's strength is not in casting away the story and doing without it, but finding another one that works in the moment, and this can help them to retain their (somewhat flighty) spark of romance longer. However, this will only work if both parties are extremely honest with each other about what is going on with them. This is the Sun's house, and light must be shed on every creature crawling in it, so that the story can be created around reality and not be a mismatched veil over hidden troubles. If there is a lack of self-awareness or unwillingness to share on either the part of the fifth-house Venus person or their partner, the story will not match the reality, and the evil troll will turn out to be a different sort of creature than first assumed, and the weapons chosen will not work against it. Of course, even the quest to discover the true nature of these inner qualities can be made into a story, and the fifth-house Venus is creative enough to come up with it.

For this placement, even a sorrowful experience can be grist for the creative mill, and the fifth-house Venus can get as many poems and songs and art pieces out of a breakup as they can out of an ongoing successful love. The partner needs to understand that the relationship with their own creativity may always, in the end, be the most satisfying one of all, and that is no fault or blame to anyone. It's just the nature of this Venus to shine with the Sun's light, and to cast those rays in a much larger circle than one drawn about two people alone.

6♀ Venus in the 6th House: Hebe

The sixth house doesn't feel like a very romantic place. Bound up with service, labor, and health, it's a place of Work, not of Pleasure, and Venus becomes very uncomfortable when she has to function in this difficult space. Her song becomes less about "Have you kissed your lover today?" and more about "Did you brush your teeth before you went off to kiss your lover today?" In the sixth house, Venus learns the process of consideration, which is often made up of small and niggling details which one must remember even if it means putting a damper on the enthusiastic urges of spontaneous love. It does no good to impulsively cook a birthday meal for your loved one if you forget that they're allergic to one of the ingredients you're used to tossing into that dish. Indeed, it can make the situation worse, not better, as nothing kills romance like having to use an epi-pen.

There's a reason why I just used an example that included both food and health, and it comes back to our reluctant sixth-house Venus heroine, Hebe the daughter of Zeus (Jupiter in Aries) and Hera (Jupiter in Libra). Hebe is the Greek goddess of health and youth, and it was originally her gift to be able to bestow eternal youth and health on the Gods of Olympus. Like the Norse goddess Iduna (Neptune in Virgo), she carried the sacred cup around the feasting-hall of Olympus, offering her gift of youth and health to all of them. Also similar to Iduna, Hebe and her gifts were closely kept by the other Gods, and she was not permitted to go running about the mortal world and handing them out to all and sundry.

Hebe was described as beautiful and glowing with health; in the early parts of her myth she is always at Hera's side, performing the tasks that would have been usual for a high-born daughter. She drew baths for them (a cleanliness practice smiled upon by sixth-house planets) and helped them in and out of their chariots. This is the house of scut-work, and people with Venus here often have a gift for finding ways to make boring jobs fun and interesting. Their Venus influence may push them not just to clean but to beautify, paying attention to the little details in a job and polishing their work to make it appear more graceful.

The sixth house rules food, and Hebe served the nectar and ambrosia (magical drink and food) to the Gods at their feasts, maintaining their health and eternal youth; her "food service" job links her not only to wellness but to service. Venus in this house often gives a strong interest in health routines, including exercise, fitness, and healthy foods. This is an earthy house, and beneficent Venus here can give these people an instinctive ability to listen to their earthly bodies and figure out what is needed. Their wellness routines will be geared to their own requirements and may not work for anyone else, but will do wonderfully to keep them in a positive physical and mental state.

However, they are known for their difficulty in refraining from commenting on other people's health routines, or lack of them. It's not done out of any kind of malice, just a generous desire to help others do and be better, given with a cheerful Venusian smile. Their advice does not always find a welcome audience, and they are often honestly surprised—wouldn't everyone want to be told how they could improve?

One of Hebe's tasks was attending on Aphrodite (Venus in Libra), the most Venusian of Greek goddesses, whose Roman form gave her name to the planet itself. Along with the three Graces, Hebe helped the Goddess of Loveliness with her daily toilet and makeup routine, emphasizing the link between health and beauty. In actual life, the sixth-house Venus has an ambivalent relationship with aesthetic beauty. Some, like Hebe, don't bother with artificial aids at all, but cultivate a clean, healthy, minimalist look. However, the Virgo rulership to this house can alternately generate anxiety about perfection when it comes to looks. Hebe may have been beautiful, but she wasn't Aphrodite, and mortals with this placement who compare themselves to other mortals with more societally desirable looks and charisma are painfully aware that they are coming up short. Some sixth-house Venus people become obsessed with bodily perfection, extreme dieting, bucketloads of supplements, or even plastic surgery to bring themselves closer to the goal of the perfect body. This practice can get even more anxiety-producing as they get older; eventually they will need to step back from perfection and find ways to become satisfied with (and compassionate about) their flawed bodies as they exist naturally.

The sixth house is traditionally ruled by Virgo, regardless of what sign is on its cusp in an individual chart, and Hebe starts out as one of the "maiden goddesses". She stays that way for a long time in the myths; unlike other Greek goddesses such as Hera, Demeter (Sun in Cancer) or Persephone (Pluto in Pisces) who learn about sexuality and relationship early, it seems at first like Hebe is meant to be one of the eternal virgins like Hestia (Sun in Virgo), Artemis (Moon in Sagittarius), or Athena (Sun in Aquarius)—or like Hebe's own older sister Eileithyia who remained single even though she was the divine midwife and goddess of childbirth. It was said that Hera, in spite of being a goddess of marriage, wanted to keep her daughters at home with her rather than giving them away to another house. Whatever the case, Hebe's long period of virginity echoes a common pattern of the sixth-house Venus, which can keep the individual single and unattached for a long time, if only emotionally. This is not a Venus that falls in love quickly and easily; in fact, they may be plagued with anxieties about all the potential problems of relationship.

One of the implications of Venus in the house of Duty and Service in more culturally repressive times was an arranged marriage. While such customs are largely out of favor today, this placement can create a situation where the individual decides to get married, or even have a love affair, because they feel that they are needed by the other person. This Venus placement shows love by serving their loved ones, and people whose lives are obviously made better by that service may be more attractive than people who inspire fireworks and passion. It may take them a few relationships, or many years, before they realize what they have been missing, and then they may be torn between duty and looking to a wider world of feeling. They may realize that they have sold themselves short, and passed by more passionate possibilities for a more practical relationship.

This brings us to the story of Hebe's sudden change of career. In one fell swoop, she went from being the virgin waitress to being the bride of Heracles (Neptune in Aries), and in this aspect she was revered as the patroness of brides, just before and just after their wedding. The tale of how this happened is not set in stone, and has a number of different variants. In one version, Hebe is bestowed on the dead Heracles after he comes to Olympus like a trophy, a marriage of Duty and a service to her family. In another version—possibly created as a morality tale about women's modesty in the 1500s—she clumsily loses her dress in the middle of serving a feast and accidentally exposes her naked body to the entire hall. After her humiliation, Zeus chooses the mortal boy Ganymede (Venus in Aquarius) to replace her as cupbearer. We've already mentioned how painfully aware this Venus placement is about their lack of perfection in natural social grace; they can probably relate to the embarrassment of making a clumsy gaffe in public which costs you the positive regard of the crowd, even when you've tried so hard to be correct.

One version of the story, however, has Hebe falling in love with Heracles from a distance, and as soon as he is martyred she gets into her chariot and flies down to retrieve his soul. Martial warrior Heracles, half-mad and trailing troubles behind him, may seem an unlikely love interest for fresh-faced virginal Hebe, but Venus in the house of service may not merely follow a needy partner out of Duty. Helping the troubled loved one past their problems and into a better state can light their hearts and open the flow of love. In one of Lois McMaster Bujold's books, she points out that "Let me help" rhymes with "I love you" in the language of the heart. By the end of his life, Heracles is in a sad state of failure after a string of disasters, and Hebe may choose him because he is a project she can improve, a barren garden she can coax into bloom. This may sound cold and inconsiderate, but only if one forgets how much Love is wound up with Service for this placement. The sixth is also the house of mentors, and one way to render service is to teach someone how to succeed when they are failing. The path of consideration consists of many small moves—what will be best for my loved one, for the long-term as well as the short term? Can I put their own good ahead of my personal inclinations and preferences? What kind of aid is most practical for the current situation? How can I make this easier for them, even if it came easily to me and I don't know what it's like to struggle with that? In this house, Venus learns how to arrange the details of Love in a helpful and practical way, and ideally find the grace in being able to move with the other person's needs instead of pushing improvement onto them in a cheerful but emotionally clumsy manner.

However, there was one more twist to Hebe which reveals another of the most humble and yet beautiful aspects of Venus in the house of work. At Sicyon, she was worshiped as a goddess of mercy and forgiveness. While we tend to think of those qualities as watery and empathic—for example, the Asian goddess of mercy, Kwan Yin, stood forward for the Moon in Cancer—not everyone has access to those qualities. This is especially true if one's feeling planets are in signs or houses that discourage the empathic flow of emotion (such as Virgo or the sixth house) or in major aspect to planets which have the same effect. It can also be a problem if the person is naturally very emotional, but their irrational fears are getting in the way of forgiving someone who has wronged them, even when they know that it's important to stop holding onto their grudge. In these situations, mercy and forgiveness must become a mental discipline, a labor of love that to plodded through one difficult step at a time.

The sixth house is traditionally ruled by intellectual Mercury; like Venus in the third house, this Venus placement has to consider the mind to be the tool that releases the heart from its spinning emotions. Hebe was associated with the eagle; she is sometimes seen feeding and caring for the pet eagle of her father Zeus, and sometimes she is shown as an actual eagle, or as a woman with wings. Eagles, like phoenixes, were thought to be able to renew and rebirth themselves, becoming young again. However, birds are also under the rulership of Mercury, and the element of Air. The eagle flies high and sees far, symbolizing the objective perspective. Surprisingly, this will come easier to this Venus than to other positions, but as it's not the first choice of any Venus, it is a practice that needs to be actively put into effect. By this road, forgiveness is achieved by honest work on one's self—starting with an awareness that carrying around negative feelings about someone is bad for one's mental (and possibly physical) health, and then a step-by-step disassembly of the anger, fear, and resentment that feed the emotions. First you view the problem from a high place and note how small it is in the greater scheme of things, and then you come down to Earth and start clearing the path.

In one legend, Zeus gives his daughter a gift of two doves that spoke with human voices. When released, they turn out to be oracular birds, and they fly immediately to the site where the Oracle of Dodona would be founded to guide confused human beings. Being able to span the distance between the height of vision and down-to-earth work can be a greater benefit to Love than the poets of passion can imagine.

7♀ Venus in the 7th House: Sif

In the last *MythAstrology* book, we met the great and popular Norse God Thor (Mercury in Taurus), who was the personification of storm and thunder for that pantheon. Here we will meet his wife Sif of the Golden Hair, and learn the tale of their courtship, love, and marriage. Her name (pronounced *Seev*) means essentially "the connection of marriage", a term used to describe specific relationships, like saying, "He is a Thorstein by marriage".

Sif, like Thor, is an Aesir goddess, meaning that she is sky-centered, one of the deities of heaven and war and civilization. She is said to be beautiful—well, many Goddesses are—and has long golden hair which pours nearly to her feet. Thor is the oldest son of Odin (Saturn in Pisces), the Lord of Asgard and the Aesir, sired on Jord the Earth Mother when Odin was only a youth looking to lose his virginity. Jord sent her son to Asgard when he was old enough to travel and seek his fortune, trusting that his father would adopt him into the family ... which Odin did, enthusiastic about his large, half-giant boy. Then, while settling into his new homeland, Thor met Sif of the Golden Hair and fell in love.

The problem was, however, that Sif was already married. While scholars debate who Sif's first husband was, the odds seem to fall on Aurvandil, the "star-hero" hunter and archer. Sif had already born Aurvandil a son—Ullr, who was soon to become a great hunter like his father—and had the baby in her arms. One assumes that she probably returned Thor's feeling, but Sif was a faithful goddess and had to wait. Ironically, Thor and Aurvandil became friends, going on adventures together and having various disasters befall them, which they helped each other out of. During one of these adventures, Aurvandil actually takes Thor to visit his first wife, Groa the giantess. At some point, both Aurvandil and Groa die; we know this because their son Svipdag has to call up his mother's ghost to get the training she had promised him while alive.

Sif is left widowed and Thor marries her, promising to help raise his stepson. On Thor's side, he has had a youthful affair with another giantess, a warrior named Jarnsaxa (Iron-sword) who has borne him two sons, Magni and Modi. So unlike most mythical couples who simply meet while young, fall in love, and have children together, Thor and Sif's house is a blended family with various stepchildren. To top off the collection, they have a daughter together—Thrud, whose name means "strength". It is said that Thor's house is the largest in all of Asgard; perhaps it needed to be that way due to the size of their blended brood. Sif, then, has been a young maiden bride, a married woman with a child, a widow, and a remarried older bride with stepchildren. She has also been a co-wife with Groa during her time with Aurvandil. As a goddess of marriage, she has seen many different forms of that relationship.

When Venus, the planet of love, falls into the seventh house of marriage, the two can't help but be completely conflated. When those with this placement fall in love, what they want most is a permanent commitment. Whether that means a legal license and a big public ceremony will depend on the cultural assumptions of the person involved. For some, it isn't a permanent commitment unless it has been legally registered, witnessed by family and friends, and property and bank accounts have all been combined. For others, the promise is enough ... but even for those who say they don't need more than a verbal commitment—so long as it is trustworthy—can find themselves yearning for some sort of public paperwork, such as a will or being put on someone's insurance.

What most people tend to forget is that the seventh house isn't just about marriage. One of its side rulerships is legal matters—contracts, suits, anything one would bring to court. Part of the reason that "marriage" is on the docket here, so to speak, is because it is a legally (or at least socially) binding contract, the sort that even in early societies would have been negotiated and whose violation would end with more than a breakup. In the beginning, tribal marriage was a survival contract. Two people would come together to create children, be a sexual outlet for each other, and divide up necessary chores so that each would have a more comfortable life, and the ensuing progeny would have a better chance of survival. It was essentially a business agreement, and collected resource trappings such as dowries and bride-prices in order to make that contract not only more attractive but safer for each party, should the union end by death or separation. While shared resources are more of an eighth-house issue, the seventh house of legalities are where they are first brought forward into the public eye, and the promise of resource combination is made. As a goddess of marriage, Sif was prayed to for not just a good husband but a good dowry, or at least a good husband who would overlook the lack of a good dowry.

The most common reason for prayers to Sif—both in ancient times and among Sif's modern worshipers—is, however, the issue of monogamy. There are a surprising variety of marriage styles in Norse/Germanic mythology—Frigga (Moon in Capricorn), another "official" goddess of marriage, is said to have slept with her husband's brothers out of hospitality; Loki (Saturn in Gemini) has two wives; Odin lays with many women and sires many children. Thor and Sif, however, pledge monogamy to each other, and become the Gods one calls upon to hold to one's vows. Here it is made clear that one can sign all the contracts and combine all the finances, but it is the heart and the will which keep the oath. Called upon singly or with her husband, Sif gives the strength to focus on one's partner through times of joy and sorrow, plenty and want ... and romance and temptation. Having Venus in this house doesn't guarantee monogamy, or even the desire for it. (I know at least two individuals with this placement who are polyamorous, but even they want consistent commitments from more than one lover, more of a group marriage than a series of flings.) But whatever style of relationship is chosen, Venus here will want Love to be yoked with Commitment.

One of Sif's myths is that Loki the trickster stole into her bedroom one night and cut off her long golden hair. Some scholars believe that Sif is associated with the earth and her cut hair symbolizes the golden grain, watered by her husband's rains and then cut down by harvesters. Others point to the custom in some European tribes of shaving the head of adulteresses, and suggest that Loki seduced her and then cut her hair to prove it to Thor. Certainly in the *Lokasenna*, the saga where the disgraced Loki breaks into the Aesir's feast party and drunkenly insults all of them, laying their faults bare, he accuses Sif of laying with him ... and she does not rebut this, although the *Lokasenna* also makes it clear that many do not believe all of Loki's statements.

We may never know if the Goddess of Monogamy was unfaithful to her husband; if she was, it may be that she understands how easy it can be to slip up in a moment of weakness, and can be compassionate to those who are struggling. Some deities are prayed to for a quality they possess in perfection, and have never done otherwise; others are prayed to because they have struggled, failed, and finally found the way through. Both paths are possible, and both are valuable. In the end, Thor forces Loki to repair the damage, and he pays the dwarves to craft Sif a wig of lifelike golden strands to replace her shorn hair until it can grow back entirely. While Thor was rightly angry at the violation of his wife's locks, he did not seem to be angry with her, so the mystery stands. One way or another, this placement of Venus will have to deal with the tangled questions of monogamy, freedom, what one can guarantee a partner and what may be unwise to promise. Part of their lesson will be learning that committed relationship isn't all pretty, loving feelings; it takes a great deal of work to sustain those first sparks and not let everything go astray.

When it comes to other problems of this placement, the seventh is the House of Projections, and any planet there may be projected onto the partner, especially earlier in life. The seventh-house person can "disown" the planet and decide that they just aren't the sort of person who does that, and then choose a partner who exemplifies the qualities of that planet. The partner then unconsciously "carries" the energies of that planet for them ... both positive and negative. When Mars is in this house, the partner is both "the brave, assertive one, while I'm the passive coward," and "the angry, aggressive, violent one, while I'm the calm peacemaker." Neptune here creates the dichotomy of "you're the compassionate spiritual one," and "you're the crazy one."

When it's Venus's turn in the seventh-house box, the individual with this placement feels like they aren't romantic. They're sensible and straightforward, but they aren't the sort who loves passionately with hearts and flowers. They also aren't the sort who gets jealous or possessive or insecure—the partner carries that for them as well. For Sif, her passionate husband Thor is definitely the Lover in the relationship, while she is the more demure Beloved. When a giant drunkenly speaks of Sif in a desirous way, Thor kills him. Eventually, over time, the seventh-house Venus learns to own that part of themselves, acknowledging that they have all the positive and negative traits of Venus in themselves as well.

Modern worshipers of Sif claim that one of her gifts is hallowing; she can spread sacred space throughout a home, a temple, a relationship. One thing I can tell you from experience is that once something is hallowed, it is under closer scrutiny from the Universe, and poorly aimed actions will come around sooner and make their karmic mark more obviously. When Sif does this to a marriage, you can bet all of its difficulties will come up in the faces of the people involved. Sif herself would likely say that this is not a bad thing, but an opportunity to clean out the dark corners and bring light and joy to all parts of it ... even if that takes a lot of work, and a lot of lost hair.

8♀ Venus in the 8th House: Kamadeva and Rati

Kamadeva, the Hindu God of love, appears as a man with skin as green as the trees, in a chariot pulled by brightly-colored parrots. He shoots a bow made of bent sugarcane, for the sweetest shot of all, and his arrows are flowers. He has many different origin stories—a number of deities want to claim siring him, and in many cases claim him as one of their forms. He has his own story, however, and it is bound up with death, destruction, and rebirth. That is why he stood forward for Venus, the planet of love, going into the house of sex, death, and transformation.

In the origin story which has him created out of nowhere by Brahma (Neptune in the fifth house), Kamadeva immediately shoots his arrows at Brahma first, making the creation god fall in love with his own daughter. The spell wore off quickly and Brahma was ashamed and embarrassed, and cursed Kamadeva to be killed at some time in the future, although not by him. When Kamadeva protested that he was only doing his job, Brahma replied virtuously that when he was killed, he would be reborn again. One can imagine that Kamadeva was not comforted by this reply.

Similar to Venus in Scorpio, what this Venus placement wants is intensity, and they may be more attracted to and interested in drama than in comfortable contentment. At least when things are riled up, they aren't boring and there's a chance of seeing underneath the calm exterior and discovering what's really going on. This Venus wants to dig down into the psyche of their partner to see what's going on there, and they want a partner who can meet them in that mutual intensity.

At some point, it was decided that a wife might calm Kamadeva and his antics, and Brahma ordered the demigod Daksha to come up with one. Daksha created Rati from a single drop of his sweat, and presented her to Kamadeva, who was delighted. (Another version of her birth claims that Brahma's daughter was so horrified at her farther making advances toward her that she committed suicide, and the other Gods reincarnated her as Rati and gave her to Kamadeva as a wife to "clean up" his mess.) However, far from calming him down, Rati eagerly leaped into her husband's adventures (and misadventures), and became his assistant and "partner in crime".

Eighth-house Venuses do fear being vulnerable in love, and when they are young, they may be a little distant, withholding their feelings (while at the same time yearning to connect deeply, make no mistake about that). When they finally give themselves in love, they give wholehearted, all-consuming, perhaps even obsessive attention to the beloved, and they expect the same in turn. This is a passionate and possessive placement, and at its worst the eighth-house Venus may be plagued by feelings of jealousy and fear of betrayal. This can create problems when it comes to actually achieving the depth of connection that they desire, and we'll get to that part of the story in a moment, because Brahma's curse would soon come true.

It started out as a simple love-mission, but it went terribly wrong. The Gods were attempting to slay a demon to whom Brahma had granted invulnerability; the creator God had left a loophole, however, in that he could be slain by one of the as-yet-unborn children of Shiva (Sun in Scorpio). After his first wife's suicide, Shiva had defected to the top of Mount Kailash where he performed austerities and showed no sign of being interested in another marriage, making that death a slim chance. The Gods appointed Kamadeva to shoot Shiva with one of his arrows in the presence of Parvati (Venus in Virgo) who was in unrequited love with Shiva. The hope was that Shiva would fall in love in return, and sire the warrior-child. Kamadeva did as they asked, but the arrow so startled the Destroyer that he reflexively incinerated the god of love with the fire of this third eye. He did fall in love with Parvati, and eventually sired not only the god Ganesha (Jupiter in Taurus) but also Kartikeya (Mars in the tenth house) who would eventually slay the problematic demon. But Shiva was furious at being so manipulated, and Kamadeva bore the brunt of his wrath. The love god dissolved into a cloud of ashes.

Rati screamed and immediately threw herself before the Gods, accusing them of sending her husband on a suicide mission and begging them to revive him. Smearing herself with her husband's ashes, she went half mad from the thought of being without him. Parvati interceded with Shiva, but because of Brahma's curse, Kamadeva could not be restored and had to reincarnate. It's not unusual for this tragic moment in the tale of Kamadeva and Rati to be echoed in eighth-house Venus relationships—not specifically the physical death of the lover, but the need for some part of the relationship to die and be reborn again, as it were. Because of their craving for deep connection rather than superficial companionship, individuals with this placement may well go through a number of partners who are not willing or able to fulfill their needs. When they do find the right person, the relationship may have to be deconstructed at some point, perhaps more than once, and rebuilt from the ground up. We are not taught, as human beings, how to have deep, soul-level relationships, and many of us must change or transform ourselves to learn this eighth-house mystery.

The Gods arranged for Kamadeva to be born to a wealthy mortal couple, and Rati went to them and offered to be the child's nurse. Over the next two decades, she raised the boy—named Pradyumna—while calling herself Mayavati (the woman of illusion). When he was old enough, she revealed to him who he had been, and who she was to him. At first,

Pradyumna rejected her, considering her a mother figure, but eventually he began to recover his memories and realized that she was the love of his life. As he grew, he recovered his powers as well, and regained his position as the God of Love.

Deities, of course, manage this death-and-rebirth thing with a lot more ease and aplomb, seemingly, than mere mortals who are trying to change themselves enough to have the profound relationship they desire. In order for the eighth-house Venus to actually achieve this, they may need to spend a fair amount of time working on themselves, transforming into a person whose trust is not so damaged, whose pride is not so unbendable, whose suspicion is not so compelling, and who can open their hands and love without clutching out of fear. Parts of them which did not mature may need to grow emotionally to full adulthood. Alternately, some external situation such as serious illness or accident may change their lives (or the lives of their partners) in some drastic way which affects the relationship, and they must learn to love again as the person they are now, not the one they had been.

This may take some time—years, perhaps—and if their partner chooses to stay through the process, they may end up being the caring support to their lover's struggles. On the other hand, at some point it may be that the partner needs to transform themselves as well, and the eighth-house Venus person takes a turn being Rati and assisting them through their own dark period. The roles may be passed back and forth over time, and the key is to accept the situation as it comes—as one accepts that death is inevitable and must be surrendered to—rather than giving up hope.

Love and passion, for this Venus placement, can actually be a healing force—first healing of old, sad feelings of being disconnected, and later in life possibly becoming a healing force to bestow on partners. This is the house of the Mysteries, and any planets here show how one connects to those forces of what is greater than us in the Universe. For this Venus placement, sex and/or love will be a channel for that greater connection. If they have a relationship with a deity (or more than one), they may have romantic or strongly devotional feelings for them. Even if they are skeptical of that sort of thing, there will be an unconscious yearning for something greater than just some pleasant exercise and a few orgasms. They may find their way to some form of sacred sexuality later in life.

This brings us around to the aesthetic connection between Love and Death, which is what happens whenever the energies of Venus and Pluto are brought together. The eighth-house Venus is fascinated by all things hidden, forbidden, and taboo, especially around sexuality. Their sense of aesthetics may be dark and morbid, but at the same time they can find beauty in broken or imperfect things which might be discarded or shunned by lighter Venuses. This can be a huge boon if the death-and-rebirth-of-relationship situation requires them to learn to see their own or their partner's beauty differently, looking to the divine spark inside rather than being hung up on external surfaces. Learning to love Death can be learning to love the marks of change, the stains of loss, the deeply engraved scars of painful transformation, and seeing them as just as beautiful as the innocent, smooth, unmarred surface which cannot truly know itself or another.

9♀ Venus in the 9th House: Atalanta

Most ancient Greek heroines are modest maidens waiting for husbands to take them away, and this is because in that culture, women were usually confined to their father's house and then handed off via marriage to be confined by their husband's four walls. Most never got to travel at all, unless something went terribly wrong, such as the decision by Antigone (Uranus in the fourth house) to follow her blind beggar-father on the road. It was sons who went out on quests and travels and adventures ... with one great exception. Atalanta waited for no man to rescue her, or for that matter to provide an excuse to go on the road. Her life was lived entirely at her own will, including her relationships ... and still, her tale is considered a love story. Well, all right, perhaps it's a combination of a love story and an adventure tale, but that's exactly what Venus in the house of far-reaching escapades wants to live out.

Atalanta's wealthy father was disappointed that she was a daughter instead of a son, so he had her exposed on Mount Parthenion. Instead of dying, she was adopted and raised by a she-bear (which some scholars take to be a metaphorical reference to forest-dwelling priestesses of Artemis). The name of the mountain comes from a word meaning "virgin", but implying a robust and athletic sort of maiden, which might have indicated one of their haunt. Another version has her rescued from the she-bear who is suckling her by a group of hunters who then raise her themselves. However she began, Atalanta comes into womanhood strong, fast, trained with weapons, and a worshiper of Artemis (Moon in Sagittarius). She wears a short tunic and sandals, eschewing women's long chitons, and when two wild centaurs pursue her with lust, she kills both of them.

Atalanta decides she wants to journey, and signs up with the crew of warriors which Jason is recruiting for his quest for the Golden Fleece. One version of the story has him turning her down, not because she is not competent, but because the men would be uncomfortable sharing a ship with her. Other versions have her going along with the Argonauts and joining in their every activity, right down to fighting next to them on Colchis, where she is wounded along with her captain and several of the other men, and eventually healed by Medea (another very independent woman).

For Venus in the house of travel, there's nothing so romantic as a road trip. (Or an ocean voyage—this is the House of Long Journeys Over Water, after all.) Atalanta may not be interested in men when she is alone in the forest, but the Argo adventure brings her a lover. Meleager, one of the Argonauts, was the son of a local prince whose grapevines are famous, and the brother of Heracles's bride Dejaneira (Mars in the twelfth house). He fell in love with Atalanta and she deigned to become his lover, although he already had an arranged-marriage wife at home. Meleager not only let Atalanta be who she was, he defended her repeatedly against men who loudly disapproved of having a woman on board a ship, much less a warrior-woman who could shoot any of them before they got their hands to their sword hilts.

After the Argo adventure was over, Atalanta bore Meleager's son Parthenopeus ("born of a virgin", or unmarried fighting woman) but allowed him to be sent to Meleager's wife to raise, as she would rather go back to traveling and had no desire to be a mother. This placement of Venus really finds nothing romantic about being a wife and mother. If other parts of the chart disagree, they can manage it, but for them love is a journey with their partner, and children can really put a damper on climbing that mountain or running off to Indonesia to do archaeology together. The ninth house is ruled by Sagittarius, one of the least domestic signs of all, and like Venus in Sagittarius, the ninth-house placement may often hear the words "settling down and starting a family" immediately followed by the clank of a ball and chain in the background.

Meleager's father then called his son home to help out with a boar problem. The Calydonian boar, a huge animal sent as a curse by Artemis, was terrorizing the land and uprooting the precious grapevines. Meleager gathered a group of adventurers to slay the boar, including Atalanta, since it was obvious this would be a multi-hunter job. When they cornered the beast, Atalanta shot an arrow and got the first wound, after which all the other hunters took a stab at it, and Meleager finished it off. Afterwards, when he was presented with the enormous boarskin as a trophy, Meleager gave it to his lover in honor of her having shed the first blood.

You'd think there would be nothing romantic about hunting down and killing a dangerous animal with your paramour and then being given a bloody trophy like another woman would be given flowers, but you'd be wrong when it comes to this Venus placement. One can only imagine how pleased Atalanta was with him at that moment. However, their joy was short lived. Meleager's uncles, who had joined in the hunt, objected to him having given the trophy to a woman whom they considered unfit even to have been there. Meleager got into an argument with them, which quickly turned ugly; they tried to wrest the skin from the victorious huntress and Meleager ends up killing both of his uncles.

Unfortunately, Meleager is an invulnerable adventurer because his mother guards a magical piece of wood; it's been prophesied that he will not die unless that stick is burned to ashes. But when his mother sees that he has killed her brothers, she throws the stick in the fire, and Atalanta literally gets to see her lover go up in flames. Magical sticks aside, the ninth-house tendency to run when matters of family and commitment are brought up has made many a relationship with such people go up in flames. There's a subtle point to the fact that her first love affair ends through a family argument inspired by her stubborn independence. It doesn't matter that in our mythic instance, Atalanta was probably quite right to be stubborn about this point; family emotions still need to be taken into account.

Grieving, Atalanta goes back to the forest of Mount Parthenion, where she lives for some years until her aging father fetches her back out. He has heard of her exploits and decides that it would be worth it to recognize his famous daughter, the Argonaut and Calydonian boar hunter. His first thought, of course, was to arrange a marriage for her, which she resisted with all her might. She did like the idea of inheriting his wealth, however, so she struck a hard bargain with him: She would marry only the man who could best her in a footrace—which she knew was nearly impossible—and the failures would be slain, to put off further suitors.

In spite of this, several would-be suitors did actually try, and were killed after failing to defeat her. One man—known as Hippomenes in the earlier texts but Melanion in later ones—had fallen in love with Atalanta and went to Aphrodite (Venus in Libra) for help in the footrace. The goddess of love gave him three golden apples and instructed him in what to do with them. When the race began, Atalanta ran on ahead of him, but he threw the first golden apple so that it rolled before her. She decided that she could afford to turn aside and grab it and still win, and she did so. He threw the next one, and she picked it up but was still ahead of him. The third one rolled to the side, and Atalanta knew that if she ran to get it, she would lose. She had a split second to decide her fate.

What the ninth-house Venus wants, above all, is someone who can keep up with them. This is the same whether it's the globe-trotting type or the college professor with multiple degrees and dozens of fields of study (this is the house of higher learning, after all, and that kind of travel is done with the mind), or just the athlete who decides to bike across the continent. If you can't keep up with their far-ranging ideas and ever-expanding interests, you will be struck off the list with deadly finality. The one who can keep up is the one they will keep. Even better, if the potential partner can hold out glittering tidbits—of knowledge, of story, of anything which expands the horizons—and keep making them a moving target, they will become even more interesting ... and worth slowing down for. Show them your journey, your fascinations, even your far-reaching beliefs (this is the house of religion as well)—whatever makes you shoot for the horizon. Then, make sure that you never allow the relationship to fall into a boring rut.

Atalanta made her choice, diving aside and grabbing for the third apple. She didn't have to do it—she could have continued and Melanion would have been executed—but she chose to see what else this clever and interesting man had up his sleeve. They married, but he forgot to make a gratitude offering to Aphrodite, so the two of them were turned into lions. They roamed the forest and mountains together for the rest of their days, hunting down interesting targets together, and while some say it was a curse, perhaps it wasn't a bad ending at all.

Venus here often has to be coaxed into love, but individuals with this placement can be surprisingly passionate and committed, once it has been proven to them that who they are will be both respected and loved (and they will need both), and that they will still be allowed to roam free in whichever ways are most important to them. And there's always the road trip, if things begin to get dull. It's not possible to run out of horizons—just ask them, they'll tell you all about it.

10♀ Venus in the 10th House: Ezili Freda

The tenth house is usually considered to be centrally about one's career, but it is more than that. It is your standing in society, the way people perceive you, how much influence you have when trying to maneuver yourself through the halls of those who consider themselves your "betters". Where the eleventh house is society as groups of friends in fellowship and shared interest, the tenth house is about social *respect*, and how one utilizes that. Unfortunately, the many factors which affect social respect are not always fair or right. People ask, "What do you *do*?" and what they mean is, what career do you identify with, and where is it in this current culture's hierarchy does it fall, so that I know how to treat you? People ask, "Who *are* they?"—usually to someone else—and what they mean is, which social stigmas or benefits do you carry, if any? Answering, "They are a nice person," often doesn't count for much. One ends up "the nice person with the disability" or "the nice person who is just on hard times right now." The tenth is the house of hierarchy, and people want to know where to place you.

Venus is particularly uncomfortable in the tenth house. What Venus values is emotional and aesthetic, and that doesn't always resonate with what's considered valuable in today's society ... with one exception, and that's appearance, which we'll get to in a bit. Saturn's house has all sorts of cultural fences for all sorts of irrational reasons, which Saturn thinks are all quite rational, at least at the moment. Venus sees beyond fences. She cares about love, not what you *do*. She certainly doesn't care about categories like race and gender ... but when she gets stuck in the tenth house, she has to take them into account.

In the Afro-Caribbean Vodou religion, there is an entire family of *lwa*, or divine spirits, whose family name is Ezili. The most popular of these—who became *the* Ezili in some places, to the point where she is sometimes just referred to as Erzulie—is Ezili Freda, the Lady of Love. The *lwa* have all taken on archetypes of specific (non-ancient) historical periods, and that must be accepted and understood if outsiders are to consider who they are as divine beings. In Freda's case, she is a mixed-race woman of the southern U.S., particularly New Orleans before, during, and after the American invasion which changed the laws and customs to much more racist norms. Being a beautiful woman poised between the categories of "black" and "white"—so crucially important at that time—meant that her options were limited. Mulatto, quadroon, octoroon; she is the woman who is too dark to marry a white man and too white to be trusted by slaves or more recently enslaved free black people. She is caught in the middle, and as she is an unadulterated romantic, that is a very hard place for her to be in. Venus wants to fall in love where she will, and in the tenth house she must stop and consider what is socially appropriate, not where the heart leads.

Ezili Freda can be a big flirt, and she uses her beauty and charisma to gain social power. Before you judge, remember that she is a spirit carrying the archetype of someone in a very powerless position; if she does not use whatever power she can get, she will end up being used, devalued, and thrown away. The sweet smile at the authority figure is a necessary defense. Her sister Ezili Dantor (Moon in the first house) carries the archetype of the woman who cannot bring herself to use that power, or is no good at it, and she has a much harder time.

Not that Ezili Freda lives in a bed of roses, even if her sacred color is bubblegum pink. Vodou practitioners host their deities through god-possession, and it is said that when Ezili Freda is at the end of her visit (after having flirted shamelessly at any attractive men) she dissolves into tears. She cries because she understands what it is to be hamstrung by unjust social rules, and she cries for all those people who also come up against the obstacle of human society's unfairness. She is a social climber because she wants better than society would otherwise afford her, and the tragedy inherent in the story is that unless she collects enough money and status in time, her luck will run out with her looks, and she is painfully aware of this.

Venus in the tenth house can manifest in a number of different ways. They may be drawn to careers which are specifically Venusian—involving art, decorating, beauty, or matchmaking. They may bank on their own attractiveness as a model or performer. More rarely, they might be "married to their work", falling in love with their career and putting human romances aside. One of the most interesting manifestations, however, is being a lover as a career. It's said that Ezili Freda is the archetype of the woman who is always a mistress and never a wife; this echoes the historical practice of rich white men in New Orleans taking beautiful mixed-race mistresses (perhaps at the same time they were married to white women, perhaps being sole lovers with them, but never able to marry because it was not legal at the time due to racist laws). Trading sexual favors and talented companionship for a nice house, pretty clothing, and money can be a kind of career whether or not there is a wedding ring involved.

Of course, this does create the issue of monetizing romance. It's the main reason why Venus is unhappy here. It also brings up the issue of social class—most people who trade that sort of behavior for money as a career may be considered prostitutes, and this goes against the grain of this Venus placement's hunger for status. They are not low-class sex workers, they are high-class courtesans. One recalls the famous Italian courtesans of the Renaissance, well versed in poetry and music, or Japanese geishas, being charming companions for those who can afford them. Venus in the house of class creates sophistication, not naïve, wide-eyed adoration. This is a Venus who has had to survive in this dog-eat-dog house environment, and they know how to play the system and make the most of it.

It's said that this placement makes Venus colder than in other houses, more likely to look out for what can be acquired as opposed to being easy and free with love. Saturn rules this house, and like Venus in Capricorn, this Venus placement is likely to be painfully aware of how easy it is to end up undervalued, objectified, and mercilessly used. If Venus here decides to do a little using first, out of an expectation that it will happen anyway, it's not surprising. Of course, that can lead to a situation without the love every Venus openly or secretly desires, having traded it for … respect. The big question here is not whether the tenth-house Venus should choose love over respect, or vice versa. It's that they need both, in equal amounts, at the same time. Giving respect is a way to show love to them, and giving love shows they are worthy of it.

Ezili Freda is known as a perfectionist—her devotees know to only give her offerings of unblemished flowers and candy. Another reason why she weeps is because she sees the imperfection of the world, which she cannot banish. The idea is that making pure offerings keeps her pure of heart, the way love should be, while blemishes and impurities encourage flaws in her behavior. Instead of gracious and charming, she will appear as the spoiled princess, spiteful, materialistic, and vindictive. It's hard for love to survive in the tenth house without becoming tainted by negative emotions. The temptation to make it transactional, to keep a careful eye on what you're getting back, to worry about whether you are seen as too slutty or too frigid or too vulnerable and thus a target … these fears can overwhelm the pure emotion of love, so the challenge for the individual with this Venus placement is to be continually mindful, instead, of keeping their love out of that muck. This means being extremely cautious about who gets invited in, which can also be read as cold and inhospitable.

Since this Venus can be charming and is instinctively skilled at navigating social hierarchies, they can do well in jobs which require a fair amount of social skills, including being in charge. However, like Freda who recoils at bad smells or wilted flowers or stained altar cloths, this Venus placement needs a work environment which is harmonious and aesthetically pleasing, and given the reins, they will try to create that themselves. Vases of flowers and nice wallpaper may be scorned by those who like a military-streamlined workplace, but sooner or later they, too, will start to miss the flowers when they don't show up.

Because they are conscious of how their relationships affect their public reputation, they may find their career or social status encroaching on their personal life to an extent that a different Venus placement would never put up with. On the other hand, partners should ideally be someone they can be proud of, and who will help them achieve their goals, whatever those may be. Like Freda who longs for the rich and powerful husband, they will be attracted to people in authority, especially if they are looked up to by others. However, if they can find a place they are respected—and don't have to fight tooth and nail for that respect—they can learn to be their own authority figure, and reign benevolently from an extremely tasteful throne.

11♀ Venus in the 11ᵗʰ House: Milda

In the wake of the great flood of forced Christian conversion, many of the tales and lore of pagan deities across Europe were lost, perhaps forever. We may never know how many stories simply stopped being passed down orally from ear to ear, never to be written down by their illiterate carriers and simply to die out in a single generation. Gods, however, have a way of finding their way forward anyway, sooner or later. They may take on new names and guises, and we may never know that we are talking about a very old deity in new clothes. They may also modernize and take on attributes which are more resonant with newer potential worshipers. Scholars and devotees alike struggle with these questions, which all bring us back to the issue of agency—that these are not just two-dimensional figures, but actual entities who can shift and change, if they so desire, to fulfill the needs and yearnings of their people. Between the lost lore and the mutable nature of Gods, it can be confusing for those who are simply drawn to the nature of a particular deity with a call that leaves no room for argument about how much of their description is "real". Deities are People, and even if they are capital-P people, they insert themselves into society and make waves. It's happening all the time, even when we don't see it.

That's a very eleventh-house discussion, weaving in questions of who is in or out of any given group, the value of "outcast" figures, and who affects social change. I'm pretty sure that's why the goddess who called out for this chapter was Milda, the Lithuanian Lady of love, friendship, and freedom. Like many parts of northern and eastern Europe, Lithuanian pagan mythology was heavily crushed by the Christian conversion, to the point where there are only crumbs of folklore which must be patchworked together. Milda is celebrated as the goddess of love and spring; her name is cognate to the old Lithuanian name for May, which—due to calendar changes—was in medieval times the even older name for April. Either way, she is linked to spring.

Milda may be linked to the Spring Maidens throughout Europe, including the medieval British May Queen who takes the Green Man as her lover, acted out in medieval times on Beltane, or May Day. She is said to never want to marry—and, indeed, to be against monogamous marriage—because it curtailed the freedom to have as many lovers as one wanted. Milda was a goddess in the old mold, belonging to no man but giving of herself generously wherever she desired, obligated nowhere but smiling on many relationships.

Some scholars believe that Milda did not exist as a goddess before she was written about in 1835 by a local folklorist. They point to a lack of archaeological evidence or trusted written sources. Lithuanian Pagans, on the other hand, fervently celebrate Milda during the spring months, and either believe completely in her authenticity or feel that it doesn't matter. Even those ranks are split, because during the early part of the 20th century, a variety of nonreligious poets and artists were inspired by the myth of Milda and made artwork of her, and slowly shifted the idea of her from a wanton love goddess who refused to marry to a deity of freedom and friendship. Her gift of love became a symbol not only of personal romance, but of transpersonal humanitarian love—*philae* as well as *eros*. The woman on the Freedom Statue in Riga, Latvia is referred to locally as Milda. More traditional Lithuanian Pagans feel that this way of viewing Milda pulls her away from her original purposes.

It seems that all love goddesses are politically controversial, but Milda is especially so. When Venus is placed in the eleventh house of friends and groups, it is often overlooked with a few sentences about how people with this Venus placement prefer to select their mates from a pool of friends or their social group, or want to be friends first, before romance comes into play. That's certainly true, but there is more to the eleventh house than your best buddy and your book club. This is the house of the future and its horizons, and of seeing humanity as brothers and sisters who must work together in order to thrive. It is in complete opposition to the fifth house of personal romance, and to imagine that Venus cannot make the leap from personal to transpersonal does not do justice to that planet's versatility. Of all the Venus placements, Venus in Aquarius (portrayed in *MythAstrology I* by the nonheterosexual Ganymede) and the eleventh-house Venus, both ruled by forward-thinking Uranus, find it the easiest to move from personal *eros* to friendly *philae* to transpersonal *agape* and back again.

This can result in the individual with this placement not only falling in love with their friends, but valuing deep friendships as much or more than romantic partnerships. Like Milda, they may resent being confined to one person not only for sex and romantic feelings, but for sharing finances, home, and children as well. The eleventh-house Venus wants to be ensconced in a loving group, perhaps with some of those bonds built in the ecstasy of the body and others built by connections of the heart or mind, but all of them (or at least most) equally valued. Sometimes they can't find that ideal and have to settle for what society offers; sometimes they find themselves most comfortable in alternative relationships such as polyamory, or living with friends who make good "nesting partners" while dating the outside romantic partner who just doesn't fit well into their home, or has their own home they don't want to give up. When they finally figure out what they want, the fact that it may not resemble the pattern they grew up watching will not deter them. They can only stay in a rigid situation for a short time, and then they will need room to breathe.

Milda is said to ride in a chariot pulled by doves, sometimes naked with only a bouquet and wreath of flowers. (An ancient statue found in Vilnius which locals claimed to be Milda was of a naked woman holding a bouquet; it was unfortunately seized and destroyed by the Church.) Her traditional May feasts are connected with delight and youth; the cuckoo—one of the first birds of spring—is her sacred animal. One glance at her naked form would make everyone begin to fall in love, not only with her but with each other. This resonates with the eleventh-house Venus, who honestly believes that everyone should get a chance at love, even if only an ephemeral one.

As this is the house of Groups, Venus here does have an ability to charm members of any group they choose to belong to, and may become the peacemaker of the group, coaxing warring parties to get over their resentments and become friends again, or at least behave courteously toward each other so as not to disrupt group harmony. This is often the position of the group matchmaker, whose belief that even the least blessed deserves to know some kind of love leads them to take it on themselves to make that happen, with or without the permission of the lonely heart in question. The eleventh-house Venus often has a wide social circle with fingers in many pies, and may actually know enough people to do some reasonable matchmaking, if idealism doesn't blind them to the actual needs of the people in question.

Even if they themselves decide to remain uncommitted or refusing society's "relationship escalator", Venus will find another way to come through. They may fall in love with a cause, or a movement, or the group itself. They are capable of being just as passionately committed to a best friend or a cause as they are to a lover, and on some level they are aware that the cause as a love object may outlast both the lover and the friend.

Milda may not have much in the way of surviving lore—if indeed she had any to begin with—but as the Goddess of both Love and Freedom, she has captured the hearts of many. She tosses away the traditional repressive assumptions about Love and urges you to choose your own adventure. She has become an embodiment of the connection between freedom in romantic love and freedom for all people out of an understanding of greater love.

I once read a quote by Olive Steiner, a short story about Life coming before a woman, with Love in one hand and Freedom in the other, and asking the woman to choose. The woman thought for a time and then chose Freedom, which Life approved. If she had chosen love, the woman was told, she would have been given that and Life would have left and never returned. However, since she had chosen freedom, Life would go away and leave her with nothing ... until the day Life returned to her. *And on that day, I will bear both gifts in one hand.* It's a lesson that this aspect of Venus knows at their core, and trusts to come true.

12♀ Venus in the 12th House: Sigyn

In *MythAstrology* I, the god who stood forth for Saturn in Gemini was Loki the Trickster God of the Norse/Germanic pantheon. In that chapter, I wrote about Loki and his Gemini tendency to love multiple people, to the point where he married two separate wives who literally lived in different worlds. The older and more senior of those wives was Angrboda, a powerful warrior, sorceress, and wolf-goddess living in the wild Iron Wood. Loki's second wife was Sigyn, who was as different from Angrboda as it was possible to be.

Not much is written about Sigyn in the patchy original sources of Norse legend. A great deal more has come out from modern devotees, and the way her worship has grown and taken shape. Her origins, like many mythic figures, have multiple possible beginnings. Some call her a minor Aesir goddess, some an orphan adopted by the Vanic ship-god Njord (Jupiter in the ninth house). The twelfth is the "house of loneliness", and people with personal planets trapped in this house often go through a lonely and rather solitary childhood. Venus in this house indicates that the Venusian qualities—charm, attractiveness, ease in loving—are hidden and don't shine through the personality. Unlike the stunning Freya (Venus in Capricorn) or stately Frigga (Moon in Capricorn) or golden-haired Sif (Venus in the seventh house) or even the icy huntress Skadi (Pluto in Sagittarius), Sigyn is not described as having particularly impressive feminine charms. She is a shy and retiring goddess who seems to have little will of her own until the most terrible choice of her life is upon her.

This chapter begins not with Sigyn's name but with that of her husband Loki, and this too is a hallmark of the twelfth-house Venus. Love does not come easily to individuals with this placement, and they often find themselves falling in love with someone unavailable, or having an affair with a lover who is married to someone else. It's as if they don't expect things to work out in any fairytale way, and they are willing to settle for anyone who will give them at least some sort of love. Once they have a partner, satisfactory or not, they have a tendency to make that person the center of their world, putting the partner's needs before their own. The twelfth house is traditionally ruled by Neptune, which discourages clear boundaries. In many ways this placement is similar to Venus in Pisces, but where that Venus is at least a fish in the moonlight, this one is trapped in a dark, lonely cave, which is exactly where Sigyn ends up.

At any rate, Loki is the center of her world. Some versions of the story have Sigyn as a random Aesir girlchild bestowed on Loki by his blood brother Odin (Saturn in Pisces) in order to bind the giant-blooded trickster-god from the wild Iron Wood to the service of the Aesir, the way that ancient chieftains would hand off a random female relative as a reward. Unassuming Sigyn seems to passively go along with this; passivity in relationships is another twelfth-house Venus tendency. Another version of the story has Sigyn as a child-bride whom Loki seduces with charming words, and courts her foster-father Njord for her hand, bringing a bride-gift of a dwarf-made armband. Either way, Sigyn seems to have little agency in the matter. She settles down as a young wife in Asgard and bears Loki two sons named Narvi and Vali.

Loki is a Jotun, one of the gods/spirits of wild nature to whom monogamy is foreign; the fact that he already has a powerful wife among his own people does not stop him from taking Sigyn as a second spouse. His polyamorous nature means that he divides his time between the two women and his two sets of children, plus random affairs with other deities. While the practice of negotiated polyamory is gaining traction in modern Western culture, the majority of its population are still attached to monogamy; through their eyes, Sigyn would be the "other woman", having an affair with an already-married man, who spends half his time elsewhere and cannot give her his full attention. As we've mentioned, this is classic for the twelfth-house Venus, who has trouble advocating for herself in love relationships, and tends to be codependent. She may find herself swept off her feet by romantic ideas and a fast-talking lover who fills her with illusions, or simply be passively carried along into a relationship because it seems like the thing to do in the face of someone claiming to care about her. The twelfth is the house of the unconscious, and she may not really know how she feels, deep down, about the people in her life that she supposedly loves … or what they actually feel about her. People with this placement can go on for a long time in the mental fairytale that they write about their relationship, making it out to be much deeper and more fulfilling than it actually is. This is known as the House of Self-Undoing for a reason.

Still, all seems to go well for Sigyn, or at least peacefully, until Loki's troubles catch up with him. After Odin attempts to murder his other wife Angrboda, imprisons his son Fenrir, enchants his serpent-child Jormundgand into a living boundary in the ocean, and forbids his daughter Hel (Pluto in Virgo) to ever appear in Asgard, Loki strikes back by arranging for the murder of Odin's son Baldur (Neptune in Libra). To make matters worse, he then walks drunkenly into the hall of Aegir (Neptune in the second house) while the Aesir are feasting, kills Aegir's servant who tries to evict him, and treats all the Gods to an insulting diatribe about their (embarrassingly true) flaws. Furious, Odin and Thor (Mercury in Taurus) chase after him, but he gathers up Sigyn and their two sons and flees. The story tells that he hides them in a little house that has windows on all four sides so that they can see enemies coming in all directions, and then turns himself into a salmon and takes refuge in the lake outside the house.

However, Odin and Thor find them anyway, and drag Loki from the lake with a net. Sigyn comes screaming out of the house with her sons, seeing her husband turned back into his ordinary form under Odin's hands and afraid that the husband who is the center of her life will be killed. Her young boys attempt to rescue their father from his furious blood brother, and Odin turns Vali into a ravening wolf who attacks and kills Narvi. Then, while the mighty Thor holds both Loki and Sigyn in his unyielding grasp, Odin tears out the dead Narvi's intestines and binds Loki with his own son's flesh. Vali runs off into the wilderness, driven completely mad, and Loki is carried to a deep cave where the other Aesir gods are waiting to imprison him. Odin cannot kill his own blood brother, and for other reasons does not wish him dead, but is determined to punish him. Loki is chained in the cave and the angry Skadi, one of his abandoned former lovers, places a poisonous snake over his head. Its poison drips down onto Loki, and causes him so much pain that his writhing triggers earthquakes.

At this point in the story, it seems that Odin and the rest of the Aesir assume that Sigyn will abandon her felonious husband and come back to Asgard to start over with some other arranged marriage. After all, her children are dead or fled; surely there is no reason to stay with him? However, in spite of their passivity, twelfth-house Venus people have great depths of loyalty in their hearts. Sometimes it takes a major romantic disaster to pull them out of the comfortable illusions of their half-lived love life and force them to make a decision. If that decision happens to be a stay-or-go choice, they may realize that neither option will lend itself to vague, boundaryless passivity. To leave will take huge strength of will as their center is ripped away; to stay will require immense loyalty and the courage to face the reality of the situation.

The twelfth house is also the House of Imprisonment, and many individuals with this placement have seen their partners jailed, or in rare cases have taken the fall for that partner and were jailed in their stead. Some have also suffered with partners who developed mental illness and were trapped in their own minds, possibly in an institution. At this moment, Sigyn makes her choice and, to the surprise of everyone watching, went to stay with Loki in the cave. It is said that she held a bowl over his body—some say that it was their wedding chalice—and let it fill with the poison dripping from the serpent. However, after a while the bowl would fill up and she was forced to go empty it, and during the short time she was gone Loki would howl and writhe in pain and cause earthquakes. It is also said that during the thousand years they were trapped together in that cave, Loki slowly went mad from the pain and sorrow, but Sigyn never left his side until they were finally released.

In modern times, she is worshiped as a goddess of compassion and endurance by her devotees, who refer to her as the Lady of the Staying Power. One said of her, "Sigyn gathers broken things to her breast." She is also the goddess of Holy Mourning—one aspect of her is the Mourning Mother who weeps bitterly for the loss of her children, and as such she comforts those who have also lost loved ones, or who have been damaged by difficult life experiences. She also offers compassion to those who are trapped in difficult places for their loyalty—perhaps caring for sick or mad or dying parents, children, or partners.

As the twelfth-house Venus person matures and learns to understand their own heart and its boundaries, their experience of giving turns from feeling swept helplessly into imprisoning situations where they unthinkingly sacrifice themselves to choosing where, when, and for whom they will give of their loving compassion. Their love stories are often fraught with trouble during their youth, and this develops understanding and sympathy for those in similar circumstances. Their dark, entombed period can teach them to find that buried love nature, especially when they must spend a great deal of time alone with themselves—this is the house of solitude—and listen to their own heartbeat until they can finally hear its voice. Once they find their way out of the dark cave that teaches them these hard lessons, their vague experience of love shifts from blind, boundaryless personal love to open-eyed, unbounded transpersonal love ... which is the place where Venus and Neptune come together at last.

MARS

♂ Mars in the 1st House: Achilles and Patroclus

Mars is the planet of the archetypal warrior. It is inner courage, motivation, the ability to act—and especially to act confidently and even forcefully. When it falls into the first house of the body and the appearance, we can assume for an assertive and perhaps even pugnacious external attitude, but there is a lot more to it than simply a loud voice and an aggressive attitude. To illustrate this, we will examine the story of a pair of brave warriors who were best friends, and possibly even each other's great love.

The first warrior, and the more famous, is Achilles, hero of the Trojan War. His mother was the water nymph Thetis, who married the mortal king Peleus. When her son was born, she feared for him as he was half mortal, and brought him to the River Styx in the underworld of Hades. Those who submerged themselves in the Styx supposedly became immune to injury, so she dipped her baby boy into the river. However, he was too young to swim, so she had to keep hold of him by one heel, and that heel didn't get the Styx treatment and was his one weak point.

Even as a youth barely past puberty, Achilles showed himself to be a brave warrior, with a strong berserker streak. He was obsessed with weapons and fighting, and trained harder than many boys older than himself. Mars was not only built into his nature, but he was well on his way to becoming a "poster child" for it. This will be familiar to people with this Mars placement—it's not unusual for them to not only practice but become associated with sports, martial arts, the military, etc. People think of them as "the Army guy", "the kung fu girl", "the jock", etc. Someone with a different but still well-aspected Mars placement who does the same activities might not necessarily get that label; first-house planets tend to stick to people's foreheads whether they like it or not. The first house is also traditionally associated with Aries, regardless of what sign is actually on it, and Aries is ruled by Mars, so in a sense this is the "purest" Mars house placement.

At some point, Patroclus was sent to the court of Peleus by his father, a minor nobleman who was looking to get rid of an extra son. Patroclus was a few years older than Achilles, and while he was well-trained in the arts of war, he did not have the younger man's talent and obsession. The two youths became fast friends, and possibly lovers. Homer writes them only as friends, but later Greek authors claim that their relationship turned sexual—an arrangement which was not unusual among Grecian men of the time—and that Achilles was the *eremenos*, or submissive lover, as he was the younger boy. Much argument erupted over this writing of the two heroes in later, more homophobic times, but it's not surprising if you look at the public-Mars aspect. Mars is sex as well as fighting, and Mars approves of a two-warrior comrades-in-arms sexual bond. If there's a way to work in some good sweaty rolling-about into the externalized "mask" of a person or character, Mars will be all over that.

When the Trojan War broke out, Thetis knew that Agamemnon the Mycenean general was looking for fighting talent to bring with him, and she had a bad feeling that if her son went to Troy, he would not return. To hide him from Agamemnon, she dressed him as a girl and stashed him amongst a group of young women. Odysseus, that crafty leader of Ithaca (Mercury in the ninth house), was sent by Agamemnon to smoke out Peleus's son and make him a private offer. He suspected Thetis's plot, and disguised himself as a peddler bringing fine goods to the court. The girls all gravitated toward dress fabric and cosmetics, but Achilles can't help himself—he goes for the weapons and starts examining the swords, thus revealing his identity to Odysseus. The clever Ithacan draws the boy aside and tells him tales of potential glory in the war to come; Achilles is dazzled and immediately signs up. His best friend Patroclus, of course, enthusiastically comes along. By the time Thetis finds out about Odysseus's victory, it's too late; they are on their way to Troy.

All forced cross-dressing aside, this little anecdote illustrates a truth about this Mars placement: it expresses itself regardless of gender. Women with a first-house Mars are just as likely as men to exhibit Mars behaviors and activities; it's just that they may be socially penalized for it, depending on the culture in which they grow up. But planets in the first house are the hardest to hide, and they may be driven in spite of themselves to metaphorically start testing out swords rather than cooing over cosmetics. This placement bestows the qualities of recklessness and self-confidence, and there's little they like better than winning, no matter what body they have.

Achilles immediately began to make a name for himself with his berserker fighting on the field, but after a few months he gets into a quarrel with Agamemnon. A couple of enslaved girls were captured, and distributed to the commander and Achilles; Agamemnon's girl, however, was the daughter of a priest of Apollo (Mercury in Leo), and a plague broke out among the Greeks at Apollo's command until he returned her. In a fit of pique, Agamemnon took away the enslaved girl who had been given to Achilles, and the young warrior went into a rage at being treated with such disrespect. He stomped back to his tent and went on strike, refusing to join the battle. Mars is driven, but also impulsive, and if he feels that he is being wronged, he is capable of blowing up the project which he was wholly committed to yesterday. Unlike Pluto which plots revenge over a long period, Mars wants vengeance *now*, in the moment, before he is distracted. He may regret the ashes of his explosion tomorrow, but today he is ready to destroy it. In the first house, this behavior is loud and public, and everyone will hear about how he has been mistreated, in all capital letters accompanied by fireworks.

Odysseus was promptly dispatched to talk Achilles back into fighting, but to no avail. Their archetypal Mars figure was sulking, and would not budge. In the meantime, the troops heard that Achilles had abandoned the battle, and were losing the heart to go on fighting. Things were looking poorly for Agamemnon's war. Patroclus knew (probably from experience) that there was no convincing Achilles until he got over his sulk, but he feared that the war would be lost while everyone waited him out. He asked his lover if he could borrow Achilles's magical armor and go out on the field pretending to be him, at least for purposes of raising military morale. The armor—which we will revisit later—was actually made by Hephaestus (Mars in Capricorn), the Olympian smith-god, at the behest of Thetis. It was stronger and more beautiful than anything mortals could make (possibly a historical reference to early iron-working during this Bronze Age battle), and also made Achilles stand out on the field. In many ways, it was another symbolic layer of the Mars Mask. Achilles agreed, and Patroclus went out dressed in his armor and crying out that Achilles was come back to the field.

While the Greek soldiers were heartened and the tide of battle turned, the problem was that Patroclus was not as skilled and powerful a warrior as his lover. The original plan had been for Patroclus to keep back and simply inspire the men, but when the entire army cheered him, he got carried away and led the charge. The Trojans killed him, and his identity was discovered as his body was borne back to the encampment. This is one of the biggest pitfalls of the first-house Mars. After embodying courage and forward momentum for everyone watching for so long, the Mars individual can begin to believe his own legend. He may enter into battles which are above his pay grade, and of course when he fails, he fails loudly and visibly. Being the Face of Mars means that overextension is both awfully tempting and openly disastrous; Patroclus's story enacts the inevitable times when the Martial drive is certain they can make the jump, but ends up going off the tracks.

When Patroclus's body is brought back to him, Achilles goes completely berserk in his grief. He cuts a huge swath of rage across the Trojan army, and kills Prince Hector—the son of King Priam of Troy whose sword cut down Patroclus. The Trojan army retreats inside the city walls to avoid Achilles's semi-divine wrath, but he is not satisfied with Hector's death. Refusing to return the Prince's body to his grieving father, he ties the Trojan hero's corpse to his chariot by its ankles and proceeds to drive around and around the city, dragging it in the dirt and screaming at the top of his lungs. It is a huge blasphemy for a culture that took decent burial very seriously so as to prevent lingering ghosts, and generally returned the dead to be buried by their families, as they wanted the same courtesy extended to them. However, when a first-house Mars crashes and burns, their response is not generally to slink away and lick their wounds. Instead, they often irrationally redouble their efforts, even under the public eye, in wrath at the Universe at having the temerity to thwart them. Bystanders may stare in bewilderment as they hammer themselves against what is clearly a lost cause. Since the first-house Mars also tends to take on leadership roles, this conflict can pour multiple followers and their efforts down a black hole until Mars finally calms down.

King Priam sues for peace and a treaty, which Agamemnon is ready to negotiate, as long as it comes with a lot of gold for his side. Priam suggests that his daughter Polyxena could marry Achilles, if the warrior would return his son's body for burial. Agamemnon, prodded by his brother Menelaus, was reminded that the whole flimsy pretext for the war was that Menelaus's beautiful wife Helen (Sun in Gemini) had run off with Priam's handsome son Paris, and Helen's return is written into the treaty. After a few days of circling the city with Hector's corpse, Achilles loses momentum and is coaxed to accept the treaty. However, when the Greeks go to the gates of Troy to bargain, Paris—not wanting to give back his lover—hides in the bushes and shoots Achilles in the heel. The warrior collapses, an infection sets in, and he dies that night.

The problem with wearing one's strength and courage on one's face is that one also wears that weak spot openly, whether the Mars individual knows that is the case or not. Mars is not only the Warrior but also the Infant, in the sense that its sign Aries is the first sign, and is connected to the innocent life stage of infancy. There is something naïve about this straightforward double-me-first placement, regardless of the sign; Mars here wants to tell it like it is, and to hell with who's watching. The consequence of this is that craftier and more strategic people can pick apart their weak points, including the famous temper, and needle them into actions they may regret later.

However, even after Achilles's death, the story of the Face of Mars isn't quite over. A fight arises over Achilles's magical armor; who is to inherit the sacred garb of the archetypal warrior? Odysseus and Ajax both vied for it; a disgusted Agamemnon decided that the Trojan prisoners of war should decide, and the two ended up giving speeches to the chained captives. Odysseus wasn't the better fighter, but he was the better speechmaker, and when he was awarded the magical armor Ajax killed himself in shame. Embarrassed, Odysseus chose to send the armor to Achilles's young son, should he turn out to be like his father.

The first-house Mars individual can inspire people to emulate them, sometimes even after they have left the scene in a cloud of dust and only their inflamed reputation is left. Whether it's Neil Armstrong, Winston Churchill, Ernest Hemingway, Mahatma Gandhi, Angela Merkel, or Johnny Rotten, the fiery afterimage they leave on people's metaphorical retinas will keep others imitating them, even when it leads to their ruin. The energy of these individuals doesn't think twice about leaping into danger, and they will battle their way to the top, leaving a tale that will continue to motivate others long after they are gone.

2♂ Mars in the 2nd House: Bishamonten

ars the Warrior is the seat of everyone's spontaneous aggressions, and Mars needs to be channeled. An undirected Mars is a danger to its owner and everyone else around, because Mars needs to

throw itself into something worthwhile or it thrashes about wildly and causes destruction. In the second house of money, possessions, and finance, the best direction for Mars is to throw itself into career goals and spend its considerable energy on making money. These are the folks who are willing to work the extra hours, go for the promotion, and make prosperity manifest by their own hands. If they are prevented from exerting themselves in this direction, they may end up manifesting whining and irritation instead, demanding to be given the bright toys and becoming piqued when they are not forthcoming.

As this is also the house of values and self-worth, the most likely culprit for blocking this Mars from its rightful quest is low self-esteem. If they have been emotionally hamstrung at a young age by being given the message that they will never amount to anything, and they actually took the message in rather than letting it bounce off, they will be a damaged warrior who sits around the fire and complains loudly, too afraid to pick up the spear and wade into the fray. The longer they sit there, the worse they will feel about themselves, and it becomes a self-fulfilling prophecy. Anger may explode out of them at various intervals, but the real culprit is not the flawed human around them but the lack of a strong purpose which returns tangible rewards.

At their best, this placement can give both forceful purpose and dignity, which are some of the attributes of Bishamonten (or just Bishamon), who is one of the Seven Lucky Gods of Japan. He is a warrior god, but unlike many other war gods he is also a giver of wealth. All the Seven Lucky Gods travel together in a great ship of riches, giving gifts of prosperity to all people, and are the patrons of various sorts of workers, depending on their other attributes. Bishamonten is the patron of soldiers, and guards the financial aspect of their lives, from the lowest-paid guard to the general at the top.

It's said that an army travels on its stomach, and many a politician over the last several thousand years has discovered to his dismay that when you don't pay your soldiers, they desert and your army crumbles. When we think about workers who need to get paid fairly for their work, we tend to first focus on those who produce some kind of physical product—farmers, artisans, those who work in industry. Perhaps we then expand our view to the vast ranks of service personnel, whose "product" is measured in actions, not items. Usually we think of doctors and cashiers and such first, and it takes a while for our minds to get around to Those Who Guard And Protect. Whether they are police, security guards, or military personnel, however, we need someone to call when humans are acting badly and endangering the safety of their property. From Bishamonten's point of view, the job is to protect people's property, and that includes their bodies and their loved ones, which also come under the rubric of "that which is mine".

Historically, Bishamonten has changed and evolved many times, as he progressed eastward across Asia. He came to Japan as the Buddhist deity Vaishravana, who in turn grew out of a wealth-god named Kubera. Vaishravana, or Vessavana in Tibetan, came to China where he was assigned the job of guarding all sacred places, protecting them from plunder and violation. He kept his wealth-god attributes, although he gained armor and weapons and became an imposing figure, sometimes mounted on a horse, with a trident in one hand and a pagoda in the other—a symbol of the sacred places he was set to guard. After coming to Japan, he gained the name Bishamonten, meaning "Guardian of the Hundred Million Gates", a Japanese pronunciation of the Chinese title *Pishamen Tian.* Those who get paid for standing guard, or are called when people need guarding, will appreciate that title, and indeed this Mars placement may make their money in Mars-type jobs such as the ones mentioned above. If they do, they will be alert for fair pay which shows the value of their skill, as well as the social value of the work itself, and they will be resentful if it is not forthcoming. Some may fight to get better pay for themselves and their comrades, as Mars here is always game for a fight over the issue of unequal wealth.

Bishamonten was the protector and patron of soldiers and guards of all kinds; of all the Seven Lucky Gods, he was the only warrior and the only one to engage in violence. Unlike other war gods, though, he was still linked with the handling of money. Sacred places such as temples were often filled with offerings and artwork which were beautiful, valuable, and tempting to thieves; much of his work as temple guardian was to ensure that no one made off with any of the gold artifacts. He was said to guard and protect the donations that people left at the temples; even if it was only the poorest beggar leaving a meager offering before an altar, Bishamonten would make sure that no one walked off with it before it could be collected by the temple keepers. Because people might come into shrines and temples at all hours and leave anonymous offerings for the Gods and spirits before going on their way, Bishamonten was cultivated as a deity who would punish anyone who interfered with the gifts of humans to the Gods. His statue, spear in hand, was usually put next to the doors of temples as a warning to those who entered to behave well or face his wrath.

Another of his names was Tamonten, which means "Listening to Many Teachings", and these last few qualities reflect the process that every Mars goes through at one time or another: finding a code of honor and learning to adhere to it. The one who guarded the doors before sacred wealth had to be above bribery, theft, or laziness. He had to cultivate the qualities of patience, steadiness, persistence, and a certain amount of implacability, along with the usual Martial qualities of courage and assertiveness. Mars energy, when left to run loose without boundaries, bulldozes over people even when its direction is chosen with good intentions. This Mars may have a problem with acting out at the job, getting angry with bosses, or being too forceful with co-workers or members of the public. Learning to be calm and patient in the face of irritation will not come easy to them, but it is crucial to acquiring that physical reward they hope for. Besides, being fired too often for acting out is rough on the self-esteem. Knowing that they can't be thrown off course by the annoying people at your job makes the folks with this Mars placement feel better about themselves, once they learn the skill of letting it roll off the armor, as it were.

Another reason for this placement of Mars to work against impulsivity is that without patience and forethought, money can roll out as quickly as it can roll in. Unlike Jupiter who spends just to have things, or Venus who spends on beauty, Mars in this house spends because something has caught their eye and they impetuously decide that it would be good to own that thing. Once they have it, they may or may not make use of it for long; it may end up sitting in the basement until they take it into their heads to sell it. They need to learn to consider the long-term picture of whether any particular object will still be interesting and useful when the novelty has worn off.

Mars is also the planet of sex, but unlike Venus in this house who may believe that she has to "sell" love, Mars tends to think that they have to "buy" sex. This doesn't have to be anything so blatant as procuring sex workers; it's more likely to have the Mars person basing their worthiness for physical intimacy on their financial status, thinking on some level that no one will want to be with them if they can't support them financially or treat them to expensive dates. They may put off the pursuit of a partner—and with Mars, it's always a pursuit—until they feel that they have enough financial stability to use as "bait". Again, it's important that they examine their values. It's not just that they need to look at what qualities they want in a partner, it's that they have to look at what qualities they want a potential partner to value in them. If they want to be desired for something more than their financial standing and security, they need to cultivate other valuable qualities and deliberately seek someone who finds those desirable. Not all value, nor all wealth, is monetary.

As this is the house associated with possessive Taurus, this Mars placement may be a bit overprotective of a partner once they acquire one. Like Bishamonten who considered it a sacred duty to protect the valuables from being stolen, they can "guard" their partner with too much fierceness, worrying that the lover themselves will walk off with the goods, so to speak, and give the treasure of their physical intimacy away to others. This can lead to angry scenes and controlling behavior if the Mars person hasn't learned patience, and learned how to earn trust … and if they choose the wrong person, of course. The right person for them will be able to advocate for their own value not just as a possession but as a human being, and leverage that value to earn the Mars individual's trust. Bishamonten understands what it is to have a sacred duty to guard something, and what the Mars individual wants to know from their sexual partner is that the lover is also willing to treat their gift of intimacy like a treasure, and also to consider it a sacred duty to keep it for the appropriate time and place—the temple of their love. In other words, they need someone who will take it as seriously as they do, and hold them to that same promise.

Over time, the pagoda in Bishamonten's hand took on the meaning of the Royal Treasury, and then his own treasure house, which he both guarded and occasionally opened its doors to give out gold to the masses. His skin was shown as yellow under his helmet and armor, to reflect his job as Guardian of the Gold. People eventually began praying to him as a defender against disease, helping the body to fight off plagues and illness, the general of the warriors of the immune system. Protector and provider, he looked out for all those who guarded, and on the side, all those whom "his" people guarded. Mars in the House of Gold will always be a guardian at heart; they need to keep in mind that Bishamonten also opened the doors and gave forth in generosity as well as keeping the treasure safe. It isn't of value unless it moves. That's a second-house Mars truth if ever there was one.

30♂ Mars in the 3rd House: Ogma

The Irish legends of the Tuatha De Danaan encompass many great fighting heroes, as warriors were highly esteemed in that culture. The god/hero Ogma was (like many others) renowned for his battle heroics, but the contribution for which he is most remembered is not his skill with the sword, but the fact that he invented a magical alphabet which is still used to this day.

This is not a book about magical alphabets or divinatory systems, so I'll just say that the Ogham (modernly pronounced *o-ham*) is an early medieval alphabet used to write likewise early Irish, and it collected a number of traditions and magical uses through the years. Modern scholars of Celtic religion continually argue about which magical uses are authentically Iron Age and which are Victorian or modern inventions. The trees associated with the letters? The birds and colors and finger positions? The possibility that Ogham was originally, or eventually, a sign language which spelled out words with the fingers laid on the hands and forearms? The tells of the Ogham colors woven into striped or tartan cloth to pass secret messages during times of oppression? The use of it as a divinatory tool at all? Indeed, many scholars have almost come to blows arguing about it. Ogma probably loves that, and so, most likely, would a third-house Mars.

Ogma has three epithets—first, "Radiant Face" or "Shining Countenance"; second, "Strongman" or "Champion"; third, "Learned Man". These sum up his nature quite nicely, and also reflect that of this Mars placement. First, brightness. Mars is fiery and the third-house placement brings that enthusiastic brightness out through language. He is "bright" as in intelligent, and "bright" as in cheerful—perhaps even overpoweringly so at times.

Second, "Strongman" and "Champion" show the warrior nature of both the deity and the placement. Even in the Mercury-ruled third house, this placement is Mars, not the airy talking-planet. It's said that Ogma was so fond of battle that others had to hold him back to keep him from rushing in too quickly and getting himself killed. He fights bravely against the Fir Bolg, but then when the new king condemns the Tuatha to servitude, he is forced to carry firewood. Undaunted, he enters athletic contests and impresses the king anyway; this is typical for the brave, determined third-house Mars who love to compete. When the king is overthrown and the old king returned, Ogma becomes his champion.

His victory is threatened by the arrival of Lugh Sun-Face (Neptune in Leo), another multi-talented shining deity. Ogma proves his strength by lifting up a great flagstone which normally took eighty oxen to move, and heaving it entirely out of the city of Tara, but Lugh heaves it right back. Clever Lugh, instead of just continuing the competition, praises Ogma and asks him to be Lugh's champion as well as the king's, and Ogma gladly agrees. Straightforward Mars just wants to be seen as a worthy winner, and the third-house placement means that he wants verbal praise … preferably heard by as many as possible.

This emphasis on the verbal praise of heroics continues in the saga. Ogma goes into battle and ends up with a magical sword, plundered from a slain enemy. Its great power is not in killing-power per se, but in heroic praise; in fact, the first thing the sword does when unsheathed is to go on a long litany of the great deeds of the heroes who have wielded it. The concept of a *talking sword* is a perfect metaphor for Mars in the house of words, and it seems to be no accident that Ogma inherits it … and promptly starts battling to be the sword's greatest hero yet.

The big problem with being a talking sword, however, is that you tend to slice people every time you open your mouth, and this is the downfall of the third-house Mars. *Argumentative* doesn't even begin to cover it. With this placement, the weapon is words, and when Mars is angry, words become blades and arrows, spears and just plain thrown rocks. This Mars is *loud*. Even ordinary speech tends to be louder, faster, more enthusiastic, and less considerate than that of other people. They are experts at the art of competitive conversation, shoving their opinions in the second the other person pauses for breath. Similarly, they love debate and lively discussion, ideally where opponents aren't afraid of a good verbal wrestling match over some interesting subject. Mars here has no time for Mercurial sleight-of-tongue; they prefer communication to be straight-forward, honest, and direct to the point. No beating around the bush, and the decibels scream upwards when they become furious, as do the harsh words. They are at their most weaponized when they are defending their ideas, the way a mother bear would defend her cubs.

At the same time, the third-house Mars does love knowledge. Unlike Mercury placements which fly about seeking it, Mars hunts it down and devours it like a wolf leaping on a rabbit. In fact, the concept of the hunt is probably the best way to get this Mars placement to learn. Couch the information as prey hiding in the bushes, needing to be sniffed out and run down, and they're interested. They can hunt knowledge down for years, intent on its trail and unwilling to give up, like a stubborn hound. However, they want that knowledge to be useful. Facts for their own sake disappoint them; they want their hard-won prey to sit up and do tricks, whether that's earning them prizes and recognition, or being put to use to make the world better. Knowledge had better be power or they will lose interest and hare off after something more purposeful.

This brings us to Ogma's third epithet of "Learned Man". In the *Ogam Tract*, he is credited with creating this magical language, which can theoretically do so many things, in order to have a tool which would set him apart from ordinary rustics and prove that he was indeed a well-educated individual. It was said that he was the father of the Ogham, and that his knife—the tool with which he carved the symbols into wood—was its mother. Again we have the combining of words and sharp things; it seems to be Ogma's theme. His name is said to come from the original Indo-European word *ag*, meaning *to cut*, referring to him cutting the symbols into slices of tree branch. The concept of *words that cut*, or alternately *words engraved into the heart*, resonates deeply with the third-house Mars.

Some scholars have argued (of course it's an argument!) that the combination of eloquence and battle-fury in the figure of Ogma stems from the old Celtic tradition of having a battle-bard who would give soul-stirring speeches, inspiring the warriors to fight harder and win. Certainly the third-house Mars is the one you'd want if you had to throw battle-rage, or at least courageous determination, into a thousand armed men facing down five thousand armed men. Mars in the Mercury house doesn't rely primarily on wordcraft to reach listeners, although they may be quite skilled in that area. Mars relies on passion, on speaking truth and letting its purity ring through the air or the airwaves. Mercury interests the mind, but Mars stirs the spirit.

The Ogham wasn't Ogma's only linguistic invention; he was also said to have invented several other languages which do not survive, and to have written a great deal of heroic poetry, and a variety of other persuasive writings. This is also reflective of this placement, as the natives often bolt from one new interest to another; having too many irons in their Martial fire is one of the complaints often heard about them. They tend to overextend themselves, believing with Martial confidence that they can handle it all—and as long as nothing goes wrong, they can. However, Life being the messy thing that it is, commitments fall off of plates and beautiful poems fall under the desk to be trampled and only remembered in wistful future lays.

It was also said that he taught humans words and eloquence through rays of light beamed into their eyes from his countenance. This brings us back around to the first epithet—*bright*—and is a picturesque metaphor for the transmission of Mars's fire through the medium of words, opening eyes and minds and creating a magical alphabet of understanding. Ogma's talking sword cuts deep, but sometimes that is necessary for the purity of an idea to fill and enlighten the chaos of a troubled mind.

4♂ Mars in the 4th House: Chantico

All over the world, the symbol of the forces which are ruled by the fourth house is the hearthfire, the warm home center which cooks the food and gathers the people. Today few of us actually have real fire in our kitchens besides perhaps a gas-stove pilot light, and we tend to gather in other areas, but after thousands of years, that symbol still holds. We tend to think of hearthfire deities as patient and kindly like the Greek Hestia (Sun in Virgo) or bustling and no-nonsense like the German Holda (Moon in Virgo), but the Aztec hearth-goddess Chantico is a very different sort of lady. While her name literally means "dweller in the house" after the central cooking fire, she is also known as "Lady of the Hot Chili Pepper" and "Lady of the Scarlet Butterfly". She is a combative warrior with a crown of poisonous cactus spikes and the warrior's green feathers, half her face painted red and the other half yellow. She is a reminder that comforting or not, throughout the ages and in many places in the world, thousands of people died when cooking fires got out of control.

We don't tend to think of cooking fires that way, but it must have been a very brave thing for humans to learn to handle fire and keep it captive. When they lapsed in their vigilance for too long, their "domestic" fire would leap up and set them aflame. "Domestic" fire has always been a risky project, because fire is just as wild as it ever was, even when confined to a stone circle or a small brick or metal box. Chantico reminds us to respect the flame and remember that what warms can also kill.

One could say the same for the fiery, aggressive planet Mars when it is confined to the small box of a home, with all one's family members. People with a fourth-house Mars placement are notorious for being kind and laid-back at work and outside interest groups, but when they come home they let their hair down and become quite loud and aggressive. It's the family and housemates who get to see their enthusiasm when they attack the mess in the garage, hear their opinionated rants about the state of the world ... and, in many cases, bear the brunt of their anger and frustration. When the hearthfire gets out of control, it's the people closest to it who get hurt. The Aztec priest Moctezuma supposedly had a life-size idol of Chantico which had a removable leg, used as a stick to pound the ground when the leader was in full wroth and raging about an attacking enemy. It was supposed to symbolize that Chantico herself was stomping her foot in anger about the situation, adding to Moctezuma's own wrath.

One of the myths about Chantico goes back to the complicated Aztec calendar of feast and fast days, with special foods being served or eschewed depending on which deity's day it happens to be. Even the Gods themselves were expected to honor these feast and fast days, as a way of paying respect to each other. Chantico decided (in a very fourth-house Mars way), that she was not going to be told what to do in her own kitchen, and rebelled against the food taboos. During a fasting day, she cooked herself a dish of fish and hot peppers (the latter being one of her sacred foods) and ate it. The scent of the food wafted out and the other Gods noted her cooking. Tonacatecuhtli, the god of food and the keeper of the food-calendar, was so angry at her that he turned her into a dog, symbolizing the dog's tendency to eat anything, scavenging garbage from midden piles.

It's also important to remember that the Aztecs kept their small hairless dogs as food animals, because they had no large livestock, so it was also a way of making her into the food which was cooked, instead of the one cooking the food. After a period of penance, he she was changed back, but because it happened on the ninth day of the month of the Dog, that was Chantico's sacred feast day from then on, and one of her titles became Nine Dogs, referring to her calendrical holiday. Besides being a good example of the fourth-house Mars's refusal to allow outsiders to have a say in what they do at home, it also echoes the loyalty of a family dog. People with this placement may bark a fair amount, but they are enthusiastically devoted to the people they live with, and dead-loyal to their family and tribe.

As the fourth is the house of ancestry and culture, their rabid loyalty may also be directed toward their ancestral heritage, and they may be the ones to "doggedly" adhere to inherited customs and cultural celebrations … and carry the anger passed down regarding injustice or oppression of their family group. It doesn't just have to be ethnic or racial; if their parents and grandparents came from a certain class or familial career, they may be moved to fight for the rights of people in that category, even if they are no longer in it. In fact, if a fourth-house Mars is taking their fight to the outside world, it's probably because they are defending a family tradition, and thus an outgrowth of their loyalty to their family itself. (That's also a useful way to reroute their aggression and righteous anger outside of the family home.)

Along these lines, the fourth-house Mars is often fiercely protective of their family. They may have an ambivalent attitude of "I'm the only one who's allowed to give them a hard time!" or if their Mars is more of an honorable warrior, they may see their family as softer beings who need their protection from the wolves outside the door. Parents with this placement will be the first ones into the principal's office when their children come home bullied, threatening the school department with all sorts of mayhem if it is not stopped. They may start feuds with neighbors if said neighbor's kid threw a punch at their own, regardless of whether their own child kicked first. Chantico's title of "Nine Dogs" resonates with the guard-dog level of a fourth-house Mars, and what those perceived as attacking the family will face.

They also expect support for their own anger and outside injustice. They can withstand a great deal of poor treatment at work if they can come home and complain loudly about it, and have their loved ones respond with supportive indignation at the unfairness of their treatment. A partner who tries to tell them how they could have behaved differently and avoided the problem will not be appreciated; the wise partner will acknowledge and sympathize with their feelings until they have calmed down before attempting to solve problems.

The fourth-house Mars was often raised in a family where the adults were hard-driving career people who expected their children to be assertive, ambitious, and do well in the world. Growing up in a military family is not uncommon, or at least a family which was run along the lines of military discipline, or a family which was very physical and bonded around sports. Alternatively, there may have been a great deal of good-natured rough-and-tumble (which might have been hard on more sensitive or introverted children) from adults who were loud and extroverted. On the more difficult side, Mars in this house can also indicate parents who were the source of loud, angry arguments or even violence.

The fourth house is indicative of the parent who sets the tone for the home, and that parent might have evidenced the Mars qualities of aggressiveness, ambition, or any of the other behaviors listed above. When the fourth-house Mars person is grown, they may unconsciously expect their home to have a Martial person in it—the family leader who gets things done, making decisions and providing direction and motivation to the rest of the family group. If the Mars person is also extroverted and assertive, they may take on this role themselves (perhaps whether the other family members agree or not), or if they are more introverted and indecisive, they may choose a partner who will fill that role for them and carry their household Mars, a Chantico they can come home to who is familiar and will allow them to relax. They will put up with a great deal of yelling and ordering about if it is done affectionately and with respect, and even enjoy it to a certain degree, but if they feel that they are being disrespected they will suddenly take back their Mars and a fiery argument will ensue. Their domestic Mars leader needs to know how far they can push, and not go over the line.

A cooking fire's main goal, however, is not to flare up but to feed and warm people, to remain the domestic fire which gives of itself to others—thus Chantico's period of time being a food animal to be sacrificed as well as an active, fiery goddess. A good way to burn off the energy of the fourth-house Mars who is well-behaved at work and then comes home spoiling for a fight is to direct them into activities which allow them to give of themselves to the family. They often end up being the ones who work in the garden, do the repair and home improvement jobs, lead the family in exercise, or throw themselves into cooking for everyone. Whatever home sacrifice they make, it is important to them to have their "workspace" to themselves, with no one interfering with their tools. If the fourth-house Mars person does the cooking, for example, all Gods help anyone else who tries to cook in it, or burns anything on one of their special pans! Chantico will rise up in wrath out of the hearthfire we thought was controlled and domesticated, reminding us again that what can warm us can also burn.

♂ Mars in the 5th House: Perseus

Perseus is one of the earliest Greek culture-hero-stories, which is why his tale is immortalized in the constellations of the sky. Like many such adventurers, he traveled around and slew a good number of monsters, but the most important one wasn't done just for the purpose of monster-ridding; it was in order to win the hand of his love. This is one of the biggest differences between Mars in this house and another one. Mars is always a warrior, always fighting and doing and deciding, but in the fifth house the end-goal is to win not fame or fortune, but love.

The hero Perseus is the son of Zeus (Jupiter in Aries) and a mortal woman—Danae, the daughter of King Acrisius of Argos. A prophecy said that Acrisius would be killed by his grandson, so rather than court future political rebellion, he locked Danae up and would not allow her any suitors. Of course, this didn't stop Zeus for a moment. It is notable that the form Zeus used to come to Perseus's mother and sire him was a shower of gold, being that this is the Sun's house, and any planet here is subtly gilded with solar energy. When Acrisius realized that his daughter had given birth and that the child had been sired by Zeus, he feared both to let his daughter and grandson live, and to risk Zeus's wrath by killing them. He compromised by shutting them both into a large wooden chest, putting it into a small boat, and sending it out onto the ocean to sink or float. They washed up on the island of Seriphos, and were rescued by a fisherman named Dictys, who raised Perseus to manhood. Dictys's brother was a rich man named Polydectes, who decided—once Perseus was grown—that he wanted to marry Danae. Perseus objected to the marriage, and Polydectes decided to get him out of the way. He sent Perseus off on a quest to get the head of the Gorgon Medusa for him.

Medusa herself has more of a part in this fifth-house Mars story than merely being a random monster. Originally a virginal priestess of Athena (Sun in Aquarius), she was raped by Poseidon (Neptune in Cancer) in front of Athena's altar, largely because the two deities were involved in a turf war at the time. Athena (who claimed to be completely rational but sometimes reacted quite irrationally) punished Medusa for being the instrument of temple defilement by turning her into a monster with living, writing snakes for hair who petrified all who looked her in the eyes. Medusa fled to the wilderness, there to nurse her grievance and create a lot of stone statues from those who came near to her. She lived with two other Gorgons whom she claimed as sisters; other women who had been divinely punished, they were equally snake-haired and fanged and clawed, but only Medusa could turn people to stone.

The inclusion of Medusa in this story is the elephant in the room of Mars in the house of romance, because it is essentially a rape narrative. Medusa has already been damaged by the worst possible ending of the planet of aggression in the house of love: she has been sexually violated, and then blamed for it. This is absolutely not to say that this placement makes people into rapists; that's only a worst-case scenario. It does, however, give them a tendency to just push a little harder for romantic possibilities which seem to be undecided, to go just a little further, to pressure just a little more and try to convince someone that they Are The One. (This behavior isn't limited to men, either; women are just as capable of this kind of pressuring.) Sometimes, of course (especially if Mars is afflicted in the chart) it might go so far as not being willing to take No for an answer, and then we have the problem which can create Medusas. Since Mars in this house isn't a terribly introspective placement, they may blame the other person for being "uptight" or "not admitting that they really wanted me" or "a weakling" or some such excuse.

Perseus, however, while being an impulsive warrior, is not a rapist. His first thought is to protect his mother, and his second thought is simply that monster-slaying sounds like a wonderful challenge. The fifth is the house of play, and Mars here is extremely competitive and finds challenges a great deal of fun. Even if the rest of the chart makes this individual into a quiet, bookish nerd, they will go into competitive overdrive when a board game and an opponent is placed in front of them. From their point of view, the quest begins not for the end-goal, but for the joy of winning against whatever is in front of them. Again, because competition is a form of play for them, they are generally good sports about losing and are probably grinning through the whole process, instead of being grim, teeth-gritted serious competitors. This competitive streak can backfire, however. Jumping ahead to later in Perseus's life, we find that he enters a discus-throwing competition while visiting a neighboring kingdom. His grandfather Acrisius is visiting and in the audience, but neither knows the other's identity. Perseus's throw goes wide, and he accidentally strikes Acrisius in the head and kills him, thus fulfilling the prophecy. When the competitive streak is aimed at loved ones who do not appreciate it, damage can happen. This placement often bestows a certain childlike enthusiasm, and their competitiveness is rarely more than that impulsiveness, but it can still backfire anyway.

At any rate, Perseus prays to the Gods for the tools to accomplish his quest, and because he is a son of Zeus, they listen and respond. His half-brother Hermes (Mercury in Gemini) appears and lends him an extra pair of winged sandals to fly with, and his *harpe*—a sword with a sickle-shaped curve on the end—with which to slay Medusa. His half-sister Athena, apparently regretting having created a monster but not wanting to deal with Medusa herself, appeared as well and loaned him a polished shield with which to view the Gorgon, and a special bag to keep the severed head safe, as she warned him it could still petrify people after its death. With these, he was able to walk backwards into the cave while the Gorgons slept, using the shield as a mirror, cut off Medusa's head and stuff it into the sack, and then fly out of the cave to leave the angry Gorgon sisters behind. He then wends his way towards home accidentally leaving a trail of Medusa-blood which creates yet more strange creatures—huge scorpions and the magical winged stallion Pegasus.

The fifth-house Mars can attempt to plan their future romantic life like a military campaign, pressing all their allies into service, plotting the battles and the eventual conquering. (They approach creative projects in the same way, but those are more amenable to being conquered.) The problem is, of course, that this subtly casts the beloved as the enemy, and as Leonard Cohen wrote, "Love is not a victory march." This placement can see "winning" the love of another person as a prize to be awarded rather than a trust to be built, and once the prize is in their hands, they may feel that they have done their job and everything should fade to the happily-ever-after. It may come as a shock to find out that this is only the beginning; that the rest of their lives together will require a give-and-take dance of earning trust in both directions, of hard emotional labor. It's almost par for the course for this placement to mean a great deal of loud arguments with one's beloved, at least in the early stages, when Mars resents having to work through all these annoying emotional issues. This can be made worse if they see attacking to be a way to get through a partner's reserve and thus reconnect, or if they find the fight-and-make-up pattern sexually attractive.

On the way home, Perseus stops at a coastal kingdom ruled by King Cepheus and Queen Cassiopeia (both now constellations in the sky), where a terrible sea monster has been terrorizing the people. Oracles claim that the sea monster will only leave when the royal couple's daughter Andromeda is sacrificed to it, so she is brought out and chained to a large rock on the shore. Perseus, hearing about this, dives down onto the rock with Andromeda and waits for the sea monster; when it arrives, he uses the Medusa head to turn it to stone and rescues Andromeda, thus winning her hand.

While she also supposedly fell in love with her brave warrior, this underlines another problematic issue of romance with this placement—the knight on the white horse who wants to rescue the damsel in distress (a trap which anyone of any gender combination can fall for). Being the rescuer is a dangerous pastime in romance. You may not actually be able to rescue them, especially from their own problems, because you're not a miracle worker or demigod. They may think they like the idea of being rescued, but then don't want to put in the work necessary to help with it. Rescuing them may create an artificial dependence which they will then need to be rescued from, and you won't be the one who can do it. There are thousands of attractive "damsels" (of any gender) in distress out there, but it isn't your job to save them. At best you might be able to create a supportive environment for them to change themselves, if they are willing. At worst you set yourself up to constantly bail them out of their continuing barrage of mistakes, and possibly get blamed for not being able to actually save them. This placement of Mars is heartbreakingly vulnerable to this trap, especially as they tend to fall very hard for people. (If they're with someone who needs help, they can dependably feel like the strong and capable warrior by comparison. If the other person always needs saving, then Mars is never the weak one who needs to be saved.)

This is the house of children, and while Mars is initially enthusiastic about the idea, those with this placement may find all the minutiae of child-rearing to cramp their fast-moving, active style. How can they do all the activities they've always jogged through when there is a crying child pulling at their hand all the time? They are better at being a "coach" for older children than a nurturing nose-wiper for young ones, and may alienate children who want more emotional comfort from them. It's been noted that those with this placement often have loud, aggressive children, and a fair amount of chicken-and-egg arguments have been made about whether this is simple astrological prediction or the reaction of a child who has to stand up to and push back against a parent with this somewhat aggressive parenting style.

Perseus gave the dangerous Medusa-head—the symbol of the destructive power of Mars's mistakes—to Athena, letting it find a home in her temple; this can be seen as placing the overly aggressive Mars nature under the control of the rational (or at least more rational) mind. But he finally comes to an accidental end when he is old and half-blind, and takes back the Medusa head to use it in a war. He cannot see well enough to aim it, and when it misses, he thinks that it no longer works after all this time. Turning it toward himself to see what is wrong, he accidentally kills himself. His son then gives the head back to Athena, who places it on her "aegis" shield to keep it away from foolish mortals, and there it stays. Some aspects of a planet are too dangerous for some individuals to keep playing with, or at least one hopes that they would grow out of that blind impulsivity in time.

At its best, this Mars placement can be the one who is willing to fight for love and for their loved ones, not as a winner-take-all but as a knight with a code of honor, who understands that the prize won with dishonorable or destructive means is not worth having. They can come to the table with an open heart, ready to share pleasure and joy, and this is the true end of the fifth-house hero's journey.

♂ Mars in the 6ᵗʰ House: Heimdall

Of all the many Norse Gods (and Goddesses) who were known as warriors, Heimdall has the most boring job of all. He is a deity who is basically a glorified security guard, and one of the patrons of anyone who holds down such a job. (The other, in this cosmology at least, is

Mordgud, guardian of the gate into Helheim, the Land of the Dead.) Heimdall is one of the sons of Odin the All-Father of Asgard (Saturn in Pisces), and as such he has a respectable place in the realm of the Sky Gods, but his task is to guard that realm day in and day out. Asgard is only accessible via Bifrost, the bridge formed by the rainbow, and Heimdall's house Himinbjorg ("heavenly castle") is located at the very top of it. Here he stands his watch, day in and day out; the trickster god Loki (Saturn in Gemini) who became Heimdall's bitter enemy once taunted that Heimdall was "doomed to have a wet back forever", referring to the hardships of standing watch in the rain.

When we think of sword-bearing warriors of ancient times, we think of them fighting on the battlefield, or perhaps sauntering around on quests. We forget that the most common job for a man-at-arms was Heimdall's own—guard duty. Without someone standing at the gate or the door or the hall outside the royal bedroom, no one was safe from attack. It was the armed servants who put their bodies—and their eyes and ears—between the skulking attacker and the helpless sleepers, and they often made the difference between life and slaughter.

When Mars passes into the house of work and service, it is the warrior's turn to work and serve. Mars often feels stifled in this house—it's not very glamorous work, after all. There's little battle-glory in it, and a whole lot of boredom, during which he must stay alert even when he just wants to lie down and sleep. The active nature of Mars wants to do great projects, but here the energy is drawn toward taking care of other people, some of whom may not even be particularly worthy of protection or care, as far as Mars is concerned. Really, the whole thing is a drag. Mars copes with this by throwing himself into his job with everything he has. People with this placement are often in danger of overdoing things, echoing Heimdall who stubbornly stood outside in all weathers, never ceasing his watch.

Heimdall's origins are mysterious; Odin dallied with the sea god's nine daughters (Neptune in the twelfth house) and Heimdall was their son. When he was born—and it is not clear which of them actually bore him; as far as Heimdall knows he was simply "born of nine mothers"—they put him on a raft and sent him floating off to Odin. He was raised by Frigga (Moon in Capricorn) and gave all his loyalties to the Aesir, rejecting his elemental water-spirit origins. Like his half-brother Thor (Mercury in Taurus), he harbors a deep suspicion of wild, elemental figures who do not bow to the civilized sky Gods, derived from their respective powerful and untamed elemental mothers. When Mars comes into this civilized, hard-working house, he distrusts the feral aspects of Nature, unbound by job and clock and regular exercise at the gym.

Heimdall has a great golden horn called the Glallarhorn, which he will blow enthusiastically to begin Ragnarok, should that horrible day ever come. Then he will commit himself to the battle, and specifically to seeking out Loki and slaying him. It's unclear when, exactly, Loki the Trickster became Heimdall's enemy, but certainly he is one of the least predictable elements of the cosmology, allied with the deities of fire and ice and wolves and serpents and death, about as far from Duty as one can get. One story relates how Loki briefly stole Brisingamen, the beautiful necklace of Freya the goddess of Love and Fertility (Venus in Capricorn). He didn't get far, as Freya raised the hue and cry, and Heimdall saw Loki leaving Asgard and running for the distant shore. Even though he hated and distrusted the ocean—it was the home of his nine uncanny mothers—he used his ocean origins to turn himself into a seal and swam out to where Loki, also in seal form, was getting away with Brisingamen. The two battled on a rock jutting out of the sea, and Heimdall bested the trickster and brought the necklace back to Freya. Somehow this grew into not merely a distrust of Loki, but a whole-hearted hatred, and if Ragnarok ever goes down, Loki will be first on the Sacred Watchman's list.

It is said that Heimdall the Watchman requires less sleep than a bird, and can see at night as well as if it were day, for over a hundred leagues. His hearing is so keen that he can hear grass as it grows on the earth, wool as it grows on the back of a sheep, and anything louder. While the sixth-house Mars person may not be quite that stalwart and gifted, they certainly attack work as if they are. Not only are they often workaholics, they are fixers, and see everything in terms of a problem that needs to be fixed, an obstacle that needs to be knocked down. Heimdall's symbolic animal is the ram, reminiscent of Aries, the sign ruled by Mars. This placement gives high energy and good health; the sixth is the house of health, but the biggest danger from this placement is accidents—often in the workplace. Individuals with this placement are happy to throw themselves into active health regimes, and may have very disciplined bodies. Regular workouts help burn off their energy while still helping them to feel that they are doing something useful.

Heimdall was said to have one of the most beautiful bodies of the Aesir, and was called "the white (or gleaming) god" and "the one with golden teeth". When it comes to bodies, this placement gives the belief that you get what you work for, and there's always room for improvement.

Mars is also sexuality, and while it may seem at first glance that this placement would push aside that whole side of the planetary influence, Mars is still Mars even when he's in service. The 6th-house Mars individual is still as fond of sex as any of the other eleven Mars placements, but for him—or her—it is placed in the service of a greater goal. In *Rigsthula*, one of the most famous Heimdall stories, he is sent by Odin to walk among humans for a year as a great lord, going by the name of Rig ("King"). The mission that is given to him is to bring divine gifts to humanity, and he does this literally by inserting those gifts into their bloodlines.

After he arrives in Midgard, he is welcomed into the rude hut of a peasant couple and convinces them to allow him to lie between them in bed at night. He couples with the peasant-wife and nine months later she births a child who will be the progenitor of the race of thralls, or serf-bondsmen. He then does the same trick with a couple who are freeborn farmer/craftspeople, and sires the progenitor of that social class. Finally, he visits a noble couple and sires the progenitor of the ruling class on the lady of the house. He adopts their son as his student, teaching him runes and the ways of rulership. When the lad reaches adulthood, Rig gives him his own title-name and leaves the realm of mortals forever.

The first thing we notice from this story is probably the class structure, and that Heimdall's efforts not only continue but cement the three-part society, which is found throughout Indo-European cultures. The story itself has long been analyzed as a class-structure justification, and it's tempting to set that aside, except that sixth-house planets—perhaps with the exception of Uranus—do tend to admire a good hierarchy, if only in secret. In the case of Mars, that hierarchy will be derived from courage, willpower, decisive action, and the ability to get the job done. The warrior-in-service wants to be in service to someone worthy, and likes to know their place—below the worthy lord or lady, but above everyone else.

In spite of this, they aren't really very good at teamwork. They easily become impatient and irritable at people who don't do things the "proper" way. (The sixth house is traditionally associated with Virgo, which definitely believes that there is a proper and improper way of doing things.) Their high energy tends to wear out their teammates, and it's best for their worthy lord or lady (or boss, or partner) to send them off to tear through some solitary job without having to deal with the messiness of other people—like Heimdall on his solitary guard duty.

However, it is also impossible to read about Rig's doings in Midgard and not notice that part of his service to Odin's goal was to have a lot of sex. He did it, of course, in service to the goal, but that didn't mean he couldn't enjoy it. The sixth-house Mars individual is usually quite happy to engage in such sports, assuming there are no other blocks in the astrological chart, but there will always be a dutiful edge to it. Sex is something one does to cement a relationship bond, or to show someone that you care, or to please them, or to make children, or to follow a socially-acceptable marital role, or even because it's good exercise, a service to bodily health and well-being. Hedonism for its own sake is not generally on their radar. If you're going to do something, why not do it for a good and useful reason?

Many people don't consider duty particularly romantic, but like Venus in this house, giving excellent service to family, clan, loved ones, and valued others is the way sixth-house placements show their loyalty and regard. This placement is rich with loyalty; like Heimdall who will stand guard over his people for as long as it takes, they will do whatever work is necessary to protect and nourish those under their care. Service has always been a meaningful way to restrain the boundless aggression of the Warrior, in archetype and in reality, and eventually they learn that some of the greatest rewards come from putting their energies toward the contentment of those they love.

7♂ Mars in the 7th House: Hercules and Omphale

In the ongoing saga of Hercules (Neptune in Aries), the great hero, one of the strangest of his trials was being sold as a slave to Omphale, the Queen of Lydia. Mars, the ruler of Aries, is more traditionally associated with the first house, which opposes the seventh—me, me, me. The seventh house, however, is about I-Thou rather than I, the concept that the dance of relationship is more important than individuality ... that you are no one and nothing until you are seen by the eyes of another. In the realm of the seventh house, if a tree falls in the forest and no one is there to hear it, it might as well not have happened.

This is an uncomfortable place for headstrong Mars to be, and it is not surprising that this myth starts out with our warrior-hero being sold into slavery. When Mars falls into the seventh, its ability do what it wants is severely compromised ... because there are other people, and their feelings and desires, to take into account. Mars chafes at the restriction, but feels compelled to check with them and gain their approval on his actions. If they don't give it, his confidence is deeply wounded, and it takes a major act of will and anger to push past their disapproval and keep going with his own path.

Hercules is sold not to any master, but to Omphale, a powerful Queen who immediately sets out to change him by turning his world upside down. Being subject to the will not only of another person but of a powerful woman is a new and humiliating thing for our macho hero. She is older and richer than he is, more intelligent, more sophisticated in her judgment, and generally outranks him in every way except that of sheer brute force. The latter category hardly matters, as she has the law on her side—recalling the seventh house's traditional association with law-obsessed Libra—and he is marched to her guarded and in chains.

For centuries, Omphale's name was poorly translated by prudish male academics as meaning "navel", as the word was referred to as being the "center of the woman". However, the stones that were referred to as *omphales* were conical rather than concave, and the current modern theory is that they actually represented the clitoris. As such, she is the embodiment of the female version of the phallus, the female active principle, which in this case overcomes the male phallic thrust. Omphale is just as assertive as Hercules—indeed, she is more than a match for him—but her active nature is focused in other areas besides war and conquest. Her kingdom is rich in trade (a seventh-house partnership activity), culture, art, and beauty (all Libran attributes).

The first thing that she does is to take away his mighty club and lionskin, and wear them herself. Then she dresses him in women's clothing, seats him among her maidens at the foot of her throne, and insists that he learn to spin. While this part of the story may, at first glimpse, seem like every bad stereotype of forced-feminization transvestite pornography (perhaps even the oldest of its genre ever written down), there is more to her treatment of him than mere humiliation. To her more experienced eyes, Hercules is two-dimensional, unfinished, naive, and shallow. The only part of his nature that he has developed is that of brute strength and raw courage, and his relationship to the other parts of life is embryonic at best. To Omphale, this lack of balance cannot be tolerated—and this placement, like any form of the opposition, is all about balance.

We must also take into account that Hercules has come to this point by murdering his wife and child in a fit of madness. Omphale decides that what Hercules needs, more than anything else, is to learn what it is to be the sort of person that he is not—feminine, restricted in his movements, dependent on another for one's very survival. When Mars is dropped into the seventh house, it is the world turned upside down. There is no way to escape the drive to be part of a couple, to have another's support in order to assert yourself and accomplish your goals, to be seen and acknowledged by the necessary other. This can be a galling thing for someone who is otherwise fairly independent, and they may both long for and resent their partner, painfully aware that their very nature cries out to be in relationship, and just as painfully aware of how much of a handicap that can be. While any seventh-house planet does poorly alone, with Mars here the individual may simply drift chaotically through life until they find a partner to anchor them. Until they are told by another that they can be a hero, they can't really believe it themselves. The point of this karmic lesson, however, is not to overcome it, but to experience it fully.

In forcing the warrior's great calloused hands to learn to spin, Omphale attempts to instill in him an appreciation for small processes that require patience and attention to detail ... like those of relationships. In this placement, the warrior is here to learn what it is to be one of two, part of an inseparable set, instead of being the lone questing wolf. Although fighting has its place in love, much more time needs to be spent carefully and considerately working things out, and this is a lesson that Mars takes hard. People with this placement may have trouble with approaching someone too directly, leaping into relationships too enthusiastically, being too pushy, trying to force their partners too roughly, and leaving too quickly when these methods don't work. Like Hercules learning to spin, they must teach themselves—or, more likely, be humbly taught by a partner with more experience in relationships—to value the graceful dance of back-and-forth, and not always try to lead.

The alternative expression of a seventh-house Mars is to indulge in that classic seventh-house pattern: projection. If we have difficulty managing a seventh-house planet or sign, one of the most popular tricks we play is to project it onto someone else, usually our partner. We may even seek out partners on the basis of how well they fit those traits that we've buried in ourselves. We then ask them to live those traits out for us, and become disappointed if they don't do it as well as we secretly think that we could do it, if we weren't busy projecting. That's part of why we are so attracted to people whose outside demeanors reflect our descendant, and the planets around it. It's not uncommon for a seventh-house Mars individual to be strongly drawn to aggressive, heroic types, either projecting a "protect-me" demeanor, or sometimes a Red Sonya-like "I'll only submit to someone who can defeat me ... please, send me someone now!" This pattern recalls Omphale's commandeering of Hercules' lionskin and club. By doing so, she assumes his Mars energy, with the implicit assumption that she will be the one to carry it for him until further notice.

Omphale also takes Hercules as her lover in order to teach him the Venusian arts of love and make him more skilled and considerate. The seventh-house Mars individual may have strong drives in this area, but they only really bloom when they are solidly in a committed partnership. At this point, however, they may find that enthusiasm is not enough, and they need to actually learn how to be a good lover to the person who has become their anchor. During one tryst in a dark cave, with both of them dressed in the other's clothing (part of learning to be a good lover is to understand what your partner feels and desires), the lustful goat-god Pan (Pluto in Aries) snuck in and tried to get in on the fun, assuming in the dark that the chiton-clad Hercules was a woman. The hero runs off the startled Pan, but in the process he learns an important lesson about women and rape, and what it is to truly live the life of a more vulnerable person. This is the lifelong lesson of the seventh-house individual, because no matter what they accomplish, they will always be vulnerable to their partner's commentary.

Finally, at the end of the story, Omphale decides that he has learned enough, and sets him loose on some of her enemies, as one would let a hound off a leash and run him at prey. He acquits himself wonderfully but does not run amuck as he has before, showing that he has learned restraint from his time at her feet. She judges him improved, and frees him from slavery. It is at this point, when he proves that he can combine the forces of Mars and Venus, that he is whole enough to truly become a hero in more than one sense of the word.

♂ Mars in the 8th House: Neith

Most warrior deities are male, but I've tried hard to provide a good complement of female warrior-goddesses as well. Mars, as an energy, is neither male nor female. What it is, is aggressive, and women have been discouraged from being aggressive for a long time, the better for them to be preyed upon. However, there are quite a few magnificent warrior-women in myth, enough to hearten all the aggressive women out there. In Egyptian mythology, one of these is Neith, a very old Egyptian goddess who dates back to the predynastic era. Her name means "terrifying one", and she was a warrior, a hunter, and a psychopomp of the Dead.

Her symbol was two arrows crossed over either a shield or a pair of bows, and it is found on some of the most ancient pieces in Egypt. She was pictured as a fierce-looking woman with the Red Crown of Lower Egypt on her head, showing that she was a tutelary deity of that region (specifically the city of Sais) before the two parts of Kemet were united. Neith made and blessed the weapons of warriors, but beyond anything else, she was the one who led their dead souls off of the battlefield and brought them to the afterlife.

There were four goddesses who performed this psychopomp duty for the people of Egypt, and they are often shown together as a quartet—Isis (Moon in Libra) who took the souls of the royalty and nobility; Nephthys (Pluto in the sixth house) who took the souls of the common man; Selket (Sun in the eighth house) whose job included beggars, criminals, and the lowest classes; and Neith who specialized in warriors. They prayed to her before going into battle to keep them whole, to guard their bodies on the battlefield until loved ones could take them away. If they died, hers would be the arms who gathered them in, and her face the first vision they would see once the body had fallen away from their souls.

Mars is our call to action, our inner warrior who protects, defends, and generally *does*. It is where we keep our motivation, and in this house, part of what motivates Mars is finding out what happens underneath comfortable and placid exteriors. Mars, however, is not a patient planet, and is more likely to rip the veil off than carefully attempt to sneak behind it. Death is the ultimate mystery, and Mars here wants to know all about it, even rushing in if that's what it will take. This placement bestows a certain amount of fearlessness; Mars leans more towards anger than fear, and this placement may actually be offended by the fact that some mysteries are beyond human understanding, and apply themselves with passion and grim determination to prove otherwise.

Neith's one foray into being a mother-figure—she was not in general a terribly maternal goddess—are pictures of her literally nursing a baby crocodile at her breast, and one of her titles was "Nurse of Crocodiles", as she supposedly cared for the crocodile god Sobek when he was an infant. Sometimes Sobek is identified as her son, although no deity really stuck with her as a consort. The Egyptians tried to pair her up with various male Gods, once they passed into their religious phase which demanded that all deities come in pairs or mother/father/child trios, but none really stayed with her and Neith remained stubbornly single. This does not mean that individuals with this house placement cannot maintain good relationships, but it does echo one point which cannot be denied. The eighth is the house of sex as well as death and mystery, and having the warrior's planet here does mean that when it comes to the intimate arts, these people do like to be in charge. This may or may not spread to the rest of the relationship as well, but it is quite likely to do so. Neith was fiercely independent—a woman who can nurse a crocodile is not faint-hearted—and while she may have dallied with other Gods, none had any hold on her.

In other creation myths, she was said to have been the mother and single parent (because she was so old that she supposedly predated reproduction) of both Ra the original sun god (Sun in Aries) and his mortal enemy Apep, the poisonous underworld serpent who attempted every night to devour the Sun as he passed from west to east again. Passionate Mars in Pluto's house can create black-and-white thinking, an all-or-nothing attitude where loved ones may flash back and forth from compatriot to enemy depending on what's going on in the Mars person's head. They have both the high-flying, fiery Sun and the serpent of the dark waters in them sometimes constantly fighting for their attention. They understand what it is to battle the honorable and the destructive within oneself, and once they have gotten control over the surging waves of that inner battle, they can be remarkably patient and tolerant of people who are fighting their own internal battles against their inner Apep who wants to kill all the light.

This echoes Neith's work as a psychopomp, leading dead, bewildered soldiers to a better place where they can find peace. One of Neith's titles is "Opener of the Way", which resonates with her psychopomp status. One can imagine that Neith had the care of a large number of people with PTSD, which comes with a great deal of anger. Neith understands rage, especially rage which comes from fighting over and over again until one is battered and scarred. This kind of work can also be both a natural fit and a balm to this Mars placement—guiding brave but beaten souls to a place of better peace, unaffected by their anger at all and sundry. This only works, however, when the Mars person has made their own journey to that place in the soul. Neith was asked to be the judge between the dueling claims of Horus (Mercury in Aries) and Set (Pluto in the eighth house), and she chose for Horus. She may have had respect for Set's troubles, but he needed to get his own anger under control before she would have placed him in a position of power.

This is a Mars placement which likes to live on the edge—again, the holding of crocodiles to one's breast—and there is a certain amount of adrenaline-seeking and little tolerance of a quiet, peaceful life. If these Mars people can't find somewhere to do battle, they will make one, perhaps frittering their great passion and energy away on arguments, especially with loved ones. They need a cause, preferably something close to life-or-death, on which to batten and dig in. They crave the challenge, the crocodile to hold and tame.

As one of the oldest deities, Neith is associated with the primordial waters and the primordial sky—the watery sea which still existed in Egyptian mythology even after millennia in the desert, from which dry land emerged, and the sky before there was day or night, Sun or Moon. She was the guardian of the sky which could not be seen because it was below the level of the horizon, gone into the underworld. On a literal level, this Mars placement may be fascinated with how things worked in prehistoric, or even pre-human or pre-Earth-as-we-know-it times. Time is just another veil they want to rip off, and see what came before it, to know what Neith knows.

A separate bane of this Mars placement is that other axis of this house ... other people's money. On some level, they have a warrior's plundering attitude toward it; the gold of others is seen as the rightful reward of the conquering army. This can lead to rash investments, callous cash extraction by any means necessary, or even in worst cases the justification of outright theft. Getting money from someone else's pocket to their own can be seen as a battle, with the fairness of the victory irrelevant to the gain. All Mars placements do better with some kind of code of honor, but the eighth house is rarely a place either of empathy or logic. Instead, the best honor code for this Mars is that of understanding the larger cycle. *What you do comes back to you, eventually, perhaps not in the exact way you doled it out, but in the way which will make an equal impact on you.* Understanding this karmic reality can make sense to them, and force them to open their minds to the future and how their actions will affect the bigger picture. This mental exercise will generally head off the more egregious mistakes with regard to monetary acquisition, and probably make a difference to the other areas of their lives as well, especially that of partnerships.

Which brings us back around to the sexual side of this house. Mars here craves deep intimacy, but doesn't always know how to get there. Mars's first line of defense is to plow through all erected walls and boundaries to plunder that intimacy, that knowledge, from the hapless object of their desire. That approach has worked on occasion, but it is far more likely to fail than be successful, especially with a guarded or sensitive person. Human hearts are not booty to be won, and this Mars may find themselves rejected, setting off another cycle of anger and retaliation.

Again, Neith holds out the crocodile, and explains the nature of true strength. *If you are really the stronger person, you will be able to show yourself openly first and not need to hide behind your own walls. If you are really the stronger person, you will be able to heal quicker from any rejection which might happen, and not be permanently harmed by it. If you are really the stronger person, you can lead through example. And if you are not truly the stronger person, you have no right to demand what should be earned. Hold the crocodile to your heart,* she says, not promising that it will not hurt, but showing the warrior that this is a test of real strength, the hardest one of all. And, because she is the eldest of warriors, she knows what that looks like.

♂ Mars in the 9th House: Scathach

The ninth house is the place of higher education, where we as adults keep learning and growing and expanding ourselves. With Mars, the urge is often aimed at skills rather than knowledge, and especially skills which are physical in nature and can eat up a lot of energy. Mars likes to move, to *do* something; this planet will not be happy sitting at a desk all the time. When Mars teaches, it's with a lot of enthusiasm, and sometimes leaping from subject to subject. Mars wants to make sure that students are going to be able to handle the big mean world out there, even if those students are in their sixties. On top of this … there's a reason why they call them *martial* arts. When Mars teaches, even gentler arts and sciences come out with an eye to how they can be used to protect and defend.

In the Ulster cycle of Irish mythology, Scathach (or Sgathaich) is the Teacher of Warriors. She appears in myth when the hero Cuchulain (Mars in Scorpio) decides that he needs more than just magical strength and berserk rage to be his best in battle. He seeks out Scathath at her stronghold on the Scottish Isle of Skye, where she lives in a high fortress at what is now Dun Scaith. (The ruins of Dun Sgathaich on Skye are said to stand on the place where Scathach had her castle.)

Scathach's name means "shadowy one", and she was said to be the daughter of Ard-Greimne of Lethra, as was her sister and rival Aoife. To get to her fortress, first one has to cross the Plain of Ill-Luck and the Glen of Peril. Then one has to cross the "Bridge of Leaping"; as one sets foot on it, the end swings up and flings them back where they came from. Few would-be students even make it across. At this impregnable castle, she trained heroes in the arts of (among other things) pole vaulting in order to assault forts, underwater fighting, and combat with a barbed harpoon of her own invention, the *gáe bolg*. Cuchulain manages to get to her castle by doing his famous "salmon leap", but even then Scathach is not terribly impressed by him at first. He threatens her with his sword, and she laughs and decides that he is worth teaching.

In many ways, Mars in this house *likes* a challenge when it comes to learning. If they do go to college or engage in some structured course of study, they may project their Mars onto some teacher whom they dislike, or whom they feel does not respect them enough. At the same time, a teacher who manages to project both belief in their ability to succeed, but also a straightforward challenge that their worth will be tested by not making it too easy, will do wonders for them. Scathach and her obstacle-course castle, and her clear assumption that just because one has a sword doesn't mean one is worthy of teaching, exemplifies this.

The ninth-house Mars lights up at the idea of a difficult quest for knowledge, especially forbidden knowledge that they are told they can't have, or the development of skills they are told they probably won't be able to master. One of the best ways to get Mars to do something is to tell them they likely can't manage it, "I'll show you!" is an excellent motivation for them. It is not known how Scathach herself learned her trade as a martial artist, but it was unlikely to be an easy road, and she is not interested in making it easy for her students. This, too, is reflected in this Mars when they (frequently) become teachers of their hard-won skills; they can challenge their students as hard as they themselves were challenged, and one of the difficulties with this placement is having a certain amount of contempt for, or at least dismissing, anyone who fails the course. *Let the prize be for those who merit it*, they would say. Unfortunately, this can leave behind those with physical or mental aptitude, but whose spirits are somewhat more sensitive and less competitive.

This is the house of one's world view, and Mars here indicates a strong willingness to defend one's own world view against that of the outer society, with fire and steel if necessary. Scathach is no demure maiden nor nurturing mother. She is a female warrior who has not only defied Iron Age Irish ideas of what a woman should be, she is sexually active with whomever she chooses. She has borne children—sons Cet and Cuar who were trained within a magic yew tree, daughters Lasair, Ingean Bhuidhe, and Latiaran—but her most notable child is her daughter Uathach who guards her castle and aids her in teaching young warriors. Like her mother, Uathach is a free woman who gives her love where she will; Scathach has passed her world view on to her children. Uathach later starts an affair with Cuchulain, even though she already has another lover; this ends in fighting and murder, but Uathach seems to come out on top anyway. For this placement, sex can be really more of a contact sport than a way to express intimacy, and as they love a good debate, the "fight-and-make-up" pattern can be exciting to them, especially before they have matured.

The world view of the ninth house Mars includes being willing to take risks exploring one's lusts and passions, because Mars is the planet of sex. I know at least two sex researchers with this placement, and they hunt down tales of sexuality with the same enthusiasm with which they pursue other pieces of information. There is reference to Scathach sexually initiating the young warriors as well, and she takes Cuchulain into her bed at the end of his training, as a reward. Before he graduates, however, he takes on Scathach's sister Aoife as part of his training, defeats her in battle, and forces her to make peace.

Scathach is also a diviner and mistress of the art of palmistry, or *imbas forosnai*—she eventually reads Cuchulain's future for him and predicts dark battles, telling him that he probably won't live past thirty. The ninth is the house of religion, and Mars's reaction to it is similar to their reaction to learning. Sometimes this placement of Mars creates a fanatic, someone who will justify violence for religious reasons or purposes. Sometimes it inspires someone to be "angry at God", shaking a fist at the Universe and asking why these challenges are thrown at them. They tend to fall into those two categories when it comes to religion—the fierce defender and the fierce rejecter. It's a rare individual with this placement who can peacefully coexist with vague spirituality, and much of that is because religion suggests that there is something larger and more powerful than you, against which you cannot battle and win. (You can, however, battle *people*, including the people who promote and represent what you dislike.) Scathach's dire warning to Cuchulain—which doesn't seem to deter him from his chosen path in the least—shows the scariest side of spirituality for Mars. Even for those who become religious scholars, there's a sense of wanting to "tame" the frighteningly powerful side of interaction with the divine, reducing it to provable equations on a page ... which, of course, never works for long.

This is the house of mind-expansion, whether through philosophy or travel or the methods already mentioned. When it comes to travel, this Mars placement plans it like a battle maneuver, and executes it the same way; they would rather climb a mountain than sit around enjoying the cuisine and culture. Philosophies will only be tolerated if they line up with this Mars's ideas about how things should go, especially if they provide justification for any social rebellion the Mars person may already happen to be doing (and also justify fighting for that philosophy). This placement of Mars can become rather self-righteous; they really need a cause to fight for, and will find specious ones if they can't manage to hang their values on a more noble one.

This is also the house of adventure, and these individuals aren't interested in a peaceful, contented life. Everything should be an adventure, from relationships to career to hobbies. With the ninth house, everything in one's life can get wrapped up in the world view, and thus the Mars nature can overrun everything unless there are other powerful forces in the chart. However, this Mars placement also has the ability, when they have matured, to laugh and shrug off the more intimidating things in life. *I've eaten scarier things than you for breakfast,* they seem to say. Like Scathach who wasn't the least intimidated by Cuchulain the berserker, but only saw the potential in him to become a greater warrior, this Mars placement can teach others a great deal about standing in your own power when pursuing the knowledge you desire.

10♂ Mars in the 10th House: Kartikeya

Warriors, in myth, may start out in boot camp or as brigands, but most burn out after years of fighting or are killed in the process of their military adventures. Only a few make it to the top as a general, and in the world of the divine (just as in the world of humanity) it helps to make it to the top as a career soldier if you have a very famous father.

In Hindu mythology, Kartikeya is the second son of the great god Shiva (Sun in Scorpio) and Parvati (Venus in Virgo), and the younger brother of Ganesha (Jupiter in Taurus). He is such a popular deity in the various regions of India that he has collected multiple names from the different areas— Skanda, Subrahmanya, Shanmukha, and Murugan. He is the patron deity of the Tamil people and their entire land, as well as their language, is sacred to him. He is either shown as a "normal" human with the ordinary number of heads and arms, or with six heads and twelve arms, each usually holding a weapon of some sort. Kartikeya has numerous different birth stories, including some where his pre-birth self traveled as fiery sparks to the Ganga river and became six boys, which Parvati seized and squeezed into one, thus explaining the greatest number of arms and heads of any deity in the pantheon.

Kartikeya is symbolized by two birds, the rooster and the peacock. Sometimes he is flanked by both; sometimes he has the rooster on a banner and is riding the peacock. The rooster is a warrior bird, the aggressive nature of Mars, and the peacock is showy and luxurious, a nod to the importance of eye-catching public image in the tenth house. His worship started as a heroic warrior and deified him as it gained traction, putting him into the Shaivite divine family. Passing into Chinese Buddhist mythology, his name changed and he went back to having only two arms, but he remained in the form of a powerful young general. In all his manifestations, he is not just a warrior but the supreme leader of warriors, the man at the top of the armies.

The tenth is not only the House of Career, but also rules authority over others, and one's public self and reputation. With the warrior planet here, it is incredibly important to the individual with this placement to be seen as an embodiment of Mars—strong, assertive, competent, action-oriented; someone who gets things done instead of merely sitting around talking about it. They may pride themselves on being the latter type of person, in comparison to those who are more process-oriented or goal-oriented. This placement is the most ambitious of any Mars, and will feel driven to make it to the top. It's not so much that they want the status (that would be Saturn's goal); it's that they want to be important enough that they can get things done without other people interfering.

While Kartikeya started out simply as the warrior-prince, over time he gained a side which was more of a thinker, and became the warrior-philosopher. This is not unusual for the tenth-house Mars; while at first the ambitious rise to the top eclipses everything else, once they are on top and stable, they begin to take time for less physical pursuits (especially if they are ones which are indicative of cultural status, as philosophy is in India). Some may remain staunchly plebeian even at the top, perhaps because they know their underlings can relate to them better if their working-roots remain. Those who didn't start out at the cultural bottom will usually embrace those indicators of high status ... but only if they don't make them look weak.

Mars here is conscious of who they had to be in order to get to the top, and they are not willing to compromise that too far. It could backfire when it comes to their public reputation. Actually, having to constantly consider their reputation is hard on Mars—they would rather be straightforward, and not have to worry about those subtleties. They are also less naturally skilled at minding their reputation than other planets, and may make overenthusiastic decisions. These can lead to them doing unnecessary and sometimes cruel things in the name of "protecting their honor".

By becoming more than a warrior—by reaching toward the light of being a philosopher-warrior—Kartikeya managed to avoid the tenth-house Mars trap of becoming someone who would defend their honor (meaning their reputation) with violence and cruelty. This, along with the callous trampling of people's rights on their way to the top, is the greatest danger of this Mars placement. Ambition is a seductive drug, and Mars can turbo-charge that. There is a reason why medieval kings encouraged their knights to learn the arts and culture of chivalry; it made them more than just armed thugs with land and money and importance. This placement of Mars needs to keep in mind that reputations founded on fear do not encourage honesty in followers, and generate the problem of surrounding oneself with lying sycophants. It also means that sooner or later, the peasants will take you down in such a way that they would not do for a more beloved leader.

Machiavelli is often misquoted as saying that it is better to be feared than loved. This is not the case; his actual words were that it is good to be loved by one's people and feared by one's military, the latter to prevent being removed by a coup. (This was Renaissance Italy, after all.) But if one had to pick only one of these, you had better choose being feared, or the throne would be taken away from you. Cultural paranoia aside, the tenth-house Mars can get caught up in so much drama with their co-workers and near subordinates and bosses that they forget about the great masses and how they see the whole situation. They need to keep a check on their short-sightedness and remember to look at the bigger picture on a regular basis.

If the fourth house is the parent who sets the tone for the home, and the tenth house is the parent who teaches the child about the outside world, then Mars in that second parent's house is indicative of a forceful, assertive parent who inculcated the child with values of hard work and success. As an adult, the child may have had to break away from the parent with a significant show of rebellion, or at least public acknowledgment of their new role. Ironically, although Kartikeya's father Shiva is an ascetic, he has immense willpower and does not respect slackers, which may resonate with the parental experience of many people with this placement.

In addition, they may feel as if they are somehow fated to make it to an important position in their community; they may be more surprised by their failure than by their success. In the story of Kamadeva (Venus in the eighth house), we learn that Kartikeya was literally preordained before his birth to be the slayer of troublesome asuras. His reputation as a great warrior existed literally before he was born, and people with this Mars placement may grow up believing that they, too, are born for a great purpose. Sometimes this can be unbearable pressure, but mostly it just drives them on with a confidence and surety which surprises others.

There is an amusing tale about a very young Kartikeya who is sent to Brahma for teachings, and asks him the meaning of Om. Brahma does not know, and sends the boy back to Shiva. Kartikeya asks the same question of his father and is told, again, that he does not know. Kartikeya informs his father that *he* knows, and if Shiva will lift him into the Guru's position—meaning placed higher than the person he is teaching—Kartikeya will tell him. Shiva lifts the boy up onto his shoulder and Kartikeya whispers the true meaning of Om into Shiva's ear, then proclaims himself the guru of his father. Given that this is a propagandistic story by Murugan worshipers who were trying to establish their favorite deity as wise and potent (Hindu sects have spent thousands of years writing stories whose prime message is basically "My patron deity is better than all the other Gods"), it does echo the parental contact of the tenth house, and give allusion to the fact that people with this placement often end up taking care of their elderly parents, or at least making the decisions for them, in a role reversal.

Kartikeya goes on to vanquish demons, challenge prideful sages, and throw around his sacred spear, the *Vel*. He never stops being a warrior and a leader of warriors, but over time his character ... well, I won't say "softened" so much as "brightened". Instead of solely a grim fighter who appeared on divine battlefields, he became someone who could walk with an ordinary person who was struggling with some personally important conundrum. He gained—or regained—the common touch, and that is what every tenth-house Mars must learn to do.

11♂ Mars in the 11th House: Gilgamesh and Enkidu

In *MythAstrology I*, I explored the (Venus in Leo) story of the Mesopotamian goddess Ishtar, and her involvement with the hero Gilgamesh. In this book we will take a closer look at the story of Gilgamesh himself, and his best friend Enkidu. It's a story of warriors, comrades in arms, and thus falls into the territory of Mars. However, instead of the lone warrior on his adventure (or the war-leader in charge of many underlings whom he must potentially sacrifice), it's a story of friendship overcoming adversarial barriers, and thus comes into the eleventh house of Friends.

The Epic of Gilgamesh is a series of long poems in different versions dating from 2100 to 950 B.C.E. Not all the pieces have survived—cuneiform clay tablets do wear away over time—but we have enough of it to understand that it is a paean to the bond of deep friendship. Gilgamesh is a warrior-king of the Sumerian city of Uruk, ascending to the throne by force of arms. He is something of a tyrant once high power is in his hands, and his people complain to the Gods about his abuse of them. Apparently the Gods become concerned about his ability to restrain himself and be a judicious king—rather than an impulsive warrior who might aggressively lead his city-state into ruin—and they decide that the best way to put a halt to this potential disaster is to create an adversary for him.

Enkidu, their creation, is the earliest literary figure of the "wild man", the antithesis of city-bred heroes who fight for the glory of their civilizations. His name may mean "Creation of Enki"—the Sumerian inventor god (Mars in Aquarius)—although some texts claim he was created by the goddess Aruru. Conversely, it may mean "Lord of the Good Place", referring to his life in the wild forests. It is interesting that even several thousand years ago, the wild was being thought of as an unscathed "good place" inhabited by protective spirits like Enkidu. He is sometimes shown as a hairy naked bearded man, and sometimes as a "bull-man" with the horns, ears, and legs of a bull.

Primitive and covered with hair, Enkidu follows the roving herds of wild sheep and deer. At one point, a hunter sees him destroying the traps laid for them, and complains to the local leaders, who report on the wild man to the city government. A sacred prostitute named Shamhat (literally "luscious") is sent out to Enkidu's watering hole, where she exposes herself to him and they have sex and conversations for two weeks. During this time, she uses her magic to civilize him, teaching him language and clothing and rudimentary civilized arts.

After this transformation, however, his animal friends run away from him—he has crossed a line and is no longer one of them. Instead, he learns to live with the local shepherds, who give him food and drink and companionship in exchange for protecting their domesticated herds from predators. Even though Enkidu is literally one of a kind, he is not a lone warrior. His heart longs to be part of a herd, whether that is of animals or humans, and this is the deep base of the eleventh house—*belonging*. When Mars comes into the house of the herd instinct, the individual often becomes a protector and guardian of their chosen people, who may see the Mars individual's courage and strength as an obligation to get between them and danger.

Shamhat, who dislikes King Gilgamesh, sees that Enkidu has great strength and encourages him to challenge and overthrow Uruk's ruler. The wild man goes to the city and attacks Gilgamesh on his way to see one of his women; the two fight brutally for hours, but finally declare a truce when both are exhausted. Gilgamesh appreciates Enkidu's strength and offers him friendship instead of being adversaries. When he brings the reluctant wild man back to the family palace, his mother Ninsun declares Enkidu the equal of Gilgamesh and adopts him into the family as another son.

Mars in the house of friends wants friendship, but the individual with this placement often has some trouble actually making and maintaining friendly relationships. Part of this is that Mars needs to see someone as worthy, and sometimes "worthy" means "able to hold their own in battle with me". The Mars person may initiate the friendship with combative words or actions, hoping that the potential friend will spar with them verbally or even physically. This validates their Martial way of being in the world, shows that they have this Mars streak in common, and proves to them that the potential friend is strong enough to hold their own and not just be run over by Mars's natural enthusiastic aggression. This approach, of course, doesn't work for everyone—some run away at the interpreted threat, some fight ineffectually and fail, and some fight well (and perhaps even win) but then refuse the friendship in anger at what they perceive as manipulation. It takes a special kind of person to come out of a mettle-measuring combat, shake hands with mutual respect, and become fast friends. It takes another warrior. What Mars wants in a friendship is someone strong and brave who will both value and inspire those qualities in them, as they do likewise.

Enkidu confides in Gilgamesh that he dislikes the city and misses the wilds, and is becoming depressed without them. His new friend suggests that they should go on a quest to the Cedar Forest, to slay the evil ogre Humbaba, whom Gilgamesh's subjects have been complaining about. With Enkidu by his side, the young king is certain that they will prevail. Enkidu warns that he has been to the Cedar Forest and seen Humbaba, and that the quest will be terribly dangerous, but Gilgamesh fearlessly decides to go. The people of Uruk are thrilled to get rid of their tyrannical king for a while, although his advisors are worried. His mother commands Enkidu to guard and protect her son, and the wild man agrees. The two comrades-in-arms set out, doing a dream-ritual at each mountain they cross on their journey. The dreams are all of Humbaba's destructive power, but they decide these are good omens anyway.

When they reach Humbaba's mountain, the ogre comes down to face them, and Gilgamesh is actually frightened for the first time on this adventure. Humbaba accuses Enkidu of betraying his relationship with the wilderness and the animals in order to be with his new friend. Furious, Enkidu encourages Gilgamesh to fight Humbaba, which he does, striking down the ogre with such power that the mountains shook. Humbaba pleaded for his life and Gilgamesh considered sparing him, but the still-angry Enkidu pointed out that Gilgamesh's reputation would be made by the ogre's death, and strikes Humbaba's head off.

When Mars makes an alliance, he takes it seriously—and when he changes to a new alliance, he wants to invest himself wholly in the new one. Sometimes this can lead to conflicts of interest, ambivalences which Mars doesn't like at all. Mars prefers a straightforward list of who is on what team, and can be resentful—or even panic a little—when ambiguities are pointed out. Enkidu's personal conflict about his shift from guardian of the wild animals to human-allied warrior nags at him internally, threatening his new friendship and joy in being adopted into Gilgamesh's family. He feels that he has to choose, and this too is a pitfall of the eleventh-house Mars. It's hard enough to find the right group which accepts you; having to choose between adversarial groups and feeling guilty about either choice is sheer hell for this placement. Facing down the evidence of his betrayal of his origins, Enkidu lashes out and silences the voice of reproach.

The two heroes return home in a procession of victory, having cut down many of Humbaba's cedar trees to be sold down the rivers, but a new challenge awaits them in the form of the goddess Ishtar. She has heard of Gilgamesh's prowess and offers him her hand in marriage ... but the hero refuses her. He has multiple reasons for this—he remembers that her last lover, Tammuz, did not have a good ending to his story, for one. Beyond that, though, the epic strongly suggests that Gilgamesh prefers the company of Enkidu to that of Ishtar. Some readings of this myths suggests that they are lovers, but regardless of whether they are ever sexually involved or simply loving comrades, their relationship is not in the Venusian-ruled territory of romance. It is entirely Martial in nature, and Mars does rule sexuality. However, the eleventh-house emphasis of this story gives a different lesson. Gilgamesh places friendship above romantic relationship. The comrade he knows will accept him exactly as he is and will follow him into danger is more valuable to him than the woman who wants romance and marriage.

This conflict is still relevant to modern people today. Does one owe more to the twenty-year friendship or the new love interest? Should one abandon tried-and-true connections because they take time away from the person one is dating? Who takes precedence, and whom should one listen to when one is in distress? Anyone might struggle with these questions, but for Mars in the house of friendship, the answer is clear. The one who shares their sexuality needs to be a friend first, and they need to accept Mars's loyalty to their existing friends and the group to whom they have sworn themselves. Romance will not triumph here simply by being romantic. They are only interested in relationships where both parties are loyal comrades-in-arms, and a love interest who can't walk that road isn't going to get far with them.

Ishtar is furious at the rejection and begs her divine father, Anu, to release the Bull of Heaven upon the population of Uruk in revenge. Anu does so and the Bull kills many people, but the two heroes come out and slay the creature. Enkidu is brave enough to grab the Bull by its very horns so that Gilgamesh can stab it. The Bull of Heaven is then cut up to provide a great feast for the people of the city, and Enkidu throws one of its severed legs at Ishtar to show his contempt for her vengeance.

At this point in the story, the Gods decide that Enkidu must die. Not only has he failed at the job he was created for—becoming Gilgamesh's adversary and throwing him down—he has allied with the young warrior-king and added to his strength. The friendship between the two was unexpected and stymied the plans of the Gods; therefore the wild man must die. Enkidu has a prophetic dream of the death goddess Ereshkigal (Pluto in Libra) telling him of this inevitability, and he informs Gilgamesh what will happen. Then he becomes ill and lies bedridden for twelve days until his death, mourning that he could not have died in brave battle. With his last breath, he asks Gilgamesh not to forget him. The young king stays with his corpse until it begins to rot.

In an earlier version of the story which has left us only a few fragments, the tale of Enkidu's death is different. In this case, Gilgamesh was given some magical items, and then a crack opened in the earth and they fell into the underworld. Enkidu offers to go down to the underworld to retrieve them, and Gilgamesh tells his friend everything he knows about how to survive on an underworld journey, including pretending to be a dead soul so as not to attract notice to one's self and be attacked. Once down in the underworld, Enkidu forgets these protocols and inadvertently reveals himself, and is killed for trespassing. His soul remains in the underworld, and Gilgamesh begs the Gods to be able to see his best friend once more. They allow Enkidu's soul to rise up and speak to Gilgamesh, although the words they speak together did not survive.

In the *Epic*, Gilgamesh goes into deep mourning for his best friend, crying out for the mountains, forests, fields, rivers, wild animals, and all of Uruk to weep for him as well. His words are a hymn to how much a good friend can mean to a passionate Mars warrior. His epic does continue after the death of his friend, with the king wandering the wilderness in a funk, dressed in animals skins—in a way, he has become Enkidu, honoring his best friend in the only way he still can.

His quest for power and glory becomes a quest to find the secrets of eternal life, as the death of friendship has shown him his mortality. The quest goes on for many stories, but ends with Gilgamesh returning to Uruk, older and wiser and understanding the nature of Life and Death. He is no longer the tyrant king, as Enkidu has changed Gilgamesh with his death. This is the legacy of a Mars friendship—to inspire each other not just to glory but to wisdom, in the end.

12♂ Mars in the 12th House: Hercules and Dejaneira

We last left Hercules back at the seventh house with his adventure with Omphale, learning how to have a balanced relationship. But while the seventh house is a difficult place for Mars, after he blows through the sexual eighth, the adventurous ninth, the ambitious tenth, and the friendly eleventh, he has to deal with the most difficult house of all, at least for the planet of action.

The twelfth house is a place of silence and meditation, of confinement, of being trapped or adapting to restricted circumstances. It's the worst possible place for Mars, because it is all about the state of being powerless, and how one copes with that. Hercules will be our Mars hero yet again, in the final phase of his mortal life on the earth. The twelfth house is also all about endings, and this is how the archetypal hero ends his life … and it is not pretty.

After amicably leaving Omphale in Carthage, Hercules wanders about the world doing random deeds and generally be a hero-assassin for hire. At some point he meets Dejaneira, supposedly a Calydonian princess or noble lady. (Various ancient writers claim different parentages for her.) Descriptions of her vary—some say that she was a warrior-princess who drove a chariot and practiced the art of war, some that she was a blushing maiden—but it seems like every myth about her involves rape, whether threatened or real. In one account, the horned and serpentine river-god Achelous wants to claim her against her will, and Hercules wanders by and challenges him to a duel in order to rescue the damsel in distress. Achelous turns into a bull in order to fight Hercules, but the hero defeats him, breaking off one of his horns and holding it for ransom. He wins Dejaneira's hand, and she is given over like a typical fairytale princess.

In yet another tale, Hercules meets her, fancies her, and rapes her himself. Then he goes off on an adventure, leaving her pregnant, but telling her that he will return eventually and marry her. As soon as he leaves, other suitors attempt to talk her father into giving her to them, including a strong suit from the centaur Eurytion. Her father agreed to give her to the centaur, but Hercules returned in time and killed Eurytion, claiming and marrying his pregnant rape victim. Leaving aside the rather dismal fate of women in patriarchal ancient Greece, Dejaneira seems to be as powerless as Hercules is powerful. She is the one who starts out embodying the victimized, trapped aspect of the twelfth house, but she will eventually pass it on to her husband.

We all know that Mars is action and decisiveness, but we forget that it is also sexuality, or more accurately, sexual aggressiveness. This doesn't have to be a bad thing—if no one ever takes initiative, people can wander around mooning over each other and no one will ever get anywhere. Someone, sooner or later, has got to speak up and say, "Hey, I like you, want to go dancing tonight?" While that has been a male prerogative in many cultures for many centuries, when the cultural chains are removed, the chasing is much more gender-equitable. In fact, most astrologers will tell you that someone's comfort with initiating the process that will eventually lead to people jumping into bed together has a lot more to do with the Mars sign and house placement of the individual than their gender. The twelfth-house Mars has it the absolute worst. With the "Hey, do you come here often?" urge locked in the basement, it may feel to them like they're standing behind thick plate glass, watching the game (and the potential targets) from a long distance away, unable to speak up.

Sexual assertiveness isn't the only thing locked in that basement, though. Mars is the power of action and decision, which makes the twelfth-house Mars person slow to do either, but it's also anger. Mars is intense—not as intense as Pluto, but definitely a close second in line. Anger has many flavors—bubbling resentment, smoldering hate, teeth-gritting frustration, slashing spite, righteous wrath, as well as the ever-feared roaring berserker rage. These can pile up in the same dark closet as action, decision, and sexuality, and spill all over each other in the close quarters. Sometimes this results in someone who stifles all of these together and lives a passive, despairing life, buffeted by the winds and the wills of others. Sometimes this results in someone who steals the image of the desired other and writes it into romantic tales with themselves as the co-star, or perhaps steals images by hovering in the bushes with a camera. Sometimes it builds up and explodes.

The twelfth house is the well of dreams and fantasies, and with Mars here, those fantasies are more likely to involve either heroism or revenge, and sometimes both. After years of soaking in those smoldering dreams, when the sexuality finally erupts, it can come out as a demon that wants to enact every repressed Mars emotion on the body or mind of the lover—or the one who rejected them. Lest we suggest that this is only the province of physical violation, let me remind everyone that emotional aggression can be just as horrific in its own way, especially if the Mars person has a longer period of time to inflict it. Sudden unexpected wounds to the heart and self-esteem can cut deep regardless of the gender combination, and can leave terrible scars.

That's why this myth is full of rapists—or, more appropriately, would-be rapists from whom the hero rescues the passive twelfth-house heroine. However, the tell-tale version where Hercules is himself the rapist still stands. It's the darkest side of Mars—aggressively taking what you want just because you can—and the twelfth house is the darkest place in the chart. In the fantasies of the twelfth-house individual, the various roles circle around and around, and they may rotate between them—passive object, evil attacker, rescuing hero who may just be another violator under the white helmet. The only way out of that maze is to acknowledge that each of these live within them. Each is a part of their Self, and the story is Self acting on Self. It's not fair to force outsiders into the story, especially while the twelfth-house person is still working it out internally (unless of course a "virtual" version of it is negotiated and the willing partner is definitely into the idea).

The final rape story involving Dejaneira has her traveling with her husband, many years and a few children later. The couple needs to cross the flooding river Euenos; Hercules decides to swim for it, but there is no way to get Dejaneira across. A wild centaur names Nessus offers to ferry her over on his back, and she agrees. However, as soon as she has mounted, he bounds off with her in the opposite direction. Hercules, in the middle of the raging river, curses and turns back to follow them. By the time he gets to the shore, Nessus—with the screaming Dejaneira—is far away. Hercules takes up his bow and the arrows he has dipped in the poisonous blood of the slain Hydra, and shoots the centaur just as he vanishes over a hill.

Nessus falls and lies dying. However, he decides with his last breath to get revenge on his killer. He tells Dejaneira that his blood is magical, and she should take his bloodstained shirt to get some of it. He claims that if Hercules ever strays from her, she should weave some of the blood into a shirt for him, and he will be hers again. Thinking that she should hedge her bets, Dejaneira takes the bloody shirt off the dead centaur and hides it, just as Hercules comes to rescue her.

Years later, Hercules's eye falls on another princess—Iole, a local princess whose father and brothers Hercules has just murdered on some flimsy pretext. He takes her as a war prize and brings her home to be his concubine, which upsets Dejaneira, but she does not dare to argue with him. Used to being passive, she cannot bring herself to confront him and demand decent treatment by her standards; perhaps she is well aware of his thinly veiled violence. Instead, she turns to sneakier means. This, too, is the track of the twelfth-house Mars, especially of the ones that repress their Mars nature. Mars is a big burning ball of fire and it's too hot to bury for long. Little fiery jabs sneak out when the opponent is least ready, in ways that can easily be excused as "nothing, never mind." It's long-term poison instead of the open thrust to the heart, a passive-aggressive slow destruction of trust and comfort.

In the myth, Dejaneira remembers the blood of Nessus that she has kept all this time, and she weaves it into a chiton for her husband. Some say that it was impregnated with the poison of the Hydra; others claim that it had a vengeful magic of its own, form the angry spirit of Nessus. At any rate, when Hercules puts on the chiton, his skin begins to burn off until his bones are showing through it. Howling in pain, he goes up a mountain and begins to rip up trees to build his funeral pyre. He knows that his artificially long life as a mortal son of Zeus is over, and suicide is the only option he can think of. However, none of his friends will light the pyre for him; they all fear to kill a divine hero. As he howls and begs, one finally stands forth and lights the pyre, burning him to death. Dejaneira feels so much guilt about what she has done that she also kills herself.

This version of the twelfth-house Mars is a painful scorched-earth story which doesn't have to end this way. If Dejaneira had been less passive, if Hercules had been less fantasy-brutal, perhaps it might have been different. The twelfth is known as the house of self-undoing, and any planet there is often busily employed in the ongoing job of self-sabotage, in lieu of more positive above-ground activities. While the first part of this myth has dealt with the mostly-imprisoned Mars that gets out in unhealthy ways, the story has ended with two dead bodies, the ultimate passivity.

This reflects the other common path of this placement, which is the oversensitive individual who manages to completely repress the entirety of their Martial nature. Since Mars is energy, this can result in physical lethargy and exhaustion; it uses up a lot of resources to keep your biggest energy source locked up. They lack confidence as well as assertiveness, and constantly talk themselves out of doing anything remotely risky. (Their standard for "risky" might be saying hello to the friendly neighbor or telling their partner that they're anything but happy today.) They are oversensitive and easily hurt—Mars is the shield as well as the sword—and find it difficult to protect or defend themselves. Everything looks like it's too much effort, and usually they just give up before they begin.

The way out, however, lies in remembering that while this may be the house that rules institutions such as prisons and hospitals (both physical and mental), it also rules monasteries and the willing sacrifices that create the peace in those holy places. The twelfth house is traditionally associated with mysterious and spiritual Neptune, and Neptune always demands a sacrificial offering. This is similar to Mars in Pisces, where Psyche had to walk down willingly to her potential death in the dark place of the Underworld. In a sense, this Mars must become a willing offering to the Universe and to the good of the world. Once this is done, the twelfth-house Mars individual may suddenly find a great flow of energy coming out, turning them into a spiritual warrior. Like a fairy tale, they will suddenly be clad in shining armor, so long as they actively pursue the quest to help people who are trapped or imprisoned in some way. This parallels the true ending of this myth, where Hercules is lifted up to Olympus after his death. Cleansed of his mortal madness, he becomes a divine hero who can be prayed to for aid.

It's not uncommon for people with this placement to end up in careers such as therapy or social work or activism, advocating for prisoners, the disabled, and the disadvantaged. Their sensitivity can focus on suffering souls other than their own, and slowly grow into Neptunian compassion. They find it much easier to fight for the rights of someone else, and it's a good place to start practicing for eventually fighting for themselves. In aiding and freeing these embodiments of their trapped Mars, they slowly loosen the locks on that basement door. It will never come easily for them, but a warrior constrained by compassion is much more of a worthy hero than a warrior imprisoned by their own fears. In the end, they must train themselves to be their own heroes, and rescue themselves in the end.

✷JUPITER✷

14 Jupiter in the 1st House: Perun

The planet Jupiter is named for the Roman version of the Indo-European thunder god who split into many similar deities and spread all over two continents. In the areas of the Slavic tribes, he became Perun, the thunder god whose rain made the crops grow. It is said that Perun is felt through the senses—in the crack of thunder, the rattle of stones, the bellow of a bull, the bleat of a buck goat, and the feel of an axe blade against the hand. Like the thunder, he is loud and rivets attention when he chooses to enter … and like the storm, he does know how to make an entrance. That quality is also found in those with the great planet Jupiter in the first house, right up front where everyone can see it. They come in with a drum roll and fanfare, and usually an entourage as well.

During the later stages of Slavic polytheism, Perun was the highest god of the pantheon, the ruler of the other Gods who took over from the original kingly deity Rod (Jupiter in the tenth house). Where Rod was dignified and fatherly, Perun was dashing and aggressive, and sometimes a little overbearing. Jupiter is the planet of royalty and nobility, and the first-house Jupiter placement often carries themselves like they are a king or queen, and Perun eventually wanted his nobility acknowledged enough that he was willing to take the chieftain's spot from Rod.

This is a way that Perun differed from Thor (Mercury in Taurus), another thunder deity who seems very similar in many ways, but who occupies a different space in his pantheon. Where Thor was the God who spoke for the common people, Perun is the God of the nobility, and the common folk are relegated to Veles (Pluto in the third house), his opposite number under the World Tree. He was also called upon by those close to the nobles—in other words, the soldiers and military—but the farmers were not his domain. Jupiter may protect the peasants and give them largesse, but his loyalty is to the "special" people, not the great run of the unwashed, unless they too prove themselves special. It's another way in which this placement can manifest as subtly or blatantly egotistical. It is important for them to remember that nobles can be taken down if there are enough angry peasants, no matter how strong or lucky they are, and a little humility is a good thing.

The great spreading oak is his tree, as it is the tree of all the other Indo-European thunder gods, because the first fire may well have come from lightning striking oak trees. Unlike other trees, oaks have very astringed wood and do not conduct electricity well, tending instead to blow apart into hundreds of flaming chunks which may have been the first fire our ancestors used and nurtured for warmth and cooking. Perun's name (which was Perkunas in Lithuania and some other Slavic tribes) comes from an Indo-European root word which meant both "oak tree" and "to strike". His bird is the high-flying eagle which looks down over all things, as the first-house Jupiter can look down on others from the height of their apparent confidence.

We say "apparent" confidence, because this placement has a wonderful talent for appearing poised and self-assured, charming and avuncular, jovial but not foolish. Underneath, they may actually be that confident or they may be faking it, but you'll never know until you have been close to them for quite some time. In reference to the eagle sailing overhead, one of the difficulties with this placement is egotism, with the first-house Jupiter feeling that they are superior to the ordinary person and thus don't have to take them seriously. They can look down on the "peasants" with that slightly patronizing smile and then move on, immediately dismissing what came out of their mouths. This can be maddening to other people, especially if they are also strongly drawn to the first-house Jupiter's warm charisma.

Jupiter is the planet of luck, and some have referred to it as having a perpetual four-leaf-clover; good things just seem to happen to them on the regular. Opportunities fall out of the sky as a reward for them just being themselves, out and proud and (usually) loud. The more they can be unafraid to put themselves out in public and express who they are, the luckier they will be. Perun lived at the top of the World Tree with the sky Gods, and every so often he would get into a fight with his underworld counterpart Veles, who would try to climb the tree in the form of a serpent and attack Perun, or steal things from him. Perun always managed to defeat Veles, and not because Veles was a weakling, but because Perun held the luck of the Gods and things just tended to go well for him. It's hard to fight someone who has Jupiter stacked against you.

This placement also likes to look good, and dresses to impress, or at least to show off. When Vladimir the Great took the throne of Kiev, he erected statues for all the Gods, but the biggest one was for Perun. It alone had a silver head and a golden moustache, the fanciest of all the idols. Similarly, the first-house Jupiter loves flash and glitter; their style can be sophisticated like royalty or glamorous like a rock star or just extroverted loud-and-bright, but they will stand out, and they're not afraid to stand out. Jupiter is the planet of expansion, however, and in the first house, as they get older they do tend to put on some weight. Jupiter's fondness for feasting, drinking, and general luxury doesn't help that tendency at all.

Perun is old enough that he was originally associated with stone weapons, and later with metal ones. His lightning bolts were thought to be stone arrows, and meteorites were said to be the evidence of these weapons falling to earth. Various Slavic countries refer to meteoric rock as "Perun's arrows" or "thunderbolt stones" or "God's finger". Perun's generosity was great, but so was his wrath; as well as his stone arrows, he had a number of magical "golden apples", which were weapons of mass destruction. He could take out large areas by throwing them at his target. These "golden apples" are thought to be ball lightning, as a couple of his carved symbols definitely represent that natural phenomenon. In some Slavic countries, "May Perun curse you!" is still a frightening pronouncement for many people. It takes Jupiter a long time to get angry—they are generally urbane enough to pass off most insults as peasant nonsense—but when their tolerance is exceeded, there will be an explosion and someone's head may come off, at least metaphorically.

The first-house Jupiter people are not just show-offs; they also have Jupiter's wandering minds and interests, often looking for deeper meanings in life. Some have an openly philosophical bent, while others are wanderers who rove the world, looking for new experiences. Some are enthusiastic and sporty, while others prefer scaling big projects, like climbing a mountain. It almost doesn't matter what it is, as long as it is big. Sometimes their big ideas overreach their practical ability to make them happen, and they may need to learn to scale back their plans, or break them down to smaller steps over a longer period. The planet of expansion wants to be free and break through restrictions, which can mean attempts at shortcuts and problems with the discipline needed for the long haul.

At the same time, if the first-house Jupiter gets into a leadership position, they may suddenly find themselves speaking for the people in power and their particular social attitude; remember that Perun was the God of the nobility? The first-house Jupiter is able to hold this ambiguity in their head—that they should have freedoms because they are right, but others should be forced to follow along behind them. The more privileged people with this placement may never get beyond that; those who have endured being thrown down by circumstances learn to be more fair and understanding of dissenting opinions. If they have a lot to lose by being thrust from the position of speaker for the elite, they may resist looking at this difficult truth.

One of the legends about Perun is that his wild huntress-daughter Devana rebelled against him, refusing to accept the female social role, and he hunted her down and subdued her, or at least forced her capitulation for a time. The first-house Jupiter has strong morals, which they may find important to embody with their public actions. Whether those morals are kind or coercive, rebellious or socially acceptable, examined or unexamined will not matter, only that Jupiter can make themselves into a poster child for these qualities. In addition, as the first-house Jupiter tends to attract an entourage, they may feel that they must represent not only their own philosophies, but also those who are orbiting them and pulled along by their gravity.

At their best, this Jupiter placement approaches the world with optimism, altruism, and faith, giving generously to others and spreading hope and good cheer. Even their thundering can be seen as the promise of good things to come—part of why Perun was so loved was that he brought the rain to the crops, thus ensuring fruitfulness and growth. It is a kind of largesse of the soul, which by simply being who one is, can rain positive thinking on all the peasants below.

24 Jupiter in the 2nd House: Hotei

Long ago, in the tenth century in China, it is said that there was a Buddhist monk named Qi-Chi who lived an exemplary life of service and generosity. We don't really know if he ever existed, or if he was invented to give a history to one of the most popular deities in all of Asia. If he did exist, like King Arthur (Mars in Libra) and other semi-historical and mostly-mythic figures, his tale has become so changed and embellished that he is now a deity … named Hotei. That's his Japanese name; in China he is Budai, in Korea he is Podae, in Vietnam Bo Dai.

His name literally means "cloth sack", because it was said that was his only possession besides his monk's robe. Now he is a god of luck and wealth and good fortune, with a huge sack on his shoulder from which he doles out gifts, especially on New Year's Day. Hotei is round and fat, in order to symbolize abundance, and often pats his great belly. Rubbing the belly of Hotei statues is considered good luck. Sometimes he is shown clean-shaven, sometimes with a full, curly beard.

Hotei also carries an *uchiwa*, a flat Chinese fan used by ancient chieftains to signal their authority, and used by other Gods and spirits to grant wishes. Sometimes he is sitting in an old two-wheeled cart pulled by children, whom he loves and protects. He is also sometimes depicted on the Takarabune, the sacred boat which transports the Seven Lucky Gods, of which he is the most lucky of all. On the first night of the New Year, children in Japan place a picture of the ship of the Seven Lucky Gods under their pillows, which is intended to bring a good dream of the New Year's happiness and beneficence.

When you read short, uncomplicated writings about having Jupiter in the second house, the first thing they say is "Wealth!" This is the planet of abundance, and it's supposed to bring lots of money into someone's life. Riches are supposed to pour out of the walls with little effort. Other people reading it are envious and decide that this must be the aspect of all the billionaires on shows about the rich and famous. The truth is a lot more complicated. Plenty of people with Jupiter in the second house are struggling financially, and it isn't because this house placement of Jupiter just doesn't bring wealth. For some people, it does—but not for all or even most. What's happening here? Isn't astrology supposed to work?

The second house is not only the House of Money—which includes possessions and other valuable resources—but the house of values as well. That includes self-value, and it's one of the reasons why, so often in our society, self-worth is tangled up with how much money you make or how many big, impressive resources you have. The fancy car, the big mansion, the valuable jewelry, all the physical objects that visibly say, "I have more to spend than anyone else, therefore I have value in this world."

It's probably not a surprise to you that this planetary placement is a deity with a big bag of gifts who is always passing them out generously. However, if you look closely at Hotei, you will notice that he is not a wealthy figure, in spite of that bag of goodies. He is a monk with a vow of poverty who owns nothing but his robe, his fan, and the sack. The only wealth he has, he gives away—Jupiter at its financial purest, so to speak. This isn't like Midas, the Sun figure of this house, a rich king surrounded by gold; this is someone who lives only to give.

This doesn't mean that everyone with this placement needs to take a vow of poverty and give away all their belongings. It's about Hotei's relationship with wealth: *It has no power over him.* When you pursue something avidly, when you lie awake worrying about it leaving your life, when your primary dreams are about having a lot of it, when it becomes the source of security and self-worth, it has great power over you. The more it preys on your mind, the more control it wields over your life. Even the most common negative manifestation of this Jupiter—overspending on luxuries—is a form of bowing to its power, because we assume that it is the first and foremost road to happiness. Hotei simply isn't under its spell.

There are a number of ways to get out from under the power of money which don't necessarily mandate a vow of poverty, but no road is that easy. The first step, however, is examining one's values. The way in which this placement *is* like the Sun living here is that the wealth won't come until the values are straightened out. The individual with this placement needs to look at how money (or the lack of it) affects their self-image, first and foremost. Then they need to ask themselves a lot of questions, and ponder each answer. What does being wealthy or being poor say about you? What standard are you using to decide whether you are rich or poor, and who made it? What physical objects have you been told your life will not be complete without? How does your wealth level affect the people with whom you feel comfortable hanging out? What do you expect from the act of being generous? Most importantly: Could you find happiness without caring about money?

In this house "enlightenment" is about the process of finding a way to remove the power that money has over your mind. Hotei was one of Buddhism's many "scattered saints", eccentric figures who likely originated as local deities and were appropriated by folk Buddhism. Budai, his Chinese version, was canonized in China during the sixteenth century, the last *bodhisattva* figure to be given that honor. The reason for this canonization was that the original monk uttered a prayer which supposedly proved that he was a living incarnation of the Maitreya Buddha. This is the Buddha of the future, who according to some Buddhist thought will be reborn and lead many people to salvation.

For those not familiar with the reincarnating Buddha beliefs, the idea is that once there was Gautama Siddartha who became the Buddha and started it all. Then after he died, various other versions of the Buddha were born and brought more wisdom to the world. The Maitreya Buddha is the future Buddha, yet to be born into the incarnation which will make a crucial difference in saving humanity. The monk who became Bodai, it is surmised, was like a sneak preview of the eventual appearance of the Maitreya Buddha. He isn't *the* Buddha, the original Gautama Siddartha, and many other "official" incarnations referred to as Buddhas aren't either. They don't need to be an incarnation of Siddartha himself to be an individual carrying the Buddha spirit. Bodai, in his particular incarnation, was referred to as the "Laughing Buddha". Wealth is one of the things he laughs at.

Ironically, Bodai/Hotei's popularity was so great, and so many prints and sculptures were made of him, that when European scholars and missionaries brought symbols of Japanese art back to the West, it was Hotei who ended up being the most common face of all of Buddhism. This led to many modern Westerners assuming that the fat, laughing figure was indeed the main face of Buddha himself, and the misunderstanding continues today. Asians understand the difference between Hotei and the Siddartha Buddha, but this is sometimes lost on those outside Asia.

On the other hand, Hotei has so much compassion for all beings that there is artwork showing him carrying demons across rivers to protect them. It is said that he could sleep outside in all weathers, because the power of his joy was so great that the rain would not touch him. In more recent times, because of his big belly and contented air, Hotei has become a kind of patron saint of restauranteurs and bartenders. His eccentricity symbolizes the idea that once you have achieved enlightenment, you no longer need to behave by standard social conventions. Is it telling that we use the term "eccentric" for people who give away more than they keep?

Jupiter in the second house wants people to learn the lesson that it's not about "giving till it hurts", it's about "learning to be someone who can give that much without being hurt". One of the lessons that is traditionally taken from the character of Hotei is that it is important to be kind to everyone, because you never know who might be a deity or saint in disguise.

Part of the Jupiterian luck of this placement is becoming the fountain from which good things flow to other people, embodying the energy of the community Jupiter whenever they can. It's their choice as to how much they give, but the more they give, the more flows back to them.

When money has no power over you—when you have freed yourself of the stories in your head about what vague or specific bad thing will happen if you are abandoned by money (and yes, look at that phrasing again)—it becomes much easier to make clean decisions about what you need and what you can do without. Prioritizing one's spending becomes much simpler. Luxuries are still alluring, but they are no longer the first fantasy of happiness. Most importantly, generosity becomes much easier, because you know what you can give, and you aren't telling stories to yourself about what you will get back for it. This does take great trust in the Universe to give you what you need, but Jupiter is all about faith and trust. With this placement, more than any other, it is possible for someone not to merely become wealthy, but to be someone for whom being wealthy is not of terrible importance, and in a lot of ways that's a better gift. With those concerns gone, it leaves a lot more room for laughter, which is Hotei's real gift to us all.

34 Jupiter in the 3rd House: Manannan mac Lir

In Irish mythology, the wizardly figure of Manannan mac Lir weaves his way in and out of other people's tales, occasionally wreaking havoc, but usually being a sort of magical faery godfather to those he drops in on. He is a mage, a trickster, a wordsmith, and a fountain of generous offerings, and this we bring forth to illustrate all-giving Jupiter when it passes through the third house of communication and short travels.

Manannan is the son of Lir, the god of the sea, and is often associated with the ocean; he has a magical self-navigating boat named "Wave-Sweeper" which he sometimes lends to mortals that he likes. His magical horse is named Aonbharr, which may mean "sea froth", and can run over the waves like a field. We don't know who his mother was, but one of his epithets is also "Son of the Soil", which indicates that his mother was an earth spirit or goddess. He is the son of both land and sea, and can move across both with ease. In one of the stories where he breezes in and regales the main character with his tales, he says that when he looks at the sea, he does not see an expanse of water, but a field of flowers across which he could easily ride.

However, while he flits about the islands and the Celtic lands, he does not make long journeys over water—the sign of the ninth house of long-distance travel. Instead, he just moves from place to place in one large area as he pleases, and here we see the aspect of the third house which is about making short trips ... which it seems is a constant state with Manannan. He is seen popping in and out, roving by, visiting and leaving, and interacting wisely and generously with many characters in other tales—but only for a short time. He never seems to settle down. In some tales it is said that when he wants to cross land in a hurry, he turns himself into a three-legged flaming wheel (like a spinning triskell) and rolls across the land. This Jupiter placement gives itchy feet, but not necessarily for long journeys. They just want to be out and about, seeing the neighborhood and looking for small adventures, and because they are lucky in that way, those adventures will come.

Mannanan is the ruler of one of the Irish Otherworlds, sometimes called the Plain of Delights or the Land of Promise—very Jupiterian titles. It is an island, not a "land under the earth", as is befitting for a deity who bridges earth and sea. The actual Isle of Man is named for him, and his three-legged triskell is on its flag.

This is the planet of luck in the house most traditionally associated with Mercury, and there is a trickster streak in this placement, as there is in the character of Manannan. Indeed, one of his bynames is Gilla Decair or "troublesome servant", a form where he changes shape a great deal and delivers his gifts with a good deal of trickery and fun. Similarly, the third-house Jupiter individual loves a good joke, although they are not malicious unless there's something else going on in the chart. It's all in good fun, and usually revealed with a flourish and a laugh. Jupiter adds excess anywhere it lives, and this placement can indicate a certain amount of hyperactivity, possibly even a neurological problem of inattention. All that dashing about, physically and mentally, can happen because it's impossible to stick to one road or thought for too long without becoming bored. Certainly Manannan has a little of this inattention—he's here today, but you might not see him again for a couple of years.

His real power, however, seems to be in abundance—literally. He owns magical swine who come back to life again after being killed and eaten, as well as a couple of cows which give inexhaustible milk, thus ensuring a permanent source of food from which he holds great feasts. Manannan is, above all else, a Gift-Giver, seeming to pull magical items out of his sleeves and give them out at random—musical silver apple-branches with golden apples, the magical Cup of Truth, a shield of sacred wood, magic javelins of scorched holly, and many pearls from his sea-father's realm. He magically repaired broken pitchers and cups of peasants whom he ran across in his daily travels, apparently on only a whim and a wish to help. His Jupiterian gifts on his many short trips are a way of spreading luck throughout his "neighborhood".

He owned a crane-bag made from the skin of a dead woman who had been turned into a crane, which was always filled with treasures. The treasures could only be seen when the bag was immersed in water during a high tide, and after he gave it away to a mortal king, it was much fought over by various rival warriors. He is also said to have pots of treasure buried in various places in wild woods, guarded by fierce serpents, as well as a barrel of gold lying at the bottom of a lake sacred to him. Supposedly mortals continually attempted to drain the lake, and the next morning the drain would have disappeared and the lake was untouched.

Manannan was later euhemerized as Orbsen, a famous merchant who studied the heavens and learned when the weather would be good or bad, and thus was able to travel only in good weather and become very wealthy. It is not surprising that the wealth of a Jupiter-figure in the house of short journeys would be hidden in many places; one of the gifts of this Jupiter placement is ingenuity, and it seems that they come up with all sorts of interesting resources, and ways of getting more resources. They are idea-people, and they are less interested in making money than in making ideas. Perhaps one in ten is actually followed; the others may drop behind them like scattered gold for others to pick up and use, and they won't mind.

Manannan has a number of children attributed to him, daughters and sons both, and even more foster children. He is often seen in the role of foster-father, rescuing the lost children of Deirdre and Naoise and raising them. He also helped to raise Lugh (Neptune in Leo), and when the time came to send him into battle, Manannan lent Lugh his horse as well as his magical sword, armor, and helmet. Jupiter often shows up as the "favorite uncle" archetype, equipping their proteges for a wide and varied life.

Other gifts of his are less physical, as Manannan can see the future, and goes about handing prophecies to people. Here we come to another gift of this Jupiter placement—the ability to look ahead and plan for the future, sometimes with inspired results. This isn't to say that everyone with a third-house Jupiter will have the gift of precognition or prophecy (although it does make those gifts more likely), but these are people who love to plan and are good at seeing the big picture and the long-term consequences. They have a talent for extrapolation, and can imagine multiple futures; Jupiter here gives them a strong intuition as to what is most likely. This means that others will often come to them for advice, which they are happy to pour out. They are inveterate students, and inveterate teachers as well, and can make a name for themselves doing either or both.

In one of his disguised byforms, he dresses as a servant and goes from manor house to manor house with a harp, playing and singing so sweetly that all the lords want to keep him for their own, but nothing can hold him in one place. He claimed to have a great reputation for reading and learning, and knows how to heal injured mortals with healing herbs. Any planet in the third house loves words and communication, and stores up knowledge like others store money. Jupiter doesn't hoard it, though; sometimes these individuals can pour it out to all and sundry at a ridiculous rate and have to asked to please stop talking for a moment. They are often very good at learning multiple languages—a nod to Jupiter's rulership of foreign countries and cultures.

They also adapt well to the different home cultures of people they visit on their little trips. Like Manannan, who can charm those to whom he speaks with his wit and wisdom, they are often very charming speakers. They usually have good social skills and can make others feel at ease, moving effortlessly through a crowd as if surfing the waters, and adapting to each person they speak to. This one gets a joke, that one a conversation on their personal interest, this one over here gets a piece of advice. Like Manannan handing out Cups of Truth and tankards of prophecy, each is a free gift scattered behind them, for the populace to fight over as they will.

In another tale, Manannan is said to have helped the besieged lady of a castle, holding the fortress single-handedly against an enemy entirely by illusory magic. He made the one man guarding the castle's battlements to look like a thousand soldiers, thus causing the enemy to retreat. In a similar tale, he drove off a group of raiding Viking ships by enchanting floating reeds to look like an entire fleet of warboats. He protected the last remnant of the Tuatha de Danann with a mist of invisibility. All these obscuratory talents point to one of the potential downfalls of the third-house Jupiter—the ability to weave a deceptive tale and mislead people. This can start off as simply a tendency to tell tall tales for the fun of it, and Jupiter's tendency toward exaggeration in all things, including narratives. Jupiter is basically well-meaning in any chart; they just get a little carried away with the stories when in this house. If you read Manannan's tales, they mostly seem to be rollicking, fast-paced adventure stories where he can do all sorts of strange feats, and this is all too often the archetype these individuals want to inhabit, at least where others can see them.

However, it can grow and shift into outright deception when the fast-talking Jupiter individual realizes that they can use this talent to get themselves out of trouble. At its worst, it can become a complicated web of lies used to hide their mistakes and weaknesses, although since this is an easily-distracted third house, they may eventually have trouble keeping all the lies straight and be caught out. (It's probably simpler just to tell the truth, and keep those entertaining tall tales on a leash.)

The only tales where Manannan loses are two later Irish stories where he goes up against Christian saints. These are obviously written to discredit a famed local deity, so we have to take them with a grain of salt, but there's still a bit of wisdom to be found anyway. One is simply Manannan going up against St. Patrick and being dispelled like a demon, but the other is more telling. Manannan mends a gold cup for St. Colum out of the kindness of his heart, and then asked him what sort of people go to hell. The dour saint answered, "People like you," and Manannan is offended. Since the Irish seem to be quite taken with Christianity, he says that he will no longer help them out until they are "weak as water", and then retired in a huff to his ocean home. This is also not uncommon for the Jupiter figure whose generosity has been devalued or rejected—well, then, I'll take my treasures, my wit and my wisdom, and go home, since I am unappreciated here.

Inevitably, though, they come back out and continue to share their knowledge, because sharing knowledge is how this placement earns luck.

Manannan continued to pop up and help people throughout the centuries, in spite of dour saints and the loss of Pagan religion, because he couldn't keep from doing it. More than anything else, this shows the power of Jupiter. A word—be it a kind word, a knowing word, a charming word, a funny word—can always be a gift, so long as words are yet spoken in the world.

44 Jupiter in the 4th House: Daikoku

Where Jupiter lies in the chart, there is always a gift. Even the weakest and most afflicted Jupiter has the ability to make some portion of life better, to ease the way through what could be a shark-infested channel. In the fourth house of home, family, heritage, and familial patterns, Jupiter bestows an interesting and more-comfortable-than-usual experience with all those things. While food in the sense of nutrition belongs to the sixth house of health, the "hearth" of the fourth house includes the actual cooking (especially shared food for families and friends), the table around which the family sits to eat, and the kitchens which, for thousands of years, have meant comfort and nourishment of heart as well as body.

I originally figured that this placement would be vied for by any number of large-bosomed mother goddesses, but the one who stood forward was Daikoku (or Daikokuten), one of the Seven Lucky Gods of Japan. We already saw a few chapters previous how a Lucky God could easily turn out to be a Jupiter figure, but it still took me aback until I learned more about this God who I had primarily known for his friendship with rats. Daikoku is a deity who has evolved and syncretized over many, many generations and multiple countries, until he bears little resemblance to his original forms. When Buddhism came to Japan, it carried a number of Hindu Gods with it who had already been through a fair amount of syncretizing with native Chinese spirits, including name changes due to verbal garbling and being moved from one phonetic alphabet to another. The god Mahakala, originally a wrathful form of Shiva (Sun in Scorpio), was considered to be a deity of darkness and fire—the "great black god of the graveyard", as he was known in India. He was dark because of the smoke of the cremation fires, but when he was incorporated into folk Buddhism first in India and then in China, the Buddhist monks started to put his dark, stern figure into the kitchens. After all, kitchens were full of smoke and fire, and it made it easier to lay out numerous food offerings before him.

In China, he was somehow syncretized with a local fertility deity who granted wealth, and whose festivals involved erect phalluses to bless those who prayed for help creating children. Here, Mahakala was no longer a form of Shiva, but just one of his servants. The combination of kitchens and wealth meant that the Buddhist monks began to pray to Mahakala to provide enough food for everyone to be well-fed, and this practice spread to the countrysides. He became less-wrathful-looking and more benevolent, and carried a golden bag of grain. Oil from the kitchen was wiped onto the faces of his statues to keep them looking dark, but now it was associated with kitchen smoke and the fertility of dark earth which grew more food. When he passed into Japan with the coming of Buddhism, he was further syncretized with Okuninushi (Saturn in the tenth house), a local deity of, among other things, agriculture and career status. He was also softened further and made into the Daikoku we know today—a broad, low-slung, plump, dark-skinned jovial man who is the God prayed to for abundance of food. His name is still the Japanese translation of "great black God", but the connotation has entirely changed.

Before we start talking more about kitchens and food, I would like to point out that this is the house of ancestry, and for many people that is a difficult and sensitive subject. When we study our ancestry, many of us note that the people of the past from whom we descend may have been either victims or oppressors, both of which can make us feel pretty uncomfortable. In addition, as this is the house which lays out the cultural and behavioral patterns that have been passed down to us through family lines, we can be shown a lot of dark, twisted, malfunctioning templates which have been forced on us. The placement of Jupiter in this house can, in some cases, indicate wealthy and important ancestors who did perhaps leave a comfortable legacy, but it can also bestow the ability to reclaim one's life and family from those old, dark patterns and build a new hearth with warmth where every person is valued. The story of how Gods evolve in the hands of humans also shows us something about their nature, and the "great dark God of the graveyard" becoming the jovial chef in the kitchen of abundance is an evolution of kindness and compassion, a story of hope coming into the domestic arena. Daikoku is went from being covered in the ashes of the dead to making that taboo substance into the joy at the center of the family home; his smoke is the kitchen warmth and the oil of a thousand tasty stir-fries is on his face.

Daikoku is the Lord of the Five Japanese Grains—rice, millet, adzuki beans, soybeans, and sesame seeds, although rice was his specialty. We might not classify all of those as grains, but they were the staple food of Japan for centuries, and thus within Daikoku's power to use to fill bellies. The mice and rats which hang around him are also symbols of abundance and generosity, because true abundance exists where there is so much food that it can be shared with vermin and still not drain the storeroom. However, childhood is not just a time of physical nourishment—your parents ideally do more than just feed you. It also involves emotional nourishment; the sense that there is enough love and affection and belonging to go around, that the ground under your feet is stable and dependable, and that you will get at least some of what you ask for when you need it. Jupiter here bestows that feeling of *enough* in childhood, so that people with this placement can bring that forward with them into the family they will eventually create.

In some cases, this Jupiter placement indicates people who do not necessarily start out to immediately form a family; they may travel a while and stay at many hearths, but are generally always welcome. Jupiter is associated with the sign of Sagittarius the far-traveler, and an afflicted Jupiter here may want to sow some wild oats for a while, before settling down with the more domestic grains. Usually when that happens, the child was sensitive enough to figure out that the solid, stable home where children could grow and flourish was paid for by parents who may have succeeded at the parental job, but sacrificed the ability to travel and see the world in order to make that happen. However, Daikoku is also a wanderer, like all the Lucky Gods; he ambles from kitchen to kitchen, dropping off bags of food and relighting cold hearths which have gone out. People with this placement of Jupiter, even before they settle down, can also find themselves working with food or child care or other domestic professions, literally spreading generosity to the cold hearths of others.

A discontented fourth-house Jupiter can also move frequently from place to place because the golden ideal of that happy childhood home just isn't available anywhere else. (The key, of course, being that one has to build it oneself.) One such individual I met lived in many different countries and cultures (Jupiter is linked to the ninth house, which is fond of foreign cultures), always renting but never buying a home, until her parents became too elderly to live alone and offered her the family home and land if she would come take care of them in their final years. It occurred to her that this was Jupiter giving her exactly what she'd longed for, fairly literally ... but that she had to pay for it in generosity. Similarly, with this Jupiter placement, if you are having trouble affording food, feed other people. That state of generosity, of trust, of "there will be enough for all" is what triggers Jupiterian changes in your life.

Besides the rice bags and the rats, Daikoku's other signifier is his magical golden mallet, with which he taps out wishes and wealth. The legend of the magical golden mallet drifts from spirit to spirit in Japanese myths, finally wending its way down to the rice god's meaty fist. The mallet may be magical, but it is still a tool, made for work. No luck or opportunity or Jupiterian change is going to work for someone if they don't reach out and take it, and then nurture it once they have it. The biggest problem with this otherwise lucky placement is that they may be too happy-go-lucky, assuming that all their needs will be taken care of, a child of privilege who is blind to others' lack. This may lead to a sort of Jupiterian selfishness where the individual is spontaneously generous to those in their adult home and family, but ignores reciprocity and does not bother to go out of the way for their more inconvenient needs. As with all things about luck, Jupiter here wants you to give at least as much as you get, or the luck begins to dribble off and the home life (in this case) becomes less emotionally nourishing and more emotionally spartan. This can simply inspire the less mature Jupiter person to get back on their wagon and abandon the situation, but the truth is that they actually abandoned it some time ago, and the dramatic leave-taking is just the end result of an inability to commit to being the giver. The likelihood is that the next home will see a reprise of the same situation, until they grow up enough to be Jupiter's hands and not just Jupiter's gaping mouth.

The cult of the Seven Lucky Gods, once it was begun, quickly gave rise to a practice called wealth-stealing, where people would steal the statues of the Lucky Gods, especially out of the homes of wealthy people, and thus magically steal their luck. Makers of statues tacitly encouraged this practice, in order to sell more statues and drive up the prices. Daikoku's statues were some of the most hotly fought over, because everyone wanted enough food and a happy home. Another form of "wealth-stealing" was throwing a stone with Daikoku's name on it into the kitchen of a rich home (usually through the window) at midnight, the hour of the Rat. Why people thought that the Lucky Gods would reward this is hard to know, but it was probably desperation. In reality, it is Jupiterian behavior which knocks over the karmic dominoes for Jupiterian return, something this placement would do well to remember. Take people in and feed them at your table, and those bags of rice will increase.

54 Jupiter in the 5th House: Uzume

Jupiter is often thought of as the planet of luck, or opportunity, or abundance, and it is all of those things. What it touches, it makes bigger. However, if one were to name the one deep spiritual quality that Jupiter carries above all things, it would be hope. From a Jupiterian perspective, every dawn is a new chance, a new possibility, a new potential healing of what has come before. Dawn is the most Jupiterian part of the day, really. You'd think it would be noon, because the Sun is so big then, but noon is the Sun's time. Dawn is the moment of the in-breath of hope, and of the moment when joy leaps up out of the ashes of the night. So when I asked about who would stand forth for the planet of hope when it occupies the fifth house of joy—traditionally ruled by the Sun—it was Uzume, the Japanese Shinto goddess of dawn.

Her full name is Ame-no-Uzume-no-Mikoto, and the etymology of that name is both disputed and interesting. *Ame* means *sky* or *heavenly*, as befits her position as a dawn goddess. *Uzume* might be a combination of words meaning *world-accept-sale*, or *ornamental-hairpin-woman*. The final part—*Mikoto*—is the same epithet many major Shinto *kami* bear, and it is an equivalent to *the great*. So she is a heavenly woman with jewels in her hair who is willing to offer herself to the whole world, just as the dawn does every morning. Other titles applied to her are "The Great Persuader", and "Heavenly Alarming Woman".

Most of her worshipers, however, simply call her Uzume. She is the goddess of laughter, and is said to be quite the comedian, echoing Jupiter as the planet of optimism and the fifth house as the center of play. It is the house of children, but also of childlike behavior—laughing together, playing games, generally having fun. Every house has multiple aspects and rulerships, and each planet there might manifest as affecting any of them, but there will generally be one aspect which each unique planetary energy is drawn to. Where a fifth-house Sun may be drawn more to the house's creative aspects, and a fifth-house Venus will go straight for the romance, and a fifth-house Moon might want to have a hundred children, Jupiter here lights up the inner child, the part that wants to laugh and play regardless of age. For Jupiter, this is the house of fun, but there's nothing shallow about it. This is the house of hope in the face of darkness, the knowledge that the sun will always rise again, and part of that armor is the willingness to find small joys anywhere you can possibly find them.

Uzume's main story is actually part of the mythos of the Japanese Sun Goddess, Amaterasu Omikami (Sun in Leo). When Amaterasu was insulted by her brother Susanoo the storm god (Uranus in Aries), she retreated to a dark cave and sulked there, fuming at Susanoo and refusing to come out. The world was plunged into darkness, and the other Gods were at a loss, milling about the cave's opening and calling futilely. Uzume, however, figured out what to do. First she overturned a tub that happened to be near the cave's entrance and got up onto it. Then she started to sing and dance ... and not just any dance but a striptease. And not just any striptease, but a comical, farcical one. Jupiter in this house is not Venus; the individual with this placement is more likely to be a playful comic than a seductive vamp, with more enthusiasm than finesse. However, Uzume knew well the power of laughter, and of dancing. In no time, she had the other Gods singing and dancing as well.

Uzume's performance was said to be the origin of the *Kagura*, the Japanese ritual dance itself, which was done to communicate an intention to the Gods, just as Uzume started dancing to communicate a message to Amaterasu, one that would pass through stone walls and get the angry Sun Goddess's attention whether she wanted it or not. The *Kagura* was used to lure and draw the Gods down, thus invoking them. (Other traditions claim that the first mortal *Kagura* was danced by a Shinto shamaness who was inspired by Uzume.) Drama may not meet the mark, seduction may fall short, but Jupiter knows that humor appeals to the child in all of us, even when we resist it.

Having pricked up Amaterasu's ears, Uzume fetched a bronze mirror and a jewel of beautiful jade, and hung them on a tree visible from the cave mouth. Then she started a long comic song about how it didn't matter that Amaterasu had vanished, because they now had an even more beautiful goddess to look at in the sky. Hearing this, the (slightly vain) Sun Goddess immediately came out to see who on earth was more beautiful than herself. The first image she saw was her own bright reflection in the mirror, which stopped her for a moment, and the Gods quickly ran behind her and stretched ropes across the cave entrance. Laughing, she saw Uzume's joke and relented, and from then on the bawdy little goddess was the keeper of the Dawn, bringing the Sun out of its darkness every day. With her laughter and cleverness, she had restored light to the Universe.

It's not that a mortal with the fifth-house Jupiter placement can't become sad or depressed, but they have a much harder time maintaining it than other placements. No matter how bad things get, they have an irrepressible optimism ready to leap out, which it will do as soon as they get distracted enough from the sorrow in front of them. With the planet of luck in the house of gambling, they are also much more willing to take risks, including with their heart … because they know that they carry an intrinsic resilience which will help them to bounce back even if the worst happens. It's not just that they don't allow themselves to look at the possible risks, or believe that they are invulnerable (like other placements); it's that they have an actual deep faith in themselves to be able to survive and make it through the worst. This recalls Uzume's title of Heavenly Alarming Woman, for her willingness to take risks to bring light into the world, not caring a whit about social propriety and decorum.

The fifth is the house of romance, of course (speaking of risking one's self), and Uzume was known as the sort of woman who flirts with many in a sort of open, easygoing way. She was said to have many lovers, and indeed that her favorite way to greet a handsome man was to open her dress and show off her breasts. This was actually another dawn-metaphor—the sunlight peeking out and flirting with human eyes—but it also reflected her generous nature. In modest Japan during some eras, Uzume's behavior was considered rather shocking, and there were intimations that she was a prostitute, although she seems less like the calculating woman who sells it and more like the easy woman who generously gives it away for pleasure. She is the Goddess of Revelry, and this too is an activity loved by the fifth-house Jupiter.

Of course, if there is a drawback to this placement, it is throwing one's self too deeply into the pursuit of joy. Jupiter's dark side is overdoing things, and even this blessed combination can go too far. Risks can turn out to be foolish and destructive, childlike fun can become childish jokes that inadvertently hurt people, humor can be a way of ignoring emotions, too much generosity in the wrong places can lead to being taken advantage of, and chasing the romantic high can lead to refusing commitment and hurting partners who may have certain expectations of love. Fifth-house Jupiters can be notorious for running from one love-drug to another and never settling down.

However, Uzume did eventually meet a man she found worth marrying. Amaterasu's young grandson Ninigi wanted to take a trip to the realms of Earth, but the crossroads between Heaven and Earth was watched by a particularly strict guardian who didn't like letting potentially-troublemaking godlets wander about on the Earth. This guard was the stern Sarutahiko Okami, the god of travel and boundaries, the leader of all the earthly kami of Nature. Amaterasu asked Uzume to accompany Ninigi, who was surprised that his grandmother had assigned him this bawdy, laughing, rather disreputable woman instead of a warrior-escort. However, when they reached the crossroads and were challenged by Sarutahiko, Uzume just started flirting with the guardian. Eventually, she bared her breasts, laughing and joking and making him smile in spite of himself. He let them pass, but later sought her out again, unable to forget her smile. The two fell in love—a meeting of Heaven and Earth—and married. (The Sarume clan of Japan considered their origin to be from the offspring of these two Gods.) It's interesting that her husband is a deity of boundaries, because sometimes Jupiter here needs a partner who will be the one to set and keep the boundaries secure. All that Jupiter energy being Large and Open and Abundant can wear a person out after a while, and it's good to have someone to lovingly step in and say, "Honey, you need to stop now."

A fifth-house Jupiter does bestow good fortune in romances, and can indicate a happy marriage as long as both parties are willing to be very generous with each other. It seems that it took Uzume the comedian to make the God of Boundaries bend and be generous, another reason why one of her names is The Great Persuader. This Jupiter placement's infectious smile and open appreciation can be very hard to resist. Another aspect of this title is her role as a mediator—she is called upon to bring harmony between warring parties, not in the way a diplomat would, but in the way a child would take the hands of two warring parties and bring them together with a smile that melts their hearts. She brings the happiness which allows people to forget their grudges.

Together, it is said that Uzume and Sarutahiko created the Noh and Kabuki traditions of Japanese theater, and Uzume became the patron of actors and performers. (Since many actors and performers were considered somewhat disreputable by the Japanese upper classes, and since some of them were nearly—or actually—prostitutes, it's not surprising that the easygoing Uzume took them on.) The fifth house rules performance, theater, and cinema, so Uzume was the perfect patroness for it. Jupiter here often gives a dramatic, theatrical bent, or at least a willingness to get up on the overturned bucket and grab the mike without shame. The fifth house rules self-expression through its traditional ruler Leo, and openly expressing themselves is second nature to people with this placement. Like the dawn, it draws our attention and gives us hope.

To this day, Uzume is a very popular *kami* in the Shinto religion, and in Japanese folk tradition. She is called upon to dispel sorrow and depression, and this gift of Jupiterian optimism is no small blessing. Like Uzume, every person with Jupiter in the Sun's house has a light-bringer within them. It is important that they believe this is a sacred task, which we all need, whether we like to admit it or not.

64 Jupiter in the 6th House: Fukurokuju and Jurojin

The Seven Lucky Gods of Japan were grouped together some centuries ago, and the population of the "lucky seven" has shifted back and forth over time and in various places. There are actually about ten of them who have moved in and out of the "lucky seven" off and on. Two of these are Fukurokuju and Jurojin, who may or may not be the exact same deity. In some tales, they are grandfather and grandson, but both elderly. In others, they are two souls who take turns sharing the same body (and while I am sure that Gods can make this work, one does wonder if this was an esoteric apologia for the fact that they may be the same deity, changed just enough from province to province that they aren't quite identical).

They are very similar in many ways. Both are shown as elderly men with high foreheads and elongated skulls. Jurojin's head is merely longer than normal-human; Fukurokuju's is sometimes half the height of his body in length, so large that he must walk with a staff in order to stay upright. Both are sometimes accompanied by cranes, turtles or black deer. All of these are symbols of longevity; cranes were thought to live for a thousand years, turtles were slow and wrinkled and said to live for centuries, and deer were said to turn black if they lived longer than two thousand years. This is because both of these Gods are givers of health and longevity.

When Jupiter, the gift-giver of the Universe, comes into the sixth house of health and labor, it may seem like a rather limited and boring place for the planet of abundance. Jupiter, however, manages to make something wonderful of anywhere he chooses to be. First, unless it is terribly aspected, this Jupiter placement tends to bestow very good health for a long time. However, there is a catch—people with this placement are particularly good at keeping the mind-body connection going strong, and that means they are better than many people at "thinking themselves well" ... but it's also possible for them to "think themselves sick" if something is going wrong in their lives. Often physical illness with this placement is a sign of too much stress, or too much serving others resentfully and not getting back what they feel they need. (Keep in mind, however, that there's a difference between having a strong mind/body connection and having psychosomatic issues, and this Jupiter placement needs to look closely at what's actually going on. Stress chemicals are valid happenings, although Jupiter here is happy to create an excess of them, because that's what Jupiter does.)

The sixth house is the sacred place of Service, and Jupiter here is often very fulfilled by serving others. They can overdo it, though—Jupiter is the planet of overdoing—and run themselves into the ground, feeling aggrieved that they are not acknowledged or given aid. Since whatever you do in Jupiter's house should be done with joy and optimism, this is another place where feelings can leak over into their health. (It may be that on some level, they know the only way they can relax and avoid their duties is by getting sick.)

Both Fukurokuju and Jurojin started out as the legend of a Chinese Buddhist monk who went about miraculously healing people, asking for nothing except what was given generously. It was said that they could even bring the dead back to life sometimes, and reincarnate people. While being this much of a bodhisattva is not required, it's important for people with this Jupiter placement to try to have a good attitude about the service they are rendering ... and set good boundaries for those times when they don't have enough to give with a whole heart. This is the planet of optimism, which is usually a good thing, but can lead them to be continually disappointed with themselves for not being able to take on superhuman amounts of work and service. It's good for them to remember that a tool functions best for the most jobs when it gets regular maintenance. After all, this is the house of maintenance, and it applies to them as well.

Some folks with Jupiter in this house can go in the opposite direction and make Jupiter's classic mistake of overdoing things in the direction of their own health, spending most of their time on unusual and esoteric health-care, diet, and exercise routines, desperately looking for even more miracle vitamins or nutrients or procedures. Like the Gods of longevity, they are willing to trade a lot of work now to get that extra year later. Fukurukuju was said to have conquered the need to eat at all, and that sort of superhuman-ness can be an unconscious yearning in the sixth-house Jupiter's heart. Imagine having created such a perfect health routine that one never needed to worry about what to eat ever again! It's probably played through their heads, perhaps as wishful thinking.

Fukurokuju may have originally been a combining of the legend of the old sage plus a squishing-together of three Chinese Gods—Fu, Lu, and Shou, gods of Fortune, Prosperity, and Longevity; the Japanese version of their names put together may have created "Fukurokuju". (Jurojin's name means "long-lived elder".) When it comes to Prosperity, those with this Jupiter placement are generally quite fine with putting in the work hours, and while they may have a lot of Opinions about how things should be done, they usually get along well with co-workers and bosses. (One of the minor gifts of Fukurokuju is popularity among one's peers, which is highly valued in Japan, and usually easy for a Jupiter person to acquire.)

Fortune, of course, is Jupiter's lucky hand coming between them and disaster, and giving them that extra push. In general, this placement tends to focus more on details, and they can overdo that as well, not seeing the forest for the trees. Like the traditional Japanese tea ceremony, a tiny detail can take on great significance. This placement can encourage individuals to specialize not just in service careers, but in jobs which require a "God is in the details" level of craftsmanship. Jurojin carries a scroll tied to his belt which contains the death date of every person, should he want to see that; Jupiter in this Virgo-associated house likes that kind of detail. To this Jupiter placement, that is a form of purification—of skill, of intent, and of motivation.

People with this placement of Jupiter firmly believe that it is best to teach a man to fish so you can get on with teaching another man to fish and not have to worry about the first one. (This contrasts with some other Jupiters who might coddle someone too much and then become upset that they cannot be independent.) They are excellent at coaxing and coaching others to manage their own self-help. They are generous with advice, but really don't want people to be dependent on them; they strive to aid in fledging, not feeding to ground-hugging fatness.

The old monk of legend who spawned both of these Lucky Gods was known as the Old Man of the Southern Pole Star, known in Western astrology as Canopus. This star is only occasionally visible in the sky in southern Japan, and is a guide to lead souls home when they die. Fukurokuju's early legend is that he was born a sickly boy whose mother worried about him living. He came across two old men sitting in a field playing a board game, and gave them a jar of wine and some dried meat. They were so pleased that they gifted him with long life. One was the Old Man of the Northern Pole Star, who had picked his date of birth while he was in his mother's womb, and the other was the Old Man of the Southern Pole Star, who changed his death date from 19 to 91 in thanks. Eventually, when he passed the death date given to him, he inherited the job of the second elder, being able to—when appropriate—give the gift that he had received to many others.

This lovely story illustrates the kind of service that the sixth-house Jupiter can render when they want to, becoming a beacon of joy that appears in the tiny details. Its essence is the meal when you are too tired to cook, the loaned mittens when you have lost your gloves, the tax help that makes sure you get back every dollar you can. It is generosity paid out in the willingness to work hard at jobs which others may scorn and wander away from, but which everyone laments about when they are not done. It is about becoming someone who cares enough about the small things to keep the big things going. Being Jupiter's hands in this way will give you the luck you need to get your own self-care done, and service will also come to you when you need it, like the polestar in the sky looking down upon us.

74 Jupiter in the 7th House: Draupadi

In the *Mahabharata*, one of the two greatest epics of ancient India, the heroine of the story is a woman named Draupadi who started out as a mortal and centuries later became honored as a goddess. She is a strong-minded person who, like Helen of Troy (Sun in Gemini), ended up being the catalyst for a terrible war. She is also renowned for having five husbands—and not one at a time, either. The *Mahabharata* has over a thousand versions, having lasted for centuries, and different accounts cast Draupadi in many varied ways, but she is never anything but an important and key part of the story. This suits Jupiter, the biggest of the planets, who can be the giver of gifts or the rain of overdoing, but is never overlooked.

Draupadi was the daughter of King Drupada; some versions of the story say that she was born out of sacred fire rather than being born the ordinary way. However that happened, she was fiery, spirited, intelligent, and independent, and said to be the most beautiful woman of the era. Her father was a canny politician caught in the middle of an ongoing conflict between multiple quarreling royal families, and he knew that whomever he married his beautiful daughter to would have to be an alliance. Choosing the path of plausible deniability, he holds an archery competition and announces that Draupadi's hand would be the prize.

The five Pandavas—exiled princes who are on the current losing side of the war—come to the competition disguised as Brahman priests; Arjuna, the best warrior of them all, shoots the arrow which wins. There is a general uproar about a Brahmin priest winning the young woman's hand, which erupts into a pitched battle, and the brothers flee with their prize. When they arrive home to where they live with their widowed mother Kunti in the forest, one brother asks their mother, "Guess what we brought home today!" She tells him that whatever it is, whoever found it must share it with all four of his brothers … and then goes outside to see Draupadi. Shocked, she considers for a moment and then reinforces the fact that Draupadi must be married to all five of her sons, to prevent jealousy.

At that time in patriarchal India, it was not uncommon for rich noblemen to take more than one wife, but vanishingly rare for a woman to have more than one husband. Jupiter, however, is the planet of abundance and cares nothing for gender boundaries. When it appears in the seventh house, it is often associated with not wanting to be tied down to one spouse, perhaps because of wanting freedom and perhaps because being limited to one human being is difficult and restrictive for them. Most of the myths used to illustrate this are stories of philanderers such as Zeus (Jupiter in Aries), but I chose to use a situation where one woman chooses to stay with five men and learns to love them all. Patriarchy aside, it is clear from Draupadi's personality that she would not have tolerated this for long if she didn't like it.

One version of the story says that in a past life (or possibly in the early stages of this one), Draupadi had asked the Gods for a husband who would have a long list of wonderful traits, which she enumerated during her prayer. Shiva (Sun in Scorpio) appeared and said that since no one man could hold all of these, she would have to be married to at least five, and that was what happened. The Pandavas were all different—Arjuna the archer and soldier, brave and thoughtful; Yudishthira was painfully honest and upright, but something of a naïve gambler; Bhima was large, strong, and hotheaded, ready to fight anyone who angered him; Nakula was quiet and shy, a tamer of horses and lover of animals, and the most handsome of the lot; and Sahadeva was brilliant and knowledgeable, an astrologer and strategist. All fell madly in love with Draupadi, and generously offered to make a rule where she could choose with whom she wanted to spend each night, and the other four would not interrupt their brother's intimate time on pain of exile. In her turn, Draupadi was faithful to her five husbands ... perhaps because with five of them, there was no time or energy to stray.

This does not mean that someone with a seventh-house Jupiter is incapable of being monogamous. For one thing, Jupiter is the House of Projections, and planets here are often mentally projected onto the partner; the seventh-house Jupiter may cast themselves as the faithful one who chooses the philanderer and puts up with their running about. More positively, they may be attracted to people who are generous of heart (like the Pandava brothers) and who will allow them a fair amount of freedom in their lives. Alternatively, they may be drawn to partners who are from foreign cultures, highly educated, or strongly religious, other Jupiterian qualities. If they must be monogamous (and being polyamorous may well have occurred to them, if not acted upon), they want a multifaceted person who can, in some sense, turn more than one single face to them.

The *Mahabharata* is long and complicated, so I will only touch on the main points here. Yudishthira, the eldest brother, gets involved in a dice game with their cousin Prince Duryodana, a political rival who hates the Pandavas and wants to destroy them. The dice are magical, and the Pandava prince is set up to fail. Foolishly, Yudishthira gambles away first his own freedom, then that of all four of his brothers. Duryodana says that he can win everything back if he puts Draupadi up as a lot; Yudishthira desperately does so and loses her as well. The whole court of Duryodana's elderly blind father has been watching this happen, and they watch as well as Duryodana has Draupadi dragged in by her hair (to the wrath of hotheaded Bhima, who cries out that he will bathe in Duryodana's blood for this) and informed that she, along with all her husbands, now belongs to him.

Draupadi, however, is not intimidated; she turns to Yudishthira and asks how, if he had gambled himself away first, he still had any claim to Draupadi and thus had the right to wager her at all. She calls upon the old King and the court to consider her words, pointing out further the traditional rules which prevent a free woman from being used as a gambling stake. (Jupiter is the planet of law and legal philosophy, which must be generous to keep from being tyrannical, and part of generosity is protecting those with less recourse in the world; the seventh house rules legal contracts, and the two together often give these individuals good fortune in legal practice.)

Duryodana and his best friend Karna call Draupadi a whore for having five husbands, and decide to publicly strip her as a way to provoke the Pandavas into violence, giving them an excuse to kill the brothers. However, in a truly Jupiterian moment of humorous overdoing, Krishna (Venus in Sagittarius) makes Draupadi's sari a thing of infinite cloth, so that after half an hour of unwinding and the general exhaustion of the unwinders, she is still clothed. At this point Duryodana's queen mother intervenes, fearing divine disapproval, and convinces the old king to put the whole matter aside. The king grants Draupadi a boon and she frees her husbands, stating that she needs no boon to be free as she was never legitimately won in the first place.

The king agrees, and they all leave together, she having rescued her five beloveds and driven her point home.

However, Draupadi is disappointed in her husbands for getting themselves and her into the situation in the first place, and not being the ones to rise up against the prince, even in his own court. One of the faults of the seventh-house Jupiter is that they may have overly optimistic ideas of what their partner(s) can accomplish—for example, expecting them to be without jealousy or indecision or other unpleasant habits. When the partner turns out to be less perfect than their Jupiterian ideals would prefer, they can feel betrayed. Draupadi demands that her husbands pay with vengeance, which of course can only lead to violence. Years later in the epic, all of this explodes into warfare and Draupadi loses her father, brothers, and five of her adult sons to the war with Duryodana, but then reigns as queen with her husbands for thirty-six years before dying.

Over the centuries, Draupadi was both lauded as a faithful and resourceful wife and demonized for being happy with five husbands; she is a powerful and larger-than-life figure (which Jupiter loves) who is in many ways too independent for traditional Indian culture. She was at once the justification that polyandry was just as spiritually acceptable as polygyny; that generosity of love and partnership was not something to be slanted in only one direction. At the end of the extremely overblown angry-Jupiter war, after Duryodana has been killed and her humiliation avenged, Draupadi manages to find enough generosity in her heart to allow the killer of her children to live, only taking from him the great jewel of which he was proud. (The seventh house is associated with Libra, and here Draupadi decides to choose beauty over bloody justice.)

Once the seventh-house Jupiter has matured out of projecting those qualities on the partner, they will be able to bring their own optimism, generosity, forgiveness, and perhaps even wealth to their partner. They will be able to accept flaws with open-heartedness, and see the divine in themselves as well. Jupiter is the planet of faith, and the best gift that the Gift-Giver can give in this house is faith in the enduring power of Love.

84 Jupiter in the 8th House: Baron Samedi

The eighth is the House of Death, and most gods and spirits of Death tend to be solemn and sober, dark presences of silence and foreboding. Not so Baron Samedi, the *lwa* of Death in the Voudou religion. He dresses fancy, smokes cigars, and laughs and jokes constantly, a downright jovial spirit of Death who doesn't give two shakes of a skeletal tail about the "decorum" expected of Death deities. A grinning, gift-giving Death God may seem a contradiction in terms, but that's what happens when you put the planet of abundance and optimism into the house of sex, death, and the mysteries.

Baron Samedi's name comes from black Louisiana patois, a slurring of either "Baron Cemetiere" (the ruler of the cemetery), or "Baron Saturday", or both. He is usually portrayed as a skeleton dressed nattily in a top hat and tailcoat, drinking a glass of liquor and smoking a cigar, as he loves the sensual pleasures of the good life. He is often shown with cotton plugs in his nostrils (part of dressing a corpse in 19th-century southern black culture) and because of this, he speaks in a high nasal voice. When he possesses devotees in Voudou ceremonies, he wears his customary hat, coat, nose plugs, and sunglasses to obscure his eyes—although sometimes sunglasses with one lens missing, symbolizing that he can see into both the material and spiritual realms. It's said that the Baron is such a cultured dandy that even his black horses wear top hats. He finds the whole concept of Death, and the seriousness with which humans take it, both absurd and humorous.

There are three "tribes" of spirits in Voudou, and Baron Samedi is the head of the Ghede "tribe", which are all associated with Death in some way; their color is black, contrasting with the peaceful "white" Radu tribe and the warlike "red" Petro tribe. The Ghede spirits are all known for their profanity, and partying, and as they are the tribe of carnality, they often do sexually explicit dances and behave irreverently. Part of this is celebrating life in the midst of death, and part is the concept that the behavioral rules which the living must follow—courtesy, decorum, dutifulness—do not apply to the Dead. The skull is always grinning, therefore the Dead can have a good time and indulge in pleasures that they may have missed during their lives. This is an eighth-house Jupiter philosophy laid out on the table; this placement is almost required to maintain hope in the face of great tribulation ... and unlike other placements, doing so will actually bring luck and good fortune to the one who clings to their faith in the goodness of life.

Most astrologers, when they talk about the eighth-house Jupiter, shy away from the aspects of death and sex and mysteries, and focus largely on this house's rulership of other people's money, pointing out that those with this Jupiter placement are often gifted in this way. Relatives may pay their way throughout much of their early years, and they may find themselves the recipients of random financial gifts throughout their life. It is true that they often have good intuition about where to put money, and some end up stockbrokers or bankers or in other careers which involve using someone else's money to make more money, and taking a cut. However, that's only one part of their intuitive senses, which also instinctively know how to seek out pleasure, how to uncover secrets, and when to drop everything and start over from scratch. This house is ruled by Pluto, the planet of rebirth and regeneration, and in spite of an early start of financial privilege, many people with this Jupiter placement find that later in life, they must start over and sacrifice what has been done already. It's almost as if, after enjoying what others have sacrificed for them, they must now turn around and be the one to sacrifice in turn. If they can do this death-and-rebirth of their life with a positive Jupiterian attitude, it will go better for them.

In spite of being married to Maman Brigitte (Pluto in the second house), the Baron is not a faithful husband. He is known to make advances toward humans, and sometimes visit them in their dreams with disturbingly erotic sexual visions. He has had numerous affairs with other lwa and orisha, and is not one whit repentant. This resonates with the planet of excess in the house of sexuality; many people with this placement will tend to see sex as a giant playground to be explored, with every attractive person being a different funhouse ride. Their expansive sexual natures may seem unable to be confined to one person, and many spend a great deal of time playing the field. At the least, they will fantasize about it, and possibly comment on it; Baron Samedi is notorious for walking up to people and making lewd and suggestive comments. His advances are crude but not contemptuous; it is simply his way of reminding people that they should enjoy life and have a good time before they go into the grave. As a deity shaped by the experiences of southern enslavement, where people's lives were often brutal and short and they had to desperately take pleasure where they could, the Baron's Jupiterian philosophy is clear. *Live while you can. Don't go to your grave regretting all the things you didn't do.*

Baron Samedi is the spirit who decides when people live or die, and he digs a grave for each of them. He can be moved by random feelings of Jupiterian generosity; it is said that no matter how much danger you are in, if the Baron refuses to dig your grave, you will not die. People pray to him for healing, as he has to power to pull someone back from the brink of death. However, he will only do so if he feels the person is worth saving, so it is important to be generous yourself and build up merit in his eyes. He has the power to undo any curse or hex, if he is so moved to help and feels that you did nothing to deserve it. Because Death inevitably leads to Rebirth through the confluence of sexuality (as does the process of the eighth house), he can also be petitioned for aid in conceiving a child, when all other methods have failed.

The Baron can also be called upon when someone wants to commune with dead loved ones, although like all Death Gods he is fairly protective of the dead souls under his care, and dislikes it when humans disturb them for specious or greedy reasons. Sometimes a Voudou practitioner who wants to do this must dig their own grave and lie in it, thus saving him some work. One of his jobs is being in charge of the veil between the worlds and making sure that nothing comes in and out which should not. He detests the practice of making zombies, which is supposedly about bringing dead bodies back to a servile half-life, because it makes more work for him and violates his strict boundaries between the living and the dead.

Jupiter is often referred to as the "favorite uncle" position, and it is said that Baron Samedi is especially fond of children, whom he would rather see live out their full lives than go early to their graves. He is frequently petitioned for the gift of saving a sick or injured child, because he is more likely to respond positively to this than to saving the life of an adult who has had a full life. This is another echo of the way this Jupiter placement, once they have figured out that they should give as much as they receive, can become a "rescuer" of others in trouble. Financial rescues aside, they often find themselves to be instinctively talented at raising hope and optimism in people who are bereaved and grieving. They are at their best when, like Baron Samedi, they are encouraging sufferers who have been avoiding life to take their first tentative steps toward pleasure and eventual joy. *Go dancing*, says the Baron. *Those whom you have lost would not want you to weep any longer.*

Any eighth-house planet will be interested in ferreting out the hidden mysteries of life and penetrating the darkness; Jupiter's talent is doing this with a sense of humor and a never-ending faith that this can make the world a better place. Eighth-house planets also demand eventual sacrifice, but Jupiter here eases this price. It's not that some sort of death and rebirth will not be required, but the planet of optimism can guide the person through it with a sense of being cared for and protected in the middle of the darkness. Baron Samedi expects to be given offerings and for you to earn merit, but he also encourages hope and joy in the face of all suffering, and so should every person with this Jupiter ... this wild dance in the graveyard.

94 Jupiter in the 9th House: Njord

The ancient name for the ninth house was "The House of Long Journeys Over Water". In those days, of course, land and water were the only ways to get places. In many cases, water was often faster than land; there were no tolls, no wars, no people getting in the way ... just the great devouring sea that could swallow up a ship and make it disappear forever, as if it had never been. We forget, these days, that boarding a ship was taking your life in your hands, although the truth of it is that the ocean is still one of the few places on Earth where we are not nearly as in control as we would like to believe.

We think of the sea in two ways: first, as a dangerous wilderness that extends a long way down to the bottom, filled with its own unusual and fascinating wildlife; and second, as a flat sheet of liquid on which to sail that connects one shore to another. In the Norse cosmology, the first view is the kingdom of the Sea Gods, Aegir and Ran (Neptune in the second house) and their nine daughters (Neptune in the twelfth house); the second is the kingdom of Njord, the god of ships, sailing, fishing, and merchant voyages. He is the original God of Long Journeys Over Water, as the Norse people had a strong maritime tradition and were some of the best shipbuilders of their era.

Jupiter is the King and the Gift-Giver, the one who has riches and thus can afford to share. Njord is the King of the Vanir, the agricultural gods of the Norse-cosmology world of Vanaheim. The various Vanir Gods include sex, love, and the production of all food under their rulership. While Njord is not a farmer, he is in charge of fishing and harvesting from the sea, which for the coastal Nordic people was a significant part of their diet. As merchant and trader, he also procured foodstuffs that could not be grown in the cold Northlands, and thus came to be seen as a giver of abundance.

Njord filled the nets with his silver-scaled flocks and herds, revealed the beds of shellfish, and sailed into the harbor with exotic food, drink, cloth, jewels, and many other riches. He stayed long enough to spend time with his Earth-goddess wife Nerthus, kiss his children, and then sail away to another distant horizon. Similarly, those with Jupiter in the ninth house tend to have itchy feet; if circumstances do not collude to send them traveling on regular journeys, they will find a way to arrange it. Travel broadens their minds, refreshes their spirits, and helps them to forget their troubles for a while. Not only that, but like the sanguine sailor-king Njord, good fortune tends to follow them on journeys.

Jupiter is also referred to as the "favorite uncle", the benign semi-parent who shows up at holidays loaded with gifts. Njord falls perfectly into that category, but he is also referred to as "Goodfather Njord", and is said to be the kindest of fathers. Certainly he is devoted to his twin children Frey and Freya (Mars in Cancer and Venus in Capricorn) and his possible foster child Sigyn (Venus in the twelfth house). It says something that in spite of being the most absent father in Norse mythology, he is still the kindest. This is Jupiter's own house, so this placement gives a big blast of Jupiterian generosity. It is similar to having Jupiter in Sagittarius, but the attitudes manifest in different ways.

People with ninth house Jupiters tend to end up in relationships with people from other countries or cultures; something in them wants to learn from the lover who sees things in a very different way. Njord himself has had two wives that we know about. One is Nerthus, the Queen of Vanaheim who is very much a homebody Earth-goddess. She is the mother of his children and she is introverted, dignified, maternal, and somewhat bloodthirsty, as she represents the devouring Earth. She contrasts with Njord's jovial, extroverted buoyancy, as well as being the eternal shore to his eternal wandering. He also ended up marrying the frosty mountain goddess Skadi (Pluto in Sagittarius) for a time, although they divorced because they were so different that they couldn't agree on where to live, and Skadi was not willing to stay with a mostly absent husband.

One of the classic and oft-quoted problems of having Jupiter in the ninth house is that the individual is so busy traveling and exploring that they don't have time to keep connections with their friends and families. Njord, of course, is a deity and his family never dies, so he has all the time in the world to sail out and back, but we human beings usually need to check in with people before they die, move away, forget about us, or become resentful at our absence. However, Jupiter here gives a great deal of independence; like Njord, the native becomes cramped after spending too long in one place, and must keep moving. It's something that loved ones are just going to have to learn to cope with. (Of course, it doesn't hurt if the Jupiterian brings them gifts from their travels.)

The ninth house represents our "inner compass" that keeps us anchored in our world view, and as the eternal sailor, Njord knows all about compasses, charting a course, and working with circumstance to skillfully get there. He also understands about faith—after all, every time a sailor climbs aboard, it's an act of faith that he will get to his destination alive. Jupiter here can give a strong, unshakable faith—in a religion, a way of being, or just in one's self. This is, of course, both the planet and the house of religion, and certainly the biggest danger of this placement is fanaticism, focusing on one's beliefs to the point where it becomes crucial that everyone else believes them, too. However, the antidote for this problem is found in the same place, as this is also the house of mind-expansion.

In older days, people grew up, lived, and died in one village, with one culture and one world view. A lucky few might get to travel, but the vast majority lived their entire lives in a ten-mile radius. That doesn't give much in the way of mind-expansion. However, the sea-travelers of old had the privilege of periodically immersing themselves in other cultures (and possibly languages as well, which definitely changes the way one thinks; remember that the third house faces the ninth). While we tend to think of Norse sailors as the violent Vikings, looking for plunder and willing to slaughter whole villages, it is important to remember that the majority of non-fishing seafarers—including the Norse—were simply looking to trade. (It's also true that if a town was too well-defended to risk attacking, the Viking horde would suddenly metamorphose into a crew of canny traders ready to cheerfully sell off some of their previous loot.)

It is a fact that the best traders are ones who can learn enough about their sales targets to be able to negotiate peacefully; the more you learn of their language, culture, religious beliefs, and world view, the more successful you will be in crafting an advantageous trade. Njord himself was said to be an excellent diplomat, one who negotiated a truce when his people fought a war with the sky Gods, and offered himself and his children as a hostage. All the better to broaden the enemy's world view, not to mention establishing some hefty trade agreements and new fishing grounds. While this might seem pecuniary, we must remember that while Njord can swing a sword with the best of them, as a Vanir god he is first and foremost concerned with feeding people, not killing them. Gift-givers function best in peacetime.

All that learning about languages and cultures and other people's religions changes you, though. First, it's an education in and of itself, and this is the house of adult education. Second, it opens you up to many different cultural and spiritual ideas, which is the basis of philosophy—another ninth-house area. Every time you absorb something from yet another new place, picking out the attractive parts to add to your world view, you pull it further away from the single-mindedness necessary for real fanaticism ... and you are more able to give, to bend, to make connections across religious and cultural divides. In fact, when facing the problem of ninth house Jupiterian fanaticism, Njord the old blue-eyed sailor would probably squint benignly at the native and recommend even *more* travel to newer and more interesting shores. After all, he might point out, it would be an education to remember.

104 Jupiter in the 10th House: The Wufang Shangdi

Jupiter is the planet of abundance, and in this instance at least, it seemed that a single deity would not be enough to encompass Jupiter's ascent to the very top of the chart. Instead, a collective of five deities—the Chinese *Wufang Shangdi*, or Five Regions Heavenly Gods— stepped forward to demonstrate the planet of good fortune passing the Midheaven. Indeed, it's very appropriate that these are Heavenly Gods, called the Five Changeable Faces of Heaven. They are referred to as "changeable" because each of them has a celestial form, a terrestrial form, and a chthonic form. This demonstrates that they have power in the heavens, on the earth, and in the underworld.

Many ancient cultures believed that if deities showed themselves to mortals in their true cosmic forms, the mortal would be immolated and destroyed by it. They come clothed in power and grandeur, and on some level this is how the individual with Jupiter in the tenth house wants to be seen. This is the planet of the King, and it bestows the gift of leadership ... and, indeed, a strong drive to put one's self on some kind of throne. The tenth is the house of Career and Reputation, and Jupiter here indicates that whatever they do, it's going to be Big, and they are going to be In Charge. This is the house of the public eye, and these people want to be seen and respected.

While it's not unusual for them to end up at the top of some business hierarchy, it's also quite possible for them to go it alone as an entrepreneur or solo artist and make it work in a big way. They need a lot of room to maneuver—Jupiter doesn't like to be crowded—and sometimes the presence of subordinates is too restricting. While they do love to tell people what to do and be obeyed, their favorite place is forging ahead in their chosen career without waiting for others to catch up.

The Five Heavenly Gods had powers which corresponded to groups of five—the five elements of Chinese medicine, the five constellations around the pole, the five directions, the five regions of China, the five sacred mountains, the seasons of the year, and the five Dragons. Their celestial forms were literally the constellations themselves, the highest stars in the sky—a wonderful tenth-house Jupiter dream. When they descended to matters of the earth, they embodied the directions, the elements of matter, the seasons, the regions of the great Empire, and the sacred mountains. In their chthonic form, they took the shape of dragons of five different colors, but they were also shown riding the dragons as mounts to symbolize their power over their own baser natures.

Jupiter in the tenth house gives many gifts, but it can also wreak a lot of damage on the world if it is afflicted and the individual allows the affliction to rule their decisions. When you wield a lot of power, you have a much stronger ability to hurt a lot of people, and you are more likely to do so accidentally just through simple propinquity. Each of the Five Heavenly Gods has specific powers and specific dangers, all of which may plague the tenth-house Jupiter at one time or another. Consider them five warnings about correct behavior, which seems to be the theme of every Chinese myth at some point.

The first of them is Huangdi, the Yellow Emperor. He is associated with the center of the sky, and his sacred stars are the constellation of the Great Chariot, which we in the West know as the Big Dipper. In terrestrial form, he rules the Chinese element of Earth, the culminating point of the sky, and the sacred Mount Song (Lofty Mountain) in Henan Province. He does not have a specific season, but is linked to the period of stillness when the weather is transitioning between one season and another. His mount is the Yellow Dragon. His mortal mother was supposedly of shamanic lineage from northern Asia, and she was impregnated by a lightning strike and took two years to carry the Yellow Emperor to term. Huangdi shapes the material world, raising mountains and deepening valleys. He is the creator of cultural laws and morality, languages, and lineage; he gets the top spot because he is supposedly the ancestor of all the Han Chinese. His name is derived from the words for "light" and "thunder", and he is able to become lightning, like the bolt which fathered him.

Being lightning is impressive—sometimes when you are the one in charge and you need to make a decision or act in an emergency, the lightning strike is good to emulate. But you can't be bright light and thunder all the time, or you will burn yourself out. The Chinese element of Earth represents stability, patience, thoughtfulness, and practicality. Lightning needs to ground itself, coming down to earth and living in reality, not just one's Big Plans and various grandiose ideas. The strike of inspiration is a good thing, but then it needs to tap into the reality of the resources one has to work with, including all their limitations which won't go away when ordered to do so. Jupiter has Big Ideas, but the tenth house is ruled by Saturn and associated with earthy, practical Capricorn, and the tenth-house Jupiter needs to respect Saturn's roots in the everyday world.

The second of the Heavenly Gods is Cangdi, the Blue-Green Emperor; he was variously known as the Green Emperor and the Blue Emperor until those names were combined. (Blue and green are often conflated in early societies, and the Heavenly Gods go back to the Neolithic Era.) He rules the eastern quarter of the sky and his stars are the Azure Dragon, which in the West is a combination of the constellations of Virgo, Libra, and Scorpio. In terrestrial form, he rules the Chinese element of Wood, the season of spring, and the direction of East and its sacred Mount Tai (Tranquil Mountain) in Shandong Province. His mount is the Blue-Green Dragon, the same as the constellation, which flew on the Chinese flag for a time. The grandson of the Jade Emperor (Neptune in Capricorn) who is the highest deity in the Chinese pantheon, Cangdi is a deity of fertility and is prayed to for the spring growth of the fields during the sowing of seeds.

To sow seeds, from a tenth-house perspective, is to begin projects and see where they go, perhaps experimentally; one knows that a certain percentage will fail, but one hopes that enough will survive to the reaping to make it worthwhile. Jupiter does tend to overdo things, and it's possible for this placement to start and abandon too many project seedlings, perhaps thinking that they are large enough to contain all those multitudes and still give them the attention they deserve. The Chinese element of Wood, however, carries the qualities of bamboo-flexibility, generosity, and cooperation. The tenth-house Jupiter needs to be able to work with others and not just order them about; they must learn to inspire others so that they will pick up and adopt the seedlings shed by Jupiter's abundant fertility, and take them in new directions.

The third of these Gods is Heidi, the Black Warrior (also called the Mysterious God). He rules the northern quadrant of the sky, and his stars are the constellation of the Black Tortoise-Snake, which partakes of pieces of the Greek constellations of Pegasus, Sagittarius, Capricorn, Aquarius, and Pisces. (Different areas of China saw it as different animals, which were later combines into a snake wrapped around a tortoise, both of which hibernate in the winter.) In terrestrial form, he rules the Chinese element of Water, the season of winter, and the direction of North and its sacred Mount Hengxi (Permanent Mountain) in Shanxi Province. His mount is the Black Dragon. When a demon king was ravaging the world, the Jade Emperor ordered Huangdi's grandson Heidi to command twelve legions of heavenly soldiers and defeat the great evil, which he did.

Getting to the top can involve a lot of fighting, and while Jupiter is not Mars and would rather be commanding than bothering with that, when the Big Planet's territory is threatened—in this case the career or the public reputation—some pretty large lightning bolts can get thrown. Those with this placement can start seeing themselves as warriors with enemies everywhere, and act accordingly. However, the Chinese element of Water is associated with wisdom, stillness, and conservation; the tenth-house Jupiter individual needs to stop and think before throwing themselves into another career war and trampling the supposed enemy, listen to the silent wisdom within them, and conserve their energy.

The fourth deity is Baidi, the White Emperor. He rules the western quadrant of the sky and his stars are the constellation of the White Tiger, which includes what Westerners would consider Andromeda, Aries, Taurus, and Orion. In terrestrial form, he rules the Chinese element of Metal, the season of autumn, and the direction of West and its sacred Mount Hua (Splendid Mountain) in Shaanxi Province. His mount is the White Dragon, which periodically spawned enormous white serpents which attacked people and had to be killed.

The serpent crawls under things, seeing the underbelly of the world, keeping secrets while sometimes "worming" its way in. It is subtle and manipulative. The tenth-house Jupiter individual, if thwarted in their attempts at ambition, may give up the direct approach and try slipping into success through dishonesty and manipulation. The Chinese element of Metal, though, contains the qualities of determination, persistence, and firmness. When things look bleak, they must stiffen their spine and keep pushing honestly—which is what Jupiter would prefer anyway—and ignore the Saturnian murmur of failure in their ears.

The fifth and final member of the *Wufang Shangdi* is Chidi or Yandi, the Red Emperor or the Fiery God. He rules the southern quadrant of the sky and his stars are the constellation of the Vermilion Phoenix, which Western astrology knows as parts of the constellations of Gemini, Cancer, Hydra, and Crater. In terrestrial form, he rules the Chinese element of Fire, the season of summer, and the direction of South and its sacred Mount Heng (Balancing Mountain) in Hunan Province. His mount is the Red Dragon, and he is a deity of science, craft, and the marketplace. He has a fiery temperament and at one point got into a war with Huangdi the Yellow Emperor. This war symbolized both fire ravaging the earth and needing to be stopped, and—more relevant—the headstrong pursuit of knowledge leading to imbalance and destruction without earthy practicality and stability to stop it. Huangdi finally defeated Yandi, but the two remain complementary opposites in the world.

This is the final lesson for the tenth-house Jupiter. It is easy to look at new knowledge and technology and think only of how it can be exploited, how much money it can make. Here the Jupiter person needs the opposing element of Earth to slow them down and make them think practically about the future for many generations to come. At the same time, they also need to cultivate the fire-element qualities of enthusiasm and creativity in order to find a good balance of the two forces.

Jupiter is the planet of luck, and this placement surely brings luck in one's public career; the big problem is the trampling of unluckier souls. Since the tenth house signifies the parent who introduces and interprets the outside world to the child, this placement can signify a parent who is well-traveled, or very religious, or highly educated, or just generous and supportive in their guidance. Often it is the presence of this parent which makes the difference in the tenth-house Jupiter person's success, putting them in a "parental" position over others in the world. They need to remember that early family luck, and pass it on by being a good mentor to as many of the less fortunate as possible. Jupiter's generosity withers if it is not spread around, and if you end up inhabiting the heavens, there's a lot of space to send it down.

114 Jupiter in the 11th House: Forseti

As long as people have been grouping themselves together in tribes—and then villages, and then whole settlements—they have continued to have violent disagreements with each other. Sometimes those disagreements turned so ugly that they gained a body count, as people took sides and slew each other. Sometimes the angry relatives and descendants of the slain continued the fight for the sake of vengeance. For that matter, the concept of vengeance is found in all ancient and aboriginal societies, because people feel pain and want those who hurt them to feel pain as well.

This question of how to keep group arguments from becoming not only lethal but widely lethal over multiple generations is an eleventh house problem. The inner planets (Sun through Mars), with their emphasis on personal relationships, tend to manifest through the eleventh house as issues between friends. When the outer planets get involved, however, the lens is widened and the focus is on group dynamics—how easy it is for the group to get out of control, and how hard it is to enforce such concepts as brotherly love for those who are not your immediate brothers.

The Germanic tribes, and later the Norse tribes which were their Iron Age descendants, started out with a vengeance system. Duels were common and feuds were ordinary; when they got bad enough, a chief or king might intervene to put a stop to the bloodshed, but he risked disobedience (and later, lack of support for his position) from angry feuders, and getting himself and his own family dragged into it if he appeared to act with bias. In general, people tended to take matters into their own hands, and it was often easier to do away with someone than to force them to atone in any way. Over time, the ruling councils pressured tribal members to bring their grievances before their lawmakers, and receive verdicts which often delineated monetary payments one party would pay to those they had wronged.

This centralized lawmaking and lawgiving changed the nature of tribal rulers. Being a Mars-type warrior who won the position through force of arms did not mean you would be any good at sorting out the nuances in legal cases. Mars is the planet of the warrior-chieftain, but the next planet out—Jupiter—is the planet of kings and queens, rulers over so many people that they did not know the names of all those under their care. Jupiter is the planet of generosity, and it requires a generous spirit to listen to hundreds of petty complaints and still want the best for everyone.

The Norse God Forseti is a latecomer to the Nordic pantheon. He is the son of the unfortunate Baldur and Nanna, and his myth is intertwined with theirs, even though it was long over before he reached manhood. His name is something of a mystery—it may come from an old word *to preside over*, or it may come from a word for "whirling stream" or "cataract", or it may come from "forbidding", or "ban". Modern Icelandic bears a form of this name as the word for "president" today, a legacy of this God. (Another similarly constructed name, *Veseti*, means "person who is in charge of or presides over the *ve*"—the hallowed space.) Jupiter is the planet of group religion, and the concept of "justice is a sacred space" was present in many cultures, and we still sometimes see an echo of that today in the rituals that surround the modern judicial system.

Some scholars feel that Forseti came from a Frisian deity named Fosite, who seems to have similar attributes. The legend involved twelve Frisian law-speakers who objected to the policies of King Charles Martel, also known as

Charles the Hammer; he told them that they must conform to his will or risk death, slavery, or being set adrift in a rudderless boat on the ocean. They chose the latter, and prayed for help as they drifted. According to the story, a thirteenth man suddenly appeared on their boat with a golden axe over his shoulder. He steered the boat using his axe as a rudder and brought them to land, then split the land with his axe and a spring came forth. He identified himself as Fosite, taught them all new laws, and then vanished. They made a shrine to Fosite at the spring on the island, called at that time Heligoland. The shrine, unfortunately, was later defiled by St. Willebrord, an overenthusiastic Christian evangelist, but the story remains of the generous figure who shared with the sincere lawmakers the knowledge of how to keep a society ethical and fair.

One-on-one legal battles are usually under the dictum of the seventh house, ruled by Libra, but the changing of an entire society to be more law-abiding is clearly an eleventh-house shift. The Nordic tale of Forseti starts with the feud between the Aesir (sky) Gods and the Rökkr (wild Nature) Gods, specifically Loki's family. Odin (Saturn in Pisces) steals and imprisons Fenrir (Saturn in Aries) the son of Loki (Saturn in Gemini) and his senior wife Angrboda. Furious, Angrboda and Hel (Pluto in Virgo) swear they will have a son for a son, and force Loki to arrange the death of Baldur (Neptune in Libra). His wife Nanna throws herself into his funeral pyre and dies. In vengeance, Odin and Thor (Mercury in Taurus) attack Loki where he has hidden himself, his junior wife Sigyn (Venus in the twelfth House), and their sons Narvi and Vali. The two young sons, who were playmates of the young Forseti, are killed and transformed into a mad, wild animal respectively. Loki is bound in a cave for a thousand years, with only Sigyn to aid him in his imprisonment.

In the aftermath of this mess—which, it was said, made such a mark on the Nine Worlds of Norse cosmology that all the birds sang of it for years—Forseti came of age, an orphan who had lost his father, mother, and childhood friends to the cycle of vengeance. He builds a hall named Glitnir, which translates to "one who shines". It had pillars of gold and was roofed with silver, and radiated light which could be seen from a great distance. Jupiter wants everything to be big, and specifically seen to be larger than all others. In Forseti's case, the reason for making a glowing, shining hall was to attract reluctant parties in conflict. Glitnir was the Hall of Reconciliation, and Forseti is its main judge.

Reconciliation is a step beyond justice. It involves generosity of spirit, and the willingness to step beyond one's own biased views. It is more than just the two sides and cutting sword of Justice. Tyr (Saturn in Aries) was the older Norse/Germanic god of Justice, but he cared little for reconciliation. On the other hand, it was said of Forseti that his was the best of courts; that he stilled all strife and put to sleep all suits, and that all those who came before him left reconciled. This is Jupiterian community work at his finest; his response to having been robbed by the system of vengeance and feud was to create a way to get beyond it. Forseti and his hall were symbolic of the growing importance of discussion rather than violence as a means of conflict resolution within the Norse tradition. He is the youngest of the Aesir gods, and his form of justice came to triumph over the older version, which had been symbolized by the original Germanic deity Teiwaz, the old form of Tyr.

In ancient times, the eleventh house was referred to as the *Bonus Daemon*, or "good spirit". This came from its association with *fellowship*—the good feeling generated when people come together in a group and become warmly connected to each other. When Jupiter, the planet of good fortune and optimism, finds its way into this house, the individual honestly loves to be part of groups—even conflicting and warring groups—and probably has a wide variety of friends, many of whom may disagree with each other. This Jupiter placement would rather overlook the differences between the friends and groups in their life, and may end up being the bridge between warring parties. Like Forseti, they see the damage that inter-group conflict does to its members, and they desperately want to solve the problem and bring everyone together.

Most people, looking at that life goal, would say that it is terribly naïve—that people are too belligerent, too cruel, too wounded to come together again and again in the face of personal pain, and possibly even generational pain. However, Jupiter is the planet which rules Trust, and the individual with Jupiter inhabiting the *Bonus Daemon* has, if they choose to use it, a gift for trusting their friends, and *inspiring those friends to live up to that trust*. Jupiter's road is to give gifts away, trusting that they will come back to you, without any evidence that will actually happen. If they are willing to put their trust in the process, the eleventh-house Jupiter person will find that when they are in need, a friend will place a gift in front of them and give them what they need. But the key is that they can't restrain their friendly efforts to a small echo chamber of people who all get along and all agree with each other. They are in the world to build bridges and inspire reconciliation, and you can't do that if you don't reach out to opposing, warring sides.

Sometimes, of course, they do overestimate someone's ability to be a friend, and they are let down by that person. The other people around them usually say that they were simply foolish and shouldn't have believed in that friend. Jupiter would say that while that friend was not a channel through which one's efforts could be returned, those efforts are marked by the Universe, and will come back through other channels. The eleventh house is a big place, with wide horizons and a lot of possibilities, and plenty of hands to give back the gift you gave out, perhaps from a direction you didn't expect.

In the end, Jupiter is the planet of hope, and the eleventh house is the home of the future. These two, when combined, remind us that *freedom* and *friendship* both come from the same root word—a word for love. The faith in humanity that Jupiter bestows can shine as bright as Forseti's hall, if we trust enough to let it.

124 Jupiter in the 12th House: The Fisher King

Jupiter is the King of the planets, the sign of royalty and nobility. In European pagan times, however, the role of kingship was not just about putting a crown on one's head and telling people what to do. The King, first of all, had a strong connection to the land he ruled—in fact, in some countries he was said to be spiritually "married" to the land, and the land would flourish or wither depending on his own health and potency.

Second, when you look at ancient European myths of kingship, sooner or later they all lead back to the Sacrificial King—the one who must die that his people may live. Some sacred kings only have to do it once and then are resurrected; others must do it every year, spilling their blood onto the crops so that more will grow again in the spring. Some stay dead and some rise again. All of them go through the darkest point of the cycle, when the King is thrown down (sometimes by a usurper) or falls of his own accord. The kingship cycle is more often identified with the Sun, sometimes through the solar cycle of waxing and waning through the solstices and equinoxes, sometimes through the golden grain which must fall and then rise again, but the Jupiter King is different from the Solar King. Jupiter is the Giver, the generous one. The peak of his reign is not glory but ultimate giving, keeping everyone fed and healthy. When Jupiter goes down, it is a mightier crash, heard throughout the land, and famine results.

The twelfth house is not an easy placement for extroverted Jupiter energies. This house relegates everything in it to the unconscious, where it cannot be pulled up and utilized by normal means. It's also the house of confinement, so any planet there feels locked away or at least fairly limited. This is not a King with great means in the outer world; it is a King in a prison, who must go within to find a realm he can master. That's why I knew at once that the right story for this Jupiter placement was the tale of the Wounded King, also known as the Fisher King.

The myth of the Fisher King was first incompletely written down by twelfth-century writer Chrétien de Troyes as part of the Arthurian cycle. Arthurian myths are often a jumbled, confused tangle of pagan and Christian symbolism, building on the virtues of pagan Gods and overlaid, sometimes clumsily or tragically, with Christian values. Chrétien de Troyes managed to die before finishing it, which gave rise to a proliferation of different versions as other authors tried to complete the story in the way they thought best, often dissonant with each other. The tale was then taken up by others in both England and Germany over the next couple of centuries, each putting their own spin on it. This proliferation of confusing tales makes this a hard myth to pin down, but that's actually not inappropriate for this chapter about the planet of abundance in Neptune's misty and mystifying house.

The Fisher King starts out with a young and rather naïve youth variously named Parsifal, Percival, or Peredur. He has seen knights passing on the road and fantasizes about becoming one, and decides to cobble together some armor and borrow a horse. Parsifal comes to a lake where a man sits fishing in a boat, and the stranger tells him to go on to the castle on the top of the hill. When he arrives, he is greeted again by the fisherman, who is a crippled king sometimes confined to bed and sometimes seated on a throne but unable to walk. He learns that the king was wounded and suffers in great pain, unable to either die or be healed; sometimes the wound is in the thigh, but usually the groin, and "thigh wounds" are often medieval euphemisms for castration. The sacred king must be generative in order for his land to thrive, and indeed in some of the later versions the Fisher King's country is a wasteland because of his festering wound and lack of ability to create children. The wounded king can neither walk nor ride, but has his servants carry him to a boat so that he can go fishing, the only pastime he can manage.

Fishing (besides all its Christian connotations) echoes Pisces, which along with the twelfth house is ruled by watery Neptune. It is also the act of reaching down into a murky, unclear place and trying to extract valuable and nourishing matter from it. This can be seen as the process by which ones deals with the twelfth house—stirring the depths, reaching down, "fishing" around as an act of faith that something good can come of this. The king's wounds also resonate with the twelfth-house placement of Jupiter; it's not unusual for people with this placement to have troubled upbringings where the parents were absent, neglectful, or (this is the Neptune house) mentally ill. Whatever the problem was, the child could not depend on them to provide physical or emotional nurturing on a consistent basis, so they turned inward for their nourishment. This placement of Jupiter can cause a lack of trust in the benevolence of the Universe; the wound of being unable to trust one's caretakers or childhood circumstances can fester into the wound of seeing the world as a fundamentally unfair and malevolent place, which one must protect oneself from by withdrawing inside.

Ironically, it is this act of withdrawing inside which leads them to the source they need. It's said that this placement bestows better access to not only the unconscious and everything there, but also to the spiritual which is connected through that part of ourselves. Spirituality invades every part of their existence, even if they don't see it that way. It may not come as an actual call from the Divine, but it definitely comes as a Calling, and something about that Calling will involve sacrifice, a search for wisdom, and transmitting that wisdom to others. In Vedic astrology, Jupiter is known as the Guru, and it's said this is one of the classic Guru placements of that planet … but first Jupiter has to heal the wound in its trust, its faith, and its belief that abundance is possible.

The "wasteland" which is the result of the Fisher King's wound resonates with the feeling of this placement that there is "not enough" … not enough time, energy, or material resources to do what needs to be done. Often they find themselves with little, and yet giving handouts to the needy people who come to them anyway. Being a wounded King with an infertile land doesn't diminish the fact that there are lines of starving peasants outside the door, and this Jupiter may despair of having enough to help all those who come to them, sensing their hidden (even to themselves) generosity. It's when they start having faith that the Universe will take care of them that the Universe begins to do so.

Young Parsifal is treated to a procession by the ladies of the castle, who walk by with trays laden with a chalice, a spear, and (in some versions) a broken sword. The chalice is the Holy Grail, the symbol of the spiritual heart. The spear is (in some stories) the weapon which made the Fisher King's wound, and can occasionally relieve his pain by being placed against the wound again in a kind of sympathetic magic. At some point in this Jupiter placement's healing journey, the individual must go into the wound and look at it fully, including looking at the weapon which caused it, and find a broader truth to the situation instead of simply wallowing in it. (This is a prelude to being able to help others with similar wounds—you can't truly help heal what you don't fully understand, and you certainly can't do it if you are still stuck in your own limited personal perception of it.) Some people with this placement turn away from the quest and pursue material success, or devolve into the Neptunian traps of alcohol or drugs; it generally only drags them deeper down and the success and/or comfort never quite seems to come, because it is distracting them from the goal.

Parsifal doesn't know what to think of all this, and stays in a confused silence. Later, one of the women asks him if he asked the Fisher King a question, and he tells her that he did not. She remonstrates with him, saying that if he had asked the right question, the king's wound would have been healed and the land restored. What "the right question" actually is varies from story to story. In one version, it would have simply been asking the king, "What ails you?" This is a question of empathy—seeing that someone is in pain, and inquiring about it in a spirit of wanting to help. Empathy may be difficult for this placement, as Jupiter either overdoes it and makes them entirely too self-sacrificing, willing to lay themselves down for unworthy causes, or it locks up the empathy where it is hard to feel it.

The "right question" in other stories is "Whom does the Grail serve?" There are probably as many answers to this one as there are human beings, depending on how you see the Grail. It is the treasure at the end of the quest, the spiritual "cup" which holds the wisdom of the heart and/or the soul. The

Grail is the point of one's karmic quest, which means that it is different for each person. Whom is served by that endgoal? It's a good question. For this Jupiter placement, the answer has to be something larger and less personal than their own material success. That Calling needs to be both tied to healing the mess in their subconscious and then generously bringing that healing to the world. Both the mental excavation and the method for transmission outwards might be classic twelfth-house means such as poetry, music, art, psychology, spiritual teaching, and service to those who are trapped or confined.

This placement has enormous imagination, which can be both a blessing and a curse. Mental escapism is definitely another potential trap; all that withdrawing to the subconscious can be a way to avoid the world and its problems, which can result in some fairly disastrous unconscious decisions. This is the house of self-undoing, and one of the ways the wound can manifest is in subtly (or not-so-subtly) sabotaging one's existence by burying one's head in the dream-world. This is the house of Dreams, and all twelfth-house Jupiter people are Dreamers, in a big way. This placement allows them to pull information out of the collective unconscious. Some will learn to "fish" their dreams out of the intangible and make them tangible, but only if those dreams are actually inspired by their true quest. Walter Mitty-style fantasizing will only lead to dead ends.

The young would-be knight, however, has failed in the first part of the quest, because he didn't ask the right question. The idea that the first step to healing those wounds is the ask the right question will reverberate, somehow, in the soul of the twelfth-house Jupiter person. If you don't ask, you get nowhere. If it's the wrong question, you'll find out soon enough. They might start, though, with "What ails me?" and then have the kind of empathy and forgiveness for themselves that they might have for others. Then it's time to look at the goal of healing, and ask who it will serve, when they are done. I'll give you a hint now: "Me" is the wrong answer. They will need to tap into the part of themselves which is the unwounded, innocent Parsifal, and ask, "What do you see? What is the simple and obvious answer which is hidden from me?"

In some versions of the story, the Fisher King gives Parsifal the broken sword and tells him to mend it, or that it will become whole when he has matured enough to be a true knight. He goes out and has his adventures, and in some stories he comes back with the sword mended, and can heal the Fisher King and his land. In others, the Fisher King dies or is not healed. True to this house, the ending isn't set, because the quest can go so many different ways. This story is about salvation, and not just the Christian kind.

This placement requires a trust-fall with the Universe and the Powers That Be. Whether or not the twelfth-house Jupiter person is religious, they need to feel that the Universe is looking out for them. One quality often mentioned about this placement is the idea of the "guardian spirit", which looks out for them, keeping them out of the worst of the destruction. It's not that bad things don't happen to them—they do, sometimes more than other Jupiter placements—but there is often the last-minute rescue, making sure the terrible thing isn't as bad as it could be. It's a strange kind of luck, only working when they are on the right path. That's why so many people with this Jupiter placement end up the center of groups with a spiritual or humanitarian bent—once the Fisher King is healed, he can hold up the Grail and teach others how to fish.

✠Saturn✠

♄ Saturn in the 1st House: Babalu-Ayé

Saturn is a tough planet to have in any house, but when it's right out front in the first house, it lays one's fears, sorrows, and general awkwardness right across the face. For some individuals with this placement, it can be an outright indicator of visible or invisible disability. The first house is linked to the body—both its physical characteristics and how one dresses it, moves it, and expresses oneself with it. When there's a big Saturn-shaped obstacle on those choices, it shows on the surface.

In the African-diaspora religion of Santeria (also called Lucumi), one of the orisha, or divine spirits, is Babalu-Ayé, the God of disease. He is descended from a number of African gods from the Yoruba tribal area, variously known as Obaluaye, Oluaye, Omolu, Sopona, Sakpata, and Anyigbato in different tribes. He began as a smallpox God, a disease which is known for permanently disfiguring some people with scarring. He himself is somewhat crippled, usually limping on a bad leg and walking with a cane or staff. He usually dresses in red, to represent both the sores of disease and the heat of fever; in Africa, offerings to him must be done during the heat of the day for that reason. Among the Ewe people, the smallpox God wanders the world at night dressed in a garment of rattling snail shells. Not only does this warn people he is coming, like a leper's bell (and more on that later), the snail is a slow limbless animal and thus special to him. He carries a broom to sweep disease into the air, or sweep the earth clean of pestilence.

Most Gods and major spirits the world over are usually shown as physically perfect. Even if they are part animal or bear the marks of their patronage (such as stars smeared over their belly or horns on their head), they are not usually obviously disfigured. After all, if one is a deity and thus has great powers, why would one choose anything other than a perfect human body to appear to human beings? Some, however, have always appeared humbly with disabilities, because that is also part of them, and that is a perfectly natural way of being in the world, even if it is difficult and inconvenient to humans with similar issues. Disease and disfigurement has always been part of Nature, whether we like it or not, and Gods work within Nature.

In some places, Babalu-Ayé is the chief deity of the element of Earth; his name in Yoruba is simply a title which means Earth Father, as his real name is not known and would be too dangerous to utter anyway. Saturn is the earthiest of planets (and often associated with the father), and one of the lessons of Earth is its physicality and limitation. Earth is slow and does not move about like the other elements. Earth, as experienced astrologically, is about the physical world and all its inconveniences—flesh, shit, decay, being forced to live inside the limiting cycle of Life, half of which is about cooling and rotting down before anything can be reborn from one's corpse. If you don't take care of the body, it will end before its time. If you don't tend to the physical needs of the world, your life will begin to fall apart ... but no matter what you do, sooner or later it will fall apart anyway. Saturn's earthy demands remind us that we are taking part in a limited, embodied world, and must find what joy we can while living inside those very narrow confines. Babalu-Ayé's limping form reminds us of the same thing, and his stories echo the concept of the body being the locus through which we experience both human limitations and divine power.

This does not mean that Babalu-Ayé is not venerated or is considered negative; in fact in some places he is one of the most popular Gods of all. He is the living embodiment of the very Saturnian phrase, "What can kill, can cure." (If this doesn't make sense to you, think of chemotherapy killing cancer.) Babalu-Ayé is prayed to for relief and prevention of all sorts of diseases, but especially skin diseases, inflammation, seizures, and anything which threatens to become epidemic. Thousands of followers in many countries make offerings to him on a regular basis, asking to be spared from their physical infirmities, or to keep their loved ones whole. If you have a body, it will fall ill sooner or later, and then you will need him.

In Santeria, he is associated with Lazarus of the book of Luke—not the Lazarus who was raised from the dead, but the beggar Lazarus who was sent to Heaven. This Lazarus was simply part of a parable and not meant to be seen as a historical person, but medieval peasantry seized upon him and drew him as a leper in folk Catholicism, with dogs following him and licking his wounds. After a time, the word "lazar" became another word for "leper"; segregated hospitals for the care of leprosy patients were known as "lazar-houses". When these illustrations were brought to the recently converted areas of the New World, they were identified with Babalu-Ayé.

Being a "leper" in some way is one of the ways in which Saturn in the house of the body can manifest. While not everyone with this Saturn placement will have a visible disability, a significant number of them will, forcing them to be embodiments of bodily limitations. It's a humbling and sometimes humiliating situation to be in, especially since human beings can often act out of triggered fear and be cruel and inconsiderate to disabled people. In Candomblé, Babalu-Ayé's face is never shown, but is covered with a mask of straw, and he is dressed in sackcloth to underscore his humility. This is a deity who knows what it is to suffer; the fact that he is always shown limping and in pain demonstrates that he understands what it is to be in that situation, sometimes permanently. While he has been known to smite people with disease—especially when they have been rude to him about his illness—he is generally a very compassionate being. When he does smite, it's usually because someone has wronged someone else, and according to legend his most common "smite offense" is to ridicule someone ill or disabled, or refuse to help them out of selfishness. Because of this, the African-diaspora religions teach that everyone should aid and be kind to crippled beggars, because any of them could be Babalu-Ayé in disguise.

The idea that Saturn shows so obviously is in itself probably a huge humiliation to first-house Saturn people. I've known quite a few people with this placement, and even if there was no physical disability, there was usually a general sense of awkwardness in the physical body, and that awkwardness showed in their movements and facial expressions. Some outright hated being "trapped" in their bodies, even if they were reasonably whole; there was a mental disconnect where they could not bear to live within the earthy limitations of a physical form, and wished to be rid of it. Others were not as openly disparaging of the "meat puppet", as it has been called, but still admitted to frequently dissociating from it. In my experience as an astrologer, it's not uncommon for the first-house Saturn placement to bestow some sort of neurological differences which show up in the affect, such as epilepsy or autism. It can also bestow neurological or neurochemical difficulties which prevent the individual from connecting with their body, and/or from being able to discern the body language of others, and respond appropriately to their movements, positioning, and facial expressions. Saturn's monkey wrench in the care and handling of the "meat puppet" can extend to the subtle art of body communication as well.

Babalu-Ayé's worship is bound up with the shift between secrecy and revelation; it carries many secrets, because the idea is that some functions of the physical world must not be spoken of or it will interfere with their actions. Silent movements, the most physical of communication, are the best road to the God of disease. This can be echoed in the first-house Saturn as well, as they have a tendency to be quiet and introverted, often uncomfortable being the center of attention or speaking out in public. Silence and observation may be their defense mechanisms. At the same time, Babalu-Ayé speaks of the permeable nature of things—sacred clay vessels made for his worship always have a number of tiny holes permeating the top and upper sides, to show that no matter what you do, disease always gets through the holes, and one must learn to be patient with that fact. For first-house Saturn people, that may ring true—no matter what kind of a polished mask they create to cover their awkwardness, sooner or later Saturn starts to show through.

The most common positive way it manifests is that they individual will come across as serious and dignified, and an authority on whatever it is they speak about. Saturn is the planet of Authority, for both better and worse; first-house Saturn people are good at expressing thoughtful gravity, and often seem older and more mature than their age. In many cases, Saturn in the forefront of their lives meant that they had to take on more responsibility at a younger age than most children or youths, and this lends them a serious (and sometimes tired-looking) demeanor. The classic first-house Saturn "look" includes a lean frame and a distinctive "craggy" face. At their best, while they do not generally come across as enthusiastic and inviting, they seem dependable—the person you would lean on to come through with the responsibility. Some end up judges or high-level bureaucrats, people in positions of trust who need to be seen as reliable and serious about their jobs.

One of Babalu-Ayé's titles is Olode, "Lord of the Outside", referring to the fact that he lives on the fringes of society and moves continually from place to place. First-house Saturn people can feel left out of group activity due to their awkwardness and discomfort with being stared at; they may well feel like outsiders. When they have matured, they may be able to be advocates for others in this position, pushing for the inclusion of "undesirables" and working to abolish the whole concept. They know intimately that looks are no basis on which to judge someone, and can push against that current in society. This is Babalu-Ayé's people sweeping away the diseases of fear, callousness, and small-mindedness, which is desperately needed.

Another of the disease god's bynames is Omolu, which means "Child of God", and this is the key to the difficulties of this placement—remembering that one is a child of the Divine, just like everyone else, and worthy of the same kindness and honor. Just because life is imperfect and one doesn't always get it doesn't mean one is not worthy of it. In fact, there is greater honor in going about the world bravely, showing who and what you are, when you don't fit the Beautiful People stereotype. We need Saturn's face in the world to remind us to practice thoughtfulness and consideration, and Saturn gives us a million chances to do that in one lifetime.

♄ Saturn in the 2nd House: Ebisu

Ebisu is another of the Seven Lucky Gods of Japan, who as a group bring treasure, wealth, and good fortune to people, and so can generally be associated with the second house of resources. Ebisu is different from the other six Gods, though—first, because he is actually an indigenous Japanese Shinto spirit, as opposed to the others who came in from Buddhism and Hinduism, and second through his distinctly interesting history.

God-legends are often patchwork and piecemeal, with different stories combined and syncretized and woven together. Ebisu's story—or at least his story since medieval times—became merged with that of Hiroku, the first child of Izanami and Izanagi (Neptune in the seventh house), and the story goes that Ebisu started out as Hiroku. The divine couple who made the islands of Japan had poor luck with many of their children, and the first one, Hiroku, came out with either no bones (according to some stories) or with no arms and legs. He was referred to as a "leech-child", and his horrified parents set him adrift on the ocean in a boat of reeds.

Saturn is the planet of obstacles and disabilities, and while the second house is usually thought of as having largely to do with money and possessions, its base meaning is that of value, and what values one places on things. Saturn placed in the house of values often indicates serious difficulties in self-worth, usually because the family did not communicate to the child that they found them worthy and valued. Hiroku starts out not only disabled, but completely devalued by his parents, who think so little of their first child that they set him out on the ocean to die. It's hard to form a good sense of self-worth when you start out being told, subtly or more blatantly, that you are not worth bothering with.

This difficulty with assessing one's own worth skews the ability to create realistic values about anything else in life, but especially the resources one needs for one's simple survival—in our modern society, wealth. Making money and acquiring possessions looms huge in the mind of the individual with this Saturn placement, pushing some of them to work long hours to hoard what they can, while others deny that money has any power over them and get themselves into debt through unwise financial choices. Sooner or later, though, Saturn calls them to account, and it's a matter of the long, long digging-out process, financial shovelful by financial shovelful.

Another story of the origins of Ebisu has him under another name as one of the two sons of the deity who ruled Izumo province. The Gods decided to hand the province over to another deity, and the father left it up to his two sons to decide whether to fight. The eldest son who would later become Ebisu chose to accept the ruling of the Gods, surrender his spear, and leave the province. This, too, is a Saturn response—*it's the rules, that's the way it works, why should I waste my time and energy fighting? I would rather lose not than lose later.* Ironically, his younger brother chose to stay and fight, and lost. Sometimes the cautious, practical Saturn response is the right choice.

Anyhow, back to the leech-child. Hiroku washes up on the shore of Hokkaido Island, where he is found by an Ainu fisherman named Ebisu Saburo. The kind man feeds him and teaches him to swim, and gives him his last name. Ebisu is associated not only with fishing—he becomes the patron deity of fishermen—but with anything that washes up on shore, whether it be treasures, logs, or even corpses, as he himself was once helpless flotsam. He keeps the ocean safe and clean of pollution, and fishermen tell of how, while he was still the leech-child, it would take seven years for screws, bolts, or umeboshi seeds to wash up on the shore, because Ebisu would carry them in his mouth and crawl along the sea floor to return them to land. (It is also said that he hates it when people pollute the ocean—it devalues the sea which has given humans so much.) It is a very Saturnian way to collect a hoard—bit by painful bit—but that is how people with this placements need to go about it. Giving up would be too easy. Persisting through each painful penny found or earned is Saturn's lesson. In addition, the idea of collecting one's possessions through found or abandoned objects will also resonate with these

Saturn individuals, who often love thrift stores, yard sales and other inexpensive piles of flotsam. One man's trash is another man's treasure, they will tell you.

Over the course of his childhood, with the help of his adopted Ainu family, Ebisu slowly grew arms and legs and learned to walk, and the abandoned leech-child became a fisherman. He is still slightly lame and a little deaf, but his demeanor is much more cheerful now. He is referred to as "the laughing god", and is depicted wearing a tall hat and carrying a rod and a large fish. It is common for Japanese fishermen to pray to Ebisu before they go out to sea, for a fine catch and a safe journey. While he began his tenure with the Seven Lucky Gods as simply a patron of fishermen, he eventually become a generalized wealth-god in his own right, as did the rest of them.

The symbolism of having to grow one's own arms and legs and learn to walk will be familiar to a Saturn placement. Ebisu's whole story is about overcoming obstacles and learning to excel at what you do, until you finally become the expert and have built your own legacy. It is said in some traditions that Daikoku (Jupiter in the fourth house), another of the Seven Lucky Gods, was so taken with Ebisu's success in overcoming his disabilities and being victorious that he apprenticed himself to the lame fisher-god to learn how to master this Saturnian skill. Similarly, those with this placement will need to "grow" their own ability to make enough money and then more than enough, slowly and patiently.

It's also said that people with this placement will not be able to accumulate any savings until after their first Saturn return at age 28-30. It's usually not that they are so profligate, but that expenses keep arising out of unforeseen necessity—obstacle after obstacle—until they have passed that first "Are you an adult yet?" point. Even then, how well their savings will go between this transit and the second Saturn return at age 58 will depend on how maturely they handle the first Saturn return, face down its lessons, and learn everything they can from it.

Since Saturn here can panic over not having a nest egg, the early period of their life can feel quite precarious, adding further to seriousness and anxieties. The older they get, though—Saturn is also the planet of old age—the easier it is for them to acquire wealth, and to be cheerful, and to think well of themselves. The growth of self-esteem will never truly happen until they have conquered the monetary demon, but once that is done, it seriously shifts their system of values. Often they become much more generous in later life, learning from Ebisu that it is better to give than to hoard. Saturn is the planet of discipline, this is the tool needed for the job. The younger they start learning to budget and keep accounts, the better.

Sometimes the lesson for people with this Saturn placement is even harder. I have known a few who were actually disabled themselves, enough that they were unable to work and limited to a fixed government income. However, even several of these managed to figure out ways to create under-the-table secondary incomes, and other ingenious ways to get what they needed. One saved money and bought a used car even though he couldn't drive, and let trusted carless friends use it in return for chauffeuring him on his own errands. All of the ones who managed to come up with alternate income reported that the first step was working on their sense of self-worth, convincing themselves that they were competent enough to do this in spite of everything.

One disabled second-house Saturn person even managed to get off disability, and I remember her triumphant declaration, "I am not a leech!" This put me in mind of Ebisu the leech-child, rejected by his parents, who just needed a kind family to give him a chance. While it is empowering to talk about "overcoming" disability, it is also important to make space for those who will not be physically able to be independent. (Not all attempts at growing limbs go to plan, and being given that financial grace is important.) Part of having enough is having enough to give. That's a difficult concept for this Saturn placement, but it's a lesson they need to learn. It's easy to judge others when you haven't walked in their broken shoes enough to know what's reasonable to expect.

Ebisu is associated with large marine fauna such as whales and whale sharks (because they also lack arms and legs), and throughout the centuries it has been the worshipers of Ebisu who have objected to the Japanese whaling industry. Whale sharks in particular are called "Ebisu sharks" because it is said that they protect fishermen and chase schools of fish closer to the shore. In later life, people with this Saturn placement can be protectors of others who lack resources, and can set up relief funds for those in poverty. Having understood what it is to be in an adversarial relationship with second-house matters, the final success is to be able to help out people who are where they've been, and replace Saturn's miserliness with careful generosity.

Finally, in terms of the positive side of divine disabilities: It is said that Ebisu is partly deaf, and that on the feast of the Seven Lucky Gods at the Grand Shrine of Izumo, he does not hear the bells which summon the other Gods, and thus is still available for prayers and worship at all times ... for his ears are never deaf to those who call out to him.

♂♄ Saturn in the 3rd House: The Seven Swans

The third house is the realm of communication, but it is also the realm of the sibling relationship. This may be because our siblings are the first people with whom we communicate on an equal or semi-equal basis. Our parents teach us how to speak and listen, but they will not be our equals until we are as tall as them. It is often our siblings, or sibling-substitutes, with whom we learn the easy conversational banter between equals that will form most of our communications later in life.

And, of course, where Saturn lies, there you find a block in the process. Having Saturn in the third house not only makes for a strong likelihood that you will not have close relationships with your siblings (or perhaps no siblings at all), it also tends to create obstacles in creating close brotherly and sisterly relationships with others later in life. The third-house Saturn individual may have friends, but not necessarily a special "chum" with whom they can share their hopes and fears. If they do have such relationships, they may be rather Saturnian—meaning that they will be centered around work, or restrictive in some way, or repressive to the true nature of the desperately seeking Saturn individual, or they may be so difficult to achieve as to require near-heroic measures.

Another situation is where the Saturn individual is made responsible for his or her siblings or sibling replacements in some way, perhaps even a way that goes far beyond babysitting and well into thankless caretaking. Sometimes the responsibility was not even thrust on them, but was willingly assumed out of some compulsion; perhaps the hope that the caretaking of these less mature ingrates will someday gain Saturn love and acceptance. It may be that the Saturn person will not be able to free themselves from that burden until they have worked through some karmic Saturnian goal and come out the other side of it.

In the tale of *The Seven Swans*, sometimes also called *The Seven Ravens*, a king has seven fine sons who are his pride and joy, and one daughter whom he ignores. Their mother is dead, and when he takes a new wife, there is animosity between the bride and the stepchildren. The new queen has sorcerous powers, and uses them to transform the seven sons into birds—swans in some versions of the tales; ravens in others. They fly away together, and the king falls deeply into mourning.

As many in other folktales, it is their sister, not their parent, who decides to follow them and save them if she can, even though she is ill-equipped for the task of adventuring. She steals out of the castle and travels aimlessly until she finds them; in the swan-version they are swimming in a lake, but recognize her and flock to her skirts, honking bitterly. A local witch tells her the way to free them, but it will be a terrible trial for her: she must spin nettles grown in graveyards into thread, and weave shirts for each of them. Most difficult of all, she must not speak once during the entire time, even though it may take months or years. Her silence is crucial to the magic.

This is the other obstacle of Saturn in the house of communication. The easy flow of words is difficult for them at best; some may have learning disabilities in the area of language, and even those who chatter constantly may be plagued with verbal tics, glossolalia, stuttering, or just tripping over their words. Some compensate by creating huge vocabularies that would make Encyclopedia Brown proud, but in the end it comes down to one stumbling block: their ability to communicate about themselves and their feelings are painfully limited.

This can result in the person who talks facts for hours on end—perhaps boring those who would have preferred the easy sibling-style conversational banter that this Saturn has difficulty learning—but when asked to speak on personal matters, they veer off into avoidance, stuttering, or silence. Third-house Saturn people find emotional processing sessions unutterably painful, as they are keenly aware of their lack of skill in this area. It is as if emotions cause some kind of shorts in their mental wiring, and they choke up. This blockage may extend itself to writing; one individual that I know read their third-house Saturn spouse's diary of many years and was dismayed to find that it was filled with detailed accounts of what was accomplished at work and what was cooked for dinner, but never once mentioned the spouse, the child, or any loved ones. It was as if a deafening silence prevailed around anything of depth, yet this was not a case of mere shallowness, but of the flow of words being choked off.

In our story, the heroic sister dedicates herself to freeing her brothers. This means that she must spend the next year or so traveling from graveyard to graveyard (the third is the house of short travels, and people with Saturn here may find themselves driven to do a lot of unpleasant commuting that they dislike but find necessary) and gathering painful, stinging nettles. She endures the pain—her brothers need her!—and processes them into thread. Making nettle-thread, or as it is called in Germany, *Nesselgarn*, is a long and arduous process similar to turning flax into linen. It requires letting it rot in stagnant water until it is soft and safe to touch, breaking off the bark and freeing the long fibers, combing out the bits of unwanted vegetation, and spinning the fibers into thread.

This can be a metaphor of just how much difficulty the third-house Saturn individual has in dealing with emotive communications. Those feelings are just too painful to speak straight out; they must be allowed to rot until they are less painful, and be processed through layers of vocabulary and rationalization. It may take them months to clearly articulate their feelings around a difficult incident, and by that time everyone else may have forgotten it and be wondering why it is being brought up now. Sometimes the words and concepts have to be broken down into small pieces, slowed to a crawl—the next step of the yarn-preparation process is literally called a *brake*—so that they can articulate them properly. Dead facts comfort them, and if they can surround the painful living truth with lifeless trivia, it can create a buffer. Spinning painful words is much more palatable when sitting in a graveyard.

During the months of searching and spinning, she maintains complete silence. One day a prince and his hunting party stumbles across her, and he is fascinated by the beautiful mute girl. He attempts to woo her, but although she is receptive, she cannot tell him what she is doing except that all the nettle-spinning is important to her. He convinces her to come home with him, and assures her that she will be allowed to continue her odd hobby. (This is the dream of the third-house Saturn—to find the person who will love them in spite of their trouble with intimate communications, who will draw them out, who will be interested enough to try to pull their deep truths to the surface and tolerant enough not to mind if those truths don't ever come up, and the partner remains a contented stranger to their most intimate depths. This way they will never see and be ashamed of their inner Saturnian monsters.) Over the next few months, he falls in love with her, and convinces her to marry him.

Of course, this being a Saturn story, the happy ending doesn't come with the wedding and the living-happily-after part. The prince's parents are furious, seeing this strange mute maiden as completely unsuitable for their son, and the local folk are uneasy about the new princess's habit of sitting for hours in graveyards, spinning and weaving strange fabrics. The rumor goes out that she is a witch, performing black magic spells. Other rumors claim that she is mad, and therefore dangerous.

This reflects again the lack of clear communication that comes with the burden of a third-house Saturn; they would generally prefer to be judged on their actions rather than their words, but without any kind of a verbal explanation, their actions may make no sense to onlookers. "Because it needs to be done" is often unsatisfactory to people who are trying to determine one's motives and get a clearer understanding of one's behavior. If the Saturn individual is unable to coherently provide an explanation that reflects their feelings and preferences on the matter, things may be wildly misunderstood. There's also a strong fear of going insane among third-house Saturn people; their mental health may be questioned by others so often that they avoid introspection and self-knowledge for fear of actually finding something wrong with themselves, which isolates them further from their emotions ... and their friends and loved ones. Since this is one of the placements that can actually indicate neurochemical or neurological problems, there may be some truth to their fears.

In our story, the king and queen decide that the rumors of witchcraft are a good enough excuse to get rid of their unsuitable daughter-in-law, and they have her arrested and hauled to the stake. In some versions her husband, too, is eventually convinced of her guilt through her unwillingness to give up her strange behavior. Even as she is deposited on the pyre of wood, she is still frantically stitching the final shirt. (Saturn is nothing if not persistent.) As the wood is lit, seven great swans fly down around her and fan out the flames with their wings. She flings the shirts onto them, and they are changed to seven handsome young men, who declare her innocence. Her task is accomplished, and she can finally speak in her defense.

This is the final dream of the third-house Saturn: she has worked hard and painfully to save her brother-figures, and they see her worth, celebrate her, and (most important) speak up for her, saving her the task of facing down the world with words. Their high-flying, birdlike (the third house is associated with airy Mercury) mental abilities have saved her from the flames of those who would misunderstand and scorn her. Of course, whether the story has a happy ending in real life has nothing to do with luck—that's Jupiter's arena—and everything to do with her hard work. Until she can painfully work through the thorns of her own sputtering mental processes, she will not have access to the high-flying part of her mind, or the ability to have true and equal intimacy with others who know her and her motivations for what they really are.

4♄ Saturn in the 4th House: Baba Yaga

Wherever Saturn goes, there's trouble and difficulty, and especially so in the house of home and family. Folktales are full of stories about dysfunctional families; one is practically spoiled for choice. In fact, it seems like there is hardly a fairy tale in existence which has a happy, comfortable family. Some scholars opine cynically that this is because if home wasn't terrible, the heroes and heroines would never leave and have adventures. Be that as it may, it's also true that outer planets in general do not sit well in the astrological place of cozy hearthfire and familial bonds, and Saturn least of all.

On the other hand, not everything about Saturn is bad. Sometimes, even as a bewildered child, the Saturn-afflicted can figure out that creating disciplines can keep you sane, and working hard can be a balm and salve, at least until one can get out and make a new life. Using Saturn's tools to blunt Saturn's effects is a tried-and-true method for survival, if only until one can do more than merely survive. And—while it is no comfort to the abused child—the hardship one has endured can teach lessons which are useful later in life.

Baba Yaga is a Slavic mythical figure who may or may not descend from some local death-goddess wearing the mask of the Ruthless Crone. She stars in a number of folktales; in some she is a kindly old woman who helps the heroes or heroines of the story, and in others she is a classic child-devouring witch. She lives in a tiny hut in the woods which walks around on great chicken-feet, and flies in a magic mortar which she pounds along the ground to keep aloft. The first half of her name means "grandmother", and the second half is still under great argument—it could be a slurred version of anything from "serpent" to "horror" to "disease" to "fury" to "wood nymph".

The most well-known tale of Baba Yaga starts out with—what else?—a dysfunctional family. The father is a widower with one beautiful daughter; he marries a wicked stepmother with two ugly daughters and then promptly leaves them to sell goods in town. While he is gone, the stepmother moves all her charges to a small cottage by the edge of the woods where it is rumored that Baba Yaga lives. She then overworks her stepdaughter by forcing her to do all the chores, in between periodically sending her off into the woods to gather various substances in the hopes that she will come to some harm.

It's classic Saturn—too much work, no way to leave and nowhere to go, and people all around who dislike you and wish you were gone. In actuality, the fourth-house Saturn may not be this bad in reality, but it may feel that way to those who have endured the unique hardships of their own childhoods. It's true that two children raised in the same home may have entirely different memories of what it was like; that's partly because they may have entirely different fourth houses. It's also because what scars one child, a more resilient one may heal from cleanly. Of course, this Saturn placement does statistically load more hard childhoods than, say, Jupiter or Venus here. Survivors—I'll call them that—of this placement's childhood relate having to take on extra responsibilities, perhaps due to poverty, perhaps due to parental disability or addiction or overwork or outright disappearance. Some recall having parents who held standards for them which were too high; they could never do anything right, and their self-esteem took the blows. The most common explanation was that they had to become adults very quickly; there was no time or space or safety to be a child.

However, the heroine (who is named Vasilisa) has a secret weapon. When her mother died, she gave the girl a little doll and told her to keep it always on her person, and always secret even to her father. When Vasilisa is too tired to work further, the doll—who speaks to her in her mother's voice—magically does the work while the girl sleeps. The doll also keeps her safe when she leaves the house as well, turning the eyes of beasts and hunters who might trouble her. Mythologically, the doll can be seen as the memory of things having been good, if only for a little while, and giving the Saturn child a rope to hang onto. *It was not always like this, every minute; if I can grow up I can make the situation be different.* That can give a great deal of energy to dealing with the Saturn slog.

The "dead mother" who helps (Saturn is a planet of Death) can also echo another positive part of this Saturn placement. Many individuals with this Saturn have related how someone in their life took the trouble to befriend them and give them advice, providing even a small and temporary anchor for them, and an example of how a healthy adult-child relationship should be. Over and over we hear that these were older adults—grandparents, aunts and uncles, older teachers or neighbors. Where Saturn puts up obstacles, it also leaves gifts ... which may resemble the best that a Saturnian figure can give. Often, these elders laid down the foundation for the internal discipline which helps the Saturn individual escape the trap of continuing to live in another version of the original home dysfunction.

One night the stepmother, tired of Vasilisa's continued resistance to dying, puts out all the fires and candles in the house. She and the stepsisters push the girl out the door and tell her to go find a neighbor and bring back some coals, and not to come back until she has them. Vasilisa wanders desperately through the woods until she comes across a hut on chicken legs which turns periodically to face a different direction. It is surrounded by a fence of bones topped with skulls at the corners; as night falls, the skulls begin to glow.

At this point, Baba Yaga comes home, riding in her flying mortar with her pestle-weapon. She asks Vasilisa crossly why she has come, and the girl relates her need for coals to light the candles and stove. Baba Yaga tells her that if she will do chores, she can take home some light. Vasilisa is then set to all sorts of chores—cleaning the house and yard, doing the laundry, and cooking a huge pot of stew which Baba Yaga eats herself in one go. She is set to separating grains of corn from rotten grains, and even separating poppy seeds from dirt. When Vasilisa flags, the doll whispers that she should take a nap, and it is done when she awakes. Unlike the bad parent-figure who was supposed to be caring but instead destroyed trust, Baba Yaga is unashamedly a "wicked" figure, who does not pretend to love Vasilisa or care if she is tired. The witch's blunt demands are almost a breath of fresh air, at least because she is honest in her agenda. Baba Yaga is still Saturnian, in that she is elderly, frightening, and demanding, but she is a slightly better form of Saturn who has nothing personally against Vasilisa. However, it is Vasilisa's experience with her terrible stepmother which has trained her to be able to survive Baba Yaga—she knows how to work hard, and how to partner with her magic doll in order to make it through hard periods.

This Saturn placement doesn't necessarily just stop being a problem once its bearers become adults. Even if the fourth-house Saturn person resists the temptation to find partners who share negative patterns with the problematic parents (which is sadly fairly common), they may find Saturn dropping other troubles on them—poverty, long work hours, depression, or disabilities which keep them home. Partners and children may also be or become disabled, requiring the Saturn individual to stay home and care for them. If the Saturn person manages to create an excellent and peaceful home life (which they probably worked very hard to manifest), they may still battle the lack of trust in other people which the Saturn childhood leaves behind.

While Vasilisa is doing chores at dawn, a rider clad all in white and on a white horse rides by the hut. At noon, an all-red rider and horse come by, and in the evening an all-black pair ride by. Baba Yaga comes home after the third rider has passed and can find no fault with Vasilisa's work. She commands three pairs of invisible hands to seize up the grain and squeeze it into oil, and then asks Vasilisa if she has any questions. The girl timidly asks about the three riders she has seen, and Baba Yaga tells her that the white rider was Day, the red rider Sun, and the black rider is Night. They could be seen because the hut and its yard is magical, and reveals the truth of what is, including the mechanisms of Nature. This little vignette in the story seems to be a useless bit of storytelling, but from the point of view of Saturn it is very telling, because it is about Time. Once out of her stepmother's abusive home, Vasilisa can see Time more clearly. It is no longer just a constant Now of misery; the future can clearly be seen.

Saturn has always been associated with the relentless March of Time—the "Father Time" figure is a leftover of the Greek Cronos the child-eater (Saturn in Cancer) who was identified with the Roman god Saturn. To a child, time seems to slog on forever or stand still, especially if bad things are happening. Adults perceive time as running faster, and once the child is an adult, they can begin to make real plans and goals. Yes, some people go on living in the moment and planning nothing, but Saturn isn't a planet who allows that, and we are speaking of people who will have experienced their childhoods as Saturnian. Once they have a goal to work toward, all the labor to bring it about isn't wasted effort that falls into a black hole of needy family members ... assuming that they don't let that happen again. Part of that work is excavating out all the childhood scars and carefully doing what is necessary to heal them, including asking for help and being patient with one's self.

Baba Yaga asks again if Vasilisa has any more questions, and she considers asking about the invisible hands, or Baba Yaga's power, but she feels the doll tremble in her pocket and thinks better of it. The witch then asks her how she accomplished all the work so perfectly. Not wanting to give away the presence of the doll, but not wanting to lie in Baba Yaga's presence either, Vasilisa says, "By my mother's blessing," echoing again the memory of a kind elder who helps one develop that discipline. Baba Yaga's reaction to this is to order Vasilisa out of her hut; the presence of a blessing means that she has no power over the girl. Saturn's discipline can keep the Saturnian figures of one's adulthood at bay, never taking their criticisms personally and never letting them define one's true self.

The witch gives Vasilisa a skull filled with magical glowing coals and tells her to take it home, and to bury it when it has done its job. The girl goes back to her stepmother's house and finds that no candle nor flame has been able to light up; coals or flames would go out as soon as they passed the doorstep. The stepmother and stepsisters have lived plunged into darkness, making literal their behavior. When Vasilisa comes into the house with the glowing skull, flames leap out and burn the whole house down, and the evil family members with it. Baba Yaga, crusty and gruff and ambivalent as she is, has repaid Vasilisa many times over for her efforts. Conscientious work after leaving the dysfunctional family has not only shed light on their darkness but burned it up, showing it to be nothing but ashes after all.

The final sentences of the folktale differ in various versions. In one version, Vasilisa goes to live with her father in town; in another, she goes to a different city and becomes a weaver so fine that she attracts the attention of the Tsar, again showing her excellent discipline. Scholars have noted that the absence of a love interest and wedding, especially with a heroine of marriageable age, makes this Baba Yaga story unusual. However, for Saturn, leaning on someone else's arm is not the point. The ultimate best ending for the fourth-house Saturn story is to become, eventually, the Saturnian elder who helped, not the Saturnian parent who couldn't. That is a victory worth scrubbing a hundred floors to obtain.

♄ Saturn in the 5th House: Gerda

Frey is one of the Golden Gods of Norse mythology, the God of Food and Farming (Mars in Cancer). He is associated with the grain that grows and is cut down, the livestock animals we kill in order to feed our families. He is a sacrificial deity who is ritually killed every year at Lammas (the first day of August when the grain harvest begins), walks the road to the Helheim, the Land of the Dead, for three days, and then is reborn to die for the people again the following year. Like his sister Freyja (Venus in Capricorn), he is a deity of love and sex, and is said to be extremely handsome and well-endowed, with a kind and sunny disposition. Given this, one would guess that he would choose as a bride someone who was as beautiful and golden as himself.

However, the myth does not go that way. While borrowing the all-seeing throne of Odin (Saturn in Pisces) for a day, he catches a glimpse of a dark, solemn giantess-maiden in Jotunheim, the land of the giants. She is gardening in her father's walled compound, which is surrounded by a ring of magical fire. He falls passionately in love with her, but is too intimidated to woo her directly himself, so he sends his elven friend Skirnir to sing his praises instead.

The maiden's name is Gerd or Gerda, which means "guard", and she is a quiet, introverted, guarded goddess, behind her high walls with all their flaming protections. In a sense, she is one of the early prototypes for the later medieval image of the Lady of the Walled Garden, difficult to access and likely to send suitors on a possibly fatal quest in order to win her regard. She is not a maiden of gaiety and good cheer, and this will feel familiar to those with Saturn, the planet of obstacles and discipline, in the fifth house of playfulness and romance.

We could say that Saturn hates the fifth house, or we could say that the fifth house dislikes his presence as much as he would rather not be there. Imagine a suited, briefcased banker, elderly and childless, plunked down in the middle of a playground full of wild urchins having a mudfight. In Hollywood movies, the banker will suddenly rediscover the childhood he never had, and start laughing and slinging mud with the brats, not caring that his good suit is ruined and that he will be late for his day at work. In real life, he is likely to sit awkwardly on a bench in the corner, praying for someone to come and rescue him before he gets hit with a mudball, painfully aware that he may not have a job at the end of the day. Fifth-house Saturn natives know that awkward, embarrassed feeling intimately. Everyone keeps telling them that they should loosen up and be more playful, but when they make their inelegant attempts to do so—often more because they think they ought to than from any genuine motivation—it tends to fall flat, sending them back into their isolated piles of books and computer programs. Sometimes, for self-protection, they develop a brusque and distant attitude, which discourages others from inviting them to social events. The walls go up with flames on the top, and they'll just stay in their well-tended little garden forever, thank you very much.

The fifth house is also the house of romance, and Saturn here can make someone feel entirely out of place here as well. Social codes of romance often expect a great deal of guessing about which romantic gestures will be welcomed, how one should act when making them, which physical boundaries it is acceptable to encroach upon, whether the target is pleased with one's efforts, and when it is appropriate to begin discussing future plans. This can all seem like walking into a mine field with a blindfold on to the individual with this Saturn placement, and their defense is generally to devalue the whole concept. Who needs all that silliness anyway? Some resort to blunt, out-front sexual display, figuring that at least they'll attract people who aren't looking for hearts and flowers; some withdraw and secretly wait for someone to breach their walled garden ... someone who won't then expect them to act like a figure in a fairytale. Saturn here can also delay the actual experience of falling in love with all those fireworks-and-swooning brain chemicals; one person I know with this placement did not fall in love until his mid-twenties (even after two serious relationships) and when it finally happened, he had to ask a friend about "these strange symptoms that seem to all be part of a syndrome of some sort."

At any rate, the courtship does not go in any way like the wooing of a fairytale princess. Skirnir, who disapproves of Frey's choice of maiden but does not want to let his friend down, starts out with a fairly blunt demand of marriage, and is met with a fairly blunt refusal. At this point he begins to threaten her with all sorts of hideous curses and magical torment that will be visited upon her if she will not meet Frey in person, outside her father's flaming walled citadel. She finally gives in, seemingly more to silence this ranting madman than out of any anticipation for it, and agrees to meet Frey at night in the Barri Woods. If she must dispense with her walls, she will settle for a dark wilderness; either way, she is not exposing herself and her discomfort to the light of day.

Frey can hardly bear to wait the few days until they meet, and while the meeting itself is offstage, it actually seems to go well. Sometimes the Saturnian individual needs a more open and effusive suitor to be the first one to confess love and desire, which allows them to explore their own feelings with less vulnerability. If the partner is willing to be the vulnerable one at first, it can even the playing field. However, it is important that they use this safer space to learn to open up; expecting the more extroverted partner to do all the heavy lifting of emotional connection and vulnerability may eventually tire out the partner and send them looking for greener and less emotionally desiccated pastures.

Gerda opens up toward Frey and agrees to marry him, but all does not end on a perfect note. There are objections toward their interracial wedding, from the Aesir who disapprove of the Jotnar, from Frey's Vanir family and from Gerda's own Jotnar family. They marry in spite of this, and modern worshipers celebrate them as marriage-gods who are willing to bless unusual or socially unacceptable pairings, as opposed to Frigga the Aesir All-Mother (Moon in Capricorn) who blesses community-supported weddings. We forget that one Saturnian obstacle to romance can be the social consequences of "improper" romances—for example, when one person is already married to someone else whom it would be disadvantageous to divorce, or when one person's career makes living together impossible ... or when one person wants children and the other does not.

The fifth house is also the house of children, and while not everyone with this placement is childless, it does often indicate some sort of physical infertility, or someone who chooses a career over having children, or that children will not come until later in life (casting them as the older Saturnian parent), or that they will end up caring for stepchildren instead of their own offspring. Even if biological children come when reproductively summoned, they may have trouble playing the part of the sensitively responsive parent, preferring instead to focus on a "teacher" or "disciplinarian" role. In Gerda's case, even though her husband is literally the God of Fertility, she is placed in a difficult bind. He is a political hostage to the Aesir, the Sky Gods who are her family's hereditary enemies, and any children she bears him will also be hostages. Faced with this dilemma, she chooses to remain barren; here her knowledge of herbs stands her in good stead. This echoes centuries of tradition where the village herb-woman—sometimes a practitioner on the edges of social acceptance, sometimes entirely an outcast—was often the only choice for desperate women who were seeking abortions, and possibly the only source of comfort in the face of that dire necessity. The Lady of the Walled Garden knows how to set Saturnian boundaries when necessary, even if she weeps alone afterwards.

Not only procreativity, but also creativity in general, is ruled by this house and thus under Saturn's touch with this placement. Fifth-house Saturn people can be quite creative, but they need to do it within a clear structure. No free verse or improv music or throwing paint at a wall for them; they flourish under rigid limitations, where the rules are all set out and they can diligently fill in the blanks. Gerda is a gardener, the patroness of walled herb gardens, which—as anyone who has ever admired a medieval knotwork garden can testify—is a patient, painstaking job that requires planning, structure, and continual upkeep. But it is beautiful, and also useful, an important Saturnian quality.

Frey is a busy deity; his fertility duties take him to Asgard, where he is a hostage, Vanaheim where he is born, and Alfheim the realm of the Light-Elves. Gerda does not wish to go with him on his travels, nor to ever set foot in Asgard (and perhaps Alfheim as well, as her people and the elves are not friends) so they spend a fair amount of time apart, she staying in her walled garden when he must travel for his duties. While the fifth-house Saturn individual can learn to open up and love deeply with the right person, tapping into the loyalty which is one of the positive attributes of Saturn, they will never be easy and comfortable with fifth-house areas. They don't like to risk, and the House of Gambling is all about risking. Generally, they will go so far, and no further, and the partner needs to be aware of this. The Lady of the Walled Garden grows treasure, in her garden and in her heart, but those walls can be necessary to protect a fragile seedling of love and shepherd it towards its rare flowering.

♄ Saturn in the 6th House: Shennong

The sixth house is the Place of Labor, and Saturn is the planet most concerned with Duty. When the Lord of Duty moves into the Virgo-associated house of Work, he becomes obsessed with it. This could be the work one does for a job, or maintaining one's health, or just keeping the house clean. It's very easy for the sixth-house Saturn to become a workhorse, pulling the plow or the cart day after day until they break, because it's no longer about just doing the work. It's about making order out of unending chaos, which is where we bring in a primordial king of one of the oldest civilizations on Earth, who set out to do just that.

In Chinese mythology, Shennong was a semidivine culture hero born thousands of years ago who became the ruler of the Yan Di people of what is now western China. At the time, the people were barbarians who did not know how to farm, and lived on whatever they could hunt and fish. Shennong set out to find better ways for them to survive, and ended up inventing many of the practical applications of civilization. His people started out weak and sickly, but by the time he was done with them, they were healthy and prosperous. In some accounts, he had the head of a bull and the body of a man, but in others, he simply had large horns of various sorts. Either way, one of his first inventions was the plow. Harnessing large animals to pull and begin the process of major agriculture, which kicked off the agricultural revolution, at least in his area of China. He also invented the horse yoke—horses need a different sort of yoke than oxen, due to the shape of their bodies—and all this being harnessed to a plow may feel very familiar to someone with Saturn in the sixth house.

Shennong also invented the wooden rake used in harvesting, the axe, and the hoe. He taught his people how to dig wells, irrigate fields, preserve seeds in boiled horse urine, and to clear the major trees on a piece of land with fire before plowing the earth. Sometimes he manifested as a great burning wind which magically cleared entire forests and made them ready for farming, with fertilizing ashes ready to be plowed in. (This is the sort of mass efficiency that the sixth-house Saturn dreams of—if only tasks could be cleared out so quickly and cleanly!) He figured out which plants were best for agriculture by testing thousands of plants on himself, and seeing if they were nourishing, uneventful, or even poisonous. In the process, he discovered the tea plant, which was to become central to Asian cooking and agriculture, mostly due to the caffeine content (which, according to the earliest texts, helps laborers get out of bed and do more work).

Like the sixth-house Saturn, Shennong certainly understood what it was to work hard, to harness himself to Duty and keep pulling. As a ruler, he honored farmers and laborers above all others; he ruled without ministers or punishments. It was said that he spoke after three days, walked within a week, and could plow a field at age three. That sounds more along the lines of godly powers rather than simple humanity, but his precocity gives a side glance to another problem with this placement—perfectionism. Saturn in the sixth house can have extremely high standards for labor, both for others (which are almost always disappointed) and for themselves. They can be miserably self-critical, thinking that they ought to be able to handle far more than they actually can, and do it better than they are realistically capable of. Something within them keeps thinking that they are failing if they can't manage the equivalent of plowing a field in childhood.

Of course, Saturn being what it is, the placement doesn't always manifest by overdoing the Saturnian duty. Instead, sometimes the individual can't bring themselves to do it at all. Saturn rules structure and processes, and the sixth-house process itself has to do with assessing the job which must be done, and how to accomplish that. For most people, that's not too hard to learn—one looks at the goal and works backwards from it, breaking it down into steps until you get to the next step. Then you work down the chain, figuring out the order of operations. However, when you have the planet of obstacles blocking this process, the individual with this placement can feel like every complex task is just a giant heap of confusion, with no idea where to start or how to find the end of the string. With this Saturn manifestation, just cleaning a room may be overwhelming, much less keeping up with the complexities of bodily maintenance. Instead of obsessing about work and maintenance, they end up avoiding it in terror.

As well as practical skills for labor, Shennong also organized and structured the days, months and years. He created the calendar, dividing the years into twenty-four sections, and then started the custom of the weekly farmer's market. The sixth-house Saturn yearns for a regular rhythm to their life; even individuals whose charts are full of Uranian free-spirit energy secretly want some kind of regular rhythm to which they can anchor themselves. The problem is that they either have a terrible time maintaining it, or they manage only by complete obsession with lists, charts, calendars, and an hour-by-hour preoccupation with efficiency. Finding an easy balance to organization and structure can be a lifetime's challenge for them.

However, giving the people food, tools, and skills was not enough to keep them healthy, and so Shennong dedicated the rest of his life to the discovery of medicine. He had already tested every plant on himself in order to discern their nourishment content; now he did it all again to find their healing uses. In the process he discovered all the most powerful Chinese medicinal plants, and taught their uses to others, becoming the first clinical herbalist. He also invented acupuncture, moxibustion, and the art of taking pulse measurements. Shennong's catalog of three hundred and sixty-five medicinal plants, or at least the catalog mythically attributed to him, became the basis for centuries of study of herbalism and botany. After this, he was known as the Medicine King.

This, too, is a title which will resonate with Saturn in the house of health. Classic manifestations of this placement include the hypochondriac who suffers from a million ailments, as well as the health nut who puts themselves on strict dietary, exercise, and medicinal regimens to the point of robbing their life of happiness in order to stay at a certain weight or stave off aging. They may experiment with hundreds of alternative medicine products and procedures to find the perfect panacea, the right combination which will make their bodies function like a well-oiled machine. Sometimes, of course, this Saturn placement manifests as disease and health problems from an early age, which the individual must suffer with or fight against. It's less often an obvious mechanical issue and more likely to be a general state of overall ill health, what they used to call "having a weak constitution".

It's said that Saturn's effect on this house is to heighten the mind/body connection, which then causes anxieties and nervous conditions—of which, in the Virgo-associated house, this Saturn placement has plenty—to afflict the physical body. The ultimate goal of this Saturn's health quest is to find that mind/body balance; they often discover that as long as they are plagued with mental distress, they will be plagued with physical distress as well. However, in the meantime, some may rival Shennong in using themselves as lab experiments for new healing methods.

The underlying goal in all of this, for the sixth-house Saturn, is purification. Organization and calendrical rhythm are attempts to purify the chaos of the outer life, and health care attempts to purify the inner one. Even the obsession with work purifies the will, distracting the individual from their anxieties, at least in the moment. It is said that Shennong could make his body turn entirely transparent, so that he could see how each food plant and medicine plant worked on each organ. In a way, this echoes the ideal of being able to see and know the mind/body connection; his transparency is also a kind of purity, using himself as a truly clean slate to sacrifice dutifully for his diseased subjects.

Except that this is a Saturn story, and those sometimes end tragically—Saturn is one of the two planets of Death, after all. According to the myths, Shennong heroically consumed seventy poisons in one day, and it was the end of him. He had made himself a magical antidote potion, and as long as he drank it immediately after noticing that the plant he had consumed was making him ill, he would be restored to health. Finally, however, he ingested the yellow flower of a poisonous weed which caused all his organs to burst before he could drink his antidote, and he died. Since he had given his life for the betterment of humanity, the cosmic Gods made him the deity of farmers and doctors, the Medicine King of Heaven. While final deification is a nice thing for a demigod, Shennong's ending is a warning tale for the sixth-house Saturn. Sometimes Duty kills. Sometimes not doing one's duty, at least to one's body, also kills. Finding the gentle balance between the two can save your life.

The sixth-house Saturn yearns for order and purification, because on some level they believe that it will calm their inner maelstrom of anxiety and self-criticism. However, like all things Saturnian, the goal is not to throw yourself at the problem until relief comes. Saturn does things the hard way, and here the hard way is to work at bringing the calm, ordered, serene mindset to the ongoing task of making the structure, injecting it little by little until the mental and physical run together. It's a work of tiny persistent steps, because that's the sixth-house way. Shennong's legacy was to bring order out of chaos, and this comes not with a great burning wind, but with a thousand small moves of patience.

7♄ Saturn in the 7th House: Penelope

The great epic story of the Odyssey is mostly about the wandering hero Odysseus, whom we met under Mercury in the ninth house. However, while he is having two decades of adventures, his wife Penelope is left at home, not knowing if he is alive or dead. I am bringing her out of the background and up to the front of the stage to illustrate both the painful and hopeful sides of the planet of obstacles living in what used to be called the House of Marriage.

Penelope is a daughter of the Greek city-state of Sparta, and is married off to Odysseus, the young king of the nearby small city-state of Ithaca. Her marriage is arranged, which was quite ordinary for high-born Greek women of the period, but it gives us our first taste of the planet of Discipline in the House of Marriage. However, she and Odysseus get along well, and she comes to love him. Odysseus, for his part, builds them a special marriage bed that can never be moved, by building the bedroom around a living olive tree coming up through the floor by a window, and making it one leg of the bed. This symbolizes, for him, the loyalty and endurance he hopes that they will have in their marriage together. This is the other, more positive side of Saturn—at its best Saturn the crystallizing planet will set a bond in stone and make it unbreakable.

But soon after their wedding, the Trojan War starts and Agamemnon calls up all the allies of Mycenae to go to war with him ... and that includes Odysseus. He tells Penelope goodbye and leaves for the war, but manages to anger a number of Gods during his tenure there. He is cursed to wander for many years before returning home, and ends up on a journey from island to island in the Mediterranean, moving forward and falling back, despairing of coming home and yet continuing the quest against all odds. This leaves Penelope alone for nearly two decades with her young son Telemachus, who grows to manhood during his father's absence. This is the most extreme manifestation of this planetary position—actual physical separation from the loved one, for an excruciatingly long period of time.

Penelope is not a cheerful or charismatic woman; she is shy, reserved, and prefers to live alone, another Saturn trait expressed in her nature. Saturn has trouble with enthusiastic emotional expression, and in the seventh house it tends to create more restrained and practical methods of showing love—

ironing the shirts instead of speaking it aloud. Indeed, her very name means "weft-face", alluding both to her talent as a weaver and the idea of the weft being hidden within the warp, concealing its true nature while enhancing the existing structure. "Weft-face", in ancient times, may have meant someone who hid themselves by weaving a particular image around their lives. Unlike Mercury or Venus or Neptune who may deliberately shift their outward demeanor to achieve a certain result (authentic or not), Saturn's "hiding" is usually out of discomfort, and the inability (or unwillingness) to bring their inner feelings out for public consumption. Saturn hides behind correctness, formality, taciturnity, and not making eye contact.

Year after year, Penelope is alone and must decide whether to hold on for Odysseus's potential return or declare herself a widow and start a new life. A seventh-house Saturn can cause long-term distance between partners, but "distance" and "separation" can come in many forms. It can, of course, be widowhood—the spouse may actually die—but Saturn can also manifest itself in other guises. The partner may need to spend a painful amount of time away from home due to money or survival issues, thinning the bonds of the relationship until both parties no longer know how to come together. They may be emotionally distant and unavailable; Saturn has a great deal of difficulty in expressing emotion. They may suffer from depression, which is also ruled by Saturn. They may divorce and leave. They may be emotionally abusive; extreme rages tend to come more usually from Pluto or Mars, but Saturn's influence via the partner can drag someone down through year after grinding year of constant negative commentary that wears away self-esteem.

Sometimes there are also other Saturnian threads that bind someone into enduring a relationship of separation rather than intimacy, including both exterior and interior pressure. Individuals with this Saturn placement are more likely to be attached to conservative, socially acceptable forms of relationship, which may include staying on for the sake of the children or because they took a vow. Saturn may push them to reduce their expectations—"At least he doesn't hit me." "At least she isn't taking the children and not letting me see them." If the marriage seems "correct" by social standards, even if there is no real intimacy and their souls are distant from each other, they may feel like they have no right to complain. After all, there are so many people who have it worse—why not be grateful for the crumbs you get? Of course, it's not that they never think about leaving—

many spend years worrying (another Saturn word!) about whether to bury the marriage and move on, or stay the course out of stubbornness or social expectation, just as Penelope did for years. Uranus in the same position would have been out the door long ago.

The situation is made more complicated for Penelope with the arrival of hordes of suitors, powerful local men who believe that Odysseus is dead and who want to marry Penelope for her wealth and position. They invade her house, eat her food, drink her wine, and press their suits; she is socially obligated to host them, but does not want to abandon her vigil for Odysseus. Persistence is one of the quite virtues of Saturn, and when lined up alongside loyalty, it can keep the individual plodding onward relentlessly for a very long time. Her son Telemachus, reaching his teenage years, is more and more resentful of these men who are taking advantage of his fatherless household.

At the same time, she has to find a socially acceptable reason to put the invaders off. Penelope is a skilled weaver, and she announces that she will not choose a suitor until she has finished an elaborate future burial shroud for her father-in-law, the elderly Laertes. Every night for three years, she undoes the weaving which she has done the day before, and thus gets no further along on it. She uses the weaving to buy herself time, but weaving itself is often a symbol of Time, and Saturn is the planet of Time—the inexorable ticking of the clock, measured in sunrises and sunsets and seasons and years. By her trick with the weaving, she tries to place a Saturnian obstacle in front of Saturn's rule of Time itself.

Far away, her husband Odysseus spent nine years with the nymph Calypso, and went back and forth about staying with her forever or trying to go back to Ithaca and rejoin his wife. He did finally leave Calypso's island, and spent some years further avoiding dangers and trying to get home, but it is implied that it was a close thing. Penelope herself, in desperation, both asks Artemis (Moon in Sagittarius) to kill her and end the situation, and considers marrying one of the suitors. Saturn closes in around her, with the threads of her promises, social expectation, stubbornness, and death. It is no coincidence that the fabric whose threads she weaves and then unweaves is a funeral shroud.

The seventh house is not just the sort of long-term relationships you might have; it's also the sort of people you are instinctively attracted to, and—on a more subtle level—it's the qualities in yourself which you pretend you don't have, and you "outsource" onto your partners. (I sometimes think that the seventh should really be called the "House of Projection".) Penelope and Odysseus do, on an archetypal level, project Saturnian qualities onto each other. He is philandering his way around the Mediterranean, having adventures, while she is his outsourced "discipline", bound to the house and to her long, patient vigil. He is the one who is unavailable, "distant", while she is present and must nurture her son. People will often choose partners who have been unwittingly tapped to "carry" the sign-and-planets energy for them, so that they can complacently continue thinking, "That's them, not me. See how different we are there?" It is not until one owns that energy in one's self that one can cleanly come to relationship with the other person, and perhaps understand what energy you are carrying for the sake of their own denial.

With Saturn here, the spouse may be the disciplined, faithful, organized, rule-following one who sets boundaries and perhaps keeps the social customs. This allows the other partner to be the opposite of all those things, confident that the partner will set the Saturnian boundaries for them. The problem is that it's easy to hate the feel of Saturn (perhaps your own most of all) and it's also easy to project that hatred of Saturn's rules onto the partner who is "being" that voice for you. Difficult seventh-house planets like Saturn, Uranus, Neptune, and Pluto (and the signs they rule) are both the hardest to bring one's self to own, and the most important to go through that process with. At the least, if the individual with this placement is stuck with an unsatisfactory (or nonexistent) primary relationship, they need to take a hard look at what inner and outer forces have brought them to this place. Saturn is the sensei of the Dojo of Hard Knocks, and he will be much easier on you if you are actively working on dismantling the roots of those obstacles, instead of outsourcing all the responsibility. This planet is all about taking on unpleasant responsibility, and that's a key point to keep in mind when dealing with Saturn problems.

The important thing to remember, if you're reading this because it's in your chart, is that Saturn is also the planet of maturity and old age. Wherever you have Saturn, you're a late bloomer. Saturn holds down progress in that area until you have reached a certain level of age and maturity—traditionally after the first Saturn return, and then full blossoming waits until after the second return. It's not that it won't come at all, it's just that you'll have to wait for it. Odysseus does eventually come home in secret, just after Penelope has come up with a new and creative ruse to get rid of suitors: the man who can marry her must bend and string Odysseus's bow. As we can see in the story of Rama (Sun in the tenth house), bending and stringing a magical bow is a common mythological trope for a woman choosing a suitor, or wanting to put one off. After stringing it, the suitors must then shoot an arrow through twelve lined-up axe heads. The newly arrived Odysseus is briefed on the situation by Athena (Sun in Aquarius), his patron deity, and comes in disguise to the suitors' shooting-test. He strings the bow and promptly starts shooting the suitors, along with the aid of his son Telemachus, whom he has previously contacted and warned about his plans.

Penelope, shocked at the sudden carnage and not recognizing the man whom she has not seen for two decades, asks him to prove that he is actually Odysseus. To test him, she tells her maid in a clearly audible aside that the maid should go upstairs and move the marriage bed into another room. Odysseus is shocked and angry; did he not make the marriage bed with one post as a living tree, so that it could not be moved? Has this symbol of his faith in the endurance of their marriage been cut down? As he protests, Penelope understands that he is really her lost husband, as no one else would not only know about the bed but understand its significance. With relief, she welcomes him back and they live out the rest of their years together. Saturn has taken their youth—and indeed at one point in the story Penelope mourns that they did not get to spend their younger years together—but Saturn's gifts come as a reward for maturity.

Astrologers often see a seventh-house Saturn in the composite charts of late-in-life marriages, after the children have all grown and flown and someone has been widowed or gotten divorced; it is the sign of a love which has already figured out what it wants and is past all of the foolish drama of younger love. In the natal chart, the full wisdom of how to be with someone else and yet still hold your own healthy boundaries can be a lesson only learned with time—and Saturn's gift here is that it will be learned, only later rather than sooner, when they are old enough to understand the full beauty of what that can be.

8♄ Saturn in the 8th House: Dhumavati

Long ago in Hindu mythology, the great god Shiva (Sun in Scorpio) lost his first wife, Sati. She burned to death on a pyre, and he mourned her and retreated to a mountaintop to become an ascetic, until his second wife Parvati (Venus in Virgo) came to him. However, a later tale relates that another goddess rose from the cold ashes of Sati's burned-out pyre. She was old and ugly, with wrinkled skin and disheveled hair the dark gray of wet ashes, sometimes turning to black. Her eyes were black and fearsome, her nose long and crooked, her breasts sagging. She had long fang-like teeth, but some had fallen out, leaving gaps in her smile. She was dressed in the rags of cremation grounds, with ornaments of snakes and skulls, and around her a low circle of fire from the cremation ground flickered as she walked, making a moving round of flame on the ground. A flock of crows followed behind her, like a cawing black cloud in the sky. She was gaunt and always hungry, devouring many things but never sating her craving. Her hands trembled, but still clutched a winnowing basket.

This was Dhumavati, who is listed as one of the ten Mahavidyas, a group of fierce goddesses led by Kali who come to challenge mortals with misfortune, in order to teach them how to overcome and evolve. All are equally likely to afflict people or help them, according to a scale of their own accounting. It is said that Dhumavati approached the mourning Shiva and asked him for nourishment, as a test to see if he would recognize the last parts of his dead wife's ashes. When he did not, she ate him, devouring him whole in one bite. Only then was she sated, holding Shiva's connection to the entire Universe within her. However, he demanded that she release him, and she had to vomit him back up. Enraged, he sent her away, and from then on Dhumavati was known as the Widow. Her name literally means "dwelling in smoke" from her origins on the funeral pyre, and she is said to be able to defeat demons by conjuring up stinging smoke. She flies across the sky in a chariot pulled by black scavenger birds, and is the harbinger of all things inauspicious—hunger, thirst, need, poverty, illness, madness, death.

Astrologers like to downplay the old title of the eighth house as the House of Death, but when Saturn—one of the two planets of Death—finds its way into this darkened house, it will be very hard to pass off this shadowed place of mystery and transformation and karma and yes, Death, as simply a house of dealing with other people's money. (It's almost amusing watching feel-good commercial astrologers try to whitewash this placement, reassuring people that at least they will probably get decent inheritances from family members.) The eighth is Pluto's house, and it is said that if Saturn has one friend in the zodiacal solar system, it is Pluto ... if only because they share some similar interests. When Saturn is here, Death will have an overarching impact on the person's life. Stories of near-death experiences, serious illnesses, caring for the dying, working in death-related industries, all about. Getting up close and personal with Death and loss is part of what Dhumavati teaches. Her ugliness and aura of all things inauspicious demands that we look closer at that which we fear, and work on it until it no longer has power over us. (Strangely enough, this placement doesn't herald an early death so much as a long, slow decline, which can be worse from some people's point of view.)

Widows, in Hindu culture, are always inauspicious, which is why there are so many cultural traditions which encourage murdering or starving them. They hold a fear which the overarching Indian culture, so worried about being married for survival, is not willing to look at. In the West, we may not kill our widows, but we still avert our gazes from outright wailing sorrow and loss, from poverty, from beggars, from illness, and from dying people. The point of the eighth house is to sit with all of these fears and to see them as an opportunity for self-work and compassion; to see the beauty behind the ugly, hungry, limping old woman. Poverty can be a special fear of people with this placement, and they can develop control issues over sharing their money with others or allowing themselves to accept donations. After all, the donations could dry up after you've become dependent on them, says Saturn, and then what would you do? Learning to trust that the fluctuations of resources are survivable and can be accepted with equanimity is a hard lesson here. The eighth house is about sharing resources, and that doesn't just mean money, but also sharing oneself. An iron fist on the finances can reflect the iron fist on every other connection.

The eighth is the house of sex, and of deep intimacy, and Saturn sets up roadblocks here as well. Saturn here is notorious for sexual repression, hangups, impotence, and other disabilities which cause sexual problems, all of which provide good excuses for avoiding intimacy. People with this placement may be so afraid of losing a loved one that they cannot open up to them, protecting their inner self from the future pain of loss. For that matter, merging with another soul means the death of the separate individual, and that vulnerability can feel like an impending disaster. This placement makes it very hard to trust other people; Dhumavati looms like a carrion crow over every moment of intimacy. She herself is said to enjoy sex a great deal, and sometimes puts on an illusion of being young and beautiful in order to get into someone's bed, only to become the old hag in the middle of it. Due to her hunger, she is never truly sexually satisfied. She is a goddess of the Tantric transgression of taboos—she devours meat and wine and people.

That hunger can also be reflected inside the Saturn person themselves. Letting go in a relationship sometimes means being overtaken by passions they have endeavored to keep under rigid control—rage, jealousy, territoriality, and the devouring hunger for another person's soul. Like Dhumavati the Widow who was rejected for her hunger, for wanting to consume Shiva's entire being, this placement bestows both a burning, passionate hunger for intimacy and a deep fear of rejection when their inner nature is seen, thus requiring unyielding repression of those feelings. Instead of being unacceptably fierce in their hoarding of their lovers, they become fierce in the hoarding of their privacy, their boundaries, any taste of their interior selves. Inside is a smoking pyre with the thin, hungry, burning-eyed Widow standing atop it, and no one, they tell themselves, wants to deal with that.

This is another planetary placement which is often—not always, but often—associated with an austere or even abusive upbringing. Saturn is associated with the disciplining parent (traditionally the father, but in some families that isn't the case) and this placement suggests that they were damaged or limited in some way; perhaps absent, dying, ill, emotionally distant, or cruel. Discipline happened, but it may have been unfair or overdone or dependent on their mood, which can bring a certain amount of hypervigilance to the adult. Randomly-descending destruction from parents are less likely to teach good habits and more likely to just teach the child that the Universe is an unfair place where terrible and undeserved things simply happen, and there is nothing we can do about it. Looking around at the world, it is very easy to find evidence to support this theory, if everything is taken at face value ... which is exactly what Dhumavati wants us to avoid. Her winnowing basket is symbolic of the discernment we must cultivate to get underneath those illusions, the stories we tell ourselves, the fears we allow to rule us. She also carries a broom, to sweep those illusions away.

As the House of Transformation, Saturn arranges both great difficulties in working through the necessary deep changes and their inevitability, often multiple times in a lifetime. *It won't come easily, it will be painful, and it will happen anyway, over and over.* It's said that this is the second most difficult of all the Saturn placements, outdone only by the twelfth house, and the individual may have many life-changing disasters and upheavals which strike out of nowhere and upend their lives. Dhumavati is also a goddess of sudden disasters, but her point, with these inflictions, is to develop emotional resilience. If you live through enough disasters, not unchanged but still upright, you learn that each new disaster can also be ridden out the same way. People with this placement may end up in counseling careers, often crisis or grief counseling, or just be the friend people informally call when that happens.

This is also the house of Mystery, and Dhumavati is said to gift her worshipers with psychic powers. She is not always a disaster-inflicting harridan—all the Mahavidyas can be benign or smiting by turns—and some say that she has a tender heart for those who can see her beauty without whitewashing who and what she is. She has two or four arms, and while she variously holds the winnowing basket, the broom, and a sword or spear, one hand is always open to grant boons. She is the power in enduring suffering, the good fortune which comes through bad fortune. She teaches the skills of patience, persistence, forgiveness, and detachment, and rewards those who work hard at them. While Saturn can set up a certain amount of fear, any planet in the eighth house will, sooner or later, start trying to strip the veil off of the mysteries and dig deep into the underworld. Understanding the mysterious is part of that house, and with Saturn it will be the mysteries behind all of Dhumavati's "inauspicious" qualities and symbolism, riddled with fear and grief as they are.

Dhumavati is worshiped in the cremation ground; to receive her blessings one needs to go to a place of death or suffering, such as a hospice. When you are willing to confront everything that is horrible inside and outside your mind, you can see through the smoke to her wisdom. Saturn, the planet of discipline, wants its eighth-house people to create a discipline of seeing through the smoke and walking willingly into the cremation ground, unclenching the iron fist and letting whatever is necessary fall to the ground. Saturn makes this house into the place of ashes, of smoke, of the grey end of all things. From this place, transformation can begin.

9♄ Saturn in the 9th House: Aeneas

So far, most of our heroes portraying the House of Travel were adventurous souls who thrilled to the journey, mastering one quest after another, and never losing their nerve. They were often driven by Gods who wanted certain actions accomplished, but while they might grumble and complain, in the end the adventure was enough. That may be true for Sun and Mercury and Venus and Jupiter, but it's not true at all for Saturn. If Saturn travels, it's because he has a duty to do it, and he'd really rather be at home. Saturn cringes at the idea of adventures—as Bilbo Baggins put it, "Nasty unpleasant things! Make you late for dinner…"—but if ordered to do it, Saturn will take a breath, pull up his bootstraps, and take on the goddamned escapade. But he won't enjoy it, and he will be hoping the whole time that after this, he'll be allowed to settle down.

The Greek hero Aeneas, mentioned briefly in Homer's *Iliad* but given a full epic story in Roman times by the poet Virgil, was the nephew of King Priam of Troy during the Trojan War. His legend claims that he was the son of Aphrodite (Venus in Libra) by Priam's brother; his divine mother gives him up as soon as he is born, but during the Trojan War she and several other Gods protect him from harm, with the implication that he has a greater destiny. He is a good warrior, but is not generally the sort of man who becomes a hero in Greek tales; he is not mighty like Hercules or courageous like Achilles or brilliant like Odysseus. Instead, the adjectives generally used to describe him are more like "pious" and "honorable" and "dutiful". In fact, later scholars have commented that being dutiful is Aeneas's greatest weakness.

When duty-bound Saturn comes into the House of World View, it's not uncommon for the individual with this placement to start out rather narrow in their focus. They may have been raised in a home with a lot of rules, where they were not encouraged to look further than those four walls, either physically or mentally or both. They may not have been exposed to much outside their family's culture, and thus they come into the greater world with a bit of a handicap. Because it's still the ninth house, they will end up being exposed over time to situations and experiences which broaden them, but it won't feel comfortable. At some point they may realize that it's worth the trouble to learn about the wider world, and set out to do so, but that plan will be methodical and well thought through. They will travel to specific places, take specific classes, or read specific philosophies, exposing themselves in small manageable amounts to new information, taking their time in integrating it into their world view.

That's the lucky ones, of course. This placement of Saturn is known to bestow trouble in the ability to take in large amounts of new information; they may have learning disabilities which make higher education study difficult, for example, an obstacle in this house of adult education. They may have trouble getting outside of their comfort zone enough to travel somewhere with a different language and very different customs and feel anything but discomfited. They may—and Aeneas certainly does—have a very rigid spiritual view of the world and how Providence works. This is the house of religion, and the ninth-house Saturn may be quite inflexible in how they see the influence of the Divine in the world. They've got a mental map of it—either the one they were first taught and have no intention of questioning, or one they developed themselves—and it will be very difficult for them to swerve away from it.

However, the Saturn process in a chart doesn't just place the obstacle of having trouble with the processes of a sign and house. It also, eventually, adds insult to injury by pushing the ill-prepared, Saturn-handicapped individual into situations which require that they overcome it. We see this again and again with Saturn anywhere in the chart, because part of Saturn's lesson is to find ways to compensate for your disabilities, and you can't do that if you never face experiences where they will be shoved in your face, and you must compensate or go down. In the ninth house, for example, this can manifest as feeling duty-bound to attend college and get a degree even if you have learning disabilities which mean you have to work ten times as hard as everyone else and miss the fun college experience.

Aeneas probably would have been happy simply living as a Trojan royal-adjacent family member indefinitely; his father had sworn an oath to Aphrodite never to reveal his son's half-divine parentage, and he seems to show no special divine gifts, so he thinks of himself as just another loyal retainer until the war destroys his home city ... and a number of Gods begin to intervene in his life, making him understand that there is something larger going on with him. As Troy is being sacked, he is informed by the Gods that he must gather any who will follow him and flee instead of staying to defend the city. Aeneas is caught between mundane duty and divine duty (a situation which will recur throughout his story), but with a heavy heart gathers what warriors he can and heads for the coast to take ship, carrying his aged, crippled father on his back.

They sail out with no idea where they are heading, which probably upsets Aeneas a great deal. He hopes to find them a place where they can settle and start a new colony as quickly as possible, but stop after stop goes wrong, usually due to hostile locals or disease. Aeneas does the best he can in his unfamiliar leadership role, but it is not a happy journey. After six years of wandering, during which Aeneas's father dies, they come to Carthage on the African coast and are welcomed. Aeneas falls in love with Dido, the Carthaginian queen, and they have a year-long affair. She gives him a fine sword and offers to let his people settle permanently in Carthage, but the Gods have other ideas. He is visited by Hermes (Mercury in Gemini) when the year is up; it was only to be a short respite to gather their health, and now they must move on to their final destiny. Again Aeneas is caught between the obligation of his own promises to Dido, and his higher duty to the Gods.

The ninth is a very transpersonal house; any planet there will place personal desires and obligations below higher obligations to the greater good. Since this is the house of religion and philosophy, fidelity to one's views about the world and one's place in it (and how those views mandate one's behavior) are going to haunt the ninth-house Saturn person. They may see the Divine as judgmental and rigid, something to be followed without question and above the needs of their loved ones. They may be so frightened of the numinous, the mysteries which cannot be fully understood, that they reject religion entirely and base their faith on scientific principles of (often limited and unempathic) rationality. Either way, their world views are likely to be utilitarian, classifying everything into concrete boxes with rules for correct behavior around each area of life.

Aeneas reluctantly sets sail with his men, abandoning Dido. She goes into a paroxysm of grief, has a funeral pyre built, climbs to the top, and then stab herself with the gift sword he had left behind. Aeneas sees the smoke of the pyre on the horizon as he sails away, and knows in his heart what has happened. Weeping with grief himself, he continues to sail on to the Italian peninsula. He and his men finally find the place where the Gods want them to go, and after a mess of fighting and treating with the locals and dutiful political marriages to make peace, he manages to start a couple of small cities. His descendants would go on to found Rome, which was theoretically the reason why he was supposed to end up in that specific place. At one point, he takes a journey to the underworld to find the soul of Dido and explain himself to her, but his justification that the Gods had taken him away does not impress her; she will not listen to him, so he must go back with the debt unfinished.

After his death, Aphrodite asks Zeus (Jupiter in Aries) to make him an immortal, and the King of the Gods acquiesces, so Aeneas ends up in Olympus. He has lost his home, his family, his love, and perhaps his honor, but he has done his duty. If he had rebelled, perhaps he would have been happy, or perhaps the Gods would have punished him, and Rome would not have been founded. He died never knowing the point of it all, and that sort of mystery is one of the things that Saturn in the house of knowledge absolutely hates—that, and the fact that the Universe is filled with ambivalent endings like these, instead of everything being sorted into neat piles of correct and incorrect. Yet the knowledge and acceptance of that understanding, while still struggling with that hatred of a messy world view, is exactly the end-goal Saturn wants.

It takes a long time and a lot of difficult work to reach Olympus, though, and one wonders if Aeneas felt that his sacrifices were worth it. The ninth-house Saturn has a love-hate relationship with the concept that there's something bigger than us, watching over us, nudging us, influencing us … loving us and yet expecting us to do hard things. Deep down, they are drawn to the idea, but they resist it as well. They need to take the long way around to it, and they may never get there, but as with all ninth-house things, the joy is in the journey. Or, if Saturn blocks you from seeing the joy, it's possible to see the good of the people you meet along the way, and reach out to them past the bars of a philosophical prison. Embracing the messiness of people is part of embracing the messiness of the Universe, and a very good first step.

10♄ Saturn in the 10th House: Okuninushi

The tenth house is ruled by Saturn itself, and associated with Saturn's sign of Capricorn, so you'd think that Saturn would be comfortable enough here to give someone a break and become a benevolent planet, rather like a more dignified Jupiter. Except you would be wrong. Saturn is still the planet of obstacles, no matter where it is, and there is no guarantee of success anywhere Saturn ends up. In the house of career, authority, and public life, Saturn is still a hard taskmaster. Some will grit their teeth and learn to push through and achieve great things, while others will simply fail. There is no destined path, even with Saturn, but you can bet there will be no easy path either.

The greatest goal of the tenth house is not just to get to the top of CEO Mountain, it is to build a nation which will live on as a legacy after one dies. "Nation" can be metaphorical, but it must involve many people and leave a mark on the world. The dream is not just to scale someone else's project but to grow your own, to become a World-Builder in a public and important way. In Japanese Shinto mythology, the deity who rules nation-building is Okuninushi, whose name literally means "Great Land Master". He didn't, of course, start out as a nation-builder, and neither do most of those with this Saturn placement. (A few do actually achieve fame at an unusually young age, but we'll discuss how that generally comes about, and what they pay for it, later in this chapter.)

Before we even get to issues of success and worldly fame, let's point out the elephant in the room with this placement. Saturn is a hard, cold planet, and its presence in a specific house can make everything to do with that house hard and cold as well. This doesn't have to be the case, but when it's not, it's either that Saturn is extremely well aspected (with nary a square or opposition in sight) or—more likely—that the individual has worked hard to get past the Saturn temptation of closing down in a hard shell of self-protection and learned to open up in spite of pain. Up there at the top of the chart, in its own house, Saturn has been known to cast a pall of callousness over the entire personality. This can show up as pure meanness, and it doesn't seem to matter whether the individual gains notoriously problematic worldly success—as in Napoleon and Hitler, both of whom had this placement—or not; one of the meanest people in my life had this placement and was prevented by disabilities from getting any career success whatsoever.

This pall of meanness can start early, as resentment for feeling held back. In order to avoid it, the tenth-house Saturn individual needs to actively cultivate sympathy for other underdogs, and never lose hold of that understanding. It should inform their every move up the ladder of ambition, lest they become the one whose success lies of the backs of all the people they oppressed and climbed over. This is the first lesson Okuninushi demonstrates, and it is his most famous—one that a nation-builder should hang onto with all their might.

Okuninushi was the youngest of eighty cruel and uncaring brothers, and was often the butt of their jokes. He was forced to be their errand boy, sent hither and thither at their whims. When they heard that the beautiful goddess Yagami-hime was looking for a husband, all the unmarried ones decided to go to her and attempt the wooing. Okuninushi was brought along as the baggage carrier, loaded with great sacks, and he soon fell behind the brothers who did not bother to wait for him. They came upon a hare which was missing large chunks of skin and was in terrible pain. Asking what had happened, the hare told them that he had wanted to travel to the mainland from his island, and thought of fooling the sharks into lining up to be counted so that he could jump across them to the opposite shore. Not being able to resist boasting of his feat as he landed on the last shark, the hare was bitten by the angry creature and much of its skin was torn off.

The cruel brothers decided to play a prank on the hare, and told it to wash itself in seawater and then let the wind dry it, and then they moved on. The hare took their advice and was made worse; it was weeping with pain by the time Okuninushi trudged up and listened to the hare's story. The youngest brother kindly advised the hare to wash itself in the nearby freshwater river, then spread the fluff from cattails on the ground and roll in it. The hare did this and was magically healed, and was grateful to Okuninushi. It declared that Yagami-hime would reject all the cruel brothers and pick him instead, which is exactly what happened when the youngest brother came to her palace. The cruel brothers were angry that Yagami-hime had chosen him, and plotted to murder him multiple times. One of their lethal attempts actually worked, and Okuninushi's mother had to bring him back to life with magic. Fearing for Yagami-hime's safety while she was with him, Okuninushi released her and went to hide in the underworld until his brothers had lost interest in killing him and moved on.

There are multiple lessons that the tenth-house Saturn can take from this story. First, the cruel brothers are examples of what happens when Saturn hardens the heart, and to counteract this, one must make an effort to be the kind one who gives compassionate aid to those in lower standing who are worse off than you. If this seems the opposite of Saturnian, remember that this is the planet which pushes us to learn the lessons that are the most difficult for us, and this is the behavior least likely to come easily to people with this placement. Turning sympathy and merciful action into a discipline both invokes Saturn's best elements and prevents its worst ones. It also tends to come back later on as rewards, which may be difficult to envision in the future when one is struggling with one's own burdens and trying to find energy to be kind at the same time.

We should also notice that many Saturn stories have a character who is disabled or wounded in some way; in this case, the hare is another aspect of this placement of Saturn. Disabilities of body and mind can prevent or at least delay the tenth-house Saturn from worldly success, and even if they manage to overcome this hurdle with slow, careful, tedious work (Saturn's favorite sort), the wounded part inside them can fester and act out once they have achieved something worth saving. They can sabotage themselves out of self-doubt, or someone else out of fear or jealousy. They can turn the pain on others to avoid seeing it in themselves—or, in the case of the rabbit, by boasting of their success to the backs they literally built a bridge out of to get them where they wanted to go. The inner rabbit must be healed, and must become wiser, for them to healthily hold power over others.

Second, Okuninushi's letting go of Yagami-hime reminds people with this placement that human beings are not trophies to be won as proof of one's success, and that being able to release someone who deserves a different life than what you can offer is generosity, not shame. Third, Okuninushi's retreat to the underworld reminds us that if everything is temporarily against you, a strategic retreat is not a failure.

Once in the underworld, Okuninushi came to the home of Susanoo the storm god (Uranus in Aries), who was living with his dead mother Izanami (Neptune in the seventh house) and his daughter Suseri-hime. The young god fell in love with Susanoo's daughter, but the storm god did not approve of the relationship and set him a number of tests—sleeping in a room first full of snakes and then full of wasps, fetching an arrow from a flaming field, picking the centipedes out of Susanoo's hair and eating them. Suserihime secretly helped him win each trial, and after Susanoo fell asleep, the couple tied his long hair to the main rafter of the house and fled for the entrance to the overworld. Susanoo awoke, tried to chase them, and pulled his house down around him. He did eventually catch up to them—no one outruns a storm god—but he rather liked Okuninushi's spunk by that time and forgave them both. Sometimes the strategic retreat results in a more fitting partnership, and changing roads does not have to be counted as disappointment.

The young god's fortunes change after this, as Susanoo gives his son-in-law magical items which help him to defeat all eighty of his cruel brothers. He finds that the land has been broken and devastated by their warfare, and tries to mend it, but it is too much for him alone. At this point the magical dwarf-god Sukunabikona appears, and offers to help him with the project. In some versions of the story, Sukunabikona reveals himself as the former flayed hare, who has been watching Okuninushi to see what sort of man he is. The two of them reform and firm up the land, and help it become repopulated. To help the people living there, they invent medicine and create remedies for plagues of birds and insects. At the end of it, Sukunabikona dies and passes into heaven, and Okuninushi mourns him. Saturn's next lesson is that it is good to depend on others, even ones whose contribution seems like it might be very small; great things can come of it. Others may have specialized expertise, and so long as the success is shared with them, one doesn't have to do everything themselves. The flayed hare becomes a competent *kami* spirit who can help build a world, another echo of Saturn rising up from the bottom of the pile. At this point, Okuninushi is called the God of the Earth Element—very much Saturn's place—and the God of Abundance, which is one of the best titles an earthy deity can have.

Okuninushi is a story of working one's way up from the bottom, which is the more common version of the tenth-house Saturn tale, but sometimes you do find people with this placement who are very young successes, and in every case it can be laid at the door of their parents. Astrologers have argued for centuries about the fourth and tenth houses, and which one is the father and which the mother. In this day and age of gendered parental roles breaking down, the best compromise I have heard is that the fourth house is the parent who sets the tone for the home, and the tenth house is the parent who teaches the child about the outside world. (Both could be aspects of the same parent, in some cases.) Saturn here can indicate great difficulty with the second sort of parent—they may be too strict, combative, distant, forcing their offspring to become an adult before their time. In some cases they push the child to early success, but most of those child prodigies fail by the time of their first Saturn return, so it can be better to start low and work up than to take the early leap and carry the anger at the parent with you ... which can mean almost certain failure later.

The story does not end at this point, though. Amaterasu the Sun Goddess (Sun in Leo) decides that the new realm needs to be taken by her family (which may be the vestigial reminder of a centuries-old struggle between different religious or political factions) and decides that Okuninushi must step down and turn his rulership over to one of her young relatives. He uses delaying tactics for many years, but eventually has to give in or start a war in heaven. Deciding that it is not worth the trouble it will cost everyone, Okuninushi agrees to give up his hard-won land and retires to the heavenly realms. He asks only that a magnificent palace be built for him which is rooted in the earth and reaches up to heaven—a fitting monument for the tenth-house Saturn.

Saturn, being Saturn, sometimes comes calling as the planet of obstacles well after success is achieved, and demands that it be given up. This can be due to health issues, political issues, or just that the structure has outgrown its usefulness (or that the person who built it has outgrown its boundaries). Saturn's ultimate lesson, even in this house is *To have is riches, but to be able to do without is power.* Real power is not only the ability to build a great edifice, but the ability to calmly lay it down and walk away, and find something new to build, even if that is one's neglected personal life. Reach to heaven ... but remember that your roots are deep in the Earth.

11♄ Saturn in the 11th House: Varuna

In the earlier eleventh house chapters, the focus was on personal friendships; Sun through Mars are the "personal" planets in the system, while Jupiter and Saturn have a wider focus, and the three outer planets are even more transpersonal. For Jupiter, we began to delve into the larger issue of social groups, and the social contracts which are enforced to keep group harmony. Friends may stick together or come and go, but when you have a large group of people who must live together in reasonable cooperation, questions of "How are we to treat each other?" become crucial. Sooner or later the group will require Rules, and enforcement of those Rules. This is the point at which Saturn enters into the eleventh house equation.

Saturn is uncomfortable in this house, at least with the personal level of it—friendship and socializing. For many people, this placement of the planet of obstacles means I Have No Friends—although that often changes when the individual grows older and enters into Saturn's time of life; they often find themselves with a decent circle of friends at that point. Others may have one or two serious friends (note the Saturnian word "serious" there) but they are not going to be social butterflies. They may be awkward with people, not knowing what to say and thus being too formal and stilted, which are common Saturnian handicaps. They despise social banter and small talk, and are often terrible at it. To them, it's a huge waste of time.

When they do join a group, it is to engage in some kind of mutual work, with some larger purpose; if they could avoid the group and do it all themselves, they would, but there are multitudinous projects which require many hands. So the eleventh-house Saturn girds themselves for the inevitable social clashing and rejection, and wades into the crowd. It doesn't take long for them to become the Arbiter of Rules, the one who is always pointing out that inconvenient bit in the bylaws about the officers of the board not using the group's funds to go on vacation. Groups without clear and sensible rules confuse them. Groups where people ignore the rules anger and sadden them, and sometimes drive them to become even more unpopular by doggedly pointing out that this behavior is not acceptable. On some level, the eleventh-house Saturn person instinctively knows that, as Robert Frost said, good fences make good neighbors. If the boundaries are not clear, people will be exploited, or be at each other's throats. Following the agreed-upon procedures is more than just a nice idea. It will make or break any group large enough to not know everyone intimately. That is why the main figure of this chapter is the Hindu God Varuna, whose original job was to hold everyone to the correct social contract, and punish them if they strayed.

Varuna's position has changed a great deal over the thousands of years India has been civilized. In the early days—even before the *Rig Veda*—he was one of the most important Gods in the pantheon. His name comes from a root word meaning "to bind", and he was the keeper of *rta* (pronounced "reeta"), a complicated concept of social order. *Rta* is generally understood to have three meanings. The first was cosmic order; the Sanskrit root word means "course", as in to run one's course. The second was moral order. The idea was that the Gods not only wanted the Universe to run smoothly and correctly, but also for human society to run smoothly and correctly as well.

Varuna was the Saturnian figure with all-seeing eyes whose job was to notice when people acted wrongly toward others, and punish it. At this point in his history, he was pictured as a handsome blue-skinned young man riding on a creature that is sometimes crocodilian, sometimes half-fish (which reminds me of Capricorn's sea-goat, another Saturnian symbol). He carried a pitcher and a noose in his hand; the noose was to catch and punish (usually with illness) those who had sinned, and the pitcher was to pour out the cosmic waters on those who repented of their sins and were forgiven. He was both a deity of punishment and of forgiveness, the enforcer of the social contract which should mirror the universal mechanism, in Vedic thought of the time.

The third meaning of *rta* is ritual correctness, and this became something of an obsession in the later Vedic period. Priests focused not on devotion, but on correctly performing the Vedic prayers and rituals over and over, the exact same way each time, for best results in propitiating deities for earthly gifts. This can sometimes be a Saturn problem—when the Rules become everything, and there is no place for compassion or sensitivity, or even flexibility in the face of Reality. Sooner or later this Saturnian flaw runs the ship aground, and when those Rules are those of a group, the fall is even harder. This Saturn placement needs to remember that enforcement must be combined with forgiveness and understanding, or it becomes a barren ritual which harms those under its yoke.

If we look back at the personal nature of this house, we notice that Varuna has one very good friend—Mitra, the Hindu version of Mithras, and I believe that it is no accident that Mitra stood forth as the Sun in this same house. Mitra was the Hindu God of oaths and promises, and the two of them together kept *rta* in order. Mitra was the sunshine of Saturnian Varuna's life, a brother-deity so close that the two of them were sometimes referred to as Mitra-Varuna. Having a best friend who stands by you in all things, keeps their word whenever they give it, and partners with you in some important work is the best heart-medicine for an individual with this placement, if they can find them.

Eventually, however, the social order itself was violently changed, and Varuna was ousted from his position and fell from popularity. Historians speculate that this was a clash between the Brahmin caste of ruling priests (to which Varuna was linked) and the Kshatriya caste of warriors. Originally, it was part of *rta* that the ruler would be a Brahmin, because it was right and proper that it be so. When the Kshatriyas took over politics and relegated the Brahmins to priestly duties, the rule changed so that the ruler was the one who could conquer and keep the throne by might. The God of the Kshatriya caste at the time, Indra (Mercury in the tenth house), replaced Varuna as the deity who decided what was right and good.

Varuna, who had originally symbolized the ocean of the cosmos which surrounded the worlds, was relegated to being the God of the physical ocean, a sort of Hindu Poseidon (Neptune in Cancer), as well as rivers, streams, and rain. He was plunged into the depths of the sea, where he broods alone. Sometimes he responds to prayers from particularly assiduous fishermen and sailors, but just as often he refuses to answer. In the *Ramayana*, Rama (Sun in the tenth house) has to strike the ocean repeatedly with lightning in order to get Varuna's attention. The way he was portrayed changed as well; he was now portrayed as a bald, ugly man with yellow eyes and protruding teeth, cruelly and judgmentally smiting people with his noose. The word for the sort of God he was—*asura*—which once meant "mighty one", came to mean "demon".

This situation may well be familiar to the eleventh-house Saturn. One tries one's level best to be an effective rule-keeper in the group, and at some point a more aggressive and charismatic person comes along and throws all the rules up in the air, and the fickle tribe follows them to victory or ruin, and You Are Out. Group members speak of you in ugly terms, reviling you, and you feel ugly yourself. The eleventh-house Saturn person usually ends up retreating in sullen resentment and frustration to isolation, and it may take them quite a long time to come out again. They stay in their cave under the sea of seclusion, and rarely come out. Why should they? Joining a group just leads to betrayal and unhappiness. They are capable of sulking in that undersea cave for years, refusing to belong anywhere. They consider themselves an outcast, and act that way, covering up a depth of loneliness in the soul with curt social rejections. Since like attracts like, their defensiveness may actually attract unpleasant people, who will then reinforce their ideas of general misanthropy and isolation.

The hard part is that they are desperately needed, awkwardness and all—and few groups will admit that fact. Saturn is rarely welcome to the party, and the person who ends up embodying Saturn for the group—if only because everyone else is dropping the ball and it needs to be done—is often resented as a party downer. Sooner or later they run the risk of becoming extremely unpopular ... if the group is determined to remain a superficial collective, refusing to look at the deeper issues. Saturn is, as many astrologers have said, the enemy of superficiality. Individuals with this placement want to dig into group dynamics and make them work, make them effective ... and make them safe. While we think of the person with Uranian energies as the whistleblower, it's likely that the most Saturnian person has already noticed the flaws in the situation, and slunk off in disgust when their initial whistleblowing attempts were shouted down as ruining the party.

What this placement yearns for is a group where people are willing to think deeply about how they should treat each other, and discuss it thoughtfully, and then stick to what is decided. Eventually they will learn that the way to be in this group is to create this group ... and that this cannot be done alone. Overtures and alliances must be made to people who will understand the eleventh-house Saturn's need for rules which keep everyone safe, and can gently show them how to temper that noose of rules with compassion and forgiveness. Varuna may sleep at the bottom of the sea, but someday yet he may emerge and become again the Emperor of Moral Congruence. In the meantime, those who inherit this placement can work on that rebirth for themselves.

12 ♄ Saturn in the 12th House: Cailleach

ailleach, or *the* Cailleach as she is known in many of the Celtic lands—more of a title than a name, which is very Saturnian in its own way—is first and foremost a goddess of winter. (Which is also

Saturnian.) Her name means "old woman" or "hag" in modern Gaelic, but comes from an ancient word meaning "veiled" or "cloaked"; she is wrapped in the cloaks and veils of winter and cannot easily be seen. In old Irish Gaelic she is Cailleach Bhéara and in old Scots Gaelic Cailleach Bheurra; the second title means "sharp" or "shrill", referencing the cold winter winds. This has become *Beira* in 20th-century Scottish folklore, and been popularized as another name for her. In some legends, she is claimed to be the aboriginal mother of all the Gaelic Gods.

It is said that she formed the mountains and hills in parts of Scotland by dropping stones from her "creel" or wicker basket as she went. Some say that it was accidental, and others claim that she built the mountains intentionally, to serve as her stepping-stones. She carries a hammer for shaping them in the ways she prefers. In most stories she is shown simply as a heavily cloaked old woman; in others she appears with white hair, dark blue skin, and rust-colored teeth. Breathing out the winter winds and glaring with her burning eyes, she stumps along the ground with an icicle-encrusted staff, and each thump of the staff on the earth freezes it solid. In some places, she was a plural spirit—"the Cailleachs" were a group of old women who brought the winter storms.

Saturn is the planet which rules old age, and many Saturnian archetypal figures are elders. The twelfth is the final house, also ruling the end of life when humans generally lose interest in worldly concerns of ambition and withdraw into contemplation. As the house of the unconscious, it holds what we don't wish to see, all the fears and hatreds and unpleasant thoughts which we have been told are unacceptable, or that we know for a fact will harm others if acted out. With the planet of obstacles here, the bearer of this placement learns early to repress, repress, repress. They may come across as smiling and helpful, but underneath may be a constant swirl of discouragement, depression, guilt, despair, and even self-loathing. It may be summer on the outside, but their subconscious is plunged into the Cailleach's winter season, and the road to their mental basement may be frozen and impassable.

This can mean that Saturn sends up a constant storm of negative thoughts and feelings, and the individual doesn't know why, or what they are all about. It's just vague, free-floating sadness and guilt. The twelfth house is traditionally associated with Neptune, the planet of vague confusion, and the combination of Saturn and Neptune can make someone feel lost in a blizzard with no visibility and no way to find the path out. They may deeply fear many of the areas of life associated with Saturn and with this house—aging, disability, abandonment, entrapment, and isolation. As the house of self-undoing, Saturn can be the cold, negative, depressing figure who seems determined to sabotage everything they want to accomplish. Many twelfth-house planets enjoy having time alone; Saturn here may be terrified of being alone with all those negative thoughts and may seek to be constantly in company, distracted enough that they can live shallowly and not look underneath.

> *And it felt like*
> *A winter machine that you go through and then*
> *You catch your breath and winter starts again*
> *While everyone else is spring-bound.*
> —Dar Williams

The Cailleach was a seasonal spirit; sometimes she is paired with a brighter goddess such as Brigid (Mars in Virgo) who rules the time between Beltane (May 1) and Samhain (October 31), while the Cailleach rules the cold half of the year. In some myths she is turned into stone during the warm season; in yet others she transforms into a young maiden herself in the spring and ages throughout the summer until she is the old woman again by Samhain. One myth recounts that by Samhain her great cloak is dirty, and so she washes it for three days in the Gulf of Coire Bhreacain until it is snow white, at which point a blizzard will come through and turn the land white as well. At Imbolc, the first of February, it is said that she gathers her firewood for the rest of the winter. If that day is bright and sunny, she will gather a lot of wood and make the winter last longer. Local belief thought it beneficent if the weather was foul, as this meant she was sleeping and would soon run out of firewood, and spring would come early. (People with Saturn in the twelfth house may nod wryly at the idea that it is easier to change the timing of the seasons than to reliably stick to a simple menial duty.)

One at a time, the freezing winds of the Cailleach must be faced down and moved through. Saturn is a planet of cold and crystallization, and one of its weapons is paralysis. If you feel like you just can't move—frozen in place—

that's Saturn waving a hand and chilling you to a stone. Even in the summer, when everything seems perfect for moving and progress, the Cailleach turns to stone. This paralysis can feel inevitable to this Saturn placement. The key is to take just one step into the fear, into the icy wind. Like someone moving through a blizzard, take one more step, and then one more. You may need to wait hours or days between steps, but eventually you will become used to the process, and know that if you just keep moving toward it, it won't be as frightening when you get there. Even if you fail the first time, give yourself praise for having been courageous enough to start. For example, when a twelfth-house Saturn person has faced their fear of isolation and being abandoned—by walking toward it and standing in it, perhaps by deliberately spending time alone and using that time to lean into the feelings and move past them—they can find solitude a peaceful place where a lot of work can get done.

On the positive side, the twelfth-house Saturn can bestow an inner strength and emotional resilience which allows the individual to stoically stand up to hardship and adversity. Saturn is the planet of karmic debts, and being in the twelfth supposedly allows the bearer to pay off more of their debt than if it was placed elsewhere, although to the person enduring this placement, that seems like little comfort. It is important to remember that the Cailleach is also a goddess of sovereignty—in some places in the Gaelic world, the king could not take this throne until she had inspected and approved of him. What does it mean to convince the Cailleach within to grant one sovereignty over one's own mind?

In the first *MythAstrology* book, I mentioned that one of the keywords for Saturn in Pisces—another combination of these two energies—is "spiritual discipline", and that goes as well for this Saturn placement. Saturn's positive side is the ability to be structured and disciplined about whatever it touches; the same walls that become obstacles can be re-formed—like the Cailleach with her hammer shaping the mountains—into boundaries and channels and structures which aid you in doing something. In the twelfth house, Saturn is "locked up" enough that the individual may feel completely at sea when it comes to disciplining themselves to get (especially unpleasant) activities done. They may be dogged with procrastination and distraction, including all the negative thoughts which tell them that it's all useless anyway, they will fail if they try … and so a self-fulfilling prophecy is created.

But when one has Neptune problems—and that includes Neptune's twelfth house—it is important to bring some form of spirituality in to heal the issue. This does not need to be religious—that's the ninth house—but it does need to create some kind of connection between the mortal and Something Bigger. As we are involving Saturn, the important part is to build the discipline which, through patient repetition, can bring them closer to the goal. You can do a lot of internal psychological work to shut up those voices, but it's much easier to do when you are also connecting to something larger and deeper and asking for aid. Spiritual discipline is the first step; over time this will draw out the positive side of Saturn—the ability to say No, including saying it to all those negative thoughts. Saturn's own tools need to be used to negotiate with Saturn.

With this placement, it's not uncommon for the father figure—or at least the parent who was or should have been the disciplinarian—to have been rather bad at it. Perhaps they were a tyrant or a martinet, rather than a firm coach; perhaps they were inconsistent or weak or even entirely absent when the time came for doing the job. The twelfth-house Saturn individual needs to create—from their own imagination—the firm but kind coach who sets wise boundaries and holds them compassionately, and then slowly make that a part of them. Transforming the internal Cailleach from judgmental, sneering force of ice to the wise grandmother who will give you hard but necessary advice in a way you can hear and accept will made a huge difference in their ability to motivate themselves.

In both Scotland and Ireland, the farmers used to have an old custom whereby the first farmer to finish his grain harvest would make a corn dolly with the last sheaf cut, referred to as "the old woman"—the Cailleach. It would be thrown into the field of the last farmer get his grain cut, the one who may have been procrastinating, and he would have to take care of it until spring. The implication was that he would have to feed and shelter the Cailleach all winter; there was a fair amount of competition to avoid getting this "prize". At the same time, the Cailleach would teach that farmer, during the winter, of methods to help them do better in the coming year.

One of the most important transformations is to turn guilt for not fixing everyone and everything about you to a healthy sense of responsibility for others ... within boundaries. People with this placement often end up in service and/or caretaking jobs for this reason, sometimes ministering to individuals who are incarcerated or hospitalized, trapped in a literal embodiment of the twelfth house, and thus representing this placement's fears of bondage. By caring for them in some way, by bringing light into the darkness of their captivity, they can slowly let light seep into their own underworld.

In a glen in Scotland, there is a small stone building with a number of vaguely human-shaped stones which stand in front of it during the summer months, and then are taken inside the structure by the locals for the winter. It is a shrine to the Cailleach, her husband the Bodach, and their children. Legend has it that as long as the local people continue this custom of bringing them in for the winter—of caring that the winter goddess and her family have shelter—the glen would be fertile and rich. The locals are still following this custom, to their benefit. It's a kind of sympathetic magic, which is a very twelfth-house process. Others become the symbol of that which you would heal in yourself, and helping them helps you. Done with patience, persistence, and discipline, it can walk you along the road out of winter and into spring.

Uranus

♅ Uranus in the 1st House: Tatterhood

I did an astrological reading for a couple once, when I was new to astrology and trying out chart-interpretation on anyone who would sit still for me. The man was a radical-punk type; the woman a softer hippie type. He had Uranus in the first house of his chart, sitting right on his Ascendant. I tried to express something about unusual appearances, and he argued with me about it. His partner put a hand on his arm and said, "But, love … you have a mohawk and a tattoo on your head."

The story that leaped out to me for this difficult combination wasn't a tale of Gods or heroes, but a Danish folktale. Like many folktales, it has multiple versions, some with different endings—not unusual for Uranus, who likes to change things up. It starts out with a king and queen who cannot have children, and are very sad about it. The Queen hears that a beggar woman is actually a hedge-witch who knows magical spells for curing barrenness; she gets the woman drunk until she agrees to teach her the right spell. The Queen is to bathe in two buckets of water and throw them under the bed, then in the morning two flowers will have sprung up—one beautiful and one ugly. She is to eat the beautiful flower, but not the ugly one, or … something will happen.

The Queen follows the instructions, and the next morning eats the lovely flower. It is so sweet that she eats the second, uglier one, in case it too is tasty … which it isn't. Then she becomes pregnant and gives birth to a daughter. The child is not pretty, and is not tractable. As soon as she is old enough, she insists on riding about on a goat, waving a wooden spoon in the air, and generally acting in aggressive, unfeminine ways. Her hair is always long and straggly, and she finds a tattered hood to wear over it to keep it out of the way, inspiring the servants to call her Tatterhood. When the Queen complains about her daughter's behavior, the little girl assures her that the next one will be prettier and nicer. She is right—the Queen gets pregnant for the second time, and this daughter is sweet and pretty and easy to manage.

Uranus is the planet of chaos and nonconformity, and this story has the Uranian child born first, taking up space in the castle and the story, and absolutely refusing to behave like a modest young maiden. She doesn't care about making herself beautiful. She doesn't care about riding a normal beast, but prefers her goat, a creature as rebellious as herself. She doesn't care about keeping her hair combed, or wearing fancy clothes appropriate to her rank. In fact, she rebels in nearly every way a medieval girl-child can, including refusing to obey her parents.

Any planet in the first house shines out as part of the "mask" of the Ascendant. When that planet is Uranus, a parent may despair of making their little rebel into a well-behaved, obedient kid who will value social rewards and conform to proper roles. The first-house Uranus's rebellion will be right on the surface, and show up in their appearance and public behavior. The specific nature of that visible rebellion will vary, but it will generally be in reaction to the messages they are being given about who and what they should look and act like. Pluto in this house may have an extreme appearance, but it will have nothing to do with outside opinions, pro or con. Uranus can't resist modeling "Don't tell me what to do—and in fact, I'll do the opposite, to prove to you that you can't make me conform!"

One way in which they may rebel, especially if it is a girl-child or if they are raised in a home with very strict roles for boys and girls, is against gender roles in general. Uranus, like Mercury, is an androgynous planet, and is a marker of androgyny in the chart unless it is overwhelmed by other planets. In the first house, it won't be overwhelmed. Not every first-house Uranus individual will ignore gender roles or create their own version thereof, but a great many do. Tatterhood's deliberately unfeminine ways contrast with those of her more stereotypical younger sister.

Uranus is also a very political planet, and Tatterhood rebels against her family's class, dressing like a peasant even though she is supposedly a princess, riding a lower-class mount, waving the wooden spoon of the laborer as if it was a royal scepter. This, too, is par for the course with this Uranus placement—they may wear their political views on their bodies, and they won't be shy about letting those views come out of their mouths. Whatever they believe, it will not be ordinary, and it will be loud. The planet of chaos doesn't manifest itself quietly; Uranus is associated with lightning.

The two sisters, however, are inseparable, and Tatterhood continually protects her younger and more passive sister. This recalls Uranus's urge for protecting the underdog, even at the risk of the Uranus person's safety. When Tatterhood and her sister are young women, a group of trolls besieges the castle. The King and Queen are at a loss, but Tatterhood says that she will go out and defeat them, as long as her family promises to stay inside and keep the doors locked. She rides out on her goat, waving her wooden spoon, and proceeds to kick troll butt. Uranus isn't Mars, but it isn't afraid to fight, either. However, where Mars fights for the joy of fighting, Uranus only fights for what they believe in. They can be pretty callous when they're facing down what they think is an enemy—Tatterhood doesn't care about her parents' feelings, and imperiously orders them to stay inside while she fights trolls. She hasn't actually seemed to care about her parents' feelings since she was born, and if the Uranus individual never develops empathy, their life can seem like one long battle with everyone, who will never understand them and who are just obstacles to the goal.

However, her sister fears for her and comes out the door in spite of Tatterhood's warnings. A troll-woman steals the pretty girl's head and replaces it with a calf's head. When the trolls are all beaten off, Tatterhood is furious that her parents let her sister out the door, but she is game to follow the trolls and get her sister's head back. She orders her parents to furnish her with a ship and supplies to last some months, and sails away with her unfortunate sister in tow, still mooing. The story of the lovely girl who is enchanted into animal form is fairly common in European folktales, but it is interesting that in this story, it is the socially-acceptable child who is forced to bear the stigma of the animal head, while the visible nonconformist was safe from the troll-magic. It is as if Tatterhood was already so far from normal that the unusual-appearance punishment couldn't even touch her, which is a remarkably Uranian trope. First-house Uranus people don't care if they are visibly unusual on multiple counts; they've already left "normal" far behind, so they might as well act as they like, and the addition of more stigmatized identities does not faze them, although it might anger them to further rebellious action or social change.

Tatterhood sails to the trolls' fortress and rescues her sister's proper head from where it is hanging from a high stone window, with a dramatic battle scene. However, the story isn't over just because her sister is pretty again. She sails to another kingdom and anchors the ship in the bay, and then proceeds to ride her goat around and around the deck, waving her wooden spoon. The people flock out to see her, all alone on the ship, because a first-house Uranus figure knows how to get attention. It isn't the deliberate attention-getting "Look at me!" of Leo; Uranus is ruled by Aquarius and the attention is more of a "Screw you! I'm being authentic regardless of what you think." (Except, of course, that it does matter. They wouldn't do it nearly so loudly if they weren't reacting against the views of the onlookers.)

The people ask if she is alone, and she answers that her sister is here as well, and that her sister is the most beautiful girl in the world. The townsfolk demand to see the sister, but Tatterhood refuses, saying that she will bring her sister out only for the King himself. When word of this reaches the King, he comes out to the ship and, true to her word, Tatterhood produces her pretty sister. The King of this country is a widower with a son about the age of the two sisters, and he has wanted to remarry for some time. When he sees Tatterhood's sister, he desires her and asks for her hand in marriage.

As the older sister, Tatterhood offers him a deal. The older man may have her if he is willing to give his son to Tatterhood as a bridegroom. The prince is horrified at the idea. When you are an all-out-in-front, no-holds-barred Uranian, finding romance isn't so easy. It's especially a problem if you're shopping in a pool full of people who expect normal expressions of gender and class, and you have demanded the freedom to ignore those social rules. It's also a problem if you are violating rules of social attractiveness—perhaps because you find them unfair, perhaps because they just cramp your style—and people don't find you attractive. First-house Uranus people tend to resent standards of attractiveness, even while they do want to be desired and loved. This can result in a lot of the Uranian sour-grapes reaction—"Never mind, I don't want it, it's all stupid anyway!"

The King wants Tatterhood's sister enough that he pressures his son into marrying the weird girl on the goat, and gets all his counselors to lay on the pressure as well. Once the deal is struck, he marries the pretty girl as quickly as possible, and then makes the plans for the prince's wedding. At this point, you may have noticed a trend which is one of the major pitfalls in this Uranus placement—an ugly little streak of hypocrisy. For all her rebellion and outward identification with the peasantry, Tatterhood still has all the arrogance and privileged world view of her noble birth. She believes that she knows what is best for everyone, and has no compunctions in pressuring them to conform to her wishes. Her sister gets no voice in these arrangements, and neither does her bridegroom. Uranus doesn't do humility or thoughtfulness very well, and the individual with this placement may end up bullying those around them into going along with their goals, becoming someone for whom the end justifies the means. They will have to look honestly at this tendency, and learn to take the actual emotional needs of others into account, or the job of making change will just get harder and harder until they have alienated everyone around. They also need to scrutinize their own privilege—Tatterhood is still someone with the power of a monarchy behind her, which she is not averse to using for her own ends.

On the wedding day, the youth shows up in fine clothing on his horse, but Tatterhood shows up in her usual rags, riding the goat. They ride together in procession to the place where the wedding will be performed, with all the folk of the town staring at them. The prince hangs his head in shame, and Tatterhood asks him why he won't speak to her. When he remains uncommunicative, she suggests that he ask her why she is riding a goat, and he unbends enough to do so.

It is the first turning point for them. Wherever you have Uranus, it's possible to feel continually alienated. What Uranus wants more even than being accepted is to be *understood*. *Ask me why I act the way I do. Ask me what I believe, what I feel is important, why I care enough to wear it on my sleeve and across my face.* Tatterhood replies that it isn't a goat at all, it's a horse as fine as his own ... and suddenly the goat turns into a graceful steed.

The prince asks her why she carries a wooden spoon; she says it's not a wooden spoon at all. In some versions of the story, it becomes a silver fan, in others a magical silver wand. He asks her why she wears the tattered hood, and she tells him it's a crown as fine as his own—and it becomes so. Catching on, he asks her why she is so ugly, and she tells him she's not ugly at all ... and becomes as beautiful as her sister.

Here the stories split into different versions. One is the sort of faerytale ending that most animal-bride or ugly-bride folktales have, where the heroine becomes a socially-acceptable pretty maiden and they all live happily ever after. Another common ending, however, has Tatterhood turning back into her original form, goat and spoon and all, and they are married that way. The prince understands that she chooses to look this way, even though she doesn't have to, and that her beauty doesn't matter. He decides that he is glad to be with her anyway. It's a very Uranian ending, and unusual for faery tales.

But it's the ending that this Uranus placement wants—for someone to see how they are beautiful even through their unusual appearance and behavior, and desiring them as they are. They are looking for someone who finds a commitment to values more beautiful than societally-accepted good looks. They want their unwillingness to follow social norms of attractiveness, wealth, success, and normal gender not to matter at all, and they want those who love them to stand with them, in public and proud. That last part is important to a first-house planet—if you can't be with me before all the people and hold your head high, defend me as I will defend you, then you can't be with me at all. I would rather be alone and free than compromise the beliefs I've been willing to be ostracized for. Be with me, be one of the outcasts with me, and I will stand by you forever.

Uranus can be a ruthless master, forcing someone to stand by their beliefs, even at the cost of exile and alienation. But without those who are willing to stand up with those beliefs emblazoned across their faces, no real change can occur. These folk are in the front line of the Uranus battle to change the world, and there is deep honor in that position.

Uranus in the 2nd House: Inari

Researching the history of Inari is a lesson in chaos and change. That's what makes it so Uranian. Aquarius's planet is never satisfied with the status quo; if there's a rule, a boundary, a "this is the way we've always done it", the time to take it down is always Now. Nowhere is this constant changing more evident than in the Japanese worship of Inari. I can't say "the Goddess Inari" or "the God Inari" because Inari could be either, or even androgynous. I can't even say *the* Inari as a singular being, because there are more than one of them. Well, sometimes. Or not. How many? It depends; that too changes like a flick of the fingers. The one thing that all the forms of Inari have in common is that their symbol is the fox ... a creature who is considered both a fortunate spirit-messenger and a mischievous trickster, although this is historically not the only animal-shape Irani may take. The trickster planet Uranus laughs at my attempts to pigeonhole this rapidly shapeshifting spirit.

One other trait besides foxes is certain: Inari is a giver of wealth and prosperity, and thus merits a place in the second astrological house of money and resources. Originally, it seems that there was a Shinto goddess named Inari, whose name comes from ancient Japanese words for "growing rice". She may have been a version of Ukemochi, another Shinto goddess of food (there would have been several local food-deities on different islands) who was able to produce silkworms from her head, rice seeds from her eyes, millet from her ears, red beans from her nose, wheat from her genitals, and soybeans from her rectum. (I've always been suspicious of soybeans.) These nothing-up-my-sleeve magic tricks (and yes, only a trickster deity would pull this off) so disgusted either Susanoo (Uranus in Aries) in one version or his brother Tsukiyomi in another that he killed her, and food grew out of her body and spread across the islands of Japan.

Inari may also be a version of the Hindu goddess Dakiniten, who is essentially a Japanese single-goddess version of all the Hindu Dakinis squished together ... or Dakiniten may be a version of Inari which the Japanese "identified" with Dakiniten. Either way, they both ride a white fox and brought rice to the people of Japan. Inari was also a goddess of fertility, and shrines were built to her in order to keep the fields growing all that rice. Eventually, her domain was extended to *sake* (rice wine) and tea.

However, at this point Buddhism enters the historical picture, and Buddhist lamas and monks seemed to not be very fond of women, or female deities. Goddesses were given sex changes by the handful; one example of this is Kwan Yin (Moon in Cancer) being forcibly reassigned as the male bodhisattva Avalokiteshwara. Inari kept the name, but was made into an elderly male god carrying rice, and his rulerships were extended again, this time to be a patron of blacksmiths and merchants. Part of this change shows that wealth was coming from places other than simple farming; as civilization and technology grew in Japan, so did new sources of wealth such as artisans and traders.

Uranus keeps pace with technological changes, more than any other planet. When the tools change up, so does this planet, and no matter what the era, Uranus wants all the new toys. In the second house, the individual will want to possess all the newest tech, perhaps only because it is new and hasn't existed before. They will also want to make their money with that new tech in some way, if at all possible. Uranus here pushes people to chase cutting-edge industries, and change them up as soon as they gain even a whiff of obsolescence. In our era of computers and cell phones, we forget that blacksmithing was once the height of technology, and that the blacksmith was the "tech" of the all-farmer era—as the traveling merchant was the corporate CEO selling the new electronic chip.

We should also take a moment to note the androgyny of Inari at this point. While Buddhism swept the land and its priests tried to masculinize all goddesses, the actual Inari-worship didn't transition so smoothly. Some people preferred the original female Inari, some preferred the male version, and at least one version could switch back and forth. The Shinto priests declared that everyone should simply worship the Inari that they preferred, and built more shrines in more places, each with a different Inari. (They all had foxes, though. Foxes ate mice and rats and thus saved the all-important grain.) This extremely Uranian declaration of religious independence and individuality expanded to Inari being more than one person—some shrines had single Inaris, some had a group of Inaris, usually three or five. Their individual names varied widely—why should they stick to a single name?—as did their rulerships, but the most popular were one *kami* (spirit) for earth, one for water, and one for grains. As time went on, they branched out into health concerns, and people came to them for medical issues as well. Soon their reach encompassed brothels and entertainers, or at least the financial aspects of those. Uranus is always searching for something new and interesting, and adding it to the collection.

Uranus in the house of money, at its worst, indicates money coming in and out very suddenly, like lightning strikes. Bang! There's a windfall. Bang! There's an unexpected financial accident or expense which eats it all up, before anyone has a chance to enjoy anything. Physical items are quickly gifted and quickly break. Remember that mischievous fox? The other symbols that Inari acquired are magical wish-fulfilling gems, scrolls of divine writing, sheaves or sacks of rice, and a whip. The whip was not often used, but it had a specific purpose: to burn down someone's rice field. Uranus is perfectly capable of gifting one moment and setting it on fire the next, making the financial history of folks with this placement completely chaotic.

When it comes to making money, these individuals do best as entrepreneurs, or if they don't have the savvy to run their own business, to be the genius tech in the back room of some other entrepreneur's start-up company. But as soon as the company becomes stable, puts down roots, and stops pushing the boundaries, things begin to go wrong for the person with this Uranus placement. It's as if the Universe won't let them be comfortable where income is concerned. They need to keep pushing boundaries, thinking outside the box, discovering the cutting edge. Their best bet is to find a job where churning out continual new research or inventions is expected; that's getting Uranus on their side.

Some folks with this placement go far enough outside of the cultural money box that they decide to become revolutionaries about money and possessions, creating communes where resources are pooled. This is Uranus working toward the survival of the group over that of the individual, not inappropriate for a single deity who doubled and then tripled, and then multiplied into an ensemble. They want to rewrite the acceptable script for distribution of wealth, and make sure that the good fortune is spread more evenly across the board. It's important to keep in mind that the second is the House of Values, and that brings us back to the other point with regard to wealth: If these people want to even out their financial profile, the first step is making sure that their work is cutting-edge and thinking outside the box. The second step is making sure that their *values* are cutting edge and thinking outside the box.

It's especially important, with this androgynous planet which doesn't believe in immutable gender, to look at the gender politics of work and acquiring wealth, and have a sufficiently Uranian opinion about that. This includes actually doing something about it, preferably on your own moneymaking home ground. With this placement, ignoring such inequalities might get Uranus on your bad side, and foxes will go on strike so that the rats eat your rice, or your field might suddenly be struck by lightning and burn down. Don't assume I'm joking; Saturn in this house can get away with that sort of thing, but Uranus won't allow it.

Inari is by no means merely an ancient figure; they are the most popular Shinto deity in Japan today, holding more than a third of Shinto shrines. Their figures are still widely varied—female, male, single, multiple. They usually have a bright orange torii gate and two stylized fox figures. Their reach has grown to include all industry, and many modern Japanese corporations include symbols or letters for Inari in their logos; one has a giant Inari shrine on top of their skyscraper. As we've said, Uranus is all about the modern and even the futuristic, and Inari shows no signs of retiring or losing popularity. Indeed, by "containing multitudes" and "being all things to all people", Inari has been able to adapt and revolutionize with the times. It's a lesson that other deities ought to take a good look at … and so should those with Uranus in the house of all things worthy.

♅ Uranus in the 3rd House: Nanabozho

The planet Uranus is one of the trickster planets, more so even than clever Mercury, and spreads an odd way of doing things everywhere it finds itself. Uranus actually enjoys being in the third house, even as it spreads difficulty and chaos throughout the brain, but perhaps Uranus doesn't think a little chaos (or for that matter a lot of chaos) is such a bad thing. This placement bestows a weird and wacky sense of humor, and a very original way of going about things. Of course, this position had to be a trickster God, and here we introduce the Anishinaabe Ojibwa trickster deity and culture hero Nanabozho, whose name literally means "the fool".

In Native American stories, culture heroes are very often trickster figures, which is rare in Europe and Asia where they tend to be adversaries. They are used, in these cultures, as teaching tools which show how things should be done—or, more likely, not done; trickster figures can be humorous warnings. Nanabozho's job, in the tales, seems to be to create problems, fall on their face, and then fish themselves out of the hole, showing listeners both the less desirable road and the way out should one go there. Nanabozho brings chaos into the situation, but then fixes what has broken as an object lesson.

One of the interesting things about Nanabozho is that they are a shapeshifter, taking on not only different human forms but multiple animal forms as well. While Rabbit is the favorite animal form, Nanabozho is notorious for taking on the animal forms of other cultural trickster deities as well, such as Crow, Raven, Spider, Wolverine, Bluejay, Porcupine, Skunk, and Coyote. In addition, Nanabozho is blatantly gender-shifting; while the majority of their stories use male pronouns, it is not uncommon for them to take on female form, and then the stories use female labels. Uranus is itself one of the androgynous planets, refusing to commit to one gender or another. Some will say that it is a masculine planet (largely because of its strong, combative nature) but Uranus has always been an indicator of androgyny in a chart, and this Uranus figure is no exception.

Another interesting quality of the third-house Uranus is the ability to make friends across a wide variety of people, usually by being willing to sit with their "tribe" and listen, and make conversation. This is echoed in Nanabozho's shapeshifting abilities; when he needs to convince a particular group of animals to do something, he simply shifts his shape into theirs, and uses that face to launch his (often extraordinary) requests. An undercurrent to his stories shows that it is the presence of others in his life who can point out foolish actions to him which anchors his success.

Nanabozho was born of a mortal mother, but his father was one of the four guardians of the directions, the Guardian of the West where the sun goes down. He grew up with his immortal spirit-father, but was sent down to earth by the spirits to help teach the Ojibwe people. His first task was to name all the plants and animals, and the natural features of the land as well. Uranus here may be strange and eccentric, but it is still in the third house, and finding names for things and situations is very important for people with this placement. They enjoy research as long as they are allowed to follow their whims and take a random trail across the plain of facts, digging here and piling up there, and sometimes forgetting how they got to where they are.

According to his legends, Nanabozho was the inventor of the Ojibwe hieroglyphic language, which is par for the course when we are talking about third-house Gods—naturally they invent languages and alphabets. Unlike other spirits who were content to scratch random petroglyphs, Nanabozho codified the pictographs into a complex system of writing. He also started the *Midewiwin* society, an initiatory group with several levels whose job it was to record the history of the tribe on birchbark scrolls, among other religious duties. It is also said that he become bored with the Ojibwe language and broke it up into numerous dialects, each used by a different tribe, which sounds like a very Uranus thing to do. Uranus often makes things more complicated just to provide interest, to the dismay of Saturnian types.

One of the stories about Nanabozho was created in response to European-descended American settler "tall tales", whose characters local Native Americans sometimes borrowed for comic relief, and which eventually found their way back into American folklore. In this case, Nanabozho was inserted into one of the stories of the huge lumberjack Paul Bunyan (or perhaps one could say Paul Bunyan was inserted into a Nanabozho story). Paul Bunyan is determined to clear-cut all of America, and Nanabozho confronts him in Minnesota and begs him to leave the state without cutting any more trees. Bunyan refuses, and a fight ensues which lasts forty days and forty nights. To end it, Nanabozho finally slaps Bunyan across the face with a huge fish, and the lumberjack falls backwards so hard that his buttocks create the hole which filled with water and become Lake Bemidji. The fish ripped off his beard, and thus the statue of Paul Bunyan at Lake Bemidji is beardless … and across the road, facing him, is a statue of Nanabozho. The fact that this trickster speaks for the trees and attempts to stop the destructive force of modern progress resonates with Uranus's tendency to side with the underdog, or at least take the part of the less socially acceptable opinion or ideology. Also, he accomplished this by fish-slapping, a trickster-style humbling if ever there was one.

One story posits Nanabozho as a creator God, coming down and seeing only waters, and then diving to the bottom for mud to place on a turtle's back and create the continent. This story is actually taken from multiple other Native American creator stories, but of course Nanabozho borrows it. The third-house Uranus, however, is actually very creative, finding unusual ways to write, sing, and even teach, as Nanabozho teaches by making a fool of himself. Their imagination is fertile and whimsical, and they have a natural leaning toward pranks and tricks, especially if they can fool whole groups of people. They tend to be excellent teachers because their sense of humor engages their students, but they also tend to wander about in their thoughts, even when teaching or lecturing, and have to be careful not to confuse the people who are listening. Their quick minds jump ahead several steps, and they may forget to fill everyone else in on how they got from Point A to Point B.

Like Nanabozho who had his own crazy ideas and often pooh-poohed the skepticism of others, third-house Uranus people can stubbornly hold onto their own plans and concepts even when others reasonably point out holes in the schemes. Instead, they plow ahead with faith that some new idea will pop up which will plug the holes and solve the problems. Sometimes that even works.

This is the house of short trips, and when the third-house Uranus gets bored or stuck, the best thing for them is a wander around the neighborhood … ideally with no specific goal in mind. Like Nanabozho who had no real home and rambled about the woods of wherever he happened to wake up today, some third-house Uranus people eschew regular living situations entirely and live in their vehicles, or with frequent stays on friends' couches. Even if they have a perfectly nice home, they will often find themselves in random diners holding forth to people who were total strangers an hour ago. Trusting to the luck of the journey to inspire them and teach them new ways of thinking, new shapes to put on and new tribes to get to know.

The third-house Uranus in the house of the brain is one of the most important indicators for neurological problems, both of the cognitive and the seizure variety. Uranian chaos can make things difficult for the neurons, and thus also the sufferer. People with this placement often have trouble in school, more with focus or unusual ways of thinking than with an inability to actually learn the material. They do best with hands-on interactive learning, and some astrologers feel that this placement bestows a special ability to flash back and forth between the right and left brain, allowing them to grasp the holistic meaning of the area they are studying. Teachers often don't know what to do with them, unless they are particularly creative and unusual thinkers themselves.

Nanabozho had so many stories that they inspired white Americans who heard them. When Henry Wadsworth Longfellow wrote his famous poem Hiawatha, it had practically nothing to do with the little-known historical figure of Hiawatha and instead was largely drawn from Nanabozho stories. Somehow it seems relevant that this very verbal trickster, inventor of alphabets and namer of All Things, should be immortalized (in a way) in an epic poem which is still recited today in this modern Uranus era … and in a different form, trickster-style.

4♅ Uranus in the 4th House: Antigone

Wherever Uranus lies in the chart, rebellion brews and chaos rains down. Some people manage to avoid it by steering clear of the arena of that house, but there is absolutely no way to avoid the fourth house. We all have childhoods, whether we like it or not. Innovative Uranus hates being in the domestic fourth house where one spends so many years being helpless and dependent. Unlike a tenth-house Uranus which can spend their adult years creating an unusual career, or seventh-house Uranus which can come up with interesting relationship structures, Uranus in the fourth house is limited to rebellion against the family—over and over and over again, until the individual gets a handle on the urge. Even as an adult when they rebel against other things, in some way they are still rebelling against the parents, the tribe, the ancestral culture. It's a very small cage for far-reaching Uranus, and excruciatingly personal. It's very difficult for Uranus to take its preferred tactic of high-flying objectivity, especially when the individual is a small child facing down their parents.

Antigone, in Greek mythology, is the daughter of Oedipus (Pluto in the fourth house) and his wife/mother Jocasta. She comes from a family history of violence: her grandfather Laius raped his friend's young son and caused his suicide, staked out his own son Oedipus to be exposed, and was in turn killed by that son who unknowingly claimed the old ruler's wife. We have no idea what her early life might have been like, except that she had two older brothers—Eteocles and Polynices—and a sister, Ismene. However, her family is no stranger to chaos and disaster, and as soon as it strikes again, she comes into her own.

Oedipus learns that he is actually the son of Laius and his wife is his own mother; his children are born of an incestuous union. Jocasta hangs herself upon discovering this truth, and Oedipus takes a brooch from his dangling wife's dead body and stabs out his own eyes. At this point he is revealed as unclean, a pariah who will bring bad luck to the city. He staggers out onto the road to expiate his sins, a blind beggar with no friends.

At this point, Antigone runs out onto the road with him and offers to be his companion, and his eyes, during his travels. While this sounds like simple selfless devotion, it is important to understand how very shocking this would have been in the actual culture of ancient Greece. High-born women were kept closely cloistered; their marriageability—and thus their main value as a human being—was based on being able to prove that they were proper, modest virgins. For a princess to decide to wander as a beggar on the roads with no protection, risking robbery, rape, kidnapping, and enslavement, was unheard of. Besides this, it is likely that Antigone had few survival skills, having been raised in a wealthy, sheltered household. She would have to endure hunger and hardship. Worst of all, Oedipus's journey is not to find a new home—no city will have him, after it is known what he has done. If she follows him, she faces permanent homelessness, until he finally dies. After that, it is unlikely that any man of rank will marry her, after her improper adventures. The faithful act of following her father is a subtle—or not-so-subtle—way of giving the finger to the entirety of upper-class Greek culture, and especially its expectations for women.

Uranus in the fourth house can manifest in a number of different ways during the childhoods of its natives. In the most positive cases, the parents weren't chaotic so much as forward-thinking and pioneering, rebels in their own way with a fascinating collection of odd friends, intellectual colleagues and bohemian happenings, interesting enough that their Uranus offspring didn't have to rebel out of boredom—although a few would still do it out of an urge to be different, usually adopting conservative values to spite their parents. (Patrick Dennis's novel *Auntie Mame* is a good fictional example of a positive fourth-house Uranus upbringing.) In more difficult cases, the parents continually moved around, perhaps due to one parent's job (or joblessness) or outside factors such as war, famine, or a poor economy. In other cases, the parents themselves were forces of chaos, perhaps neurotic, addicted, or just flighty with poor judgment. Some are overly intellectual, perhaps brilliant but with no empathy for their partners or children. Whatever the fourth-house Uranus upbringing is like, it won't be the "white-picket-fence" or its cultural equivalent by which "normal" childhoods are measured.

However, in some cases, fourth-house Uranus individuals admit that the force of chaos in the home was ... them. I've met with ones whose neurological problems (Uranus rules neurology) caused enough disruption in the family that everything had to revolve around keeping them on some semblance of an even keel. I've met with ones whose urge to rebel was so strong that it blew apart their whole immediate family and left scars on their siblings. Uranus can be brilliant, idealistic, and original, but its force is not empathic. Uranus loves humanity in the theoretical state, but up close Uranus doesn't much like actual people at all. They are messy and irrational and their rules are terribly oppressive, and so of course one has to fight to get out, by any means necessary.

The chaos that descends on the royal house of Thebes gives Antigone the chance to differentiate herself as unique among high-born women—her sister Ismene dutifully stays behind to be a "good" princess—and she takes it, to embark on a long journey that is Uranian for its very randomness and purposelessness. Unlike Jupiterian journeys which seek some kind of goal (if only an idealistic fantasy) Uranian journeys exist to experience new situations, not to get anywhere. One has to wonder if at least part of Antigone's motivation in running after her father was because it might be the only chance she would get to see the world.

Oedipus finally dies at the shrine of the Furies at Colonnus, and Antigone's sister Ismene comes to fetch her back to Thebes. In the meantime, however, Oedipus's two heirs Eteocles and Polynices have come to grief. They argued over which one would rule, and each had half of the city behind them. It was agreed that they should switch back and forth, but after the first one had his turn he refused to give up the throne, and the other raised a rebellious (Uranian) army and attacked the city. Both fought to the death, and both were slain in the battle. Antigone and Ismene, being women, would never be considered heirs in patriarchal Greek culture, so the crown went to Creon, the younger brother of Jocasta. Creon is a conservative and canny statesman—Oedipus accused him of being manipulative behind his stolid, apparently faithful exterior—and his first objective is to get Thebes into a state of peace, whatever that takes. He decides that one of the brothers must be lionized while the other one is used as a bad example to stop further revolt and rather randomly chooses Polynices. His corpse is to lie unburied where it fell outside the city gates, and no one is to attempt to bury it, on pain of death.

This is more than a symbolic punishment. In ancient Greek belief, if the body lay abandoned and unburied or unburnt—perhaps even devoured by wild beasts—the soul would wander mournfully and aimlessly, finding no rest. Antigone returns to Thebes immediately after Creon's decree, and she is even welcomed by her first cousin Haemon, Creon's son. Haemon loves and admires her in spite of—or perhaps because of—her courage and adventurousness, and wants to marry her. She seems to like him as well, but after having survived years of freedom, she chafes at the idea of going back to the protected cloister, to spend the rest of her life bearing children and obeying her husband in all things. However, there is no other choice for her in that culture. Without the minimal protection of her sacred-outcast father, she has nothing left but the family that would yoke her into a traditional feminine harness.

So Antigone makes her choice. She goes outside the city late at night and covers her brother's body with dirt. The next morning, when it is discovered, Polynices is uncovered again and a watch set on the body. She makes another attempt the following night and is caught. When she is brought to Creon, she openly admits that she did the deed, and would do it again, and will protest his unfairness to the end. *Just because he was the loser,* she says, *is no reason to punish him so horribly.*

One of my old friends has Uranus in the fourth house, and his childhood was rocked by a fierce and bloody parental divorce that dragged on for four harrowing years, complete with nasty trumped-up charges on both sides. He lived with his grandmother while his parents fought each other for custody and property, and he remembers constantly switching his ideas about which parent he wanted to live with. While this could easily be excused as the ambivalence of a child who does not want to choose between parents, in retrospect he realized that his sympathy was with whoever was currently on the losing side, being knocked down by their opponent. After the dust settled, he spent his adolescent and college years rebelling against one parent and going to live with the other one, only to reverse the process in a few months. As an adult with a wife and three children, he found to his discomfort that he was always more sympathetic to the child who was troubled. Two of his children figured this out, and made sure to have their father's affection by competing for which one could be more troubled. Uranus always gravitates toward the underdog, on principle—sometimes even if the underdog is the one causing all the trouble.

It may well be that Polynices was not so much Antigone's favorite so much as Antigone's excuse; it is also difficult to judge her motives from this century. Since Sophocles' play *Antigone* was written, the story has been retold in dozens of different ways, each one with a different political slant. (How Uranian!) In some it is her piety that drives her to the deed and she tells Creon that she is upholding divine law in caring for her brother's corpse. In other versions it centers around her love for her brother, and in yet others it illustrates various political views about tyrants and the unfairness of political expedience. Some versions are set in ancient Greece and others in a more modern era. Every single one is all about the values and effectiveness of rebellion—in other words, every one of them is a Uranian story. While Creon and Antigone are often posed as the archetypal Politician and Young Rebel, there is no escaping the fact that they are also uncle and niece. It is unlikely that Antigone would have mounted this doomed resistance for the distant ruler of a different city-state. She resists Creon not only because he is the one who is harming her brother's soul, but because her family is determined to railroad her into an existence she cannot bear, and she can see no other road. Better a martyr's death than the living death of decades of oppression by family, tribe, and culture.

Creon, not wanting her blood on his hands, has her walled up alive. His son Haemon tears down the stone wall and finds her dead, having killed herself rather than slowly starve. He is desolate and stabs himself with a knife. His mother Eurydice, who has been weaving throughout the whole story—symbolizing the Fates, and the idea that Creon and Antigone are doomed to this ending—hangs herself in despair over the death of her only child. Creon is left to rule alone, devastated, among the bodies of his dead family. While Antigone failed in her attempt, she did manage to ruin his life. Uranus crashes through the crystallized family patterns like a whirlwind and leaves it all shattered in its wake.

Of course, there is also one other version, by the Greek playwright Euripides. When looking at myths for their archetypal value as astrological parables, it's important that multiple versions aren't seen as "right" or "wrong", but simply as potential alternatives. We don't have access to the full text of Euripides' play—only commentary about it—but in his version the Gods avert the disaster at the last minute, unbend Creon's heart and Antigone marries Haemon. This is almost a Disneyesque rewriting of Antigone's dramatic last stand, and one has to wonder if it is the one where the fourth-house Uranus person gives in and wearily accedes to "normal" life, perhaps to rebel again in ten or twenty years when they just can't take it any more. When astrologers describe this placement, they usually throw in a warning to potential or current partners of the fourth-house Uranus person: *If you let them have their freedom, they will love you for it; if you try to pin them down, you will become the past that trapped them.*

The gun-shy nature of this placement when it comes to "settling down" behind that theoretical white picket fence cannot be overestimated. Just the thought of it can make the whites of their eyes show. In order to have a lasting relationship, they may have to be allowed to come and go as their nervous Uranian natures allow. Home needs to be, literally, wherever they are hanging their hat at the moment, and the right partner will be able to cope with that in whatever way works for both parties. Just as the seventh-house Uranus person will sneer at the idea that relationships "must" be a certain way, with a certain number of people, this Uranus placement will snarl at the idea that home "must" be in one specific place, with nuclear family members ensconced there at all times. *Home is where the people who accept you happen to live,* says the fourth-house Uranus, *even if that is in many places at once. And family is those people, regardless of whether they are bound to you by blood. And culture is what you make of it … by any means necessary.*

One of the biggest arguments around the various versions of the enduring myth of Antigone is the question of whether she really rebelled for a purpose, or just for the sake of rebelling. What we astrologers need to understand is that to Uranus, there is no difference. Rebelling can be a cause in itself, a way of being that constantly challenges everything that is thought to be set in stone. Uranus, Neptune, and Pluto all have one thing in common: They all tell us that permanence is an illusion. It is a temporary castle of sand that we desperately build against the tide. This Uranus placement tells us exactly how easy it is to sweep away our earliest experience of that sand castle, and that it is possible to stand in the shifting tide and anchor yourself, instead, to the winds of change.

5 ♅ Uranus in the 5th House: Kokopelli

Uranus is the ultimate trickster of the planets. (Well, Mercury is a close second, but Uranus is just plain wackier.) Uranus operates like a lightning strike—ZAP! Something happens, chaos tumbling into order, good or bad at random, whether we like it or not. *Every curse is a blessing in disguise, and the reverse is true as well,* says Uranus. *It's all in looking at the gift in your lap in a new way.* When Uranus goes into the house of fun, romance, children, and risk-taking—all things Uranus loves—it becomes a party animal. That doesn't mean it's always fun and games for the individual with this placement, of course, but they are definitely able to see more fun and games in the craziness than most people.

Among many of the Native American cultures of the southwest desert regions—such as the Hopi and Zuni—one of the most beloved trickster Gods of all time was Kokopelli. Even to this day, modernized versions of his pictographs abound as graphic art. He was the Spirit of Music, playing on his magical flute, and when he played, everyone sang and danced and forgot their troubles for a time. The fifth house is associated with Leo, one of whose archetypes is the Performer, and planets in this house often find an outlet in performing for others. Uranus is no different with regard to those urges, although those with a fifth-house Uranus may perform in radically unconventional ways. It was probably someone with this placement who invented the idea of "performance art" which involves audience participation and/or eccentric and shocking themes. Another possibility, given Uranus's trickster nature, is comedic performance of some kind. Whichever is chosen, it will be heartfelt and unexpected—the fifth-house Uranus is great at improvisational acts.

Kokopelli lived as part of no tribe, but was welcomed by all, which echoes Uranus's need to belong and contrasting need to be a unique individual, beholden to none. He went wandering through the land, staying at this place and that, moving constantly between groups and giving them his blessing. He is one of the oldest known deities of the southwest peoples, with versions of his picture going back to the ancient Pueblo civilization. Some scholars believe that he was originally a deified version of traveling Aztec traders, who walked the land with goods from the southern Mexican regions, a large pack on their shoulders. (This has been given as one explanation for the humpbacked silhouette of Kokopelli.) There are legends that such traders announced themselves with flute-playing as they approached new tribal lands, to declare themselves as friendly. They would have been welcomed not only as a source of goods, but also news and entertainment.

In addition, they often left new genetic material behind. Kokopelli was known as a Casanova figure in his own right, seducing the women of a tribe whenever he came through. His flute-playing could also mesmerize them into bedding him in spite of his strange humpbacked appearance. The original Kokopelli figures had large erect phalluses to imply this; modern versions have emasculated him and removed all visual references to genitalia, but he was formerly a deity of love and lust, appropriate to the fifth house of romance. Uranus in this house of falling in love, of course, will find an unconventional way to manage that as well. In older times, this placement was notorious for loving and leaving partners and for being unfaithful; in modern times, they may be drawn to the practice of polyamory, or some form of negotiated non-monogamy which allows them to have new experiences with a lower ratio of dishonesty or heartbreaking.

The biggest problem, romantically, for these individuals is not the ability to fall in love, which can hit like Uranian lightning. It's the ability to *stay* in love, finding ways to connect once the fifth-house excitement has worn off and it's time to move on to the more tedious parts of commitment. Kokopelli, being a deity, solves this by never sticking around ... and it's not uncommon for humans with this placement to walk the same path, at least in their youth. Love affairs tend to start and end suddenly with them, but they can be uncommonly comfortable about it, shrugging and moving on. After all, there's always another tribe just over that mountain.

Some legends say that the bag on Kokopelli's back was actually full of unborn babies, and that he could disperse these offspring to any women who heard his flute, without even having to bed them. Because of this talent, it was said that girls were often frightened of him and would hide when they heard the sound of his flute, lest he give them an unwanted pregnancy. Of course, this propensity also meant that a vision of Kokopelli was a good excuse for a sudden pregnancy; one wonders how many of those were blamed on him by girls who found themselves with child and with no father willing to take responsibility.

This is the house of children, and unconventional Uranus here is far less likely than other placements to become a parent. In fact, it often seems that Uranus wants to put all that creative potential into some outlet other than procreation; raising children can become boring very quickly and the "romance" of babies wears off faster than any other fifth-house placement (except perhaps Saturn, who may never have experienced the baby romance to begin with). It's more pleasant for Uranus to play with other people's children and then give them back after a few hours. If they do become a parent, Uranus's chaotic nature gives them a slightly higher chance of abandoning their child, having it removed from their custody, or in some cases just leaving their spouse to be the full-time parent while they check in jovially from time to time. Kokopelli certainly didn't claim any of the children he sired on all those women; he left the tribe and went on to the next adventure, and the idea of child support was unknown in those cultures.

Of course, Kokopelli was a fertility deity, and fertility Gods often have a rampant, casual, devil-may-care attitude toward spreading the gift of Life. The fifth-house Uranus may feel that way as well, thinking that if it happens, it's just another adventure. This planet isn't the best at taking the feelings of others into consideration—for that you want Moon or Venus involved—and individuals with this placement may forget that a living child grows up to be a person with opinions and needs, who may be unhappy with their charming but unreliable parent. Kokopelli himself was welcomed by tribes because he could bring fertility to the childless, and also because he could bring the rains with his flute-playing, and sing the crops up from the ground. His music could chase away the winter and bring the spring, and he also bestowed fertility on the game animals, which provided meat for the tribe. Animal friends such as wild sheep and deer followed in his wake as companions. For traditional peoples, fertility was just as much about food as it was about human babies, and perhaps even more so.

One of the reasons for the high rate of unplanned pregnancy with this placement is that this is also the house of risk-taking and gambling, and you can imagine how much fun Uranus has with that. The excitement of a pregnancy risk, or just the excitement of not worrying about it, can leap out at the most inconvenient moments when the planet of chaos is involved. If there are other ways to get this energy out, it may be best to stick to those; as this is the house of play, Uranus loves to be a wild, wacky party creature and is often sought out due to their outrageous sense of humor. No matter how strange-looking they are—and Uranus can delight in looking pretty strange—everyone lights up when they hear the flute-playing coming over the hill. Drugs and money-gambling may be a problem for this placement, mostly because they are another way of having fun and taking risks, and Uranus here blithely assumes everything will go well and their luck will hold. It's just another iteration of the traveling salesman's life—if your existence relies on the attitude of the next town, that's like an eternal rolling of the dice.

Kokopelli was said to be the best storyteller of all the Gods, and when he performed, he jumped into it with his whole body, expressing each character in a spellbinding way. One of his titles was "Joy-Bringer", and as this is the house of Joy, Uranus's placement here can presage just the kind of ephemeral joy that shows up just when we need it. If it doesn't hang around, that's all right—it's done its job. Those with a fifth-house Uranus are here to be joy-bringers, and it's the archetypal nature of joy-bringers to come and go with the weather. With a slightly crazy smile, they tell the magical story and leave you to puzzle it out. *Give them a dose of joy,* says Kokopelli, *and keep moving. The rest will take care of itself.*

6♅ Uranus in the 6ᵗʰ House: Hanuman

Earlier in this book, we met Rama (Sun in the tenth house) and his wife Sita (Moon in the tenth house); the story of how Sita was kidnapped by the demon Ravana and her husband had to get her back as best he could. While Rama and Sita are technically the main characters of the *Ramayana*, it's now time to tell the tale of the character who really steals the show, who leaves the biggest impression on the audience, and is in many ways the most beloved of all. That would be, of course, Hanuman the magical monkey warrior.

We bring him forth to illustrate the otherwise apparently incompatible combination of the freedom-loving trickster planet Uranus when it's found in the sixth house of work and service. It is certainly true that Uranus isn't fond of the sixth house at all, and finds it boring and imprisoning. Generally the best astrologers can do with this combination is to focus on the sixth house's rulership of health maintenance and Uranus's rulership of technology and say cautiously that perhaps the native might find a fulfilling career in medical tech and alternative health care. While this is certainly a distinct possibility and a not uncommon way for the careers of such individuals to go, they rarely have anything positive to say about how to handle the wayward and freedom-loving Uranus in a houseful of rules and scrub brushes. The planet of chaos can rattle around disturbingly in this house of submission to duty, rebelling and breaking things. Hanuman the monkey warrior understands these problems, and took the huge leap to get past them.

Hanuman is one of the oldest Gods in India, possible dating to a proto-Dravidian monkey god who existed before the Indo-European invasion many thousands of years ago. After the invasion, he was incorporated into the legends of Vishnu (Neptune in the first house) in order to embed this ambivalent trickster figure into a more rigid, caste-based religious world. He is a member of a magical race called the Vanaras, half-monkey and half-human, living wild in the forests and jungles. They had protruding monkey faces, a tail, and sharp claws, and were exceedingly tough and agile. His mortal parents were two Vanaras named Kesana and Anjani, but like many legendary heroes, he had a third divine parent who also affected his genetic qualities. Vayu the wind god stole some sacred pudding which had been offered to the Gods and dropped it into the hands of Kesana and Anjani, thus allowing his own energy to go into the child they conceived. Hanuman's Vayu-derived divine parentage gave him super-Vanara abilities, including leaping over mountains and across huge stretches of ocean.

Later, it is told that he saw the Sun in the sky and decided it looked like a ripe fruit, and tried to leap high in the air and grab it. Surya the Sun God (Sun in the seventh house) complained, and the god Indra (Mercury in the tenth house) punched Hanuman in the jaw with a thunderbolt, knocking him back to earth. In some versions he is killed by the impact, and his spiritual father Vayu threatens to remove all of the air from the world if his son is not resuscitated and given extra pay for his killing. Shiva (Sun in Scorpio), the God of destruction and rebirth, revives Hanuman on a whim, and Indra relents and agrees to give him yet more special qualities. He makes Hanuman's body as strong as one of his thunderbolts, and convinces Agni (Jupiter in Sagittarius) to make him immune to fire and Varuna (Saturn in the eleventh house) to make him immune to drowning.

The problem is that Hanuman is an inveterate trickster, and promptly uses his magical gifts to play pranks on people. The practical jokes go on for some time and get worse, until his people murmur that something needs to be done in order to control him. This is a situation that Uranus is familiar with—strongly Uranian people often have a wacky sense of humor, but this planet isn't so good at compassion and noticing when people have been hurt by what they perceive to merely be a hilarious joke. Eventually people do get tired of being good sports when stung, and lash out. In the house of work, this inappropriate joking can show up at one's job or interfere with the daily maintenance of others. ("Whoops! Didn't mean to knock that on the floor! Well, I guess you're going to have to get out the mop!") This is especially an issue when the sixth-house Uranus person sincerely volunteered to help with something, but then gets bored and can't resist stirring things up in an unhelpful manner. It's made worse by the fact that sometimes this Uranus placement figures out how to improve on a situation by testing it mercilessly and looking for its flaws.

Hanuman eventually plays a nasty prank on a sage with some magical powers, continually interrupting the man's attempts to meditate. Furious, the sage strikes him with a curse, saying that he will forget he has these powers and will think himself nothing more than a simple Vanara. For the next several years Hanuman lives without his special powers, and his tribe breathes a sigh of relief. Even without them, he becomes an excellent warrior who can tumble with great agility through the trees, and is given a high rank in the Vanaran army. Eventually Rama and his younger brother Lakshmana meet the Varanas and ally with them. When Rama's wife Sita is captured, Rama asked Sugriva, the king of the Varanas, to send out scouts in all directions. Hanuman is sent out as one of the scouts, partnered with a supernatural bear named Jambavan. They traveled to the very tip of India and suspected that Sita was being held on the island of Lanka, but neither monkeys nor bears have boats and they could not get across the water.

Jambavan knew about Hanuman's forgotten powers, although he had been sworn to secrecy about it. He knew that Hanuman would have been able to jump across the ocean to the island and begs Sugriva to lift the curse for this purpose. It is agreed, and Hanuman is allowed to remember his divinely-bestowed talents. He flew across the channel to Lanka, turned into an ant, and infiltrated the palace of the demon king Ravana. This situation may be familiar to the sixth-house Uranus, whose companions or co-workers may deem them too erratic to be allowed to help with many activities, but when some out-of-the-box problem-solving is needed, suddenly they become useful and are called in.

Hanuman steals into the grove of trees where Sita is being kept, and offers to spirit her out. For her own reasons (discussed in her chapter), Sita refuses and says that only Rama may rescue her. This irrationality frustrates Hanuman so much that he starts tearing up the grove, alerting guards and getting himself captured. The sixth is the house of routines, and although Uranus here generally hates routines and is a disruptive force any time the Uranus individual attempts to force themselves into one, it's different when they have actually come up with the brilliant plan themselves. Everything is supposed to go like clockwork, except here Uranus appears in the feelings of the other people involved and clog up the great scheme. Uranus may tend to blow up when this happens, because it is the planet of sudden and violent change.

Ravana's guards capture Hanuman and drag him to their lord, but the monkey warrior defiantly tells the demon king that Rama is coming and he had better beware. Ravana merely laughs at the monkey-man and orders his guards to set Hanuman's tail on fire. At this point, Hanuman breaks free of his bonds and leaps out the window, jumping from building to building all over Ravana's city and setting all the roofs on fire with his flaming tail. Once the whole place is ablaze, he leaps into the ocean to put out his tail and then jumps back to the mainland, flying back to Rama and Sugriva with his news.

Rama and Sugriva gather together the army and attack, and the Battle of Lanka commences. Hanuman acts as one of the generals, and during the war he is able to observe Rama and develop a great admiration for him and for his courage. At one point during the fighting, Rama unveils powers that Hanuman recognizes as divine, and he realizes that Rama is actually an incarnation of Vishnu. After the fighting is over and Sita is rescued, Hanuman swears loyalty to Rama and asks to be his servant. This is an unusual move for the chaotic monkey, as it would be an unusual move for the sixth-house Uranus, but not unheard of. Any planet in the sixth house—even the planet of chaos and freedom—desires to serve in some way; Uranus is just extremely particular about where that service is rendered. The person or cause must see and appreciate their unique gifts, and not set rules that hem them in to the point of compromising their creativity or making them feel bored. Uranus respects intelligence, innovation, and talent, and will want to see that in their leadership. With the right boss and the right boundaries, they can put their brilliance toward a surprisingly loyal and sustained effort.

At one point along the way, Lakshmana was badly wounded, and the field doctors opined that he could only be cured with a special herb which grew on one Himalayan mountain. Eager to help, Hanuman flew to that far mountain, but could not figure out which herb was the right one. Not wanting to delay, he picked up the entire mountainside and carried it to Lanka, where the physicians could pick out the plant they needed and save Lakshmana's life. That Hanuman is here associated with unique and innovative ways of finding medicine is another key to this Uranus placement. We mentioned at the beginning that the sixth house rules medicine and health maintenance, and finding entirely new ways of making and keeping people healthy can become a glorious obsession with these individuals.

After the war is over and Rama is brought back to his father's city, the restored prince pays all his volunteer soldiers, giving them gifts of wealth. Hanuman was given his gift, but immediately threw it away. The court officials were taken aback by the inappropriate behavior of this monkey-man, and asked why he would so dishonor his lord's gift. Hanuman replied that he did not need a gift to remember Rama, because the divinely incarnated prince would always be in his heart. When the disapproving court officials challenged him on this claim, Hanuman tore open his chest to reveal an image of Rama and Sita, sitting over his heart chakra. Rama came forward and sealed up Hanuman's chest again, healing him, and said that he would bless him with immortality. Hanuman said that he didn't need immortality, but only a place to sit at Rama's feet. Touched, Rama blessed him with immortality anyway, and the already powerful monkey-man became a demigod.

Hanuman appears in various later writings, sometimes adding in more feats to save Rama in his war, sometimes helping others who run across him. While his advice and prophecies are useful, he often begins them with some sort of prank in order to test the patience of the receiver. After Rama kills himself the faithful monkey-man retires to the forest and is rarely seen, echoing this Uranus placement which has a tendency to live alone and prefer solitude. His worship spread across Asia as far as Japan, and he was beloved by many generations of Hindus, Buddhists, and others who may not even have known where his myth came from.

He is considered to be a wonderful example of *bhakti*, or devotion, especially as he doesn't seem like the sort who would go for the Bhakti path. Hanuman finding the one place he could fully dedicate himself, in spite of his trickster nature, is used to illustrate the idea that no matter what sort of person you are, you can still touch spiritual devotion. That's a difficult lesson for high-in-the-mind Uranus—to whom it rarely occurs to bother with emotions such as love—in a house that seems prosaic and by-the-book. But even though these two energies are strange bedfellows who seem like they would never get along, and that neither would get along with devotion, when they come together a weird and wonderful alchemy can occur, as Hanuman demonstrates. High, cold Uranus can become a force of inspiration, the sixth house can become service that fulfills the soul, and devotion can bind them both together. All it takes is finding the right target and making the great leap.

7♅ Uranus in the 7th House: Maeve

Irish mythology is full of pseudo-historical figures who all seem to be chaotic, pugnacious, warlike and generally troublemakers, constantly instigating feuds against each other. It's often difficult to tell them apart in their continual obstreperous behavior. That's not just limited to the men, either; female characters are just as bad. One who stands out above the others, however, is Maeve of Connaught.

Scholars argue as to whether Maeve was a historical figure, a mythical heroine, or a euhemerized goddess of sovereignty, reduced to a mere human queen in later post-conversion stories. If she is, or once was, a goddess, she is tied to the old custom of the earth-goddess's priestess representing the land, and if the King wanted to truly rule that land, he had to at least couple with the goddess's representative and ideally partner with her. Sex, in this system, became larger than a sharing between two people; it was symbolically the intertwining of humanity (and human agendas) with Nature.

Be that as it may, humans will be humans, and you can imagine the chaos wreaked by the remains of this system, once it had faded to the point where it could still be invoked well after the original divine connection had faded. That chaos would come down on the relationships between these important figures, and struggles in those relationships would reverberate out over the land and the people. Love and desire has often been wrapped up in excuses for warfare in myths and folktales (while in real historical life, the reasons were likely to have been more along the lines of greed and/or economic hardship and/or religious intolerance), but when you add in the idea that a woman's sexual and romantic regard could make the difference for an ambitious ruler, the chaos spills all over seventh-house matters of partnership.

Uranus thinks this is great. *Shake it all up. Tear down boundaries and rules around who goes to bed with whom, and why. Emphasize freedom of choice at all costs. Trickery is a valid method to get what you want. Who cares if some people get trashed in the process? The future will change, and that's all that matters.* Leaving aside the lack of empathy in the Uranian perspective, there's also the issue that human beings aren't often well-trained in how to overcome their emotional baggage, nor how to cope when they are triggered beyond equanimity. Uranus, as an airy planet, likes to believe that emotions don't come into it—that decisions made from the Uranian viewpoint are wholly logical—when in point of fact Uranus is notorious for having periodic lightning-strike defensive rages. These blow over quickly—it's not like Pluto's scorched-earth tactics or Mars's angry punch—but they happen. In the house of partnerships, Uranus's biggest delusion is that other people ought not to indulge in jealousy, while the Uranus person is wholly free of that demon. And, of course, it's not true.

Maeve was the daughter of Eochaid, the High King of Ireland, and her name—Medb in Old Irish—is related to the root-word for "mead", the sacred drink which was passed around in the hall on important occasions. So her name is either "mead-woman" (perhaps associated with the goddess of sovereignty giving the new king an alcoholic drink to confirm his title) or "intoxicating woman". She was strong, passionate, violent, scheming, highly sexual, and hated to have her freedom curtailed. As soon as she was old enough, her father married her off to Conchobar, the King of Ulster, but the marriage immediately soured and the two became hard enemies. It's important to remember that the seventh house is not only about marriage and business partners, but it was also called The House of Open Enemies. Maeve divorces Conchobar, and her father gives him her sister Eithne as a replacement.

Many ancient cultures didn't allow divorce, and even in Old Ireland the ability to divorce might have depended on economic circumstances. Maeve is rich and high-status, and her ability just walk away is lucky … but she can't resist giving in to jealousy. When Eithne becomes pregnant and seems happy with the husband Maeve didn't want, Maeve becomes jealous of her happiness and has her killed. (Her son, however, is cut from her womb and lives on.) This clinches Maeve and Conchobar's relationship as Open Enemies.

Maeve goes through a number of different lovers, insisting on her sexual freedom. For a woman at that time, anything other than virginity or monogamy was unheard of, and generally punished. Uranus in the house of partnerships, however, insists on freedom and sovereignty over one's body and actions. Just because someone is a spouse does not, in the view of Uranus, allow them to tell you what to do. This doesn't mean that a seventh-house Uranian can't be monogamous, but it means that they must freely choose it for themselves for personal reasons, not because it's what society expects …

or what the other partner expects. Even if they agree to sexual exclusivity, they are going to want a lot of freedom in the rest of their life. They may travel, and expect the partner to be sanguine about being alone for periods of time. They may have outside interests, or groups of friends, whom they refuse to deprioritize just because it intrudes on the marriage. The right partner for them will understand, and have their own independent lives as well.

The gender roles in traditional heterosexual relationships will also go by the wayside, or at least the seventh-house Uranus person will cherry-pick the ones they like and toss the rest. In demanding her sexual autonomy and the right to have as many lovers as she wants, with none of them claiming exclusivity over her body, Maeve rebels against the accepted role of women in her culture. Uranus is one of the androgynous planets (along with Mercury), and will not be told that behavior is mandated by the luck of the biological draw. This works for more than just women—I've seen men with this placement who are stay-at-home husbands supported by working wives. Uranus wants to look at both parties in a commitment as unique individuals with their own collection of needs and desires, which cannot be assumed from their external characteristics, and thus a unique custom-built relationship is the only ethical choice.

Maeve swore that she would never marry again unless she found a man who was without fear, meanness, or jealousy, and would let her sleep with whom she chose. She finally marries the chief of her guards, Ailill, who claimed that he could hold to this promise, and for a time he did. Meanwhile, her father had deposed the king of Connaught (after Maeve had taken him as a lover and he had got himself killed), and installs Maeve in his place to rule. She and Ailill have seven sons and two daughters, most of whom come to bad, chaotic ends. At one point, she meets her ex-husband Conchobar during a yearly law assembly at Tara, and he rapes her in revenge for her sister's death. Maeve's hatred for him grows even stronger, and she consults a Druid to ask if any of her seven sons will kill Conchobar and give her vengeance. The Druid tells her that a son named Maine will do it; none of her sons bear that name, so she renames them all Maine, with second names to tell them apart. (The irony is that eventually one of her sons does kill a man named Conchobar, but it's a different Conchobar and not her arch-enemy. Uranus laughs and chaos rules.)

One night, Maeve and Ailill are laying in bed after lovemaking, and they begin comparing whether they are truly equal. They both have equal amounts of land, money, servants, resources, etc.; but Ailill has a white stud bull which is far more valuable than anything in Maeve's herds. For some reason, that bull becomes Maeve's symbol of how she and her husband are not complete social equals, and it galls her. The seventh-house Uranus can become obsessed with having a partnership which is completely equal in every way that counts (and what ways actually count will be subjective to them), ignoring the fact that humans are all more or less fortunate or skilled in many different areas. They can also ignore the fact that true equality is in what kind of recourse each person has in the relationship, which comes back to how they treat each other, not who makes more money or can find more dates.

At the same time, Uranus is often deeply aware of politics and social inequality, and can react to this global injustice by attempting to create artificial equality in relationship. This rarely works, because it is, in the end, artificial and based on a biased, idiosyncratic standard, but it is a common Uranus mistake. "If only I had more money, or they were better-looking, or we owned the house in common and only had one car apiece..." This mistake happens because Uranus is still thinking in terms of independence, and maintaining that state even in a partnership. Actual interdependence weaves together one person's weak areas with another person's strengths, and both help hold each other up as a unit.

Maeve decides that the only way to get equality in her relationship is to get hold of the Brown Bull of Cooley, which is equal to her husband's animal. Its owner wouldn't sell to her, so she embarked on the infamous Cattle Raid of Cooley, which created a local war, involved lots of heroes killing each other, and ended with more chaos all round. She does finally manage to steal the bull, but as soon as she gets it home to the pasture, the two bulls start fighting. Ailill's white bull gores the Brown Bull of Cooley to death and then dies of its own wounds, proving that the whole enterprise was for nothing.

Around this time, things go sour for Maeve and Ailill. He has been patient with all her lovers and shown no jealousy, but Fergus was the exception. Fergus was the former king of Ulster, deposed by Conchobar and wandering the countryside with his household, and it was said that it took thirty men to sexually satisfy Maeve, or one night with Fergus. In spite of his promise, Ailill becomes jealous of Fergus and has him killed. At the same time, Maeve is becoming jealous of Ailill's affairs with other women, and so has her husband killed. Her rejection of the normal human emotion of jealousy prevents her from either being sympathetic to her husband's single failure and mediating the problem before it came to murder, or acknowledging that she herself was just as prone to jealousy, and indeed murderous jealousy.

Sometimes it is hard for the Uranus person to face that they are not as evolved or advanced as they think they ought to be, and if that is the case, they should not be so intolerant of the flaws of others. This can lead to inhuman standards for both parties, which sets everyone up for failure. Add in the fact that Uranus in this house is attracted to partners who are brilliant, independent, chaotic, and ideally more radical and socially evolved than they are, and it may be a race to see which one will be the first to fail at being perfectly enlightened.

This placement of Uranus generally indicates that "normal", unquestioned relationships are just not in the cards for the individual, and that each joining must be custom-built and carefully thought through. Maeve lived in an era long before the rainbow of consensual, negotiated alternative relationships we have today, and her story reflects this lack of choice, but modern lovers have less of an excuse. Human connections need to be assembled with human failings clearly visible and accounted for, and at its best, this placement of Uranus is in a good position to do that—problem-solving rather than simply reacting.

Maeve is eventually killed while bathing in a lake by her dead sister's son, who has planned his revenge for years; thus her first act of jealousy comes around to haunt her. This Uranus placement, so quick to cut and run when their freedom is threatened, needs to remember that you can't run away from your past poor relationship decisions. Every new relationship is a chance from the Universe, not to avoid them, but to understand and work through them. Every new connection is an opportunity to change a little of the great sea of past injustices, including those visited domestically on each other ... if only by embodying that hope and clear-sightedness in the love you build, and continually rebuild, with each other.

♅ 8 Uranus in the 8th House: Number Eleven in the Village of Death

The eighth house is a scary place. Planets that get stuck there are often loaded with karma, stifled by gloom, made heavy with the associated Plutonian power of the place. It's like living permanently in a haunted house, where ghosts chill their way down the halls and disturb you while you're on the toilet or trying to make love to your partner in the bedroom. The inner planets often have a hard time dealing with the situation, and become depressed or fearful. The outer planets, on the other hand, have larger ways of coping. They take the long view of things. To a transpersonal planet, ghosts are nothing to be afraid of, sex is always a vehicle for something bigger, and karma is what's for breakfast.

Uranus, especially, is not fazed by the haunted house. He makes faces at the ghosts and tries to get them to form an ethereal kazoo band. He's probably the guy whose Rube Goldberg machine creates Pluto's supply of Instant Karma Beverage Powder. Uranus's sojourn in the eighth house is echoed in the Ashanti story of Number Eleven, one of the famous ancestor-gods of their people.

The tale begins with a mother whose eleven voracious children eat so much that she cannot get food herself, and is starving. She decides to kill a few of them off, so that there will be more food to go around. At this point, we can recognize the devouring-mother figure of legend. In the eighth house, which deals with psychological depths, all parent figures are devouring, or cold, or otherwise unloving, and all children are voracious and unsatisfied. This is the house where we struggle with that which we fear, and Bad Parent and Evil Child are just some of the ghosts floating through the halls. In the story, the mother makes a deal with a tree-spirit, under whose branches she has planted a gourd patch: when the children are sent to pick the gourds, the tree will drop its branches on them and kill them.

The youngest child of the lot is different from the other ten. He is brilliant, imaginative, fearless, and a trickster figure. He has no name; his mother had run out of names by the time he was born, and he is only called Number Eleven, which is reminiscent of this trickster planet's rulership of Aquarius, the eleventh sign. He overhears his mother's plotting with the tree, and tricks it into dropping its branches too early, so his siblings manage to eat the gourds safely.

Seeing that her plan did not work, the children's mother complains to their absent father, who is a sky god. He agrees that the children have to die, and orders them to take a trip to the Village of Death, supposedly to obtain four items that Death has hoarded—a pipe, a snuffbox, a chewing-stick, and a whetstone, all made out of gold. When they arrive at the village, they find it populated by Death and her brood of children. Death is a tall old woman with sharp red teeth who greets them eagerly, intending to eat them once they are asleep. She prepares sleeping mats for them, bedding each of them down with one of her children.

Number Eleven is suspicious, and refuses to go to sleep. Seemingly unafraid of Death, he lingers at the campfire, harassing her. This is the sort of Uranus trickster energy that is perversely convinced of its own immortality. The person with this placement may be the one to take death-defying risks, testing his ability to skate near the edge. Death tries to convince the irrepressible child to go to sleep, but he nags her for a smoke from her pipe. When she allows it, he pockets the pipe. Then he asks for a pinch of snuff, then a chewing-stick, then finally some food. The Uranus person likes to get closer and closer to danger, almost daring it to touch him: if I do this, will I survive? I survived that, what about this? Will this be pushing it too far? There's something about daring Death to smite you, he's found, that makes you feel so very alive, lucky, and blessed. It's an attitude that may horrify onlookers, who aren't quite so sure of his ability to evade consequences.

In the tale, Death takes her whetstone and sharpens her knife, and goes to prepare some food. Number Eleven has secretly cut holes in her water calabash in order to delay her. He pockets the whetstone, runs to where his siblings are sleeping, and wakes them. Herding them all up into a tree, he replaces their sleeping forms with piles of blankets. When Death comes in, she kills all her own children, thinking that they are the intruders.

The individual with Uranus in the eighth house may be fascinated with Death, and worrisomely unafraid of Her. He's the one who wants to put Death under a microscope while keeping himself at a safe distance, whether through laboratory testing or occult study. Many famous scientists have had this placement, unfortunately including two who were noted Nazi experimenters. In their cases, Uranus was quite happy to sacrifice the children that were not related to him for the sake of the children who were, and echoes of this coldness can penetrate into other less extreme folks as well. The Uranus individual with this placement needs to remember and respect every life that is placed in danger or sacrificed that he might gain knowledge, and be careful not to consider some lives more expendable than others simply because he is not invested in those specific people.

This placement can give a strange combination of hot passion and intermittent coldness; Uranus is not entirely immune to the eighth-house energy and soaks up some of its Plutonian emotional extremity. Number Eleven is willing to take great risks for his siblings, but he is also willing to endanger them out of his own pride. When Death walks under the tree, he cannot resist urinating on her. The children are discovered, and Death shrieks with rage. She utters a spell that causes them all to fall out of the tree and break their necks. Number Eleven, guessing what the spell might be for, jumps down before it finishes and is spared. His taunting of Death has now cost him his siblings.

However, one of the useful things about this placement is its ability to utilize the tools of the enemy, turning them against the oppressor. This is the person who will learn the system well enough to manipulate it, perhaps with the eventual goal of bringing it down. Number Eleven plays dead while Death climbs the tree, making sure that all the children have fallen. He repeats the spell as he has heard it, and she falls out of the tree and breaks her neck. Elated, he reverses the spell, and brings his siblings back to life … but Death, also, comes back to life with them.

It's a hard lesson. Under all his pokings and proddings and risk-taking, the Uranus individual really hopes to control Death, and karma, and taxes, and all those other inevitabilities that come along with it. (He may also want to control some of the other uncontrollable parts of eighth-house experience, including sexual feelings and deep emotions. They're often so inconvenient, after all.) That which he values should live; that which might destroy what he values should go down. It's a very human need, to control the world around us, and in the eighth house Uranus wants to be able to change the very mysteries of the cycle of life around at will. It is a terrible disappointment to him when he realizes that he cannot change those inevitabilities; that they will always come back, in this form or another one. The predator is killed; the species overpopulates and dies of disease. The virus is exterminated; another one evolves. The check and balance of the cycle of life cannot be overrun by anyone's desires.

A friend of mine runs an occult shop, and she has told many an amusing tale of customers who come in, buy items that are clearly for the purpose of doing harmful magic to others, and then ask if she could recommend a spell for them to avoid the consequences of their actions. She has to tell them, again and again, that a spell to change the orbit of the Earth would be more effective. Sometimes, these folk have read elaborate spells written by past magicians in the hope of avoiding the consequences that they so richly deserve, and they are always disappointed when these spells are debunked. From childhood on, we hope to be able to "get away with" things that we know ought to have consequences … but on the universal scale of things, if you think you're getting away with something, you can be sure that it will come around anyway, whether you recognize it or not. In our story, Number Eleven and his siblings run screaming to the river, where they attempt to cross before Death can get to them. She is in hot pursuit, and catches up just as the second-to-last child crosses over. Number Eleven is left to face her alone, in all her wrath.

At this point, Number Eleven is desperate, so he resorts to a Uranus trick—shapeshifting. In our lives, shapeshifting can be done in many ways, but in its simplest form it's about fitting yourself (with whatever difficulty) into the perspective of someone or something else. The catch, of course, is that doing it even for a hour will change you irrevocably. Nobody shapeshifts and gets away unchanged. In his terror, Number Eleven changes himself into a stone by the riverside, and then realizes that he has made himself into everything he is not—passive, helpless, slow as a stone, utterly unlike the quick Uranian problem-solver that is his normal way of being. This part of the story, though, is the key to understanding the goal.

Uranus will not master the House of Death until he really understands Death intuitively, not just intellectually. Part of that is coming to terms with the inherent helplessness of the mere mortal against Death, and the force of Karma, and all the rest of it. Even sexuality cannot be fully controlled, or all you're doing is stifling it. To master sexuality, you need to learn to surrender—not necessarily to another, but to the power of your own flesh and feelings. You need to relax and lean back and let it take you where it will … even if that's a scary place. Even if, with Uranus in this house of deep psychology, you are almost guaranteed to hit some feral urges that you cannot control.

What happens in the story is that Death decides to throw a stone at the escaped children, and she picks up—of course—the rock that is Number Eleven. Up until this time he's managed to remain just out of reach of her clutches, but here he is, finally, helpless and in her hands. At this point he gives up and consigns himself to Death ... and it's about time, too. Everything he's tried to escape the Greater Powers has failed, and now he is reduced to everything he fears...

...and Death flings the stone across the river at the children, and Number Eleven flies to safety. He turns back into himself and flees with his brothers and sisters, and the story ends. They do not go back to a happy life; the Devouring Mother and Indifferent Father still await them, but Number Eleven has learned something about the nature of direct confrontation with fears. Dancing around them at arms' length, trying to control them from a distance ... this doesn't work. They simply come back again and again, cutting the ground out from beneath your feet. You need to get up close, personal, and vulnerable with them in order to finally be set free.

Uranus in the 9th House: Sun Wukong

One of the most memorable and enduring characters in all of Chinese folklore is Sun Wukong, the Monkey King. An irrepressible trickster, a dedicated rebel, and a general loose cannon, his is the tale of how a monkey tried to storm heaven, and what became of it. The story spans Taoism, Buddhism, Confucianism, and indigenous Chinese polytheism, showing what a religious melting pot China became, which is highly appropriate for the entrance of chaotic Uranus into the house of religion ... and of higher education.

The worship of sacred monkey figures in China is attested back to the first century, so it is not surprising that the story of a particularly magical monkey would come about. Mainstream Chinese Buddhism denies that he has any standing in that faith, but the common people still revere and honor him as part of folk Buddhism. (Uranus is often unsettling to, and shunned by, the dogmatic mainstream.) Sun Wukong is no ordinary monkey; he is born out of a magic stone sitting at the peak of the Mountain of Flowers, already endowed with great talents. He had amazing strength and could support large weights on his shoulders while running with the speed of a meteor, or so it was said. He had vast memorization skills, and when he met the ordinary monkeys and they made him their king, he could remember the name of every one of them.

As he crawled out of the stone at his birth, two golden beams of light shot out of his eyes, and for a split second penetrated the palace of the Jade Emperor of Heaven (Neptune in Capricorn), who sent down a couple of messengers to check it out. They returned, saying that a stone monkey had been born, but it was nothing special. The Jade Emperor shrugged and forgot about it, not knowing that this strange monkey would one day be one of the greatest thorns in his side. Hierarchical spirituality was unimpressed by this Uranian strangeness.

When Sun Wukong realized that the ordinary monkeys were mortal and he began to lose several of his friends to old age, he decided to make a quest to find the way to beat death. He wandered into the human lands, stole some clothing to hide his monkey body, and walked about watching the humans and their foibles. A peasant was singing a religious chant, and Sun Wukong was drawn to it; he asked the peasant about it and was told that it had been taught by an ancient sage living in a temple in the woods, Sun Wukong, goes to find this man, a sorcerous Taoist sage and martial artist named Puti Zushi, but the sage refuses to teach a monkey. The Monkey King camps on his doorstep for three months, trying to convince him, and finally the sage gives in and teaches him for a year. Sun Wukong learns the Seventy-Two Earthly Transformations, which give him seventy-two separate magical powers, including the ability to transform into a man or various animals or objects, become invisible, freeze people in place, make temporary copies of himself, turn his hair into small weapons, and become a skilled martial-arts fighter.

Sun Wukong then threatens and extorts a local Dragon King into giving him a weapon; he is given a magical staff which can shrink down to the size of a sewing needle when not used. He also demands fine clothing, and the Dragon King gives him a golden mail-shirt and a magical crown of phoenix feathers. Sun Wukong then hears that the Demon King of Confusion was kidnapping his monkey subjects, so he returns home, rescues them, and slays the demon king. This makes several other Demon Kings and

Animal Spirit Kings rally around him, hoping to be his allies. Before he knows it, he has become a leader of a large and chaotic group.

At some point, Death comes to collect his soul, and he asks to be shown the book wherein everyone is listed, so that Death knows whose time has come. When Death is not looking, he wipes his name out of the book, along with that of every monkey known to him. This saves him from Death, but draws attention to him from Heaven, and the Jade Emperor decides that perhaps this monkey has gotten too powerful, and needs a job to discipline him. Sun Wukong is invited to Heaven, but once there is given low-status tasks which do not have the importance he feels he deserves, and he is treated patronizingly. Enraged, he goes back to his forest (but not before stealing and drinking the Emperor's magical wine of immortality), rallies his troops, and decides that he will attack Heaven itself and topple the Jade Emperor.

When Uranus comes into the house of higher education, the individual with this placement may have an erratic time of it, perhaps preferring alternative education or having an unusual or spotty record. It is highly appropriate for rebellious, political Uranus to then take that education and use it to defy the state. Those with this placement may be drawn to philosophies which preach freedom and distrust hierarchy, which makes no friends with those involved in such chains of command. They may find themselves in leadership positions due to their education, knowledge, or philosophy, and then build systems for their group which they may end up destroying and rebuilding over and over again, trying to find the right system which gives everyone enough freedom and yet has some kind of accountability. With idol-toppling Uranus in the House of World View, all pyramidal groups may be seen as evil; the top of any system may be seen as something (or someone) to be thrown down.

The Monkey King and his army of allies attack the Kingdom of Heaven, and for a while Sun Wukong looks like he is actually winning. A powerful warrior god in service to the Emperor finally vanquishes his troops, and Sun Wukong gets trapped in a magical sigil, but he escapes a few weeks later and goes to face the Emperor and fight him single-handedly. At this point the Jade Emperor decides to call on a higher power, and he and his courtiers call for the Buddha to come help them keep from being slain by the ever-more-powerful Monkey King.

Sun Wukong has learned many skills, but he lacks wisdom and keeps going mostly on sheer chutzpah. He has little sense of strategy, but a great deal of overwhelming luck. While Jupiter is usually the giver of luck, Uranus can offer a species of "trickster luck", which can, of course, turn on you at any moment. The Buddha sends a message to Sun Wukong with a wager, saying that he cannot escape from Buddha's hand, and that he should meet the Buddha in a particular place to test this. If he can do it, the Buddha will allow him to attack the Jade Emperor.

Sun Wukong confidently takes the wager and goes to the indicated place, to find it empty except for five pillars of stone pushing into the air. Seeing no one about, he cries out a challenge and pisses in the middle of the stone circle. Then, as it rises and the pillars bend and close in around him, he realizes that he has been standing in the Buddha's hand all along, and the pillars of stone were his fingers. The hand closes around Sun Wukong, and he is placed under a mountain with only his head and hands outside it, to meditate on his life choices for five hundred years. The Buddha arranges for two earth spirits to feed him iron pellets when he is hungry and molten copper when he is thirsty.

Uranus is an impatient planet—perhaps even more impatient than Mars—and wants change to come immediately, in the way Uranus wants, and will knock over as many applecarts as seems likely to get the job done. However, now Sun Wukong must learn patience, watching five hundred years and all their attendant history go by. At the end of all this, he is much chastened and has finally learned some wisdom. He begs for release, and to be apprenticed again to a teacher who will show him how to behave wisely and well.

Kwan Yin, the Goddess of Compassion (Moon in Cancer), offers to free Sun Wukong on one condition. The Buddhist sage Tang Sanzang wishes to undertake a journey to the West to find the lost sutras of legend, but he is a peaceful man who cannot defend himself against human bandits who want to rob him, and demons who think that eating his flesh will give them magical powers. If Sun Wukong will serve him and be his bodyguard until the legendary sutras are found and brought back to the Jade Emperor, the monkey hero will be freed. Kwan Yin knows that he will be hard to control, so she puts a magical circlet on Sun Wukong which will incapacitate him when Tang Sanzang says a certain word, but the sage never needs to use it.

Sun Wukong becomes the disciple of the patient old man, defending him through eighty-one troublesome adventures until their long quest is over. By that time, he has learned enough wisdom to achieve enlightenment, and comes into his power with compassion and joy, no longer a loose cannon, nor obsessed with destroying a heavenly hierarchy which he does not need to deal with any longer.

It's par for the course that a ninth-house Uranus would learn best while on a long road trip adventure; that's when their minds are most awake to change. The best teacher for a ninth-house Uranus is one who is well-traveled, either literally or metaphorically—who has seen a great deal and can become a patient anchor for them while they go through their mental and spiritual gyrations, yet at the same time honoring their skills and talents and neophilic philosophy. If they stick with the spiritual and/or philosophical education long enough, sooner or later they do become some species of enlightened. (We can see this in Gandhi, who had this placement and moved from rebel to resister to sadhu during his many travels.) They may develop an uncanny insight into future trends, being able to see down the "long road" of life into the future itself. All they have to do is put down their cannonballs and see the greater picture, the force of change in the place of World View.

10 ♅ Uranus in the 10th House: Daedalus

Where Uranus strikes, we have both genius and chaos; when it lands in the tenth house, one's career is abundant with both those qualities. This is the story of a hero whose career was, quite literally, being a genius. He is the greatest inventor in Greek legend, the most brilliant figure of all. Uranus is the planet of technology, and the tenth-house placement often gives those who carry it a love of tech careers; Daedalus is the first serious tech-geek in Greek myth.

Stories of the birth and parentage of Daedalus abound in ancient Hellenic cultures, and they are all different. It seems that every city-state wanted to claim him for their own, so they decided that he'd been born there and gave him parents with plausible names for their regions. In other words, his origins are shrouded in chaos. One thing is always certain, though—unlike other heroes such as Hercules or Theseus who were attributed some kind of divine as well and mortal parentage, Daedalus is always the child of two mortals. His genius is purely human, and as such it epitomizes the way in which humans use technology to be the equal of the Gods.

The tales of his inventiveness were also legion. He supposedly invented the art of carpentry and tools such as axes and glue. He carved wooden mannequins which could move in lifelike ways and were carried around the countryside as ritual figures called *daedala*. The Athenians claim that he began in Athens, designing buildings and creating new technology, and was lauded as the most brilliant man in the city. This echoes the path of the planet of innovation when it lands in the house of career; people with this Uranus placement do best in careers which are unusual, don't follow the clock, and make use of their unique ways of thinking.

However, there was a worm in this apple of fame, and that was intellectual pride. This isn't unusual for Uranus, which often knows (or at least believes in) its intelligence and originality. Any planet in the tenth house of career and public opinion wants to be praised by society, and when Uranus is here, it wants to be known as the greatest and most original genius of them all. The planet of electricity has a temper, and wherever Uranus lies, one has a tendency to be mentally erratic and fly off the handle at (perhaps imagined) slights. In the tenth house, Uranian voltage can erupt at bosses, co-workers, and anyone else who gets in the way of the Great Work, perhaps with irritating and contemptible tirades about how there isn't enough funding for the project, or how that advertising won't appeal to the public, or that this experiment is animal cruelty. It can also erupt at those who deny Uranus's brilliance, or—at its worst—turn out to be more brilliant than them.

At the height of Daedalus's fame, his sister apprentices her son Talos to the great inventor, and the boy immediately starts to follow in Daedalus's footsteps. Studying a toothed seashell on the shore, he notches a piece of metal and creates the first saw. Riveting two pieces of iron together, he creates the first compass. This goes on for a while until Daedalus begins to fear that his young protégé may steal his fame, at which point he throws the boy off of the Acropolis in a fit of rage and kills him. Athena (Sun in Aquarius), the goddess who loves brilliant thinkers, saved the boy by turning him into a partridge before he hit the ground. Daedalus is charged with murder anyway, and flees Athens, taking refuge with King Minos of Crete. Chaos has struck, and Uranus must have an immediate change of scenery.

The inventor spends his time with Minos inventing better masts and sails for the island king's navy and building a magical dance floor for his daughter Ariadne (Jupiter in Scorpio), but the strangest task of all was set him by Pasiphaë, the wife of Minos. She had been cursed by Aphrodite (Venus in Libra) and Poseidon (Neptune in Cancer) to have an obsessive sexual passion for her husband's sacred white bull, in revenge for Minos withholding the bull when he had promised it as a sacrifice to the sea god. She asked Daedalus to help her mate with the dangerous creature, and he fashioned a hollow wooden cow covered in real cowhide so that the queen could have her way. She then gave birth to the Minotaur, a half-human half-bull child with a homicidal temper, and Daedalus was commissioned to create the famous Labyrinth to house him.

Later, when Theseus (Pluto in the eleventh house) came as a tithed bull-dancer to Crete and fell in love with Ariadne, the two plotted to kill the Minotaur and flee together. Daedalus gave Ariadne the idea to give Theseus a ball of string in order to get in and out of the Labyrinth, and after their flight Minos becomes enraged with his personal inventor who has aided and abetted so much trouble over the years. This is also a problem with tenth-house Uranuses; having the planet of change and chaos in the house of authority means that they are not generally impressed with the social order, nor those at the top of it. They will have their own quirky and unusual moral code, which may or may not be socially progressive and probably isn't particularly socially acceptable. When they've decided on the right thing to do, they cease to care what the people who give orders are going to think of it. Daedalus's willingness to take great risks in the name of science, even if it costs him his patron, is an example of this Uranian disdain for the Establishment.

Any planet in the tenth house affects one's public reputation, and with Uranus here, they may inadvertently build a reputation for being erratic, open-minded, and socially unconventional. Some individuals with this Uranus build on that outlet and specifically point their careers at the goal of making social change, but even with that focus, technology will likely be involved somewhere. On the other hand, scandal is often involved as well; their very disregard for social rules can create situations where they become the center of horrified gossip. Fortunately, they rarely care.

Minos locked his wayward inventor up in his own Labyrinth, and he was not allowed to leave. According to Minos's plan, there Daedalus would stay, chastened and meekly turning out inventions for his master. Uranus, though, is the hardest planet of all to keep contained. By this point Daedalus had married a Cretan woman who had given him a son and then died, and the youth Icarus is locked up with his father, as an extra lever for good behavior. There was no way to leave the island nation by ship, as Minos knew every boat which entered and left, so Daedalus created two pairs of wings from bird feathers, threads from blankets, and beeswax. He instructed Icarus not to fly too close to the ocean in case the dampness might clog his wings, nor too close to the sun in case the heat might melt the wax, and the two of them took flight over the ocean from Crete. Unfortunately, Icarus was just as arrogant and risk-taking as his father had been in his younger days, and in his delight flew too close to the sun. His wings melted and he fell into the sea and drowned.

Horrified, Daedalus took the body of his son and buried it on a nearby island. As he was burying the boy, a partridge appeared and cackled at him; the inference was that the spirit of Talus was punishing him for his earlier murder. This is the point in the story when Daedalus is humbled; he realizes that there are limits to what mere technology can do, and also sees that his intellectual arrogance has pushed him into unwise choices. His determination to be free no matter the price has now cost him his only son. This Uranus placement often comes with drastic ups and downs in one's career which can reverberate into the rest of one's life. Usually, the reaction is to pack up and move on, as if moving on can erase the chaos that has been left behind. Sometimes they will change their entire career suddenly, throwing away decades of training and qualifications to start anew in some completely different field. After all, when it gets old, why not move on?

Daedalus next went to Sicily where he was employed by King Cocalus, but the furious Minos tracked him across the Mediterranean. Minos went from city to city with a spiral seashell, saying that there would be a reward for anyone who could figure out a way to wind a string through the spiral without breaking or opening it. He knew that Daedalus would be unable to resist the intellectual challenge, and he was correct. When Minos came to the court of Cocalus with his puzzle, the king immediately brought it to his new inventor. Daedalus solved the problem by tying a string to an ant and letting it work its way to the center of the shell, and Cocalus come out in triumph with the string-wound shell. Minos then knew that his escaped inventor was at the Sicilian court, and demanded that he be returned at once. However, Cocalus wasn't interested in giving back his new court genius, and he convinced Minos to take a bath in the new tub with plumbing which Daedalus had invented for him. Boiling water was poured through the pipes, and the great King Minos was murdered in the tub.

For the rest of his days, Daedalus moved from city to city, avoiding places where he was actively wanted by the law. His fame kept growing and his death, like his birth, was claimed by multiple cities. Alone among well-known Greek heroes, his story is not one where he ever raised a sword. Instead, he hummed with Uranian energy and poured out his creativity into his work, striving ever to make the world a better place through science and learning. While his life was by no means peaceful, individuals with this Uranus placement aren't usually looking for peaceful. They're looking for change in the outer world, and they are quite likely to be the cause of it.

11♅ Uranus in the 11th House: Momotaro

Uranus is a planet of chaos, a trickster, a jokester, a force which thinks new and different is always better than old and probably stagnant, at least in this planet's view. Uranus is the true ruler of the eleventh house, which we think of as the House of Friendship ... and also the house of groups, whether political or social or interest-oriented. Yet we also think of Uranus as the most independent of planets, the classic I-don't-need-anyone loner who goes his merry eccentric way. All that is truth, but the truth underneath is more nuanced. Uranus is extremely concerned with being in or out of the group. Just because Uranus may choose to be exiled rather than compromise their own path doesn't mean they aren't full of secret desires that they might find the group which is "different the same as me", who will welcome them and not require that they be something they are not.

Part of being in a group is accepting the group culture, or challenging it. Uranus both longs for the group and is willing to walk away from it, which is important; while loyalty to the group is an excellent thing (and is illustrated by other planets in this house), someone has to be the person who points out the flaws and the ugly bits, and is willing to vote with their feet if the group refuses to clean up their act. The eleventh-house Uranus person may also end up being a force of chaos in the group itself, trying the patience of people with their insistence on new, untested, and possibly socially unacceptable activities.

Group theory leads, inevitably, to political theory. What tribe you belong to, and what tribe won't accept you, go back as far as humanity to create the basis for most political disagreements. Even wars fought over scarce resources come down to "I'm not sharing with anyone who isn't my tribe, and my tribe needs to come first." Uranus is an intensely political planet, because it indicates how much someone is willing to go along with the status quo, and where they will rebel and try to make change. The eleventh house, beyond being about friends and groups (and all the politics involved in those), is also the house of the brotherhood/sisterhood of humanity, and how any given person sees that condition. All this means that we are not getting out of this chapter without talking about politics.

But first, the story: An elderly Japanese couple, childless and long past childbearing age, live by a river in a small village. One day the old woman is washing laundry in the river when a huge peach floats by, and she fishes it out and brings it home for dinner. In one version of the story, the couple eats the peach and both become younger; the woman promptly gets pregnant and names their son after the magical peach itself. In the more famous version, they cut the peach open and find a baby boy inside, and adopt him as their son. Either way "Momotaro" is Peach Boy, and he grows quickly into a strong, quick, and very mischievous child, constantly getting into trouble and playing tricks on people, a very Uranian individual.

The village is periodically raided by a group of *oni* (ogre-demons) who live in on a nearby island named Onigashima. One day when he is fifteen years of age, Momotaro announces that he is going to Onigashima to defeat all the *oni* and discourage them from attacking the village again. His parents beg him not to go, but he is adamant. Instead of asking for weapons (or even taking any), he asks his mother to make him the largest millet dumplings she can cook for food on the journey.

As he travels toward the island, a large dog approaches him and asks to share the large millet dumplings. Momotaro gives the dog half a dumpling and tells him of his plan to go defeat the *oni*, and the dog likes the idea and asks to come along. Further on, they meet a monkey who has heard of Momotaro's quest, and asks to accompany him. The dog objects, as dogs and monkeys are supposedly enemies, and the two start a fight. Momotaro breaks it up, tells them that if they want to come along that they must act courteously toward each other, and gives the monkey some of the dumpling. They travel along for some time—Momotaro periodically breaking up fights between the two of them—and meet a large pheasant, who also wants to come along … but who does not get along with either the dog or the monkey. Again, Momotaro remonstrates with them all, feeds them all more millet dumplings, and herds his little band of argumentative misfits toward the goal.

This is a very common situation for the eleventh-house Uranus. They don't mind making friends from different levels in society, and in fact the stranger and more unusual a person is, the more interested they are in making their acquaintance. It's a truism that they like their friends a little weird (or more than a little). At the same time, they will not tolerate contempt and bickering among their friends or any group where they have influence, especially if the dislike is aimed at the sort of person they are, as opposed to some wrong which one might have done to another. Uranus isn't afraid to force people to be peaceful with each other if necessary, which sounds like a non sequitur but makes perfect sense to this chaotic planet. "You will all be brothers and sisters together, or I'll punch you all in the head until you see some sense!" is the rallying cry of the eleventh-house Uranus child, and in more elaborate terms, the adult as well.

Momotaro and his odd little group make it to Onigashima, and make friends with two captured human laundresses who are weeping by the shore. They cannot resist Momotaro's friendly overtures, and show him a back door into the *oni* castle. Momotaro sends the pheasant around to the front of the castle to create a distraction, telling the bird to taunt the band of *oni* with threats, but fly about quickly and avoid being a target. While the pheasant does his performance, Momotaro (along with the dog and the monkey) sneak into the castle and attack the *oni* from behind. Most are vanquished (of course) and the *oni* chieftain finally offers the hero all the plunder from the villagers if Momotaro will spare him, which the boy-hero does. He returns triumphantly to the village with the spoils, returning them all to the villagers from whom they had been stolen. His parents welcome him back, knowing that as a sacred child he had a good chance of survival, and all live happily ever after … except that the villagers periodically roust Momotaro whenever there is a destructive supernatural entity to be dealt with.

The earliest Momotaro stories were written down in the sixteenth century, long after they had circulated as a standard sort of hero-tale, largely aimed at children. Artwork of Peach Boy came along soon after, and it is interesting to see how he shrinks from being portrayed as an adult in his prime to being a youth, and then a child, over the centuries. At some point, the Momotaro stories started to be used as children's morality tales— portraying filial piety, courage, and most importantly the significance of getting diverse and disagreeing people to come together for a single cause. This latter moral grew in stature as Japan became less of an island divided into small warring fiefdoms, and the Emperor became a stronger central leader.

Similarly, the *oni* started out as just supernatural beings with no particular crime to their name (except perhaps having a treasure trove of wealth to steal); one killed *oni* because they were *oni*. At some point, the stories add that they have been plundering the villagers, and thus must be stopped; this part of the story became popular during the Japanese war with China, and is obviously aimed at Chinese foreigners. Over time, the *oni* took on more foreign qualities until one Japanese writer asked plaintively if the tales were meant to teach Japanese children that all foreigners were devils. In 19th-century versions, the *oni* enumerate their wrongdoings and make a solemn promise never to do them again ... and the wrongdoings were very pointedly wrongs of the current political scene as it gradually changed.

During the half-century leading up to the second World War, the Momotaro stories became more and more propagandized, subtly characterizing the dog, monkey, and pheasant as various factions within Japan whom, the ruling court felt, ought to drop their differences and band together in one army. Then things got more blatant, as Momotaro was illustrated for books. During Japan's war with Russia in the early 20th century, a book version came out which showed the *oni* as Russians. By World War II, early films and cartoons showed Peach Boy as representing the imperial Japanese government, and the *oni* became the Allies. After the defeat of Japan, Momotaro media suddenly dropped off the face of the earth in a massive silence, and only recently has it been acceptable to find him again in children's books.

The irony of using a story whose goal is group cooperation as wartime propaganda for a corrupt government is a discomfiting thorn. One wonders what Peach Boy himself thought of it. Perhaps as a Uranian figure, he took comfort in being able to hold it all up as a deeply painful lesson to the future. That's the sort of thing Uranus lies in wait to teach us, once all the hullabaloo has died down and we must face our mistakes, not as people of a tribe, but as human beings.

The ultimate goal of this placement of Uranus is to learn to see all human beings as brothers and sisters, even the ones which annoy you, or with whom you vastly disagree. That's not an easy call, and not every eleventh-house Uranus will ever get there. On the other hand, Momotaro also teaches us to set boundaries at the same time we are compassionately seeing warring people as siblings and friends, all part of the same wave of humanity. *If you want to be my friend, you're all going to have to find a way to get along, because I don't want friends who hate my friends for who they are. I'll help you, but you'll have to find a way.* Because there will always be a Uranus ... which is what we deserve, and what we need.

12 ♅ Uranus in the 12th House: Iktomi

While we met the Ojibwe trickster hero Nanabozho in Uranus's third-house position, here we take a look at a different Native American trickster spirit—Iktomi, the Spider Man of the Lakota people. Iktomi was originally a deity of wisdom and the intellect—he invented language, stories, games, and named many things, much like Nanabozho—but he enjoyed playing tricks on people so much that he lost touch with what would harm and what would not. His tricks embarrassed several Gods to the point that they complained to Skan, the god of motion who judged all things. Skan decreed that because of the misuse of his knowledge, Iktomi would be condemned to never again sit at the feasts of the Gods, to sit alone in the wilderness without a friend, and that his cunning would only entrap him. Skan pronounced these words and Iktomi became a spider, spinning his webs to entrap people, but mostly managing to entrap himself.

The twelfth house is the strangest place in the astrological chart, ruled by vague and mysterious Neptune who never told anyone anything in a straightforward manner. It includes not only one's personal "underworld", or subconscious-to-deep-unconscious, it also includes the collective unconscious of humanity and everything contained therein. We can define the collective unconscious as the experiences we have simply from the effect of being human and living in this world, with perhaps another piecemeal layer that includes meta-experiences common to specific cultures. Uranus, with its trickster nature, finds itself a little out of its depth when it comes to the twelfth house. The other Uranus placements can spread their uniqueness and chaos about in various areas of the world, but in the twelfth house, when the Uranus person indulges in this, the one who is affected is ... them. On top of that, because of the way the unconscious works, sometimes they don't know that the wave of discomfort rolling through them is due to their own devices until much later.

This constant roiling in the psychological basement can come across as a person who needs a lot of solitude in order to work things out in their head. Twelfth-house Uranus people are often antisocial; they can appear to be unfriendly or awkward or lack social skills. Sometimes, even though that nonconformist planet is buried in the twelfth house, they will come across as weird and unusual. Unlike other Uranus placements who flaunt their difference in the area of that house, the twelfth-house Uranus is just vaguely weird whether they like it or not, and is often uncomfortable with the weirdness bubbling up from places unknown, but doesn't know how to stop it.

The Lakota Spider Man differs from the other trickster figures in that he has been condemned to be alone, without friend or tribe, stuck in his own head. This sums up the most difficult part of this Uranus placement—they have to spend a good deal of their lives stuck in their heads. The truth is that this is Uranus's goal in the house of the unconscious—to explore it with the same risk-taking spirit that the ninth-house Uranus books a plane to somewhere they know nothing about. It is part of their destiny to explore that lonely and wild place within, and they can't do that without a lot of time alone, without distractions.

The twelfth house also rules places of restraint that have strict rules and may not be easy to leave—such as prisons, mental institutions, hospitals, ships, monasteries, and ashrams. While it is by no means guaranteed that a twelfth-house Uranus will end up in one of these, many have found themselves in such a place of confinement and realized, ironically, that it gave them the quiet place to do the inner work they needed.

Iktomi sometimes appears as a spider, but sometimes also shows up as a human being. When he does, his face is usually painted with red, yellow, and white paint with black rings around his eyes, dressed in skins of deer and raccoon. He is shown with a round body, spindly arms and legs, and powerful hands and feet, just like a spider. He often sits with his knees drawn up to his chin, mimicking the spider's bent-legged posture. It is said that he first started his tricks because people laughed at his awkwardness and strange looks, which in many cases is something that the twelfth-house Uranus can relate to. He spins intricate plots which tend to backfire and fall into ruin, but as a mythic figure he teaches morality by messing it up. The Iktomi stories are amusing, and listeners can quietly examine their actions and motivations without feeling called out—when Iktomi falls on his face, it's all right because it's not them.

Sometimes the twelfth-house Uranus finds themselves in the position of the scapegoat as well, a problem which many twelfth-house planets fall into. Planets in the twelfth house (especially if they are close to the Ascendant) can be a complete mystery to the owner of the chart, but may sometimes be vaguely sensed by other people, who react to them in uncertain ways. Something about the individual doesn't quite seem right, although they may not be able to put their finger on it. When it's chaotic Uranus, the seemingly harmless person may be perceived as being a vector of hidden chaos, even if there is no outward evidence of that.

The spider trickster knows how to spin magical threads which hook onto people and can, if they are not particularly self-aware, make them dance like puppets. He also brews potions to control similarly blind and blundering humans. On the other hand, he sometimes sees that something will go wrong in the future and attempts to help humans by warning them. Usually they ignore him and things go wrong, which will also resonate with the twelfth-house Uranus. This placement can bestow the ability to glimpse the guiding patterns of history and consequence, the ways of human society as they have evolved over the millennia, and the way they will likely move in the future. Because this comes out of the twelfth house, it is often less an analytical reasoning and more of a vision which leaps full-blown to their minds. If Uranus is badly afflicted, the vision may be tainted with their own fears and neuroses, but sometimes a clear picture does come through. Getting humanity to listen to them, however, is a much more difficult proposition, which can lead them to attempt to address the problem themselves, alone in the world. Iktomi sometimes reacts to being disbelieved by then working to make the disaster come true on a quicker schedule, largely so that he can say, "I told you so."

In one story where Iktomi meets Coyote (Uranus in Leo), Coyote is sleeping so soundly on the prairie that Iktomi thinks he is dead and decides to cook and eat him. Slinging Coyote over his shoulder, he carries him back to camp and builds a fire. Coyote wakes up, but continues to play dead because he is curious about what Iktomi will do. When Iktomi slings him into the fire, Coyote explodes back out of it in a shower of sparks and coals, burning the Spider Man. Then Coyote laughs and tells Iktomi that he should make sure his prey is dead before he tries to cook it, and runs away. The twelfth-house Uranus sometimes has trouble figuring people out, seeing if they are honest or deceitful, even though they themselves can be strangely deceitful on occasion if they feel it is necessary to achieve their goals.

Iktomi is associated with the Dreamcatcher, which was originally called the "spider-spell". The twelfth house is the place of Dreams, ruled by dreamy Neptune, and it is said that Iktomi can put out a thread through any dreamcatcher which is not made in the traditional way (which is nearly all modern dreamcatchers of the sort sold in gift shops) and hook into the one who sleeps beneath it, if he so chooses. Traditional dreamcatchers are the ones which are able to take the nightmares and not let the Spider Trickster through. This placement of Uranus is often remarkably skilled at the arts of lucid dreaming, as long as they don't try too hard—Uranus magic is the sort where one has to just let go and jump in, and let it work or not.

The mature twelfth-house Uranus can learn enough about the inside of their own heads that they can learn how to read other people's subconscious patterns. These, too, come to them as sudden insights rather than systematic consideration, and since Uranus is not the most diplomatic of planets, they may be a bit rough in their delivery … but they can become very useful at helping people to figure out how to get free of their own internal potholes. They may be renegades, independent and often untrusting, but for those people who have made the effort to be patient and wait out their gruff spider-dance, they can be extremely loyal and find unusual ways to make their lives better. In the end, after the years of internal deep-diving, the twelfth-house Uranus finally comes around full circle to reach the goal they didn't know they had—to make connections with other human beings who do not have to be arranged, manipulated, or tricked into just being there and being friends. This requires them to learn to trust, which Iktomi can tell you is one of the hardest lessons in the world.

NEPTUNE

1♆ Neptune in the 1st House: Vishnu

Hindu deities, unlike European Gods, are much more nebulous in their boundaries. They combine and recombine and get muddled up with each other to the point where it's very difficult to assign them discrete qualities at all. Their worship is spread over so many people in so many culturally different areas over so many centuries that it's almost impossible to make more than generalizations about many of them, and one has to wade through descriptions of every one of them being the sun, moon, stars, and the whole world while you're at it. On top of this, ever since the Muslim invasion where Hinduism had to play down its polytheism and emphasize that all Gods are just the shifting face of one deity, seeing them as separate entities with separate agendas has been unfashionable, and instead focusing on transcendence is emphasized.

Vishnu, the second of the male triumvirate of Brahma/Creator, Vishnu/Preserver, and Shiva/Destroyer, is probably the best example of this. He is the most popular god in India, and a fair amount of effort has been put in by his followers to paint him as the Big God Of Whom All Other Gods Are Merely Pieces, But Vishnu Is His Real Face. This is helped by the fact that Vishnu has a history of incarnating in various human and animal bodies, so it is common for his worshipers to decide that any enlightened and vaguely historical human is actually another Vishnu incarnation—for example, the Buddha. (Buddhists apparently feel differently about the matter, I am told.) He has become so big, so vague, and so many-faced that he is not really the God of anything specific any more, except of generally being great and helping people to follow the Hindu path to enlightenment and getting off the wheel of death and rebirth. Even his "preserver" title seems to be not much more than a generality now.

If there is a planet which also embodies vagueness, lack of boundaries, and transcendent spirituality all rolled up into one, it's Neptune. The more I researched Vishnu and became chagrined at how nonspecific he has become, the more I heard Neptune laughing softly in my ear. Look at that word "embody". *How do you embody something when you are spread too big and wide to have a single body? When one body is not enough? How do you balance being here and not-here at once?* After I started listening closely instead of simply searching books and articles in vain for more specificity, I realized that embodying multitudes is what Neptune does when it's in the first house of the physical form.

People with the planet of indistinctness in the house of how you look to the world are often chameleons. They don't even necessarily do it consciously; they just have a sensitivity to what people want them to be, and they automatically move in that direction. They will wear one face for one person, and another for the next one, and it's not deliberate deceit. It's Neptune telling them that they should just merge with this person and their desires and everything will go better. When they don't have someone else's clear desires to merge with, they don't seem to act like anyone in particular; it's as if they are "on hold". They often seem spacy and distant, like they are daydreaming or their head is up in the sky.

The sky, where Vishnu lounges on the "Sea of Time". The more I look at Vishnu-the-overarching-deity, the more his incarnations come into sharp relief. He's been a fish, a turtle, a boar, a half-man-half-lion, and a number of human beings. Some of his incarnations are specific enough that they have their own separate chapters in this book series—Krishna is Venus in Sagittarius and Rama is the Sun in the tenth house. The form of each incarnation seems to depend on what is needed in the world at the moment—fierceness, compassion, ingenuity, playfulness, leadership, or just rescuing people. When he's not incarnating, he's vague and boundaryless. When he takes on a temporary face, it's as if it gives him purpose and sharp edges for that moment.

This is a situation which will be very familiar to people with Neptune in the first house. When they are with someone else—especially someone who has very strong and obvious needs, or who has a strong personality, they know who they are, who they have to be, and where their edges are. The rest of the time, it's as if they don't need to be anything, and live mostly in their imaginations. As Neptune is the planet of drugs and madness, a certain percentage will end up merging with the bottle, or the pills, or the tinfoil hat—and since this is the first house where everything is laying out for people to see, it will definitely be visible in some way. Of course, the running joke among astrologers is that people with first-house Neptunes look like they're stoned even when they're not.

Eventually, at least in the ones who haven't merged in those negative ways, there will be an identity crisis. *Who am I when I'm not around people? Who am I when nobody needs me to be something?* Strong personalities will blink at this and have trouble relating to it. I'm who I am. Yes, sometimes I may have to add or subtract some as I grow and change and gain new information, but I'm still pretty much the person I know to be me. Not so the ones with Neptune up on the windshield. Even when they attempt to build a unique style or mode of self-expression, there's always the danger that the presence of other people will push them back into chameleon-hood and their self-made mask will be washed away and replaced with whatever those people want them to be (or, to be fair, what they believe those people want to see).

Some will borrow heavily from Neptunian fantasy, taking on the personas of fictional characters or animals. Some will copy others whom they respect, until they drift away from that person or fail to live up to the expectations of others who expect them to remain that person. Because no matter how reflexive and appropriate the mask, if people stick around, sooner or later they will figure out that there's someone else behind it. They might even get a clearer idea of who that person is than the person themselves. Some will treat this as a betrayal or dishonesty, not understanding how the first-house Neptune can work on an unconscious level, and this reaction simply discourages the Neptunian from attempting to show who they are inside. Some will have the patience and discernment to work their way past this diffuse layer to find what's trapped behind those vague mists, often when they find themselves disinterested in this purely surface connection, and can appreciate what they find.

Strangely enough, one of the places where Vishnu actually seems to get some clear edges is when he is with his wife Lakshmi (Moon in the second house). Even though their relationship is somewhat unequal—she sits at his feet, and is often shown much smaller than he and doing some domestic duty like rubbing his feet—this small window of homely affection seems to make him less of a limitless deity and humanizes him. This is also something which will be familiar to the first-house Neptune people; having a partner can be like having someone else around whose love (and constant presence) gives them enough "weight" that they can drown out the tendrils of other people's needs, and the Neptune person can spend most of their time being what the partner wants. In the end, though, this is just a helpful stopgap to the work of figuring out who you are and what your authentic face actually is.

The answer to most Neptune problems is discouragingly similar: this is the planet of spirituality, and it is to some form of spiritual understanding that they must turn. It helps if the spiritual understanding is fairly clear; if it is too vague, the first-house Neptune person will simply merge with it and wander around, not truly connected to it, any more than they are truly connected to anything else. A regular and sustained practice to back up the spiritual world-view can be useful here, because it becomes an anchor.

Besides fantasy, vagueness, and whatever-you-want, another classic way for this placement to manifest is through being a visible example of some kind of spiritual path. This can entail putting on the "uniform", or just letting it be known that they are committed to this path. Over time, people think of them as "the person of Spirituality X", and this becomes an anchor they can use to hold their own against the pressing needs of others, which constantly attempt to pressure them into "embodying" what they need. That's because they are anchored into something bigger, higher, and deeper than human needs. If they can manage it at all, this can be a wonderful "shape" for the first-house Neptunian, and one which will feel fairly natural, once they find the right path.

Somewhere during my Vaishnava research, I asked someone who had done a lot of reading Hindu philosophy if there was one quality Vishnu had which set him aside from all the other Gods. (Well, besides his wife Lakshmi.) I was told, "Purity." This makes a certain amount of sense; whatever incarnation he plunges himself into, it is done wholly ... and consciously. The ability to appear as the face people need is a rare talent when used consciously and mindfully, and for the highest good. It's a talent that many spiritual masters have learned, or perhaps Neptune granted it along with being the public face of a path of spirit. It can help seekers who come for advice by becoming the one face or voice whom they are most likely to hear—including the face of pure Neptunian compassion which does not judge, because we're all like everyone else anyway, only more so. Deliberately embodying the pure essence of an archetype, but being able to let it go just as cleanly when the advice has been delivered and the seeker is gone, can be a way to separate out the true face. Vishnu doesn't teach this by telling you; he teaches it by being ... and hoping that you will take the time to see.

♃♆ Neptune in the 2nd House: Aegir and Ran

The ocean is both a great and generous giver of life—our very existence is said to have started there—and an implacable taker, as any sailor will tell you. I live within two hours' driving distance of the ocean and visit there when I can; I grew up reading the names of men lost at sea on the brass plaques next to beach monuments. That combination of "great giving" and "great taking" is a hallmark of Neptune, the planet named for another god of oceans, and here we explore Neptune's oceanic attitude toward physical resources—all that stuff in your second house.

In Norse mythology, the ocean is ruled by Aegir and Ran, a marine power-couple whose kingdom is everything beneath the surface of the sea. (Boats, and all man's efforts to travel in and on the water and not drown, are under the oversight of Njord the Ship-God of sailors and fishermen—Jupiter in the ninth house in this book.) Aegir, whose name is simply one of the words for "sea" in Old Norse—possibly stemming from an Indo-European root word which may be cognate to the Latinate *aqua*—is renowned for his hospitality. He is referred to in many old texts as "the Ale-Brewer" and is said to have a giant cauldron eternally filled with ale. This comes from the idea that the foaming tides looked similar to foaming ale, but it also echoes Neptune, the planet that rules mind-altering substances and especially alcohol.

Aegir was known for his generosity. His greatest task, it is said, is seeing that all the bellies in his vast kingdom of creatures are fed. This includes hapless human souls who end up there—in his undersea castle of Aegirheim ("Aegir's Home") is a banquet-hall where he eternally feasts drowned sailors and fishermen. His undersea hall was dark except for scattered piles of gold, salvaged from sunken ships and enchanted to constantly give off light. The sagas refer to this pile of glowing gold as "the fire of the sea."

He also feasted the Aesir—the sky-gods of war and civilization—and they are often depicted as utilizing his undersea palace almost as a convention center, a place to have a good time and discuss important issues. According to one of the old sagas, it is unclear whether Aegir has a choice in hosting them, as there are implications that he was forced to provide periodic feasting and drinking for their entertainment. This, too, parallels the problems of Neptune in the second house of resources. Where Neptune lies in your chart, there you are often taken advantage of by others. You are moved to sacrifice for them, or to feel pressured to give too much. Alternately, a Neptune placement might swing in the opposite direction and take too much from others, assuming that they can spare it so they ought to give it to you. Some strongly Neptune-ruled people might engage in both sacrifice and selfishness by turns. Aegir may be forced by the Aesir-gods to hold feasts for them, but he takes in the dead sailors out of sheer generosity, not to mention all those fish.

People with Neptune in the second house tend to fall one of two ways. Either they allow others to take advantage of their generosity, or they take advantage of the generosity of others. If Neptune is afflicted, they might bankrupt themselves trying to help other people out, or resort to pressure and emotional extortion to acquire their riches. The other side of this dichotomy is revealed by Aegir's wife Ran, whose name descends from the Old Norse word for "robber".

Ran is green-eyed and beautiful, with long hair that lies in all the seaweed of the northern ocean, and sharp teeth and claws. She is the mother of their nine daughters, the Undines who represent the Powers of Water (Neptune in the twelfth house). In contrast to her generous and fatherly husband, she is portrayed as the capricious and devouring aspect of the ocean. She and her daughters were said to blow up the storms at sea, wrecking ships so that she could help herself to their treasures, and—if she felt like it—their souls. Drowned men were feasted by her husband until she grew bored with them, and then they were sent to the realm of Hel (Pluto in Virgo). Any ship bobbing perilously on the surface could attract her attention, and she would reach for it like a child desiring a new toy and drag it down to the bottom of the ocean. She owned a magical net once borrowed in an emergency by Loki (Saturn in Gemini) which she uses to drag men down to their deaths, like Neptune at its most fascinating and confusing.

Both Aegir and Ran—in fact their whole family, but especially Ran—were often liberally bribed by ancient sailors to keep their ships safe. While Aegir would take bread or meat thrown in to feed his small subjects, Ran preferred gold. Uncountable pieces of gold were dropped overboard to sate her thirst for its glow and to prevent her from starting storms. When she grew bored with the precious coins and jewelry as well, her husband enchanted it to create light for his hall.

The second house is the place of money and wealth, and it is telling that Ran was literally propitiated with monetary treasure in order to stay her greed. It's a perfect metaphor for Neptune in the house of riches … precious gold falling into the depths of the sea. There is something about this Neptune placement that expects the money, the wealth, the possessions, to do something magical for the individual's life. It's supposed to bring happiness, or fulfillment, or status, but the way these trophies flit through their minds isn't about practical goals—"I'd like a house to raise a family in, and a better car so I could go on a road trip." It's more nebulous than that. Unlike the Sun in this house who collects wealth to raise their own value, Neptune collects objects to raise the value of life and make it worth living. Second-house Neptune people believe, on some level, that if they have enough money and stuff—or if they manage to find the *right* stuff—it will make the unpleasant physicality of this world worth bothering with.

Neptune is the planet of idealism and merging, and it has trouble being confined to a physical body in a life of Saturnian limitations. Neptune makes us chase idealized versions of the situations expressed in the house where it is found, but when we catch what we think are those people or places or achievements—or, in this house, objects—we find that they don't give us what we want, and we toss them aside, like Ran with her "toy" human souls. On the other side, we might hold onto those things for a long time, unwilling to admit that they aren't doing the magic that we feel they ought to be giving us … the door that helps us make peace between the division of flesh and spirit.

That's why many people with this placement are strongly prone to becoming hoarders. *Surely this object will open that door, be the thing that heals this division within me.* There are a lot of astrological reasons why people hoard, just as there are many reasons why they might lean in the opposite direction and become completely unattached to possessions, but for this placement it's about seeking, through possessions, a way to fully possess one's body and one's place in the world.

Yet it is important to remember the fairytale ending to all that gold. Unlike Fafnir the Dragon-Dwarf, Ran does not sit on her gold, nor hoard her souls forever. Neptune's attention is vague, not focused, and physical objects often seem to wash away on the tide. Another way in which this placement manifests is in people who never seem able to hold on to their wealth and possessions. Money slips through their fingers, expensive things break or are stolen, they are evicted and all their possessions must be thrown out or given away or put onto the street to be taken. While carelessness, inattention, and sometimes downright poor financial judgment are part of it, with this placement one can often see extreme and unplanned outside circumstances washing over the individual, knocking them down in the tide and stealing their prosperity with the ruthlessness of Ran's salty fingers.

But when Ran was finished playing with her wealth and dropped it, her husband Aegir turned it into light, illuminating the feast-hall where he spread his hospitality to dead men and living gods. Part of Neptune's "gold", as it were, is in that generosity. Neptune wants sacrifice, done out of compassion for others, and this is a way to transform riches into something that lights the lives of those less fortunate. At the same time, this planet also allows the second-house Neptune person as much compassion for themselves as for others, so long as they keep a sensible share for reasonable comfort, not hoarding or greedy fantasies. Like the Sun placement here, generosity keeps them sane and turns the tide of their unlucky wealth.

The blessed aspect of Neptune in the second house is when the individual learns to feel wealthy no matter how much money or how many things they have; when whatever is given to them is enough, and they have faith that enough will come. For them, that faith may actually bring wealth, once they have learned the tide-like rhythm of give and take, ebbing and flowing in moderation. Once they have mastered this rhythm, Neptunian intuition kicks in and they may well be able to "sense" wealth, developing a nose for what financial exploits are lucrative. As long as it's something they can let go of—letting a spiritually healthy amount of it pass through their fingers—their faith and their intuition can lead them into the real flow of riches, where they can learn to give and take like the ocean. Give like you are the source of Life, take what Life puts into your open hands.

3♆ Neptune in the 3rd House: Kui Xing

The planet Neptune spreads confusion wherever it goes. Whichever house you may have which is graced by Neptune, there will be illusion and confusion and possibly some madness. It's a well-known truism that the best way to cope with Neptune issues is to lean into spirituality in that area, as if Neptune spreads its dreamy insanity in order to force us into the corner from which only a spiritual path can free us. When Neptune comes into the third house of the Mind, the consequences can range from disruptive to disastrous. This placement is notorious for vagueness, distraction, and what some would call "woolly thinking"—the feeling that the head is full of wool and the thoughts are tangled. It is an indicator for both neurological difficulties and neurochemical thought or personality disorders, as well as speech impediments. While not everyone with this placement will have any of these, it's a common enough problem to have been noted by multiple astrologers. In the house of short trips, third-house Neptunes are notorious for having trouble with schedules, showing up late or forgetting to show up entirely.

On the other hand, the third-house Neptunian has excellent intuitive powers, and can often sense the undercurrents and hidden nuances of any given situation they are in. They have an extrasensory ability to extract not only the subtleties of a conversation, but the greater ideas which are being generated, and in some cases even a flash of the secret divine intention behind the connection of minds. They can pluck ideas seemingly out of nowhere, tapping into the great mystery of knowledge itself. This is the payment for the clear, concise mind and way of speaking which they have sacrificed to one extent or another. Of course, if the Neptunian problems are great enough, those magical flashes of insight may be distorted or misinterpreted, but with enough time and meditation, this tendency can often be ameliorated.

In Chinese mythology, there is a whole bureaucracy of Gods, imitating the bureaucracy of Chinese government and education (or perhaps on some meta-level, the Chinese system imitates those Gods—a very Neptunian thought). Those who attempted to rise in the ranks with minds instead of swords or marriage faced an arduous ladder of examinations, and any failure would cast them back down. The third-house Neptune person, while possibly even brilliant, is not at their best in a world of written tests of memorization, and would probably be one of the desperate students who would call on Kui Xing, the Lord of Stars and the God of Examinations.

The assistant of Wenchang Wang (Mercury in the fourth house), Kui Xing's name refers to the four stars of the handle of the Big Dipper, or the Gourd Ladle as the Chinese called it; these are his special stars. Literally, his name means "Spirit of the Ladle", and from his position high in the sky, he looked down on those who found themselves doing less than well with the (often unfair) system. He was said to be bent and crippled, shaped like an actual calligraphy character, but in spite of that he was very powerful. His hair sticks up in hornlike clumps all over his head, and his face is ugly and usually has a wild expression. His feet are bare and his robes disheveled, like someone who has not gotten enough sleep. Over time, he grew from being a deity of composition and examinations to being a kind of saint of human fortune, prayed to for any dilemma which involved the bureaucracy, where a hapless mortal required mercy.

Mercy and compassion are the qualities of Neptune's best side. Those with this Neptune placement often find that they are at their best, conversation-wise, when they are sympathizing with someone and passing out Neptunian compassion to them. Somehow when it comes time to reach out and be empathetic, much of their normal woolly-headedness seems to clear up; it's a Neptune gift for being that planet's hands in the world in the best possible way. It has been noted that one of the best concepts for the third-house Neptune to ponder is the saying that without love, the mind becomes a pair of scissors which cuts itself to pieces.

Of course, there are other Neptunian pitfalls to this placement as well. It is possible for the third-house Neptune—who wants very much to live in a perfect world where everyone is kind and gentle—to mentally idealize people and situations, and then demonize them when they turn out to be flawed. This kind of black-and-white thinking, like other Neptune problems, can be overcome with a spiritual and compassionate focus that the Neptune person brings themselves back to, again and again, when they feel that pattern coming up. Because they sometimes miss details when they speak, thinking they've said it all but forgetting important points which they think others also know, they may unwittingly spread Neptunian confusion, and then be confused themselves by the result which comes back.

The (originally Taoist) story of Kui Xing starts with him as a mortal who was a brilliant but ugly and physically crooked dwarf; he passed all the emperor's examinations far ahead of everyone else, but was denied a job due to his looks. Crushed, he tried to commit suicide by flinging himself into the ocean, but was suddenly borne up by either a giant fish or a giant sea turtle, which carried him up to heaven. He was then informed that his great brilliance and virtue had earned him a place as an immortal in the bureaucracy of the Jade Emperor (Neptune in Capricorn) to give aid to those who are working against the odds. As well as helping the ones who have trouble with the tests, he also benevolently aids those who are considered too unbeautiful to get the jobs they have earned, and soften the looks-obsessed interviewers who judge them. This echoes the third-house Neptune person's ability to see below the obvious surface and appreciate the gifts which are underneath, missed by most people who can only see the outward form.

It also echoes the third-house Neptune's struggle with clear thinking, and in some cases with mental illness. Many people suffer from discrimination and the cruelty of the world, but most do not respond with suicide, even in Asian cultures where it is generally more accepted as a practice. It is telling that the only path out of his self-destructive madness was the intervention of Heaven, to place him on a path of compassion and aid to others … the flip side of Neptune.

Kui Xing is usually pictured standing on either the giant fish or the giant turtle who gave him a ride to his new job; part of this is acting out the Chinese phrase "to stand lonely on the turtle's head", meaning to score at the head of examinations, thus setting oneself apart from the rest. The fish/turtle can also be seen as a watery Neptunian symbol, so it is particularly interesting that sometimes the fish is in the process of turning itself into a dragon. This symbolizes the student who was originally a struggling fish becoming, with effort and the right study habits, a true dragon of knowledge. Kui Xing is an expert in helping people figure out how best to study, and what learning style is most effective for their unique brains … plus helping with the difficult situations of working with a teacher whose teaching style doesn't match you, or a less-then adequate study situation. Even as a deity who administers tests, Kui Xing is far from a stern martinet. In fact, he is quite compassionate with those with deficiencies, so long as they are willing to work hard.

Once the third-house Neptune individual has figured out their mental quirks and put some sort of compensatory discipline in place, they can be absolutely brilliant at helping others to figure out and compensate for their own mental oddities. Their compassion for the imperfect mind means that they are far less quick to judge the struggling brains of others, and more likely to offer aid from long experience. They can often recognize when someone is having a brain problem while everyone else is assuming it is just a failure of will.

The God of Examinations is usually shown with a brush and ink block in his hands, and sometimes with a container identified as a brush-washer (in one unusual statue, he is standing on one foot with the brush-washer balanced on the heel of the other one). This symbolizes the need to keep one's instruments of communication clean, which is something the third-house Neptune should bear in mind. Neptune rules alcohol, drugs, and addiction, and in the third house the main cause of indulging in mind-altering substances is frustration with one's mental quirks. However, adding actual liquid or pill-form Neptunian confusion to the matter does not help, and can even make things worse. Kui Xing reminds us that periodic cleaning out of the mind, with meditation or deep breathing or taking a walk or just sitting in a beautiful and quiet place can create excellent benefits for the mind, as well as not imbibing substances which make the fog worse, even if they temporarily do away with difficult memories.

Known as the "starry-eyed God", Kui Xing resonates with Neptune's third-house dream of a place where all learning is easy, because the right teachers appear and the world looks kindly even on the difficult students. Like all Neptune placements, once a spiritual discipline is achieved, the planet becomes a gift-giver in its own right, and not just a dilemma. In the third house, the individual needs to look at spiritual disciplines of the mind. Kui Xing points to the tests which are not only of the mundane world, but of higher ones—tests of one's character, the place where we look skyward at the Universe and see how small these mundane examinations are in the greater scheme of things. The real test is the ability to calm the thrashing waves of the brain, which threaten to carry the third-house Neptune away, and rise gently up to Heaven, to look down over the great plain of one's life and find understanding.

4♆ Neptune in the 4th House: Orestes

When you read descriptions of having Neptune in the fourth house in your birth chart, there always seems to be a lot of careful misdirection, focusing on the positive, being cautious so as not to scare anyone. (How Neptunian!) There's usually one sentence in there about how it can sometimes mean a dysfunctional childhood, or something about growing up with secrets, or with parents who had "problems" or were "confusing", and then the description rushes on to talk about intuition and psychic powers and ancestry.

It's not that these other points aren't true (and we'll get to them later), but as an astrologer, three out of four people I know with this placement had childhoods full of secrets, lies, abuse, mentally ill or alcoholic or addicted or very ill parents, and nightmarish things that happened behind closed doors which no one was supposed to talk about. Most had to assume adult duties and responsibilities well before their time, caring for erratic parents or younger siblings. When dreamy Neptune crosses over the nadir, something deep and dark happens to it. It is rarely a healthy childhood companion, and it often leaves deep scars of hypervigilance and mistrust of the world.

The Greek myth that called out to me for this placement was that of Orestes, the son of Agamemnon and Clytemnestra. His story is told not only in the *Oresteia* by Aeschuylus, but in several other myths, and must be pieced together. His family is descended from the House of Atreus, which has been cursed by the Gods; madness and violence and feuding come down through the family line, appropriate in this house of ancestry. (It is not unusual for difficult planets in the fourth house to show up as genetic problems, and with Neptune here, inherited mental problems are a distinct possibility.)

Orestes's mother was a woman traumatized by her brutal husband Agamemnon, and her full story is told in the chapter on Orestes's older sister Iphigenia (Moon the in twelfth house). When she bears Agamemnon's son, she decides to kill the baby. However, Orestes is smuggled out of the tower and the country by his nurse and his teenage sister Electra, who is none too sane herself. Electra idolizes her brutal father, taking his side against that of her victimized mother.

Orestes grows up on Mount Parnassus in the house of the local lord, raised by Electra who tells him tales of his evil mother and wonderful father. It's not unusual for people with this Neptune placement to be raised with distorted stories about family members and their behavior. *These terrible things are normal and even desirable. Those outsiders who disagree are evil. It's all for your own good. Don't talk about what happened to you. Everything is just fine.* Later, they may either idealize or demonize the family in their mind, and it will be a hard road to see them clearly and compassionately.

When Agamemnon comes home and Clytemnestra's lover murders him, Electra begins to groom Orestes to become his father's avenger and slay his own mother. The young prince is caught between two changing eras of culture—the older matriarchy and the newer patriarchy which was quickly conquering and replacing it. The Gods themselves were taking sides, and Orestes ends up caught in the middle of their conflicting opinions. Neptune is the planet of sacrifice and surrender, and where this planet lies, one may feel as if one is beset by outside forces against which one is helpless. In the fourth house, one's whole childhood can feel like a losing battle with powers who want you passive and compliant, willing to be sacrificed. In Orestes' case, when he is still in his teens, he is approached by Apollo (Mercury in Leo) who orders him to go along with Electra's plan. Cornered between a deity and his mad savior-sister, he reluctantly raises an army, rushes into Mycenae, and kills his mother and her new husband.

However, this is only the beginning of his troubles. The Erinnyes, or Furies—serpent-haired hag-goddesses of vengeance who are fiercely matriarchal and punish matricides above all others—pursue him in rage and torment him, appearing in his dreams with their screaming and slowly driving him mad. This plague of nightmares is also a Neptunian curse—the legacy of that childhood where reality was distorted to cover up familial delusions.

Orestes, in desperation, goes to Apollo and begs for help, since Apollo was the one who had demanded he do the deed to begin with. Apollo sadly tells him that he cannot stop the Furies, but that Orestes must be tried by the Gods for his crime. He orders the boy prince to travel to Athens, where Athena (Sun in Aquarius) will judge the trial. Feeling unfairly set up, Orestes goes to Athena and pleads his case in front of all the Olympians. What he does not fully understand is that it isn't just his divinely-ordered deed which is being judged; the cultural change of the Western world is hanging in the balance.

The Gods vote on Orestes' guilt, and the Olympians are split half and half. Athena casts the deciding vote, and absolves Orestes with a speech about how she was born of a father only, and thus a mother is less important to her. (One wonders, at this point, if it was brought home to the hapless defendant what greater ramifications his acquittal would have in the world, and how thoroughly a pawn he was in these matters.) At any rate, Aeschuylus writes that the Furies are appeased at this point, paid off with a temple and a new ritual, and become the Eumenides (or Kindly Ones). The author Euripides, however, casts them as still angry and refusing to back off from tormenting their prey. Another deed must be done to mollify them.

Apollo instructs Orestes to steal the statue of Artemis (Moon in Sagittarius) from Tauris and bring it back to Mycenae to set up a temple. He travels there with his best friend Pylades, whom some accounts treat as his lover. Of all his relationships, Pylades seems to be the healthiest; he was said to be entirely devoted to Orestes, and Orestes to him. The two young men are arrested when the get to Tauris, because the temple's custom is to capture and sacrifice travelers to Artemis. In a poignant writing by the Roman author Lucian, Pylades cares for Orestes, whose Fury-induced madness now makes him fall on the ground in seizures, and both young men plead to be the one who remains to be sacrificed, while the other should flee and save himself. Neptune's forced martyrdom is replaced by Neptunian compassion; it is not unusual for people with this Neptune placement to build their own families out of people not related to them, who do not spark the memories of their blood kin. While Orestes eventually marries Hermione, the daughter of Helen of Troy (Sun in Gemini), his same-sex relationship is the beginning of a chosen family.

Here the story takes a turn and the high priestess of Tauris figures out that one of these young men is her lost brother. Iphigenia takes the statue and escapes with Orestes and Pylades, bringing the cult of Artemis to Mycenae and setting up a temple. Artemis was the sister of Apollo, but they had been on opposite sides of the vote in that trial. This was a way of appeasing her by spreading her cult, and it also appeased the matriarchal Furies. The relationship of the divine brother-sister pair is healed by the deeds of a mortal brother and sister, working together. As another sacrifice of the family of Atreus, but this time by one who became a priestess, Iphigenia's entry into Orestes' life heralds the Neptunian upward shift from self-absorbed madness to higher spirituality. The other angry rift that is healed is that between human and divine. "Why did you let this happen to me?" cries the hurt child, and it is a long time before they can see the long, confusing, Neptunian view of the situation, the view of the Gods who plan and weave for the future.

Orestes rules the land of Mycenae for many decades, until he is bitten by a snake while hunting in Arcadia in his old age, and dies. This recalls the serpent-haired Furies one last time—were they biding their time to finally strike him down? The problem with Neptune's scars of confusion, when delivered via one's childhood, is that they can jump out and recur throughout one's life, forcing the native back to the work of cleaning out their depths and removing yet more poison.

Neptune rules, among other things, the collective unconscious, and in the house of ancestry, Orestes' trial rules on the shaping of an entire people. This, too, is reflective of the experience of the fourth-house Neptune; as well as the "traditional" suggestion of inherited ancestral psychic powers, the shaping of their childhood often puts them in touch with wider patterns which are unconscious or unseen by most people. Their intuition is highly developed—possibly as a defense mechanism to survive their early family life—and serves them well as they begin the necessary transition from victim to repatterning their own psyches, and then applying their hard-won knowledge to the rest of the world.

5Ψ Neptune in the 5th House: Brahma

Back in Vishnu's chapter on the first-house Neptune, we mentioned (somewhat repeatedly) Neptune's ability to be vague and merge like a transparent mist with whatever it comes across. When that dreaminess comes into the house of creativity and romance, it can bestow both unearthly beauty or confusing inertia, and sometimes both at once. The Hindu deity we will be examining here is Brahma the Creator, the first of the Trimurti (divine triumvirate) we discussed in Vishnu's chapter. He is almost as nebulous as Vishnu, but not quite … and it is his flaws which set him apart and make him his own person.

Brahma's name comes from the same root word as the Sanskrit words for "priest" and "Universe". According to the legends, Brahma created himself in a golden cocoon and came forth, and then began to create all manner of other beings and places and things. He is said to be a deity of passion, which fits with the fifth house of areas which spring from passion—romance, children, play, taking risks, and of course creativity. In his case, the passion to create filled him and overflowed from him.

Anyone with a strong fifth house will understand this feeling. Brahma is said to embody the sacred quality of *rajas*, or the passion that burns forth, and creative people know that when it's trying to burst out of you, the best thing to do is to get out of the way and let it come into the world. The Creator God made all types of beings upon the world, including the other Gods, the demons, the good ancestral spirits, and humans. Of course, through centuries of the three Trimurti followers attempting to one-up each other, plus the Goddess-worshipers doing the same, there are multiple stories in which Vishnu or Shiva (Sun in Scorpio) actually create the other two members, including Brahma who then creates things. Explaining this, centuries after the infighting was long forgotten, resulted in a vague (and very Neptunian) teaching about how all three kept dying and being reborn and creating each other in endless cycles.

Brahma created for the sake of creating, not caring so much as to what he created as that it simply came into being where it hadn't been before. This is also a fifth-house Neptunian gift; the mind-altering bliss of creating is more important than what is actually made. That changed, however, when he created a bunch of his own children, and the youngest daughter was Sarasvati (Mercury in Libra), the goddess of knowledge, music, and the arts.

When she came into the world, Brahma was hypnotized by her beauty and immediately fell in love. Unlike any of his other creations, she riveted his attention. It is said that when he saw her dancing, he grew all his extra heads as a way to keep watching her as she moved. He determined that they must marry and share that love, but Sarasvati was not interested in marrying her father. She tried subtly to get away from him, but he kept after her and would not leave her alone.

This is where the fifth house turns to romance, and with Neptune here, you can bet that it will get confusing. Individuals with this placement can live in a fantasy world about who loves them and who they love. Some simply make up stories in their heads about how that person over there would love them passionately if only they could bring themselves to approach them. Some go further and imagine whole relationships, sure that the other person is also secretly involved with them, and become stalkers. Some have lovers, but those lovers are idealized in their minds and fitted into the fantasy roles they have mentally prepared. This lasts until the lover refuses to act the part (remember that the fifth house is also theater) and then the Neptunian feels betrayed and leaves them. Some keep going with the denial even if the partner is incompatible or abusive, although they are less likely to fall into this pattern than a seventh-house Neptunian, and more likely to leave in disappointment and rail about how evil the former partner was. It is very difficult for the fifth-house Neptunian to really see lovers as they really are, at least until they have been together for some time and the relationship moves out of the fifth-house falling-in-love period. It's also true that when this happens, they may lose interest entirely. Being a realistic partner to a real human being is a challenge they will have to master.

Brahma's sons try to tell him that he must not pressure their sister to marry him, but he does not listen. It's not so much the incest that is the main issue—many divine stories have siblings or other family members marrying each other. The Gods are exempt from our rules on this subject, and of course this placement does not assume for incestuous longings; don't take that literally. The problem seems not to be so much that Brahma desired his daughter as that he did not see her, in the beginning, as someone distinct from himself, with her own desires and agenda. She was not another entity with agency, but simply an extension of himself, which would of course want what he wanted. The actual sutras describe the problem as Brahma being too attached to his creation. This happens to all of us, especially those of us who are creators of many things. Our creations are our children—it's not an accident that both of these dwell in the same house—and we bleed to watch them used and changed by others. I've often warned new writers who have just finished their first book that the editing process will feel like someone is mutilating their new baby, and they must resist the urge to grab it and run for the hills. We may identify with them so strongly that we can't separate them from us in our minds.

Sadly, the same thing can happen with the children of our flesh and blood. It is not uncommon for parents to build fantasies of who the child will be when they grow up (which will be, of course, someone who holds the same values and desires as the parents) and then refuse to see them as separate individuals from themselves, who may actually be quite alien in some ways, and the parent is expected to give them their freedom and love them anyway. People with Neptune in the house of children are particularly prone to this struggle with allowing the child to be someone else with entirely different ideas, and may cling on or be resentful for some time. Their children may have to break away in dramatic ways, and even then they may go on for years pretending as if the child really wants what they want down under it all, and simply needs to be guided in order to realize that.

The fifth-house Neptune person can also err by being too lenient and passive, and letting the children walk all over them, or can forget about them once they are out of sight and out of mind. This absent-mindedness can hurt a child when they are young, and even adult children can be miffed when they realize how little they matter in the day-to-day thinking of their dreamy parent. Neptune's romanticism and passivity—and perhaps on some level the Brahma-like urge to create—can actually end up bringing unintended children into the world. It's said by some astrologers that individuals with this placement have more accidental pregnancies than other placements, and more of those children will end up neglected. Brahma is a creator, not a preserver.

At any rate, Brahma was duly punished for his treatment of Sarasvati. Shiva cut off one of his five heads in disgust, and he lost his power as the central creator; his sons had to take over for him. It was decreed that all of his temples would be destroyed, and his worship left to fall into the dust. There are actually a few Brahma temples in existence, although far fewer than most of the other Hindu Gods, and his worship is not entirely gone, but he is mostly appended onto the prayers of multiple deities. (The actual historical reason for all this was political and religious coups between different sects, but that's not a story for this book.) The end result was that Sarasvati did marry him, but she was much more powerful than her husband/father, with widespread worship and many temples. In their married relationship, she is most certainly the dominant partner; there is no sitting submissively at the husband's feet like Vishnu (Neptune in the first house) and Lakshmi (Moon in the second house). Instead, Brahma depends on her for most of his in-depth mentions; he is Sarasvati's husband before he is anything else.

Neptune can sometimes be a very passive and "go-with-the-flow" planet, and this can indicate being drawn to romantic relationships where they are the more passive person, allowing the active partner to set the goals, say how the relationship will be, and lead them down the road. They can also end up with partners who act as a Muse to their creativity, and Sarasvati the all-talented lady of arts and music certainly makes a very good Muse. The fifth-house Neptunian deeply understands that there is no controlling the

Muse, and may end up fairly dependent on the inspiring partner to help them do what they love to do most.

Another "read" on the issue of Brahma's fall from popularity is the concept that as the Creator, he is what happened in the past, while Vishnu the Preserver is the present, and Shiva the Destroyer is the future. The past is behind us, and we don't think about it any more. Perversely, this can be a problem for the fifth-house Neptunian, who has a tendency to become distracted in the middle of one creative project and move on to another, forgetting that the first one existed until they find it in a pile of old boxes years later.

Coming back to the truism that Neptune problems can be addressed spiritually, this placement at its best can produce sacred artists, musicians whose songs move through them from a higher or deeper level of existence, writers who channel the words of the Gods, builders who are drawn to sacred architecture, and artisans whose creations have their own special spirits. The process of spiritualizing one's Making also bestows better focus, more persistence in following it to the end, and a beautiful legacy left to the world. If this can work with songs and stories and clay pots, it can work with lovers and children. The fifth-house Neptunian needs to consider what partnering or parenting would look like if it was a holy journey with a sacred trust, and thus carry all forms of creativity down the highest Neptunian road.

6♆ Neptune in the 6th House: Kamrusepa

The sixth house is a very practical place. It's the home of simple labor, maintenance, service ... and health. (That's because health is something you maintain with work.) Medicine falls here, because it is health as a service rendered to others. It looks like it's as far away from misty, drifty Neptune as it's possible to get, and it's true that this is one of Neptune's least favorite houses to be in. The mysterious cosmic merger doesn't work well in a place which requires precision, scheduling, and hard, boring work. Still, one-twelfth of humans will be afflicted with this placement, and will have to fight against the dragging vagueness of Neptune in order to cope with all the sixth-house matters which will be thrown into their laps.

Neptune rules the sign of Pisces, and the sixth house is associated with the sign of Virgo, and those two are in opposition in the zodiac. Neptune wants merging with infinity, and the sixth house's Virgo energy specializes in cutting things apart into their component bits—what, after all, is diagnostic analysis anyway but that? Neptune tends to drift apart into pieces only so that it can come back together in a better and more whole-making way, and the sixth house likes to have everything intentionally sorted into little boxes and labeled. Neptune is spiritual and the sixth house is practical. Only one of these basic urges can win, and what will likely happen with the sixth-house Neptune is that one will be dominant for a bit, and then the other will take over, and back and forth. That can apply to anything from getting one's electric bill paid to cleaning the nasty floor to making sure one takes one's meds on time. The individual with this oppositional placement will have to be very aware of themselves and their motivations, and find a balance point between the two.

Neptune/Pisces and the sixth house/Virgo do have one thing in common, though, and that is selfless service. They render service in very different ways, but the underlying concept is the same. Sometimes when this Neptune placement finds itself in a place where it is serving others, the middle ground becomes clear and the balance point is achieved. It's not unusual for these people to end up in service jobs for that reason; the problem is when it's themselves. The best advice for this is to take a step away from the personal nature of the problem (both of these energies are good at distancing themselves, although they do it in different ways), and consider maintenance done for themselves as a sort of "cleaning the company car", because they are an important component of their work for the world.

There's another place where, ironically, the spiritual nature of Neptune and the precise character of the sixth house come together, and that is magic. Not vague wave-a-wand-in-the-air magic, but the sort where recipes and formulas are carefully put together and prayed over when the stars are correct. We forget, in this day and age, how much of medicine was magic in ancient times. While our forebears did indeed have traditions of healing plants and minerals and manipulations, gathered over the millennia by trial and error, they were always overlaid with prayer and magical ritual, and sometimes the components of a potion might also include substances for sympathetic sorcery. To us, these are in different camps; to our ancestors for thousands of years, they were one and the same.

The ancient Hittite peoples of Anatolia left their home and swept across the Mediterranean area, conquering lands as they went and spreading tales of their Gods. We don't know as much about them as we would like, but a few important faces stand out, described by some of their more literate conquered people. One of their goddesses was Kamrusepa. the goddess of both medicine and magic. For her, as for the rest of the ancient cultures, the two were the same. Every substance had a magical power and a medicinal one … and a spiritual one, as it was linked to a deity or spirit in the world. Keeping all of that straight requires both Neptunian intuition and sixth-house mental organization. Knowing what to do with all of them requires bringing those qualities together into one way of working in the world.

While Kamrusepa could name the medicinal and magical properties of thousands of items, her name means "Mistress of Clouds" or "Mistress of Smoke". That seems to be a reference to the use of steam or smoke in healing, but it's also a wonderfully Neptunian name. Most deities from the tribes of that area who ruled over magic were associated with the underworld, but Kamrusepa was a heavenly goddess, flying across the sky in a chariot drawn by white horses. This was because she was perceived as clean and purifying—qualities loved by the sixth house. She had a domestic role as well, as one of the goddesses who is a keeper of the hearth, but her domestic role was less about caring for children and family and more about keeping the fire-area and the house clean.

This Neptune placement can often interfere with the regularly-scheduled cleaning and maintenance of one's home space which is required for cleanliness (and which the sixth house needs to be doing), distracting the individual with mind-fog or difficulty motivating. Adding a spiritual aspect to it—"My home is a sacred temple and I am purifying a temple space," or "As I clean these dirty dishes, so I purify my stressed-out mind"—can bring Neptune more fully into the picture and provide a surprising amount of joyful motivation. The other extreme, of course, is when Neptune goes into demonization mode and cleans obsessively, trying to purify their lives by constantly scrubbing the toilet but only becoming stressed and frustrated.

We have only a few texts from Hittite mythology, but Kamrusepa holds an important role in them … generally assisting the other Gods when they run into problems. She helps out the storm God Tarhunna, the Sun Goddess Arinnanda, and her son the sea God Aruna. She is the protective tutelary divinity of multiple cities. People wrote prayers to her that she might turn away oncoming plague. In the myth of Telipino, the fertility God by that name is furious because he wants to stay sleeping peacefully and people keep waking him up. He flies into a rage and starts the rivers flooding everything, and the other Gods aren't sure how to handle him. Kamrusepa begins to sing a song of peace to him—a song which names off several substances which some scholars feel is actually a potion of some sort. She names the powers of cedar essence, tree resin, wheat, sesame, figs, olive oil, and wine. Then she sings that his rage is as barren as the malt which cannot be planted for seed or use for bread, and that it will fall away very soon. Telipino finds that he suddenly feels much better and stops storming about.

Once they have matured, this double talent of learning many details and using intuition to figure which to use can be exceptionally healing to other people, regardless of whether it takes the form of medicine or something else. They are often extremely sensitive to substances, and may need less of something to get the same effect, or they may have a great number of food sensitivities. (The sixth is the house of food as nutrition, as opposed to food-sharing as an emotional activity, which lands in the fourth house.) Their nervous systems may also be more sensitive than most people, and they may need to "purify" their environment of stressful stimuli. Because of this sensitivity to the merging of body, mind, and energy, they can be deeply aware of the spiritual concept of the body as a sacred space. This may bring them into alternative health care practices, which comes one step closer to the merging of medicine and magic, if we think of "magic" as harnessing the energetic essences of spirit to heal the physical realm. For this Neptune placement, both the physical and the spiritual have to be respected in some way and to some extent.

Kamrusepa is said to have invented all the medical procedures the Hittite people had, and she passed them all on; she also invented the tools of medicine, including herbal remedies, razors, scalpels, knives, and lancets (and communicated them to humans through Neptunian dreams and visions). Creating procedures and tools is a sixth-house delight; even Neptune can get in on the game, as long as the tools are used towards compassionately relieving pain and illness. Compassion is the quality which will get Neptune working towards the goal; it's not normally a sixth-house quality, but it should be for someone with this placement. When it comes to the workplace, for example, it's not unusual for the person with this Neptune to be the one co-workers come to for compassionate counsel, although it's also not unusual for them to be ignored or passed over by authority figures. (Neptune can place a mist over one's efforts in a particular house.) This placement can also indicate that one's job, even if menial, can give a great deal of emotional and even spiritual satisfaction, and uplifting rapport with those who work alongside you.

Beyond just her remedies and incantations, Kamrusepa was also a celestial midwife, bringing life into the world. On the other end of creation, she shepherded lost dead souls along to the underworld, as part of the physician job which often requires seeing someone die in pain. So while she could pay great attention to the sixth-house details of tools and formulas, she could also pay attention to larger, more Neptunian functions like the sacred cycle of birth and death. Like Kamrusepa, those with this Neptune placement do best when they are of service, utilizing their gifts in a way which brings everything together, and which magically heals the world in some tiny way. This kind of magic can even come to magically heal the world overall by helping others one at a time—the perfect combination of Neptune and the sixth house.

7♆ Neptune in the 7th House: Izanami and Izanagi

In the Shinto mythology of Japan, the first divine couple was Izanagi ("Man who invites") and Izanami ("Woman who invites"). Being the first divine couple is a lot of responsibility on a mythic level. You are expected to be a perfect example of how a marriage ought to go, to be eternally happy together. Somehow, though, stories of first couples often seem to go very wrong, more often than they go right. Like Adam and Eve, Izanami and Izanagi are set up to be the Father and Mother of All Creation, and yet in spite of that, they fail. Part of why they fail is circumstance, but another part is their attitude toward those circumstances, and their refusal to accept anything but the perfect ideal.

This is one of the pitfalls of Neptune, the planet of dreams and idealization, in the house of partnerships. Neptune spreads confusion in whatever house it falls into, but in the seventh house it is particularly difficult, because it clouds the view of what relationships should be, how they should go, and the nature of the ideal partner. This house placement lends a dreamy and often unrealistic cast to the search for love, which can backfire terribly when the reality of other human beings intrudes into the quest.

According to Shinto legend, the first deities of Heaven made two beings, a divine man and woman, and charged them with creating land on the Earth below, which was all water and mist. To help them do this, they were given a magical spear decorated with jewels, and sent to the bridge between Heaven and Earth. Here they dipped the spear into the water, and the drops falling off the blade created the first islands. The famous 19th-century painting by Kobayashi Eitaku showing them dipping in the spear has them surrounded by mist and clouds over the ocean, very Neptunian for its dreamy, watery veils.

"Between Heaven and Earth" is a good image for seventh-house Neptune relationship challenges. There's the Heaven of the ideal relationship in their head, and then there's the Earth of reality—who the person in front of you really is, what baggage they've come with, and what flaws and insensitivities you will have to learn to cope with. The job of the seventh-house Neptune individual is to find that balance, taking inspiration from the dream but not allowing it to rule their reaction to the reality. Staying in the middle of that bridge is difficult, because they always want to float upward to Heaven, and yet they need to spend as much time on the Earth dealing with the ordinary negotiations and troubles that circumstances lay on a relationship.

It was decreed by the older Shinto Gods that the pair should be married, and that they should build a ritual pillar on the site where this would happen. The two of them built the pillar named Ame-no-Mihashira, and then circled around it. When they met at the other side, Izanami smiled and greeted her husband-to-be as if she had just met him for the first time, but he immediately became disgruntled that she had spoken first. The two lay together anyway, and Izanami bore two children. The first was Hiruko, who later became Ebisu (Saturn in the second house), the god of fishermen. He was born either with no bones or no arms and legs or both, and the parents were horrified. They set him afloat on the ocean in a boat of reeds, assuming that he would drown, and tried again. The second child, Awashima, was also deformed or undesirable in some way, and again they put her into the ocean (and she, also, eventually became a worshiped deity in her own right, in spite of this). Here Neptune's power makes its first major failure. At its best, this is the planet of compassion and sacrifice, and the couple could have turned the Neptunian energy into lovingly caring for their disabled children (both of whom, by the way, floated away to eventually have good lives with other parents who cared for them and helped them to prosper). Instead, they let their anger at the loss of the Dream of Perfection have its way, and rejected what could have been a compassionate learning experience.

Izanagi asked their progenitor-Gods what could have happened to make everything go wrong with their marriage, and was answered that it should have been Izanagi who spoke first. This is another Neptune moment, when Neptune chases the ideal, is disappointed, and then grasps for ways to recapture it. *If we only do this, or don't do that; if we go on that romantic cruise or have another baby, everything will be all right.* Instead of addressing down-to-earth concerns, Neptune tries to create a magic formula that will remove all problems. This is a particular problem when the seventh-house Neptune individual chooses someone who looks good on the surface but turns out to be incompatible or even unpleasant, and Neptune goes into denial and blames themselves. *If I am only a perfect spouse, they will love me and treat me well.* The problem is that there is no magical formula, and eventually there will be a fall off of that bridge and a crash to earth.

The couple repeated their marriage ceremony, this time with Izanagi speaking first, and then settled down to have more children. At first things went well—Izanami birthed all the islands of Japan—but things were about to take an even worse downturn. Seeing that the people below needed warmth, they decided to make a baby who would heat them, and Izanami birthed the fire-deity Kagutsuchi. The fire-infant burned her out from the inside, and she died in childbirth. In her death throes, she also bears the fire-kami's twin Mizuhanome, a water-kami who can pacify the fire-kami, but she also brings the first death into the world. Raging in grief, Izanagi beheads the fire-child and hacks his body into eight pieces, which promptly become the eight volcanoes of Japan and threaten the people.

Izanami's body is buried on the side of a mountain, and her soul goes to the empty shadow realm of Death. Izanagi is determined to bring her back, and enters the shadow realm. Neptune often has trouble accepting when a relationship is over, and may trail after the lover, stalking them from a distance or just refusing to let go in their heart and start over, carrying a torch for years. After all, they did all the right things according to the magical mental formula! How could it have all gone so wrong? When Izanagi found the shade of his dead wife, she was seated in dark shadows and he could not see her; she made him promise not to look upon her. He asked her to return with him, but she told him that it was too late—she had already eaten the food of the Underworld, and could not return to the land of the living. Izanagi protested that he had come to rescue her, and she had to leave, but she refused him. It's not unusual for this placement to see themselves as the rescuer, and want to pull lost objects of desire out of their terrible circumstances, not thinking about how that might go wrong for everyone.

When Izanami was turned away, Izanagi took the wooden comb out of his hair and set it on fire, creating light that pushed back the shadows. He saw his wife as a rotting corpse crawling with maggots, and cried aloud in disgust and horror. Izanami shrieked as well, this time in outrage, and chased after him, but he ran out of the Underworld and pushed a large stone across the door. This is the moment when the Neptune individual sees the worst of their idealized partner—the internal trouble and struggle that we all have, the none-too-pretty parts of us. It dashes the last of their dreams, and they run in horror at darknesses that could have been approached with compassion and patience. No one actually helped a partner out of their personal Underworld by refusing to see what kept them there. If Neptune is too stuck in the cloud-land of dreams, reality can be pretty dark by comparison.

For some with this placement, repeated iterations of this pattern will finally mature into the ability to see their partner's deepest flaws and reach out with compassion, but not with the hubris that they can "save" this person. The more common reaction, at least the first time, is closer to Izanagi's. When the dream is dashed, the rose-colored glasses through which they had been viewing the partner flip to blood-colored, and suddenly they are The Worst Person Ever, and many horrible tales will be told of their transformation into a monster, having cruelly deceived the innocent Neptune person. Neither idealization nor demonization, however, is accurate; nor is either the road to real compassion for someone's flaws, whether or not they choose to stay together.

In one version of the story, Izanagi goes to cleanse himself after the shock of seeing Izanami's corpse-form, and while washing his face, three children run out of his eyes and nose—Amaterasu the Sun Goddess (Sun in Leo), Tsukiyomi the Moon God, and Susanoo the Storm God (Uranus in Aries). In another version of the story, the three children were born to Izanami and Izanagi before the fire-kami killed her. The two versions of the story are telling—when there are children involved in the bitter ending of a relationship, there is always the Neptunian temptation to decide, "These are *my* children, not yours; you have lost the right to them by hurting me." Amaterasu is the "golden child", but Tsukiyomi's oversensitivity and Susanoo's outright temper tantrums make Izanagi tear his hair out, and eventually he ends up banishing Susanoo entirely. No matter what fantasies one has wrought, sooner or later the test will be coping with the difficult reality.

While this story is full of tragedy, it doesn't mean that the seventh-house Neptune individual is doomed to unhappiness forever. The story is a map of mistakes, one piled atop the other, and if they can be understood and prevented in the future, the positive side of this aspect is the ability to create a relationship of mutual compassion, tenderness, patience, and realistic engagement with the other person's darknesses. First, though, one has to come down off the bridge and be content with the limited earth and its denizens, and Life which gives you imperfect creations and undeserved disasters. Real relationships require good boundaries and an appreciation of authenticity, even when that means it's not as pleasant as you wanted.

As it goes with Neptune problems, turning to spirituality is the best solution, if it can be done cleanly. All those conscious dreams hide an unconscious desire: to have a truly spiritual relationship. It's difficult to know what that looks like, though, and most people's ideas about it will simply be illusions. It can only come when the illusions are thoroughly in ruins and the real people are revealed ... and loved for who they are, including their flaws. That's the challenge of this Neptune placement—embracing the divine through another deeply flawed human being, without any illusions about what they are. It's a dichotomy that Neptune is uniquely prepared to solve.

8♆ Neptune in the 8th House: Yarilo and Marzanna

When I first came across Yarilo, the Slavic god of summer, fertility, and love, I thought he was a Venus figure. His name means "summer" or "strong life force". He is said to have been revered as a god of erotic sexuality—a fair young man on horseback, crowned with flowers and carrying a sheaf of wheat. While the Christian church stamped out his worship, his name survived as the label for the spring festivals which featured feasting, dancing, and young people courting each other. He rode a white horse, the symbol of a bridegroom, and carried eight swords—one for each of the seven months of his rule, and an extra one to fight with, should he need to do so. The various Slavic tribes prayed to him for the growth of their crops.

That sheaf of wheat should have tipped me off, though. As I learned more about him, I discovered that he was a dying-and-reborn grain god, an agricultural deity who died in the autumn with the crops and was born again with the new shoots in the spring. That's not the path of Venus, but of Neptune, which walks the road of sacrifice. Like so many Neptunian Gods, Yarilo burns bright only to be slain and spill his sacred blood onto the earth.

His story is more complicated, however, because his wife Marzanna is a much darker deity, appropriate for this eighth house of death and mystery and transformation. Yarilo himself has a rather dark past. He was the son of Mokosh the Earth Mother and Perun the King of Thunder (Jupiter in the first house), but he was stolen from them as an infant by Perun's archenemy Veles (Pluto in the third house) and raised in the underworld, the realm of Death. Trickster Veles raised him to be wayward and appreciate dark humor, which would be his undoing. Eventually he grew to manhood and came to the upper world, where he was celebrated by Perun and everyone else as a beautiful young golden God who rose in the springtime.

The first being of the upper world whom he came across on his early explorations, however, was Marzanna. They became attracted to each other and, over that first month, fell in love and married on the summer solstice, when the year was at its height. It was only when Yarilo came before Perun that he realized that his wife was actually his sister, who had not recognized him. (The wedding between brother and sister to make the crops flourish is found in many European cultures.) Their union also brought temporary peace between Perun and Veles, upper world and underworld, and created peace and balance. Marzanna was also the daughter of Mokosh and Perun, and also a goddess of agriculture ... but her nature was different. She was brooding, passionate, and possessive, echoing Pluto, the traditional ruler of this house. Putting her together with bright, ephemeral, drifting, Neptunian Yarilo was guaranteed to end in tragedy.

When Neptune, the planet of spirituality and madness, enters the dark eighth house of sex, death, and transformation, its vagueness and confusion magnifies those already emotionally charged areas. In older times, it was said that individuals with this placement had a much more tenuous grasp on life and might die suddenly at any moment. Ethereal Neptune in the house of death was supposed to make the veils between their life and their death thinner and more fragile, and they were also more prone to suicide. They were advised not to resort to the Neptunian solution of drugs or alcohol, because it could lead them all the faster towards death. More modern astrologers note that people with this placement tend to glamorize death, perhaps vaguely yearning for it or thinking that it will fix all their problems. Some find a more compassionate way by entering service professions which deal with the dying. On a higher level, it is said that this fascination with death is really a sort of "divine homesickness", with the eighth-house Neptune ultimately wanting to join with the divine. Neptune erases boundaries and merges souls, and wanting to merge into the Great Divine is a yearning for every placement of this planet. Here, death is one of the more attractive ways to fantasize about it.

It's not the only fantasy for this house, though. This is also the house of sex, and Neptune here can gift them with a natural talent for accessing spiritual sexuality. At the other extreme, the planet of sacrifice can lead to over-idealization of sex and love, to the point where no real human being is good enough to fulfill the fantasy. Some go the route of denying sexuality altogether, embracing celibacy or directing their sexual urges toward the divine. The most common route for most eighth-house Neptunes, however, is to follow Yarilo's pattern. They will fall madly in love with someone and decide that they are the perfect sexual partner, but sooner or later Neptune's wandering tendencies may lead them to notice the beautiful spirits in other bodies, and want to merge with them as well.

This placement is notorious for promiscuity, but its source is not a craving for novelty so much as the Neptunian Urge to Merge. Sex, for them, is a way to lose their boundaries or engulf those of another, a way to forget themselves and their troubles, to escape from their inner loneliness, and to be swept away on a sacred tide. Some find Neptunian solace in sexually serving their partners, or using sex to heal them. They do have a tendency to long for the unavailable, sometimes simply because they *are* unavailable. If they actually get the desired object, it's often a disappointment compared to their fantasies, and they slip away.

According to what can be painstakingly excavated about this myth, Yarilo was repeatedly unfaithful to Marzanna. She reacted badly, enacting as she does the Plutonian rulership of this house, associated with intense, possessive Scorpio. In a fit of jealous rage, she killed Yarilo and sent his soul back to the underworld from where his body had once emerged. This played out the death of the golden grain and handsome livestock animals during the fall harvest; where once Yarilo had made the fields lush wherever he walked, now his journey echoed their descent into barren stubble as the summer's food supply was brought into the home. One well-known Neptunian trap is first seeing someone or something they love through idealized rose-colored glasses, and then the flaws are seen and they flip to blood-colored glasses of demonization; Marzanna tears down this path with Plutonian intensity, but further on she will, in turn, be the demonized one.

In a bizarre turn of the story, Marzanna dismembers Yarilo's dead body and uses its pieces to magically build a house of bones for her to live in. This is a different kind of merging, and one which happens to the eighth-house Neptune rather than the one Neptune might seek. The house of transformation strips them down slowly over time, divesting them of their illusions and forcing them to see the bare bones of reality underneath. This is a different kind of merging; facing the reality of death and loss—the real cost of living in the world—can plunge them into a deep depression. At the same time, that reality is the "house" they must live in, learning to find comfort in the ephemerality of all things, including one's hopes and dreams.

This is what happens to Marzanna, and now the story pivots to her role in the myth. Her name—Marzanna or Morana according to different Slavic people—comes from the root word for death. After murdering her lover, she becomes a bitter, angry, cold hag and transforms into the Goddess of Winter, holding the world hostage with her sorrow and rage. At this point, she is often referred to as the Death Crone, and her name lived on in some regions as that of an evil spirit who came into the house and snuffed out people's lives. The snow falls and ice covers everything; winter wins over summer for another season. This, too, can be a part of the psychological cycle for the eighth-house Neptune—when all the fantasies of sublime sacrifice and ecstatic merging crumble into dust before the onslaught of reality, they too can become bitter and angry, living among the dead bones of their dreams.

Marzanna also had a yearly festival in the spring, called the *Topienie Marzanny* or the *Jare Swieto*, but it celebrated not her life but her death. All over the Slavic world, around the time of the spring equinox, people would gather with cut-off branches of evergreen trees decorated with ribbons and trinkets. This was called "walking the copse", and the crowd would process through the village like a herd of moving trees, celebrating the green to come. An effigy of Marzanna would be carried at the forefront of the parade; this varied from a simple doll of straw (when the ceremony was carried on largely by children, who were less likely to be chided by Christian priests who had banned the ritual) to a large stuffed figure of the Winter Hag.

In some places, the Marzanna effigy was dipped and "drowned" in every puddle of melting slush on the way to the lake where she was finally thrown in; other regions simply processed her to the largest lake in the area and ceremonially sacrificed her to the spirit of the unfreezing water. The ritual was also called "walking with the Queen", and afterwards the living copse went back to celebrate the ending of winter with music and feasting. Days or weeks later, Yarilo's spring festival would come again, and he would rise from the underworld for the new beginning of the cycle. Marzanna would also be reborn as her younger and more innocent self, and the story would start over.

It's an agricultural myth, like many others around the world, but those with the planet of spirituality in the house of transformation may find themselves living it over and over again, until they have transformed enough to be able to see the sacred in the ordinary, the flawed, the imperfect, the we'll-make-do-with-this daily reality. Until then, they will cycle through the times of winter—depression and perhaps even despair, and then back to clutching at bright illusions again. Neptune hates to live in the real world, but in the grip of the Plutonian eighth house it has no choice. Ironically, it would seem that the "house of the mysteries" would be a place where Neptune could wallow in a spiritual fountain forever, but the eighth is more like a cremation ground, strewn with the burning bodies of one's hopes and dreams ... and this, too, is wholly sacred. When the eighth-house Neptune person can see and understand this, and sit with it serenely, then real rebirth can finally get through.

9♆ Neptune in the 9th House: Merlin

hen we think of Merlin, we mostly think of the Arthurian-legend figure who was the teacher of young King Arthur (Mars in Libra). Some consider him to be a Druid, others just a sorcerer. However, the Merlin figure we know today was woven together from many different strands by the 12th-century fiction author Geoffrey of Monmouth. Untangling those strands gives us a deeper look at the figure which is Merlin—or Myrddin, as the name was originally known in ancient Britain.

Scholars generally agree that there are multiple strands of myth twisted together to form Merlin the great teacher. The first one is Myrddin Emrys, or Merlin Ambrosius, a seer in the old Arthurian tales who prophesied before King Vortigern. Little more is said about him except for his prophecies, but that's still a Neptunian thread. The second one is Myrddin Silvestris (Merlin of the Woods) or Myrddin Willt, who pulls Neptune's energies in a different direction.

The original name of these twisting threads may come from an old French word for "blackbird", or it may come from an old Welsh word for "madman". Here we need to remember that Neptune is the planet of madness. Astrologers who don't believe in spirituality tend to see Neptune entirely through its negative aspects, and one of those is Neptune's ability to merge ... with the bottle, the drug, the tinfoil hat. A madman is always at least partly Neptunian, at least at the point where they begin to seriously diverge from consensual reality. At the same time, those people who don't believe in spiritual power may see that also as insanity. The truth (a ninth-house quest!) is that people can be insane, and people can be psychic, and some people can be both.

The most obviously Neptunian figure making up the Myrddin myth is Myrddin Willt, or Wild Myrddin, a figure in medieval Welsh legend. He was originally a renowned bard, poet, and warrior, but in the middle of the Battle of Arfderydd, watching his friends slaughtered, his mind snapped. One version of the legend is that he saw a horrible portent in the sky which robbed him of his wits; another is that after seeing all his loved ones killed, his mind broke in a kind of post-battle PTSD. Either way, he uses the ninth-house method of escape: he runs away. In this case, far away into the woods, where he is not seen for many years. He emerges periodically to hurl prophecies at the populace, which of course they never believe until they come true. Some of those prophecies anger the people who were trying to hide their secret business; having a madman proclaiming it in the marketplace is not what they want, and Myrddin is mostly shunned.

The local lord, Rhydderch, hears about this strange mad seer living in a tree in the woods, and has him coaxed to his court, but the stress and crowds makes Myrddin try to run back to his forest, and Rhydderch finds it necessary to put him in chains. There is a young boy at court, and Myrddin prophesies that he will die soon. To test him, the boy is sent to him three days in a row, but dressed very differently each time, and he is asked how the boy will die. First he says that the boy will die in a fall from a rock, then that he will die in a tree, and then that he will drown. Rhydderch decides that Myrddin is of no use as a prophet and lets him go. However, soon thereafter the boy falls from a rock into a river where a large tree has fallen in, becomes entangled in its underwater branches, and drowns.

Back in the woods, Myrddin watches the stars in a homemade observatory, and hides from humanity. The bard Taliesin (Mercury in Sagittarius) visits him and engages him courteously, and finds that the prophetic madman is quite learned. Myrddin holds forth on subjects from cosmology to the habits of fishes and cranes to the islands of the world. Taliesin decides to stay with him and learn from him, even though he is mad. The story ends there, but later Geoffrey wrote another book of prophecies which he attributed to Merlin.

The ninth house rules adult education, including both spiritual and mundane education. It rules gurus and religious mentors and teachers of philosophy and any specialized esoteric knowledge. Beyond everything else, Myrddin/Merlin ends up in the archetype of the teacher who trains those who will go on to be in positions of power and influence. It's said that individuals with Neptune in the ninth house seek the ultimate guru, the perfect special teacher, the one who will reveal to them the secrets of the Universe. However, the Universe being what it is and functioning in the way it does, whether or not they ever find that Merlin figure, if their Neptune manifests in its healthiest and best way, they may end up becoming that archetype for others.

Any planet in the ninth house activates someone's desire for mind-expanding learning—not just "how to do X", but "Why does X work this way? What are the unseen mechanisms behind X, and what else might they explain?" Neptune, however, is the planet of vagueness and distortion … and madness, as well as higher spirituality. Where you have Neptune, the process of that house is made more challenging due to its constant layers of confusion. The key is to apply spirituality to the problem, although even this is not a guarantee of clarity. It's quite possible to be deluded about one's spirituality and have pseudo-spiritual experiences with the sock puppets in one's head. Neptune has no guarantees. Neptune will be Neptune, and try to erase boundaries wherever it goes. (That's why we have Saturns, after all.) However, a focused link with the Universal wisdom or Holy Powers or whatever you want to call it has historically been the best way to dissolve at least some of the Neptunian mists and bring clarity to the situation.

Neptune is also very good at finding places to insert madness and delusion in the areas of any house, but some houses (the fourth, eighth, twelfth, seventh, and yes, the ninth, for example) rule parts of life which have particularly tempting fields in which to plant Neptunian seeds of delusion. Religion and philosophy especially come to mind. Myrddin is a man of learning, a trained bard and priest, and yet when the moment of emotional panic comes, he interprets a great portent in the sky as being a sign for him to run away to a wild place and avoid humanity. Perhaps it was a true omen, and perhaps it was only a manifestation of his fear and shock at the horrors of war, but his education made it easy to dress it up in a costume of religious omen. Either way, humanity was robbed of a learned teacher.

Other areas of higher learning can also be affected by Neptune's vagaries—political study, for example, or psychology or sociology. The ninth-house Neptune individual has probably delved deeply into many fields of knowledge—ninth-house planets giving one such cravings—and this floaty, in-the-mind world may be where they live. It's more comfortable than the real world, certainly. When this airy intellectual world is invaded by the boiling waters of strong emotions, the result can be a mist that distorts and misleads, making a jumble of what would otherwise be useful knowledge. Since this is the house of World View, this confusion can become downright cosmological and pervade every aspect of the individual's life.

This placement, as we've said, comes with a hunger for finding the Right Teacher. One of its more common pitfalls is getting involved in cultish situations with unhealthy guides. Sometimes the ninth-house native tries to rigidly emulate the spiritual teacher in every way—acting, dressing, speaking like them—in the mistaken belief that if they act like an enlightened person, they will become enlightened. This has been referred to as "buddha disease". Ironically, in a Neptunian twist, some psychologists who study cults and their disciples have noted that the more likely the disciple is to resort to this tactic, the more likely they are to be gullibly fooled by a spiritual teacher who is an alcoholic, or addict, or actively mentally ill. In other words, afflicted Neptune calls out to afflicted Neptune, and sets everyone involved up for a life lesson. One could conjecture that it's actually better, at that point, to be alone in the woods. At least one has fewer distractions for the work of hearing one's own psyche.

Neptune's ultimate goal is transpersonal compassion. That's a term which makes a lot of people roll their eyes—"What New Age nonsense!"—but in the end, that's where Neptune wants us to go. It's the place where we can clearly see both the beauty and the damage of every person and every world view, including ourselves and our own world view, and be in a place of understanding and spiritual mercy rather than harsh judgment. The ninth house is traditionally ruled by Sagittarius, and this sign seeks Truth … but usually has to settle for a series of smaller lower-case-truths, which will only assemble themselves into a Great Truth when each has been seen realistically and with transpersonal compassion. You can't always back up far enough to see the connections when you're face down in the mess.

It is no accident that it is Taliesin, the Sagittarian Mercury figure, who makes the first real breakthrough with the mad Myrddin. Instead of seeing him as just a lunatic, or wanting to use him for his prophetic powers, Taliesin reaches out to share knowledge. As another figure who is highly educated and has also struggled with controlling "magical" and prophetic (read: Neptunian) powers, and who has also reacted to crisis in the classic Sagittarian/ninth house way (running away), he has sympathy with the wild man's plight. It is in the meeting of minds that Myrddin comes to a place of sanity, and this gives us a key to the healing of this placement.

The two traps for this Neptune are, first, isolation with one's own ideas (which can turn into isolation with one's own mental sock puppets over time), or being part of a group which is an unhealthy echo chamber, a place where shared illusions can fester. It's important to remember that this is also the house of travel and mind-expansion, and any planet in the ninth house does better when it is moving and changing its external reality. Taliesin is a breath of fresh air, a figure from a faraway place who bonds with Myrddin on shared intellectual knowledge, but whose experiences have been different. He is the outside perspective, and this Neptune placement needs lots of outside perspectives. If they are from different cultures and world views, even better. Neptune here needs to lean in to the views of as many others as possible; stagnation means corruption for this placement, and outside views blow away the mist and vapors.

This older-and-wiser-and-more-perspective figure is the one who matures into a different story—that of Merlin the teacher of Arthur, the wise man who trains the promising youths. The Arthurian Merlin is said to be the child of a mortal mother and an incubus/demon, which explains his magical powers. In some of these stories, he is a good force; in others an evil half-demon who misleads Arthur. In some he is both, struggling against the two sides of his nature to force wild powers and precognition into a lawful mold, and sometimes failing. He is less of a prophet and more of a wizard, in that his powers are less overwhelming visions and outbursts, and more controlled manifestations which can be used for good. He shapes the young King, and thus shapes the court and the country, spreading wisdom.

However, even the Arthurian Merlin has to beware of Neptunian interference. His apprentice Viviane/Niniane/Nyneve/Nimue (depending on the story), a powerful sorceress, casts an evil spell over him and seals him up for hundreds of sleeping years in a cave (or tree, or island, or stone). In some stories she does it to fend off his lustful desires, in others because she is jealous of his relationship with another sorceress, and in yet others it is simple ambition for his job. This points to the fact that one can be just as confused and deluded in a relationship with a damaged student as with a damaged teacher, a point which the ninth-house Neptune needs to keep in mind.

The single line which sums up Merlin's complex, many-stranded archetype (and this Neptune placement itself) better than any other is from T.H. White's *Once and Future King*, one of the more modern versions of the Arthurian tales. At one point Arthur asks his mentor about the solution for sadness, and the wizard says: "The best thing for being sad … is to learn something."

10♆ Neptune in the 10th House: The Fisherman and His Wife

he tenth house is an extremely concrete place. It is bound up with career ambitions, being seen by the right people, getting ahead in the human world. The Midheaven—the crucial first cusp of the tenth house—is specifically the part of the chart one looks at in order to find out what one's real-world, physical-life goals should be. It is traditionally ruled by Saturn and the sign of Capricorn, neither of which have any patience with nebulous woo-woo. That's why it's one of the worst places to have Neptune, the planet of booze and drugs and madness and delusions and imagination and spirituality.

The story of *The Fisherman and His Wife*, collected by the Brothers Grimm, is sometimes referred to by scholars as an anti-fairytale, in that it does not end with a happy, utopian situation. It has multiple variants from different countries, some more positive than others. It starts with a poor fisherman in a boat on the ocean, who pulls up a fish (usually a huge flounder) larger than anything he has ever seen. (Neptune is ruled by Pisces, the sign of the Fish.) The fish speaks, and begs to be spared; it tells the fisherman that it is a magical fish, and can grant any wishes the fisherman might want. The fisherman, a kindly sort, releases the fish and says he will go home and ask his wife about wishes. The fish gives him a little rhyme to recite when he wants the fish to come to him.

Going home to his tiny hut, the fisherman tells his wife all about the day's magical adventure, and his wife insists that he go back the next day to ask the fish for enough money to buy a nice house and have enough to eat at all times. The fisherman returns to the shore and recites the rhyme to call the fish, although he is disturbed by the ocean being rougher than the day before, when it had been calm and clear. He asks the fish for what his wife has requested, and the fish tells him it is already done, and he should go home and see for himself. Returning home, he finds that his hut has become a nice house and there is food in the cupboards and money on the table.

If the story stopped there, it would be a second-house tale, and would probably have had a happy ending. However, the wife is not satisfied, and after a couple of weeks she sends him back to the shore to ask to be a great lady in a palace. He does so, and the fish grants the wish, although the sea is rougher and the fisherman is worried. Days later, she decides that she wants to be king and rule over the land. He tells her that he does not want to be King, but she says that even if he does not want to, she wants a crown on her head, so he goes back to the shore and tells the fish, who grants again his wish. When he returns to the palace, his wife is seated on a throne as King, and all the local lords are fawning over her. The fisherman can only stand there and stare at her; when he finally speaks, it is to say that she shouldn't need to ask for anything else now. She tells him that she is now feeling restless and wants more to do, and she sends her husband back to the shore to ask for her to be emperor.

With the choice to become King, the issue is no longer about wealth; it has become a matter of temporal power, which moves everything to the tenth house. This is especially true when the wife demands the move to emperor, implying that she is already bored with the job of being King and desires something more challenging. Neptune in the house of career often has dreamy ideas about what the career will be like, and the difficulties in the early stages can be worked through by assuring themselves that it will all be better when they get to the top. Generally, though, the Neptunian individual either washes out significantly before that point due to boredom, stress, or other personal issues, or—rarely—they make it to the "top" and discover it wasn't at all what they thought it would be. This can manifest as never being satisfied and always chasing something bigger and further in the hopes that this will yield the idealized situation they have been dreaming of, although the more common ending is that Neptune will demand a sacrifice, as we will see later in the story.

The fisherman goes down to the sea, noting that every time he approaches it, the waves become darker and more violent. He calls the fish and tells it that his wife wants to the emperor, and the fish grants the wish. He goes home and stands there in the imperial palace which was once his small hut, watching his wife on the throne, surrounded by high lords and minor kings, crowned and carrying a sceptre. As soon as she sees him, she tells him that she wants to be Pope, and orders him to go out the next morning and call up the fish again.

At this point, Neptune is beginning to make an appearance for more than just delusions of grandeur. Being Emperor is temporal power; being Pope (even in the Middle Ages) is about spiritual power as well, and perhaps even more so. The Pope figure wields both kinds of power, but in this case the fisherman's wife comes to Pope from Emperor. The urge to do something spiritual with one's career, to have a calling which goes beyond just one's interest and talents, is subtle but strong with this Neptune placement. It's not uncommon for them to start out with the mundane career and then feel the "call" later in life … and be unwilling to sacrifice all their success to follow it. Instead, they convince themselves that the mundane career can be spiritualized if they just get high enough. Perhaps, if they are successful enough, they will have the recognition to start talking about spirituality and make people listen.

As with all things Neptune, the question is whether you can combine some form of actual spirituality with the areas of the house in question. Neptunian spirituality doesn't have to mean religion, and in fact organized group religion is under the purview of Jupiter, not Neptune. Neither does it require belief in a specific divinity. Neptune just wants you to reach out and make a connection with something larger than the world of human assumptions, culture, and values. That could be the natural world, or just the Universe. It could be embracing a career which helps others, even if it is at your expense, and requires a great deal of compassion to be successful.

It's quite possible to bring spirituality into one's career, depending of course on what it is, and how well it fits with the spiritual values you hold. But the problem is that this is Neptune, and Neptune demands sacrifice … and pushes for compassion. Just as knowing how to be a CEO requires starting underneath and working your way up, so does spiritual authority, but on a different road. One doesn't just skip all the years of deep, hard spiritual work and jump from CEO to Famous Spiritual Leader. Neptune, of course, can whisper that this is exactly what one should try. It's not that Neptune believes this is true; it's that Neptune wants to prove to you, without a shadow of doubt, how very wrong you are. Neptune loves to set people up for the big fall from hubris, and this is something that anyone with this placement should keep in mind.

The fisherman argues with his wife, telling her that he is sure this will go poorly for them. He has had doubts about every step past the first request, and now he begs her not to make him ask for this. However, he embodies the other dark side of Neptune: passivity. He is yet another manifestation of the tenth-house Neptune; he is content with his tiny lot and has no ambition. Working his way up a career ladder seems like entirely too much work, and he might have to deal with assertiveness and standing up for his desires. Neptune's laziness and conflict-avoidant passivity is bulldozed by his strong-willed wife, and he sadly goes down to the shore in a gathering storm and calls the magical fish. The fish sadly agrees to make his wife Pope, and he returns to see a large church surrounded by palaces. Inside are thousands of lit candles, and his wife is seated on a throne with heads of state kissing her slippers.

The fisherman stands and watches her for a long time. According to the myth, he looks as if he is squinting into a very bright sun. The heads of state all leave in time, and she stands there in the middle of the room, completely motionless, staring at nothing. It is as if the spiritual responsibility she has shouldered is finally striking her, and she realizes what she has taken on, and that she does not have the resources to do a good job at it. Neptune has two answers for someone in this position—for example, someone who started out as a mental health provider and began to integrate a few spiritual practices into their client work, and suddenly their clients are treating them as a guru and asking deep cosmic questions of them. One answer is real—start again from the bottom and learn this road the hard way. The other is the illusory answer, and of course the wife chooses it—skipping ahead to supposedly gain the insight and power necessary to do the job, in one fell swoop. Many spiritually-oriented classes promise this, if you give them enough money, but real Neptune pathways aren't so easy.

The fisherman finally asks her if it is good that she is Pope. She does not answer. He tells her that there is nothing higher she can become, and thus she should be satisfied, but she still does not answer, and the two of them go to bed. He sleeps soundly, but she cannot sleep at all, turning over in her mind what she should do. Finally dawn breaks, and she sits in her bed watching the sun rise, and has an idea. Waking up her husband, she tells him to go ask the magical fish to give her divine powers. She wants to be able to make the sun and moon rise and set; to become a God.

Her husband is so surprised that he falls out of bed. He argues with her, but the changes wrought in her by the fish's wishes make her very fearsome, and he is afraid of her. She screams at him and kicks him, and the fisherman gives in because he is used to being passive with her. He goes down to the shore in a terrible storm, with winds overthrowing peasant cottages and tearing up trees. It is so bad he can hardly stand, but he stands by the heaving, ripping waves, and calls the fish. When he delivers his wife's latest demand, the fish is angry, and tells him to go home, promising nothing. When he returns, everything is gone except for the little hut, and his wife standing empty-handed within it.

There are several other versions of the story from other countries, and in some of these the fish's final question is to ask the fisherman what he wants, rather than what his wife desires. He tells the fish that he only wants her to be happy (a very Neptunian attitude). This creates a less harsh and at least somewhat more satisfying ending, where he returns home to find her in the little hut, but happy and content with her lot.

While some individuals with this Neptune placement will be so confused by different career options that they will never really get started, others with end up enacting the riches-to-rags story. Sometimes it is voluntary, such as the person who realizes that their life feels empty and their career goals, once achieved, are not filling the hole, and quits to go live in an ashram or sell seashell crafts at the beach. Sometimes it all goes terribly wrong and crashes down, often because the individual has been in denial about poor choices they are making. Neptune doesn't mind if you crash and burn. Neptune is the planet of humility, and one of the best ways to truly understand humility is to get there from hubris, preferably very fast and with great violence. It is the road of the Sacred King (Sun in Pisces) who is lifted up just so that they can be thrown down.

The healthiest way to cope with this placement is to invest yourself in a career in which you give of yourself to the world, with as much selflessness and compassion as you can manage and still stay physically and emotionally solvent. (That's what you have a Saturn for—setting those boundaries.) It's also important not to confuse spiritual and temporal power; for your own good, you should probably keep them quite separate. The best ending to this story, though, is to learn to be content with what you have at any given point, whether that ends up being a palace or a hut by the ocean. After all, magical fishes don't come by every day—perhaps fortunately for us.

11♆ Neptune in the 11th House: Damon and Pythias

Neptune is the planet of sacrifice and martyrs, and also the planet of idealization. Neptune's energy can be beautiful and compassionate and spiritual, and it can also be confusing and insane. Neptune is the planet of dreams, and it holds the ideal dream of everything in the world, realistic or not. We all carry some of those ideal dreams inside us, and we strive for them. Sometimes we even achieve them, if only for a moment, if only for one area. We tell each other stories about these beautiful ideals, to inspire ourselves and each other.

In the eleventh house, it's the Dream of Friendship. The myth of Damon and Pythias is such an iconic tale that it has become a metaphor for that Neptunian dream. However, at the time it was basically created as a piece of propaganda for the Pythagorean school of philosophy. Damon and Pythias both belong to the secret society created by Pythagoras, and their idealized behavior was intended to be an example of how evolved and spiritual the society's members were.

Even this little twist is more Neptunian than we might think. While we like to think that when we are striving for the Compassionate Neptunian Dream, we will have no ulterior motives or agendas, but this in and of itself is a Neptunian illusion. It's better to acknowledge that there might be an agenda present, and thus be able to look at how it affects the situation. Perhaps it doesn't actually matter so much in the face of the positive results, or perhaps it is actively poisoning the process, and we can't deal with that if we can't look at it honestly.

Damon and Pythias were two Pythagoreans who traveled to Syracuse and lived there for a while, spreading the word and wisdom of Pythagoras. (But only bits and pieces of it, because it was a secret society and all the juicy education was only open to the small number of people who were allowed in.) One day Pythias was suddenly accused of plotting against the tyrant Dionysius who ruled the city, arrested, and sentenced to death. He asked to be allowed to make one last trip home to settle his affairs and say goodbye to his family, promising to return in a limited time to face his execution. Dionysius did not trust him and refused, but Damon offered himself as a hostage, accepting that if Pythias does not return, he would be executed. With this agreement, Dionysius allows him to leave.

What neither Pythias nor Damon knew was that the charge had been set up by Dionysius because some of his courtiers didn't believe that Pythagoreans actually lived the beliefs that they espoused, and felt that when they were in a tight place, they would revert to the average grasping person. They picked out Pythias and decided that he would be their test case. The date for his execution comes and goes, and Dionysius decides to wait a couple of days just to make sure. When Pythias still does not arrive, he decides that it is killing time, and has Damon dragged out in a public place to be executed.

Just then Pythias pushes through the crowd. He explains that his ship was attacked by sea raiders and wrecked, and he had to swim to shore and make his way to Syracuse as quickly as he could. He stands before Dionysius and asks him to trade his friend again for him, and that he will face his sentence. Dionysius is so impressed by the strength of their friendship that he decides to release both of them.

Neptune in the house of friends puts this myth of perfect friendship—"I would die for you!" into the world view of the individual with this placement. They want to experience the Dream of Friendship, of *philae* as the Greeks labeled it—brotherly love. When they are younger, they approach apparent friends with this trusting naïvete, and are deeply hurt when that absolute fidelity is not returned. The friend who goes away for the summer and finds others to hang out with, who moves away and stops writing, who finds a romantic partner and has no time for the buddies; these stab them to the heart like knives of hot iron. Eventually they may become cynical, but even then part of them longs to offer themselves wholly to a close friendship, to create something which will last until death. Even romantic partners may come in second to best friends, perhaps to their chagrin.

Of course, the story of Damon and Pythias has a happy ending. Let's compare that to a myth which doesn't. In Vergil's Roman epic *Aeneid*, Nisus and Euryalus are two soldiers serving in the Trojan army who are best friends. After the sack of Troy, their captain sails away to find a new country, and many of his men follow. They come accidentally onto the shores of the Italian peninsula, and promptly get into a big battle with the locals, who don't like a pack of armed strangers sniffing around their land. Nisus and Euryalus offer to make a daring nighttime raid and kill as many of the local warriors as they can, Euryalus making his comrades promise to care for his elderly mother as their own should he perish.

Nisus is the older of the two, and is an experienced hunter and thrown-weapons expert. Euryalus is younger—only a teenager by our standards—and looks up to Nisus. He was trained young as a warrior by his father, who died at Troy. His mother has traveled with him, but he is too cowardly to tell her he is leaving for a dangerous mission. Earlier in the Aeneid, the two friends competed in a footrace; Nisus was in the lead and Euryalus two behind. Nisus slipped and fell, and knowing that he could not get up in time, tripped the next runner to allow Euryalus to win. It's interesting to look at the cultural differences around perfect friendship between the first story and the second—the Greeks would not have gauged Damon and Pythias's loyalty by how much they were willing to cheat in order to help each other, but the Romans were fine with that. It is only a small vignette, but it shows that Nisus is willing to do anything for his friend.

The raid goes reasonably well, with a lot of gruesome killing, but as they ran from the camp Euryalus could not resist taking a fancy helmet from one of the corpses as a trophy. In the dark, in the light of the torches, it was the light glinting off the helmet that allowed the pursuing local warriors to see and catch him. Nisus realized that his best friend was not behind him and turned back; to his horror he saw that Euryalus had been caught and held. He threw his javelins and killed a couple of them, but failed to free his friend. He screamed at the men that it was all his doing, that Euryalus was innocent and should be freed, but they stabbed the boy anyway. Nisus then ran straight up to the warriors and took several of them down before he was also slain and fell across his dead friend's body.

The warriors cut off their heads, mounted them on pikes, and went back into battle the next day with their gruesome trophies. This sacrificial friendship story is very different from that of Damon and Pythias, and not just because it doesn't have a happy ending. These are not morally perfect friends; they are flawed people who have more courage than common sense. They get themselves into unwise situations which turn out badly, and it does not sway their loyalty to each other. The floating agenda behind Vergil's tale was to showcase the horrors of war and lament the deaths of all the young men who would go down, perhaps for less than prudent reasons. It's still part of the Dream of Friendship, though; a grittier take, perhaps, but still a story of friends who would die for each other.

Bringing the eleventh-house dream onto a larger stage, people with this Neptune placement also have dreams about the Right Group—the one that's more like an extended family you aren't related to, where everyone has everyone else's back, and no one ever throws anyone out for not fitting in. Maybe the ideal group has a humanitarian focus (very eleventh-house), or a spiritual one (very Neptunian). Maybe the people in it should be willing to die for each other. Certainly the stories of groups which change the world are often veneered with perfect loyalty and kindness (with an agenda of attempting to inspire groups of people to sacrifice themselves for political systems). The Neptune person will go into the group ready to open up and sacrifice themselves for the people who, surely, will give that sacrifice right back.

Inevitably, the group does not turn out to be a roomful of Damons and Pythiases, and the eleventh-house Neptune individual is crushed. The worst part of Neptune's idealization is that when it is damaged, it can turn to demonization. In this house, the friend who disappointed becomes The Worst Person Ever, and I Will Never Trust Anyone Like That Again! The group which turns out to be imperfect becomes Those Horrible People, and I Just Don't Fit Into Groups, I Shouldn't Even Try! Sometimes the entire process of friendship and belonging becomes demonized. Neither idealization nor demonization is realistic, and it will take some time and experience and consideration to find a middle ground of authenticity. Eventually the ideal stories of the Dream of Friendship get overwritten by actual experiences of people reaching out to each other, having each other's back, connecting in sincere and satisfying ways ... but you have to keep reaching out, making friends, joining groups, risking yourself, in order for that to happen.

12Ψ Neptune in the 12th House: The Nine Undines

The twelfth house is Neptune's own house, regardless of what sign happens to be on the cusp, and it gives Neptune great strength. When other planets are locked up in the twelfth house of confinement, they are difficult to access except through right-brain means like poetry, music, and meditation. When Neptune lands here, however, it is able to open the gates of the unconscious (at least some of the time) and flood the individual with images, feelings, and all manner of nebulous concepts. In fact, it's difficult to close those gates, even when you're dealing with everyday matters and need to keep from being distracted. The problem with having better-than-usual access to the unconscious is that the unconscious all has better-than-usual access to you.

It also seemed that whenever I'd look at a description of this Neptune placement, in books or on the Internet, there was a better-than-usual chance that I'd find a visual or literary reference to a mermaid. Something about this extra-watery placement just brings up that image, front and center. At first I dismissed it, but eventually I gave in and asked: *Mermaids?* And I was answered not by a single voice, but by nine-voices—the Nine Undines of Norse Mythology.

Their parents, Aegir and Ran, the King and Queen of the oceans, have already been described in the chapter on Neptune in the second house. These two ocean deities spawned nine mermaid daughters, demigoddesses in their own right. However, these were not the pretty, seductive, delicate mermaids of pop art. Aegir and Ran are members of the Jotun race of Gods and spirits, who symbolize Nature red in tooth and claw, and their daughters followed this pattern. They were known to reach up with a clawed hand and haul a man from his boat, devouring him and spitting out his bones. Like their parents, they had to be propitiated with offerings so as to keep them in a good humor. However, unlike their parents, also they were known to capriciously save a drowning sailor who had given them offerings in the past; they could be suddenly generous as well as suddenly cruel.

They were known, also, as the Nine Waves. This name echoes the idea that unlike their deep-sea parents, they flirted with the land and its denizens. Indeed, some of them have names which describe ways in which the ocean touches land—the tides, the breakers, the great wave. Even while we stand on a beach, we tend to think of land and sea as being separate worlds, when we are probably walking on land that belongs more to sea than to the earth where we make our homes. Does the ocean not own everything up to the high tide mark, and perhaps more besides, since the oceanic spray affects the soil and plant growth for some yards inland? Beaches and saltmarshes are a middle ground, a liminal space that is not quite sea or land, and people with

Neptune in the twelfth house spend a fair amount of time in the corresponding liminal zone between the solidity of consciousness and the vague, watery realm of the unconscious.

Each of the Nine Undines reflects one of the mysteries of the ocean, the archetypal Powers of Water. We can look at these as a kind of shorthand for the various ways in which the subconscious bubbles up in the mind of the person with this placement. The first and eldest sister is Kolga, whose name means "Cold One"; she is the spirit of the northernmost arctic waters which freeze into ice. The arctic is a cold and lonely place, far from human habitation and the warmth of community, and certainly one of the twelfth-house Neptune states of mind is a kind of cold, bleak loneliness and alienation. The twelfth-house Neptune person knows that they are, in some way, indefinably different from everyone else. They can be extremely sensitive, and perceive what others miss, and yet—unless there are Mercury connections—they may not be able to express any of this. Someone asks "What's wrong?" and icy silence descends, even as they long to communicate behind that wall. On the positive side, they may also have an instinct for keeping a cool head as a form of supportive compassion, and may develop that skill to the point where it can be a professional attribute.

The second sister is Duva, Kolga's twin, whose name means "Hidden". She is the spirit of the ocean mists that confuse ships and sailors, as well as all that is hidden from us at the bottom of the sea. She is a mistress of ocean islands, and pearls hidden within shellfish. Like Duva the veiled mermaid, people with a twelfth-house Neptune often feel like large parts of them are hidden from the world. At the same time their strong intuition gives them clues about secrets hidden by others, and they may be fascinated by "occult" or hidden knowledge. They can learn to see the currents of the unconscious like sunken treasure to be dived for and rediscovered.

The third sister is Blodughadda, whose name means "Bloody-Haired"—the lady of the sharks who smell blood and attack, and of the place where the river meets the sea. She reminds us that all the blood in our veins is seawater with iron-based additives. It's not unusual for people with this Neptune placement to have a history of victimization. As children, their unusual sensitivity can draw damaged people looking for someone vulnerable to hurt, like sharks scenting blood in the water. It can also be one possible indicator for a childhood riddled with adults who had alcohol, drug, or mental illness issues, especially if there was huge secrecy around their problems and the trouble they caused.

However, Blodughadda's point that blood is simply a kind of seawater can be a comfort for the adult with this placement, even with a violent history. Blood, the metaphorical vulnerability that draws sharks, is also just another form of Neptune's waters of compassion. The lesson here is that sometimes the best way to heal past damage is to use the compassion gained from that pain to help others in similar need.

The fourth sister is Hronn, whose name means "Whirlpool" or, more literally, "Sucking Water", and who is the emotional power of Fear. The sucking whirlpool of terror will also be familiar to people with this Neptune placement, especially if they had the aforementioned childhood of pain and confusion. Some will continue the process using the coping mechanisms they saw demonstrated—alcohol, drugs, or martyrdom—and some will discover those for themselves; anything to dull the fear and let them pretend that the whirlpool didn't suck them in, that they are drifting on the surface rather than tumbling in the depths. Hronn demands that the fear be acknowledged and spoken, and only then can they begin to swim free of the sucking depths. Sometimes they must hit the bottom and move through that in order to escape from her clutches.

The fifth sister is Hevring, whose name means "Heaving". The twin of Hronn, she is the sorrow that complements Hronn's fear. It is repeatedly said that people with this placement feel not only their own sorrows, but those of the whole world. This is more than just an empathic ability to see (or imagine) people in pain and being able to understand what that feels like. It is a deeper ability—that of being able to tap straight into the sorrows of the collective unconscious itself, often without any idea that this is happening. Anything Neptunian blurs the boundaries between you and another, you and anything that is not-you. This placement heightens that issue, which means that the individual may feel the sorrow of any given negative experience far more strongly—strangely and inappropriately strongly, some would say—than another person might respond. It's because they have inadvertently moved beyond their own personal sorrow and somehow tapped into the great throbbing well of general human suffering, and may not be able to tell the difference.

This is especially a problem when they are children; well-meaning parents may compound the problem by telling them that this is an overreaction and it's foolish to make such a fuss. This kind of early message can cause even more doubt around already confusing emotional tides. The adult with this placement needs to simply accept that they may inadvertently fall into sorrow that does not belong to them. When it happens, the best response is to say a prayer for others who are suffering and then redirect the mind to finding some small joy to counteract it.

The sixth sister is Bylgja, whose name means "Breaker", those waves that those of us who grew up on a coast were warned about as children. *They can grab you and drag you down,* we were told. You could be washed out to sea if no one rescues you. By now the pattern should be clear—the waves of Neptune in the twelfth house can carry someone away if they do not have the strength or resources or will to stay afloat. Here the problem is less about coping with fear (Hronn's lesson) and more about fighting free of the drowning rush of mental illness. Some folks with this placement will have other points in their chart which mitigate against this, but with the planet of madness in the house of institutions, it's not uncommon for someone to end up spending some time there. Of course, Neptune's compassion may lead them, instead, to work voluntarily in such places rather than being trapped in them.

The seventh sister is Bara, whose name means "Big Wave", the goddess of the tsunami that slams into the land and tears away whole sections of what we thought was safe earth. This huge whale-goddess holds the relationship between sea and land, which is that the sea wants to wear away and steal as much of the land as possible. Twelfth-house Neptune people usually have excellent imaginations, perhaps even full-sensory ones, and can become "swept away" by a dream—Neptune is the planet of Dreams—without checking to see how much of it is illusory. They might make wonderful poets and artists, though. Being able to make something concrete out of that imagination requires that they respect the practical element of Earth, and keep it under their feet.

The eighth sister is Unn, the Undine of the Tides. Inexorably, the tide moves back and forth, encroaching on the land and then backing away, but getting a little further each time. Eventually it turns and begins to slowly recede, leaving the beach swept clean. People with this Neptune placement need to get used to the idea that these waves from the unconscious will come in a rhythm—in and out—and it is necessary to accept and adapt to wherever the tide is currently moving. If a particular emotional state is distressing, waiting it out while being gentle with yourself is the most helpful reaction. Like the tide, it will pass. Unn is also said to be in love with Mani the Moon God, and it is important to check for aspects from this hidden Neptune to the natal Moon, as the emotional Moon can be strongly affected by Neptunian tides.

The ninth sister is Himinglaeva, whose name means "Sun Shining Through", the spirit of Fair Weather. After all these warnings, there's a purely positive side to this placement here, and it has to do with spirituality. By "spirituality" we don't mean organized religion—that's the ninth house—and indeed someone with this placement is more likely to find their spiritual path in solitude rather than among other people and their opinions. So long as their spiritual practice and values focus on compassion and mindfulness, anything else will simply be the manifestation of their own deeply-felt intuitive knowledge. They will find that they have a gift for being purposefully alone—as opposed to aimlessly solitary—and that their creativity and connection to the Universe increases when they are able to find a comfortable haven in which to do their work. It's as if they need to be away from the psychic noise of the human crowd in order to hear the spiritual depths of their twelfth house clearly ... but once they find that haven, the clouds of confusion part and the sun shines through. The sun shines off the water, and they can become mirrors which reflect the Divine to those stranded on lonely shores.

 # PLUTO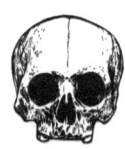

1♀ Pluto in the 1st House: Pele

Astrologers agree that the first house is a very difficult place to have Pluto, because it means that the struggle with your personal demons—and with this placement, the individual will have a great number of personal demons—keeps pushing itself out where others can see. First-house planets in general can be devastating to private people, because it's impossible to keep them hidden, The more you try, the more they surface, and that's especially rough when it's a planet as explosive as Pluto. It's like a calm ocean that one day erupts in a volcano which then creates a lava-spurting island. Many islands in the oceans once started as volcanoes, and most are still volcanoes today. Perhaps they are dormant for a time, but sooner or later they will go off again, wreaking destruction. Pluto in the first house is like that. The intensity that frightens others will, sooner or later, erupt in devastation.

In Hawaii, the goddess of volcanoes—said to be living in Kilauea, the largest one—is Pele, whose home volcano is by no means fully dormant, and one could say the same of her reputation and worship. She is known for her power, passion, jealousy, and strong emotions—anything she feels, she overdoes. When she becomes enraged, her volcano explodes with lava … or the metaphorical equivalent. On the modern Big Island of Hawaii, there are signs on Kilauea's lava beaches warning tourists not to pick up the black rocks and take them away, because they are Pele's rocks, and she will punish thieves. American tourists being what they are like, they take them anyway. Every year the Hawaiian tourist office gets hundreds of black rocks back in the mail from people describing the terrible fortune which has befallen them, and begging to have the rocks returned to Pele so that she will be merciful. The volcano goddess does not sleep, and she knows how to make lives erupt with problems.

Astrologers write about the many first-house Pluto charts they have read where the individual's struggle with their demons started very young. Many had extremely dysfunctional childhoods, often with medical issues that created intense physical or emotional pain. Problems with parents are frequent, but in the first house of the body, there was often some medical issue of the child's which disrupted the family, or which the family did not know how to cope with. "Like a natural disaster for everyone," is a frequent comment from the families of first-house Pluto people. The family's reaction can deeply wound the child, causing shame and guilt; some may develop major insecurities as a result of this. They may attempt to hide the evidence, which creates conflicts between the inner and outer selves, and in spite of that Pluto breaks through anyway.

Pele has several life myths. In most of them, she starts out the child of a divine couple with multiple siblings, usually very close to the element of fire. In one version, it is said that she stayed close to the hearth and the hearth-tender, playing with the fire. Then, inevitably, one of her siblings suddenly decides that Pele is going to destroy them all, and probably the land they live on. They object to her intensity, which no matter how hard she tries to hide, still shines through. People with this placement embody Pluto's transforming power, and they need to find a reasonably comfortable way to publicly embody it. If they don't, Pluto will choose the manifestation, and it might not be comfortable. People who are feeling belligerent may suddenly feel like they have to pick a fight with the Pluto person. People who are frightened of something else may project that fear onto them. They constantly get told they are intimidating, no matter how innocuous they try to be, and often find themselves the scapegoat. On the other hand, they also give off an aura that tells sufferers that they are strong enough to hear their troubles, so people might also suddenly pour out their predicaments to their Plutonian ears.

In some versions of the story, Pele is forced out of her homeland by her family, who fear her ambition or destructive nature. In other versions, she sets out on her own, perhaps accompanied by siblings whom she jettisons on various islands along the way. In these stories, her sisters all seem to be goddesses of rain and frost, and are her rivals. One of them—Namaka—chased her from island to island, putting out the fires she started, and finally attacked her when they reached Hawaii. They fought for several days and Namaka finally killed her, which simply transformed her into the spirit of volcano fire itself. Her body was made of lava and steam, and could appear in many different forms; she died only to become immortal.

This is the planet of violent transformation, and the point of these periods of eruption in the Pluto person's life are first to force them to look at and deal with all the magma-hot emotions in themselves, and then to slowly transform them into someone whose volcano is under control. They may go through multiple extreme physical changes, often in response to something going wrong with their body, in this house of physical form. Some astrologers point to the Pluto/Pluto sextile transit as the time when the real transformation begins, and the Pluto-Pluto square as the point when it's complete ... for a while, anyway. Then the cycle starts over again. Pluto's transformation goes deep, destroying who people believe they are, and some don't survive the destruction of their idea of themselves. Some people with this placement report repeated "Everything I know is wrong" moments, where the idea of themselves and their future was torn down, and then later in the next episode of destruction, they find out that their beliefs about the last episode were also at least partly wrong, and so on. Pluto forces them to break everything down and rebuild it, but on a stronger base.

Pluto is both a creator and a destroyer, and it is important for these individuals to acknowledge both sides of this dichotomy in themselves. It's said that those who deny their own destructive urges may unconsciously provoke other people—and sometimes their own bodies—to engage in "de-structuring" them. It's easy to read that and think, "This is paranoia-inducing blame-the-victim mentality, except that so many first-house Pluto people who write about it in their later lives agree that was exactly what happened ... and that it was what needed to happen. Pluto will use anything when it thinks everything is too stagnant and transformation is not happening fast enough. The way to stop this from happening is to meet every aspect of Pluto in one's psyche, face to face, and offer to actively engage with the change it wants instead of waiting for unconscious triggering ... even if that means looking strange to the outside world.

It's said that the most common reason for this unconscious triggering is that the Pluto person notices something which makes them feel vulnerable. Remember that Pluto is about power, and first-house Pluto people are very, very sensitive to currents of power and where they are running, the way that elephants feel an earthquake through the ground. Sometimes the feeling of not having power over the situation hits their sense of safety and security, and Pluto deals with it ruthlessly, "killing" the whole situation before it can kill them. It is also said that the answer to this is to build an internal sense of safety and security which cannot be easily triggered, and then the unconscious process itself will become transparent and manageable.

One of the most challenging goals is to develop compassion for people who are overreacting and scapegoating them. This wouldn't be easy for anyone, and it's hard to be a saint with a volcano right in (and on) your face all the time. In one story, when Pele left the island, her earth-goddess mother gave her the latest infant, a baby sister, to take care of ... because Pele needed someone to raise and love in order to learn compassion. Pele loves her little sister and raises her with care, but when Hi'iaka, as she was known, became a young woman, their relationship hit some rocks. Pele went into a trance for nine days to the sound of drums, and Hi'iaka watched over her. After nine days she became worried and chanted to call her older sister back. Pele returned, but was unhappy because her soul had been having a mad affair with a beautiful young man named Lohiau, who lived on a different island.

Hi'iaka offered to travel to Lohiau's island and bring him back for Pele. The volcano goddess agreed, but warned Hi'iaka that she must not fall in love with him, and she must be back in forty days. Hi'iaka made Pele promise to protect her small piece of land and her lover Hopoe, and traveled to Lohiau's island, only to find that the young man has killed himself in despair that he would never again see the exciting goddess in his dreams. Hi'iaka had to bring him back to life with songs and chants, which took a while, and then had to convince him to come with her, and then had to guard him on the journey. It is more than forty days by the time they get back, and Pele has lost patience.

The challenging side of Pluto means being prone to fits of jealousy and sometimes even paranoia. Pele decided that Hi'iaka must have stolen Lohiau and gone to live with him, and she burns Hi'iaka's land and kills her lover Hopoe. When Hi'iaka returns with Lohiau to find her home devastated, she becomes angry and throws her arms around Lohiau to spite Pele, who then promptly kills Lohiau with another spurt of lava. After this, Hi'iaka explains everything and Pele realizes that between them, they have killed the two people they love the most, and make up.

Pele apologetically brings Lohiau back to life, but now that he has seen her up close, he no longer wants her. Pele tells him that he can choose between herself and Hi'iaka, and she will bless whatever choice he makes. He chooses Hi'iaka, whom he has grown to love on their long journey, and the chastened Pele blesses his choice. Hi'iaka becomes the goddess of the hula dance, and promises that the first hula dance will always be a tribute to Pele, so the ability to apologize and reconcile has provided a constant cultural honor which still continues to this day. Several of the most common traditional hula dances are done for Pele, usually with fast, intense movements which challenge the dancer's skill and abilities.

People with Pluto in the first house challenge others by their very nature. They may bring out the worst of people, and catalyze transformative change in them, which few like and fewer can endure for long periods of time. Trusting is hard for them, because their early life has not given them much in the way of a safe space. They anticipate disaster, feeling that they must continually barricade and protect themselves against doom and destruction. When you walk around mistrusting life, anything could be an enemy. Disaster could erupt like a volcano at any time, and one's peace and security could be wiped out with a lava flow. Think about the hypervigilance of people who live on the slopes of an active volcano, and the kind of magical patterns they create to ward off the inevitable, or at least to allow them to escape again the next time ... and then come back to rebuild all over again.

But over time, their own transformations can bring them to a place of great power. They learn to use their ability to see below the surface in ways not distorted by fear. They learn to roll with the punches and achieve amazing resilience. They learn grounded security in themselves and become nearly untriggerable. They learn to use their excellent intuition to follow the right path up and down the volcano's sides, and get good at jumping over the lava flows. They learn the psychological hula dance that calms the fury within. They learn to respect and channel their destructive drives into places which don't destroy the village, and they learn how powerful they actually are. They embrace the future, whatever it holds. Pele, after all, likes people best when they dance for her ... in joy.

♇ Pluto in the 2nd House: Maman Brigitte

ossibly the most unusual of all the Voudou *lwa*, or divine spirits, is Maman Brigitte ... because she is the only *lwa* who is portrayed as a white woman. Scholars have had great arguments over the origin of her name, and that she is shown as a Caucasian woman with red hair and green eyes ... but, of course, the face of a skull, or sometimes even a face which is half skull and half decaying flesh peeling back. One theory is that Irish indentured servants sometimes worked alongside the

black enslaved people who had brought African religion to the Americas, and shared with them the story of St. Brigid, who was originally the pre-Christian Irish goddess Brigid (Mars in Virgo). Others point the fact that besides the coloring and the name, Maman Brigitte shares nothing in common with Brigid, and claim instead that the name was simply a convenient and randomly-assigned syncretism using St. Brigid to hide a Voudou *lwa*, and the coloring got picked up over time through common usage. No one knows for sure, as enslaved people were often illiterate and even if they could write, would not have wanted to put down anything dangerously incriminating, like the details of their forbidden religion.

What we do know is that Maman Brigitte is the wife of Baron Samedi (Jupiter in the eighth house), who rules the Ghede tribe of *lwa*—all death-spirits who tend to be foul-mouthed, carnal, and happy to party. Maman Brigitte is said to be all of these things as well. When graves are dug in Voudou practice, graves for women are dedicated to Maman Brigitte and graves for men are dedicated to her husband. She wears brightly-colored, overtly sexual clothing over her skeletal form. She drinks rum infused with peppers, and is said to love sex, much like her husband. Also like her husband, she can be called upon to help children who are very ill; it is said that if you are too afraid of the Baron to ask, you should ask his wife, as she is more approachable.

She is often symbolized by a black rooster, even though the rooster is a male bird, because it shows off its plumage. It's also said that the rooster's cold stare is like Maman Brigitte's cold stare, which is a known Pluto phenomenon. The rooster has also been a symbol of France, who founded the island country which would become Haiti, and so the black rooster symbolizes black French-speaking people.

Besides being a Death Goddess, Maman Brigitte is also the *lwa* of money, and how it is used in society. In this way, she is similar to Hades/Pluto (Pluto in Capricorn) whose Roman name literally means "wealth", and who was said to own all underground wealth of metal and stone. In Maman Brigitte's case, while she can certainly be prayed to for a quick influx of cash in desperate situations, her rulership over money is more complicated than that. She expects people to fully respect transactions of money, not attempting to subtly cheat the other person, nor allow yourself to be cheated (which means actually finding out what something normally costs before claiming that it is overpriced). She is called upon to get people to honor their side of financial deals, and to pay money owed to others. Being honorable about how you handle your finances is important, as is finding out if something you bought cheaper was so cheap because it was made by exploited people who had no recourse. She is also a spirit who believes very strongly in justice, so financial justice is something you should be practicing, at least somewhat, before you call upon her.

At the same time, she also emphasizes that money and material possessions should not have too strong a hold over you. This is part and parcel of the need for honorable financial behavior; if you are so desperate that you feel you cannot act honorably and still survive, then the money owns you, not the other way around. If you cannot do without the fancy car to show your status in society, then the possessions own you, and have great power over you. As a Death Goddess, Maman Brigitte reminds us that we can't take it all with us, and it is best to hold money and possessions lightly. Death doesn't care about your wealth; Death has seen it all go down to dust. She sometimes "steals" Baron Samedi's hat and cane in order to prove this point to people.

This is a good thing, because when Pluto goes into the second house, all sorts of issues with money crop up and come into the light. Pluto is the urge to control, and Pluto is also purification, which can include letting go of that which no longer serves you. People with this Pluto placement are notorious for having unhealthy relationships with money. They may obsess about getting it and hoarding it (and since Pluto is also the house of movable possessions, they may act the same way about valuable physical items, buying and then hiding them). They may go without luxuries in order to desperately save more cash for that "rainy day emergency", and years later realize that they have passed over many experiences they could have had. If Pluto is especially afflicted, they may use money as a weapon to control others, extorting them or holding it over their head in order to get their way.

Obsessing over finances is made worse by the fact that this Pluto placement can actually have a repressive effect on someone's ability to make money, especially when they are in an unhealthy relationship with it. The more they obsess, the harder it is to make. Conversely, the more they relax and spend sensibly but not compulsively, the better the flow will be. On the other hand, where you have Pluto, you sometimes have great reversals which "clean out" the mess that has piled up. In the second house, that can mean financial crashes, or giant house fires which reduce one's material objects to ashes ... or in some cases, midlife crises which cause one to sell everything and head for the coast to start a new life. If you've become identified with your bank account and your big house, Pluto invites you (with a sinister glare) to start basing your identity on something not so easily removed from you. So for this placement, it is particularly crucial to hold what you have in an open hand, and not base your life around it.

Another of Maman Brigitte's powers is helping people who are in abusive relationships or suffer from bouts of domestic violence. This brings us to the second house's higher axis of meaning, which is values ... and how much you value yourself. This is the house of self-worth, and almost inevitably when someone is enduring domestic violence without leaving (and perhaps also excusing the abusers) they are likely also suffering from a low sense of self-worth, and do not value themselves highly enough to stop exposing themselves to the situation. Maman Brigitte helps adult abuse victims to see that they are worth enough to save, enough to not have to put up with hurtful, dysfunctional behavior. Maman Brigitte herself is a good model of self-value; she has no patience with idiots and will unleash a tirade of profanity against those who displease her.

Maman Brigitte can also be called upon for healing, and is especially a healer of sexually transmitted diseases (Pluto is a highly sexual planet, and Maman Brigitte's touch is purifying). She is also called upon as a goddess of fertility, because the other side of Death is Rebirth, which happens (at least among human beings) through sex and procreation. This is Pluto's gift of seeing every piece of destruction as clearing and fertilizing the space for the new life which will fill it.

This will resonate with the nature of the second-house Pluto person, because one of the things this Pluto placement is good at is recycling. Even if they don't work in any field related to recycling, many of them are particularly skilled at taking old, discarded objects and altering them so as to give them a new life, or finding new homes for them which will appreciate them more than the ones who threw them out. Their homes are often waystations for items which will get passed on when the right person walks in the door; they often gift people with their found objects, and this is another way of not allowing the possessions to own you, but freely passing them on.

This can lead to them seeing people who are considered less valuable by others, perceiving the special qualities in each of them, and perhaps helping them to be "recycled" and come into lives which will better foreground their unique specialness. Maman Brigitte, as a Death Goddess, says: *Don't worry about losses. Reclaim what you can. It is all grist for the mill of the future.*

♇ Pluto in the 3rd House: Veles

Words have power, and where there is power, Pluto is interested. Pluto is drawn like a moth to a flame when it comes to power, and in the third house of communication, it's the power of words which get studied under Pluto's microscope. Pluto is also one of the planets of Death, and that combination—Death, power, and words—makes a fascinating mythological creature. In Slavic mythology, the god Veles (or Volos) is just such a mythological creature, as he spends half his time in the form of a dragon. To the Slavic peoples, a dragon was a cross between a bear and a serpent with bulls' horns—a chimera who lived in low places such as swamps and caves, and could either protect or devour a farmer's livestock.

Many cosmologies have Gods of eloquence, singing, writing, and other communicative and performative arts. In this book and the last one in the series, you read about many of them. Somehow, though, they all seem to have high origins—they are sky Gods, heavenly Gods, deities whose words lift up all those who hear them to those same celestial realms. All except Veles, that is. He is one of the few Gods of song and eloquence who is also a Death Lord, a King of the Underworld—a God of low places.

Veles was the rival of Perun the Thunder God (Jupiter in the first house), and the two were polar opposites in all things. Perun ruled the nobility and warriors while Veles was prayed to by the peasant; Perun smote his foes with death in battle while Veles hit them with disease. Perun was the God of Air and Fire (sky and thunder/lightning), while Veles was the God of Water and Earth. He slept as a dragon under the roots of the World Tree, on a bed of black sheepskins, and all caves and low, swampy areas were his sacred places. In fact, when the pagan king of Kiev erected statues to all the Gods, he made sure to put Perun's on the highest hill above the city, while Veles's statue was in the marketplace where the ordinary peasants could easily make offerings to him.

This fascination with low, dark, watery places is something which will be familiar to the third-house Pluto. Whenever you combine Pluto and Mercury energies—whether it is this combination, Mercury in Scorpio, Mercury in the eighth house, Pluto in Gemini, or even aspects between the two planets—you combine the incisive mind with a strong interest in anything hidden, forbidden, mysterious, or even horrific. If it's dark and/or socially unacceptable, they're interested. Pluto is associated with the sign of Scorpio, which many people forget is a water sign, and bogs are a very Scorpionic place because they were once considered gates to the Underworld. (That's why people dropped the bodies of human sacrifices into them.) You can't see through the water of a swamp, because there's too much earth and plant matter in it. The joining place of earth and water ... that is Veles's territory. It's opaque and mysterious and might lead to another world. Perun's tree was the tall oak, but Veles had the flexible, twisting willow tree which grew on riversides and whose roots can bore through anything ... like the relentless penetrating mind of a third-house Pluto on the trail of an interesting research hunt.

Pluto, in astrology, is associated with death (as is Saturn); the planet is even named after the Roman God of Death. Veles was the Lord of the Underworld in Slavic mythology, called the Shepherd of the Dead—thus his bed of black sheepskins. Veles was also known as the Lord of Animals, similar to the Gaulish Cernunnos. In his human form, he often appeared as a bald man with cow horns carrying a harp, and he was specifically a protector of the cattle and herds of peasants. However, he also protected the wild animals, and could take on the form of a bear or wolf. He maintained the balance between wild and domesticated, caring for everything in the animal world, and he was a shapeshifter who could take on many forms. Understanding—and crossing—the boundary between human and animal is another shaman-gift, bringing the mind and the spirit into the pure intensity of an animal experience. It's another forbidden place for the third-house Pluto to delve.

Veles was the deity of singers, musicians, and writers; at pagan Lithuanian weddings the musicians would not begin singing until the bride or bridegroom had poured out a toast onto the ground to him, ideally on the roots of a nearby tree. Once their patron deity had been honored, they could play. He bestowed eloquence, knowledge, and deep wisdom learned from his many lives. Like Odin (Saturn in Pisces, or more relevant here, Mercury in the eighth house) and the Morrigan (Mercury in Scorpio), he was associated with black birds such as ravens and crows in his aspect as a God of wisdom; they were his messengers and gave him news from faraway places. One of the gifts of Pluto in this house is the ability not only to seek out mysteries, but to find words to describe them to people who have never delved into the darkness. They can bring readers, listeners, and students into that world and send chills down their spines, placing searing images into their minds. It's the gift of that flash in the crow's black eye.

The classic rivalry tale of Perun and Veles starts, inevitably, with Veles taking on his dragon form and creeping up the World Tree toward Perun's domain at the top. In some versions he steals Perun's wife or child; in more of them he steals his cattle. Perun retaliates, there is a huge battle, and Veles is blasted apart, his blood falling as rain on the earth which will fertilize the fields. Being a serpent-dragon with all the powers of regeneration that implies, he is then resurrected and retreats to his dark, damp kingdom to go about his business until the next foray upwards on the Tree.

It's important to remember that Veles is and was not considered evil—most of the peasantry worshiped him, and he was one of their most popular Gods. Why, then, this continual and impotent initiation of battle? All simplistic nature-myths aside, most sacrificed Gods are Neptunian sorts—bright solar types who must be cast down, or warriors more like Perun than his rival. Sly, shrewd Veles seems an unlikely sacrificial deity … but if we broaden our search, we can find sly, shrewd, dark Odin who hung himself on the Tree for wisdom, and Dionysos (Neptune in Scorpio) who is himself a dark trickster like Veles, coaxing people into the Maenad dance to get torn apart, but willing to go under the sacrificial knife himself. That's where the Plutonian sacrifice diverges from the Neptunian one. Veles is a Lord of Death who is periodically driven to experience Death himself. He understands the Dead he cares for because he has been one of them. His resurrection through his skin-shedding dragon form is not a matter of Neptunian spiritual surrender, but of active, wrenching, personal transformation and rebirth—very Plutonian.

This begins to make sense from an astrological perspective when we remember that Pluto is an obsessive, driven planet. In the third house, it is driven to seek knowledge and wisdom, at any price. If this means passing beyond the ultimate mystery, then so be it. If the average third-house Pluto had Veles's ability to resurrect, Death would probably become their playground just to find out how it works. If, as a side effect, one is also able to save a lot of people by becoming a rainstorm, so much the better. One is reminded of a surgeon or microbiologist who is willing to plumb the mysteries of Death to save lives, a very third-house Pluto career, perhaps more than the usual assumptions of detectives and journalists. Being driven to periodically creep toward Death (and, for that matter, any forbidden realm) makes much more sense from that perspective. (There's also that Veles is a trickster God, and tricksters are often driven to go where they are not wanted, just on principle.)

Veles is also the god of magic and the patron of magicians, another forbidden area of knowledge which he has plumbed and which he teaches to others. Magic, sooner or later, approaches that line between the physical aspect of Life, and the mysterious darkness beyond, of which Death is the greatest conundrum. Veles has been animal and human, alive and dead, above-ground and underground, air-breathing and underwater, and all this has given him a strong understanding of how the world works ... and how to dance with, and even sometimes bypass, that working. This Pluto placement understands that Words Have Power—the power to shape thoughts, which is a kind of magic. One of the problems with this placement, however, is the ability to use words as a weapon, and sometimes little compunction in doing so. Pluto, when angered, can strike deliberately to cut deep, and this house holds some of the best of those weapons. The wild beast has teeth, and may not care who it hurts when it is hurting.

One of his myths recounts a shepherd-magician who makes a bargain to learn from him, and to keep a great number of special taboos and prohibitions for the rest of his life. He also sacrifices his best cow to Veles. As part of the bargain, he asks Veles to do something about the ghosts who continually escape from the Deathrealms and wander about the world, causing trouble and disease. Veles, on the other hand, retorts that he doesn't want curious mortals stumbling into his realm either. They come to an agreement that a magical border will be created between the realm of the living and the Dead, so as to keep both better into their places. Veles plows a furrow in the earth with his own hands, and next to it the shepherd-magician cuts a swath in the earth with a knife. This is supposedly why the world today no longer has as many spirits in it, and why it is harder to cross to the

Otherworlds, or communicate with them. While the third-house Pluto wants to cross that line, they don't always want other people mucking about in there. Making it harder to get there can feel worth it to keep out the fools and despoilers.

Like Hermes who guided souls in and out of Hades's realm (another Mercury/Pluto combination), this Pluto placement can be, in their deepest (we won't say *highest*, not for this planet) form a psychopomp, guiding others to knowledge. They make excellent counselors once they have plumbed their own psyches and those of others, and can lead others through and out of the mire in the same place. They are not afraid of transformation, and use the tool of mind and concentration to get there. Like Veles, the darkness is not frightening to them. It is their familiar home, and the most fascinating library ever.

4♀ Pluto in the 4th House: Oedipus

When volatile Pluto, the planet of dark secrets and painful revelations, falls into the fourth house of home and family, the result can be either purifying or devastating or both. One thing that it won't be, however, is easy … or safe. Individuals with Pluto looming over their childhood home will experience it, more often than not, as a place where they did not feel safe. Sometimes there may be abuse, but often it is subtler—manipulative uses of power, dark silences about family secrets, sudden rages and savage words. Not uncommonly, there is some kind of terrible "shock" from the outside which destabilizes the family's safety and casts them adrift—perhaps the death of a family member, an ugly divorce, or an uglier secret being brought to the light and disillusioning everyone.

What I asked about this house placement, the figure that appeared to me was the Greek hero—or antihero—Oedipus, made famous by several ancient plays, notably those by Sophocles. Oedipus was made even more famous in modern times by Sigmund Freud, who used his myth as a rather inaccurate catchword for mother-son incest. Oedipus's story is a tragedy, but its main theme reflects the religious culture of ancient Greece in a way that may be rather alien to modern readers. It is all about the inevitability of prophecy and destiny, and how one can never escape it.

This is a problem for astrologers, whether we like it or not. Arguments abound as to how much freedom we have to resist our natal charts, which often turn on disputes over whether they primarily indicate internal psychology or external circumstances. Modern astrologers push for the idea that we can mindfully adjust and overcome our astrological tendencies, even as outsiders who know little about astrology beyond tabloid Sun Sign columns accuse us of accepting predestination and setting aside free will. The ancient Greeks who left us their knowledge of astrology certainly believed in this divine fatalism, as is repeated constantly in the tale of Oedipus. However, Pluto—named for the Roman God of Death—is often bound up with events that cannot be escaped, because they must be transformed and an escape would prevent that necessity.

Of all the planetary energies, Pluto is the most implacable. When it lands in the house of family and ancestry, it drags in not only questions about the psychological patterns that are passed down in families, but the very genetic inheritances themselves, and whether those genes create behavior that continue abuse through generations. Which is more inescapable—nature or nurture? It's a frightening question, our own modern version of the debate around divine predeterminism, and it's a question that Pluto will not let us ignore.

Oedipus is the first-born son of Laius, the King of Thebes, and his child-wife Jocasta (it was not unusual for twelve-year-old girls of noble birth to be married off to much older men, and to find themselves pregnant at thirteen or fourteen). Laius is an unpleasant individual who was once a guest in the home of another noble, where he raped the noble's young son and the boy killed himself in shame. In Greek culture, the violation of the youth was a lesser infraction compared to the violation of hospitality, which was sacrosanct. (Hospitality is an issue pertinent to fourth-house questions around inviting people into one's home, but the child-rape sets the scene for a past history of familial violence.) Laius was cursed for his deeds by the Gods, and an oracle states that a son of his will kill his own father and marry his mother.

Laius looks at his newborn son and orders Jocasta to slay the infant. She refuses in terror, so Laius puts a nail though the infant's feet and gives him to a servant to stake out and expose in the way that many unwanted infants were disposed of in ancient times. The servant takes the child, but instead of nailing him up on the mountain, he gives the baby to a passing shepherd who is traveling to Corinth. The shepherd takes the child to Polybus and Merope of Corinth, who are childless and raise him as their own son. He is named Oedipus, meaning "swollen foot" due to the injuries on his feet.

As an adult, Oedipus seeks his fortune at an oracle, only to be told that he will kill his father and marry his mother. Horrified, he leaves home so as not to harm Polybus and Merope. On his way to Thebes, he meets an unpleasant older nobleman with several retainers, and a quarrel ensues. Oedipus kills the man in anger, beats off the retainer, and flees, not knowing that he has just murdered his biological father Laius. Further down the road, he is waylaid by the Sphinx, a woman-headed lion-bodied winged monster with a penchant for riddles. She asks Oedipus a riddle, making it clear that if he can't answer it, she will kill and eat him. This echoes Pluto's warning: "What do you know? If you don't know, you'll be in trouble, so you'd better find out. It's always better to know."

The famous riddle is "What goes on four legs in the morning, on two legs at noon, and on three legs in the evening?" Oedipus guesses the answer, which is Man—crawling on all fours as a baby, walking on two legs afterwards, and with a cane as an elder. He is apparently the first person to guess it, and the Sphinx flings herself to her death in rage and shame. The riddle foreshadows Oedipus's own end and hints at fourth-house tropes of childhood and the progression of growth and maturity. However, some alchemists later interpreted the Sphinx's riddle as referring to sacred geometry—the solar square of the four elements yielding to the two-line crescent of the Moon, which yields in turn to the triangle of Mercury. Alchemy is the magical science of transformation, using chemical changes to transmute inner and outer circumstances, turning spiritual lead into spiritual gold. One of its tenets is that stasis gets you nowhere, and that in complete change is your hope of heaven—a very Plutonian ideal.

Later scholars have seen the Sphinx as a symbol of the older pre-Olympian (and possibly pre-Indo-European) religion of the region, with its devouring half-animal matriarchal goddesses, and Oedipus as one of the transitional figures who puts down the old ways and institutes the worship of the Olympian Gods over all others. If this is the case, the Sphinx is an old reverberation of many ancient Plutonian goddesses like Ereshkigal (Pluto in

Libra), Lamia, and Kali (Pluto in Scorpio). In a way, the Sphinx warns Oedipus with her own death of the waste and devastation in meeting Plutonian failure and humiliation with Plutonian self-destructive overkill, but he ignores her. Pluto's initial whispers that something is not right with the family are usually ignored, sometimes even in the face of overwhelming evidence. For the moment, though, Oedipus goes on his way.

When he arrives in Thebes, he discovers that Creon, the brother of Jocasta, has announced that any man who can kill the vicious Sphinx will be made king of Thebes and will be given the recently-widowed Queen Jocasta as his wife. Oedipus finds himself unwittingly married to his own biological mother, and they have four children together—their sons Eteocles and Polynices, and their daughters Ismene and Antigone (Uranus in the fourth house). Decades later when Oedipus is an old man, a plague strikes the city and the oracle says that it is revenge against the killer of Laius, who must be made to suffer. Oedipus calls in the androgynous prophet Tiresias (Neptune in Aquarius), who advises him to leave the matter alone, Angered, Oedipus pressures Tiresias until the irritated prophet blurts out the truth.

This is the Plutonian moment when the outside circumstance hits the family interior, but at first Oedipus responds with anger and denial. He accuses both Tiresias and Creon of plotting against him and spreading lies. Jocasta intervenes at this point and tells him about her long-gone sacrificed son. Terrified, Oedipus summons the now-ancient servant who tells him about giving the child with the pierced feet to the Corinth-bound shepherd to be placed in a home. Oedipus sees his own guilt in the very marks on his flesh, and even in his own name. Although he tried to run away from it, his destiny managed to come true. Pluto tears the veil off of the family secrets and demands that everyone look at them.

At this point, we come back around to the arguments over our reactions to crisis moments, and whether those reactions are simply programmed by our genes, our culture, and our upbringing, or whether we have the power to reshape them and choose a different path. While the story up to this point is about the chain of outside circumstance leading inexorably to the shock of discovery, theoretically Oedipus has a choice about what he does next, even though every choice is ambivalent and difficult. Individuals born with Pluto in the fourth house face this choice over and over throughout their lives. Something horrible comes up that reminds them of the abuses of power they have witnessed in the past, but because this is Pluto, every instance is offered with a choice of responses. Will they deny and ignore it, or copy the abuse themselves? Will they run in terror, or will they mindfully seek a way out? There are many roads out of this one predestined point, but all too often only one is visible, especially when the intense Plutonian emotions—anger, pain, horror—are running high.

The first tragedy from the revelation is that Jocasta, realizing that her husband is her son and she has committed incest with him, goes to her room and hangs herself. Oedipus's story varies depending on the tale—in some versions, he continues to rule Thebes even after everything is known, and his sorrow over his wife's death relieves the plague. In another, he is attacked, blinded, and possibly killed by an old servant of Laius. However, in the most popular version—memorialized in Sophocles' play—he has a complete psychological meltdown. Taking a large brooch from the dead body of his wife/mother, he jabs out his own eyes and abdicates the kingship of Thebes. As a patricide and an incest-committer, he is now considered unclean by his culture, so Creon and Oedipus's two sons exile him from Thebes. He goes wandering on the road, a blind beggar with a staff.

This is definitely overkill, and it is a problem with Pluto in the house that contains the ghosts of the past. This isn't Saturn which freezes the individual in place, or Neptune which makes them helpless and passive in the face of those triggers. This is Pluto, and the response to pain of an immature Pluto can be to blow everything up so thoroughly that the mistake cannot be repeated, because there is nothing left to do it with. Like the Sphinx's rageful suicide in Oedipus's wake, he ruins himself and his life, spending the rest of it in an anguished attempt at self-immolation. He ceases to care about his citizens or his family, obsessed with his own incest-guilt.

Of course, Pluto is also the battle for self-control and self-will, and sometimes where one has Pluto, one has to find the road to controlling one's intense responses to the areas of life ruled by Pluto's sign and house through rather excessive means. It's Pluto's way of bringing you to the middle road by first forcing you into the extremes until you've had enough of them. The fourth-house Pluto person may have to experience extremes of emotion—burning and freezing—around the secrets of their past until they can harness their own power and hold the wild chariot-horses to a straight road.

Centuries after the tales of Oedipus were told, Sigmund Freud created the term "Oedipus complex" to describe young boys' fantasies of sex with their mother. His justification for using the story of an unwitting adult incest-marriage as a metaphor for adult-child sexual fantasies came from a single line in Sophocles' play, where a character refers to mother-son incest as something that any normal man might innocently dream about when young, but that one should not attach much importance to it. At the same time, he coined the phrase "Electra complex", based on an even less relevant myth about a daughter risking her life to bury her dead father's body, to describe women fantasizing about sex with their fathers. At the time, he was surprised at the numbers of his clients who talked about childhood experiences of sex with their parents. At first he actually took them seriously, but eventually so many of his clients reported memories of childhood sexual abuse that he shut his ears in denial. Such happenings could not be so frequent and commonplace in proper and upright Victorian Europe; the former children must simply be fantasizing, and all such memories must be dismissed as such. His writings encouraged the repression of such Plutonian secrets, and aided and abetted the continuation of fourth-house abuses of power. Finally, in the twentieth century, the truth of childhood sexual abuse exploded outward with the pent-up rage of centuries, and we are still dealing with the ongoing repercussions today.

As for Oedipus himself, in Sophocles' second play he is shown wandering from city to city with his daughter Antigone as his guide, seeking a place where he can lie down and die. An oracle of Apollo (Mercury in Leo) has given him yet another prophecy: that because of his terrible self-punishment and self-expiation, if he dies at any place sacred to the Furies—three terrible goddesses of vengeance—he will bring permanent good luck to that land. At this point, cities literally start competing to have him die on their property. Creon decides that Oedipus must be lured home to die, and sends the old man's daughter Ismene and his now-exiled son Polynices to convince him to come home. They find him at Colonnus, a village on the outskirts of Athens, in a grove sacred to the Furies where beggars are allowed to pitch their camps. Finding out that Eteocles and Polynices have gone to war with each other, he curses his sons for ruining their birthright and says that he will not go home.

Theseus, the king of Athens (Pluto in the eleventh house), comes out and promises that Oedipus can stay and die near the shrine at Colonnus. Oedipus speaks about how he has come to understand that he is not responsible for what happened to him, but that his expiation of guilt was necessary anyhow. The story ends with Oedipus being immolated in sacred flame by Zeus (Jupiter in Aries) as a sign of his forgiveness, and his ashes are buried in a secret place by Theseus. From a powerless figure, he has become someone so powerful that his choice of death-site can bring good luck to a city. It's a Plutonian twist, where dealing with darkness brings magical power, but only after the experience of giving it up. "To have is riches," goes the proverb, "but to be able to do without is power." Oedipus ends with only one family member standing by him, but it is the daughter who would not abandon him even in his uncleanness. To walk away entirely from the tangle that produced the pollution is sometimes the only road out for this placement—or, perhaps, to walk away and to see who follows you out, even in the face of a future of family loss that can feel, at the moment of walking out, like little more than the promise of a peaceful death.

All these dark threads weave themselves together into a cord that the fourth-house Pluto individual can use to pull themselves up out of the darkness, inch by inch. Burn and freeze, burn and freeze—like the smith forging metal, like the alchemist combining chemicals that bubble and solidify by turns, that sometimes release foul gases and sometimes even burst from their container, the path of this Pluto seeks to transform the lead of the past into the powerful gold of the future.

5♇ Pluto in the 5th House: Tlazolteotl

The planet Pluto is the place of purification, the cremation ground where everything is burned down and new growth can come from the ashes. That sounds good, but in reality no one likes it when Pluto stomps across some part of our chart, destroying and burning and generally rubbing our faces in everything we don't want to look at. People forget that before you can purify anything—especially parts of a human soul—you first need to acknowledge that there are substances which need to be removed. You need to look at where the contamination is, and how it got there, and what it's doing, before you can begin to face the hard task of scrubbing it out. It's a process that no one wants to go through, really. It can be humiliating and painful, and all our defense mechanisms assemble to prevent us from having to do that work. Fear. Pride. Ego. Righteousness. Rage. Did I mention fear? And these defense mechanisms are usually first on the hangman's list for Pluto, because they so often turn out to be part of the problem.

The Pluto process seems especially out of place in the fifth house of fun and games, romance and creativity, children and risk-taking. This is supposed to be the meadow of hearts and flowers, not a cremation ground ... and yet one-twelfth of the population will have the Destroyer in this place, and have to go through periodic burn-downs until Pluto is satisfied with the results. Fifth-house activities, by their very nature, tend to be areas we idealize and hold onto, and refuse to see where they are going sour. The dirt can creep up while we're hiding behind those rose-colored glasses, pretending that everything is fine and we have a perfectly healthy relationship with all of it. This is fertile ground for Pluto to get in there and show us what unhealthy really means—and, by process of elimination, healthy as well.

Tlazolteotl is one of the most discomfiting deities in the Aztec pantheon. White writers dismissed her as a goddess of lust, vice, and prostitutes, which misses the point of her unusual designations. Like all deities, she could be kind or cruel, depending on whether you were doing what she felt you ought to do. She had several functions: fertility, childbirth, adultery and forgiveness thereof, spinning and weaving cotton, protecting prostitutes, and of course her most important function, filth-eating. Her name itself basically means "garbage-goddess", and as such one of her symbols is compost—garbage which has rotted down and can now create fertility, which is one of her other gifts. She is the embodiment of the truth that nothing grows until something rots.

Let's start with her most uncomfortable aspect up front, as that's the way Pluto likes it. Tlazolteotl's secondary title was *Tlaelcuani*, which literally means "eater of filth". She shares with a small number of other Gods around the world the ability to rip the sin and negativity out of human souls and devour it. She was sometimes shown with black rubber face paint around her mouth, emphasizing that she can devour everything terrible, if we will only let her in and give it to her. Of course, having one's filth divinely removed means that we have to admit it's there—which we may be too embarrassed or fearful to do—and then be willing to let go of it. Often our unhealthy behaviors exist because they are (or were once) defense mechanisms, allowing us to survive in some way. This, along with the cement trap of habit, makes it hard to unclench our fist and let them go, even when they are hurting ourselves and our loved ones.

When it comes to the fifth house, we have plenty of unhealthy behavior to look at. Jealousy toward our lovers, grabbing for power over each other without consent, possessively controlling our children and other creations and being unwilling to let them pass into the world, taking foolish risks which can cause pain to others—we've all done them, and this placement of Pluto is especially prone to doing them with special intensity. This is the negative Pluto pattern, and it's all about wanting control which was not granted to you, because you fear letting go and having it all fall apart. Pluto lets the individual with this placement mess around in these mud puddles for some time, and then the jaws close in. Something happens which shows them the unhealthiness of these patterns, and they either learn or refuse to look—which means gearing up for another round. Eventually, things will get so bad that they will be forced to see it, and must transform or spend life as a very lonely failure.

It's important to have a healthy sense of power and worth, but that doesn't mean you must trespass on the rights of others. The hardest place to maintain those boundaries, without doubt, are your lovers and your children. Tlazolteotl seems to have a rather sideways view of social mores, based less on what is considered to be proper in any society and more on the basic truth underlying the situation ... which, again, is what Pluto likes. Adultery was held as a terrible evil in Aztec society, punishable by the death penalty. All sorts of folk customs were instituted to discover it—if rats broke in and chewed the sleeping mats, or the chickens all died and fell upside down, it was assumed that one of the adults had been unfaithful, and a community investigation would begin. When adultery happened, it was said that Tlazolteotl had caused it to happen, and that she would protect the adulterers from shame and legal action. It seems that she was a sort of divine objector to the strict sexual laws, and felt that they did more harm than good. Those who strayed outside of (especially arranged) marriages were following their instincts, and following one's heart was a purer thing to her than staying monogamous out of pure fear. Pluto is the planet of control, but control should be over one's self and not over a nonconsenting partner, and this is the first lesson for this Pluto placement.

Adultery itself is taking a risk, especially in a culture where the risk is death. The fifth house is the place of gambling, and understanding that all love, in the beginning, is a gamble. Risking one's self for love can be a great and noble act of authenticity and protest, or it can be a self-sabotaging or self-indulgent foolishness; Tlazoteotl, who was a patroness of gambling, asks us to look at it and figure out what is actually going on when all the pretty delusions are cleared away. Supposedly, if she didn't like your motivations for breaking the rules, she would smite you with sexually transmitted disease. Her yearly celebration included confessions to her priests where people knelt and told their sins, and were forgiven. It also included a great deal of cleaning of one's house and possessions, to clear away the invisible, energetic dirt so that new growth could come.

Tlazolteotl is also a goddess of fertility, to whom people prayed to bring them children, and of safe childbirth. One of her most famous statues is her sitting with her legs spread and face grimacing, giving birth. Children, being our creations (at least physically, and in many other ways as well), can also induce feelings of possessiveness and the urge to control everything about them. Even if this is done out of wanting to protect them, it still comes from a place of fear, and it is still unhealthy. Children belong to the future, says Tlazolteotl, demanding that we give up our overprotectiveness and allow them to be the individuals they are. She understands that the pain of childbirth is nothing to pain of letting them go after years of care, at least for this placement of Pluto, but the hands must be opened and they must leave.

On the other hand, the act of having children at all, with this placement, can be a life-changing decision which will reach out to affect everything else, and perhaps require that the life be started anew. This is true to some extent with every parent, but the reverberations here are further-reaching. The best outcome for children with this placement is the parent being a role model of self-control balanced by unflinching self-honesty.

Another area of the fifth house is creativity, and here Tlazolteotl is a goddess of spinning and weaving, especially the cotton which was a staple in the area. Creative projects often feel like children to many artists and artisans, and they may have the same possessiveness, suspicious about letting them out into the world where others can see them. This is especially the case as

Pluto's intense death-vibes can make the subject matter rather morbid or grotesque, or at least determined to expose the dark underbelly of life. Pluto would say that this is not a bad thing—human beings need to see and face their inner darkness—and Tlazolteotl the filth-eater would say the same.

Creative artists and musicians with this placement do find that the more they delve into and clean out their psyches, the more steadily their creative flow comes through. Some fifth-house Plutos have created amazing works based on the plumbing of their own inner selves, transforming inner "filth" into art. The reverse is true as well—the more they ignore or whitewash or deny their own darknesses, and the less they are willing to undergo the process of cleaning out their own internal dirt, the more blocked their creative impulses will be. In fact, for this placement, such blockages should be a warning signal that it's time to go down into the basement and have a hard look at yourself again.

The dark Aztec love goddess shows us Pluto's transformational power, using our nearest and dearest relationships as a burning ground to practice reshaping bad situations or motives or behaviors into positive ones. You can't transform these things until you have fully "digested" what they are about and where they came from, and you can't do that until you're willing to devour the situation with courage and brutal self-honesty … no matter how much it stinks. Your lovers and children will thank you for it, because otherwise that stink will be their problem. Real joy, after all, includes being able to shine light into every corner and find nothing to be ashamed of, and it's better to do a fifth-house scrub-down than a burn-down, any day.

6♀ Pluto in the 6ᵗʰ House: Nephthys

In the surviving mythology of ancient Egypt, a great deal of energy is expended on the stories of Isis (Moon in Libra), the "favorite goddess" of the later tales. Little is said of her younger sister Nephthys, or Nebet Het as she would have been called in the original land of Kemet (and how I shall refer to her occasionally throughout her essay). But Nebet Het was also an important goddess, even if we know less about her than we do about Isis, or Hathor (Venus in Taurus) or Bast (Moon in Leo). She has been referred to as Isis's darker sister, in the sense that Isis was bound up with daytime and the experience of being birthed into this physical world, while Nephthys is bound up with nightfall and being birthed into the next world, through Death. As such, she is a Death Goddess, and they generally carry the energy of either Saturn or Pluto, both associated with the transition at the end of life.

She and Isis often stood on either side of the flat-topped trapezoidal doorways to the temple courtyards, which symbolized the horizon line. Isis was the eastern horizon, where the Sun rose, and Nephthys was the western horizon of sunset. One of the prayers from the Pyramid Text reads: "Ascend and descend; descend with Nephthys, sink into darkness with the Night-Bark. Ascend and descend; ascend with Isis, rise with the Day-Bark." Prayers like these show that she was just as important as Isis in her own way, as the night in ancient Kemet was merciful, alleviating the relentless heat of the daytime. She was said to bestow the gift of "seeing that which is hidden by moonlight"—perceiving faint clues in the darkness by psychic means, or intuitively noting the less obvious "daylight" wisdom.

Isis and Nephthys are actually two of a reaper-goddess-foursome, which also includes Neith (Mars in the eighth house) and Selket (Sun in the eighth house). Each gathers in the dying souls of a particular stratum of society. Isis's bailiwick is that of the nobility—the royal pharaohs and their wealthy courtiers and administrators and priests, the sort of people who left tombs full of gold and jewelry and priceless artifacts. Nebet Het, on the other hand, was the Death who reached out her hand to the working classes, the hundreds of thousands of peasants who chiseled out stone for those tombs, painted their insides, crafted the treasures they could never afford to keep for themselves, ploughed and irrigated the fields, baked bread and milked cows and fished in the Nile, and generally kept the entire society of Kemet moving and maintained.

It's a myth that the great pyramids and temples and tombs were built by teeming hordes of slave. They were built by average workmen during the flood season when they could not work their fields, and wanted to make a bit of income, or pay their taxes in labor instead of barley. Their wives and children accompanied them, and did smaller jobs while maintaining their camps. We have scribal writings from the period recounting how, when their promised bread and beer did not arrive, the thousands of workers downed tools and went on the earliest recorded labor strike in history, much to the chagrin of their wealthy masters. These were the people who knew that Nebet Het would welcome them to the peace of the afterlife with her gentle hands, and thought no less of them for their comparative poverty and work-roughened hands. She was the Death who advocated, in the next world, for those who performed hard labor, and as such she is a Death Goddess whose story lives in the sixth house of labor itself.

When the planet of intensity finds itself in the house of Work and Service and Health, all these areas of life become intensely important to the individual with this placement. The sixth house is traditionally ruled by Virgo, the sign of perfectionism, and that quality may invade their preoccupation with sixth-house areas. They may work themselves half to death doing the perfect job or serving in the best possible way, although ironically the quality which is most likely to keep them from actually ruining themselves might be a similar obsession with perfecting their health. Nephthys, intensely focused on the working man, understands the importance of labor, and especially the often-invisible labor of all the humble hands who make the people at the top look good and function smoothly. One of her epithets is "The Useful Goddess", which sums up the goal of individuals with this placement: They want to be supremely useful in their work and their lives. To be called "useless" is the greatest shame of all to them.

Nebet Het's name technically means "Lady of the House", but that translation is misleading as the term "house" here has a double meaning. It refers both to the house in the middle of an enclosing courtyard, or the temple in the center of a similar courtyard. Nebet Het is both "Lady of the House" in the sense of the working woman who cooks and cleans and maintains the family, and "Mistress of the Temple" who serves in the temple—again, cleaning and maintaining and supporting the ritual work of the priests. In the House of Service, Nephthys looks out for those who serve, both in mundane and in sacred work.

In the tale of the Ennead, Nephthys is the fourth of Ra's grandchildren, and is married off to her brother Set (Pluto in the eighth house); their child is Anubis, the jackal-headed psychopomp who guides lost souls to the Underworld (Uranus in Scorpio). In a sense this trio—warlike Set, reaper Nephthys, and psychopomp Anubis—are the darker (as in death-oriented as opposed to life-oriented) version of the trio of Osiris (Pluto in Taurus), Isis (Moon in Libra), and Horus (Mercury in Aries). When Set kills his brother Osiris, Nephthys has a hard choice to make—to continue on in loyalty to him, or to leave him and follow her wronged sister. She chooses to leave Set, at least until he is thrown down by his nephew Horus and must work to redeem himself by being the after-dark bodyguard of Ra (Sun in Aries). We don't have writings about what happened to their marriage after this, but we do know that all the temples of Set, even in the days of his demonization, were accompanied by temples to Nebet Het right next door. Neither do we have writings about how the Egyptians of that era reconciled Nephthys's place in both Set's temple complexes and those of Osiris and Isis, but apparently they understood that the nature of deity was not always to take things in a straight line and obey human laws of timing and linearity.

Applying this to the human perspective however: The individual with Pluto in the house of service will always want to serve, down to the bottom of their soul. However, they may be extremely choosy about who, and under what circumstances, they are willing to serve—and this is not a bad thing. Pluto in the house of finding perfection holds those they serve to a high standard, as well as balancing their place in the hierarchy of need. In order to feel comfortable serving, they must see the person or group or project move in a positive direction according to their own high standards, and they must feel like contributing to this person or group or project's progress is the best place for their competence and effort. If one or the other of these goes sour, they can make it work for a while … but if both go down, they will walk away. Because Pluto is also the planet of "burn it all down and start over", when they decide that this is a lost cause, their defection can be sudden and implacable.

Nephthys decides that serving as Set's wife, once he has murdered his brother, does not live up to her standards. At the same time, her sister Isis is not only the wronged party, with the higher moral ground, but is also in greater need—she is widowed, and eventually has a small child to care for. The sister wins on both counts, at least until Set shows her that he has changed enough to meet her standards again (and perhaps, one wonders, if his campaign to redeem himself needs her support). Nephthys is shown helping Isis assemble her husband's corpse in preparation for temporary reanimation, and then wet-nursing the infant Horus.

This is another way in which she serves, and it also reflects the Virgo-ruled nature of this house. Nebet Het is actually a mother in her own right—of Anubis—but she offers to be Horus's wet-nurse. In ancient Kemet, a woman of wealth and high standing would hire another woman to take on the task of nursing the baby for her, and often to be its "nanny" to some extent, at least while the child was young. Pharaohs were often shown seated in the lap of either Isis or Nephthys, and both were addressed by them as "Mother". However, Isis was considered the Pharaoh's spiritual mother, and Nephthys was considered the spiritual wet-nurse. On a ritual level, Isis gave birth to them, and Nephthys changes the diapers, so to speak. Like the Virgo Moon which is more often the archetype of the stepmother than the birth mother, Nephthys serves by taking on the role of surrogate nurturer. It's a working woman's role rather than that of a woman of privilege, and she sees no shame in that. It's also one step away from the Cancerian/Lunar mysteries of giving birth, and is closer to the Virgo role of caretaking as a job.

As Set was moved from being a deity of storm and rain to being a god of the infertile and hostile Red Desert, so Nephthys became the one who symbolized the edge of the desert, which was sometimes made fertile with particularly good flooding or irrigation. These areas were generally home to poorer people who had to work harder to eke a living out of the semi-fertile areas; Nephthys, who knows what it is to work hard and beautify the unbeautiful, blessed them all. As the one who beautifies the unbeautiful and makes the useless useful again, she reflects her husband Set's quality of being able, with great effort, to redeem the unredeemable. She is also the Mother who doesn't quite fit into the lush, fertile, lunar tides of emotional motherhood. She is the Mother who works for a living, to eke out the support of her children (or stepchildren) and considers that to be gift enough.

Speaking of jobs—it's said that individuals with this placement are drawn to work at jobs which are bound up in some way with Death, and especially with the grubby details of death which no one else wants to deal with. I knew one person with this placement who picked roadkill off the rural highways for the state police, and another who worked in hospice. Pluto placements are always drawn to the dark side, but in the sixth house, after you're finished being fascinated, you are compelled to ask, "How can I help with this mess?" As for Nebet Het herself, another of her epithets was "Queen of the Embalmer's Shop", and "Nebet-Het of the Bed of Life", the latter referring to the embalmer's table where bodies were prepared for their next life. Not many deities are specifically the patrons of undertakers, but it is a beautiful conjunction of Plutonian and sixth-house energies.

This is also the House of Health, and the title of Nephthys which seems the most appropriate here is "Lady of the Winnowing Basket". Isis was a mistress of magical fertility, making the grain spring forth; Nephthys was the process of weeding out, of separating the grain from the chaff. She is spoken of as a healer, along with her sister, but while Isis's powers were to give good health, Nephthys's were to show where poor habits needed to be cast off in order to maintain that health. It's not uncommon for sixth-house Pluto people to throw themselves into rigorous health routines and disciplines, periodically paring down their indulgences in order to find the magic key to that health-maintenance. (Of course, because this is Pluto, the planet of All or Nothing, they may also swing back and overindulge, and so the cycle begins again.) Nephthys's wisdom is that of the common man's common sense—if it doesn't serve you or the future, maybe you should drop it?

Finally, her last title was Protector of the Bennu Bird—the magical bird on whom the Greek legend of the dying-and-reborn Phoenix was based. She was the caretaker and guardian of this uniquely Plutonian symbol, and this too is linked to her wisdom as Lady of the Winnowing Basket. It's work to keep sweeping that floor, cleaning that pot, winnowing that chaff, polishing that soul ... but it is work that supports the eventual regeneration of all Life.

7♀ Pluto in the 7th House: Circe

When Pluto, the planet of power struggle, intensity, and transformation finds itself in the house of relationships, neither the planet nor the individuals afflicted with it are going to be comfortable. In fact, comfort is something Pluto scorns. If a situation has become comfortable, it must mean that something has gone wrong inside it, and it must be immediately and ruthlessly dissected to show the inevitable rot at the core ... and, hopefully, excise it. If there's nothing to find and excise, then perhaps the whole structure is wrong somehow and must be transformed, by force if necessary. If this Plutonian way of looking at the world makes you the opposite of comfortable just thinking of it in general, think of what it's like to have that worldview ruling your relationships.

One of the great femme fatales of mythology, the sorceress Circe (originally spelled, and correctly pronounced, *Kirke*) first appears in Homer's *Odyssey*, and then makes the occasional cameo in other Greek and Roman writings, at least as a reference. Most sources have her as the daughter of the sun god Helios and a nymph named Perse, who was supposedly renowned as a healer. Odysseus (Mercury in the ninth house) called her a "great and cunning goddess", and like many divine children it is unclear if she is goddess or mortal, or if it matters. Like all children of Helios, she was said to have golden eyes which could shoot out rays of light, and fiery hair. Her mother had taught her the arts of using herbs and making healing potions ... but she turned that art to making magical philters which could do all manner of good and evil sorceries. She wielded a magic wand or staff whose power was to transform one thing into another. Her magical powers became famed in many lands, but her reputation was mixed and rather frightening.

Wherever she had been raised, at one point she decided to make her home on the island of Aeaea—whose very name sounds like a wail of torment—because she had seen it one day while riding in her father's golden chariot with him across the sky. He obligingly moved her and all her sorcerous belongings to the small island via that same golden chariot, and she made it her own. When people came to her island on their boats and ships, she judged them harshly to see if they were good and honorable, and if they did not pass, they paid a terrible price. The seventh-house Pluto judges prospective partners according to high and rather arbitrary standards which perhaps they do not live up to themselves, and if they fail—sometimes even by being human—they will be cast aside.

When Odysseus and his ship of lost Achaian warriors washed up on shore, they found Circe in a large house with a stone wall all around it. Wolves and lions lolled about outside, but when the contingent of men sent to scout the territory approached the beasts, they were friendly and rubbed against them like great cats and dogs, for Circe had entirely tamed them with her magic. They knocked timidly on her door, as they had already seen many of their comrades killed in previous adventures. Inside, Circe was weaving on a loom, making a tapestry so beautiful and full of so many colors that only one with divine powers could have created it.

She welcomed them cheerfully and bade them come inside and eat; the men were relieved and entered, except for their captain who stayed outside in suspicion. Circe sat them down and gave them food, and offered them all the drink they could stomach. In no time they were thoroughly drunk and became rowdy and offensive ... and then, after the usual vomiting, passed out around the table. While they slept, Circe turned every one of them into pigs—a blunt commentary on their behavior. The captain saw her driving the pigs into a pen and throwing them some acorns to eat, and returned to Odysseus to tell his tale in horror.

This is not the first time Circe had done such a thing. In other stories which mention her, she turns an Italian named Picus into a woodpecker for rejecting her advances. In another story, she fell in love with the sea demigod Glaucus, but he left her for the naiad Scylla. In a jealous rage, Circe found the inlet where Scylla bathed and poured a magical potion into it. When her rival immersed herself, she transformed into a monster—huge, wild, and toothed, with a long serpentine tail instead of legs, and three to six partial dog-bodies extruding from where her thighs would be. She also had a terrible appetite for human flesh. Horrified at her own body, Scylla went mad and lived by the narrow strait across from the whirlpool Charybdis, snatching sailors out of passing boats and devouring them.

This is not to say that every individual with a seventh-house Pluto is necessarily this rabidly jealous, but jealousy is a very common problem for them. As Pluto is the planet of—among other things—power and control, individuals with this placement tend to be suspicious and untrusting of partners unless they feel they are in control of the situation, and jealousy is a common response to feeling out of control in your relationship. It can be fear of abandonment, or anger from the insult of rejection, or vengeance for "stealing" a lover whom they saw as their possession, or betrayal from a partner they were hoping was more perfectly faithful. Mature seventh-house Plutos don't act on these feelings, and can use logic to talk themselves through them, but those emotions (or similar ones) have certainly banged around in their heads and tempted them to evil.

What this Pluto placement wants is emotional intensity in relationships. Easy, relaxed, complacent unions just stir up their paranoia. What they may not know that they want is for the partner to open up for them to the very core, to show themselves in all their pain and glory, and to be able to do that themselves as well, and be seen and loved. That soul-deep connection of pure honesty with no secrets is their (probably) unconscious desire, although they may never have seen a model of it and thus have no idea of how to go about obtaining it. Instead, they may semi-consciously attempt any number of destructive methods which usually just cause more damage, and further hurt their trust that such a union can ever be achieved. Obsession with a lover is another common seventh-house Pluto trap; one woman with this placement admitted to me that she would chase the object of her desire obsessively until they gave in, and then turned cold. She'd recently figured out that it wasn't Uranus or Mercury who just get bored and lose interest; in her case what she really wanted was for them to turn around and chase her with the same obsessiveness, showing her that they could respond with the same level of intensity. Merely holding out a hesitant hand wasn't nearly good enough … and, of course, she was often disappointed.

Like Circe, people with this placement are often magnetically attractive, perhaps even with a whiff of exciting danger about them. Also like Circe, being around the emotional cycles of an immature seventh-house Pluto can drive someone to beastly behavior, which the Pluto person's paranoia will cynically see as them being unworthy, and thus deserving of less than fair behavior. *After all, if I could make you act like that, you're less powerful than me, and I'm the one in control.* In addition, since this is the House of Projections, they may well project all these Plutonian thoughts and actions onto the partner, allowing themselves to smugly justify everything.

Odysseus decides he must get back his men, and starts on his way across the island. Partway there, he finds Hermes (Mercury in Gemini) lounging against a tree, appropriate for this exceptionally Mercurial hero. Hermes first taunts him, then relents and says he will protect him from Circe's sorceries. He gives him a magical herb called *Moly* which only the Gods can pick, a guard against all magics aimed at oneself. He also tells Odysseus that if he threatens Circe with his sword, she will want to bed him, and advises him to take advantage of the situation and do it.

The hero goes ahead and follows Hermes's advice. Circe gives him a goblet of wine, but the *Moly* in his tunic prevents the potion from working. She strikes him with her wand in order to transform him, but when it doesn't work, he leaps up and presses his sword to her throat, demanding that she release his men from her spell. Circe then changes her tune entirely, telling him that Hermes once told her that a hero would come who was not affected by her spells, and that she should give herself to him for one year. He orders her to take a solemn oath not to harm him or his men again, and to set them free, both of which she does. Then he stays with her for a full year as her lover and sires two children upon her. When he decides to attempt to sail home a year later, she gives him a great deal of useful advice on how to get past the various magical traps in the ocean.

All this can be tossed off as a conquering-hero story with the otherwise assertive heroine suddenly falling for the man with the sword and becoming uncharacteristically submissive, and perhaps it is exactly that, but from an astrological perspective it cannot be denied that power is an aphrodisiac for those with this Pluto placement. Some find very sexy the concept of an unequal relationship where they are in charge or someone is in charge of them. Some simply want a partner who is as powerful as they are, or more so, even if the relationship is quite egalitarian. Some are projecting power onto the partner because they have yet to own the Pluto nature in themselves. The reasons vary, but it all comes down to the hope for someone who can match them in intensity.

The mature way for a seventh-house Pluto to approach a relationship is to accept the fact that this will bring up all their issues around human interaction, and the partnership needs to be looked at as a tool to work out those problems ... ideally without harming the partner in the process. This does require a generous amount of honesty and patience on both sides, and not everyone is up to using their relationship as a tool of mutual personal transformation, but that's Pluto's ultimate goal in this house of balance and cooperation. Becoming someone who sees all the traps and knows better than to fall into them, who can give and receive wholly without holding back, and who can compassionately keep their loved one's feelings in mind will require a great deal of painful emotional resculpting.

Before Odysseus sails away, Circe gives him one last gift. She tells him that before he attempts to get home, he must consult the shades of the Dead to find out what is going on with his wife and child, his Achaean comrades, and the deities who are angry with him. This will require him to visit the Underworld, but not get trapped there among the ghosts. She tutors him in the dangers of the Deathrealm and the rituals needed to get safely in and out. This Pluto placement can, if they have learned their own lessons, help others to get in and out of their own underworlds with fresh information on their loved ones and relationships. This can include helping their own partners, if they are willing to share the road and the pitfalls. It takes someone who has been to the darkness and back to find the light to guide others out, even—and perhaps especially—in matters of the heart.

8♇ Pluto in the 8th House: Set

Classic Egyptian mythology tends to focus on the saga of Ra (Sun in Aries) and his two children and grandchildren, and five great-grandchildren, and their various adventures. This religious grouping was referred to as the Ennead in later Roman writings, meaning "group of nine", and it dates from the fifth dynasty in Awanu (which the Greeks knew as Heliopolis). In this story, the god Set was the villain, the evil killer. We forget that centuries before, Set was an honored deity. We forget, also, that human politics sometimes rewrites religious stories to suit their purposes.

Originally, Set (or Sutekh) was the tutelary deity of Upper Kemet (the Egyptians' actual name for their land), which refers to southern area of the Nile Valley. Lower Kemet got its name because it was a flat, rainless desert which eased into the Mediterranean delta, but Upper Kemet had hills and some mountains, was less of a pure desert, and actually had some rainfall. Set started out as a god of storms, which were entirely unknown in Lower Kemet; his rains brought much-needed water to the region, and started the flooding which would continue down the entire Nile.

Set's associated animal is a strange creature which has been much argued about—it might be a desert aardvark, a gazelle, a wild dog, a fennec fox, a donkey, a conglomerate creature, or an extinct one. What must have been obvious in the realm of ancient Kemet has now become a mystery, not inappropriate for a story taking place in the House of Mysteries.

When Pluto, the planet of intensity and power struggle, is in its own house of death and mystery, its Plutonian characteristics become even stronger, for better or for worse. In the case of Set's story, it starts out with power struggle in the form of competition, and then gets stranger and unhealthier. First, Set and Horus the Elder—the tutelary hawk-god of Lower Egypt (Mercury in Aries)—are shown binding together the two Nile countries into a single nation. However, they must then compete to see which one will be the primary deity of the entire Nile valley, a competition organized by and judged by Ra. This story definitely feels like echoes of an millennia-old religious power struggle—whose popular deity was going to be the mascot? Horus wins, although both Gods try all sorts of underhanded magical ways to sabotage each other.

Set is relegated to representing the barren desert, ironic for the God who was originally the rain-giver. (One of his later titles is "Lord of the Oasis Town".) He was then said to have had reddish hair, which showed not a Caucasian origin but was instead seen as the color of a donkey's hide, and the color of the barren red desert as opposed to the black, fertile Nile. However, the main rulership of Kemet had now moved to Lower Kemet, and those who had never known rain would not value or worship a storm deity.

The problem was made historically worse by Kemet's invasion and conquering by the Hyksos, people from Asia Minor who came from a country with storms, and decided that Set was the same as their own main deity, a storm-god. From this period, Set gained the epithet "Lord of Foreigners", which did not help his reputation when the Hyksos were overthrown and driven out. In spite of the fact that several Pharaohs revered Set and named themselves after him, his reputation continued to decline until the Greeks, conquering the Egyptian Empire in its very late stages and writing down versions of their myths, identified Set with Typhon, a nasty demonic figure from their own mythology. This alienation from his own people echoes the eighth-house Pluto individual, whose natural tendency to be aloof and introverted about their ambitions—playing their cards close to their chest—can make them feel like they don't belong to the masses of "happy people" who find it easy to be open about their personal thoughts and feelings.

In the Lower-Kemet Ennead story, Set becomes the enemy and the murderer. The eighth is the house of death, although it is concerned with much more than just the eventual hour of our physical demise. With intense Pluto here, the individual may be prone to hidden, seething rage when they are thwarted, and may be tempted to coldly manipulate situations in order to gain what they see as necessary power. There are many ways to deal little deaths and endings to others, and until Pluto matures, these are all whispering temptations surrounding every perceived failure. The Ennead rewrites the family story to cast Osiris (Pluto in Taurus), Isis (Moon in Libra), Set, Nephthys (Pluto in the sixth house), and Horus the Elder as the five great-grandchildren of Ra. Osiris and Set marry their slightly younger sisters (giving rise to the genetically disastrous Pharaonic practice of kings marrying their sisters), and Osiris, as the eldest, is given the kingship. Set is envious and considers this unfair, and so attempts to murder his brother.

Set gathers seventy-two accomplices, and inducts the local Queen of Ethiopia into his plan, commissioning her to make a lovely carved coffin made to fit Osiris's body. (In Egypt, because of the huge emphasis put on funerary rites, people often had their coffins made while they were still alive, and showed them off as works of art and beautiful pieces of furniture.) Osiris laid down in the box to see if it fit him, and Set's accomplices rushed up and nailed the cover on, sealing the box with lead, and threw it in the Nile. His wife Isis managed to find his body and temporarily resurrect it, but Set tracked the body down, cut it into fourteen pieces, and scattered them all across the land. One piece was eaten by a fish, so his brother could not be resurrected again. Set takes the throne, but lost his wife Nephthys, who abandoned him in horror to aid her widowed sister and fatherless nephew.

It is interesting that the eighth is actually the house of resurrection, and Set's increasingly desperate attempts to keep his brother from being resurrected seem to lay bare his own fear of the process. Pluto is the planet of transformation and rebirth, and when it is in the traditionally-Pluto-ruled house, there is a double likelihood that the individual will be faced with a Plutonian destruction of all they are, and a rebirth or rebuilding into a new person. Feeling the shadow of that process coming down the path can make someone fairly paranoid, and while they are still unevolved, they can strike out at those who seem to have mastered or even lived through this change. It's too frightening to face down, until the Universe arranges for it to happen to them personally. Set's response was a frantic attempt at control over the act and time of Osiris's death, and in turn Death itself.

Anyhow, Isis raises her son Horus (named after his uncle) to be his father's avenger, and when he is old enough, Set is faced with a battle with yet another Horus. He loses and is cast down, and one would think he has simply become yet another "villain" defeated by the "hero". However, the story does not end there. After Set is deposed, Ra—who had favored him in the original Set/Horus competition, and thus must have seen his positive qualities—gives him the job of nighttime bodyguard. Ra must travel through the Underworld in his Boat of Millions of Years every night, reaching the eastern horizon at dawn, but the Underworld had become full of terrible creatures who continually attacked Ra's boat. The chief of these was a terrible serpent named Apep, who was determined to eat the Sun. Ra asked

Set to defend his sacred boat, because—as he points out—Set is the only one strong enough to do the job.

If Set is an ambivalent figure cast as the bogeyman, Apep is a much more specifically evil figure. Its gaze was said to hypnotize Ra into inaction, which left him vulnerable, but Set is unmoved by the serpent's gaze. When the eighth-house Pluto individual stops seeking grimly for external power at any cost, and instead dedicates themselves to achieving internal power with that same intensity, Pluto can then get behind them and push them forward. Pluto says: *Far more important than controlling others is controlling yourself. Far more important than protecting yourself from the hard realities of the world is transforming yourself at will into someone who cannot be harmed by them. The way to control fear is not to attempt to control what is frightening, but to become someone who is not afraid of them.*

Everyone with Pluto has to face this down eventually, perhaps during a Pluto transit, but the individual with this placement must face it again and again as one of the main themes of their life. The secret goal, of course, is that there is huge emotional liberation in becoming the person who has control over themselves and their inner processes, and is free of the insecurities that beset them. One could almost hear the voices in Set's mind during his earlier story: *People love my brother more than me; does that make me lesser? Perhaps if I eliminate him, they might love me instead? He and his wife have more power than me; I am helpless in comparison! If I take their power, I will no longer be helpless. He keeps coming back to life—how can I fight that except with more killing? His wife was loyal, and mine abandoned me; does she not see that I am more lovable now that I am more powerful?* However, now his job is to travel into the Underworld every night and fight real destruction, something too great to be killed which can only be fended off again and again. Set understands smooth deception, with the teeth of destruction behind it. He has walked that path until its bitter, ugly end; Apep's hypnosis does not fool him.

The process of transforming and rebirthing oneself is not fast or easy; in fact, it's painful and seems to go on forever, until you finally come out the other side. The eighth-house Pluto process requires bringing up every unpleasant part of you and reworking it, fending off that serpent of destruction again and again—every night—until it loses its power over you and becomes power within you. Set's story begins with joining and the birth of a new nation, but then moves into killing, and people with this placement cannot help but have some kind of an intense relationship with Death. Some are fascinated by it, some are terrified (at least until Pluto comes for them), but the journey into darkness to see what it contains and master it is a necessary eighth-house road.

It is also important that Set cannot make this journey until his race to become the one in power is over and Ra extends his hand. As the house of other people's resources, the turning point where Pluto goes from seizing external power to pursuing inner power sometimes needs the aid and wisdom of others. Doing it all on your own is very seductive to aloof, introverted Pluto, but learning to be interdependent with those you respect is part of the process.

This is also the house of sex and deep bonding, and it is no accident that Set's bad behavior loses his wife. We have no writings about whether they came back together after Set had been thrown down and took on the work of redemption on the Boat of a Million Years, but we can only hope it might be the case. We do know that Nephthys continued to have temples built to her next to Set temples, even in the days after Set was demonized and his temples became fewer. However, in the human realm, wanting control over one's sexual partners is a common side effect of this placement; this is a desire which, if handled poorly and unempathetically, can go very badly for everyone involved. This is especially true if the Pluto individual has not yet gained control over their inner self, and uses control over their loved ones as a way to divert attention from that fact, or attain environmental control in the face of inner chaos. Eventually they may learn that the best relationship for them is with someone who is not afraid of transformation, and can show them how a relationship can transform both people involved.

As a "demonized" deity, Set has been commandeered and worshiped by many "adversary" religions, such as Satanism or chaos-focused ceremonial magick, but few of those practices emphasize the redemption of a deity of strength and power redeeming themselves and learning inner control by becoming a protector through the Underworld. This, however, is the ultimate lesson of the planet of power in the house of the Mysteries: not only learning the depths of the darkest places, but protecting those who also walk down into that darkness.

9♀ Pluto in the 10th House: Etain

The ninth is the house of World View, our basic philosophy of life, and to have the planet of destruction here means that the entire view of life will be influenced by the disasters that strike, taking the ground out from under you and transforming everything ... for better or worse. If the individual with this placement cannot see the "better" part, then every upheaval will be conceived of as "worse", and fatalism will ensue. To have one's world view shaped by constant transformation and still remain steady in one's faith in the essential sacredness of the Universe is the goal of this Pluto placement.

We illustrate this upheaval with the old Irish story of Etain (pronounced *Ay-deen*), whose tale ranges over a thousand years. We know that she was born a stunningly beautiful daughter of the Tuatha de Danaan, the sacred children of Danu. Who her parents were vary from tale to tale, but the version that rings the most true for this telling is that she was the daughter of Diancecht the healer, and sister to Miach and Airmid (all of whom are Mercury in the sixth house). Midir, a prince of the Tuatha de Danaan sees Etain and falls in love with her, although he is already married to a Tuatha sorceress named Fuamnach. He takes Etain as a second wife and promptly begins attending to her and ignoring his first wife, at which point Fuamnach flies into a rage and hurls a series of spells at Etain. First she transforms Etain into a pool of water, but the water glows like the sun, so Fuamnach then transforms her into a worm, which begins to become a butterfly. Finally Fuamnach transforms her into a fly, or a flying beetle of some sort, but the fly is jeweled and glitters like a treasure. The transformed Etain flies straight to Midir, who is enchanted by the lovely thing and lets it settle on his shoulder. He does not know that the fly is his wife, but he loves it and carries it with him everywhere ... and his interest in Fuamnach remains quite low.

Furious, Fuamnach sends a great wind to blow the fly away, and to follow and torment Etain for seven years, only allowing her to alight on the rocks of the ocean shore so that she cannot move inland. At one point, Aengus mac Og, the god of love and summer and poetic inspiration, comes down to the ocean and Etain alights on his sleeve. He recognizes her, but cannot figure out how to free her from the spell, and as his family is currently at war with Midir, he chooses not to return her. However, he does bring her home and keep her in a tiny chamber with open windows so that she can come and go at will, either hanging in his sheltered garden or carried with him for safety. This goes on for several hundred years, but Fuamnach eventually finds out about Etain and sends another wind which blows her away, preventing her from alighting anywhere for another seven years.

The Etain-fly accidentally falls into a glass of wine and is swallowed by a mortal woman, who becomes pregnant immediately afterwards. She bears a daughter who looks very much like Etain; by this time it has been almost a thousand years since she was taken away from her husband. The girl grows up to be exquisite-looking, and is claimed in marriage by Eochaid the High King.

At this point we'll pause for a moment and look at the story thus far. It isn't over, but it does provide a blueprint for how this placement manifests in the world. The force which attacks Etain and makes her change is Fuamnach; while the sorceress's motives of jealousy, possessiveness, rage, and loss are unfortunate, they are also very Plutonian—the shadow side of Pluto. The ninth-house Pluto may find themselves, sooner or later, up against Pluto's shadow side, embodied in others or in their own internal attitudes.

As for Etain, we must remember that the Tuatha are a near-immortal magical people, tied to the elements and living in enchanted mounds under the earth. They live in a world of music, beauty, and sorcerous artistry, and do not have to endure most of the problems and misfortunes of mortals. The Plutonian force smashes her innocence, her assumption that she will live as a pampered queen in a realm of magic, and thrusts her into a millennium of tumult. Even in Aengus's garden, she is not safe, and her view of the world has been radically changed by her forced travels. In the house of both world view and travel, one of the driving forces of the ninth-house Pluto is the quest to find meaning in everything, including misfortune. If Etain cannot do this, she will not survive.

Sometimes this urge goes sideways, of course. In the house of religion, Pluto may be intolerant and fanatical, with a vengeful Plutonian version of the divine in their heads and a mistaken mandate to carry out that projected deity's will. In the house of higher education, they may be drawn to rigid and dogmatic ideas about any area of study. In the house of foreign cultures, they may idealize or demonize foreign customs or peoples, ignoring that they, too, are just ordinary human beings doing the best they can. On the other hand, when a more positive manifestation occurs, religion can be a purifying source which drives the convert to question themselves on a deep level. The adult education may bring them to a challenging teacher who pushes them in the same direction; and traveling to other places in the world can teach them a great deal about themselves.

At each transformation, Etain manages to make something more lovely out of her misfortune. The pool of water glows like the sun; the worm becomes a butterfly; the fly is jeweled and beautiful and makes men want to keep it for a companion. Pluto's gift is not just to transform a steady situation into a violent upheaval, it also holds the ability to transform the upheaval, by force of will acting on one's attitude, into something better ... usually a learning experience. This does not come easily, but Pluto's search for meaning can take them there, if they will allow it into their minds. At the end of this time of tumult, Etain is literally born again into a different life—the ultimate Plutonian transformation. Her soul may still be Tuatha de Danaan, but she has endured enough that she is a different kind of Tuatha, and one who can come to a mortal life with understanding and compassion.

Returning to Etain's convoluted story, the new Queen of Tara settles with reasonable contentment into her married life, including bearing a daughter to her husband who is named after her. But something is missing, although she does not know what it is. In her dreams, she contacts a strange man who reaches for her, but then fades away. Then Eochaid's brother Ailill reveals that he is madly in love with her, and begs to see her alone. She goes to the meeting place and meets with a man who looks like Ailill, but she senses that it is someone else wearing Ailill's face. He does not touch her, but speaks of his love for her in strange terms. The next day, she speaks to Ailill only to find that he has forgotten all about his supposed love for her. Etain realizes that something very strange, and probably spirit-touched, has happened.

What has actually passed is that Midir has found her, even though she has been reborn a thousand years after her disappearance. He approaches her a second time and tells her of who she used to be, and of their love, and promises that if she will come back to him, he will make her immortal again. She flees him, not ready to face the reality of her more-than-human past. After a few days, though, her memories begin to come back and she meets with Midir again. Etain finds herself caught in a difficult moral dilemma, as she now remembers her love for Midir, but she has given her hand and her word to the mortal Eochaid. She tells Midir that she can only go with him if Eochaid gives her permission.

The Tuatha, being of the faery sort, are just as tricksy as their relatives the Sidhe or the Alfar, and Midir decides to win Eochaid's permission by subterfuge. He goes to Eochaid's hall disguised as a wizard from far away, and offers to play chess with him, with the loser giving rich gifts to the winner. Midir deliberately loses to Eochaid multiple times, and pays by using his magic for the good of the land of Tara; he reclaims fields, cleared forests, and built causeways across bogs. Eochaid figures out that Midir is a being of great power, and keeps setting him greater tasks, perhaps hoping that he will get tired and go away. The final gamble is that Midir may have an embrace and a kiss from Eochaid's wife. Midir wins that round, and when he puts his arms around Etain the two of them turn into swans and fly away together.

It's often said that the road of Life eventually brings us back to the place where we started—if not literally, than in some other way, such as coming around to our early experiences and deconstructing them mentally, once we have the distance to do so. The point, though, is that we come back to them as different people, and our choices are changed. Much as she loves Midir, Etain stands by the principles she has learned in her human life and the torturous years before it. She demands that he do right by her husband in some way, and will not budge in the face of his seductive wooing. She has been transformed, and Midir too must transform in order to be worthy of her. For at least a time, he becomes a force for good in the mortal world. Then, when he has earned her back, the two of them can fly away together. If the turmoil does not lead to a wider meaning and a longer view—the gifts of the ninth house—then the homecoming cannot be achieved.

Some scholars have attempted to trace Etain back to being a Sun goddess, or a Moon goddess, or a sea goddess, or a horse goddess, or a fairy, before she was swept up into euhemerized stories. In modern-day American Paganism, interest in the old stories has resurfaced, and some of the gods have grown and shifted, becoming more than they had been. Some Pagans honor Etain as a goddess or demigoddess of transformation and rebirth, helping us to see how the tumultuous changes forced on us can be ridden out, and with faith, can end as positive experiences. Etain's story brings her fully around to where she started, but as a different person who can see the starting point with new eyes, and begin a different cycle. It is a Plutonian lesson whose happy ending is less about the circumstances and more about the internal attitude, which is the goal for the house of Wide Understanding.

10♀ Pluto in the 10th House: Yama

The tenth house is not only the House of Career, it is the Place of Authority. If you want to know how someone will handle being in authority, and what their ideal authority figure looks like, look at their tenth house and any planets within, as well as their Saturn's sign and house, as that stern planet rules this house. Pluto, on the other hand, is one of the two Death planets, and is named for the Lord of the Underworld. If one was going to choose an underworld God whose career had led him to be in authority over the greatest number of souls, there would be no question that Yama would be the one. Yama started out as the God of the Dead throughout India, but with the advent of Buddhism and its subsequent march across Asia, his name was borrowed, spread, and took over the same role in China, Tibet, Bhutan, Thailand, Sri Lanka, Cambodia, Myanmar, Laos, Korea, Vietnam, and Japan. He is the most widely successful Death God in the world, ironically a tenth-house accomplishment.

Yama is the son of Surya (Sun in the seventh house) and his wife, and his name means "restraint" or "self-control" or "one who binds". (Sanskrit words all have dozens of meanings, as they shifted over many centuries.) In his Hindu form, he is usually shown as a dark-skinned man riding a black buffalo or horse, carrying a noose with which he captures the souls of the newly dead. Sometimes, though, he appears in a fiercer mode with fangs, flames, and a wrathful expression. In East Asian countries, he appears as a scowling man with a long beard, dressed in traditional robes and wearing a judge's cap. His face appears on Hell Money, the artificial bills which Chinese mourners burn to ensure that their deceased relatives will be financially secure in the afterlife.

In some Indian myths, he is the first mortal man, meaning that he chose to die in order to open a way and create a safe space for all those who would die after him. He is considered the Father of the Dead, which resonates with Saturn, the ruler of this house and the signifier of the Father in an astrological chart. He is also the Judge of the Dead, assessing the worth and future of each soul as it comes into his territory, and this function grew and became more important as his reputation spread to the East, throughout Asia. Yama is characterized as stern but wise, often teaching devotees about the way the Universe works.

In China, he is known as Yanluo Wang; "Yanluo" is the Chinese translation of "Yama Raja", or King Yama, and Wang is the Chinese word for King again. (Having two out of three names mean a title of authority is a very tenth-house situation.) Here he is the ruler of ten levels of judges, which oversee the judging of many different kinds of souls, and sentence them to either rebirth, Heaven, or one of 136 hells. Souls can work their way up through the hells if they work hard and are diligent and willing to endure suffering. (The Chinese afterlife has been characterized as extremely corporate, mirroring the extensive government bureaucracy of Chinese culture, another ironic tenth-house situation.) In Japan, he is called Enma (a transliteration of Yama) and looks and acts similarly to his Chinese face. Those whom he judges to be unworthy are sent to one of sixteen regions of fire or ice for a set period of time, but that time can be shortened by the prayers of living descendants.

Having Pluto, the planet of power and intensity, in the house of career is going to give a great deal of ambition. When the individual with this placement chooses a career, they commit with their whole soul, and it can become the central focus of their life. Plutonian careers need to be absorbing, intense, and ideally something in which they can obtain some kind of authority. It need not be a leadership position at the top of a hierarchy (although this will be a great draw for them), but at least they need to be in a position where their expertise is honored. If there is a "top", they will be headed there, unless the juiciest work is at the hands-on rather than the managerial level. The small minority of tenth-house Pluto people who claim to be unambitious have generally been demoralized at a young age regarding their worth and competence, and are so frightened of failure that they dare not try for success. Eventually, as Pluto comes into its own (in the Saturn-ruled house, things often happen later in life), they will get over it.

This brings us to the fact that this is one of the two houses which indicate one's experience with the parents. Just as the fourth house indicates the parent who set the tone for the home, the tenth house indicates the authority figure of the family, the parent who connects the child to the outside world and teaches them what can be expected there. With Pluto here, what the child mainly saw of this parent was how they wielded power. They may have watched power struggles between parents, or the authoritarian figure had a heavy hand in emphasizing their power to the family. Later in life, this may make them very sensitive to the currents of power in their job. The least skillful and mature may grab for power at all costs, becoming the tyrannical parent in their career; the more evolved will want power, but will be moved to use it for good.

Those with this Pluto placement may have to overcome the fear of being powerless in life in order to relax and have a healthy relationship with their job and co-workers, or on a subtler level they may have to overcome the fear of not having a worthy life purpose. Either way, they often end up in positions where they have to judge the performance of a number of people, and have the authority to promote, demote, or fire them. Pluto here can make that task particularly intense, and they may struggle to be objective about it. With great power comes great responsibility, and this truism should become a mantra for this placement. While Yama's judging of the Dead is heavily informed by cultural norms in each society where he holds court, he does attempt to be discerning and fair whenever possible. Deciding people's fates is a stressful and ugly job, and yet it is those people who find it casual and easy who are the worst ones to hold it.

Some individuals with this Pluto placement will, like Yama, choose a career which brings them close to death in some way. This might be as obvious as the funeral industry or as subtle as grief counseling; other Plutonian careers might include emergency medicine and surgery, medical research into serious diseases, law that specializes in wills, or activists working for euthanasia rights. Those with this placement will be drawn to fields which shed light on dark, mysterious places such as psychology or the occult.

We must also remember that Pluto is the planet of transformation and rebirth, as well as death. Yama/Yanluo/Enma has the power of reincarnating souls who must come back to earth, and similarly the individual with this Pluto placement may be the catalyst for some kind of of great regeneration in their field—a new discovery which changes everything, or a reorganization which breathes new life into its purpose, or in some cases a destructive move which brings down the whole edifice, or the regeneration of a supposedly lost cause from the ashes of its destruction. If the change is personal rather than part of an organization, they may throw away their entire career and start over with a new one which is more healthy and integrated with their life path. Part of Plutonian transformation is purification, and ideally these radical changes should clean up the karmic mess that collects around any system which has been unexamined for too long.

People with this placement often have a strong intuitive feeling about their career and public-life path which feels like guidance from a parental figure, and in return they can often become that parental career-mentor for others. While some people simply proceed step-by-step in their career paths, the tenth-house Plutonian will sometimes have flashes of insight which will allow them to skip steps and get to the "top" faster. The trap of becoming power-hungry can be alleviated by closely examining one's relationship with one's childhood authority figure, and perhaps taking steps in one's personal life to address this situation and keep oneself humble. One person I know with this placement undertook years of training in a career which would put him in a position of power and influence, but the entire time he was also caring for his aging father in the old man's last years of life to remind himself of compassion and the duty to be kind.

Yama/Yanluo/Enma has to balance sternness and understanding, personal judgment with objectivity, and the implacability of Death with compassion for those who were in his power to change with a mere decision. This ambivalent placement can do great good or great evil, and those born under it will need to make that decision on a regular basis, knowing that a single choice can affect a whole tribe of people, and thus deserves the best judgment they can give.

11♇ Pluto in the 11th House: Theseus and Pirithous

Some stories of bonded best friends end well, and some don't. Failure, of course, is a subjective concept, and in the eleventh house, failure is not counted by the tragic ending of a person's life. Tragic endings happen all the time, and are a matter for other houses. The question is simple: are you a friend all the way to the end, in spite of any foolish mistakes your best buddy might make? Are you a comrade through thick and thin? Would you follow them to the gates of hell and beyond, even if neither of you gets out alive? If so, then the goal of the eleventh house has been met, and there was no failure.

Pluto is equally exacting, in any house it happens to be in. Whatever you do, says Pluto, you do it to the fullest, holding back nothing, charging in with teeth bared even in the time of desperation. Mars may be great at rushing in with immediate courage, but it takes Pluto to give their all when there may be no hope and no way to fool yourself that the road will ever lead home. This is the planet of All Or Nothing, and Pluto has no patience with slackers. In the House of Friendship, Pluto has the capacity to hold to one friend with the strength of iron, loyal to the bitter end. Even if that ending is disaster.

The tale of the great hero Theseus has many parts to it, but this chapter will concentrate on one segment of his story—his enduring friendship with Pirithous. Theseus may be best known for his role in the slaying of the Minotaur of Crete, finding his way through the labyrinth, and seducing and then abandoning Ariadne (Jupiter in Scorpio) to her promised husband Dionysos (Neptune in Scorpio). That all happens while Theseus is a young man; later, when he has inherited the kingship of Athens from his father, another young leader named Pirithous comes to test his mettle.

Pirithous was the chieftain of the Lapiths, a wild and hardy mountain tribe who were known for their strength and pugnaciousness. His mother was related to the tribe, but married elsewhere; when he was old enough he deserted his more civilized family and went to live with his wilder relatives, quickly rising to the position of chief. Pirithous had heard all about Theseus's exploits—not just the adventure in Crete, but his prior days of scouring bandits off of the shore road from Troezen to Athens. He wanted to see for himself if the reality matched the legend, so he decided to test Theseus by cattle-rustling the giant herd which the Athenian king grazed on the plain of Marathon. The young king of Athens reacted immediately, pursuing Pirithous (who couldn't exactly hide an enormous herd of cattle) and engaging him in single combat. The two fought each other furiously, but at some point both were so impressed by the courage and grace of the other that they ceased to fight and made a bargain: Pirithous would apologize for stealing the cattle and help Theseus drive them back to their pasture, and Theseus would honor him as a friend and brother. Before long, they ended up taking an oath of immutable friendship which would last until the end of at least one of their lives.

Pluto is by nature suspicious, and each potential friend will be scrutinized for flaws. Often they will be held to a higher standard than the Pluto person themselves, because on some (possibly unconscious) level, they are looking for an example to lead them into personal evolution. Pluto is the planet of transformation, and in the eleventh house that will come through their friends and the groups they cautiously enter. This "testing" of anything related to Pluto's sign or house can also been seen in Scorpio planets; it has long been observed that Mars in Scorpio people can subtly set up a "moral takedown" from someone with higher standards than they have. In general, Pluto is not comfortable with groups, or even with the easy camaraderie of friendship, but once they have committed to them, they are in for the long haul ... or until everything is destroyed. They may reject individuals as friends or groups as being appropriate for strange and sometimes unfair reasons of their own; had Theseus not managed to take back his herds even through no fault of his own, Pirithous might well have considered him too weak to be worth befriending.

Once their friendship is made fast, the two of them join a group of heroes who have gathered to hunt the Calydonian Boar, including Jason (Sun in the ninth house), Castor and Pollux (Sun in Gemini), and Atalanta (Venus in the ninth house). The boar had been rampaging through the countryside, laying waste and killing peasants, until the heroes grouped together to slay it at the behest of the region's lord. When Pluto joins a group, it had best be doing something serious and important; sitting around and swapping tales does not go deep enough for them to bother. If exertion and/or violence is involved, so much the better; another favorite group activity is hunting anything, perhaps looking to uncover information.

The boar hunt succeeds in its goal of slaying the creature, but the hunt itself is a disaster in other ways. Heroes accidentally kill each other during the chase, and afterwards there is a huge argument about who should get the trophy which spills over into multiple murders. This is another danger of this placement, not so much because the Pluto person chooses negative people, but because with Pluto energy present, all the cracks and splits of a group will come to the surface. Often it is the Pluto person who cannot help pointing them out, or by their refusal to take part in drama, they make others in the group feel ashamed or lesser in comparison. This can end up with the Pluto person treated as a scapegoat, blamed for betraying the group, when in fact it is the group which has betrayed them.

Theseus and Pirithous make it home unscathed, though, and get on with their lives. Theseus marries Phaedra, a young local princess still in her young teens, largely for political reasons; he has to put aside his former wife Hippolyta the Amazon to do this, even after she has borne him a son, Hippolytus. The angry Amazon attacks the wedding party where Pirithous is standing up for Theseus and is killed. Later Pirithous weds Hippodamia, and Theseus comes to his wedding. Pirithous has invited a local tribe of centaurs, who get drunk and attempt to carry off the bride and several of the female wedding guests. Again, Theseus and Pirithous lift swords together and slay the centaurs, rescuing the guests. The fact that both have tumultuous weddings is notable; Pluto's intense bond with a friend can cause problems with their partners, who may feel as if they are getting the short end of the deal.

This is reinforced by the Greek writers who report that Phaedra feels jealous of Theseus's bond with Pirithous, complaining that her husband spends all his time hunting and riding with his best friend and gives her little attention. Due to this neglect, her eyes turned to her stepson Hippolytus, who was dedicated to Artemis (Moon in Aquarius) and had taken a vow of chastity. Phaedra attempted to seduce him to no avail, and in revenge accused him of raping her. Theseus cursed his stepson to die, and Hippolytus's horse trampled him; Phaedra was so guilty that she killed herself. Hippodamia died in childbirth soon after, and the two friends had a drunken pity party and decided to find new brides. They came up with the idea that they would both wed daughters of Zeus (Jupiter in Aries). Theseus decided that he would kidnap Helen of Troy (Sun in Gemini), who was currently only about twelve years old, and keep her until she was old enough to marry.

This was at least a workable plan, if not particularly ethical, but Pirithous, not to be outdone, decided that he would steal Persephone (Pluto in Pisces) from Hades (Pluto in Capricorn) and marry her. Theseus tried multiple times to talk him out of it, but Pirithous was determined, so Theseus said that he would follow his friend even into the underworld. This is the point where Pluto's loyalty to their best comrade becomes a test of fire: will they follow them into Death itself? If the person with this placement is not particularly Plutonian in other ways, they may be attracted to friends and groups who have a Plutonian aura, perhaps outcasts who engage in risky activities and don't care about social opinion, or even criminals. The darkness tempts them through their associates, and they may not be able to resist even when it is against their better judgment. Their friends may encourage them into worse behavior, or they may be the one encouraging friends to embody that darkness for them.

The first part of the plan goes well—Helen is duly kidnapped by the two men and left with Theseus's mother to care for. The plan to raid the underworld, however, is disastrous. Theseus and Pirithous are used to going up against heroes, not Gods, and no sooner are they in the realm of Death than Hades traps them. The two sit down for a moment and find that they cannot move; the "sleep of death" is an easy trick for the Lord of Death. They are forced to wait there for many months in the darkness, unmoving and taunted by the Furies, until Hercules (Neptune in Aries) is sent to the underworld as his twelfth penitential labor in order to free them. He manages to free Theseus, after the hero apologizes to Persephone, but Hades refuses to let Pirithous leave, and has him fed to the great three-headed hound Cerberus (Pluto in the twelfth house). The friendship bond between these heroes ends there, although the two were both honored together as great warriors in temples of heroes.

When he returns to Athens, Theseus finds that in his absence, Helen has been rescued by her brothers and his throne has been usurped. He has paid for his Plutonian devotion with all his hopes and successes. The eleventh house is more than just friends and groups; it can also be, in its highest manifestation, the brotherhood of all humanity. Experiencing loyalty and betrayal, the sharing of paths positive and negative, is simply the training ground for the dedicating oneself to social change in a way that is not swayed or distracted, that can walk through fire and darkness to get the job done. That's why it is so important for Pluto in the eleventh house to learn the skill of discernment, because whether the road they follow leads to success or disaster will depend on the merits of the people to whom they dedicate themselves, and whom they allow to transform them. On the other hand, sometimes this Pluto can also transform another person or a group through their dedication, and thus learn to aim that transforming power at the larger world.

12♀ Pluto in the 12th House: Cerberus

While this adventure again stars the archetypal hero Hercules (Neptune in Aries), the main character of this story is not him but the foe he fights, who turns out not to be a foe at all. Cerberus is the guardian dog of Hades, the lord of the Greek underworld named after him (Pluto in Capricorn). Both Hades and his queen Persephone (Pluto in Pisces) seem to have a close relationship with Cerberus, who fawns on them—and especially on his master—but he is vicious toward any living humans who attempt to get into the realm of the Dead. While dead souls could walk by him toward their doom without him turning an eye, any live human who tried the gates of the inner realms would have Cerberus at their throat. He was equally fierce toward dead souls who attempted to leave.

Cerberus's name has been given a number of etymologies, but the most likely is from *ker* and *erebos*, meaning "death in the dark". He was usually pictured as a great hound with three snarling, toothed heads, a whipping poisonous snake for a tail, claws as large as a lion's, and a mane of more snake-heads on his shoulders and each of his three necks. His red eyes flashed fire and his hearing was incredibly acute. When facing down humans he is shown as coming up to their shoulders—the size of a pony—but when pictured with Hades he comes only to his master's knee, and looks up in adoration. He was the son of Typhon and Echidna, two monsters of the Titans who fought against Zeus (Jupiter in Aries) and were locked up under Mount Etna for it. Typhon was a dragon with a hundred heads, and Echidna a half-serpent half-woman. They had numerous monster children together, including the Sphinx, the Lernean Hydra, the Chimera, the Nemean Lion, the Caucasian Eagle who ate Prometheus's liver (Saturn in Aquarius), the Colchian and Hesperidian dragons, the Crommyonian Sow, and of course Cerberus. He was claimed by Hades as a puppy and thus escaped the fate of his parents and siblings, who were all eventually killed.

If this sounds like a litany of horrible monsters, that's par for the course when we are dealing with Pluto, the planet of intensity and destruction and passion and transformation ... down in the dark basement of the unconscious where it does not see the light. Pluto indicates the primal urges in us—power, animal passion, fury, fascination with death and destruction, and the ability to transform oneself by sheer force of will alone. Pluto is both greedy for power and understands that real power is the ability to do without. It is a planet of extremes, and does nothing halfway. Those with Pluto locked up in their personal underworlds fear the Beast Within, and will do whatever they can to keep it from getting out.

Of course, planets in the twelfth house do actually manifest sometimes in the upper world. If other planets in the chart are aspecting them, their energy can come out through that aspect. When planets in the sky transit them, they may suddenly come blazing out for a short period of time. The same phenomenon may happen when another person interacts with the twelfth-house individual, and one of their planets or points contacts the hidden planet. Either situation can trigger the twelfth-house person to act surprisingly—and sometimes distressingly—out of character, bringing up all that is hidden in their musty, foreboding mental cellar.

When that planet is Pluto, one of the most distressing eruptions can be rage. The twelfth-house Pluto may not think of themselves as an angry person, although the placement of their Mars may also have a lot to do with that, but suddenly they are wracked with fury and fantasizing destruction. One individual I know had a very physically abusive upbringing; both parents had twelfth-house Plutos and their child's Ascendant was right on top of them, bringing them to the surface with every interaction. Their siblings also suffered, but the brunt of the sudden screaming rage was usually directed at them. Afterwards, it was as if nothing had ever happened. Pluto sank down into his basement to skulk until the next triggering.

Not every Plutonian eruption is about rage; great creative and transformative energy may also be released, as well as sexual passion, obsessions, and a strong attraction to death and all things taboo and forbidden. Pluto forces us to face down all our darknesses, our greed, our selfishness, and of course our fears. When its force is hidden in the subconscious, it makes it easier for the individual to ignore and deny those parts of themselves ... and it also means that more of it than usual will silt up down there, because it has no regular outlet.

Cerberus, the Death in the Darkness, echoes the Beast in all of us. Any planet can manifest, in its own way, as a Beast, but Pluto's Beast is the most frightening of all. Even so, heroes have come down into Hades's realm for different purposes, and dealt with Cerberus in a variety of ways. Orpheus (Mercury in Pisces) sang a song of sleep and peace, and the great hound fell into a doze. The sibyl-guide of Aeneas (Saturn in the ninth house) threw Cerberus a honey-cake spiced with sedative herbs. These approaches suggest using drugs (or fantasies, or music, or other mind-altering actions) to temporarily quiet the Beast and get to the treasure behind it. While they are expedient, they do not actually clear the way. The Inner Guardian is still there, and cannot always be drugged senseless.

The twelfth labor of Hercules, on the other hand, put the strongest of heroes face to face with an awake snarling Cerberus. Eurystheus, the ruler who had passed the sentence on Hercules, kept sending him out on more impossible errands in the hopes that the next one would kill him. He ordered the warrior to go down into Hades and bring up Cerberus for display. Hercules asked Hades, rather respectfully, to be allowed to borrow his pet with the promise of returning it immediately afterward. Hades and Persephone told him that he must first defeat Cerberus in combat, but he must not use any iron or bronze weapon to do it. Iron is the metal of Mars, and this is not a place for the outer warrior, but the inner one. Bronze is the copper of Venus mixed with the tin of Jupiter, and this is not a place for those energies either. Pluto wants raw flesh on flesh, or it will not respect the process.

This is in parallel to the idea that in order to get through the fear of the inner Beast, one must meet the Beast on its own terms, and come to appreciate it for what it is. Ignored and locked up, the inner Beast has only the individual it inhabits to prey on. Fear of one's baser instincts can create immense self-hatred; the twelfth-house Pluto individual can judge themselves harshly and unmercifully, expecting impossible inner saintliness. They may live a life of powerlessness, because their internal power is locked away, and they cannot believe that one could be powerful and not corrupt. They may turn that self-loathing outwards with manipulative behavior and vengeful sabotage, fearing that others will turn against them the power they fear to wield openly. Each of these fears and negative behaviors must be bravely faced down, wrestled to the ground, and made to submit ... which is exactly what Hercules did with Cerberus.

The hero took off his lionskin—made, ironically, of the invulnerable skin of Cerberus's own brother—and wrapped it around the hell-hound's neck and heads. Although he was stung repeatedly by the snake-tail, he held on until Cerberus was rendered temporarily unconscious. Then he bound him with chains of adamantine and brought him up to the surface. He also managed to get Theseus (Pluto in the eleventh house) out as well, and when the great hound balked at coming out of the underworld entrance and up into the light, the two of them were able to drag him out together. Once in the upper world, Hercules took the hound first to Eurystheus—who was so horrified that he jumped into a large jar to hide—and then on parade, showing him off to the cheers of the crowds. After that, he returned the hound to his master in the underworld, and Cerberus was very glad to come back.

The Beast must be brought into the light—perhaps through internal meditative exploration, perhaps through writing, perhaps through acting it out in safe contexts, perhaps through therapy. Once the inner Cerberus is displayed, it is easier to figure out what he was set to guard and why, and whether it is necessary any longer. To become a hero who can wrestle down Cerberus takes time, and that transformation is not a simple or comfortable thing. Some people have found that one of the best preparations is strenuous and disciplined physical activity, such as martial arts, yoga, or heavy exercise. Others have prepared for the "ring of combat" with meditation and mental disciplines. Either way, this is something one trains for ... and then holds firm, even when it hurts.

Once this has been achieved, even partially, the equivalent of parading Cerberus through the streets is being able to share the experience with others, and perhaps show them how to brave their own underworlds. The mature twelfth-house Pluto who has already been down there and back, won the battle and proved to the judgmental fears he has inherited—embodied in this story by Eurystheus—that he is powerful and can force Cerberus to yield, can transform into someone to whom others go when they are facing down a similar journey. There need be no more hate or anger or fear toward the Beast; they can be calm and serene about it, as well as powerful. Pluto now has the ability to sense what is in the underworlds of others—Cerberus had a potent nose and ears—and this gift can help them when the Universe makes them a guide dog for others, rather than only a guard dog for themselves.

www.ingramcontent.com/pod-product-compliance
Lightning Source LLC
Chambersburg PA
CBHW021756220426
43662CB00006B/81